T0135158

Lecture Notes in Information Systems and Organisation

Volume 46

Lecture Notes in Information Systems and Organization—LNISO—is a series of scientific books that explore the current scenario of information systems, in particular IS and organization. The focus on the relationship between IT, IS and organization is the common thread of this collection, which aspires to provide scholars across the world with a point of reference and comparison in the study and research of information systems and organization. LNISO is the publication forum for the community of scholars investigating behavioral and design aspects of IS and organization. The series offers an integrated publication platform for high-quality conferences, symposia and workshops in this field. Materials are published upon a strictly controlled double blind peer review evaluation made by selected reviewers.

LNISO is abstracted/indexed in Scopus

More information about this series at http://www.springer.com/series/11237

Frederik Ahlemann · Reinhard Schütte ·
Stefan Stieglitz
Editors

Innovation Through Information Systems

Volume I: A Collection of Latest Research on Domain Issues

Editors
Frederik Ahlemann
Faculty of Business Administration
and Economics
University of Duisburg-Essen
Essen, Germany

Reinhard Schütte
Faculty of Business Administration
and Economics
University of Duisburg-Essen
Essen, Germany

Stefan Stieglitz
Department of Computer Science
and Applied Cognitive Science
University of Duisburg-Essen
Duisburg, Germany

ISSN 2195-4968 ISSN 2195-4976 (electronic)
Lecture Notes in Information Systems and Organisation
ISBN 978-3-030-86789-8 ISBN 978-3-030-86790-4 (eBook)
https://doi.org/10.1007/978-3-030-86790-4

This Springer imprint is published by the registered company Springer Nature Switzerland AG
The registered company address is: Gewerbestrasse 11, 6330 Cham, Switzerland

Preface

Business Information Systems Engineering is a vital scientific discipline, which has objects of investigation that can hardly be more timely: the design, use, and management of information systems (IS). The discipline's wide range of topics is impressive, which is also documented through the contributions submitted to the 16th International Conference on Business Information Systems Engineering (WI21). Innovation through IS has been the guiding theme for the conference, representing both the present and the future. The coronavirus pandemic has made it clear to individuals, companies, and society as a whole that the digitalization trend will not lose its power for a long time to come. Areas of society long known for their slowness to adopt digital technologies, such as health, education, and government services, are opening up to the use of modern digital IS. The massive expansion of online shopping and the increased acceptance of digital customer touchpoints will stay even when the pandemic has ended. Moreover, virtual teamwork and working from home concepts are now implemented in many companies that were reluctant to embrace these trends before the pandemic started. Altogether, the past year has enabled a new level of digitalization and is driving companies to take further steps to digitalize products, services, and business models.

Digitalization is changing our world faster than ever, and Business Information Systems Engineering as a discipline has the potential to play a major role in understanding and shaping this development. Not only does Business Information Systems Engineering combine technical and economic knowledge in its origins, but also its intrinsic interdisciplinary nature gives it a great position to continue and extend collaboration with other disciplines, such as business economics, informatics, communication science, and psychology. In recent years, it has become clear that addressing complex organizational and societal problems requires theoretical and methodological approaches used in different disciplines. Making visible how rich, wide-ranging, and practically relevant the outcomes of our discipline are is a major goal besides contributing to the academic discourse of our community.

Business Information Systems Engineering as an established discipline gains its profile from three constituent aspects. *First*, Business Information Systems Engineering research presupposes an *information technology artifact*. This technical artifact is at least fundamentally understood (and not merely represented as a black box). This implies an understanding of the design process as well as the context of use. *Second*, the use of the technical artifact *takes place in a system that has social elements*. The integration of socio-organizational aspects is necessary because the appropriation and use of the artifact by people influences its mode of action. *Third, resource constraints can be observed in all actions in organizations*. Economic considerations are required if an organization's goal is to be achieved in the best possible way. This implies the need for economical design, use, and management of information technology (IT) artifacts as well as the question of added value that arises from their use. For example, Business Information Systems Engineering is not just about the issue of developing software according to user requirements but also about the successful use of software in organizations, which is reflected in economic dimensions.

It is a mark of great success that our discipline actively addresses a wide range of urgent research fields by submitting so many research articles to WI21. In these proceedings, we have structured the accepted papers in the areas of *domain, technology,* and *management* and a *general* area on innovative, emerging, and interdisciplinary topics and methods, theories, and ethics in Business Information Systems Engineering. The high number of papers submitted has made it necessary to publish several volumes. We have used the conference structure to divide the conference proceedings into three volumes. The first volume contains the domain-related tracks, supplemented by the two general tracks. In the second volume, the tracks on technology are summarized, and the third volume contains the management tracks. A total of 267 full papers and 80 short papers were submitted for the conference, of which 93 were accepted as full papers and 28 as short papers, resulting in an acceptance rate of 35% for the full papers and for the short papers. All the accepted papers passed a double-blind peer-review process.

The details of the short papers can be found in the table of contents and the brief introductions to the tracks; they are not detailed in this preface. The student track's interesting and diverse contributions, a clear indicator of the discipline's attractiveness for students, have also been included in the conference proceedings.

In the following, we briefly summarize the articles submitted for the different domains. In doing so, we aim to highlight the wide range and diverse nature of the contributions that characterize our academic community.

Volume I: Domain

Domain represents that part of the discourse that is of scientific interest, which has become highly differentiated due to problem specificity in research. This structure largely follows the divisions in management consultancies, standard software manufacturers, the software product-related organization of IT in companies or, in the area of research, also the call for applications-oriented research programs by the Federal Ministry of Economics in Germany. The domains contain their own "language games" with deviating application architectures and economical problem definitions. The five tracks on creating value through digital innovation in healthcare, retail, digital services and smart product service systems, and smart city and e-Government examine a broad spectrum of current technology use in specific domains.

At the time of the conference, hardly any area is more present from the point of view of the digitization discussion than *Digital innovation in healthcare*. This is also documented by the contributions accepted in this track. The role of patients in the value creation of digital innovations often depends on the patients. One paper focuses on their attitudes toward apps for chronic disease management and another discusses in an empirical study how satisfied elderly people are with telemedical remote diagnostic applications. In the third paper, the evidence about patient engagement tools and their integration in patient pathways is analyzed. The transformation path from research to clinical practice for data-driven services is the subject of the last paper in this section, which analyzes how a third party can take part in less digitalized domains like health care.

The *Retail* domain is subject to two requirements as a result of digitalization: the improvement of internal and network-like value creation processes and the implementation of omnichannel customer requirements, including diverse customer touchpoints. The customer interface capabilities are essential for companies, especially after the pandemic experiences of the past year. The three selected contributions are dedicated to this topic. In the first contribution, the impact of the coronavirus pandemic on local retailers and local retailer shopping platforms was investigated with interviews. The role of personality traits and gender roles in choosing a consumer channel was investigated in a laboratory experiment with the result of significant differences in channel evaluation. The third paper discusses digitalization of luxury retail by assessing customers' quality perception of a digital sales desk for jewelry stores.

In a sense, a symbiosis of old material and new informational worlds is explored in the track *Digital services and smart product service systems*: A maturity model for manufacturers with five areas (strategy, culture, structure, practice, and IT) is used to show the stages from a pure product to a product service system provider, existing methods for the design of a digital service in operational practice are evaluated, a conceptual framework for tools for the development of digital services is designed, and requirements for augmented reality solutions for safety-critical services are formulated.

The *Digitalization and society—even in times of corona* track discusses societal challenges and the role and usage of information technologies. An empirical paper on an online survey conducted in March 2020 examines if willingness to release private data increases if fear of the crisis exists. The role of trust in government also has an impact on voluntary data provision, as shown in the paper. The perceived stress of knowledge workers working at home in COVID-19 times is investigated in another empirical study. The third paper reviews online platforms for cultural participation and education and develops a taxonomy. The differences in the challenges of digital transformations between industrial and non-profit organizations in the areas of business processes, business models, and customer experience are investigated using a grounded theory approach. The fourth paper discusses the success factors of pandemic dashboards and the development of dashboards for the specific requirements of COVID-19 data. The last paper in this section discusses the impact of digitizing social networks on refugee decision making in Germany.

The *Smart city and government track* contains both conceptual and empirical contributions. An empirical paper on competence requirements for the digitalization of public administration analyzes job advertisements, while a literature review on requirements for blockchain-based e-government services represents the status of the scientific debate on e-government blockchain approaches. The future of cities in the South Westphalia region in Germany is the subject of a scenario-based paper that examines how we can prepare cities against uncertain future circumstances. The potential uses of smart city data in smart city projects are explored through a taxonomy of such projects that provides guidance for real-world projects. The focus on sustainable urban logistic operations is directed in a contribution that offers a design-oriented strategic decision support approach. In the last contribution of the track, an explicable artificial intelligence approach is demonstrated as a support for public administration processes.

The two general tracks on innovative, emerging, and interdisciplinary topics and methods, theories, and ethics in Business Information Systems Engineering and the students' track conclude the first volume.

The track *Innovative, emerging, and interdisciplinary topics* includes five papers that address the influence of organizational culture on idea platform implementation, a taxonomy for data strategy tools and methodologies in the economy, the design of an adaptive empathy learning tool, an empirical study of secondary school students' openness to study Business Information Systems Engineering, and the altered role of 3D models in the product development process for physical and virtual consumer goods.

The track *Methods, theories, and ethics in Business Information Systems Engineering* includes three full papers on ethical design of conversational agents, a framework for structuring literature search strategies in information systems, and the design of goal-oriented artifacts from morphological taxonomies.

The *Student* track, which has been part of WI conferences since 2016, comprises 16 selected full papers and another 13 contributions accepted for the poster session. These contributions are listed in the table of contents. The program chairs consider the strong involvement of students as a distinguishing feature of Business Information Systems Engineering. For this reason, the student challenge became part of the WI2021 in Essen to bring students and companies together and to emphasize the application orientation as a further strength of Business Information Systems Engineering.

Volume II: Technology

The second volume is dedicated to the core of change in organizations, information *technology*. The five tracks of the second volume are data science and business analytics, design, management, and impact of AI-based systems, human–computer interaction, information security, privacy, and blockchain, and social media and digital work, which represent the wide range of technologies investigated in Business Information Systems Engineering.

The first track in the technology section is dedicated to the perspectives of *Data science and business analytics*. Hardly any area is associated with as much expectation in operational practice as the possibilities for using as much data as possible. A wide variety of contributions were selected that report on managing bias in machine learning projects and the design of hybrid recommender systems for next purchase prediction based on optimal combination weights, present a holistic framework for AI systems in industrial applications, use natural language processing to analyze scientific content and knowledge sharing in digital platform ecosystems demonstrated for the SAP developer community, and realize information extraction from invoices based on a graph neural network approach for datasets with high layout variety.

The second technology track, *Design, management, and impact of AI-based systems,* also covered a wide range of topics. The first paper presents a socio-technical analysis of predictive maintenance. The evaluation of the black box problem for AI-based recommendations is empirically investigated on the basis of interviews in the second paper, and the role of influencing factors and the challenges of chatbots at digital workplaces is the subject of the third contribution. Another empirical work examines the relationships of AI characteristics, project management challenges, and organizational change. The challenges for conversational agent usage through user-specific determinants and the potential for future research are the subject of the fourth paper in this track. A design science perspective is used for an augmented reality object labeling application for crowdsourcing communities and also to construct an artificial neural network-based approach to predict traffic volume. A hybrid approach is used at a German bank by combining leveraging text classification with co-training with bidirectional language models. The eighth and final paper in this track contributes to explaining suspicion by designing an XAI-based user-focused anti-phishing measure.

One research direction that has been established in Computer Science longer than in Business Information Systems Engineering is *Human–computer interaction*. Four contributions were accepted, which deal with the influence of the human-like design of conversational agents on donation behavior, state-of-the-art research on persuasive design for smart personal assistants, a conversational agent for adaptive argumentation feedback, and insights from an experiment with conversational agents on the relation of anthropomorphic design and dialog support.

The five papers accepted in the *Information security, privacy, and blockchain* track consider data protection challenges and their solutions with regard to blockchain technologies from the perspective of German companies and organizations, a survey of private German users about the relationship between IT privacy and security behavior, cyber security challenges for software developer awareness training in industrial environments, the hidden value of using design patterns to whitebox technology development in legal assessments, and an analysis of the user motivations driving peer-to-peer personal data exchange.

The last technology track focuses on *Social media and digital work*. In the first accepted contribution, the design principles for digital upskilling in organizations are analyzed. A comparative study on content and analyst opinion, crowd- or institutionally oriented, is the subject of the second contribution. The third paper is dedicated to a no-code platform for tie prediction analysis in social media networks. The track on social media and digital work is rounded off with problems and solutions in digital work, exploring measures for team identification in virtual teams.

Volume III: Management

The third volume of the conference covers *Management* aspects and has the largest number of tracks. The volume includes tracks on data management and data ecosystems, digital education and capabilities, digital transformation and business models, digital innovations and entrepreneurship, enterprise modeling and information systems development, the future of digital markets and platforms, IT strategy, management, and transformation and, finally, management of digital processes and architecture.

Data management and data ecosystems form the starting point for value creation processes, which are expressed, among other things, in data-as-a-service considerations. In the first paper of this track, the authors design a data provenance system supporting e-science workflows. A taxonomy for assessing and selecting data sources is designed in the second paper, which also discusses aspects of the efforts for data integration in a big data context. Another literature-based paper develops four types of hybrid sensing systems as a combination of high-quality and mobile crowd sensing systems.

The *Digital education and capabilities* track includes four papers. In the first paper, a literature review about digital credentials in higher education institutions is presented. The interplay between digital workplace and organizational culture is investigated using a multi-case study in the second paper. The current performance of digital study assistants and future research fields are subject to state-of-the-art investigations in the last paper of this track.

The track *Digital transformation and business models* has been particularly topical and not only since the coronavirus pandemic. The first article takes a long-term look at which strategic orientations are identifiable, and digital business model patterns are investigated. In the second article, digital leadership is analyzed through a literature review. The path from the producer to the holistic solutions provider is an empirically oriented investigation of digital service development in an automotive environment, while the fourth contribution focuses on the success of digital transformation and asks, using the notion in IS literature, what is meant by digital transformation success. The last article in this track explores IT artifacts in people analytics and reviews tools to understand this emerging topic.

Digital innovation and entrepreneurship, the fourth management track, comprises four papers, which deal with the impact of business models on early stage financing, structuring the different capabilities in the field of digital innovation, structuring the digital innovation culture using a systematic literature review, and the question of how to recombine layers of digital technology to create digital innovation.

The track *Enterprise modeling and information systems development* as a traditional research field of our community includes three papers this year. The first is devoted to language-independent modeling of subprocesses for adaptive case management. Challenges of reference modeling are investigated in the second contribution by comparing conventional and multi-level language architectures. The last contribution is dedicated to how dimensions of supply chains are represented in digital twins by presenting a state-of-the-art survey.

With eight contributions, the *Future of digital markets and platforms* track indicates the enormous interest that our community is showing in this topic. This track also presents systematizing literature work in the form of literature reviews, taxonomies, and empirical work. The first paper undertakes a literature-based review of 23 digital platform concepts, leading to eight research focus areas. The second paper develops a taxonomy of industrial Internet of Things (IIoT) platforms with architectural features and archetypes. The third paper explains that existing reviews matter for future reviewing efforts. The reviewing effort, measured by the willingness to write an evaluation and how long the textual explanations are, is negatively correlated to the number of existing reviews. In an experiment with 339 participants, it was investigated how different evaluations are between anonymous crowds and student crowds in terms of their information processing, attention, and selection performance. The role of complementors in platform ecosystems is the subject of a literature-based review. In another paper, an empirical examination from social media analytics about IIoT platforms describes currently discussed topics regarding IIoT platforms. The principles for designing IIoT platforms are presented, analyzing an emerging platform and its ecosystem of stakeholders with a focus on their requirements. The track is rounded off with a contribution on how data-driven competitive advantages can be achieved in digital markets, which provides an overview of data value and facilitating factors.

Strategic IT management, which forms the core of the *Information technology strategy, management, and transformation* track, is also one of the traditional pillars of Business Information Systems Engineering at the interface with business administration. The first contribution considers the problem of how the design of IS for the future of leadership should be structured. The role of open source software in respect to how to govern open-source contributions is a case study-oriented research contribution of the second paper. The third paper analyzes feedback exchange in an organization and discusses the question of whether more feedback is always better. The impacts of obsolescence in IT work and the causes, consequences, and counter-measures of obsolescence are the subject of the fourth paper in this track. Chief digital officers, a significant role in the organization in times of digitalization, are reviewed, and a suggestion for a research agenda is presented in the fifth contribution. An empirical investigation of the relationship between digital business strategy and firm performance is presented in paper six, and the role of IT outside the IT department is discussed in paper seven of the track. The last paper analyzes the requirements for performance measurement systems in digital innovation units.

The final track, *Management of digital processes and architectures*, concerns the connection of digital processes and architectures. Consequently, the first contribution to the track asks the empirically motivated question: How does enterprise architecture support the design and realization of data-driven business models? Event-driven process controls, which are important in business reality, are related to the Internet of Things (IoT) in the second contribution. This combination of the technical possibilities of IoT systems with the event-driven approach defines the purpose and attractiveness of IoT architectures and scenarios. Based on a literature review, an outlook on a future research agenda is given, and the final contribution in this track is dedicated to the status quo of process mining in the industrial sector and thus addresses the use of an important method of Business Information Systems Engineering in industry as a domain.

Due to the restrictions of the coronavirus pandemic, the International Conference on Wirtschaftsinformatik 2021 will be held as a purely virtual event for the first time. This is clearly a drawback, because meeting colleagues and getting into face-to-face discussions is one of the highest benefits of this conference. Also, we are sadly missing the chance to present the University of Duisburg-Essen and the vibrant Ruhr area to our community. However, the conference's virtual design has huge potential for the whole community to use and reflect on digital communication and collaboration and to invent new concepts of interaction for the future.

The Conference Chairs would like to thank our sponsors who made the WI2021 possible and gave valuable input for innovative ways of virtual interaction and collaboration. Furthermore, we want to thank the Rectorate of the University of Duisburg-Essen for supporting the event. Moreover, we want to thank all those researchers who contributed to WI2021 as authors, those colleagues who organized conference tracks and workshops, and those who supported the track chairs as associate editors, session chairs, and reviewers. We are aware that all these services for the community are time-consuming and mean substantial efforts to make such a conference a successful event. We are especially grateful for the support of the scientific staff involved. In particular, we would like to thank Jennifer Fromm, Dr. Erik Heimann, Lennart Hofeditz, Anika Nissen, Erik Karger, and Anna Y. Khodijah.

In these special times, we would like to close the preface with the words of Friedrich Schiller (in German):

Einstweilen bis den Bau der Welt
Philosophie zusammenhält
Erhält sich das Getriebe
Durch Hunger und durch Liebe

April 2021

Frederik Ahlemann
Reinhard Schütte
Stefan Stieglitz
Conference Chairs WI 2021

Contents

Digital Retail

Digital Services and Smart Product-Service Systems

Creating Value Through Digital Innovation

Introduction to the WI2021 Track: Creating Value through Digital Innovation in Health Care

Lauri Wessel[1], Hannes Rothe[2], and Eivor Oborn[3]

[1] European New School of Digital Studies, European University Viadrina, Frankfurt (Oder), Germany
wessel@europa-uni.de
[2] Digital Entrepreneurship Hub, Department of Information Systems, Freie Universität Berlin, Berlin, Germany
hannes.rothe@fu-berlin.de
[3] Warwick Business School, Coventry, UK
eivor.oborn@wbs.ac.uk

1 Track Description

COVID-19 has significantly impacted on societies and healthcare sectors worldwide. New needs in terms of research, diagnostics, treatments, and care emerged in rapid pace and brought with them substantial implications for value creation [1]. While significant change in how value was being created and captured in health care was already underway before the pandemic [2, 3], it accelerated this dynamic and brought to the fore the timeliness of rethinking the relationship between digital innovation and value creation in health care. On the one hand, the availability of increasing amounts of data is often associated with positive outcomes as data can inform genomics, medical imagery, and enable patients to self-manage their own health [4–8]. On the other, studies are also beginning to point out that some of these innovations can have detrimental impacts on how patients may organize their lives [9], that certain digital innovations may be in conflict with values that medical professionals advocate [10] and that digital innovations can generally lead to unexpected changes in health care organizations [11, 12]. As digital technologies are used in health care with wider scale and scope, this calls for a nuanced inquiry into the relationship between digital innovation and value creation in health care and to attend to how digital innovation changes what, why, and for whom value is being created.

The abovementioned area of interest stands somewhat in contrast to the trajectory along which research on health care IT has developed within the information systems (IS) discipline. While IS researchers have studied topics related to health care IT for many years [13], their primary interest was in understanding and managing the numerous challenges involved with making HIT work in organizations [12, 14–17]. This work has provided important and nuanced insights into how health care IT can be organized so that independent professionals comply and use it faithfully. Yet the technological and organizational developments referred to above indicate that it becomes important to widen the focus of research to include a range of new and recent phenomena such as the spread of data that becomes available for managing health in both research and practice, the shift towards patient self-management and with it the question of how to engage patients in value creation in health care. Our track was devoted to capture state of the art research in these areas of interest.

2 Research Articles

We received 18 submissions in total out of which we selected 14 for the peer review process and included seven in the conference program. Our AEs played a key role in this selection process. We would like to express our sincere gratitude to all of them! We discuss the articles that we included in the conference proceedings in three steps.

2.1 Entrepreneurship and the Exploitation of Data for Creating Value Through Digital Innovation in Health Care

The availability of data is central for effectively leveraging digital innovation in whatever setting [18]. Yet in health care, data is particularly crucial because its effective use is likely to influence patients' wellbeing. The paper "Third-Party Venture Legitimizing Research Data Application in Healthcare Practice" by Penninger and Lindman addresses how entrepreneurial ventures can work towards the translation of data-driven services from research to clinical practice. This is a cutting-edge topic.

2.2 The Role of Patients for Creating Value Through Digital Innovation in Health Care

Digital innovations enable patients to become active contributors to their own health [7, 8]. While this is particularly important for including elderly people or managing chronic conditions [9], changing the role of patients not only creates opportunities but also obstacles for care. In their paper "Patients' Attitudes toward Apps for Management of a Chronic Disease", Alpar and Driebe find, for example, that education of patients regarding the potency of apps is critical. Elderly people are at the center of Pflügner and colleagues' paper "When are Elderly People Satisfied with Telemedical Remote Diagnosis Applications?". Finally, Burkard and colleagues' paper "Managing My Bladder Dictates My Daily Routines" taps into self-management of health in patients' private lives; a key area of digital health.

2.3 Integrating Patients and Organizations When Value Through Digital Innovation in Health Care

The final set of papers integrate the more recent focus on patients with established knowledge of health care IS in organizations. Hickman and colleagues' "Let's get engaged" looks at patient pathways in care networks. Care networks can be seen as promising organizational forms to address complex chronic conditions, in turn, designing effective pathways is critical to integrate patients into care processes on the organizational level. Scheplitz's paper "Pfade schaffen das!" dives deeply into design of pathways. Finally, the importance of hygiene has been accelerated by the COVID-19 pandemic and is at the center of the paper "A Feedback Information System for Improving Hand Hygiene on a Personal and Organizational Level" by Stingl and colleagues who address hygiene on personal and organizational levels.

References

1. Thomas, O., et al.: Global crises and the role of BISE. Bus. Inf. Syst. Eng. (2020). https://doi.org/10.1007/s12599-020-00657-w
2. Porter, M.: What is value in health care? - supplementary appendix 2. N. Engl. J. Med. (2010). https://doi.org/10.1056/NEJMp1011024
3. Porter, M.E., Olmsberg Teisberg, E.: Redefining health care: creating value-based competition on results. Harvard BUsiness Review Press, Boston (2006)
4. Vassilakopoulou, P., Skorve, E., Aanestad, M.: Enabling openness of valuable information resources: curbing data subtractability and exclusion. Inf. Syst. J. (2018)
5. Jarvenpaa, S.L., Markus, M.L.: Data perspective in digital platforms: three tales of genetic platforms. In: Proceedings of the 51st Hawaii International Conference on System Sciences, pp. 4574–4583 (2018)
6. Rothe, H., Jarvenpaa, S.L., Penninger, A.A.: How do entrepreneurial firms appropriate value in bio data infrastructures: an exploratory qualitative study. In: Proceedings of the 27th European Conference on Information Systems (ECIS), Stockholm & Uppsala, Sweden (2019)
7. Barrett, M., Oborn, E., Orlikowski, W.: Creating value in online communities: the sociomaterial configuring of strategy, platform, and stakeholder engagement. Inf. Syst. Res. 0, null (2016). https://doi.org/doi:10.1287/isre.2016.0648
8. Dadgar, M., Joshi, K.D.: The role of information and communication technology in self-management of chronic diseases: an empirical investigation through value sensitive design. J. Assoc. Inf. Syst. 19, 86–112 (2018). https://doi.org/10.17705/1jais.00485
9. Wessel, L., Davidson, E.J., Barquet, A.P., Rothe, H., Peters, O., Megges, H.: Configuration in smart service systems: a practice-based inquiry. Inf. Syst. J. 29, 1256–1281 (2019). https://doi.org/10.1111/isj.12268
10. Ologeanu-Taddei, R., Wessel, L., Bourdon, I.: Persistent paradoxes in pluralistic organizations: a case study of continued use of shadow-it in a french hospital. In: 40th International Conference on Information Systems (ICIS) (2019)
11. Barrett, M., Oborn, E., Orlikowski, W.J., Yates, J.: Reconfiguring boundary relations: robotic innovations in pharmacy work. Organ. Sci. 23, 1448–1466 (2012). https://doi.org/10.1287/orsc.1100.0639
12. Wessel, L., Baiyere, A., Ologeanu-Taddei, R., Cha, J., Jensen, T.B.: Unpacking the difference between digital transformation and it-enabled organizational transformation. J. Assoc. Inf. Syst. (2020)
13. Baid, A., Angst, C.M., Oborn, E.: Research curation: health information technology. MIS Ouarterly (2018)

14. Lapointe, L., Rivard, S.: A multilevel model of resistance to information technology implementation. MIS Q. 29, 461–491 (2005). https://doi.org/10.2307/25148692
15. Kohli, R., Kettinger, W.J.: informating the clan: controlling physicians' costs and outcomes. MIS Q. 28, 363–394 (2004)
16. Davidson, E.J., Chismar, W.G.: The interaction of institutionally triggered and technology-triggered social structure change: an investigation of computerized physician order entry. MIS Q. 31, 739–758 (2007)
17. Davidson, E.J.: Technology frames and framing: a socio-cognitive investigation of requirements determination. MIS Q. 26, 329–358 (2002). https://doi.org/10.2307/4132312
18. Yoo, Y., Henfridsson, O., Lyytinen, K.: Research commentary—the new organizing logic of digital innovation: an agenda for information systems research. Inf. Syst. Res. 21, 724–735 (2010). https://doi.org/10.1287/isre.1100.0322

Third-Party Venture Legitimizing Research Data Application in Healthcare Practice

Anna Auguste Penninger[1(✉)] and Juho Lindman[2]

[1] Freie Universität Berlin, Business Information Systems, Berlin, Germany
[2] Applied IT, University of Gothenburg, Gothenburg, Sweden
juho.lindman@ait.gu.se

Abstract. Especially in the area of genomics, global research institutions constantly provide new insights. Yet today we lack insight on how the use of research data in clinical practice is facilitated. Our study researches an entrepreneurial venture as complementing actor in the international health context who bridges data use from research to science. In this paper, we present a three-step framework how the venture legitimizes data-driven services to facilitate research data use in clinical practice. Our findings illustrate that the venture managed to adjust to clinical needs by using three mechanisms: 1) assessing and aggregating, 2) allowing for ambiguity and 3) assuring clinical assistance. This study adds to the understanding of new ventures' services legitimation scaling across traditionally national healthcare with local systems. Moreover, our framework is of interest to entrepreneurs and investors, who seek entrepreneurial opportunities and information about ventures that have been able to navigate this field.

Keywords: Healthcare · Venture · Genome data services

1 Introduction

Genome data and genetic medicine have promising global advancements such as personalized medicine, new diagnostic methods and new disease treatment that are of relevance to humankind [1–3]. Genetics is a field that benefits greatly from the digitalization of research data. Borders between research and application are blurring in genetics, because the ongoing research efforts have direct relevance in healthcare practice [4]. It is thus becoming increasingly relevant to integrate highly international and research-centered efforts into local (national) medical practice [5]. This is not an easy task, as scientific research and healthcare institutions currently work separately from each other, pursue different goals and use different information systems [6]. Information systems (IS) researchers have pointed out these challenge and the need to include the field of genetics to advance IS research [7–9].

How to use the ubiquity of (research) data? That is a relevant question, it has only played a minor role in health IS research which has often discussed national projects in context of national healthcare. We follow an earlier research call to explore how research flows into clinical applications [5] and show the novel possibilities that

F. Ahlemann et al. (Eds.): WI 2021, LNISO 46, pp. 7–21, 2021.
https://doi.org/10.1007/978-3-030-86790-4_1

entrepreneurial ventures can take in healthcare [10], serving new and complex needs of various stakeholder groups.

We are especially interested in new venture-provided services in biological, specifically human genome data [11, 12]. Our study researches a data-intensive, young firm (entrepreneurial venture) as a complementing actor in international health services [9, 13]. Our research question is: *How can a third-party venture legitimize new data services to facilitate research data use in healthcare*? In our empirical case study, we explore a venture that supports sharing and generating insights between international researchers and healthcare practitioners. We explain how the venture establishes new services for a heterogeneous range of stakeholders.

2 Background

2.1 From Traditionally Local to International Context of Healthcare

In today's IS health literature, the "durability and central role of existing practices, conventions, tools and systems" [14] is often central to studying the challenges along the lifecycle of building, adapting and evolving local health systems and information infrastructure in national healthcare [15–18]. Healthcare research seldom refers to international projects that establish or adapt healthcare related services with digital technology. The focus on a siloed setup in local healthcare settings ties traditional healthcare research to addressing challenges with a rather localized view [15, 19–21]. But comparably new and recent fields for medical treatment rely on cross-institutional and cross-national collaboration and data exchange [22, 23].

Data-related problems impact healthcare sector globally: Western countries as well as developing countries experience difficulties in ensuring that data are standardized [24] are safely shared [21, 25], available [26] and lead to legitimate services [20, 27]. For analysis in clinical diagnosis, the representation of health-related problems in data is paramount: In data-heavy fields like genomics, access to these data and the need for sharing initiatives are the desired path to advance clinical practice [2, 4, 28, 29]. Little standardization exists, and large datasets grow incessantly [30–32]. The shift of attention from local healthcare concerns to global communities is appropriate as data digitization is transforming healthcare [24, 33, 34] as it removes limitations of physical access while also "*dissolv[ing] product and industry boundaries*" [35].

2.2 The Role of Data in Clinical and Research Context

Today, healthcare and research institutions are working with different stakeholder groups. Healthcare institutions involve distinct stakeholders—patients, insurance companies and medical practitioners—relying on the existing prevalent clinical problems and proven diagnostic guidelines [15, 17, 18]. In contrast, research institutes take up risks to find methods, diseases and cures that are unknown to date and explore large sets of new data in collaborative and country-spanning programs [6, 36]. Indeed, researchers have often distinguished between clinical institutions (healthcare, as in hospital or care institutions) [14, 18, 19] and research institutions [37–39]. This separation conveys the impression that they are not connected, yet as mentioned in the previous chapter, data is the blood that runs both in the veins of research and healthcare institutions [30, 40, 41]. Thus, we do not believe that the division of discovery and application to different kinds of organizations is the best way to approach this issue [21]. Surprisingly, data as a resource is only infrequently discussed in health IS literature on research and clinical institutions. Scientific institutions could not directly care for the data (re)use in healthcare [6], and while international patients exchange forums (Patients Like Me) are rather common by now [42], we know little about the involvement of clinicians and researchers in such areas. We think the assumptions behind this rather limited view of health-related matters should be challenged [5]. Data are the basis for both of these activities (research and clinical) and should be focused on [29, 33, 37, 43].

2.3 The Role of Third Parties in Serving New Healthcare Needs

As digitization and data sharing across countries facilitate the collaboration of multiple organizations, third parties can also take a role in previously less digitized fields such as healthcare [11, 44, 45]. A third-party firm as incumbent might act as an intermediary, as the involvement of third-party firms has several interesting benefits to healthcare:

First, with digital services, the venture is likely to aim for growth of its user base [46, 47] and establish a proposition to fit more than one organization. If successful, the complexity of adapting to the broad range of healthcare stakeholders could be avoided, and healthcare would be freed from the burden of deeply local IS transformation projects [13, 17, 21]. Meanwhile, it could have a greater effect—that is, reach more communities in healthcare overall. Second, ventures seek to establish new services and innovative solutions [48] and might compensate for limitations that existing healthcare institutions would have been hindered from overcoming once principles for their local IS systems are defined [14]. Third, while digital technology ventures have an interest in quickly appropriating value from their work and achieve growth [46, 49, 50], they also seek legitimacy from existing structures [51, 52]: experimenting and probing with the right standards of digitized data and technology in a strictly regulated field, can be applied with existing procedures that are key to healthcare organizations, too [52–54]. Within the realms of entrepreneurial ventures in other sectors, we find different strategies used to navigate in such new markets [54], but in healthcare, we know little about how such industry-spanning ventures bring different requirements together.

2.4 The Context of Genomic Health

In healthcare, all diseases are somehow mirrored in genetic components, and knowledge regarding genetic pathology is constantly growing [3]. Technological progress has lowered the cost of genome sequencing over time, and an increasing number of healthcare practitioners now use genetic data for diagnostics [44, 55].

Research institutions have access to large scalable infrastructure for use in basic research because sharing, collaborative problem solving and open experimentation are crucial for scientists when tackling complex questions [37]. The existing IS systems in research are tuned toward processing large amounts of data to find new patterns.

Data governance and quality in the related science repositories are not necessarily suitable for healthcare organizations [7]. Healthcare institutions need data from research to verify their findings [56, 57]. They may risk ignoring new knowledge or over- or underestimating the impact of their findings by finding other, similar cases [58, 59]. A genetic diagnosis that has not been validated primarily affects patients who run the risk of receiving an inaccurate diagnosis, living with uncured pain, or succumbing to death. Reference systems could be provided eventually, but would be general in purpose; establishing those will take years to come [23]. The activity of firms that prepare data and offer their exclusive services for commercial fees [7, 29] is not beneficial for countries that have little means to afford such access. However, the interest in simultaneous research and diagnostic use has increase the interest in entrepreneurial ventures in health [9, 13].

3 Case Description

Our case investigates an entrepreneurial venture in Switzerland that leverages openly available scientific data to support the intersection of research and healthcare practice. Established in 2013, the company provides services to over 200′000 users across the globe, namely Asia, North and South America and Europe. The case company vision is to create a genome data service for various interest groups with most essential information on genetic variants and their documentation, annotation, connection and classification. Users can access all services online via a web-based search application that leverages data pre-processed primarily from research sources, including more than 50 internationally acknowledged data repositories. These include RefSeq, ClinVar (National Center for Biological Information), gnomAD with more than 120 single investigators and contributing projects, and numerous additional data sources. The venture runs its service across 33 billion data points.

4 Methodology

Our goal is to provide explanations [60] that allow a better understanding of research data use in healthcare, second, for the role of entrepreneurial ventures in gaining legitimacy to establish the respective services to facilitate the data use. Thus, an in-depth understanding of the phenomenon requires us to consider multiple sources and means of data collection, as well as a long preparation phase in which we understand the context of the science, healthcare and genome data infrastructure. We present an unusual and revelatory case in health IS that is best understood using an embedded case study [61]. The uniqueness of our case shows in distinctive attributes, compared to other small ventures. First, there is the market success of this venture. It has enjoyed a two-digit growth rate in the last five years and has reached by now over 200′000 users. These users come from over 120 countries and underline that the venture's services address global needs. In this study, we expect to observe the factors that resulted in the venture's legitimacy, as the. We understand that the opposing needs and settings of science's and healthcare's data use are complex to address. In contrast to other entrepreneurial ventures that operate either for healthcare or science, our case company refers to both worlds and bridges a gap that is hardly visible in previous papers. This has been confirmed once we had talked to users, who refer to this venture's services as their main reference points. Finally, the venture has a pioneering status due to its comprehensiveness for over 50 data sources from different data sources and ease of use.

Having gathered extensive background knowledge from the industry, we observed the firm as a first unit of analysis for 2 years and included the users as a second unit of analysis. Hence, we exclude with relative certainty the possibility that "the issues that motivate our study are (sometimes) stated as imaginary pseudo-problems" [62].

4.1 Data Collection

The interview data were collected during semi-structured interviews, which were held in English. The questionnaire for the first round of interviews focused on the role of the employees (all in the leadership team), their motivation, and the description of the product and its function, users, as well as their relationship to research institutions and clinical institutions. Review meetings were held to confirm that the information collected was still valid as stated in the interviews and to ensure that users could be contacted. From 100 requests to users, 5 users signaled their willingness to participate in interview. These users were asked about their role, the module and actual use of the product and what they had used as a solution before they found it. All audio interviews were recorded and transcribed.

Table 1. Data collection

Level	Date	Description	Durat.	Record
Industry	02/2017–03/2020	Seminars on human genome diagnosis; shadowing laboratory staff in Germany	50 d (400 h)	Notes
	09/2018–08/2020	Workshops, attending product demos, roundtable with IS researchers in health in three countries	30 h	Rec.
Firm	10/2018–12/2019	Interview with CEO, 10/18	70 m	Rec.
		Interview with CTO, 02/19	30 m	Rec.
		Interview with PM, 02/19	45 m	Rec.
		Update with CEO, 04/19	30 m	Notes
		Update with Product manager, 12/19	20 m	Notes
Users	01–03/2020	Interviews with current users (MDs, researchers) of the firm's services in Mexico, France, Turkey, Spain and Iran	5 × 30 m	Rec.

4.2 Data Analysis

The analysis of all material was performed with MaxQDA. Applying inductive principles of Gioia [63], we created a rich set of codes, resulting in a pattern and a set of 1st order themes close to the informants' expressions. Though iterative literature and data analysis, higher-level, 2nd order themes were created. Finally, aggregated dimensions helped us explain how new services were created and legitimized by the ventures. Findings were also discussed with two non-authoring researchers.

5 Findings

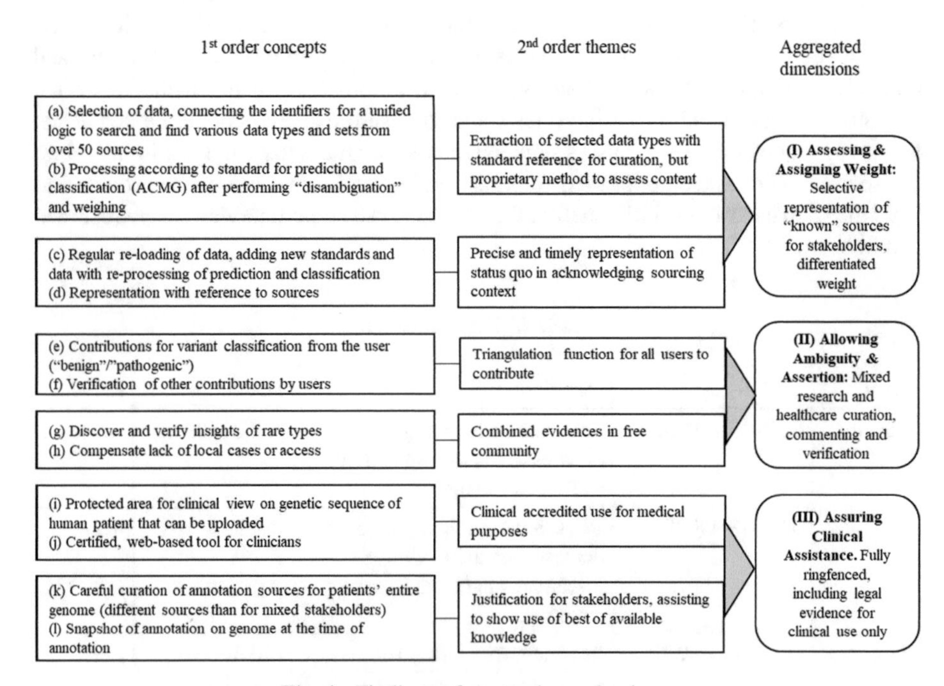

Fig. 1. Findings of venture's mechanisms

We present our findings referring to the 1st order concepts and proceed with the explanation of the aggregated dimensions in the next chapter.

5.1 Establishing Common Ground

The firm downloads the data from research repositories and processes all data in their proprietary physical servers in Switzerland. This data dump is then transformed to fit one database model with consolidated metadata (handled in what is like a mapping of different databases). This requires disambiguation, transformation of formats and cleansing of data. The firm stores the data and the associated meaning, including comments and relationships, in separated structures for faster retrieval of the required data in context of the command entered by users. Disease prediction mechanisms are applied and re-calculated daily, based on the insights from single databases.

(a) *One of the classic problems whenever you deal with sequences in biology each database has its own identifier. So, the same gene can be known in at least 20 different ways. (…) So, we will have tables that combine this information to allow me to go from ensemble transcript identifier to a the equivalent refseq identifier. That is a data process that we will set up. (…) That tells me where the gene is located, the start position the end position the exomes et cetera were found. literally an own table in the MySQL database. So, what we will add is the table that links the different identifiers that helps us communicate between the different data sources and databases.* (PM).

The service provides a threshold by which it shows disambiguated results for a disease-causing meaning of the variant, in addition the variant meaning is classified with an applied standard by American College of Medical Genetics (ACMG) for healthcare. All services in their Product (Product A) access the two structures but returns depending on the services. The CEO would not want to interfere with the domain knowledge of genetics. Instead, they engage with stakeholders of the platforms like ClinVar to ensure their offering is adjusted to a common understanding of the "industry standard". Based on the industry understanding and new tools being created, the users (often medical doctors, but also researchers at the same time) would see the firm provided updates in the service to do justice to new best practices in the community. All available data and analysis tools in the web interface include relationships to classification for healthcare, clinical meaning and various other attributes. Once the results were returned, there appeared numerous options for a drill down and exploration, which always returned the respective associated knowledge from different sources. The new information first went to the interface for researchers and free users: That interface was free to access, the firm uses it to test and validate new functions, standards it had imported and data it loaded.

(b,c) *It gives the – prediction average of 21 prediction tools. It makes an average. And I already, I trust its rather than a mutation tester (…) because revel includes an average prediction. So, I am very pleased to see Product A to include it in recent months* (User from Turkey).

5.2 Encouraging Global Contributions from Researchers and Clinicians

When users access the services, they do not only see the result and a visualization of the attached meaning (variant finding related information for example from a specific ethnographic group, publication on the variant, suggestions for variant-associated diseases, prediction tools for the variant effects…). The user would also be able to common on the finding with own contributions. In fact, finding comments of other medical professionals or researchers would be useful to verify the retrieved information and also correct the data where meaning (classification = pp is pathogenic, disease causing) could be put into context. That is important to know, because users would come from various backgrounds and the meaning of a variant in, say, leukemia would be different from a variant that is researched related to kidney cancer. Also, phenomena that span the globe could be identified and shared, as a user (researcher and medical doctor) from Mexico explained.

(e) *I have seen that others, other people in other laboratories, many Asian, they have seen some of our variants that we classified, I guess they are seeing them or they are recommending them also because that is a linked with their patients and our patients in these variants of uncertain significance* (User from Mexico).

This effect was carefully deployed by the venture due to its supporting effect for both quality and legitimacy in the community. A researcher who found others' comments (mostly also with a short note on the affiliation and background of the individual) would allow them to see which legitimation it had in eyes of other researchers of similar or other disciplines. Both firm and users explained us that the free services are "tuned" towards a reinforcement of clinical use – to both encourage contribution and to avoid too much free riding. Once the limitation of 100 free searches is consumed, the firm requests users to contribute back to the community with a classification of a variant. While the user is not forced to contribute, the firm leverages the implication (speed decreases) to encourage the user to contribute.

(f) *It actually helps a lot because all the feedback we get from the community helps us make it better. Especially as I said when there is a lot of room for interpretation of any data. We launched it here first. We get feedback from a thousand people let's say. It's of course a variant quality and we have to use our judgement to see who is liked and who is most likely to be more reputable* (CEO).

The set-up of the services considers possibilities of discovery, with is relevant where new insights appear (so called "de novo" findings, with little experience and data to refer to). The community was required to assess and contribute, either in the sources that the firm pulls in, or in the actual service interface to converse about the clarification and generation of new knowledge. For established findings on variants with associated diseases, the services encouraged refinement and re-use of knowledge which exists in various existing platforms through their commenting function and daily loads of new information. A user from France who faced a very rare condition in a patient was able to contact the respective user who had contributed to the classification of the candidate gene, who then allowed him to achieve a confirmation of the phenotype and diagnosis.

(g) *So today, we've been able to identify a new candidate gene, thanks to Product A, another variant which was disturbing because, the phenotype was quite severe and did not know if the variant was really pathogenic. And Product A was really useful to connect to the patient with the same variant* (User from France).

In addition, we found that the researcher and medical community included less privileged participants. Being deprived of other possibilities, the user from Iran regarded the possibility to collaborate via webservice as a unique opportunity to share his knowledge and benefit from a wider range of contributors he would otherwise not have access to.

(h) *Users can see my classification and it's easy for them to decide if a variant that they identified is pathogenic or not. I always try to do this, because I think it's helpful for others. But we are underdeveloped country, it is very hard for us to manage or design a system to help people, people in the country. But you as a developed country it's easy for you, you can collaborate all around the world.* (User from Iran).

5.3 Accounting for Distinct Clinical Requirements

Another service that the firm offered was specifically built for clinical use in diagnosis, it also had to be In Vitro Diagnostics (IVD) certified and was only available for a fee. This service serves as an extension to diagnostic analysis for doctors who had an entire patient sequence available. The firm checked for personal data attributes (names, address, etc.) and would delete such attributes if contained. The genome then could – only with one click- be annotated (show the different assessments and degrees of pathogenic variants, the associations with diseases and reference data from various sources). Then, the venture had ensured that the user would receive a snapshot which annotations at the time of the upload and annotation. As the knowledge of the human genome still progresses, the user needs a justification that he used the knowledge available at the time.

(l) *This is an advanced clinical platform. For example, it contains pictures such as audit trails. In other words, it tracks your uses of the platform in case there's ever any legal issue. (..) On Product A here, we keep updating the data. Here we keep updating the data for new analysis of new patients. If you have analyzed a patient the data is frozen exactly to the state of the day of the analysis, so that there's no issue afterwards. The knowledge that was available on that day allowed us to produce this report. You can also create a diagnostic report* (CEO).

6 Results and Discussion

Our study looks at a venture that uses more than 50 large genetic research sources to facilitate its use in a medical context. We find that the third party uses three mechanisms to legitimize their services [64]: 1) assessing and assigning weight, 2) allowing for ambiguity and assertion, and 3) assuring clinical assistance. These mechanisms are prerequisites that must be fulfilled for the venture to legitimize these data services. The venture applies them sequentially (1, 2, 3) and independently in order to successfully achieve legitimacy. We describe them in more detail.

6.1 Assessing and Assigning Weight

The venture represents itself as a partner to organizations to reduce uncertainty and provide support in standard-setting. In lack of one standard, they consolidate standards to apply with hand-selected, curated and processed data sources, which reduces also the uncertainty for the venture: A combined reference may be a factor enhancing timeliness and disambiguation as more contributions – also contradicting ones- are included [8, 65]. In overcoming the rigidity of a one-standard-system that would hold data in a local healthcare infrastructure, the venture as arbitrator separates the data itself from the context they are used in (literally saving them in different places) and shows data even when there are contradicting insights that come from various groups (example: from a rather breast-cancer-focused database from research, applying a data standard that mostly clinicians use). Data silos are a problem which is well known in clinical context, the low transparency of the related silos producing data [21, 66] is mitigated with this third party involvement. Leveraging known standards in their innovation of IS [67, 68] they can ensure a reference point of "known" trusted settings from clinical settings and at the same time keep generativity of data high [24].

6.2 Allowing for Ambiguity and Assertion

The users of the venture's services also work at the intersection of the institution types (as researchers and laboratory workers for clinical labs, or as medical doctors who pursue research interests, too). For the venture, research and practice are just as closely intertwined as genetics [5, 69]: This ambiguity of roles is acknowledged as the data can be enriched with new interpretations. In a dynamic field as genetics where new data and classification are added [70] the venture can only prove its legitimation of the service when it allows references to be established by its users who are discovering and using the data themselves in various settings [45, 52]. The online exchange on the venture's webservice are openly and globally accessible and allow of diverging opinions, uncertainties and connections like a non-medical or non-professional online forum [15, 33, 71]. That also provides a non-threatening context to clinicians and researchers, where they are not judged.

6.3 Assuring Clinical Assistance

Finally, the clinical service of the venture seeks to transfer physical medical standards to digital processes. The In Vitro Diagnostics (IVD) certified procedure, for which also humans have the responsibility in the end. Attaching evidence of the references used (data sources, annotated reports and justification documents for data used) it is closest to the procedure clinicians know [52]. Task-related procedures instead of fully integrated systems could support also external providers. Activities of such complexity, split into modules as the venture does, then, would only lead to small transformations that do not affect existing healthcare information systems [14].

In sum, that brings a totally new perspective to healthcare research, moving away from additions to the local healthcare practice to cross-border service that can fit into any healthcare system. Thus, the legitimation of new services can scale across sectors and countries. Instead of holding one person right away accountable for a comment, the venture promotes easy access for exchange [72]. The peer validation and feedback mechanisms remind us of the open source movement. The meaning of different findings is discussed and validated in the context of each user. That context can be very different and diverse, but with global contributions, weighs more [73]. Local healthcare information systems are much less flexible [8, 14]. There, a change project for installed base systems is likely to span years and would be unlikely to generate such scale as they work local, are locally regulated and have a limited set of data, too [14, 21].

7 Conclusion

Within a dynamic and data-rich environment, where research and clinical borders blur, third parties add to the healthcare landscape by offering new services. In our study, we observed a venture that addresses both research and healthcare stakeholders, who usually find themselves working in segregated systems without touchpoints. We find that the venture brings stakeholders from both sides together via their new services. The case shows that different mechanisms of legitimation are enabled through digital technology through mirroring what has been considered a relevant reference (e.g. framework, certification) in clinical practice. Moreover, as the three mechanisms work independently from established national healthcare systems but greatly enhance the work of clinicians, we see these as modular elements that can scale legitimation of new services. With these contributions, we call for more research on the role of ventures as intermediaries within healthcare in a dynamic and complex field such as genetics.

Our findings have clear limitations. In our single case study, we reveal first mechanisms that help us understand how a venture uses technology, both scientific and healthcare communities and established certifications to legitimate its services. More research on other organizations increases the external credibility of our findings; focusing on a single case by necessity leads into questions about transferability of findings to other cases. As our findings may not apply to all ventures, we add three boundary conditions that describe how to identify "similar" cases. We hope they help guide other researchers on how to determine the applicability of our findings [74]:

- (1) Use of technology is appropriate and configured by one or more stakeholders (decide how it should be done)
- (2) Involvement of communities is feasible and allowed (to delegate the legitimation mechanisms in part to others)
- (3) The necessity of validation and achieve legitimacy is open to a range of legitimacy values (in our study: either clinical, scientific exploration etc.)

If one of these prerequisites is not met, the degree of legitimation we have shown in our study needs to be re-assessed. However, we see no reason to not to believe that the mechanisms identified in this single case study would be dramatically different in other potential organizations. Thus, we hope to deliver a basis for future work on data ventures.

References

1. Fichman, R.G., Kohli, R., Krishnan, R.: The role of information systems in healthcare: current research and future trends. Inf. Syst. Res. **22**, 419–428 (2011). https://doi.org/10.1287/isre.1110.0382
2. He, K.Y., Ge, D., He, M.M.: Big data analytics for genomic medicine. Int. J. Mol. Sci. **18**, 1–18 (2017). https://doi.org/10.3390/ijms18020412
3. National Institute of Health: Understanding Human Genetics. https://www.ncbi.nlm.nih.gov/books/NBK20363/.
4. Matthijs, G., et al.: Guidelines for diagnostic next-generation sequencing. Eur. J. Hum. Genet. **24**, 2–5 (2016). https://doi.org/10.1038/ejhg.2015.226
5. Romanow, D., Cho, S., Straub, D.: Editor's comments riding the wave: past trends and future directions for health IT research. Manag. Inf. Syst. Q. **36**, iii–x (2012)
6. Ribes, D., Finholt, T.: The long now of technology infrastructure: articulating tensions in development*. J. Assoc. Inf. Syst. **10**, 375–398 (2009)
7. Vassilakopoulou, P., Skorve, E., Aanestad, M.: Enabling openness of valuable information resources: Curbing data subtractability and exclusion. Inf. Syst. J. **29**, 768–786 (2019). https://doi.org/10.1111/isj.12191

8. Vassilakopoulou, P., Skorve, E., Aanestad, M.: A commons perspective on genetic data governance: the case of BRCA data. In: Proceedings of the 24th European Conference on Information Systems (ECIS) (2016).
9. Rothe, H., Jarvenpaa, S.L., Penninger, A.A.: How do entrepreneurial firms appropriate value in bio data infrastructures: an exploratory qualitative study. In: Proceedings of the 27th European Conference on Information Systems, p. 17 (2019)
10. Recker, J., von Briel, F.: The future of digital entrepreneurship research: existing and emerging opportunities. In: Proceedings of the 40th International Conference on Information Systems, pp. 1–9 (2019)
11. Benner, M.J., Tushman, M.L.: Reflections on the 2013 decade award - "exploitation, exploration, and process management: the productivity dilemma revisited" ten years later. Acad. Manag. Rev. **40**, 497–514 (2015). https://doi.org/10.5465/amr.2015.0042
12. Lakhani, K.R., Panetta, J.A.: The principles of distributed innovation. Innov. Technol. Governance, Glob. **2**, 97–112 (2007). https://doi.org/10.1162/itgg.2007.2.3.97
13. Blaschke, M.: Socio-technical complexity in digital platforms: the revelatory case of helix nebula: the science cloud. In: Urbach, N., Röglinger, M. (eds.) Digitalization Cases. Management for Professionals, p. 427. Springer, Cham (2019). https://doi.org/10.1007/978-3-319-95273-4_9
14. Aanestad, M., Grisot, M., Hanseth, O., Vassilakopoulou, P.: Information Infrastructures and the challenge of the installed base. In: Aanestad, M., Grisot, M., Hanseth, O., Vassilakopoulou, P. (eds.) Information Infrastructures within European Health Care, p. 263. Springer, Cham (2017). https://doi.org/10.1007/978-3-319-51020-0_30
15. Aanestad, M., Jensen, T.B.: Building nation-wide information infrastructures in healthcare through modular implementation strategies. J. Strateg. Inf. Syst. **20**, 161–176 (2011). https://doi.org/10.1016/j.jsis.2011.03.006
16. Grisot, M., Vassilakopoulou, P.: Infrastructures in healthcare: the interplay between generativity and standardization. Int. J. Med. Inform. **82**, e170–e179 (2012). https://doi.org/10.1016/j.ijmedinf.2012.08.010
17. Rodon, J., Silva, L.: Exploring the formation of a healthcare information infrastructure: hierarchy or meshwork? J. Assoc. Inf. Syst. **16**, 394–417 (2015). https://doi.org/10.17705/1jais.00395
18. Thorseng, A., Jensen, T.B.: Building national infrastructures for patientcentred digital services. In: 23rd European Conference on Information Systems (ECIS 2015), 2015-May, 0–15 (2015)
19. Constantinides, P., Barrett, M.: Information infrastructure development and governance as collective action. Inf. Syst. Res. (2015). https://doi.org/10.1287/isre.2014.0542
20. Bernardi, R.: Health Information systems and accountability in Kenya: a structuration theory perspective. J. Assoc. Inf. Syst. **18**, 931–958 (2018)
21. Bygstad, B., Hanseth, O., Le, D.T.: From it silos to integrated solutions. a study in e-health complexity. In: 23rd European Conference on Information Systems (ECIS 2015). 2015 May, 0–15 (2015)
22. Yoo, Y., Henfridsson, O., Lyytinen, K.: The new organizing logic of digital innovation: an agenda for information systems research. Inf. Syst. Res. **21**, 724–735 (2010). https://doi.org/10.1287/isre.1100.0322
23. Birney, E., Vamathevan, J., Goodhand, P.: Genomics in healthcare: GA4GH looks to 2022. bioRxiv. 203554 (2017)
24. Grisot, M., Vassilakopoulou, P.: Infrastructures in healthcare: the interplay between generativity and standardization. Int. J. Med. Inform. **82**, 170–179 (2013). https://doi.org/10.1016/j.ijmedinf.2012.08.010

25. Moorthy, V., Restrepo, H., Ana Maria Preziosii, M.-P., Swaminathan, S.: Data sharing for novel corona virus (COVID-19). Bull. World Health Organ. **98** (2020). https://doi.org/10.2471/BLT.20.251561
26. Braa, J., Hanseth, O., Heywood, A., Mohammed, W., Shaw, V.: Developing health information systems in developing countries: the flexible standards strategy. MIS Q. **31**, 381–402 (2007). https://doi.org/10.2307/25148796
27. Gebre-Mariam, M., Bygstad, B.: Digitalization mechanisms of health management information systems in developing countries. Inf. Organ. **29**, 1–22 (2019). https://doi.org/10.1016/j.infoandorg.2018.12.002
28. Eichler, G.: A recipe for insights (2018)
29. Jarvenpaa, S.L., Markus, M.L.: Data perspective in digital platforms: three tales of genetic platforms. In: Proceedings of the 51st Hawaii International Conference on System Sciences, pp. 4574–4583 (2018)
30. Middleton, A.: Society and personal genome data. Hum. Mol. Genet. **27**, 8–13 (2018). https://doi.org/10.1093/hmg/ddy084
31. Sittig, D.F., et al.: Grand challenges in clinical decision support. J. Biomed. Inform. **41**, 387–392 (2008). https://doi.org/10.1016/j.jbi.2007.09.003
32. Ayorech, Z., et al.: Publication trends over 55 years of behavioral genetic research. Behav. Genet. **46**(5), 603–607 (2016). https://doi.org/10.1007/s10519-016-9786-2
33. Kallinikos, J., Tempini, N.: Patient data as medical facts: social media practices as a foundation for medical knowledge creation. Inf. Syst. Res. **25**, 817–833 (2014). https://doi.org/10.1287/isre.2014.0544
34. Barrett, M., Oborn, E., Orlikowski, W.: Creating value in online communities: the sociomaterial configuring of strategy, platform, and stakeholder engagement. Inf. Syst. Res. **27**, 704–723 (2016). https://doi.org/10.1287/isre.2016.0648
35. Yoo, Y., Boland, R.J., Lyytinen, K., Majchrzak, A.: Organizing for innovation in the digitized world. Organ. Sci. **23**, 1398–1408 (2012). https://doi.org/10.1287/orsc.1120.0771
36. Nelson, B.: Empty archives. Nature **461**, 160–163 (2009)
37. Dougherty, D., Dunne, D.D.: Digital science and knowledge boundaries in complex innovation. Organ. Sci. **23**, 1467–1484 (2012). https://doi.org/10.1287/orsc.1110.0700
38. Mc Namara, P., Baden-Fuller, C.: Shareholder returns and the exploration-exploitation dilemma: R&D announcements by biotechnology firms. Res. Policy **36**, 548–565 (2007). https://doi.org/10.1016/j.respol.2007.02.012
39. Perkmann, M., Schildt, H.: Open data partnerships between firms and universities: the role of boundary organizations. Res. Policy. **44**, 1133–1143 (2015). https://doi.org/10.1016/j.respol.2014.12.006
40. Kodama, Y., Shumway, M., Leinonen, R.: The sequence read archive: explosive growth of sequencing data. Nucleic Acids Res. **40**, 2011–2013 (2012). https://doi.org/10.1093/nar/gkr854
41. Vassy, J.L., Korf, B.R., Green, R.C.: How to know when physicians are ready for genomic medicine. Sci. Transl. Med. **7** (2015). https://doi.org/10.1126/scitranslmed.aaa2401
42. Kallinikos, J., Aaltonen, A., Marton, A.: The ambivalent ontology of digital artifacts. MIS Q. **37**, 357–370 (2013). https://doi.org/10.25300/misq/2013/37.2.02
43. Tuomi, I.: Data is more than knowledge : Implications of the reversed knowledge. J. Manag. Inf. Syst. **16**, 107–121 (2000)
44. November, J.: More than Moore's mores: computers, genomics, and the embrace of innovation. J. Hist. Biol. **51**(4), 807–840 (2018). https://doi.org/10.1007/s10739-018-9539-6
45. Gao, C.: Strategy and Entrepreneurship in Nascent Industries (2018)
46. DeSantola, A., Gulati, R.: Scaling: organizing and growth in entrepreneurial ventures. Acad. Manag. Ann. **11**, 640–668 (2017)

47. Siegel, R., Siegel, E., Macmillan, I.C.: Characteristics distinguishing high-growth ventures. J. Bus. Ventur. **8**, 169–180 (1993)
48. Rindova, V., Barry, D., Ketchen, D.J.J.: Entrepreneuring as emancipation. Acad. Manag. Rev. **34**, 477–491 (2016). https://doi.org/10.5465/AMR.2009.40632647
49. Boudreau, K.J., Lakhani, K.R.: Using the crowd as an innovation partner spotlight. Harv. Bus. Rev. April 2013, 61–69 (2013)
50. Miric, M., Boudreau, K.J., Jeppesen, L.B.: Protecting their digital assets: the use of formal & informal appropriability strategies by App developers. Res. Policy **48** (2019). https://doi.org/10.1016/j.respol.2019.01.012
51. Ruef, M.: The emergence of organizational forms: a community ecology approach 1. Am. J. Sociol. **106**, 658–714 (2000)
52. Navis, C., Glynn, M.A.: Legitimate distinctiveness and the entrepreneurial identity: influence on investor judgments of new venture plausibility. Acad. Manag. Rev. **36**, 479–499 (2011)
53. Bremner, R.P., Eisenhardt, K.M.: Experimentation, bottlenecks, and organizational form: Innovation and growth in the nascent drone industry. Working paper, Stanford Technology Ventures Program (2019)
54. McDonald, R.M., Eisenhardt, K.M.: Parallel play: startups, nascent markets, and effective business-model design. Adm. Sci. Q. **65**, 483–523 (2020)
55. West, J.: Open source platforms beyond software: from ICT to biotechnology. Entrep. Innov. Platforms. **37**, 337–30 (2017). https://doi.org/10.1108/S0742-332220170000037011
56. Cook-Deegan, R., Conley, J.M., Evans, J.P., Vorhaus, D.: The next controversy in genetic testing: clinical data as trade secrets? Eur. J. Hum. Genet. **21**, 585–588 (2013). https://doi.org/10.1038/ejhg.2012.217
57. Cook-Deegan, R., McGuire, A.L.: Moving beyond Bermuda: sharing data to build a medical information commons. Genome Res. **27**, 897–901 (2017). https://doi.org/10.1101/gr.216911.116
58. Davis, C.: mBLAST: keeping up with the sequencing explosion for (Meta) genome analysis. J. Data Mining Genom. Proteom. **04**, 1–31 (2013). https://doi.org/10.4172/2153-0602.1000135
59. Merton, R.K.: Sociology of Science. Polit. Sociol. **1**, 115–126 (1942)
60. Gregor, S.: The nature of theory in information systems. MIS Q. Manag. Inf. Syst. **30**, 611–642 (2006). https://doi.org/10.2307/25148742
61. Yin, R.K.: Case study research and applications. Design and method. Sage, Los Angeles (2018).
62. Van de Ven, A.H.: Grounding the research phenomenon. J. Chang. Manag. **16**, 265–270 (2016). https://doi.org/10.1080/14697017.2016.1230336
63. Gioia, D.A., Corley, K.G., Hamilton, A.L.: Seeking qualitative rigor in inductive research: notes on the gioia methodology. Organ. Res. Methods. **16**, 15–31 (2013). https://doi.org/10.1177/1094428112452151
64. Star, S.L.: The ethnography of infrastructure. Am. Behav. Sci. **43**, 377–391 (1999). https://doi.org/10.1177/00027649921955326
65. Yang, S., Lincoln, S.E., Kobayashi, Y., Nykamp, K., Nussbaum, R.L., Topper, S.: Sources of discordance among germ-line variant classifications. Clin. Var. Nat. Publ. Gr. **19**, (2017). https://doi.org/10.1038/gim.2017.60
66. Kohli, R., Kettinger, W.J.: Informating the clan: controlling physicians' costs and outcomes. MIS Q. Manag. Inf. Syst. **28**, 363–394 (2004). https://doi.org/10.2307/25148644
67. Garud, R., Schildt, H.A., Lant, T.: Entrepreneurial storytelling, future expectations, and the paradox of legitimacy. Organ. Sci. **25**, 1479–1492 (2014)
68. Garud, R., Tuertscher, P., Van De Ven, A.H.: Perspectives on innovation processes. Acad. Manag. Ann. **7**, 775–819 (2013). https://doi.org/10.1080/19416520.2013.791066

69. Goes, P.B.: Editor's comment: big data and IS research. MIS Q. **38**, iii–viii (2014)
70. Gao, C., McDonald, R.M.: Shaping Nascent Industries: Innovation Strategy and Regulatory Uncertainty in Personal Genomics, Harvard Business School Publication, Barcelona (2020)
71. Alaimo, C., Kallinikos, J.: Computing the everyday: social media as data platforms. Inf. Soc. **33**, 175–191 (2017). https://doi.org/10.1080/01972243.2017.1318327
72. Schlagwein, D., Conboy, K., Feller, J., Leimeister, J.M., Morgan, L.: "Openness" with and without information technology: a framework and a brief history. J. Inf. Technol. **32**, 297–305 (2017). https://doi.org/10.1057/s41265-017-0049-3
73. Krogh, G., Von Spaeth, S.: The open source software phenomenon : characteristics that promote research. J. Strateg. Inf. Syst. 16, 236–253 (2007). https://doi.org/10.1016/j.jsis.2007.06.001
74. Rodon, J., Sesé, F.: Towards a framework for the transferability of results in IS qualitative research. Sprouts Working Paper Information System, p. 8 (2008)

Patients' Attitudes Toward Apps for Management of a Chronic Disease

Paul Alpar[1(✉)] and Thomas Driebe[2]

[1] Department of Mathematics and Computer Science, Philipps-University of Marburg, Marburg, Germany
alpar@staff.uni-marburg.de
[2] School of Business and Economics, Philipps-University of Marburg, Marburg, Germany
driebe@staff.uni-marburg.de

Abstract. We model the intention of patients to use a telehealth app for the management of a chronic disease. Our model integrates the health belief model with a model of information technology acceptance to reflect the technology- and health-related parts of the intention. The intention of non-using patients to use the app is influenced by their hedonic motivation and social influence. An analysis of sub-groups reveals deeper insights: Patients without access to the app would use it based on the expected performance and their self-efficacy. Patients who do not use the app despite having access to it would use it if influenced by their social environment and if they perceive their disease to be severe. A third group does not even know whether they can use the app. The results show that proper education of patients and people influencing them is necessary even in the case of chronic diseases.

Keywords: Chronic disease management · M-Health · Telehealth · Technology adoption · Patient behavior

1 Introduction

Treatment of chronic diseases has been continuously improved over the last decades, with an increasing focus on patient self-care [1]. Chronic diseases differ from acute diseases (that last only a short time) in their impact on patients as well as on the healthcare system and are the most common cause of death worldwide [2]. M-health is well suited to support chronic disease patients [3] and it is expected to improve their treatment adherence [2]. It has also been shown analytically that m-health can be superior to the office-visit model with respect to patient's average life expectancy and expected total lifetime utility [4]. The benefits come mostly from additional opportunities for intervention by the health care provider. We concentrate on hemophilia, as an exemplary chronic disease. It is often "neglected" by research on m-health [5] because the number of patients is comparably low at 400,000 hemophiliacs [6] vs. 400,000,000 diabetics [7] worldwide. The hemophilia treatment is named replacement therapy because it replaces the blood clotting factors missing in hemophiliacs. Clotting factors help to close wounds

F. Ahlemann et al. (Eds.): WI 2021, LNISO 46, pp. 22–37, 2021.
https://doi.org/10.1007/978-3-030-86790-4_2

and stop internal bleedings. The required substance for hemophilia treatment, a synthetic blood clotting factor, is costly and prone to overconsumption, since the precisely needed dose is difficult to determine, but overdosing has no negative health consequences [8]. In a study regarding the outpatient expenditures for 34,000 children with chronic diseases in California, only 145 children from this group had hemophilia but they accounted for 41% (195$ million) of the state spending for this group [9]. M-health supported documentation offers advantages to patients and the health care system, as they provide data about the success of different therapy approaches and allow for a more precise dosage and thus less overconsumption. This study uses combined models from health psychology and information systems to analyze which conditions facilitate the application of m-health for support of chronic diseases, esp. hemophilia.

2 Background

2.1 Hemophilia

Hemophiliacs are prone to longer bleedings after injuries and possible internal bleedings, e.g., inside joints or the brain. This may result in disabling arthropathy and, in severe cases, death [8]. Regular treatment (replacement therapies) produces better results concerning the prevention of arthropathy (compared to on-demand), but patients may not comply with the therapy and health care providers are hesitant to finance it [8]. This study researches hemophiliacs in Germany.

Chronic disease management (CDM) apps, here specifically for hemophilia treatment, are an example of m-health support. Since September 2020, hemophiliacs in Germany receive their prescription from hematologists and their factor supply in pharmacies. Hematologists are organized in hemophilia treatment centers (HTC), which range from big comprehensive care centers with approx. 40 patients and with specialized personal to individual physicians with some hemostaseological experience. They are required by the German blood transfusion law to report their patients' factor usage to the German Hemophilia Registry (DHR). For this purpose, HTCs depend on an accurate documentation by the patients or their legal guardian. Patients also report relevant occurrences like joint bleedings.

Now, most patients document their factor usage in a paper notebook, which the nurses in the HTC use to update the patient data on each visit. This paper-based documentation is prone to several errors. Adherence to documentation and treatment is difficult to verify, since the only time patients must show their records is when visiting their physician, which can be just once a year. Patients often make updates just before the visit, which can result in wrong dates, for example. The notebooks do not provide a standardized way of recording joint bleedings. Therefore, patients improvise and often do not enter information that is precise enough.

Alternatively, two apps have been separately developed to facilitate the documentation via easier input (scan of the factor charge number) and digital data transfer to the centers. These apps offer additional features and advantages. For example, physicians can utilize them to monitor patients' adherence to regular prophylactic therapy. Disabling arthropathy as the most common consequence of hemophilia is also easier prevented by CDM apps, since they allow to precisely record the bleedings: the patient simply taps the location of the bleeding on a body drawing, which provides the physician with an overview of all occurrences. In addition, the data can be immediately forwarded to a hematologist. The collected data can also help to better monitor the cost effectiveness of different treatment regimens [10]. HTCs need to have the corresponding infrastructure, and therefore, support only one of the apps or none at all. Both apps are certified medical products.

To summarize, hemophilia is different from chronic diseases like diabetes, because on one hand an exact tracing of the medication taken is needed (in the past blood transfusions were sometimes contaminated with diseases of the blood donors). On the other hand, overdosage "only" burdens insurances and society but not patients.

2.2 Research Problem

There is no law in Germany that mandates the use of an app. Even if an HTC supports an app, it is not allowed to demand its use from a patient or to put a non-user into any disadvantage compared to patients who use the app. Also, no physician can deny treatment if a patient does not want to use the app. Each patient can decide absolutely freely whether to use the app. Models of technology acceptance are well-suited to describe this voluntary use of an app. One of the most advanced and comprehensive of such models is UTAUT2 (Unified Theory of Acceptance and Use of Technology 2). It is based on several previous behavior models like the technology acceptance model (TAM), TAM2, and the theory of reasoned action (TRA) [11]. Its constructs cover IT aspects as well as some psychological aspects. However, it does not contain health-related constructs which can be very important in the context of chronic diseases.

Psychology of medicine has developed models that take health believes into account, specifically related to an illness or behavior which can lead to an illness. These models can be used to measure intentions of people to change their behavior or to measure the effectiveness of activities that try to make people adhere to medical advice. The measures need not demand any use of technology by patients. For example, warnings about consequences of smoking on cigarette packages do not expect any technology use. For such purposes models like the health belief model (HBM) have been developed [12]. The HBM was originally developed to explain and predict the acceptance of medical recommendations [13]. It assumes that, health-related actions depend on an individual's perception of his own health status and assessment of these actions. This perception is formed by how threatened individuals feel and how beneficial the possible action may be. The threat is determined by the perceived seriousness and susceptibility of the disease, and the decision is further weighted against costs and benefits of the action. Additionally, the decision is influenced by cues to action, represented by health events or physician advice [13].

Our research goal is to systematically develop an adoption model for the use of an app in the context of a chronic disease. The app helps to manage a life-threatening disease. The resulting model can be applied to gain knowledge in this specific context. Modeling the use of treatment-supporting apps for (chronic) diseases, requires consideration of IT and health-related issues [14].

In some cases, older acceptance models are used despite the existence of newer models with better conceptual coverage. Leanness of the combined model was often achieved by simply omitting some constructs. This is problematic because important concepts may be missing, and explanations of the problem can be biased. TAM and HBM show conceptual similarity between their constructs (e.g., perceived usefulness) [15]. We create a combined model systematically by combining constructs which are conceptually similar but retain the conceptual coverage of HBM and newer acceptance models. This way, we achieve an adequate conceptual coverage and a relatively lean model.

3 Model Building

We start with health-related constructs provided by the HBM, then continue with shared constructs and discuss the technology-related constructs from UTAUT2 at the end.

The HBM-exclusive part of the model contains the health-specific constructs perceived susceptibility and perceived seriousness. They may be viewed as an individual's threat appraisal, which is part of several HBMs [12]. It is an essential part of health behavior, since every coping behavior (e.g., using an m-health app) needs to be induced by a perceived threat [16]. The versions of HBM are not consistent in the operationalization of the links between susceptibility, seriousness, threat, and behavior [17]. Following previous studies, we measure susceptibility and seriousness as separate dimensions to achieve a more differentiated prediction [16]. High values of susceptibility and seriousness, positively influenced the behavioral intention in other cases [18]. The construct of perceived threat originates in psychological research about fear, where the influence of fear on behavior change is described in various contexts, including health [16]. The perceived seriousness is viewed as the most common variable [16] and has consistently been found to facilitate behavior change [19]. Accordingly, we hypothesize that a hemophiliac perceiving his illness as more severe will more likely use the digital documentation:

H1: Perceived seriousness has a positive effect on usage intention.

Perceived susceptibility constitutes the second component of fear [16, 20]. E.g., it is used in the research of preventive breast cancer mammography [20]. The construct has consistently shown to facilitate behavior change, the more a subject was aware of and felt susceptible to a disease [12]. It does not make sense to consider the fear of getting hemophilia, because it is hereditary. In our study, threat is specified as the threat of disabling arthropathy caused by joint bleeding since this is a common and dangerous consequence of hemophilia. If a patient perceives himself as more susceptible to suffer from joint bleeding, he is more likely to switch to m-health documentation in order to better monitor and prevent the bleedings Therefore, we propose:

H2: Perceived susceptibility has a positive effect on usage intention.

Self-efficacy describes the degree of a person's ability to perform an intended behavior [21]. It is an effective predictor of behavioral intention and has been later added to the HBM [12], while it was included in the Protection Motivation Theory (PMT), an alternative to HBM, from the beginning [16]. Users confident in their ability to effectively use technology will be more likely to use that technology. This positive influence has been validated in general models of technology acceptance [22] as well as in studies focusing on m-health [12]. It has also been found to be the most decisive predictor in studies researching long-term health behavior, e.g., dietary behavior [23]. Here, self-efficacy describes a patient's ability to intuitively use smartphone apps. It is assumed that a patient, who perceives himself as efficient in the use of apps and smartphones in general, is more likely to also use the smartphone-based documentation.

H3: Self-efficacy has a positive effect on usage intention.

Next, we discuss constructs that are found both in HBM and UTAUT2. The integration of these models allows for a reduction of latent constructs where they conceptually overlap. The similarity of the constructs can be derived from their definition and operationalization. The HBM constructs are viewed as easy to adapt for specific use [17] and they have been shown to be valuable predictors using alternative operationalizations [13].

Performance expectancy is defined as the degree to which an individual believes that using a system will help him to increase performance [22]. It proved to be a strong predictor of behavioral intention in studies with a healthcare context [24]. Perceived benefits in the HBM were defined as the likelihood of an action to be taken depending on an individual's perception of the effectiveness of the action [13]. Therefore, both are perceptions about effectiveness, differentiating only between an action and (IT) system. In our study, the action is defined as using a system (the app), therefore the constructs are similar. This notion of benefit has been used by various researchers to predict health behavior [13, 18]. Here, benefits provided by the app are, for example, improved bleeding monitoring and facilitated exchange with hematologists. An extensive literature review in the domain of telehealth treatment of chronic diseases identified perceptions of effectiveness as a possible facilitator to tele-homecare programs [25]. We assume, therefore, that an increase in the perceived benefits of an app-based documentation will increase a patient's intention to use it.

H4: Performance expectancy has a positive effect on usage intention.

Effort expectancy describes the ease of using a technology [11]. Perceived barriers are defined as potential impeding aspects of a health action [13]. These can be described as "difficulty of use" which is the opposite of ease of use. However, both descriptions are guided by the same idea and can be operationalized in the same way. Documentation apps face two types of barriers: the software must match the technical abilities of users and their health knowledge. Technical barriers can be slow loading and responses while a medical barrier may be the use of terms the patient is not familiar with. The apps need to present easy interactions that give medically and technically clear instructions. We assume that if the user expects such problems, his intention to use the app will decline.

H5: Effort expectancy has a negative effect on usage intention.

Social Influence (e.g., advice from family, friends, or physicians) has been found to be another strong predictor of behavior intention [11]. In a recent study on patient adoption decisions of a diabetes management app, it had the strongest positive influence [26].

Concerning social influence, it is described as the degree to which an individual perceives that important others believe he or she should use a new system [22], while the cues to action encompass influence exerted by significant others [17]. Thus, the constructs may be considered to be similar. Social influence is also found in general behavioral theories like TRA and TPB, where subjective norm is included as perceived social pressure to perform a certain behavior [27]. Advice is usually a positive, awareness-raising factor and will, therefore, exert a positive influence [12]. In previous studies, social influence has sometimes not been an important factor for determining behavior regarding health technology [28], but those studies mainly applied UTAUT to health care professionals. As this study focuses on patients, who normally heed their physician's advice, social influence is expected to take a more significant role. Another study showed physicians to be viewed as reliable sources concerning health app suggestions [29]. In sum, this study assumes advice from physicians and/or friends to increase the intention of patients to use smartphone documentation, since they want to satisfy their social group's expectations.

H6: Social influence has a positive effect on usage intention.

The technology-exclusive part of our model consists of the UTAUT2 constructs facilitating conditions and hedonic motivation. Facilitating conditions describe the availability of physical resources aiding in the use of m-health (e.g., smartphone) as well as support by friends or an introduction course given by the care center [11]. They have been found to reliably predict behavior intention in a health-care context [12]. Here, facilitating resources specifically include an easy to use smartphone and the possibility to ask for help when using the app. We assume that better resources and support will increase the likelihood of using an app-based documentation.

H7: Facilitating conditions have a positive effect on usage intention.

Hedonic motivation describes the fun or pleasure derived from using a technology [11], m-health in this case. It represents an intrinsic motivation within UTAUT [11]. Although our study is conducted in the context of CDM, hedonic motivation may be present because apps represent a much newer technology than paper-based documentation. Patients may find satisfaction in using new technology for managing their disease. Therefore, a patient experiencing more pleasure in using apps is expected to be more likely to use an app-based documentation:

H8: Hedonic motivation has a positive effect on usage intention.

UTAUT2 further proposes price value and habit as constructs. Price value is excluded, since the sample only used m-health apps distributed by the HTCs free of charge. Habit was dropped from the model, since there is no possibility for patients to use a similar app before adoption and develop correlated habits. While fitness or health tracking apps also serve tracking purposes, their use is not in a life-threatening context. The consequences of not using them for days are usually not severe. All moderators proposed by UTAUT2 were included except gender, because hemophilia only affects males.

Figure 1 presents the complete research model while making the origins of concepts explicit. It also shows where previous models are overlapping and can be made leaner in our case.

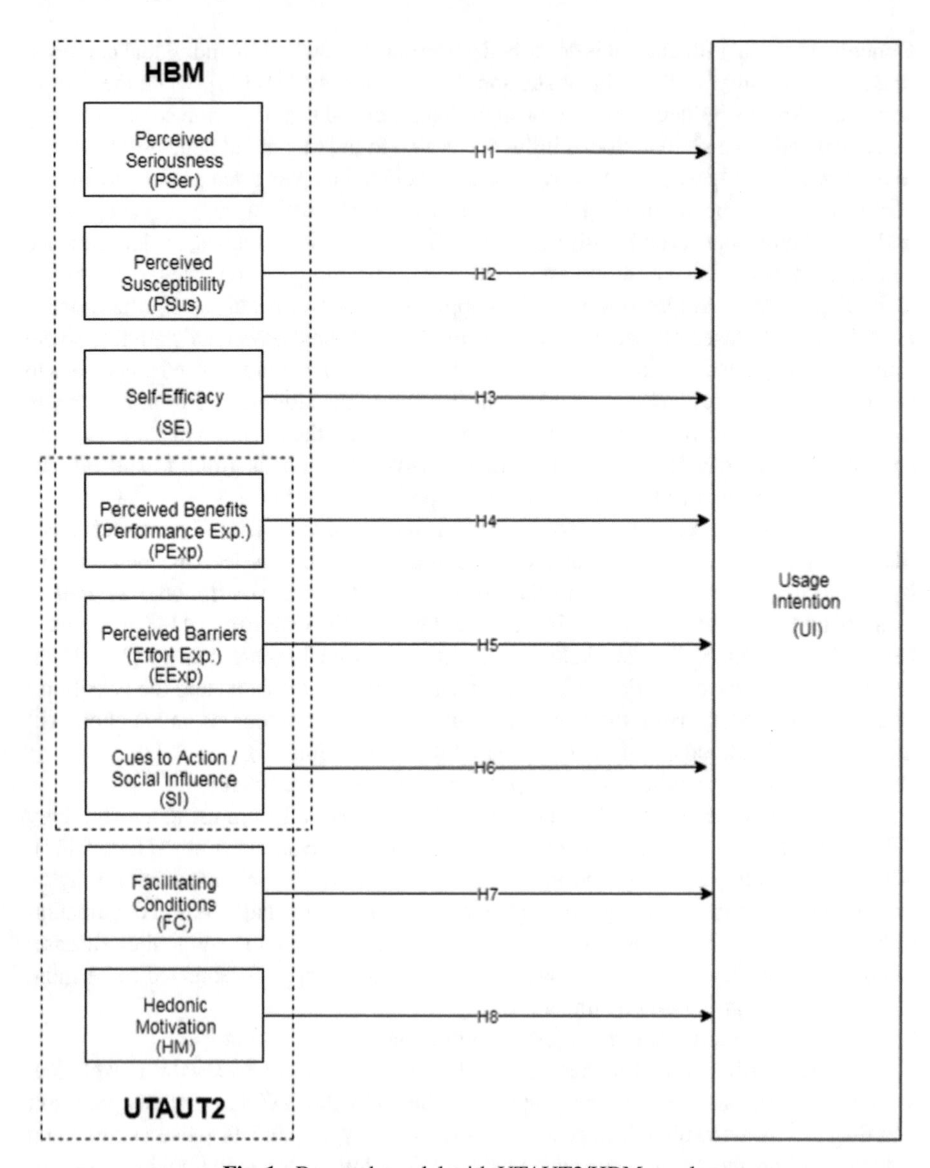

Fig. 1. Research model with UTAUT2/HBM overlap

4 Sample and Data Collection

To test the proposed model and hypotheses, a survey was conducted with support of the two major German hemophilia associations of patients. They have more than 3250 members in sum [30, 31] which includes patients, their relatives, and physicians. The unique number of patients is not exactly known; we estimate it, based on talks with experts, at about 3000. The associations aided in distributing the survey to their members via mail, e-mail, or as a link on their home page but no follow-up was possible because respondents were absolutely anonymous. The e-mail contained a link to the online version of the survey, while the mail contained a printed version with a return envelope. We received 144 responses in total. This amounts to less than 5% of the population of unique patients in both associations. There are three possible reasons for the relatively low return. First, most current users of the app did not care to participate since they are aware of m-health in this case. Second, patients with the mild or moderate form of hemophilia rarely use hemophilia medication and barely document anything. Third, due to the rare occurrence of hemophilia relative to other chronic diseases, the patients are frequently asked to participate in surveys for medical research. The survey was designed to differentiate between users and non-users and contained accordingly different questionnaire sections for them. From the total, 71 respondents were using an app. These patients perceive to have a significantly better knowledge about hemophilia than non-users. In this research, we were interested in the 73 respondents who do not use any app to document their illness, yet. Eleven responses were excluded because of suspicious answer patterns (always the same answer) and contradictory answers to reverse questions, leaving n = 62.

5 Measures and Instruments

In addition to the questions related to the above research model, several socio-cultural and health-specific items were asked. The additional questions include whether the survey was answered by the hemophiliac himself or his legal guardian, the age, and the way they document their disease now (app or paper). Furthermore, information on an individual's knowledge about hemophilia was collected since it was determined as a possible variable in health behavior [32]. The participants were also asked to state their objectively measured severity of hemophilia. Table 1 provides insight into the sample.

Table 1. Sample statistics

Variable	Mean (SD) / distribution	Measurement
Age	39.6 (19.84)	
Knowledge by severity	Mild: 2.33 (0.71) Moderate: 2.71 (0.76) Severe: 2.94 (0.73)	Not existing (1) – Perfect (5)
Degree of hemophilia	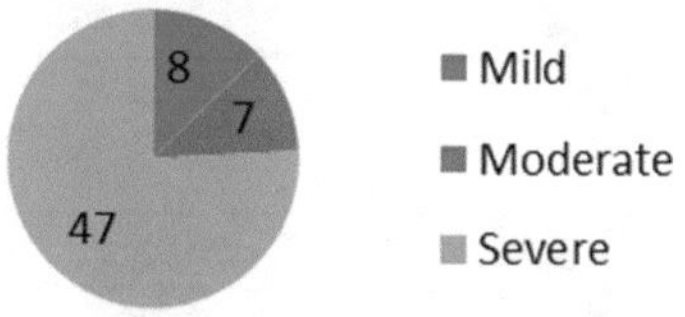 8, 7, 47 Mild Moderate Severe	Mild (1), moderate (2) and severe (3)
Health status	73.45 (24.13)	Bad (0) – Perfect (100)

The (perceived) knowledge about hemophilia rises with the severity of the disease. When adding non-users (62) and users (71), the percentage of severe cases in our survey is 80%. This is higher than in the general population where the share of severe cases of all hemophilia cases is estimated to be at 60%. First, the number of severe cases among association members is probably bigger than in the general population because these patients are more concerned with their disease and its treatment than patients with mild or moderate hemophilia. Second, the interest of patients with severe hemophilia in new CDM approaches is probably bigger than of other patients so they are more likely to answer a related questionnaire.

Most model constructs were tested using scales derived from previous research. We used the HBM's main constructs perceived susceptibility, seriousness, benefits, and barriers [33]. The measurement of perceived barriers and benefits is also used to represent effort and performance expectancy, these constructs overlap with UTAUT2. We follow previous studies in the e-health domain [34] and view self-efficacy as the ability to use e-health applications. The scale was taken from a previous study [35] and altered to specifically apply to CDM apps. The scales for measuring the factors facilitating conditions and hedonic motivation are based on a previous UTAUT2 study [11]. The scale for the integrated social influence/cues to action construct is adopted from a study that also combines UTAUT and HBM [36].

It was necessary to decrease observation dropout due to missing values given the small size of the sample. Therefore, Markov-Chain-Monte-Carlo imputation was used to provide viable substitutes for missing values. The missing values were tested to be missing at random. Ten values from eight respondents were imputed. Table 2 sums up the used constructs and Cronbach's α within the present study. The recommended threshold for Cronbach's α is 0.7, with values lower than that acceptable in exploratory studies [37]. Only Social Influence does not provide a satisfying α but it is considered close with a value of $\alpha = 0.69$. Facilitating Conditions and Self-Efficacy score the highest means (Table 2), suggesting that the confidence and support to use digital documentation is present.

Table 2. Variables

Variable	Abbreviation	Cronbach's α	Mean (SD)
Usage intention	UI	0.96	3.67 (1.66)
Perceived susceptibility	PSus	0.95	3.51 (1.64)
Perceived seriousness	PSer	0.88	3.05 (1.23)
Performance expectancy	PExp	0.88	2.76 (1.14)
Effort expectancy	EExp	0.88	2.05 (0.88)
Social influence	SI	0.69	2.47 (1.10)
Facilitating conditions	FC	0.77	4.25 (1.14)
Hedonic motivation	HM	0.90	3.59 (1.37)
Self-efficacy	SE	0.89	4.99 (0.90)

6 Analyses

Further analyses are conducted with PLS-SEM in SmartPLS3 and with Stata 14.1. First, a correlation analysis is conducted to detect possible antecedents to behavioral intention. While not providing predictive ability, the correlation analysis allows to determine possible relationships. Second, a PLS-SEM is calculated to test the research model. Third, several multiple regression analyses are carried out to extract more information concerning relevant subgroups of the sample because their size is too small for a PLS analysis. The correlation matrix between the variables given in the previous chapter and behavioral intention is presented in Table 3.

Table 3. Correlation matrix

	UI	PSus	PSer	PExp	EExp	SI	FC	HM	SE
UI	1								
PSus	0.16	1							
PSer	0.26*	0.50***	1						
PExp	0.47***	−0.09	0.00	1					
EExp	−0.29**	−0.21	−0.21	0.02	1				
SI	0.39***	0.08	0.10	0.29*	−0.01	1			
FC	0.06	0.07	0.07	0.04	−0.32**	0.22*	1		
HM	0.67***	−0.07	0.14	0.60***	−0.44***	0.28**	0.17	1	
SE	0.26**	0.09	0.11	−0.00	−0.67***	0.09	0.56***	0.34**	1

***$p < 0.01$; **$p < 0.05$; *$p < 0.10$

Concerning the correlations, it is evident that the antecedents behave as intended towards the outcome variable, with Effort Expectancy as the only antecedent with negatively phrased items presenting the only negative correlation. Apart from Perceived Susceptibility and Facilitating Conditions, all predictors show a significant correlation. Hedonic Motivation and Performance Expectancy correlate best with Usage Intention and show the highest level of significance together with Social Influence. It is, therefore, likely that these factors are significant predictors of Usage Intention.

Several antecedents show a high and significant correlation with each other, therefore the VIF is calculated to test for multicollinearity. As Table 4 shows, no VIF in the regression analysis is greater than ten, indicating no relevant multicollinearity within the regression analysis [38]. In the PLS-SEM, no VIF exceeds 3.3, which indicates that multicollinearity and common method bias have no relevant influence there [39]. We further used Shapiro-Wilk to assess normality of the data, and several non-normal distributions were found. While this will not impact the nonparametric PLS, robust estimators were used in the regression analyses to address it. The assumptions of linearity and homoscedasticity were tested for via plotting and the Breusch-Pagan test. Both assumptions are fulfilled.

A PLS-SEM analysis is conducted to determine the relationship between antecedents and Usage Intention. It is based on N = 62 with results shown in Fig. 2. The antecedents account for a variability of 68% of the Usage Intention ($R^2 = 0.679$). This R^2 makes the sample size of 62 sufficient for a statistical power of 80% and with 5% probability of error [40]. The significant positive predictors include Social Influence and Hedonic Motivation. Therefore, H5 and H8 are supported. The antecedents Perceived Susceptibility, Perceived Seriousness, Performance Expectancy, Effort Expectancy, Facilitating Conditions and Self-Efficacy showed no predictive power for Usage Intention. Therefore, hypotheses H1, H2, H3, H4, H7 and H6 are not supported when analyzing the full sample.

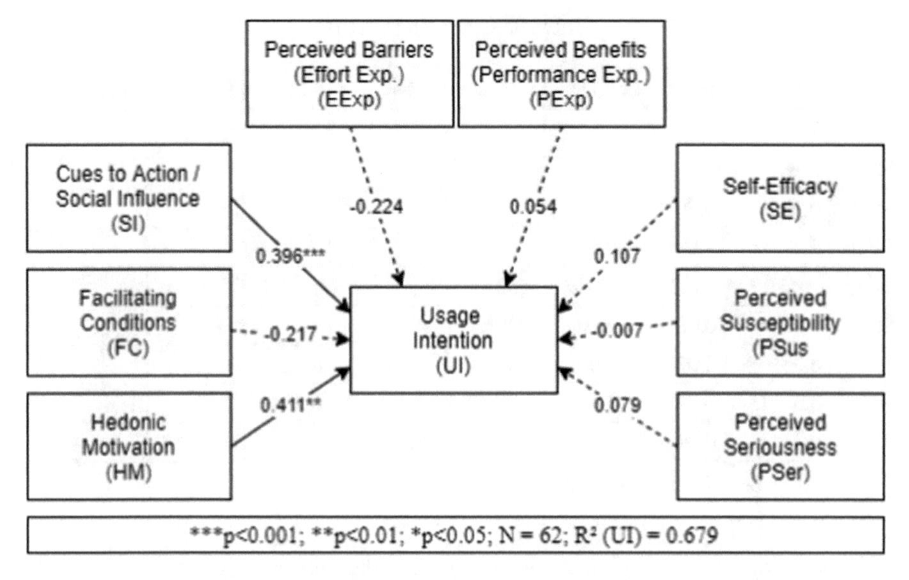

Fig. 2. Path coefficients and significances in the PLS-SEM analysis

However, the full sample is not homogenous with respect to the availability of an app for documentation. On one hand, there are non-users who may want to use digital documentation, but their HTC is not supporting it. On the other hand, there are non-users who do not use an app although their HTC supports it. The situation of the two groups of patients is objectively different so that a separate analysis is needed. A third group is formed by patients who do not know whether their HTC offers an app. We expected that hemophilia patients would be well informed about the disease and the possibilities for its management (see also Table 1) but almost 30% of respondents crossed the "do not know" option. Accordingly, the participants could be split in a sub-sample that does not use digital documentation despite its availability (Group DU), another sub-sample with no access to it (Group NA) and a third group not knowing whether it is available (Group DK). Due to the smaller sample size of the subgroups (given in Table 4), we can only search for a large effect size and accept a higher probability for Type II errors. Also, since smaller sample size can decrease the significance level, we set the significance threshold to 0.1 in the regression analyses [41]. Table 4 presents the different multiple regression analyses.

Hedonic Motivation is the only significant antecedent for the non-informed group. It means that they do not understand what value the digital documentation may have and, therefore, would only use it as a more entertaining way to document. Participants with no current access to digital documentation expect it to be useful (Performance Expectancy) and consider themselves to be well-prepared (Self-Efficacy) for it. Lastly, participants who do not use digital documentation despite having access to it are significantly influenced by Social Influence and Perceived Seriousness. The influence by Facilitating Conditions has an unexpected negative sign which we suspect to be a Simpson paradox, which was validated by additional single variable linear regression [42]. Hence, we will exclude Facilitating Conditions from further discussion. The non-adoption by this group is surprising at first. A look at the illness severity in this group explains this behavior to some extent. because 44% of participants do not have the severe form (in other groups the share is only 21% and 12%) and do not really need much documentation. If we add to this group app users, the share of severely ill patients rises to 78%.

Table 4. Multiple regression analysis

Variable	Group DK	Group DU	Group NA
Perceived susceptibility	0.14	−0.28	0.10
Perceived seriousness	−0.07	0.73*	0.05
Performance expectancy	−0.05	−0.52	0.64*
Effort expectancy	0.44	−0.01	−0.08
Social influence	0.18	0.80**	0.07
Facilitating conditions	0.08	−0.70*	−0.42
Hedonic motivation	0.79**	0.97	0.05
Self-efficacy	0.49	0.62	0.88*
R^2	0.77	0.74	0.59
Adj. R^2	0.58	0.51	0.39
MaxVIF	3.52	6.42	4.76
N	19	18	25
% severe	78	56	88

***$p < 0.01$; **$p < 0.05$; *$p < 0.10$

7 Discussion and Conclusions

The present study examined the factors determining the intention of patients to use m-health for a chronic disease. Suitable factors from UTAUT2 and HBM were analyzed in a PLS-SEM and in several multiple regressions. The analysis of the full sample of non-users reveals that Social Influence and Hedonic Motivation are significant predictors. The significant positive relationship of Social Influence confirms the relevance of the social environment in deciding whether to use digital documentation. The more suggestions patients receive from their friends, family members, or physicians, the more inclined they are to use digital documentation. It shows a significant difference between the role of Social Influence for professionals and patients: while professionals seem to be little concerned about others' opinions [28], patients seem to rely more on advice, which makes sense given their lack of professional knowledge. These results are in line with other studies researching m-health usage from the patients' perspective [12, 24], confirming that Social Influence should be considered when researching m-health usage intention.

Hedonic Motivation shows to be the strongest and most significant predictor, which matches the results of other adoption studies [5, 11]. It suggests that m-health apps need to exceed their utilitarian value and provide additional features to gain the patients' interest. This may seem surprising given the serious nature of chronic diseases, but also fits the observed scenario: Patients will document their factor usage either way. Digitalization cannot be achieved by only simply digitalizing the process, but it must keep the patient engaged. M-health users value supportive functions like integrated reminders and tracking [29].

The analysis of the full sample does not disclose perceptions of patients in a specific situation. The sub-samples are small but still lead to some interesting and statistically significant findings. The group with no access to digital documentation shows a significant influence of Performance Expectancy on Usage Intention. This implies that positive expectations about m-health are likely to lead to an increasing demand for such possibilities. Given the close and often long relationship between physicians and their patients, we do not believe that patients will switch to another physician (and HTC) for that reason but we think when patients look for a new physician (e.g., because of relocation) the opportunity to use an app for documentation will play a role. For the group of patients with access to digital documentation but who do not use it, the concern about hemophilia consequences (Perceived Seriousness) raises UI. For patients with severe hemophilia in this group, it is probably just a question of smartphone skills, cost, or time till they switch. Since they are open to Social Influence, some relating advice may help to persuade them to switch to an app. The third group which is not informed about the support of their HTC with respect to apps is puzzling. Whatever the real situation in their HTC may be, they did not care to find out. This is understandable for mild and moderate forms but not for the severe form of hemophilia (79% in this group!). These people should know about the existence of apps for documentation from their association (or other sources).

The present study offers several theoretical contributions and practical implications. By combining UTAUT2 and HBM, the specific behavior in the health context is represented in more detail than previously [43]. It follows the appeal to explore theory-based additions to health-IT use [14]. In comparison to studies on healthcare professionals [12], our study shows that patients are different from professionals with respect to m-health. This should be recognized when trying to persuade both groups to use m-health or when conducting studies in this domain.

Compared to previous studies [44], our study shows the necessity of utilizing the full UTAUT2 model instead of TAM or only parts of TAM2, since significant predictors like hedonic motivation may be overlooked otherwise. Our study also shows a direct impact of social influence on adoption intention instead of just an indirect one via perceived usefulness. In other words, even if a patient does not perceive an app as useful, he may still use it if the treating physician recommends it. We can also add that the perceived usefulness, which was a central predictor to adoption attention in previous studies [44], is only a significant predictor for patients who currently have no possibility to use the respective CDM app (due to their treatment center). The study also provides some insights useful to m-health providers and healthcare professionals on how to get patients to adopt m-health. The significance of Social Influence demonstrates that app providers need to reach out to treating physicians and the patients' social environment, which in the case of rare chronic diseases could be done via patient associations. App providers should implement engaging and interesting additions to their apps. There are already abundant implementations of such functions in the context of general health applications. Similar features can be applied in the context of chronic diseases, where the serious nature of the disease needs to be respected, but nonetheless information should be presented in an interesting manner.

The limitations of the study are based on the measurement of intention rather than use, the small sample, and the specific context. Participants with the intention to use an app still must install and actually use the app. Therefore, a longitudinal design to track actual usage after the intention has been formed is more reliable. Unfortunately, this is especially difficult when respondents' privacy must be assured without any compromise. The number of respondents is a methodological restriction. Hence, the findings of this study can only be considered as exploratory. A higher number of participants would also allow for structural relationship modelling in subgroups, since multiple regressions cannot fully map the factors' relationships with each other.

Disease specifics do not allow a simple extension of the findings to other diseases. Hemophilia patients already have the disease. Perceived susceptibility may play a bigger role with a disease that can be contracted (e.g., various forms of cancer). The download of the app cannot be done via an app store, but it must be provided by the HTC due to the sensitivity of the data handled and the needed cooperation with the HTC/physician. If an app can be offered via an app store, the rank of the app, its public rating by other users, and similar factors may influence the adoption of such apps.

References

1. Estrin, D., Sim, I.: Open mHealth architecture: an engine for health care innovation. Science **330**, 759–760 (2010)
2. Viswanathan, M., et al.: Interventions to improve adherence to self-administered medications for chronic diseases in the United States: a systematic review. Ann. Intern. Med. **157**, 785–795 (2012)
3. Bauer, U.E., Briss, P.A., Goodman, R.A., Bowman, B.A.: Prevention of chronic disease in the 21st century: elimination of the leading preventable causes of premature death and disability in the USA. Lancet **384**, 45–52 (2014)
4. Agnihothri, S., Cui, L., Delasay, M., Rajan, B.: The value of mHealth for managing chronic conditions. Health Care Manage. Sci. **23**(2), 185–202 (2018). https://doi.org/10.1007/s10729-018-9458-2
5. Wang, J., et al.: Smartphone interventions for long-term health management of chronic diseases: an integrative review. Telemed. e-Health **20**, 570–583 (2014)

6. Brooker, M.: 2010 WFH Global Survey Report. https://www1.wfh.org/publication/files/pdf-1427.pdf
7. WHO: Diabetes. http://www.who.int/news-room/fact-sheets/detail/diabetes
8. Fischer, K., et al.: The effects of postponing prophylactic treatment on long-term outcome in patients with severe hemophilia. Blood **99**, 2337–2341 (2002)
9. Dowd, B.E., Swenson, T., Parashuram, S., Coulam, R., Kane, R.: PQRS participation, inappropriate utilization of health care services, and medicare expenditures. Med. Care Res. Rev. MCRR **73**, 106–123 (2016)
10. Berntorp, E., Shapiro, A.D.: Modern haemophilia care. Lancet **379**, 1447–1456 (2012)
11. Venkatesh, V., Thong, J.Y.L., Xu, X.: Consumer acceptance and use of information technology: extending the unified theory of acceptance and use of technology. MIS Q. 157–178 (2012)
12. Sun, Y., Wang, N., Guo, X., Peng, Z.: Understanding the acceptance of mobile health services: a comparison and integration of alternative models. J. Electron. Commer. Res. **14**, 183 (2013)
13. Janz, N.K., Becker, M.H.: The health belief model: a decade later. Health Educ. Q. **11**, 1–47 (1984)
14. Holden, R.J., Karsh, B.-T.: The technology acceptance model: its past and its future in health care. J. Biomed. Inform. **43**, 159–172 (2010)
15. Huang, J.-C.: Remote health monitoring adoption model based on artificial neural networks. Expert Syst. Appl. **37**, 307–314 (2010)
16. Rogers, R.W.: A protection motivation theory of fear appeals and attitude change1. J. Psychol. **91**, 93–114 (1975)
17. Abraham, C., Sheeran, P.: The health belief model. Predicting Health Behav. **2**, 28–80 (2005)
18. Harrison, J.A., Mullen, P.D., Green, L.W.: A meta-analysis of studies of the health belief model with adults. Health Educ. Res. **7**, 107–116 (1992)
19. Khorsandi, B., Khakbazan, Z., Mahmoodzadeh, H.A., Haghani, H., Farnam, F., Damghanian, M.: Self-efficacy of the first-degree relatives of patients with breast cancer in the prevention of cancer: using the health belief model. J. Cancer Educ. **35**(5), 977–982 (2019). https://doi.org/10.1007/s13187-019-01551-0
20. Gilfoyle, M., Garcia, J., Chaurasia, A., Oremus, M.: Perceived susceptibility to developing cancer and mammography screening behaviour: a cross-sectional analysis of Alberta's Tomorrow Project. Public Health **177**, 135–142 (2019)
21. Bandura, A.: Self-efficacy: toward a unifying theory of behavioral change. Psychol. Rev. **84**, 191 (1977)
22. Venkatesh, V., Morris, M.G., Davis, G.B., Davis, F.D.: User acceptance of information technology: toward a unified view. MIS Q. 425–478 (2003)
23. Orji, R., Vassileva, J., Mandryk, R.L.: Modeling the efficacy of persuasive strategies for different gamer types in serious games for health. User Model. User-Adap. Inter. **24**(5), 453–498 (2014). https://doi.org/10.1007/s11257-014-9149-8
24. Diño, M.J.S., de Guzman, A.B.: Using partial least squares (PLS) in predicting behavioral intention for telehealth use among Filipino elderly. Educ. Gerontol. **41**, 53–68 (2015)
25. Radhakrishnan, K., Xie, B., Berkley, A., Kim, M.: Barriers and facilitators for sustainability of tele-homecare programs: a systematic review. Health Serv. Res. **51**, 48–75 (2016)
26. Zhang, Y., et al.: Factors influencing patients' intentions to use diabetes management apps based on an extended unified theory of acceptance and use of technology model: web-based survey. J. Med. Internet Res. **21**, e15023 (2019)
27. Ajzen, I.: The theory of planned behavior. Organ. Behav. Hum. Decis. Process. **50**, 179–211 (1991)
28. Chau, P.Y.K., Hu, P.J.-H.: Information technology acceptance by individual professionals: a model comparison approach. Decis. Sci. **32**, 699–719 (2001)

29. Funk, C.: Mobile Softwareanwendungen (Apps) im Gesundheitsbereich: Entwicklung, Marktbetrachtung und Endverbrauchermeinung. ibidem-Verlag (2013)
30. DHG: Über die Deutsche Hämophiliegesellschaft zur Bekämpfung von Blutungskrankheiten e.V. https://www.dhg.de/organisation/ueber-uns.html
31. IGH: Informationen und Ziele. https://www.igh.info/inhalte/ueber-uns/informationen-und-ziele/
32. Maiman, L.A., Becker, M.H.: The health belief model: origins and correlates in psychological theory. Health Educ. Monogr. **2**, 336–353 (1974)
33. Champion, V.L.: Instrument development for health belief model constructs. Advances in Nursing Science (1984)
34. Cho, J., Quinlan, M.M., Park, D., Noh, G.-Y.: Determinants of adoption of smartphone health apps among college students. Am. J. Health Behav. **38**, 860–870 (2014)
35. Bhattacherjee, A., Perols, J., Sanford, C.: Information technology continuance: a theoretic extension and empirical test. J. Comput. Inf. Syst. **49**, 17–26 (2007)
36. Thomas, M.A., Li, Y., Oliveira, T.: Nuances of development contexts for ICT4D research in least developed countries: an empirical investigation in Haiti. Telematics Inform. **34**, 1093–1112 (2017)
37. Hair, J.F., Black, W.C., Babin, B.J., Anderson, R.E., Tatham, R.L.: Multivariate Data Analysis, vol. 6. Pearson Prentice Hall, Upper Saddle River (2006)
38. Menard, S.: Applied Logistic Regression Analysis. Sage (1995)
39. Kock, N.: Common method bias in PLS-SEM: a full collinearity assessment approach. IJeC **11**, 1–10 (2015)
40. Hair Jr., J.F., Hult, G.T.M., Ringle, C., Sarstedt, M.: A Primer on Partial Least Squares Structural Equation Modeling (PLS-SEM). SAGE Publications (2016)
41. Cohen, J., Cohen, P., West, S.G., Aiken, L.S.: Applied Multiple Regression/Correlation Analysis for the Behavioral Sciences. Routledge (2013)
42. Hernán, M.A., Clayton, D., Keiding, N.: The Simpson's paradox unraveled. Int. J. Epidemiol. **40**, 780–785 (2011)
43. Akter, S., D'Ambra, J., Ray, P.: Development and validation of an instrument to measure user perceived service quality of mHealth. Inf. Manage. **50**, 181–195 (2013)
44. Dou, K., et al.: Patients' acceptance of smartphone health technology for chronic disease management: a theoretical model and empirical test. JMIR mHealth uHealth (2017)

Medical Teleconsulting Applications: An Empirical Study on Elderly Peoples' Satisfaction

Katharina Pflügner(✉), Florijan Hrovat, and Christian Maier

Information Systems and Services, University of Bamberg, Bamberg, Germany
{katharina.pfluegner,christian.maier}@uni-bamberg.de, florijan.hrovat@protonmail.com

Abstract. Medical teleconsulting applications improve the accessibility, increase the quality and reduce the costs of healthcare services especially for elderly people. Despite these benefits, such applications are still at an early state of diffusion. As the intention to use teleconsulting applications depends on the users' satisfaction, we aim to reveal the application features of teleconsulting applications that lead to user satisfaction. Based on the theory of attractive quality, we argue that application features can be classified into different categories, depending on how well they achieve user satisfaction. We identify 17 application features and conduct a quantitative study with 87 elderly people for categorization. The results show how each application feature affects elderly peoples' satisfaction and dissatisfaction with teleconsulting applications, and we derive recommendations for future teleconsulting application development.

Keywords: Telemedicine · Elderly people · Kano analysis · Theory of attractive quality (TAQ) · Application features

1 Introduction

Overburdening the health care system through excessive visits to physicians, a shortage of specialists and health workers [1], an increase in chronic diseases due to the demographic change [2], and a global pandemic – the challenges that face the health care system are manifold [3]. A digital solution in the form of medical teleconsulting applications are a possibility to relieve the burden on the health care system as these applications have several positive potentials: improve the accessibility, increase the quality, and reduce the costs of healthcare services [4]. For the US, it is expected that 4.3 billion US dollars can be saved annually [5]. However, not all studies confirmed these positive effects [6], highlighting a need to better understand the use of teleconsulting applications. Teleconsulting applications, connecting physicians and patients, offer a virtual visit to a physician via the mobile smart device and physicians can examine and make a diagnosis of patients describing their symptoms, which might be supported by live video and further application features [5]. Teleconsulting applications become increasingly important in the existing Covid-19 pandemic [7] as they prevent infections

F. Ahlemann et al. (Eds.): WI 2021, LNISO 46, pp. 38–54, 2021.
https://doi.org/10.1007/978-3-030-86790-4_3

associated with person-to-person visits to physicians, but their widespread implementation in daily practice is still pending and several promising applications are at an early stage of diffusion [4]. For elderly people, teleconsulting applications are a double-edged sword as their usage decreases the risk of infection, but their usage comes with challenges due to the new technology [8]. A key factor for the success of technologies, i.e. teleconsulting applications in daily practice, is that the users, i.e. patients, need to be satisfied with the technology [9]. There is a consensus in previous research showing that only satisfied users have intentions to use the technology, so that it is relevant to unfold which factors drive user satisfaction [10].

Therefore, our approach is to examine the factors that are relevant for user satisfaction by identifying and categorizing different application features of teleconsulting applications. In terms of potential patients, we focus on the baby boomer generation (1946–1969), a subpopulation of the elderly people, which already represents a large part of the population [11] and will be a major challenge for health systems in the future due to age-related health problems [12]. Thus, we ask:

Which application features are relevant for elderly peoples' satisfaction with teleconsulting applications?

We base on the theory of attractive quality (TAQ) [13] to reveal how the application features are related to user satisfaction and dissatisfaction and conduct a Kano analysis, which enables to reveal unexpressed wishes of the elderly people regarding the application features. The findings on the respective features make a relevant contribution to the design of teleconsulting applications, the exploitation of the potentials of teleconsulting, and the improvement of the application development.

2 Theoretical Background

In this section, we will outline prior research in the stream of telemedicine and illustrate specific aspects of elderly people that are relevant for the satisfaction with technologies such as teleconsulting applications.

2.1 Telemedicine

Telemedicine refers to the delivery of health care services from a distance, where health care professionals and patients exchange valid information for diagnosis, treatment and prevention of diseases and injuries by using technologies [14]. Thus, telemedicine enables the evaluation, diagnosis, treatment, monitoring, counselling and follow-up care of patients without geographical limitations [15]. There is evidence of the feasibility of telemedicine as a clinically effective substitute for personal care in an increasingly wide range of applications and environments. In terms of diagnostic accuracy, for example, there is substantial empirical indication of the equivalence of virtual and personal physician visits [16].

A more specific form of telemedicine are teleconsulting applications, which belong to mHealth [15], i.e. medical and public health services that are supported by mobile smart devices such as smartphones [17]. With teleconsulting applications, a virtual visit to the physician is made possible via the mobile smart device as this system offers physicians the possibility to examine patients' symptoms by real-time interaction, e.g. video conferencing [5, 18]. Thus, the teleconsulting application supports the remote exchange between the physician and the patient. This form of telemedicine has reduced the technological barriers and costs for the development of telemedicine applications, as a smartphone is available to an increasing part of the population.

2.2 Elderly People and Technologies

An important user group of teleconsulting applications are elderly people, as they already represent a large part of the population [11] and their health provision will be a major challenge for health systems in the future due to the demographic change and age-related health problems [12]. Elderly people differ from younger people in terms of technology adoption and usage as on average especially elderly people are more likely than younger ones to try to maintain their status quo [19], e.g. person-to-person visits of physicians, evade new innovations due to fear of technology [8]. Moreover, although elderly people are a diverse societal group and there are interindividual differences, research finds that they are mainly driven by utilitarian factors, e.g. effectiveness and utility of the technology, rather than hedonic factors to adopt and use technology [8]. Research highlighted the importance of age-sensitive design of technologies as an important aspect of IS research [20]. In terms of teleconsulting applications, the design can differ between the applications due to the implementation of different application features, e.g. whether patients can exchange their experience with other patients who have a similar state of health in the application.

Due to these aspects, we focus on elderly people as one user group of teleconsulting applications and aim to reveal application features that lead to user satisfaction of elderly people. User satisfaction increases the intention to use the technology [9], which is the requirement for the widespread deployment of the teleconsulting potentials. In specific, we focus on the baby boomer generation, a subpopulation of elderly people, of which 81 percent use a smartphone [21] and thereby have an access to the teleconsulting application. To reveal how the application features are related to user satisfaction, we rely on the theory of attractive quality (TAQ) and conduct a Kano analysis, which is an established way to study factors relevant for satisfaction and dissatisfaction.

3 Theory of Attractive Quality

Kano [13] developed the theory of attractive quality (TAQ) to better explain the influence of different attributes on customer satisfaction. The theory is based on the assumption that customer satisfaction is not necessarily proportional to the functionality of a product. This means that customers are not necessarily the more satisfied the more functional the product is or the more dissatisfied the less functional the product is [22]. An essential feature of this theory is that it categorizes different attributes according to how well they are able to achieve customer satisfaction [23]. The attributes can be grouped into five different categories, each of which has a different impact on customer satisfaction [24] (see Fig. 1). Customers take must-be (M) attributes for granted as long as they are fulfilled. However, if the product does not sufficiently meet these attributes, customers will be dissatisfied. In the case of one-dimensional (O) attributes, their fulfilment is positively and linearly related to the degree of customer satisfaction. The higher the degree of fulfillment, the higher the degree of customer satisfaction and vice versa. The fulfillment of attractive (A) attributes, leads to a disproportionate level of satisfaction. However, the absence of these attributes does not lead to dissatisfaction, as customers do not expect them [23]. Indifferent (I) attributes are indifferent towards the customer, i.e. the customer is neither satisfied nor dissatisfied with whether the product meets this attribute or not. Reverse (R) attributes indicate that the judgment of functional and dysfunctional was the opposite of what the customer expects. With questionable (Q) attributes, there is a contradiction in the customer's answers to the questions [22].

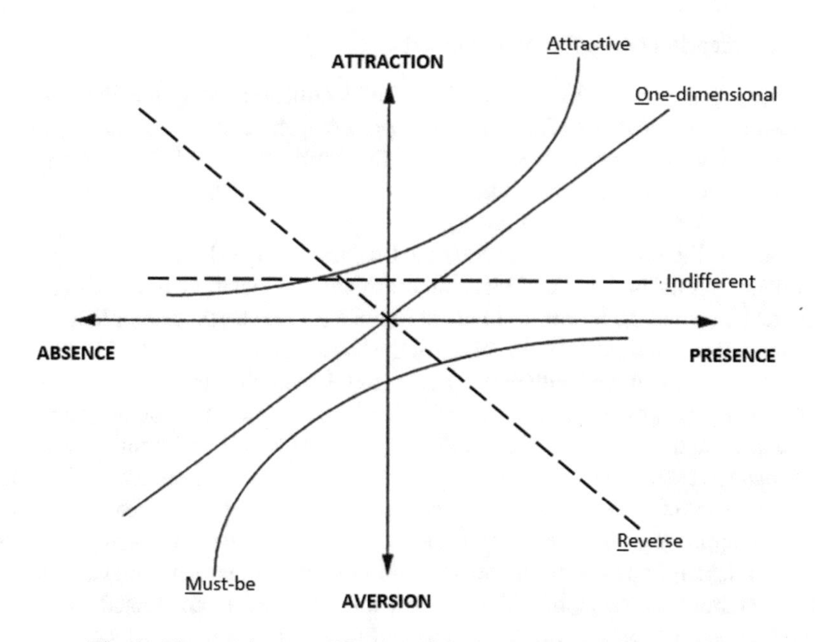

Fig. 1. The supplemented Kano model of customer satisfaction [22]

The TAQ offers an opportunity to investigate attributes that lead to satisfaction with a product and provides a valuable orientation in tradeoff situations during the product development phase to achieve satisfaction [25]. Existing research has shown the usefulness of basing on the TAQ for studying product features and their influence on user satisfaction in information systems research such as mobile feedback tool features [26] as well as mobile security and antivirus features [27]. In our paper, we focus on attributes, i.e. application features, which lead to customer satisfaction, i.e. user satisfaction with the product, i.e. teleconsulting applications. A high level of satisfaction has a positive effect on the acceptance and the intention to use the teleconsulting applications. Accordingly, meeting the application features that are relevant for user satisfaction is an important means for the diffusion of teleconsulting applications.

4 Method

To study application features that are relevant for the satisfaction of elderly people with teleconsulting applications we base on the TAQ and follow the main steps of a Kano analysis [28]. The Kano analysis is an appropriate means to identify application features of teleconsulting applications and to study the also non-proportional relationship between the features and user satisfaction. This is based on the fact that the analysis is theoretically grounded in the TAQ and enables the categorization of the application features into the different before mentioned categories. Closely linking theory and method provides an essential understanding of the features' relevance for user satisfaction from a research, but also a practice perspective [29].

4.1 Identification of Application Features

The starting point for the Kano analysis is the identification of application features of teleconsulting applications. For doing so, we took a three-step exploratory approach consisting of a literature search, review of the applications and their functionalities available in the application store and expert interviews, which led to a comprehensive list of application features (see Table 1).

Within the literature search, the database Business Source Ultimate, the Top 3 Health IS Journals (Journal of American Medical Informatics Association, International Journal of Medical Informatics, Journal of Medical Internet Research), the Senior Scholars' Basket of Journals as well as the proceedings of the conferences ICIS, ECIS, HICSS, PACIS and AMCIS were searched with the search terms telemedicine, mobile applications, and remote diagnosis to extract relevant application features. Based on the literature search, we identified and focused on one article [30] to be especially relevant for identifying the application features due to its content relevance and publication in a leading Health IS journal (JAMIA), where the major contributions are likely to appear [31]. The list of relevant application features was extended based on a review by reading through the functional descriptions inside the teleconsulting applications that are available in the application store. Subsequently, three expert interviews were conducted to verify the application features of the two prior steps and to identify further application features. Two of the interviewees do research in the field of telemedicine and one interviewee is responsible for the strategic assurance of a telemedicine project in practice. The main areas of responsibility of the latter interviewee include the operative project management of the telemedicine project, i.e. operation, further development, problem solving, preparation and support. An overview of all identified application features is given in Table 1.

4.2 Construction of Kano-Questionnaire

After the identification of application features, we develop a questionnaire to classify each feature. We ask a functional question "What would you say if the application met [feature x], how would you feel?" and a dysfunctional question "What would you say if the application did not meet [feature x], how would you feel?" [29] for each feature with the five answer alternatives "I like it that way", "It must be that way", "I am neutral",

Table 1. Overview of identified application features

#	Identified application feature
#1	Emergency service/outpatient call button that makes a direct request for medical assistance [2, 3]
#2	(Push) notifications of further individual information/recommendations on the diagnosed disease [2, 3]
#3	Reminder messages about the times for taking medication [2, 3]
#4	Information possibility about data protection [2, 3]
#5	Adding data on health status (e.g. blood pressure, sugar) and medication [3]
#6	Transmission of messages/information to the own family physician [2, 3]
#7	Exchange of experience with other patients who have a similar state of health [1, 3]
#8	Information on health care facilities and pharmacies in the surrounding area (e.g. address, occupancy) [3]
#9	Direct orders from online pharmacies [2, 3]
#10	Reminder messages about required examinations/post-treatments [2, 3]
#11	Issuing (online) prescriptions [2, 3]
#12	Time graphs with progress and objectives for the patient [1, 3]
#13	Possibility of sending image/video material to simplify the diagnosis for the physician [2, 3]
#14	Evaluation of the physician/physician contact [2, 3]
#15	Summary display of the examination results [1, 3]
#16	Practical/clear menu navigation [3]
#17	Choice of diagnostic paths in the form of a chat, telephone call or video call [2, 3]

Note: [1] Literature search; [2] Review of applications; [3] Expert interviews; # number of application feature

"I can live with it that way", and "I dislike it that way". In addition, the user evaluates how important the application feature is ("self-stated importance") (from 1 to 5) to derive priorities for product development and improvement measures [28]. At the beginning, the questionnaire contained a short introduction to the topic, explanations on the use of data and processing instructions.

4.3 Data Collection

We collected data in the form of a paper-based survey from 87 persons of the baby boomer generation (see Table 2). To recruit participants, we followed two approaches. Participants of the respective target age group were recruited based on own contacts and forwarded based on a snowball sampling strategy. In addition, questionnaires were laid out in a physician's practice, which were filled out while waiting for the physician appointment. Our sampling resulted in a total of 100 completed questionnaires in the period from February to March 2020. Due to incomplete data sets and inconsistent user statements, the final sample consists of 87 questionnaires. All participants are from Germany, but more precise information about the particular residential area was not recorded.

Table 2. Demographic data of survey participants

Age (in years) Mean: 57.5, SD: 5.12	Minimum	50	Experience with medical teleconsulting applications	Yes	3.5%
	Maximum	72		No	96.5%
Sex	Male	63.2%	Health status	Excellent	3.5%
	Female	36.8%		Very good	27.9%
	Diverse	0.0%		Good	55.8%
Average duration of smartphone usage per day (in hours)	<1	35.6%		Less good	12.8%
	1–2	48.3%		Poor	0.0%
	2–3	13.8%			
	>3	2.3%			

5 Results

The evaluation approach for the collected data consists of five main steps [32, 33], which are explained in the following sub-sections.

5.1 Categorization According to Classification Scheme, Frequencies, and Rules

First, the 17 application features are categorized according to the classification scheme provided by Kano (see Table 3) [22] for each participant based on the answers to the functional and dysfunctional questions.

Then, the frequency of each category per application feature is calculated across all participants. Usually, a particular application feature is assigned to the category with the highest frequency, as this is the predominant view of the participants. If features cannot be uniquely assigned to one of the six categories because two or more frequencies are close together, the following evaluation rule is applied: M > O > A > I.

The feature is assigned to the category that has the higher rank in the hierarchy according to the evaluation rule [33]. The basis of the evaluation rule is the assumption that decisions on product development should primarily take into account those features which lead to dissatisfaction in case of non-fulfillment [34]. According to the classification scheme, the frequencies, and the evaluation rule, no application feature is categorized as attractive, five are categorized as one-dimensional, three as must-be, and nine as indifferent (see Table 4).

Table 3. Evaluation table according to Kano [28]

Application feature		Dysfunctional question				
		Like	Must-be	Neutral	Live with	Dislike
Functional question	Like	Q	A	A	A	O
	Must-be	R	I	I	I	M
	Neutral	R	I	I	I	M
	Live with	R	I	I	I	M
	Dislike	R	R	R	R	Q

Note: A = attractive; I = indifferent; M = must-be; O = one-dimensional; Q = questionable; R = reverse

Table 4. Initial categorization of application features (absolute frequencies)

#	Attrac-tive	One-dimen-sional	Must-be	Indif-ferent	Reverse	Ques-tionable	Rule	Category
#1	8	37	18	19	2	1		O
#2	10	14	14	35	13	0		I
#3	8	26	12	29	11	0	X	O
#4	4	14	36	29	3	0		M
#5	12	20	13	29	12	0		I
#6	8	31	17	24	2	4		O
#7	4	7	4	44	25	2		I
#8	11	22	13	36	3	1		I
#9	9	12	9	42	15	0		I
#10	13	16	18	31	7	1		I
#11	18	19	11	31	7	1		I
#12	10	5	9	52	10	0		I
#13	7	28	17	20	13	1		O
#14	6	11	14	48	6	0		I
#15	7	24	26	20	8	1		M
#16	2	26	44	13	1	1		M
#17	16	24	15	26	5	0	X	O

Note: # = number of application feature; X = evaluation rule was applied

5.2 Category Strength and Total Strength

Two further measures help to evaluate the assignment of an application feature to a category [35]: category strength (Cat) and total strength (Tot) [32, 36]. The former is used for quantitative analysis of the strength of assignment of an application feature to a category [33]. The formula is defined as the percentage difference of the highest category above the next highest and can be represented as follows: *Cat = most frequent denomination – 2nd most frequent denomination* [*0%; 100%*]. The larger the Cat, the clearer the assignment of an application feature to a specific category. A Cat of at least 6.0% shows a statistically significant difference between the most frequent and the second most frequent category at a confidence level of 90.0%. A Cat of less than 6% requires a new mixed category to be created, meaning that the application feature cannot be statistically assigned to one of the classic Kano categories. At this point, however, the Tot must also be considered [33]. The Tot is defined as the total percentage of attractive, one-dimensional and must-be answers [36]: $Tot = A + O + M$ [*0%; 100%*]. The higher the Tot, the higher the percentage of respondents for whom this feature is generally relevant, regardless of categorization. By combining the Tot and the respective category assignment of the features, the order in which the features should be implemented or offered can be determined [33]. If the Cat of an item is less than 6.0% but the Tot is at least 60.0%, the attribute must be assigned to the mixed category [32]. The results of the present study show that two features must be classified in a mixed category (see Table 5).

Table 5. Extended evaluation of the categorized application features

#	Category	Better index	Worse index	Category strength	Total strength	Fong test	Importance (SSI)
#1	O	0.55	−0.67	21.2%	74.1%	–	4.15
#2	I	0.33	−0.38	24.4%	44.2%	–	3.55
#3	O	0.45	−0.51	3.5%	53.5%	X	3.44
#4	M	0.22	−0.60	8.1%	62.8%	X	4.07
#5	I	0.43	−0.45	10.5%	52.3%	X	3.81
#6	O	0.49	−0.60	8.1%	65.1%	X	4.19
#7	I	0.19	−0.19	22.1%	17.4%	–	2.56
#8	I	0.40	−0.43	16.3%	53.5%	–	3.59
#9	I	0.29	−0.29	31.0%	34.5%	–	2.69
#10	I	0.37	−0.44	15.1%	54.7%	–	3.64
#11	I	0.47	−0.38	13.8%	55.2%	–	3.32
#12	I	0.20	−0.18	48.8%	27.9%	–	3.15
#13	O	0.49	−0.63	9.3%	60.5%	X	3.75
#14	I	0.22	−0.32	40.0%	36.5%	–	2.93
#15	M(X)	0.40	−0.65	2.3%	66.3%	X	4.07
#16	M	0.33	−0.82	20.7%	82.8%	–	4.47
#17	O(X)	0.49	−0.48	2.3%	64.0%	X	3.83

Note: A = attractive; I = indifferent; M = must-be; O = one-dimensional; Q = questionable; R = reverse; # = number of application feature; (X) = mixed

5.3 Statistical Significance of Categorization

In order to test the statistical significance of categorization, the Fong test is carried out. This test is used in cases where the evaluation according to the frequency shows only minor differences between the two most frequently mentioned categories [33]. The results show that for seven features the Fong test is significant (see Table 5) and therefore there are only minor differences between the two most frequent category assignments. Thus, it is advisable to examine the self-stated importance to make a classification [33].

5.4 Self-stated Importance

The self-stated importance (SSI) is especially helpful if the users' answers are equally distributed over two or more Kano categories [23]. The SSI allows to draw attention to the most important results [22] and to set priorities for product development and improvement measures [28]. The SSI is determined by the weighted average value from 1 (refers to not important at all) to 5 (refers to very important) from the survey data. In the present study, all must-be features can be confirmed to be important (see Table 5). Moreover, the one-dimensional and indifferent categories can each be placed in a priority hierarchy from high SSI to low SSI.

5.5 Better Und Worse Indices

As suggested by previous research [22], we calculated the satisfaction coefficients, which indicate whether the satisfaction can be increased by fulfilling a certain application feature or whether the fulfilment of this feature only prevents the user from being dissatisfied [36]. Thus, the determination of the satisfaction coefficients is suitable for providing additional information in case of ambiguous category allocations [33]. There are two satisfaction coefficients [33]: The better index indicates whether satisfaction increases by fulfilling a specific application feature. The worse index indicates whether user satisfaction decreases if the application feature is not met. The better index ranges from 0 to 1: the closer the value is to 1, the higher the influence on satisfaction. The worse index ranges from 0 to -1. An index of -1 indicates that the influence on the dissatisfaction is particularly strong if the analyzed application feature is not fulfilled [28]. Values from 0.5 for the better index are considered as significant, while values from -0.5 for the worse index are considered as critical. The satisfaction coefficients should always be interpreted in relation to each other [33]. Looking at the results of this study (see Table 5), the emergency service/outpatient call button that makes a direct request for medical assistance proves to be particularly significant, which points to an indispensable implementation of this feature in the application.

5.6 Summary of Results

With the help of the Kano analysis, this paper shows how each application feature affects satisfaction and dissatisfaction with teleconsulting applications. The application features can be classified into four categories: must-be, one-dimensional, indifferent, and mixed. The results show that two features, i.e. information possibility about data protection and practical/clear menu navigation are classified as must-be, which means that teleconsulting applications should offer these features, as they are a decisive competitive factor [34]. If they are not fulfilled, the user will have no interest in the teleconsulting application. Four attributes are categorized as one-dimensional: Emergency service/outpatient call button that makes a direct request for medical assistance; reminder messages regarding the times for taking medication; transmission of messages/information to the own family physician; and possibility of sending image/video material to simplify the diagnosis for the physician. The higher the degree of fulfilment of these application features, the higher the user satisfaction and vice versa. Features that have been assigned as one-dimensional are explicitly requested by the user [37]. Moreover, nine attributes are classified as indifferent, which means that they have no influence on the satisfaction with the application: (Push) notifications of further individual information/recommendations on the diagnosed disease; adding data on health status and medication; exchange of experiences with other patients who have a similar health status; information on health care facilities and pharmacies in the surrounding area; ordering directly from online pharmacies; reminder messages about required examinations/post-treatments; issuing (online) prescriptions; time graphs with progress and objectives for the patient; evaluation of the physician/physician contact. In addition, two features, i.e. summary display of the examination results; and choice of diagnostic paths in the form of a chat, telephone call or video call, were assigned to the mixed category in the course of the evaluation method [22, 32, 33].

Figure 2 shows a summarized graphical representation of the results in the coordinate system.

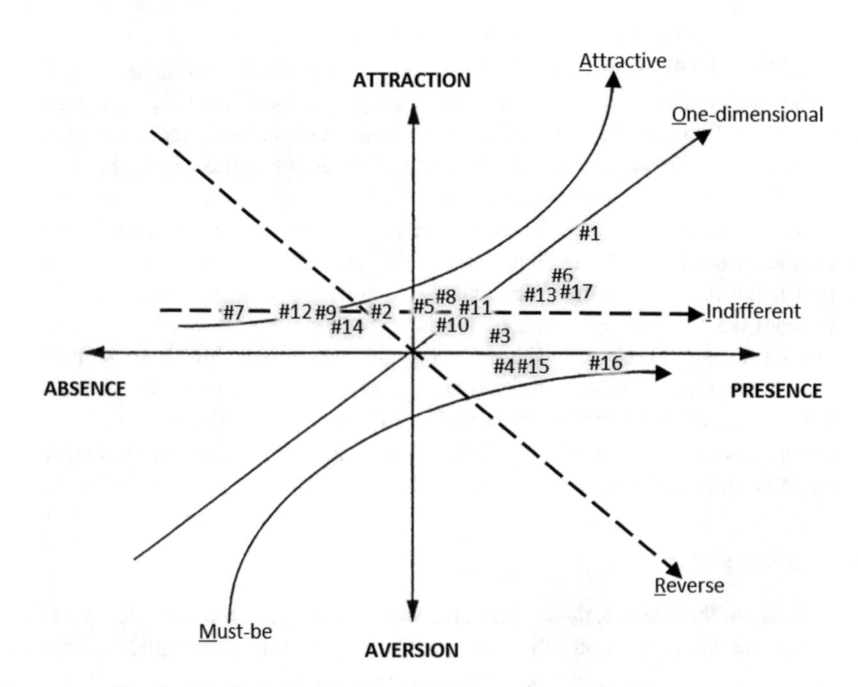

Fig. 2. The Kano model of satisfaction supplemented with our results

6 Discussion

We aim to provide an understanding on the attributes that form user satisfaction of teleconsulting applications of baby boomers generation. Based on the theory of attractive qualities (TAQ) [13] we develop a general understanding of elderly peoples' expectations of teleconsulting applications regarding application features. For this purpose, 17 application features were identified by literature search, review of teleconsulting applications available in the application store, and expert interviews. These were then evaluated and categorized with the help of a Kano questionnaire from participants belonging to the baby boomer generation.

6.1 Research Contributions

Research in the stream of telemedicine has revealed the effectiveness, e.g. the diagnostic accuracy, of teleconsulting as comparable to personal physician visits in a wide range of applications and environments [16]. Building on these promising results, we examine how these effective applications achieve user satisfaction that – together with other factors, e.g. social or cultural factors [38] – in turn leads to users' intention to use the technology and the exploitation of its potential. Focusing on technological aspects, we identify 17 application features of teleconsulting applications, which sheds the light on possible ways how to design the applications.

Thereupon, following similar approaches in IS research studying product features [26, 27], we introduce the Kano analysis [13] as an appropriate methodological approach to evaluate the relevance of these application features for the elderly peoples' satisfaction with teleconsulting applications. The results reveal that the application features can be classified into different categories, namely must-be, one-dimensional, indifferent, and mixed category. We contribute that the application features do not necessarily have a proportional relationship with user satisfaction, i.e. for the features categorized as must-be. The presence of the application features information possibility for data protection and practical/clear menu navigation prevent elderly people from being dissatisfied with the application, but they take these features for granted, meaning that their presence does not result in satisfaction with the application. Moreover, not all application features are relevant for the elderly peoples' user satisfaction as they do not influence the satisfaction, i.e. the indifferent application features. Thus, we highlight that the application features can be placed in a hierarchical order depending on their relevance for creating user satisfaction, namely by considering their assigned category as well as the better and worse indices [39]. For some application features, user satisfaction increases significantly with only a small improvement in the application performance, while for some other features it increases only slightly, even though the application performance has been greatly improved.

Further, we focus on elderly people, i.e. the baby boomer generation, which is an important user group of teleconsulting applications as they already represent a large part of the population [11] and their health provision will be a major challenge for health systems in the future due to the demographic change and age-related health problems [12]. Research highlighted the importance of age-sensitive design of technologies as an important aspect of information systems research [20]. Thus, we contribute by revealing elderly peoples' needs and expectations towards application features of teleconsulting applications and derive age-sensitive recommendations for the design of these applications. Moreover, elderly people are more likely to maintain their status quo [19], i.e. person-to-person visits of physicians, and evade new innovations. Features that are categorized to the attractive category lead to attraction to a specific product [13] such as teleconsulting applications and thereby lead to an abandonment of the status quo. Our result did not reveal an identified application feature to be attractive. Thus, we highlight that there is a need to design further application features and study the factors leading an application feature to be attractive in the view of the elderly people.

6.2 Recommendations for Future Teleconsulting Application Development

The results of the paper at hand have implications for the design and development of teleconsulting applications as they allow the derivation of recommendations for how user satisfaction with these applications can be increased. Identifying and categorizing the critical features for user satisfaction by the Kano analysis helps to focus on the important features for increasing satisfaction [36], namely where users notice their impact the most [22]. If developers know to what extent an application feature influences the user satisfaction and are aware of the relative importance of this feature, a satisfaction portfolio can be created and appropriate measures be taken.

Fulfilment of Must-Be Features and Competitiveness in One-Dimensional Features. A general recommendation in line with the TAQ [13] for application development is to strive to meet all must-be features and to be competitive with the market leaders in the one-dimensional features. The improvement of a must-be feature that has already reached a satisfactory level is not productive compared to the improvement of a one-dimensional or attractive one. Accordingly, application developers in the field of teleconsulting applications should ensure that the must-be features, i.e. practical/clear menu navigation, information possibilities for data protection, and a summary display of examination results, are implemented. They should then focus on the one-dimensional categories, with special attention to the respective satisfaction coefficients and SSIs. Factors that have both low satisfaction and low importance are of low priority. Top priority is given to application features that the user considers important and those that have disadvantages compared to competitors' products [37]. A similar approach is recommended for the application features with an indifferent classification, although these generally have the lowest priority.

Research and Implementation of New Features of the Attractive Category. For application developers, it may not be enough to satisfy users under the current highly competitive conditions by simply meeting the essential features. Thus, we recommend application developers to implement new and innovative features perceived as attractive that meet user needs and differentiate from the competitors, because none of the identified features in our study is an attractive feature for elderly people. To come up with new features, the potential users that are selected to present a variety of different user needs should be involved in an early stage of the product development process. New features to gain attractiveness should especially address the utility of the application, because elderly people are mainly driven by utilitarian factors rather than hedonic ones to adopt and use technology [8]. According to the TAQ [13], the same feature may change category over time, i.e. attractive features can become one-dimensional and ultimately must-be, because the user needs towards the application features are dynamic rather than static [39]. In other words, products that were perceived as innovative and attractive are no longer considered so, and user satisfaction may no longer be achieved. The timely development and introduction of a teleconsulting application with innovative features is therefore important [39].

6.3 Limitations

The present study is not free of limitations. The majority of participants has not used a teleconsulting application yet. Future research could investigate whether the evaluation of application features changes when users have gained experience with these applications or how individual differences shape the evaluation of a technology [40, 41].

Moreover, we focus on possible patients, i.e. the elderly people, as users of teleconsulting applications. Further users of the applications are the physicians. The physicians might evaluate the distinct application features differently, implicating that there are differences between patients and physicians in which application features lead to satisfaction and dissatisfaction.

We base our study on the TAQ and the KANO analysis to prioritize teleconsulting application features. However, there exist further approaches for prioritization such as analytic hierarchy process or quality function development, which may supplement the results of our study.

Furthermore, we did not distinguish between less and more severe diseases, although user might evaluate the features differently depending on the severity of the disease, e.g. might value specific features only in the case of severe or chronic diseases. This is relevant for studying baby boomers, because within the generation there might be great variety in the severity of the diseases, with some potential users having chronic or multiple comorbid diseases.

Finally, we evaluate the application features in terms of their relevance for creating user satisfaction, while not accounting for their relevance for medical effectiveness, although those two might be related. Future research could account for both evaluation criteria, i.e. user satisfaction and medical effectiveness, and specify to which degree recommendations resulting from the user satisfaction perceptive overlap or do not overlap with recommendations resulting from a medical effectiveness perspective.

7 Conclusion

In this paper, we conducted an empirical research to investigate the application features of teleconsulting applications that influence the satisfaction of the baby boomer generation. We identified 17 application features in existent literature, by reviewing existing teleconsulting applications and by interviewing experts. Subsequently, 87 persons of the baby boomer generation were surveyed to evaluate the previously identified application features according to the Kano analysis. The present research shows that the application features can be categorized into four categories, which has implications for application developers in their endeavor to ensure user satisfaction.

References

1. Hasebrook, J.P., Hinkelmann, J., Volkert, T., Rodde, S., Hahnenkamp, K.: Securing the continuity of medical competence in times of demographic change: a proposal. JMIR Res. Protoc. **5**, e240 (2016)
2. Hoque, R., Sorwar, G.: Understanding factors influencing the adoption of mHealth by the elderly: an extension of the UTAUT model. Int. J. Med. Informatics **101**, 75–84 (2017)
3. Reis, L., Maier, C., Mattke, J., Creutzenberg, M., Weitzel, T.: Addressing user resistance would have prevented a healthcare AI project failure. MIS Q. Executive **19**, 279–296 (2020)
4. Jansen-Kosterink, S., Dekker-van Weering, M., van Velsen, L.: Patient acceptance of a telemedicine service for rehabilitation care: a focus group study. Int. J. Med. Informatics **125**, 22–29 (2019)
5. Khairat, S., Liu, S., Zaman, T., Edson, B., Gianforcaro, R.: Factors determining patients' choice between mobile health and telemedicine: Predictive analytics assessment. JMIR Mhealth Uhealth **7**, e13772 (2019)
6. Williams, C.W., Oetjen, D.: An ethical analysis of telemedicine: implications for future research. Int. J. Telemed. Clin. Pract. **1**, 4–16 (2015)
7. Mueller, B.: Telemedicine arrives in the U.K.: '10 years of change in one week'. https://www.nytimes.com/2020/04/04/world/europe/telemedicine-uk-coronavirus.html
8. Maier, C., Laumer, S., Eckhardt, A.: Technology adoption by elderly people – an empirical analysis of adopters and non-adopters of social networking sites. In: Proceedings of the 10th International Conference on Wirtschaftsinformatik, pp. 85–110 (2011)
9. DeLone, W.H., McLean, E.R.: The DeLone and McLean model of information systems success: a ten-year update. J. Manage. Inf. Syst. **19**, 9–30 (2003)
10. Laumer, S., Maier, C., Weitzel, T.: Information quality, user satisfaction, and the manifestation of workarounds: a qualitative and quantitative study of enterprise content management system users. Eur. J. Inf. Syst. **26**, 333–360 (2017)
11. Tennant, B., et al.: eHealth literacy and web 2.0 health information seeking behaviors among baby boomers and older adults. J. Med. Internet Res. **17**, e70 (2015)
12. LeRouge, C., van Slyke, C., Seale, D., Wright, K.: Baby boomers' adoption of consumer health technologies: survey on readiness and barriers. J. Med. Internet Res. **16**, e200 (2014)
13. Kano, N., Seraku, F., Takahashi, F., Tsuji, S.: Attractive quality and must-be quality. J. Jpn. Soc. Qual. Control **14**, 39–48 (1984)
14. WHO Global Observatory for eHealth: Telemedicine: opportunities and developments in Member States: report on the second global survey on eHealth. World Health Organization, Geneva (2010). https://apps.who.int/iris/handle/10665/44497
15. Abby, S.K., McLeod Amy, C., Wager Karen, A.: Telemedicine in an international context: Definition, use, and future. In: Menachemi, N., Singh, S. (eds.) Health Information Technology in the International Context, vol. 12, pp. 143–169. Emerald Group Publishing Limited (2012)
16. Bashshur, R.L., Shannon, G., Krupinski, E.A., Grigsby, J.: Sustaining and realizing the promise of telemedicine. Telemed. J. e-health **19**, 339–345 (2013)
17. World Health Organization: mHealth: new horizons for health through mobile technologies. World Health Organization, Geneva (2011). https://apps.who.int/iris/bitstream/handle/10665/44607/9789241564250_eng.pdf?sequence=1&isAllowed=y

18. Wootton, R.: Twenty years of telemedicine in chronic disease management - an evidence synthesis. J. Telemed. Telecare **18**, 211–220 (2012)
19. Kim, H.-W., Kankanhalli, A.: Investigating user resistance to information systems implementation: a status quo bias perspective. MIS Q. **33**, 567–582 (2009)
20. Pak, R., Price, M.M., Thatcher, J.: Age-sensitive design of online health information: comparative usability study. J. Med. Internet Res. **11**, e45 (2009)
21. Deloitte: Deloitte Babyboomer-Studie Digitaler als ihr Ruf: Die Babyboomer im technologischen Wandel. https://www2.deloitte.com/de/de/pages/presse/contents/Deloitte-Babyboomer-Studie.html
22. Berger, et al.: Kano's methods for understanding customer-defined quality. Center Qual. Manage. J. **2**, 3–36 (1993)
23. Ting, W., Ping, J., Clegg, B.: Understanding customer needs through quantitative analysis of Kano's model. Int. J. Qual. Reliab. Manage. **27**, 173–184 (2010)
24. Matzler, K., Fuchs, M., Schubert, A.: Employee satisfaction: does Kano's model apply? Total Qual. Manage. Bus. Excellence **15**, 1179–1198 (2004)
25. Chen, C.-C., Chuang, M.-C.: Integrating the Kano model into a robust design approach to enhance customer satisfaction with product design. Int. J. Prod. Econ. **114**, 667–681 (2008)
26. Stade, M., Seyff, N.: Features for mobile feedback tools: applying the KANO method. In: Mensch und Computer 2017 - Tagungsband, pp. 171–180. Gesellschaft für Informatik e.V, Regensburg (2017)
27. Yao, M.-L., Chuang, M.-C., Hsu, C.-C.: The Kano model analysis of features for mobile security applications. Comput. Secur. **78**, 336–346 (2018)
28. Bailom, F., Hinterhuber, H.H., Matzler, K., Sauerwein, E.: Das Kano-Modell der Kundenzufriedenheit. Marketing ZFP **18**, 117–126 (1996)
29. Witell, L., Löfgren, M., Dahlgaard, J.J.: Theory of attractive quality and the Kano methodology – the past, the present, and the future. Total Qual. Manage. Bus. Excellence **24**, 1241–1252 (2013)
30. Cronin, R.M., Conway, D., Condon, D., Jerome, R.N., Byrne, D.W., Harris, P.A.: Patient and healthcare provider views on a patient-reported outcomes portal. J. Am. Med. Inform. Assoc. **25**, 1470–1480 (2018)
31. Webster, J., Watson, R.T.: Analyzing the past to prepare for the future: Writing a literature review. MIS Q. **26**, xiii–xxiii (2002)
32. Sauerwein, E.: Das Kano-Modell der Kundenzufriedenheit. In: Sauerwein, E. (ed.) Das Kano-Modell der Kundenzufriedenheit: Reliabilität und Validität einer Methode zur Klassifizierung von Produkteigenschaften, pp. 27–55. Deutscher Universitätsverlag, Wiesbaden (2000)
33. Hölzing, J.A.: Die Kano-Theorie der Kundenzufriedenheitsmessung. Eine theoretische und empirische Überprüfung. Gabler Verlag/GWV Fachverlage GmbH Wiesbaden, Wiesbaden (2008)
34. Sauerwein, E., Bailom, F., Matzler, K., Hinterhuber, H.: The Kano model: How to delight your customers. In: International Working Seminar on Production Economics, vol. 1 (1996)
35. Lee, M.C., Newcomb, J.F.: Applying the Kano methodology to meet customer requirements: NASA's microgravity science program. Qual. Manage. J. **4**, 95–106 (1997)
36. Löfgren, M., Witell, L.: Kano's theory of attractive quality and packaging. Qual. Manage. J. **12**, 7 (2005)
37. Matzler, K., Hinterhuber, H.H.: How to make product development projects more successful by integrating Kano's model of customer satisfaction into quality function deployment. Technovation **18**, 25–38 (1998)
38. Mohamed, A.H.H.M., Tawfik, H., Al-Jumeily, D., Norton, L.: MoHTAM: a technology acceptance model for mobile health applications. In: Developments in E-systems Engineering, pp. 13–18 (2011)

39. Shen, X.X., Tan, K.C., Xie, M.: An integrated approach to innovative product development using Kano's model and QFD. Eur. J. Innov. Manage. **3**, 91–99 (2000)
40. Pflügner, K., Maier, C., Weitzel, T.: The direct and indirect influence of mindfulness on techno-stressors and job burnout: a quantitative study of white-collar workers. Comput. Hum. Behav. **115**, 106566 (2021)
41. Pflügner, K., Maier, C., Mattke, J., Weitzel, T.: Personality profiles that put users at risk of perceiving technostress: a qualitative comparative analysis with the Big Five personality traits. Bus. Inf. Syst. Eng. **63**, 389–402 (2020)

Managing My Bladder Dictates My Daily Routines – A Model for Design and Adoption of mHealth in Lower Urinary Tract Symptoms Management

Michael Burkard(✉), Jannik Lockl, Tristan Zürl, and Nicolas Ruhland

University of Bayreuth, Wittelsbacherring 10, 95444 Bayreuth, Germany
{michael.burkard,lockl.jannik,tristan.zuerl,
nicolas.wolfgang.ruhland}@uni-bayreuth.de

Abstract. Lower urinary tract symptoms (LUTS) are prevalent urological health issues affecting billions of people worldwide. While conventional aids have unhygienic and cumbersome attributes, mobile health (mHealth) solutions have the potential to significantly improve the quality of life. However, knowledge of how LUTS patients adopt mHealth and how these solutions should be designed is scarce. In this study, we present an adoption model to explain and support the adoption of mHealth solutions by patients suffering from LUTS, and derived design principles to guide future developments of such mHealth. We, therefore, conducted a systematic literature review of 67 papers and followed an action design research approach with 32 expert interviews and a confirmative survey to build, refine, and evaluate the *ex-ante* model. The *ex-post* model consists of five categories and 28 sub-categories of mHealth adoption.

Keywords: Action design research · inContAlert · Literature review · mHealth · Technology acceptance

1 Introduction

Lower urinary tract symptoms (LUTS) are prevalent urological health issues estimated to currently affect 2.3 billion people worldwide [1–3]. Conventional aids to counteract these symptoms predominantly contain unhygienic and cumbersome attributes [4, 5]. Mobile health (mHealth) solutions have the potential to significantly improve both the quality of life and care of those suffering from LUTS [6–8]. The number of mHealth solutions and the amount of respective research are quickly growing [6, 7, 9]. However, mHealth regularly lacks in user acceptance and fails when entering the market [9, 10]. Designing mHealth with the objective to ensure later user adoption needs further guidance and structure [12, 13].

In this study, we present a model for the adoption of mHealth solutions by patients suffering from LUTS and derived principles for designing such mHealth. We developed and evaluated the model along *inContAlert*, an mHealth device to support patients suffering from LUTS in their daily routines and prevent harmful incidents.

F. Ahlemann et al. (Eds.): WI 2021, LNISO 46, pp. 55–61, 2021.
https://doi.org/10.1007/978-3-030-86790-4_4

At the outset, we conducted a systematic literature review [14, 15] to build an *ex-ante* adoption model of factors that positively affect the intention of patients suffering from LUTS to adopt the intended mHealth solution. Subsequently, we applied an action design research (ADR) approach [16] to revise the adoption model and develop an mHealth solution, which noninvasively determines the filling level of the urinary bladder and displays the filling level to a digital end-device. Equally split in the α- and β-cycle, we conducted 20 semi-structured interviews [17–19] with patients suffering from LUTS and twelve with selected experts in various LUTS-related fields. To evaluate our constructs in a larger setting, we conducted a confirmative survey [20] as the last part of the β-cycle. We concluded with the *ex-post* adoption model that we call the *Chronic Disease mHealth Adoption Model* (CDmHAM) and derived principles for designing such mHealth.

2 Background

LUTS occur as a consequence of diseases affecting the urinary bladder and the urethra [21]. Many patients suffer from perturbing symptoms influencing their health-related quality of life and life expectancy [21, 22]. LUTS come along with high stigmatization and psychological problems for those affected [1, 23]. Conventional aids to manage LUTS include absorbent and draining aids, medicaments, surgeries, and strengthening training for pelvic floor muscles. They have in common that they contain unhygienic or cumbersome attributes [4, 5]. Due to their widespread appearance and insufficient means to counteract their symptoms, LUTS have a huge socio-economic impact [23, 25]. Meanwhile, experts predict that digital technologies, such as mHealth applications, have the potential to reduce the overall healthcare costs, further extend life expectancy, and improve the quality of life of those affected [7, 8].

As multiple LUTS result from missing knowledge on the filling level of the urinary bladder [21], an mHealth solution to digitally output that information would be of significant value. Unwanted spontaneous micturition and backflow of urine to the kidneys can be avoided. Yet, under which conditions patients would adopt such an mHealth solution and how it should be designed remain unclear. For this reason, though still grounding on seminal technology acceptance models (i.e., TAM [26], TAM2 [27], and UTAUT [28]), we investigate the adoption and design of such a sensor system.

3 Methodology

3.1 A Literature Review to Build the *Ex-ante* Model

To build the *ex-ante* adoption model, we conducted a systematic literature review following recommendations from vom Brocke et al. [15] and Webster and Watson [14]. We applied title, abstract, and keyword search in the seven online databases PubMed, IEEE Xplore, AISeL, Epistemonikos, Web of Science, ScienceDirect, and EBSCOhost with the search terms *mHealth*, *mobile health*, *noninvasive*, *chronic disease*, *chronic illness*, and *health care*. We limited our search to peer-reviewed research papers and reviews written in English and published between January 2006 and January 2020 [15, 29]. A total of 302 papers was suitable for analysis.

To sort the sample of papers, one co-author reviewed the abstracts in-depth to obtain a detailed overview and assessed the papers with a four-point Likert scale. Articles of score 4 were dropped before a second co-author reviewed the papers with score 3 to drop or give them the score 2. A third co-author read all those with score 2 to finally ex- or include them for the in-depth analysis, concluding in 60 papers with a score 1 [15, 30]. Finally, we found another seven papers relevant for our purpose after a backward/forward search [14]. The so-identified 67 papers were the base for our in-depth analysis, during which we analyzed the papers with open, axial, and selective coding. Identifying basic constructs, we grouped them in superordinate categories and simultaneously built sub-categories between the constructs and categories to implement an additional abstraction level [29, 31, 32].

3.2 Action Design Research to Build the *Ex-Post* Model

The α-cycle

Within the α-cycle of our ADR approach, we developed large parts of the *ex-post* model and the sensor system. To gain an in-depth understanding of the intention of potential users to adopt our mHealth solution, we conducted semi-structured interviews [17–19] with users and practitioners. In the α-cycle, we iteratively interviewed ten patients suffering from LUTS. To include a representative group of interviewees [33, 34], we decided to involve patients suffering from diseases associated with LUTS, such as multiple sclerosis, paraplegia, Parkinson's disease, spina bifida, or stroke. Further, we interviewed six practitioners from urology, neuro-urology, paraplegiology, physiotherapy, or medical technology. We stopped the interview process of the α-cycle after these overall 16 interviews since we realized that new knowledge emerged only marginally and conceptional saturation had been achieved [35]. We conducted all interviews via telephone taking from 25 to 50 min each. The overall structure of the explorative interviews reached from open to more specific questions about the adoption model and the α-version of the sensor system. We analyzed the interviews qualitatively using coding techniques from grounded theory [29, 32, 36], hence revised the *ex-ante* adoption model, and developed the β-version of the sensor system.

The β-cycle

During the β-cycle, we evaluated, incrementally enhanced, and confirmed the results of the α-cycle to conclude with the CDmHAM and derive design principles from the so-built sensor system. To ensure the generalizability of our findings, we interviewed ten new patients suffering from LUTS in the β-cycle [17–19]. This time, the sample consisted of individuals suffering from congenital LUTS, multiple sclerosis, paraplegia, prostate cancer, or stroke. Furthermore, we interviewed six practitioners from urology, paraplegiology, physiotherapy, daycare of demented patients, or medical technology. We again stopped the interview process in the β-cycle since we realized conceptional saturation [35]. In the β-cycle, the interviews were of confirmatory nature to appropriately evaluate the initial findings, although, all interviewees were invited to complement with new insights. Building upon these findings, we concluded with the CDmHAM, developed the final sensor system, and derived a catalog of principles for designing mHealth solutions.

Finally, we conducted an online survey to validate our previous findings in a larger setting [20]. We applied this quantitative approach, as we sought to weight our sub-categories regarding their relevance to allow for a better focus of later research and practice [18, 37]. In the survey, we asked participants to rate our sub-categories concerning their relevance on a scale from 1 to 7 where 1 means the sub-category is not important at all and 7 means the sub-category is very important. Patients suffering from LUTS as well as care assistants supporting respective patients were allowed to take part in the survey. In the end, a total of 387 individuals participated. We analyzed the survey examining mean scores, standard deviations, and variances of the ratings.

4 Results

As a result of the literature review, we identified factors affecting the intention of potential users to adopt mHealth solutions in general. Our *ex-ante* adoption model consisted of five superordinate categories (i.e., *User Factors, Perceived Benefits, Hard- and Software, Data Factors, Environment*) and 21 sub-categories. Building upon the generic *ex-ante* model, we developed the α-version of the sensor system. Within the α- and β-cycle of our ADR approach, we specified our perspective on LUTS patients and practitioners. We confirmed the five categories and enhanced them to conclude in 28 sub-categories. The *ex-post* adoption model (i.e., the CDmHAM) in Fig. 1 depicts the interrelations between the categories, the adoption intention, and the design of mHealth devices.

In the following, we provide an overview of the identified sub-categories and list them adding their mean scores obtained from the survey to illustrate the relevance of each. First, the category *User Factors* is characterized by *Accessibility* (5.96), *Customization* (6.12), *Initial User Briefing* (6.20), and *Constant User Consulting* (5.78). Second, *Perceived Benefits* are split into *Usefulness* (6.14), *Autonomy* (6.38), *Convenience* (6.37), *Comfort* (6.30), *Mobility* (6.54), and *Unobtrusiveness* (6.23). Third, *Hardware and Software* build upon *Safety* (6.39), *Reliability* (6.52), *Performance* (6.32), *Durability* (6.28), *Hardware Fixation* (5.60), *Design* (4.78), *Interoperability* (5.23), and *Connectivity* (5.26). Fourth, in terms of *Data Factors, Generation and Integration* (5.14), *Storage and Access* (5.13), *Analysis* (5.27), *Feedback on Usage* (5.66), *Transfer* (5.19), and *Privacy* (5.73) are relevant. *Environment*, fifth, is determined by *Ongoing Maintenance* (6.01), *Costs* (5.89), *Health Insurance Involvement* (6.19), and *Provider Involvement* (6.12). *Perceived Benefits* is the most important superordinate category, and its sub-categories all belong to the top ten of the most relevant ones. Noticeably, the category *Data Factors* obtains the lowest relevance by far. On the sub-category level, *Design* shows the lowest mean of all sub-categories.

Resulting from the β-cycle, the final version of the sensor system comprises an mHealth sensor device, a monitoring app, and an additional drinking protocol app. Furthermore, we derived a catalog of 26 design principles guiding future developments of mHealth for LUTS and other chronic health issues. Design principles addressing the hardware comprise *Miniaturization, Flexibility, Soft Materials, Lightweight Construction, Smooth Surface, Wireless Device, Transparency, Washability, Biocompatibility*, and *Durable Components*. Addressing both the hard- and software, *Plug-and-Play, Reduction of Manual Input, Clearness, Voice Assistant, Multiple Interfaces, Energy Efficiency*,

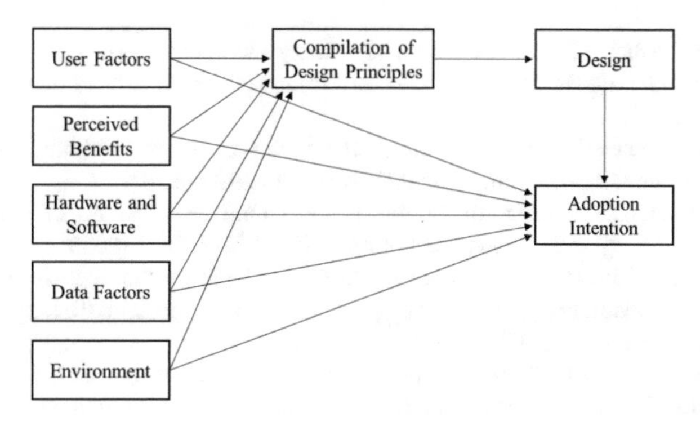

Fig. 1. The chronic disease mhealth adoption model

Internal Data Storage, and *Cost-Effectiveness* are relevant. In terms of the software, *Readability*, *Intuitive Operating Steps*, *Appropriate Language*, *Graphic Visualization*, *Mobile-Friendly Software*, *Cloud Computing*, *Alert Mechanism*, and *Learning Algorithm* are pivotal determinants to be considered.

5 Discussion

As research provides little knowledge on mHealth adoption with urological health issues, we followed a multi-method approach to build both the CDmHAM and catalog of design principles. Integrating patient and expert interviews, we ensured the applicability of our generic model for the specific case of LUTS. Our study thereby contributes with a comprehensive model of mHealth adoption [cf., 26–28].

Our study faces limitations as we investigated neither dependencies between factors nor the influence of moderating variables [38]. Hence, we invite future studies to investigate whether the factors depend on each other, to identify specific moderating variables, and to probe their effect within the CDmHAM and on the catalog of design principles. Since potential users assessed the relevance of the adoption factors, we suggest focusing on the most relevant ones while investigating mHealth adoption and developing mHealth devices.

Concluding, we obtained an adoption model as well as a catalog of design principles specifically applicable in LUTS management and supposed to apply to other chronic diseases as well. The comprehensiveness of factors and principles and the proven applicability for LUTS are valuable for research. We invite researchers to build upon our findings and validate and enhance both the model and the catalog.

References

1. Irwin, D.E., Kopp, Z.S., Agatep, B., Milsom, I., Abrams, P.: Worldwide prevalence estimates of lower urinary tract symptoms, overactive bladder, urinary incontinence and bladder outlet obstruction. BJU Int. **108**, 1132–1138 (2011)
2. DeMaagd, G.A., Davenport, T.C.: Management of urinary incontinence. Pharm. Therapeut. **37**, 345–361H (2012)

3. Rizvi, R.M., Ather, M.H.: Assessment of urinary incontinence (UI) in adult patients. In: Alhasso, A., Bekarma, H. (eds.) Synopsis in the Management of Urinary Incontinence. InTech (2017)
4. German Continence Society: Heil- und Hilfsmittel. https://www.kontinenz-gesellschaft.de/Heil-und-Hilfsmittel.187.0.html?&L=872. Accessed 29 June 2020
5. Toye, F., Barker, K.L.: A meta-ethnography to understand the experience of living with urinary incontinence: 'is it just part and parcel of life?' BMC Urol. **20**, 1 (2020)
6. Dou, K., et al.: Patients' acceptance of smartphone health technology for chronic disease management: a theoretical model and empirical test. JMIR mHealth uHealth **5**, e177 (2017)
7. Silva, B.M.C., Rodrigues, J.J.P.C., La Torre Díez, I., de López-Coronado, M., Saleem, K.: Mobile-health: a review of current state in 2015. J. Biomed. Inform. **56**, 265–272 (2015)
8. World Health Organization: mHealth. New horizons for health through mobile technologies. World Health Organization, Geneva (2011)
9. Jiang, Y., West, B.T., Barton, D.L., Harris, M.R.: Acceptance and use of ehealth/mhealth applications for self-management among cancer survivors. Stud. Health Technol. Inform. **245**, 131–135 (2017)
10. Krebs, P., Duncan, D.T.: Health app use among us mobile phone owners: a national survey. JMIR mHealth uHealth **3**, e101 (2015)
11. Pan, A., Zhao, F.: User acceptance factors for mHealth. In: Kurosu, M. (ed.) HCI 2018. LNCS, vol. 10902, pp. 173–184. Springer, Cham (2018). https://doi.org/10.1007/978-3-319-91244-8_14
12. Bernard, S., Boucher, S., McLean, L., Moffet, H.: Mobile technologies for the conservative self-management of urinary incontinence: a systematic scoping review. Int. Urogynecol. J. **31**(6), 1163–1174 (2019). https://doi.org/10.1007/s00192-019-04012-w
13. Noorbergen, T.J., Adam, M.T.P., Attia, J.R., Cornforth, D.J., Minichiello, M.: Exploring the design of mhealth systems for health behavior change using mobile biosensors. CAIS 944–981 (2019)
14. Webster, J., Watson, R.T.: Analyzing the past to prepare for the future: writing a literature review. MIS Q. **26**, xiii–xxiii (2002)
15. vom Brocke, J., Simons, A., Riemer, K., Niehaves, B., Plattfaut, R., Cleven, A.: Standing on the shoulders of giants: challenges and recommendations of literature search in information systems research. CAIS **37**, 205–224 (2015)
16. Sein, M.K., Henfridsson, O., Purao, S., Rossi, M., Lindgren, R.: Action design research. MIS Q. **35**, 37–56 (2011)
17. Myers, M.D., Newman, M.: The qualitative interview in IS research: examining the craft. Inf. Organ. **17**, 2–26 (2007)
18. Malterud, K.: Qualitative research: standards, challenges, and guidelines. Lancet **358**, 483–488 (2001)
19. Curry, L.A., Nembhard, I.M., Bradley, E.H.: Qualitative and mixed methods provide unique contributions to outcomes research. Circulation **119**, 1442–1452 (2009)
20. Dillman, D.A., Smyth, J.D., Christian, L.M.: Internet, Phone, Mail, and Mixed-Mode Surveys. The Tailored Design Method. Wiley, Hoboken (2014)
21. International Continence Society: Fact Sheets. A Background to Urinary and Faecal Incontinence (2015)
22. Damián, J., Pastor-Barriuso, R., García López, F.J., de Pedro-Cuesta, J.: Urinary incontinence and mortality among older adults residing in care homes. J. Adv. Nurs. **73**, 688–699 (2017)
23. Neubauer, G., Stiefelmeyer, S.: Economic costs of urinary incontinence in Germany. In: Becker, H.-D., Stenzl, A., Wallwiener, D., Zittel, T.T. (eds.) Urinary and Fecal Incontinence, pp. 25–31. Springer, Heidelberg (2005)
24. Subak, L., van den Eeden, S., Thom, D., Creasman, J.M., Brown, J.S.: Urinary incontinence in women: direct costs of routine care. Am. J. Obstet. Gynecol. **197**(596), e1–596.e9 (2007)

25. Nitti, V.W.: The prevalence of urinary incontinence. Rev. Urol. **3**, S2–6 (2001)
26. Davis, F.D., Bagozzi, R.P., Warshaw, P.R.: User acceptance of computer technology: a comparison of two theoretical models. Manage. Sci. **35**, 982–1003 (1989)
27. Venkatesh, V., Davis, F.D.: A theoretical extension of the technology acceptance model: four longitudinal field studies. Manage. Sci. **46**, 186–204 (2000)
28. Venkatesh, V., Morris, M.G., Davis, G.B.: User acceptance of information technology: toward a unified view. MIS Q. **27**, 425–478 (2003)
29. Wolfswinkel, J.F., Furtmueller, E., Wilderom, C.P.M.: Using grounded theory as a method for rigorously reviewing literature. Eur. J. Inf. Syst. **22**, 45–55 (2013)
30. Bandara, W., Furtmueller, E., Gorbacheva, E., Miskon, S., Beekhuyzen, J.: Achieving rigor in literature reviews: insights from qualitative data analysis and tool-support. CAIS **37**, 154–204 (2015)
31. Wiesche, M., Jurisch, M.C., Yetton, P.W., Krcmar, H.: Grounded theory methodology in information systems research. MIS Q. **41**, 685–701 (2017)
32. Corbin, J.M., Strauss, A.: Grounded theory research: procedures, canons, and evaluative criteria. Qual. Sociol. **13**, 3–21 (1990)
33. Barrat, H., Shantikumar, S.: Methods of sampling from a population. https://www.healthknowledge.org.uk/public-health-textbook/research-methods/1a-epidemiology/methods-of-sampling-population. Accessed 19 Aug 2020
34. Etikan, I.: Comparison of convenience sampling and purposive sampling. AJTAS **5**, 1–4 (2016)
35. Briggs, R.O., Schwabe, G.: On expanding the scope of design science in IS research. In: Jain, H., Sinha, A.P., Vitharana, P. (eds.) DESRIST 2011. LNCS, vol. 6629, pp. 92–106. Springer, Heidelberg (2011). https://doi.org/10.1007/978-3-642-20633-7_7
36. DeCuir-Gunby, J.T., Marshall, P.L., McCulloch, A.W.: Developing and using a codebook for the analysis of interview data: an example from a professional development research project. Field Methods **23**, 136–155 (2011)
37. Venkatesh, V., Brown, S.A., Bala, H.: Bridging the qualitative-quantitative divide: guidelines for conducting mixed methods research in information systems. MIS Q. **37**, 21–54 (2013)
38. Cohen, J., Cohen, P., West, S.G., Aiken, L.S.: Applied Multiple Regression/correlation Analysis for the Behavioral Sciences. Erlbaum, Mahwah (2003)

Let's Get Engaged: On the Evidence of Patient Engagement Tools and Their Integration in Patient Pathways

Emily Hickmann, Peggy Richter(✉), and Hannes Schlieter

Chair of Wirtschaftsinformatik, esp. Systems Development, Technische Universität Dresden, Dresden, Germany
{emily.hickmann,peggy.richter2,hannes.schlieter}@tu-dresden.de

Abstract. Patient pathways are a means to structure the care process for patients with complex and long-term diseases in integrated care networks. Simultaneously, they have a stronger emphasis on the patient perspective and engagement than related pathway concepts. Still, there are no common mechanisms for patient engagement concepts in patient pathway models. This paper therefore explores the state-of-the-art of patient engagement tools as well as evidence on their effectivity and feasibility, picking the Option Grid, the Patient Diary, and the Question Prompt Sheet (QPS) as representative examples. Based on this, we propose recommendations for the representation of such tools in patient pathway models and demonstrate them with the application of the QPS in a colorectal cancer patient pathway. To conclude, the evidence on patient engagement tools is still diverse but promising. Anchoring successful tools in patient pathways holds the potential to support their broader application and enhance individualized care.

Keywords: Patient engagement · Patient pathway · Shared decision-making · Literature review

1 Introduction

Current challenges in the health care sector, including sectoral boundaries, the financing system and demographic changes, result in an increased need for a transparent and well-organized coordination of patients through their individual care processes. At the same time, an efficient distribution of resources has to be ensured. The recreation of processes is a central strategy to combat these challenges, as a well-designed process can for instance promote continuity of care, ensure an efficient resource allocation and support the decision-making process [1]. In the health care sector, a common tool used to design processes is the pathway.

In medicine, there is no standardized definition for the term pathway. Küttner and Roeder (2007) [2] describe three main components of pathways that seem to be prominent in all definitions: They refer to a specific patient group, are used by an interprofessional treatment team and define a diagnostic and therapeutic action corridor [2]. A major concern regarding pathways in medicine is that they could foster depersonalisation,

F. Ahlemann et al. (Eds.): WI 2021, LNISO 46, pp. 62–78, 2021.
https://doi.org/10.1007/978-3-030-86790-4_5

as they may be based too heavily on the requirements of an average patient, leaving diminutive space for individual needs and decisions. Even though a main aim of pathways is to reduce variations and therefore guarantee all patients the same level of a high-quality treatment, they also have the potential to foster individualization. These concepts may seem contrary at first, however a well-designed pathway must be flexible enough to be personalized to individual cases in a standardized manner [3]. For example, a pathway can incorporate steps where the patients are systematically asked for feedback or input on the respective health issue. This information could then decide the further route that is taken in the pathway. It therefore needs to enable the users to navigate patients through different options and stages, depending on the individual decision-making process [4]. Compared to other pathway approaches, patient pathways have a very prominent focus on individualization [5]. Therefore, the concepts of patient engagement and shared decision-making (SDM) need to have a central part in the design and implementation of the pathway process.

There is no widely accepted definition of the term patient engagement, however a comprehensive definition by Higgins et al. (2017) defines it as *"the desire and capability to actively choose to participate in care in a way uniquely appropriate to the individual, in cooperation with a healthcare provider or institution, for the purpose of maximizing outcomes or improving experiences of care"* [6]. An important aspect of this definition is a patient's capability to participate. In order to be capable, patients must acquire the necessary knowledge to decide, which is an integral part of patient empowerment. Other characteristics include capacity building, gaining control over the situation, motivation, self-care and trust [7]. SDM is an integral part of engaging patients into their health care process. It implies an active engagement of the patient and the physician in the decision-making process by sharing information and personal values [7, 8].

Actively engaging patients yields multiple benefits for all stakeholders along the care process. Engaged patients have a better awareness and understanding of their condition, leading to an enhanced communication with their health care professionals [9]. As a result, compliance is fostered and the health status improves. Different authors [9–11] agree that patient engagement has the potential to reduce health care costs and enhance a more appropriate and effective usage of resources. The quality of health care delivery is enhanced further, as less treatment errors tend to occur when patients are engaged in the process [9–11]. When combining the concepts of patient pathways and patient engagement a higher quality of care can be guaranteed throughout the health care process. Patient pathways will become more individualized, therefore putting more emphasis on patient's individual needs. Simultaneously, patient engagement concepts are not yet represented in patient pathways to support these aims.

Therefore, the research objective of this paper is to explore how patient engagement tools (i.e. an item that supports the user in enhancing patient engagement, similar to an instrument or a utensil) can be integrated into patient pathways. In order to do this, diverse patient engagement tools will be analyzed and opportunities for their practical implementation into patient pathways will be shown. Two research questions (RQ) are to be answered: *RQ1: What is the evidence for the effectivity and feasibility of patient engagement tools?* The effectivity of the respective tool refers to the extent to which the goals, or characteristics of patient engagement are enhanced through its implementation or usage. Feasibility refers to how practical and acceptable the tool is for all stakeholders involved in the process. *RQ2: How can patient engagement tools be used in patient pathways?*

Accordingly, the remainder of this article is structured as follows: The used method of a literature review is described in Sect. 2. The review results are given in Sect. 3. In total, three out of nine evaluated tools are presented in this paper (selection criteria explained in Sect. 2.1). These are the Option Grid, the Patient Diary, and the Question Prompt Sheet (QPS), which are described in Subsect. 3.1 (referring to answering RQ1). In Sect. 3.2, a representation form for the utilization of patient engagement tools in patient pathways is proposed (referring to answering RQ2). For demonstration purposes, the representation of an engagement tool in a colorectal cancer patient pathway is used as an example. The paper closes with a conclusion and discussion in Sect. 4.

2 Method

2.1 Preliminary Study on Patient Engagement Tools

A preliminary study, with the objective to present the current state-of-the-art on tools to engage patients into their health care process was conducted. For this purpose, a literature review in the scientific database PubMed was performed in November 2019. The search string consisted of alternative terms for "patient engagement" in combination with the terms "method", "tool", "aid", "instrument", "strategy" or "implementation". In total 772 articles were identified. From 228 full-text articles that were assessed for eligibility, 53 records were included in the final preliminary study. A study was included if any kind of tool (including the alternative terms used above) was used to involve patients in their own treatment or care. Extraneous topics, such as training programmes or challenges of patient engagement were excluded. The results are a mixture of specific tools, but also diverse strategies that either the physician or the patient can utilize to enhance patient engagement. When only considering the concrete, practical tools (strategies were generally too concrete for a broad evaluation) the following nine could be distinguished: Adaptive Conjoint Analysis (ACA), Best Case/ Worst Case (BC/WC), Decision Box, Option Grid, Patient Empowerment Tool (PET), Patient Diary, Patient Portals, Question Prompt Sheets and the Roulette Wheel. These were evaluated and due to space limitations only three of them were selected for a detailed result presentation in this paper. The Option Grid, Patient Diary and Question Prompt Sheet were chosen for this purpose, as they are intensively considered in literature, can be used in diverse health settings and at different points in time along the patient pathway (i.e. diagnosis, treatment, rehabilitation). The results on the other tools are summarized only shortly in Sect. 3.1.

2.2 Literature Review on the Evidence of Patient Engagement Tools

To answer RQ1, a literature review following the guidelines proposed by Rowley and Slack (2004) [12] was conducted. In the first step, a quick scan on the respective tool was performed, in order to gain a general understanding about its operating mode and possible alternative terms that are used in literature. This information was used to create the search string for the tools, which is depicted in Table 1. A separate search was conducted for each tool and the search string was partially adapted depending on the functionalities of the respective database. Furthermore, the search string for patient portals and personal health records was adapted to include an outcome component to specify the results. This was not necessary for other tools, due to their low prominence in literature.

Table 1. Search string used for literature review

<table>
<tr><td>Patient OR Patients (PubMed)
Patient$ (Web of Science)</td><td>AND (PubMed)
NEAR/4 (Web of Science)</td><td>Empower* OR Engag* OR Involv*</td></tr>
<tr><td colspan="3">OR</td></tr>
<tr><td colspan="3">Shared decision making</td></tr>
<tr><td colspan="3">OR</td></tr>
<tr><td colspan="3">Patient participation [MeSH Term] (PubMed only)</td></tr>
<tr><td colspan="3">AND</td></tr>
<tr><td colspan="3">Adaptive Conjoint Analysis</td></tr>
<tr><td colspan="3">Best Case/ Worst Case</td></tr>
<tr><td colspan="3">Decision Box*</td></tr>
<tr><td colspan="3">Option Grid* (PubMed)
Option Grid$ (Web of Science)</td></tr>
<tr><td colspan="3">Patient Empowerment Tool</td></tr>
<tr><td colspan="3">Diary OR Diaries (PubMed)
(Patient$ OR Symptom$) NEAR/4 (Diary OR Diaries) (Web of Science)</td></tr>
<tr><td colspan="3">(Personal health record* OR Patient portal*) AND (Outcome* OR Effect* OR Consequence*) (PubMed)
(Personal health record$ OR Patient portal$) NEAR/6 (Outcome* OR Effect* OR Consequence*) (Web of Science)</td></tr>
<tr><td colspan="3">Question Prompt Sheet* (Pub Med)
Question Prompt Sheet$ (Web of Science)</td></tr>
<tr><td colspan="3">Roulette wheel* OR Dart board* OR Pie chart* (PubMed)
Roulette wheel$ OR Dart board$ OR Pie chart$ (Web of Science)</td></tr>
</table>

During the literature selection process, any record that addressed effectivity or feasibility of patient engagement, as defined in Sect. 1, was included. Publications focusing on extraneous topics were excluded. For example, articles not referring to the tool, as described in Sect. 3.1, were excluded. This was, however, seldomly the case, because the individual search string already contained the specific name of the tool. The literature selection process is summarized in Table 2.

After completing this process, the information retrieved from the review process was structured and is summarized in Sect. 3. As the records selected have very different study designs and therefore levels of reliability, the Oxford scale of evidence was used to put the obtained information into context. The evidence level (EL) of each included study is noted in brackets behind the references of the study and an overview is given in Table 3. Levels could be graded down on basis of study quality, imprecision, indirectness, because of inconsistency between studies or because the absolute effect size was very

Table 2. Literature selection process

	Records identified through database search	Records after duplicates were removed	Records screened in title and abstract	Records assessed in full-text	Records included
ACA	12	9	9	8	7
BC/ WC	9	5	5	4	4
Decision Box	15	8	8	6	2
Option Grid	32	21	21	13	9
PET	2	1	1	1	1
Patient diary	53	51	51	12	6
Patient portal	73	70	70	26	14
QPS	13	10	10	6	4
Roulette Wheel	4	3	3	3	3

small. Studies could be graded up if there was a large effect size. Systematic reviews were generally assessed as better than individual studies [13]. They will also be referred to in the individual summaries for each tool, when answering RQ1.

Table 3. Number of sources used assessed with the oxford scale of evidence

EL	ACA	BC/WC	Decision box	Option grid	Patient diary	Patient portal	PET	QPS	Roulette wheel
I	0	0	0	0	1	1	0	0	0
II	1	0	0	0	1	3	0	3	0
III	2	0	0	2	1	5	0	0	1
IV	4	4	2	6	2	5	1	1	1
V	0	0	0	1	1	0	0	0	1

I: Systematic review of randomized trials or n-of-1 trials
II: Randomized trial or observational study with dramatic effect
III: Non-randomized controlled cohort/follow-up study
IV: Case-series, case-control studies, or historically controlled studies
V: Mechanism-based reasoning

3 Results

3.1 Evidence-Based Patient Engagement Tools

Option Grids. An Option Grid is a one- to maximum three-page summary of all available healthcare options for a specific treatment decision. The information is categorized in form of patients most frequently asked questions when considering different treatment options. For example, likely outcomes, risks and benefits are commonly discussed.

Providers can also choose which options they want to present to the patient and can customize the grid with patient-specific data [14, 15].

Three of the included studies were conducted on Option Grids for knee osteoarthritis. During the first study, a step-wedged trial with a population of older patients (with lower than average health literacy), the Option Grid led to higher knowledge levels of the patients about the osteoarthritis and its treatment possibilities. Furthermore, an increased readiness to decide for one of the options and an overall improvement of the SDM levels could be observed. This enhanced patient engagement was achieved without prolonging the duration of the encounters [16] (EL: III). During the second study, clinician interviews were performed before and after adoption of the knee osteoarthritis Option Grid. After initial concerns before adoption, the usage of the tool was generally seen as acceptable and helpful for the communication process during the patient encounter, while simultaneously helping clinicians take on a more neutral position. Additionally, they experienced that the patients had a more active role, asking more questions during the consultation [17] (EL: IV). In the third study by Kinsey et al. (2017) interviews with patients using the Option Grid during consultation and a control group were performed. The patients in the intervention group showed an increased awareness of the different treatment options, while the patients in the control group were less clear about the fact that different treatment options had been discussed. The physicians working with the control group also seemed to focus the discussion on risks and benefits concerning the (for them) most likely option. Acceptability of the tool for patients was rated as high. Most patients in the intervention group felt more involved in the decision-making process, however both groups felt that they had finally made their own treatment decision [18] (EL: III).

In a further study by Smith et al. (2019) an Option Grid for knee replacement surgery was evaluated. The Option Grid made patients feel better informed and provided them with a starting point for further individual research. This is an important aspect for the development of patient engagement [19] (EL: IV).

Two studies focused on Option Grids for breast cancer. Both studies concluded that the Option Grid was acceptable and feasible for facilitating patient involvement and for improving the perceived understanding of patients. The study by Hahlweg et al. (2019) (EL: IV) highlighted the importance of training physicians on the usage of the Option Grid in order to promote acceptance [20, 21] (EL: IV). In a further study, an Option Grid for the usage of antipsychotic medication was evaluated positively. In interviews the tool was perceived as usable, context appropriate and feasible in psychiatric consultations by patients, psychiatrists, family members and administrators [22] (EL: IV). This is supported by the opinion of a general practitioner and professor of primary health care, who concludes that the information in Option Grids is presented in a format that allows both reflection and dialogue. In contrast to other SDM-tools the physician also sees the benefit in the simplicity of Option Grids, stating that *"neither the patient nor the clinician needs to be a geek to use them"* [23] (EL: V).

Only one study was found, in which an Option Grid did not have an influence on the degree of SDM. This was a pre-post intervention study by Scalia et al. (2018), in which over a time period of three months the Option Grid tool was used for diverse conditions in a clinical setting [15] (EL: IV).

Patient Diary. A Patient Diary is a simple tool that can be used by patients for self-monitoring. For example, symptoms, body weight, blood pressure or activities can be recorded and, when necessary, presented to health care providers [24].

Several records evaluated the feasibility of Patient Diaries. For example, feasibility and acceptance of internet-based and telephone-based diaries were tested in a study by Cherenack et al. (2016) amongst a population of 61 young HIV-infected men. Diary data and qualitative interviews showed that the internet diaries were preferred by 92% of the population with a completion rate of 78% over a 66-day measure. Generally, keeping the diaries was described as promoting self-reflection and behavior tracking [25] (EL: IV).

During a study with 393 rural patients, who recorded symptoms on heart failure, it was found that participants actively using a Patient Diary lived longer. For example, patients with a "very high" diary usage, were 39% less likely to die due to heart failure compared to patients using no diary [26] (EL: III). Using the diary is closely connected to self-management skills and treatment adherence, due to which these results can be partially explained.

Hodge (2013), a family physician and clinical instructor explains that Patient Diaries have a series of advantages. These include that keeping diaries gives patients a sense of control, therefore engaging them more into the treatment process. Furthermore, in terms of feasibility, it takes physicians less time to review the one-page diary than to verbally interview a patient for the same information [27] (EL: V). This opinion is supported by a study of Himes et al. (2016). It was found that self-management programs that include diaries, compared to those that do not, are associated with a higher disease control, enhanced life quality and fewer hospital visits [28] (EL: IV).

In direct contrast to this, are the results of the study by Schmidt et al. (2015). A trial comparing length of hospital stay and quality of life (one year after hospitalization) in a group of 652 patients concluded that the diary did not have an effect on these aspects. Participants were randomly assigned to receive either standard care or an information booklet and a diary. Their mean age of the patients was 72 years. Patient empowerment through booklet and diary did, however, have a positive influence on patient's short-term well-being, such as postoperative pain [29] (EL: II). Also, a systematic review by Ullman et al. (2014) concludes that there is minimal evidence from randomized controlled trials that Patient Diaries do any benefit or harm. This review was set in the context of patients in the intensive care unit [30] (EL: I).

Question Prompt Sheet. QPSs are lists of frequently asked questions that patients can take into a consultation. They are specified to the respective disease or condition the patient is in. Additionally, space is given for patients to take notes or record further questions. Their goal is to animate the patient to become a proactive customer by asking more questions during the consultation and therefore also gain more knowledge on their condition [31, 32].

Arthur et al. (2017) tested the QPS in a palliative care setting. In total 100 patients and 12 physicians received the tool and were interviewed on their perception of its helpfulness. Overall, both patients and physicians had a positive connotation towards QPS. Most stated the tool was helpful for communicating with the physician (77%), clear to understand (90%) and they would use a similar tool in the future (76%). Physicians perceived QPS as helpful for 68% of encounters and 73% stated it did not prolong the duration of the consultation. Acceptability and feasibility of this tool are rated very positively in this study. Additionally, patient anxiety was measured before and after consultation. Results indicated a significant decrease in patient anxiety after consultation. The results were, however, not compared to a control group, that did not receive QPS. This makes it difficult to link the usage of the tool to reduced anxiety, as patients could generally be less anxious after a consultation [33] (EL: IV).

The information obtained in Arthur et al. (2017) is supported by the study of Brown et al. (2001), which concludes that QPS, which are actively addressed by the physician during consultation, enhance information recall, reduce anxiety and shorten the length of the encounter. In order to reach these conclusions 318 patients with cancer, seeing their oncologists for the first time, were randomized to receive or not receive a QPS. The group that received the tool was again divided into patients, whose physicians would actively address the prompt sheet in the consultation and patients, whose physicians would not. The consultations were audio-taped and standardized questionnaires and interviews used, to gain information from the patients. The results indicated that patients with QPS asked more questions on prognosis and therefore received more information from their physician on the topic. If the tool was, however, not directly addressed by the physician, it had a negative impact: increasing patient anxiety after the encounter and prolonging consultation duration [34] (EL: II).

In 1999 the same author was already part of an intervention to promote question-asking behaviour in patients. The effectiveness of QPS was compared to coaching sessions exploring benefits and barriers to question-asking as well as rehearsal techniques. It was found that the QPS (addressed by the doctor) had a significantly greater effect on promoting patients to ask more questions, thus involving them in the consultation [35] (EL: II).

In contrast to this, a study by Butow et al. (1994) found that the QPS did generally not increase the number of questions asked, however questions on prognosis increased from 16% in the control group to 35% in the intervention group. In this randomized controlled trial 142 patients either received a QPS or a general paper informing them of available services in the institution [36] (EL: II).

Further Patient Engagement Tools. Due to space limitations, the results of the other six patient engagement tools that were evaluated are not displayed in detail. Instead, a short summary is given in Table 4.

Discussion of the Evidence on Patient Engagement Tools. When considering the results obtained, the effectivity and feasibility of the three patient engagement tools, Option Grid, Patient Diary, and QPS seems to generally be high. Especially for the Option Grid and the QPS both measures can be evaluated positively.

When summarizing the information obtained for the Option Grid, it can be concluded that there is no study displaying any negative impacts through the usage of Option Grids. Effectiveness, in terms of increasing SDM and patient engagement, was present in multiple studies. Feasibility is partially given, if the encounter is not prolonged through usage of the tool, which was measured and positively evaluated in one study. This is, however, surely dependent on the design of the Option Grid and training of the physicians. Acceptability of the tool seems to be very high, especially for patients.

Table 4. Overview on effectiveness and feasibility of further patient engagement tools

Tool	Effectivity	Feasibility	Representative sources
ACA	+	++	[37] EL: IV; [38] EL: IV; [39] EL: III
BC/WC	++	+	[40] EL: IV; [41] EL: IV
Decision box	0	+	[42] EL: IV
PET	0	0	[43] EL: IV
Patient portal	0	+	[44] EL: III; [45] EL: I; [46] EL: II
Roulette wheel	+	0	[47] EL: IV; [48] EL: V

++ Evidence for effectivity/feasibility is present to a large extent
+ Evidence for effectivity/feasibility is generally present
0 Evidence is controversial or there are no sources available
- Evidence for effectivity/feasibility is generally not present
-- Evidence for effectivity/feasibility is not present to a large extent

Results for the effectiveness of Patient Diaries, in the sense of enhancing patient engagement, are controversial. Monitoring personal symptoms is already a form of engaging oneself with the individual health status. Self-reflection is fostered and decisions that need to be made with the physician are more informed, which can have a positive impact on SDM. Still, the two studies with the highest levels in the Oxford Scale of Evidence for Patient Diaries, both portrayed only marginal proof of benefits the tool may generate, so that a decisive conclusion is not possible without any further research on the topic. There is no evidence that Patient Diaries can have a negative impact. Feasibility seems to be present to a large extent. Acceptance for the Patient Diary was proven amongst a population of very young adults, in an online format of the tool. Feasibility is also fostered by the expert's opinion that retrieving the information from a Patient Diary is faster, therefore shortening the duration of consultations.

When summarizing the results of the studies found for the QPS, it can be concluded that acceptability and feasibility for the tool are high. Duration of the encounter (when used in the correct manner) is shortened through the QPS, which suggests a high feasibility. Helpfulness was also rated positively by patients and physicians. Effectiveness and therefore patient engagement is the extent to which patients are more involved in consultation and therefore ask more questions to gain an increased understanding of their condition. This is also the basis for SDM to take place. As shown in the studies, QPS are generally very effective for promoting question-asking behaviour. For this tool, it is noticeable that the records are comparably old. The most recent study from 2017, however, also reflects the positive results obtained in the other sources.

When considering the obtained results, it can be concluded that evidence for the effectivity and feasibility of Option Grids and QPS is present to a large extent. Evidence for these two criteria in Patient Diaries is at least given partially. It can therefore be derived that an enhanced usage of some patient engagement tools in practice has the potential to yield multiple benefits associated with patient engagement. Furthermore, the possibility that other patient engagement tools may also prove to be effective and feasible is conceivable.

3.2 Representation and Utilization of Patient Engagement Tools in Patient Pathways

Recommendation for Representation. In order to answer RQ2, two main areas of interest need to be discussed. First, it must be considered to which patient pathway elements the tools can be linked. Second, a meaningful representation of the tools in patient pathways, including variations for diverse characteristics, is necessary.

The Business Process Model and Notation (BPMN) is a domain-independent conceptual modelling language, commonly used as a visual representation of complex business processes in economy and industry. However, BPMN is also used for modelling care processes and is an established approach in health care practice [49, 50]. There are healthcare-specific BPMN extensions for pathway modelling such as BPMN4CP [51]. For this reason, we choose BPMN4CP for patient pathway representation and patient engagement tool inclusion.

When considering the purpose of diverse patient engagement tools, it becomes clear that they are generally used to support specific tasks, e.g. communication or self-management. Also, SDM is a task, which needs to be performed at some point in the process jointly by the physician and the patient. It is therefore clear, that SDM tools can be attached to this specific task, which will be prominent in all patient pathways, as these already have a focus on individual patient planning and management. What also supports the idea of attaching patient engagement tools to particular tasks, is that such tools always need to be introduced or handed over to the patient in some form. This means that someone must actively correspond with the patient about the tool. Tasks in patient pathways often already incorporate an interaction between the patient and a health care professional, through which the further integration of a tool at this point does not lead to additional efforts.

It should also be considered when, not only where, patient engagement tools can generally be used. Many cannot be used in every kind of pathway (depending on the condition) or with any type of patient. As an example, SDM tools can only be utilized for conditions in which there are multiple, reasonable different treatment options, these options are sensitive to preferences that patients may have (involve trade-offs) and the evidence for choosing one option over another must be uncertain [52]. Additionally, not all patients want to be involved in their care or in decision-making processes. Preferences can differ dramatically, meaning that a patient's personality must also be considered when deciding if and what kind of patient engagement tools to use [53]. Furthermore, a pathway should not be overloaded by diverse patient engagement tools. Some can be combined in a manner that makes sense, but for example using multiple different SDM tools for the same decision may only confuse the patient. Therefore, which tools fit best to the different workflows for conditions described through the pathways, needs to be thought through and tested individually.

The symbol proposed for the representation of patient engagement tools in patient pathways is depicted in Fig. 1. It can be connected to the element in the patient pathway using a dotted line.

Fig. 1. Symbol for patient engagement tool[1]

Different features that patient engagement tools possess can be depicted in the patient pathway through alternations of the patient engagement tool symbol. Depending on the type of patient engagement tool, the color of the symbol could change. SDM tools are depicted in orange, communication tools in yellow, self-management tools in green and tools for patient education are depicted in blue. If necessary, further color schemes could be added. Additionally, patient engagement tools in the form of documents (that could for example be printed, filled out together or handed out to the patient) should be distinguished from other types of tools by the form of a paper with a bent edge around the symbol. If the tool can be independently configured and therefore adapted to the individual patient through a health professional, it should be depicted through a screwdriver icon centrally placed at the top of the symbol (Fig. 2).

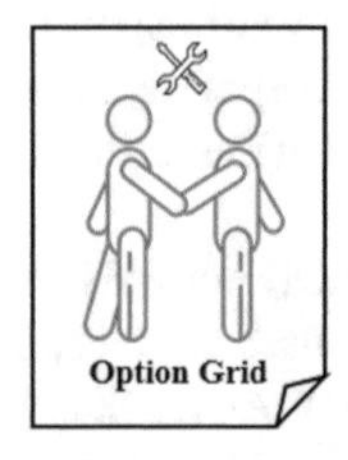

Fig. 2. Engagement tool symbol for an adaptable Option Grid in the form of a document[2]

Additionally, further information to the user should be depicted in an extra view named "details", which opens when clicking on the patient engagement tool symbol. A practical example is given in the following section by applying the integration of QPSs in patient pathways to the oncology use case.

Application Example – Question Prompt Sheets. In order to demonstrate and test the recommendations for representation of patient engagement tools, a tool will be explored

[1] Icon made by Freepik from www.flaticon.com.

[2] Icons made by Freepik and Becris from www.flaticon.com.

in the context of a colorectal cancer patient pathway for comprehensive cancer care networks. The QPS was chosen as an example, because evidence levels regarding its effectivity and feasibility are high and it is a tool that should fit into most pathways, unattached to the specific condition. The used patient pathway for colorectal cancer patients was developed as part of the large-scale European Joint Action iPAAC (Innovative Partnership for Action Against Cancer)[3], aiming to develop and implement innovative approaches to cancer control.

The QPS is used by the patient and the physician during consultation. Especially for complex diseases, such as cancer, several consultations take place. QPS are not a typical tool for SDM, as they do not focus on different treatment alternatives. Questions about these could be included, but the main aim is to promote general question asking behaviour (and therefore increase the amount of information obtained) by patients on their specific conditions. Especially during the first consultation after diagnosis patients often need a lot of information on their condition, due to which the integration of the tool during this task makes sense. When referring to the colorectal cancer patient pathway template, the QPS will be integrated at the initial "patient consultation" for patients that have a confirmed histological finding, which is depicted in Fig. 3. This approach is supported by information in the study of Lambert et al. (2019), in which feedback from patients indicates that the QPS would be less valuable to them in review consultations [54]. For the QPS, a details-view with more instructions and further information on its usage can be retrieved (see Fig. 4).

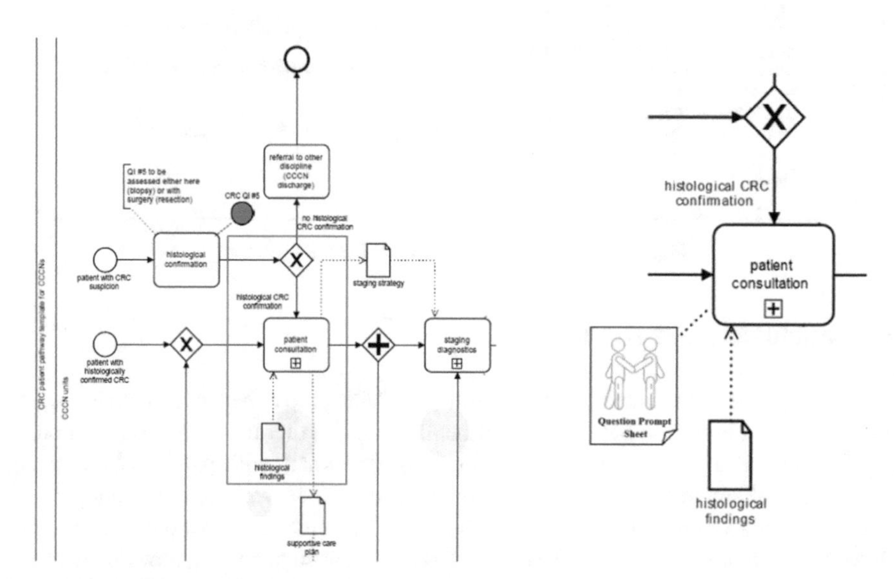

Fig. 3. Representation of QPS in patient pathway for colorectal cancer (left: patient pathway model without QPS integration, right: detailed view on integrated QPS)

[3] URL: https://www.ipaac.eu/ (accessed 25.08.2020).

▼ **General information**

Question Prompt Sheets (QPS) are lists of frequently asked questions that the patient can use during consultation as a memory and prioritization aid. They are specified to the respective disease or condition the patient is in. Their goal is to animate the patient to become more proactive by asking questions during the consultation.

Sources: Moloczij et al. 2017, p. 1084; Stacey et al. 2008, p. 296

▼ **Operating procedure**

The QPS was already handed out or sent to the patient before consultation. In this context it was explained to the patient that it is intended for them to make the most of their time with the physician by asking questions that are most important to them. To help them the QPS is a list of questions, which other patients found helpful in their situation. Furthermore, they were asked to highlight questions that are important to them, note down any further questions in the blank space provided and bring the sheet with them to consultation.

Studies suggest that the QPS should be actively addressed during the consultation, therefore:

- Ask patients what questions they highlighted or are important for them from the QPS
- Ask if they noted down or came up with any further questions, they might like to discuss

Sources: Lambert et al. 2019, p. 6; Brown et al. 2001, p. 248

▼ **Recommendations**

None

▼ **Documentation**

Following text can be used and adapted for documentation in the patient record

"The patient brought the question prompt sheet to the consultation. The sheet was actively addressed and we used it together to discuss the questions that were of special importance to the patient."

▼ **Useful links**

- "Promoting patient participation in the cancer consultation: evaluation of a prompt sheet and coaching in question-asking" (Brown et al. 1999)
  https://pubmed.ncbi.nlm.nih.gov/10390003/
- "Promoting patient participation and shortening cancer consultations: a randomised trial" (Brown et al. 2001)
  https://pubmed.ncbi.nlm.nih.gov/11720460/
- "Perception of Helpfulness of a Question Prompt Sheet Among Cancer Patients Attending Outpatient Palliative Care" (Arthur et al. 2017)
  https://pubmed.ncbi.nlm.nih.gov/27744019/
- "A Systematic Literature Review on Question Prompt Lists in Health Care: Final Report" (Sansoni et al. 2014)

▼ **Data collection**

None

Fig. 4. Example of a details-view for the QPS tool

4 Conclusion and Discussion

Tools for patient engagement and SDM offer possibilities to enhance the active integration of patients into their own process of health care. Furthermore, their integration of specific tools in the form of concrete working instructions at specific pathway steps seems more practical and goal-oriented than a general proposal of working in a more patient-centred manner through a general explanation of the concepts of patient engagement. However, evidence for how well these tools foster patient engagement, how fluently they can be integrated into the process and how acceptable they are to patients and health care professionals needed to be explored. Therefore, a literature review was conducted to find out what evidence for the effectivity and feasibility of patient engagement tools exists (according to RQ1). Overall, it can be summarized that there is evidence for at least some patient engagement tools, including the Option Grid and the QPS. It must, however, also be considered that there is a lot of contradictory information. Furthermore, studies were often performed in very diverse setting, for example with different medical conditions, treatment options and participant groups. Also, the quality of the tool usage varied immensely depending on how and when it was put to action. Comparability between studies is therefore limited. It can also be concluded that research on patient engagement tools is only beginning to develop. Nearly all sources used for the review were published in the last five years.

Despite evidence for the effectivity and feasibility of some engagement tools, reports of their usage in practice remain rare. When embedding engagement tools in the already well-established concept of pathways, they may also gain more prominence and acceptance. This approach is a chance to close the gap between research and practice and therefore to eliminate inefficiencies through a suboptimal execution of health care services, which is the case if patients do not receive the chance of being involved. Only through patient engagement individual needs and preferences can be elicited and a better understanding of the condition by the patient leads to higher compliance and an enhanced communication. All these aspects ultimately lead to better health care outcomes and a higher quality of care. Therefore, we explored how patient engagement tools could be represented in patient pathways (according to RQ2). The proposed recommendations for representation where applied to a patient pathway for colorectal cancer using the QPS as an example. The goal was to demonstrate and test the recommendations given. After application, no further changes needed to be made to the initial representation format or to the general statement of where these tools can be connected to the pathway.

The results of this paper contribute to the mounting evidence that the usage of patient engagement tools in practice should be enhanced. The integration of these tools into patient pathways could be a substantial part of putting theory into practice. Several new research areas become prominent through these results. For example, the evaluation of patient engagement tools in practice, would be of interest to support the findings of this paper. The representation of patient engagement tools in patient pathways will be made possible by developing a BPMN extension to represent patient engagement tools in patient pathways. Furthermore, in the context of patient pathways, the active engagement of patients during their development could be exploited. These topics are of high interest to research and concrete plans for their realization are in progress.

Acknowledgements. This article was partly funded by the European Union's Health Programme (2014–2020).

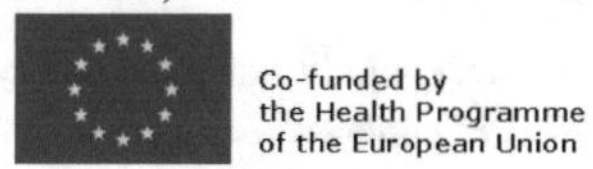

References

1. Vanhaecht, K.: The Impact of Clinical Pathways on the Organization of Care Processes. Technical Report, Katholieke Universiteit Leuven (2007)
2. Küttner, T., Roeder, N.: Klinische Behandlungspfade. Deutscher Ärzte-Verlag, Köln (2007)
3. Gand, K., Schlieter, H.: Personalisation and Dynamisation of Care Pathways – Foundations and Conceptual Considerations. Research-in-Progress Report 68 (2016)

4. The Value Collaborative: Putting Patients at the Center of the Clinical Pathway Debate. https://catalyst.phrma.org/putting-patients-at-the-center-of-the-clinical-pathways-debate. Accessed 10 Nov 2020
5. Richter, P., Schlieter, H.: Understanding patient pathways in the context of integrated health care services - implications from a scoping review. In: Proceedings of the 14th International Conference of Wirtschaftsinformatik (2019)
6. Higgins, T., Larson, E., Schnall, R.: Unravelling the meaning of patient engagement. A concept analysis. Patient Educ. Counselling **100**, 30–36 (2017)
7. Cerezo, P., Udina, J., Eulália, P., et al.: Concepts and measures of patient empowerment: a comprehensive review. Revista da Escola de Enfermagem da USP **50**, 0667 (2016)
8. Doherr, H., Christalle, E., Kriston, L., et al.: Use of the 9-item shared decision making questionnaire in intervention studies: a systematic review. Plos One **12**, 1–16 (2017)
9. Keddem, S., Agha, A., Long, J., et al.: Creating a toolkit to reduce disparities in patient engagement. Med. Care **55**, 59–69 (2017)
10. De Santis, M., Hervas, C., Weinman, C., et al.: Patient Empowerment. National Center for Rare Diseases (2018)
11. Walker, D., Sieck, C., Menser, T., et al.: Information technology to support patient engagement: where do we stand and where can we go? JAMA **24**, 1088–1094 (2017)
12. Rowley, J., Slack, F.: Conducting a literature review. Manag. Res. News **27**, 31–39 (2004)
13. Howick, J., Chalmers, I., Glasziou, P., et al.: The Oxford Levels of Evidence 2. https://www.cebm.net/index.aspx?o=5653. Accessed 09 Oct 2020
14. Nijhuis, F., Elwyn, G., Bloem, B., et al.: Improving SDM in advanced Parkinsons disease: protocol of a mixed methods feasibility study. Pilot Feasbility Stud. **4**, 1–8 (2018)
15. Scalia, P., Elwyn, G., Barr, P., et al.: Exploring the Use of option grid patient decision aids in a sample of clinics in Poland. ZEFQ **134**, 1–8 (2018)
16. Elwyn, G., Frosch, D., Kobrin, S.: Implementing shared-decision making: consider all the consequences. Implement. Sci. **11**, 1–10 (2016)
17. Elwyn, G., Rasmussen, J., Kinsey, K., et al.: On a learning curve for shared-decision making: interviews with clinicians using the knee osteoarthritis option grid. J. Eval. Clin. Pract. **24**, 56–64 (2018)
18. Kinsey, K., Firth, J., Elwyn, G., et al.: Patients views on the use of an option grid for knee osteoarthritis in physiotherapy clinical encounters: an interview study. Health Expect. **20**, 1302–1310 (2017)
19. Smith, S., Alvand, A., Locock, L., et al.: Partial or total knee replacement? Identifying patients information needs on knee replacement surgery: a qualitative study to inform a decision aid. Qual. Life Res. **29**, 999–1011 (2019)
20. Hahlweg, P., Witzel, I., Müller, V.: Adaptation and qualitative evaluation of decision aids in breast cancer care. Arch. Gynecol. Obstet. **299**, 1141–1149 (2019)
21. Alam, S., Elwyn, G., Percac-Lima, S., et al.: Assessing the acceptability and feasibility of encounter decision aids for early stage breast cancer targeted at underserved patients. BMC Med. Inform. Decis. Mak. **16**, 147 (2016)
22. Zisman-Ilani, J., Shern, D., Deegan, P., et al.: Continue, adjust, or stop antipsychotic medication: developing and user testing an encounter decision aid for people with first-episode and long-term psychosis. BMC Psychiatry **18**, 142 (2018)
23. Greenhalgh, T.: Option grids: an idea whose time has come? The British journal of general practice. J. R. Coll. Gen. Pract. **63**, 147 (2013)
24. Wright, S., Walsh, H., Ingley, K., et al.: Uptake of self-management strategies in a heart failure management programme. Eur. J. Heart Fail. **5**, 371–380 (2003)
25. Cherenack, E., Wilson, P., Kreuzman, A., et al.: HIV/AIDS interventions: the feasibility and acceptability of using technology based daily diaries with HIV-infected young men who have sex with men. AIDS Behav. **20**, 1744–1753 (2016)

26. Park, L., Dracup, K., Whooley, M. et al.: Symptom diary use and improved survival for patient with heart failure. Circulation. Heart Failure **10** (2017)
27. Hodge, B.: The use of symptom diaries in outpatient care. FPM J. **20**, 24–28 (2013)
28. Himes, B., Weitzman, E.: Innovations in health information technologies for chronic pulmonary diseases. Respir. Res. **17**, 1–7 (2016)
29. Schmidt, M., Eckardt, R., Scholtz, K., et al.: Patient empowerment improved perioperative quality of care in cancer patients aged 65 years – A randomized controlled trial. PloS One **10**, e0137824 (2015)
30. Ullman, A., Aitken, L., Rattray, J., et al.: Diaries for recovery from critical illness. In: Cochrane Database of Systematic Reviews, vol. 4 (2013)
31. Moloczij, N., Krishnasamy, M., Butow, P. et al.: Barriers and facilitators to the implementation of audio-recordings and question prompt lists in cancer care consultations: a qualitative study. Patient Educ. Counselling **6**, 1083 (2017)
32. Stacey, D., Samant, R., Bennett, C.: Decision making in oncology: a review of patient decision aids to support patient participation. ACS J. **58**, 293–304 (2008)
33. Arthur, J., Yennu, S., Zapata, K., et al.: Perception of helpfulness of a QPS among cancer patients attending outpatient palliative care. JPSM J. **53**, 124–130 (2017)
34. Brown, R., Butow, P., Dunn, S., et al.: Promoting patient participation and shortening cancer consultation: a randomised trial. Br. J. Cancer **85**, 1273–1279 (2001)
35. Brown, R., Butow, P., Boyer, M., et al.: Promoting patient participation in the cancer consultation: evaluation of a prompt sheet and coaching in question-asking. Br. J. Cancer **80**, 242–248 (1999)
36. Butow, P., Dunn, S., Tattersall, M., et al.: Patient participation in the cancer consultation: evaluation of a QPS. Ann. Oncol. ESMO Open **5**, 199–204 (1994)
37. Streufert, B., Reed, S., Orlando, L., et al.: Understanding preferences for treatment after hypothetical fit-time anterior shoulder dislocation. AOSSM **5**, 2325 (2017)
38. Dunlea, R., Lenert, L.: Understanding patients' preferences for referrals to specialists for an asymptomatic condition. SAGE J. **35**, 691–702 (2015)
39. Hess, L., Litwiller, A., Byron, J., et al.: Preference elicitation tool for abnormal uterine bleeding treatment: a randomized controlled trial. Patient **8**, 217–227 (2015)
40. Chesney, T., Deveon, K.: Training surgical residents to use a framework to promote shared decision-making for patients with poor prognosis experiencing surgical emergencies. Can. J. Surg. **61**, 114–120 (2018)
41. Taylor, L., Nabozny, M., Steffens, N., et al.: A framework to improve surgeon comm. in high-stakes surgical decisions: best case/worst case. JAMA Surg. **152**, 531–538 (2017)
42. Giguere, A., Labrecque, M., Haynes, B.: Evidence summaries to prepare clinicians for shared decision-making with patients. In: Implementation Science (2014)
43. Lastinger, A., Gomez, K., Manegold, E., et al.: Use of a patient empowerment tool for hand hygiene. Am. J. Infect. Control (2017)
44. Dendere, R., Slade, C., Burton-Jones, A., et al.: Patient portals facilitating engagement with inpatient electronic medical records: a systematic review. JMIR **21**, e12779 (2019)
45. Ammenwerth, E., Schnell-Inderst, P., Hoerbst, A.: The impact of electronic patient portals on patient care: a systematic review of controlled trials. JMIR **14**, e162 (2012)
46. Fiks, A., Mayne, S., Karavite, D., et al.: Parent-reported outcomes of a shared decision-making portal in asthma: a practice-based RCT. Pediatrics **135**, e965–e973 (2015)
47. Scalia, P., O'Malley, J., Durnd, M., et al.: Presenting time-based risks of stroke and death for patients facing carotid stenosis treatment options: patients prefer pie charts over icon arrays. Patient Educ. Counselling **102**, 1939 (2019)
48. Hoffmann, J., Wilkes, M., Day, F.: The roulette wheel: an aid to informed decision making. PLoS Med. **3**, e137 (2006)

49. Scheuerlein, H., Rauchfuss, F., Dittmar, Y., et al.: New methods for clinical pathways-BPMN and t.BPM. Langenbecks Arch. Surg. **397**, 755–761 (2012)
50. Zerbato, F., Oliboni, B., Combi, C., et al.: BPMN-Based representation and comparison of clinical pathways for catheter-related bloodstream infections. In: International Conference on Healthcare Informatics, pp. 346–355 (2015)
51. Braun, R., Schlieter, H., Burwitz, M., et al.: BPMN4CP revised - Extending BPMN for multi-perspective modeling of clinical pathways. In: Proceedings of the 49th Hawaii International Conference on System Sciences (HICSS), pp. 3249–3258 (2016)
52. National Health Service England: When and where is shared decision making appropriate? https://www.england.nhs.uk/shared-decision-making/when-and-where-is-shared-decision-making-appropriate/. Accessed 10 Nov 2020
53. Fredriksson, M., Eriksson, M., Tritter, J.: Who wants to be involved in health care decisions? Comparing preferences for individual and collective involvement in England and Sweden. BMC Public Health **18**, 18 (2018)
54. Lambert, K., Lau, T., Davidson, S., et al.: Development and results on the feasibility of a renal diet specific QPS for use in nephrology clinics. BMC Neph. **20**, 48 (2019)

Pathway Supporting Health Information Systems: Interdisciplinary Goal Integration - A Review

Tim Scheplitz(✉)

Chair of Information Systems, Dresden University of Technology, Dresden, Germany
tim.scheplitz@tu-dresden.de

Abstract. Care pathways and implementing information systems increasingly permeate the discipline of Health Information Systems Research (HISR). It explores the conception, modelling, realisation and impact of pathway-supporting HIS and strives for the best possible harmonisation of interdisciplinary goals from technology, medicine and public health research. A systematic literature review with qualitative content analysis is dedicated to this integrating character. It examines the interdisciplinary network of objectives associated with care pathways and pathway-supporting HIS in the HISR literature of the past decade. The research-in-progress paper presented here describes the background, methodology and interim content analysis results. Alternative questions and analysis strategies to this status are outlined in conclusion as a basis for discourse. In this way, adjustments to the research strategy of this project will be sought in a targeted exchange with researchers from the HISR.

Keywords: Care pathways · Health information systems · Literature review · Qualitative content analysis · Research-in-Progress

1 Introduction

Medicine describes complex sequences of interventions of defined patient groups in defined time periods as care pathways in order to promote the organisation and decision-making of care processes [1, 2]. Terms have been established to emphasise intra-organisational ("clinical pathways"), cross-institutional ("integrated care pathways") or patient-centred ("patient pathways") orientations [3–5]. Business informatics, domain-specifically named Health Information Systems Research (HISR), also conducts research with and on "care pathways" and investigates the conception, modelling, realisation and impact of pathway-supporting Health Information Systems (HIS) [3, 6–8].

It can be observed that the research and development work seek to bring original motivations from the process perspective in line with the requirements of other views or disciplines. For example, it is discussed how patient integration can be intensified along care pathways [8], how data analytics methods can describe care pathways retrospectively [9] or how data mining approaches can contribute to the individualisation of care

F. Ahlemann et al. (Eds.): WI 2021, LNISO 46, pp. 79–87, 2021.
https://doi.org/10.1007/978-3-030-86790-4_6

plans [10]. Experiences from practice-oriented digital health research projects confirm the observation that the objectives of care pathways and pathway-supporting HIS go beyond the traditional process perspective.

The research presented here builds on these observations. It examines the thesis that the objectives of research and development of care pathways and pathway-supporting HIS are becoming increasingly interdisciplinary. It therefore explores the question of what objectives are associated with work on this research topic. Such a consolidation can serve to describe the solution space for pathway-supporting HIS, to derive design implications and to point out disciplines and professions to be involved. It thus extends the knowledge from previous reviews on the characterisation of patient pathways [3] and on the support of clinical pathways by health information technologies [11].

This RiP paper shows the current status of a systematic literature review with qualitative content analysis. It presents the research strategy, descriptive and first content-analytical results. Although the material review and interpretation have not been completed, the current evaluation status motivates a discussion of alternative questions and analytical approaches. Selected options are outlined first for the search strategy and then for the evaluation strategy in order to initiate the scientific discourse.

2 Search Strategy and Amount of Analysis

A systematic literature review [12–14] was opened for the above-mentioned question. The databases of the following ISR or HISR publication bodies were selected: AIS Senior Basket, Proceedings of the AIS Conferences, recommended eHealth Journals of the AIS SIG Health. After abstract and full text screening, 49 articles were selected as the final set for analysis. Only articles that prominently mention care pathways as a research context were included. Details of the review process are given in Fig. 1.

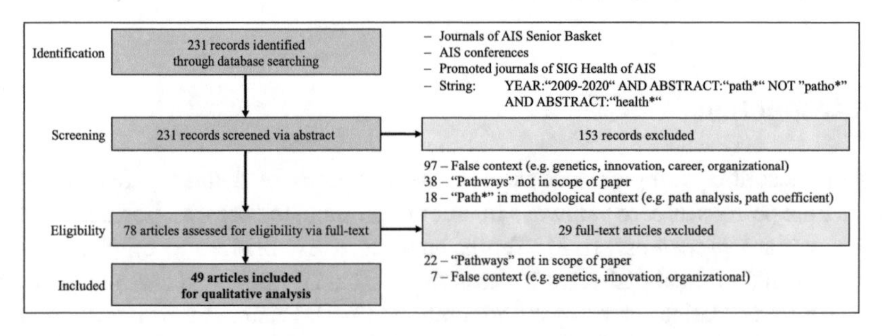

Fig. 1. Review process description according to PRISMA recommendations [14].

The identified articles are distributed relatively evenly over the past years (see Table 1). With regard to the distribution across the publication organs, it can be seen that the majority of the articles found are published in HISR journals recommended by the AIS Health SIG (n = 37). Here, 14 articles could be found in the *International Journal of Medical Informatics* alone and 12 papers in the journal *BMC Medical Informatics and Decision Making.* A total of 11 papers were identified in the proceedings of the AIS conferences, and only one article in the AIS Senior Basket.

Table 1. Publication distribution by year and publication organ

		09	10	11	12	13	14	15	16	17	18	19	20	Σ
AIS Senior Basket	EJIS						1							1
AIS Conferences	ICIS				1	1								2
	AMCIS			1										1
	ECIS				1				2	1		3		7
	HICSS										1			1
TOP 5 Journals suggested by AIS SIG Health	JAMAI			1					1		1	1		4
	IJMI	1		1	2	2				1	2		5	14
	JMIR								1			1		2
	Health Systems								1	2		2		5
	BMC MIDM					1	3	4	2	1			1	12
	Σ	1	0	3	4	4	4	4	7	5	4	7	6	49

3 Discussion of the Search Strategy

The high exclusion rate and the inherent uncertainty as to whether the relevant literature could be comprehensively identified also call the **search strategy** into question. With backward and forward searches, while maintaining the time and journal restrictions, additional articles are to be included. The inclusion of additional journals according to known journal rankings [15, 16] can also contribute to the expansion of the analysis set. The configuration of the search string could also counteract the exclusion rate. For example, terms such as “care pathway”, “treatment pathway”, “patient pathway” or “clinical pathway” could lead to a result set with similar quality, although indication-specific care pathways would then escape the search. Likewise, the integration of process terms (e.g. “process” or “workflow”) could identify adequate contributions that would remain hidden, especially when searching the journals of the AIS Senior Basket or the AIS conferences. Given the number of alternative search strategies, the discussion with SLR-experienced colleagues from the HISR will address the question of how an advantageous degree of differentiation can be determined for the research question of this project.

4 Content Analysis and Evaluation Alternatives

From the abstracts of all identified contributions, initial information was gathered on background, contributions and the relationship of the content to the object of study. Methodologically, an inductive, qualitative content analysis [17] follows for comprehensive interpretation. Following the process model of a summarising content analysis with inductive category formation [18], the analysis material was reduced to those text passages in which goals or contributions of the presented research are described with reference to care pathways or pathway-supporting HIS. Paraphrases were constructed for these passages (see Table 2 for examples) and structured interpretatively. This process step has so far been carried out for the contributions of the years 2017 to 2020 (n = 22, see Table 3). The remaining contributions are referenced here: [19–45].

The interim results support the observation of increasingly interdisciplinary work with and on care pathways. Pathway-supporting HIS for clinical workflow support and interorganisational coordination are being developed and evaluated in the field. Innovative data-based predictive models are tested with them and combined with management task areas. They also provide structuring support for consolidating research contributions, so that the impression arises that care pathways take on the function of a "lingua franca" in practice-oriented research and development projects. An impression that motivates separate exchange and additional analytical approaches.

Table 2. Examples of paraphrases

Research contribution [reference]: Paraphrase for description
Askari et al. 2020 [46]: Study on the professional assessment of the effectiveness and efficiency of clinical pathways and pathway-supporting HIS in medical care
Kempa-Liehr et al. 2020 [47]: Modelling tool for care pathways and prediction models based on data mining methods and machine learning models

Consideration of the multiprofessional objectives also raises the fundamental question of whether drivers of interdisciplinary work on pathway-supporting HIS are to be found in medical care practice or in its research. Possibly there is also a recursive, mutually reinforcing interrelationship. To approach this question, alternative analytical strategies are presented. Their presentation primarily serves as a discourse stimulus for the concrete object of study and the presented interim results, but suggests a generalisability to other research objects of HISR.

A first, alternative analytical approach is devoted to the genesis of identified publications. A detailed examination of the **author team's background** could describe the interdisciplinarity of the research. So far, articles have been analysed in terms of the average number of authors (mean = 5.18; median = 5, modal = 3). However, these numbers do not provide information about the diversity of expertise involved. With the information on author details, the institutional background (with subject area) could be collected. In this way, the following questions, among others, could be addressed: Which scientific disciplines (e.g. IS, medicine, health services research, etc.) are involved in the research of pathway-supporting HIS and how? How are medical and ICT practice involved in research projects? Which sub-disciplines of ISR discuss the research topic?

Another alternative evaluation is the **classification in the HISR landscape**. Current meta-studies of HISR could be used to deductively investigate the following questions: In which subfields of HISR does research with and on pathway-supporting HIS contribute [67–70]? For which current challenges and trends does this research show particular potential [67, 69]? What is the analytical focus and methodological orientation of the contributions [68–70]? Which health information technologies and which user groups

Table 3. Interim results of content analysis

Category of contribution to care pathways or pathway-supporting HIS: Examples
Evaluation and assessment of pathway-supporting HIS: - Studies on effectiveness, efficiency and user experience [11, 46, 48–51] - Usage analyses for coordination around communication [48, 50, 52, 53]
Data-driven path modelling and integration of data-based predictive models: - Modelling methods or tools for deriving care pathways from electronic case record data [47, 50, 54–56] - Development of data-based predictive models (data & process mining, machine learning, deep learning) for medical decision support [47, 50, 56, 57] - Data-based analysis and decision models from data pathway-supporting HIS for care and hospital management [55, 58]
Conventional modelling of care pathways: - Development of process-oriented modelling languages for care pathways [59] - Presentation of modelling tools for supply pathways [47]
Conceptual integration of the management perspective: - Intersection analysis of expertise from information systems, operational research and industrial engineering for problem solving in connection with supply paths [60] - Method conception for embedding quality management in care pathways [61] - Path-based data analysis for tactical and strategic hospital management [62]
Care pathways as a structuring aid of HISR: - Analyses of the status quo of the digital transformation [63, 64] - Studies on the potential analysis of telemedical measures [65] - Studies on the personalisation of HIS services [66] and technology support [11]

are the focus [69, 70]? In what relation are theories of ISR and health care discussed [68]? Resulting findings can uncover research potentials as well as suggest suitable compositions for research and development consortia.

Furthermore, an **investigation of the health care contexts** could determine and describe those health care scenarios that motivate the development of pathway-supporting HIS or benefit particularly from them. From the results, characteristics and possibly types of care scenarios could be derived, which in turn could be linked to concrete care goals. This investigation could include the following focal points: care setting (outpatient, inpatient, rehabilitation); medical specialty (e.g. oncology, emergency medicine); indication (e.g. COPD, depression); role of the patient (autonomous vs. paternalistic) or degree of multiprofessionality or number of institutions involved. The analysis of the abstracts showed that only half of the contributions named specific care contexts. An adjustment of the content-analytical approach could help to collect the information sought also from the implicit statements about the care context of the 23 contributions with a generic approach. Thus, in addition to the interim results shown, this RiP contribution concludes with an equal amount of research questions and approaches that are available.

References

1. EPA: "Care Pathways," Eurpean Pathway Association: Care Pathways (2019). http://e-p-a.org/care-pathways/
2. Vanhaecht, K.: The Impact of Clinical Pathways on the Organisation of Care Processes. Katholieke Universiteit Leuven, Leuven (2007)
3. Richter, P., Schlieter, H.: Understanding patient pathways in the context of integrated health care services-implications from a scoping review. In: Presented at the Wirtschaftsinformatik 2019, Siegen, February 2019
4. Kinsman, L., Rotter, T., James, E., Snow, P., Willis, J.: What is a clinical pathway? Development of a definition to inform the debate. BMC Med. **8**, 31–33 (2010)
5. Vanhaecht, K., Panella, M., van Zelm, R., Sermeus, W.: An overview on the history and concept of care pathways as complex interventions. Int. J. Care Pathways **14**(3), 117–123 (2010). https://doi.org/10.1258/jicp.2010.010019
6. Raphael, H., Lux, T., Martin, V.: State-of-the-art process-oriented hospital information systems. Bus. Inform. **2**, 689–698 (2009)
7. Burwitz, M., Schlieter, H., Esswein, W.: Modeling Clinical Pathways - Design and Application of a Domain-Specific Modeling Language, Wirtschaftsinformatik Proceedings 2013, January 2013. http://aisel.aisnet.org/wi2013/83
8. Benedict, M., et al.: Patient integration through pathway systems. In: Presented at the Wirtschaftsinformatik (WI 2019), Siegen (2019)
9. Prokofyeva, E.S., Zaytsev, R.D., Maltseva, S.V.: Application of modern data analysis methods to cluster the clinical pathways in urban medical facilities. In: 2019 IEEE 21st Conference on Business Informatics (CBI), Moscow, Russia, pp. 75–83, July 2019. https://doi.org/10.1109/CBI.2019.00016
10. Schlieter, H., Benedict, M., Gand, K., Burwitz, M.: Towards Adaptive Pathways: Reference Architecture for Personalized Dynamic Pathways, pp. 359–368, July 2017. https://doi.org/10.1109/CBI.2017.55
11. Neame, M.T., Chacko, J., Surace, A.E., Sinha, I.P., Hawcutt, D.B.: A systematic review of the effects of implementing clinical pathways supported by health information technologies. J. Am. Med. Inform. Assoc. **26**(4), 356–363 (2019). https://doi.org/10.1093/jamia/ocy176
12. Schryen, G., et al.: Literature reviews in IS research: what can be learnt from the past and other fields? Commun. Assoc. Inf. Syst. **41**(1), 759 (2017). https://doi.org/10.17705/1CAIS.04130
13. Paré, G., Trudel, M.-C., Jaana, M., Kitsiou, S.: Synthesizing information systems knowledge: a typology of literature reviews. Inf. Manage. **52**(2), 183–199 (2015). https://doi.org/10.1016/j.im.2014.08.008
14. Moher, D., Liberati, A., Tetzlaff, J., Altman, D.G., PRISMA Group: Preferred reporting items for systematic reviews and meta-analyses: the PRISMA statement. Ann. Intern. Med. **151**(4), 264 (2009). https://doi.org/10.7326/0003-4819-151-4-200908180-00135
15. AIS SIG Health: Health IS Journals. International Journal of Medical Informatics (2020)
16. Serenko, A., Dohan, M., Tan, J.: Global ranking of management- and clinical-centered E-Health journals. Commun. Assoc. Inf. Syst. **41**(1), 198 (2017). http://aisel.aisnet.org/cais/vol41/iss1/9
17. Mayring, P.: Qualitative content analysis: theoretical foundation, basic procedures and software solution. Klagenfurt (2014)
18. Mayring, P.: Qualitative Content Analysis: Fundamentals and Techniques, 12th Revised Edition. Beltz, Weinheim Basel (2015)
19. Donald, M., et al.: Development and implementation of an online clinical pathway for adult chronic kidney disease in primary care: a mixed methods study. BMC Med. Inform. Decis. Mak. **16**, 1–11 (2016)

20. Gand, K., Schlieter, H.: Personalisation and dynamisation of care pathways-foundations and conceptual considerations. In: Proceedings of ECIS 2016. Research-in (2016)
21. Gibbs, J., et al.: The eClinical Care Pathway Framework: a novel structure for creation of online complex clinical care pathways and its application in the management of sexually transmitted infections. BMC Med. Inform. Decis. Mak. **16**, 1–9 (2016)
22. Meng, F., Ooi, C.K., Keng Soh, C.K., Liang Teow, K., Kannapiran, P.: Quantifying patient flow and utilization with patient flow pathway and diagnosis of an emergency department in Singapore. Health Syst. **5**(2), 140–148 (2016). https://doi.org/10.1057/hs.2015.15
23. Schriek, P., Türetken, O., Kaymak, U.: A maturity model for care pathways. In: Proceedings of ECIS 2016. ResearchPaper127 (2016)
24. Smith-Strøm, H., Iversen, M.M., Graue, M., Skeie, S., Kirkevold, M.: An integrated wound-care pathway, supported by telemedicine, and competent wound management-Essential in follow-up care of adults with diabetic foot ulcers. Int. J. Med. Inform. **94**, 59–66 (2016). https://doi.org/10.1016/j.ijmedinf.2016.06.020
25. Evans, R.S., et al.: Automated identification and predictive tools to help identify high-risk heart failure patients: pilot evaluation. J. Am. Med. Inform. Assoc. **23**(5), 872–878 (2016). https://doi.org/10.1093/jamia/ocv197
26. Flott, K., Callahan, R., Darzi, A., Mayer, E.: A patient-centered framework for evaluating digital maturity of health services: a systematic review. J. Med. Internet Res. **18**(4), e75 (2016). https://doi.org/10.2196/jmir.5047
27. Barbagallo, S., et al.: Optimization and planning of operating theatre activities: an original definition of pathways and process modeling. BMC Med. Inform. Decis. Mak. **15**(1), 38–53 (2015)
28. Gkatzidou, V., et al.: User interface design for mobile-based sexual health interventions for young people: design recommendations from a qualitative study on an online Chlamydia clinical care pathway. BMC Med. Inform. Decis. Mak. **15**(1), 1–13 (2015)
29. Boehler, C.E.H., de Graaf, G., Steuten, L., Yang, Y., Abadie, F.: Development of a web-based tool for the assessment of health and economic outcomes of the European Innovation Partnership on Active and Healthy Ageing (EIP on AHA). BMC Med. Inform. Decis. Mak. **15**(1), S4 (2015)
30. Wagner, S., et al.: Analysis and classification of oncology activities on the way to workflow based single source documentation in clinical information systems. BMC Med. Inform. Decis. Mak. **15**, 1–13 (2015)
31. Bouamrane, M.-M., Mair, F.: Integrated preoperative care pathway - a study of a regional electronic implementation. BMC Med. Inform. Decis. Mak. **14**(1), 1–32 (2014)
32. Li, W., Liu, K., Yang, H., Yu, C.: Integrated clinical pathway management for medical quality improvement - based on a semiotically inspired systems architecture. Eur. J. Inf. Syst. **23**(4), 400–417 (2014). https://doi.org/10.1057/ejis.2013.9
33. Hurwitz, J.E., Lee, J.A., Lopiano, K.K., McKinley, S.A., Keesling, J., Tyndall, J.A.: A flexible simulation platform to quantify and manage emergency department crowding. BMC Med. Inform. Decis. Mak. **14**(1), 1–20 (2014)
34. Bouamrane, M.-M., Mair, F.S.: A qualitative evaluation of general practitioners' views on protocol-driven eReferral in Scotland. BMC Med. Inform. Decis. Mak. **14**(1), 1–24 (2014)
35. Sung, K.H., et al.: Application of clinical pathway using electronic medical record system in pediatric patients with supracondylar fracture of the humerus: a before and after comparative study. BMC Med. Inform. Decis. Mak. **13**(1), 1–8 (2013)
36. Eason, K., Waterson, P.: The implications of e-health system delivery strategies for integrated healthcare: lessons from England. Int. J. Med. Inform. **82**(5), e96–e106 (2013). https://doi.org/10.1016/j.ijmedinf.2012.11.004
37. Hao, A.T.-H., et al.: Nursing process decision support system for urology ward. Int. J. Med. Inform. **82**(7), 604–612 (2013). https://doi.org/10.1016/j.ijmedinf.2013.02.006

38. Paulussen, T., Heinzl, A., Becker, C.: Multi-agent based information systems for patient coordination in hospitals. In: ICIS 2013 Proceedings (2013)
39. Ryhänen, A.M., Rankinen, S., Tulus, K., Korvenranta, H., Leino-Kilpi, H.: Internet based patient pathway as an educational tool for breast cancer patients. Int. J. Med. Inform. **81**(4), 270–278 (2012). https://doi.org/10.1016/j.ijmedinf.2012.01.010
40. Husain, M.J., et al.: HERALD (health economics using routine anonymised linked data). BMC Med. Inform. Decis. Mak. **12**(1), 24 (2012)
41. Juhrisch, M., Schlieter, H., Dietz, G.: Information systems engineering in healthcare - an evaluation of the state of the art of operational process design. Int. J. Organ. Des. Eng. **2**(4), 420–444 (2012). https://doi.org/10.1504/IJODE.2012.051444
42. Gooch, P., Roudsari, A.: Computerization of workflows, guidelines, and care pathways: a review of implementation challenges for process-oriented health information systems. J. Am. Med. Inform. Assoc. **18**(6), 738–748 (2011). https://doi.org/10.1136/amiajnl-2010-000033
43. Schuld, J., Schäfer, T., Nickel, S., Jacob, P., Schilling, M.K., Richter, S.: Impact of IT-supported clinical pathways on medical staff satisfaction. A prospective longitudinal cohort study. Int. J. Med. Inform. **80**(3), 151–156 (2011). https://doi.org/10.1016/j.ijmedinf.2010.10.012
44. Juhrisch, M., Schlieter, H., Dietz, G.: Model-supported business alignment of IT-conceptual foundations. In: Proceeding of AMCIS 2011 (2011)
45. Wakamiya, S., Yamauchi, K.: What are the standard functions of electronic clinical pathways? Int. J. Med. Inform. **78**(8), 543–550 (2009). https://doi.org/10.1016/j.ijmedinf.2009.03.003
46. Askari, M., Tam, J.L.Y.Y., Aarnoutse, M.F., Meulendijk, M.: Perceived effectiveness of clinical pathway software: a before-after study in the Netherlands. Int. J. Med. Inform. **135**, 104052 (2020). https://doi.org/10.1016/j.ijmedinf.2019.104052
47. Kempa-Liehr, A.W., et al.: Healthcare pathway discovery and probabilistic machine learning. Int. J. Med. Inform. **137**, 104087 (2020). https://doi.org/10.1016/j.ijmedinf.2020.104087
48. Andellini, M., et al.: Experimental application of business process management technology to manage clinical pathways: a pediatric kidney transplantation follow up case. BMC Med. Inform. Decis. Mak. **17**, 1–9 (2017)
49. Appari, A., Johnson, M.E., Anthony, D.L.: Health IT and inappropriate utilization of outpatient imaging: a cross-sectional study of U.S. hospitals. Int. J. Med. Inform. **109**, 87–95 (2018). https://doi.org/10.1016/j.ijmedinf.2017.10.020
50. Shivers, L., Feldman, S.S., Hayes, L.W.: Development of a computerized paediatric intensive care unit septic shock pathway: improving user experience. Health Syst. **8**, 1–7 (2019). https://doi.org/10.1080/20476965.2019.1620638
51. Toy, J.M., Drechsler, A., Waters, R.C.: Clinical pathways for primary care: current use, interest and perceived usability. J. Am. Med. Inform. Assoc. **25**(7), 901–906 (2018). https://doi.org/10.1093/jamia/ocy010
52. Platt, N., Tarafdar, M., Williams, R.: The complementary roles of health information systems and relational coordination in alcohol care pathways: the case of a UK hospital. In: ECIS 2019 Proceedings (2019)
53. Øvrelid, E., Sanner, T., Siebenherz, A.: Creating Coordinative Paths from admission to discharge: The role of lightweight IT in hospital digital process innovation (2018)
54. Cho, M., et al.: Developing data-driven clinical pathways using electronic health records: the cases of total laparoscopic hysterectomy and rotator cuff tears. Int. J. Med. Inform. **133**, 104015 (2020). https://doi.org/10.1016/j.ijmedinf.2019.104015
55. Baker, K., et al.: Process mining routinely collected electronic health records to define real-life clinical pathways during chemotherapy. Int. J. Med. Inform. **103**, 32–41 (2017). https://doi.org/10.1016/j.ijmedinf.2017.03.011

56. Ye, X., Zeng, Q.T., Facelli, J.C., Brixner, D.I., Conway, M., Bray, B.E.: Predicting optimal hypertension treatment pathways using recurrent neural networks. Int. J. Med. Inform. **139**, 104122 (2020). https://doi.org/10.1016/j.ijmedinf.2020.104122
57. Cochran, A.R., Raub, K.M., Murphy, K.J., Iannitti, D.A., Vrochides, D.: Novel use of REDCap to develop an advanced platform to display predictive analytics and track compliance with Enhanced Recovery After Surgery for pancreaticoduodenectomy. Int. J. Med. Inform. **119**, 54–60 (2018). https://doi.org/10.1016/j.ijmedinf.2018.09.001
58. Greenwood-Lee, J., Wild, G., Marshall, D.: Improving accessibility through referral management: setting targets for specialist care. Health Syst. **6**(2), 161–170 (2017). https://doi.org/10.1057/hs.2015.20
59. Trajano, I.A., Filho, J.B.F., de Souza, F.R.C., Litchfield, I., Weber, P.: MedPath: a process-based modeling language for designing care pathways. Int. J. Med. Inform. **146**, 104328 (2020). https://doi.org/10.1016/j.ijmedinf.2020.104328
60. Aspland, E., Gartner, D., Harper, P.: Clinical pathway modelling: a literature review. Health Syst. 10, 1–23 (2019). https://doi.org/10.1080/20476965.2019.1652547
61. Richter, P.: Bringing care quality to life: towards quality indicator-driven pathway modelling in health care networks. In: ECIS 2019 Proceedings (2019)
62. Demir, E., Gunal, M.M., Southern, D.: Demand and capacity modelling for acute services using discrete event simulation. Health Syst. **6**(1), 33–40 (2017). https://doi.org/10.1057/hs.2016.1
63. Berntsen, G., Strisland, F., Malm-Nicolaisen, K., Smaradottir, B., Fensli, R., Røhne, M.: The evidence base for an ideal care pathway for frail multimorbid elderly: combined scoping and systematic intervention review. J. Med. Internet Res. **21**(4), e12517 (2019). https://doi.org/10.2196/12517
64. Hufnagl, C., Doctor, E., Behrens, L., Buck, C., Eymann, T.: Digitisation along the patient pathway in hospitals. In: ECIS 2019 Proceedings (2019)
65. Gaveikaite, V., et al.: Challenges and opportunities for telehealth in the management of chronic obstructive pulmonary disease: a qualitative case study in Greece. BMC Med. Inform. Decis. Mak. **20**(1), 216 (2020). https://doi.org/10.1186/s12911-020-01221-y
66. Korhonen, O., Isomursu, M.: Identifying personalization in a care pathway: a single-case study of a finnish healthcare service provider. In: ECIS 2017 Proceedings (2017)
67. Ho, S.Y., Guo, X., Vogel, D.: Opportunities and challenges in healthcare information systems research: caring for patients with chronic conditions. Commun. Assoc. Inf. Syst. **44**(1), 39 (2019)
68. Haried, P., Claybaugh, C., Dai, H.: Evaluation of health information systems research in information systems research: a meta-analysis. Health Inform. J. **25**(1), 186–202 (2019). https://doi.org/10.1177/1460458217704259
69. Samhan, B., Crampton, T., Ruane, R.: The trajectory of IT in healthcare at HICSS: A literature review, analysis, and future directions. Commun. Assoc. Inf. Syst. **43**, 792–845 (2018). https://doi.org/10.17705/1CAIS.04341
70. Davidson, E., Baird, A., Prince, K.: Opening the envelope of health care information systems research. Inf. Organ. **28**(3), 140–151 (2018). https://doi.org/10.1016/j.infoandorg.2018.07.001

A Feedback Information System for Improving Hand Hygiene on a Personal and Organizational Level

Carlo Stingl(✉), Sebastian A. Günther, and Thorsten Staake

Chair of Information Systems and Energy Efficient Systems,
University of Bamberg, Bamberg, Germany
{carlo.stingl,sebastian.guenther,thorsten.staake}@uni-bamberg.de

Abstract. Hand hygiene plays a key role in the prevention of infections. However, there is still a lack of hand hygiene practices among both healthcare professionals and the public. Electronic hand hygiene monitoring systems have the potential to improve the situation by giving an accurate assessment of hand hygiene behavior and by placing digital interventions, but such systems are used only in a small number of healthcare facilities. Barriers that limit their large-scale adoption include high costs, privacy concerns, and usability. In this paper, we present a novel real-time feedback system that aims to overcome the existing barriers and supports hand hygiene on a personal and organizational level.

Keywords: Hand hygiene · Real-time feedback · Health information system

1 Introduction

Proper hand hygiene is one of the easiest, cheapest, and most effective ways to contain the spread of infectious diseases [1]. It is a particular concern in the health sector, where hospital-acquired infections constitute a massive threat to patient safety and cause large economic damage (average cost of 14,000$ per infection [2]) that would often be preventable. Despite large-scale efforts to improve hand hygiene practice (e.g., the "Clean Care is Safer Care" campaign by the WHO), the compliance with guidelines remains below 50% [3] and only 8.5% of healthcare workers perform correct hand hygiene technique according to guidelines [4]. The COVID-19 pandemic underlines the need for good hand hygiene outside of hospital systems and highlights the importance of hand washing everywhere, from kindergartens to elderly care facilities.

Electronic hand hygiene monitoring systems (EHHMS) can improve this situation for two reasons: First, an information system (IS) can provide a scalable, extensive, and objective method to measure and assess hand hygiene performance and identify situation- or location-specific problems. EHHMS have major advantages over human observers, as they can measure behavior permanently and less affected by the Hawthorne effect (people changing behavior due to feeling observed) [5]. Second, EHHMS can deliver digital interventions to induce behavior change towards better hand hygiene.

F. Ahlemann et al. (Eds.): WI 2021, LNISO 46, pp. 88–94, 2021.
https://doi.org/10.1007/978-3-030-86790-4_7

Such interventions may comprise for instance performance feedback, "nudges" such as goal setting and the activation of social norms, and may also place reminders, which are all key elements of the WHO multimodal hand hygiene improvement strategy [6] and effective at improving hand hygiene behavior.

We see potential in such IS that a) address barriers of adoptions that current systems face and are b) more versatile and accessible than previous systems for application areas beyond healthcare facilities. In this paper, we outline a novel IoT-based feedback IS that tracks hand hygiene behavior at the place of action only (faucet and sink for hand washing) and thereby does not rely on costly personal tracking devices. It trades more advanced tracking capabilities for a cheaper and more accessible system, while maintaining capabilities to measure and improve hand hygiene on a personal and organizational level.

2 Related Work on EHHMS

Prior research on EHHMS has mostly focused on the medical field and utilized a wide range of technologies. For instance, simple electronic soap and disinfection dispensers record frequency and time of activation, but can only inform about rough trends in hand hygiene behavior [7, 8]. More technically advanced systems use wearable tracking devices that deliver real-time feedback to improve HH compliance of healthcare workers [9–13]. This approach has led to promising results: the number of hand hygiene procedures were increased by 23% [9] and relevant nosocomial infections were halved [13]. Other systems set a focus on monitoring correct handwashing techniques which can be implemented using wristbands [14], smartwatches [15], or camera-based systems [16]. The measurement of hand hygiene behavior works well with state-of-the-art EHHMS: they detect compliance with high accuracy of over 90% [17, 18], while detection rates of hand washing poses is possible with an average accuracy of 90% for both camera based systems [16] and wrist-worn technology [15]. In addition to the papers with a technical focus, a small number of studies exist that apply concepts from behavioral economics to induce behavior change. To this work, insights from IS research may make important contributions when the objective is to build scalable yet powerful EHHMS. Examples of relevant work from IS includes studies on injunctive social norms [19], gamification in combination with social comparison [20], priming [21], and goal setting [22]. We intend to bring both fields together and build a system that allows us to test and deploy powerful interventions.

3 Methodology

We conducted an extensive qualitative screening of the literature concerning existing technical solutions, digital and behavioral hand hygiene interventions, and best practices for implementation[1]. From this literature, we identified critical barriers that limit

[1] The literature screening was conducted with search engines of PubMed, ScienceDirect, and Google Scholar. Search terms included e.g.: "hand hygiene AND intervention AND hospital" or "hand hygiene monitoring system".

the widespread adoption of EHHMS (see Sect. 3.1). To address those barriers, we derived requirements for the design of future systems (Sect. 3.2). The requirements are underpinned by detailed analysis of the existing literature, the described barriers for adoption, and interviews with major stakeholders of such systems. Unstructured and semi-structured interviews (n = 14) were conducted mostly in a one-to-one setting in German hospitals and included healthcare workers (n = 7), a hygiene officer (n = 1), clinic maintenance and building services (n = 3), engineers and salesperson from the sanitary sector (n = 3). Subsequently, we present a prototype of a feedback IS that implements the derived requirements (Sect. 4).

3.1 Barriers of Adoption for Previous EHHMS

Cost: Several studies have named high cost of EHHMS as a barrier for adoption [23–25]. Studies that report the costs of their EHHMS estimate them between 30000$ and 50000$ for small hospital units of 20 beds or less [9, 26, 27]. In a survey of 56 hospitals, 79.8% named cost the primary reason for non-adoption [28].

Privacy of users: Healthcare workers have expressed concerns that their location is continuously monitored using personal tracking techniques [11, 29] and data of individual hand hygiene performance might be used for punishment [29].

Usability: Systems with personal tracking devices have also been found to be inconvenient [30] and disrupt the workflow of healthcare professionals [11, 23], hence the usage of systems can decrease over time [11]. Perceived inaccuracy of tracking devices has caused frustration of users and even led to manipulation of systems [31].

Accessibility: Many systems require dedicated personal hardware (e.g. badges, wrist worn sensors, or smartwatches) and thus limit accessibility, as the systems capabilities are only available to a predefined group of users equipped with hardware.

3.2 Requirements for Our Feedback Information System

R1: *The system shall cost considerably less than previous solutions and have low operating cost.* This limits the sensors and ICT-hardware to relatively low cost versions and shifts complexity from measurement hardware to scalable software (Barrier: Cost).

R2: *The system shall preserve privacy and not track individual behavior.* Privacy concerns are a critical barrier for the adoption of EHHMS and may lead to resistance against the introduction of such systems, especially by healthcare workers. By omitting personal tracking devices, the system emphasizes collective improvement instead of surveillance (Barrier: Privacy).

R3: *The system shall deliver real-time feedback in situ.* Feedback has been one of the most common and effective methods in inducing behavior change. As research from other areas such as energy conservation has shown, feedback may be most powerful at changing behavior when delivered at the place of action and in real time [32] (Barrier: Usability).

R4: *The system shall be easily integrable into existing sanitary installations.* To keep the system versatile for applications outside of healthcare, the system shall be integrated into faucets and dispensers for soap or disinfection agent. For the user, the only visible difference to a common sink is a feedback device for delivering digital interventions, which supports usability (Barriers: Usability, Accessibility).

R5: *The system shall assure legionella prevention by automatic flushing of stagnating pipes.* Water quality plays an important role for hygiene, as Legionella reproduce in stagnating water pipes at temperatures between 25 and 45 °C and may cause pneumonia when inhaled via aerosols. Hospitals and semi-public buildings invest considerable effort into prevention and the associated documentation.

R6: *The systems (wireless) technology shall not interfere with medical equipment at healthcare facilities and drinking water regulations.*

3.3 System Architecture of Our Feedback Information System

With consideration for the identified barriers and requirements, we developed an IoT-based feedback IS for improving hand washing, as pictured in Fig. 1. A single installation consists of a touchless faucet (a), a soap sensor (b), a feedback display for user interventions (c), and a gateway (d), which connects to devices (a-c) via Bluetooth and relays data to a cloud infrastructure (e). Connected IS, such as dashboards to monitor hand hygiene (f), can access the system via this cloud infrastructure.

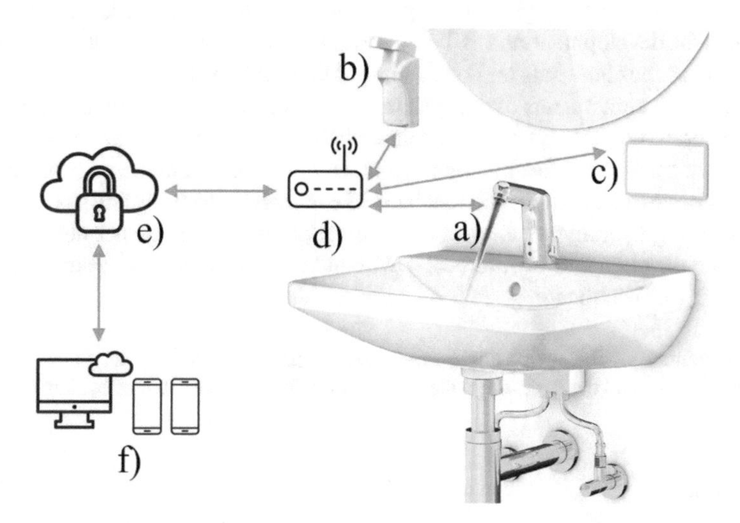

Fig. 1. Architecture of our feedback information system

The system measures individual hand washing performance using the duration of the hand wash, usage of soap or disinfection agent, and the application duration of cleaning product. Thus, the adherence to the widespread five step process for hand washing [33] can be observed. We will validate the accuracy of behavior tracking with ground truth data from field experiments, which is still work in progress.

Individual users of the IS can be targeted by arbitrary messages on the feedback display, which may contain instructions, reminders, or feedback on individual behavior. To support hand hygiene on an organizational level, the system measures hand hygiene of users at all equipped faucets. Depending on the location of such faucets, this enables tracking of hand hygiene behavior across different organizational units, e.g. the wards of a hospital, or different user groups such as patients, visitors, and healthcare workers. Such behavioral data may reveal a need for action and support resulting information campaigns for improved hand hygiene.

The lack of personal tracking hardware or vison-based technology results in some limitations of this system: Only behavior of users that interact with the installation (e.g., use of water or soap) can be tracked or influenced, while non-compliance (no hand hygiene performed) cannot be detected. Furthermore, the system is unable to differentiate between fine-grained handwashing movements and poses that e.g. vision-based systems can detect.

4 Conclusion and Outlook

EHHMS have great potential to monitor and improve hand hygiene behavior in a reliable and scalable way, but cost and complexity of existing systems limit their application to selected healthcare facilities. In this paper, we have presented a prototype of a novel IoT-based handwashing system that addresses critical adoption barriers of existing systems and supports hand hygiene on a personal and organizational level. This system is currently in development and is being evaluated in an ongoing field study with 40 installations at four hospitals and one semi-public building. In future work, we plan to use the feedback components of our system (i.e., the display next to the sink, email based reports generated by the system) to evaluate behavioral interventions (nudges such as descriptive normative feedback) targeting hand hygiene in a randomized controlled trial. Furthermore, we explore how such feedback IS can assist in forming and sustaining good habits regarding hand hygiene. With this evaluation, we aim to gather design implications for the development of future EHHMS and support a more widespread adoption in and outside of healthcare.

Acknowledgements. This work has been funded in part by the Bavarian State Ministry of Education, Science and the Arts within the framework "TechnologieAllianzOberfranken (TAO)".

References

1. Bloomfield, S.F., Aiello, A.E., Cookson, B., O'Boyle, C., Larson, E.L.: The effectiveness of hand hygiene procedures in reducing the risks of infections in home and community settings including handwashing and alcohol-based hand sanitizers. Am. J. Infect. Control **35**, S27–S64 (2007). https://doi.org/10.1016/j.ajic.2007.07.001

2. Stone, P.W., Larson, E., Kawar, L.N.: A systematic audit of economic evidence linking nosocomial infections and infection control interventions: 1990–2000. Am. J. Infect. Control **30**, 145–152 (2002). https://doi.org/10.1067/mic.2002.121099
3. Erasmus, V., et al.: Systematic review of studies on compliance with hand hygiene guidelines in hospital care. Infect. Control Hosp. Epidemiol. **31**, 283–294 (2010). https://doi.org/10.1086/650451
4. Tschudin-Sutter, S., Sepulcri, D., Dangel, M., Schuhmacher, H., Widmer, A.F.: Compliance with the world health organization hand hygiene technique: a prospective observational study. Infect. Control Hosp. Epidemiol. **36**, 482–483 (2015). https://doi.org/10.1017/ice.2014.82
5. Boyce, J.M.: Hand hygiene compliance monitoring: current perspectives from the USA. J. Hosp. Infect. **70**, 2–7 (2008). https://doi.org/10.1016/S0195-6701(08)60003-1
6. World Health Organization: WHO guidelines on hand hygiene in health care: first global patient safety challenge: clean care is safer care. World Health Organization, Patient Safety, Geneva, Switzerland (2009)
7. Boyce, J.M., Cooper, T., Dolan, M.J.: Evaluation of an electronic device for real-time measurement of alcohol-based hand rub use. Infect. Control Hosp. Epidemiol. **30**, 1090–1095 (2009). https://doi.org/10.1086/644756
8. Scheithauer, S., Bickenbach, J., Heisel, H., Fehling, P., Marx, G., Lemmen, S.: Do WiFi-based hand hygiene dispenser systems increase hand hygiene compliance? Am. J. Infect. Control **46**, 1192–1194 (2018). https://doi.org/10.1016/j.ajic.2018.03.026
9. Marra, A.R., et al.: The use of real-time feedback via wireless technology to improve hand hygiene compliance. Am. J. Infect. Control **42**, 608–611 (2014). https://doi.org/10.1016/j.ajic.2014.02.006
10. Radhakrishna, K., et al.: Real-Time feedback for improving compliance to hand sanitization among healthcare workers in an open layout ICU using radiofrequency identification. J. Med. Syst. **39**(6), 1–8 (2015). https://doi.org/10.1007/s10916-015-0251-1
11. Al Salman, J.M., Hani, S., de Marcellis-Warin, N., Fatima Isa, S.: Effectiveness of an electronic hand hygiene monitoring system on healthcare workers' compliance to guidelines. J. Infect. Public Health **8**, 117–126 (2015). https://doi.org/10.1016/j.jiph.2014.07.019
12. Storey, S.J., et al.: Effect of a contact monitoring system with immediate visual feedback on hand hygiene compliance. J. Hosp. Infect. **88**, 84–88 (2014). https://doi.org/10.1016/j.jhin.2014.06.014
13. McCalla, S., Reilly, M., Thomas, R., McSpedon-Rai, D., McMahon, L.A., Palumbo, M.: An automated hand hygiene compliance system is associated with decreased rates of health care-associated infections. Am. J. Infect. Control **46**, 1381–1386 (2018). https://doi.org/10.1016/j.ajic.2018.05.017
14. Galluzzi, V., Herman, T., Polgreen, P.: Hand hygiene duration and technique recognition using wrist-worn sensors. In: Proceedings of the 14th International Conference on Information Processing in Sensor Networks - IPSN 2015, pp. 106–117. ACM Press, Seattle, Washington (2015). https://doi.org/10.1145/2737095.2737106
15. Mondol, M.A.S., Stankovic, J.A.: Harmony: a hand wash monitoring and reminder system using smart watches. In: Proceedings of the 12th EAI International Conference on Mobile and Ubiquitous Systems: Computing, Networking and Services. ACM, Coimbra, Portugal (2015). https://doi.org/10.4108/eai.22-7-2015.2260042
16. Llorca, D.F., Parra, I., Sotelo, M.Á., Lacey, G.: A vision-based system for automatic hand washing quality assessment. Mach. Vis. Appl. **22**, 219–234 (2011). https://doi.org/10.1007/s00138-009-0234-7
17. Filho, M.A.O., et al.: Comparison of human and electronic observation for the measurement of compliance with hand hygiene. Am. J. Infect. Control **42**, 1188–1192 (2014). https://doi.org/10.1016/j.ajic.2014.07.031

18. Doll, M.E., et al.: A comparison of the accuracy of two electronic hand hygiene monitoring systems. Infect. Control Hosp. Epidemiol. **40**, 1194–1197 (2019). https://doi.org/10.1017/ice.2019.209
19. Gaube, S., Tsivrikos, D., Dollinger, D., Lermer, E.: How a smiley protects health: a pilot intervention to improve hand hygiene in hospitals by activating injunctive norms through emoticons. PLoS One **13**, e0197465 (2018). https://doi.org/10.1371/journal.pone.0197465
20. Marques, R., Gregório, J., Pinheiro, F., Póvoa, P., da Silva, M.M., Lapão, L.V.: How can information systems provide support to nurses' hand hygiene performance? Using gamification and indoor location to improve hand hygiene awareness and reduce hospital infections. BMC Med. Inform. Decis. Mak. **17**, 15 (2017). https://doi.org/10.1186/s12911-017-0410-z
21. King, D., Vlaev, I., Everett-Thomas, R., Fitzpatrick, M., Darzi, A., Birnbach, D.J.: "Priming" hand hygiene compliance in clinical environments. Health Psychol. **35**, 96–101 (2016). https://doi.org/10.1037/hea0000239
22. Diefenbacher, S., Fliss, P.M., Tatzel, J., Wenk, J., Keller, J.: A quasi-randomized controlled before–after study using performance feedback and goal setting as elements of hand hygiene promotion. J. Hosp. Infect. **101**, 399–407 (2019). https://doi.org/10.1016/j.jhin.2019.02.001
23. Conway, L.J.: Challenges in implementing electronic hand hygiene monitoring systems. Am. J. Infect. Control **44**, e7–e12 (2016). https://doi.org/10.1016/j.ajic.2015.11.031
24. Boyce, J.M.: Current issues in hand hygiene. Am. J. Infect. Control **47**, A46–A52 (2019). https://doi.org/10.1016/j.ajic.2019.03.024
25. Edmisten, C., et al.: Implementing an electronic hand hygiene monitoring system: Lessons learned from community hospitals. Am. J. Infect. Control **45**, 860–865 (2017). https://doi.org/10.1016/j.ajic.2017.03.033
26. Armellino, D., et al.: Using high-technology to enforce low-technology safety measures: the use of third-party remote video auditing and real-time feedback in healthcare. Clin. Infect. Dis. **54**, 1–7 (2012). https://doi.org/10.1093/cid/cir773
27. Sahud, A.G., Bhanot, N., Radhakrishnan, A., Bajwa, R., Manyam, H., Post, J.C.: An electronic hand hygiene surveillance device: a pilot study exploring surrogate markers for hand hygiene compliance. Infect. Control Hosp. Epidemiol. **31**, 634–639 (2010). https://doi.org/10.1086/652527
28. Durant, D.J., Willis, L., Duvall, S.: Adoption of electronic hand hygiene monitoring systems in New York state hospitals and the associated impact on hospital-acquired C. Difficile infection rates. Am. J. Infect. Control **48**, 733–739 (2020). https://doi.org/10.1016/j.ajic.2020.04.005
29. Ellingson, K., et al.: Healthcare personnel perceptions of hand hygiene monitoring technology. Infect. Control Hosp. Epidemiol. **32**, 1091–1096 (2011). https://doi.org/10.1086/662179
30. Levin, P.D., et al.: Obstacles to the successful introduction of an electronic hand hygiene monitoring system, a cohort observational study. Antimicrob. Resist. Infect. Control **8**, 43 (2019). https://doi.org/10.1186/s13756-019-0498-2
31. Dyson, J., Madeo, M.: Investigating the use of an electronic hand hygiene monitoring and prompt device: influence and acceptability. J. Infect. Prev. **18**, 278–287 (2017). https://doi.org/10.1177/1757177417714045
32. Tiefenbeck, V., et al.: Overcoming salience bias: how real-time feedback fosters resource conservation. Manage. Sci. **64**, 1458–1476 (2018). https://doi.org/10.1287/mnsc.2016.2646
33. Centers for Disease Control and Prevention: When and How to Wash Your Hands. https://www.cdc.gov/handwashing/when-how-handwashing.html. Accessed 14 Aug 2020

Digital Retail

Introduction to the WI2021 Track: Digital Retail

Jörg Becker[1] and Axel Winkelmann[2]

[1] Westfälische Wilhelms-Universität, European Research Center for Information Systems, Münster, Germany
becker@ercis.uni-muenster.de
[2] Julius-Maximilians-Universität Würzburg, Faculty of Business Management and Economics, Würzburg, Germany
axel.winkelmann@uni-wuerzburg.de

1 Track Description

Retail faces many challenges. The ubiquitous competition in the form of Amazon and Co. is leading to a tendency towards declining sales for stationary retailers. This is even getting more evident in "Corona-times". At the same time, the stationary retailer must also be well-positioned in the multi-channel and omni-channel in order to be able to trade economically in the future. This raises the question of the optimal business model in retail: only digital, only stationary, which hybrid form? Is the medium-sized retailer capable of surviving on its own, or does it have to think in terms of cooperation in order to survive? These can be "physical" cooperations (cooperatives) or "virtual" ones (integration into the platform economy). The question of both the business model and the cooperation has an impact on the IT design of the retailer and the integration of the IT components (ERP system, e-commerce system, platform integration). As such, the Digital Retail Track encompasses a broad field of topics concerned with retail and its digitalization, such as retail strategies, business models, IT integration strategies, and retail in smart cities.

2 Research Articles

As digital retail has been more important than ever, we are excited to announce five research articles as part of the Digital Retail Track.

2.1 Discovering Geographical Patterns of Retailers' Locations for Successful Retail in City Centers (Philipp zur Heiden, Daniel Winter)

As digital retail does not limit itself to business transactions over electronic channels, this short paper offers interesting insights into what factors influence city centers' success consisting of brick-and-mortar stores using machine learning techniques. The authors analyze 40 cities and over 30,000 entities within these city centers. Findings show that their success especially relies on the centrality of the shops within the city centers.

2.2 E-Service Touchpoints for Jewelry Retailers: Customers' Perceptions of a Digital Sales Desk (Cara Michelle Pfabe, Benjamin Barann, Ann-Kristin Cordes, Andreas Hermann, Torsten Gollhardt)

Luxury goods such as jewelry and watches are still mainly sold in retail outlets, as customers appreciate direct contact with customer advisors. Nevertheless, luxury stores can benefit from digital solutions. This full paper raises the idea of a digital sales desk which supports the watch advisory service. The authors conducted a survey regarding the potentials and future orientation of such services. The survey showed that most participants agreed with the prospect that digital sales desks would benefit the retailers and address the expectations of the customers. In addition, the survey results were investigated for two different customer groups with low and higher willingness to pay.

2.3 Local Retail Under Fire: Local Shopping Platforms Revisited Pre and During the Corona Crisis (Sören Bärsch, Lars Bollweg, Peter Weber, Tim Wittemund, Valerie Wulfhorst)

As the COVID-19 pandemic especially affects local retail, the authors investigate whether the pandemic has influenced the development of Local Shopping Platforms as well. The full paper draws from a content analysis regarding the development of Local Shopping Platforms between 2016 and 2019 and interviews conducted during the pandemic. Results show that the crisis heavily accelerated the implementation of Local Shopping Platforms.

2.4 Towards the Digital Self-Renewal of Retail: The Generic Ecosystem of the Retail Industry (Timo Phillip Böttcher, Lukas Rickling, Kristina Gmelch, Jörg Weking, Helmut Krcmar)

The challenges imposed on brick-and-mortar retail by e-commerce have to be addressed by traditional retailers. As digital retailers have many advantages, such as extensive knowledge of their customers' purchase patterns, the authors argue that retailers need to leverage the advantages of inter-organizational collaboration to create value. In this short paper, the authors present an e3-value model consisting of the German retail ecosystem.

2.5 The Effect of Personality Traits and Gender Roles on Consumer Channel Choices (Dennis Hummel, Tobias Vogel, Alexander Mädche)

As each customer is different, the authors of this full paper investigate a little-explored topic: How do personality traits and gender roles influence (digital) channel choices? The authors try to answer this question by conducting a lab experiment. The experiment results show that some personality traits and gender roles have a significant impact on trust, perceived risk, and perceived benefits, which in turn influence the channel choice significantly.

Discovering Geographical Patterns of Retailers' Locations for Successful Retail in City Centers

Philipp zur Heiden(✉) and Daniel Winter

Paderborn University, Paderborn, Germany
philipp.zur.heiden@upb.de

Abstract. City centers and resident retail businesses have to react to the continuous growth of online retail. However, some city centers are far more successful concerning the total turnover in relation to its inhabitants. Using machine learning and data analysis methods, we investigate the types and locations of retail businesses inside the city center, comparing successful and unsuccessful city centers. Our results show that success does not come with particular types of shops, but rather with centrality and bundled shopping areas. We provide insights for planning and developing successful retail in city centers to compete and interact with online retail.

Keywords: Machine learning · City center · Retail · Clustering · Centrality

1 Introduction

The rise of digital retail continues to pressurize retail in German city centers [1, 2]. The downwards spiral of fewer customers and fewer retail businesses inside the city center further increases the number of vacancies in many formerly successful retail areas in city centers [3, 4]. This primarily affects medium-sized cities and smaller retail businesses because they more often cannot focus on increasing their customer experience as a central element of high street retail [5]. Retail businesses are not the only businesses affected by this transition, but also other types of businesses common in high streets, e.g., the service industry, restaurants, and businesses for entertainment and amusement. We continue to use the term businesses to refer to all different types.

With machine learning and data-driven studies transforming whole industries [6], we see new ways to discover novel insights for the planning and development of city centers to strengthen the advantages of city center businesses. Manual and conventional analysis of geographical data cannot deliver insights on comprehensive patterns of business locations. With machine learning, however, one can analyze geographical data and information about businesses making up retail in different city centers by using novel methods. We suspect more factors than the sheer size of the city and its inhabitants to influence the success some city centers have, whereas others fall behind. Therefore, we focus on the following research question: *Which geographical patterns of retailers' locations enable successful retail in city centers?*

F. Ahlemann et al. (Eds.): WI 2021, LNISO 46, pp. 99–104, 2021.
https://doi.org/10.1007/978-3-030-86790-4_8

2 Theoretical Concepts: City Centers and Machine Learning

City centers are network models of different entities, comprising housing, employment, and transportation [7, 8]. Different indices are able to estimate the success of different city centers. One common index for measuring retail success in Germany is the retail centrality index, defined by the percentage value of the quotient of spending capacity of the resident population and turnover of the local retail businesses [9, 10]. A percentage bigger than 100% shows that a city attracts more customers spending money in the city center from its vicinity than it "looses" customers to other cities. The retail centrality index is only calculated once per city and does not indicate the success of different types of retailers. Naturally, bigger cities and regional centers—e.g., Berlin, Munich—will have a significantly higher retail centrality index [9]. Thus, while comparing different cities based on their retail centrality index, one should always assure that the cities' populations are even.

Machine learning, in general, describes the automatic extraction of algorithms for data analysis purposes [11]. Research in machine learning revolves around the development and application of new methods to analyze vast amounts of data to gain otherwise hidden patterns and insights [12]. Machine learning comprises three types of learning strategies: supervised learning, unsupervised learning, and reinforcement learning [12]. In our study, we rely on supervised learning to investigate differences between successful and unsuccessful cities. We apply decision trees [13, 14], random forests [15], and support vector machines [16] to answer our research question, using types and locations of businesses as input variables and success classification based on the retail centrality index as our output variable.

3 Research Method

Analyzing vast amounts of data has become a popular research method in the IS discipline, as it not only serves to gain insights but also to develop theory to extend the knowledge scope of IS [17]. In this study, we apply the research method of utilizing big data sources and advanced analytics by Müller et al. [18]. They picture the research with unstructured data as a process of four phases: framing a research question, collecting the necessary data, the computational analysis, and, finally, interpreting the results [18].

As our study already proposed a research question in Sect. 1, we continue with our data collection and analysis steps. First, we have to decide on the highly and poorly ranked cities in terms of success. We focus on middle-sized cities (20,000 to 100,000 inhabitants) in Germany and use the retail centrality index to define successful and unsuccessful cities (cf. Sect. 2)[1]. We use a total of 40 cities for our analysis—20 of them having highly valued retail centrality indices. The other 20 cities have the lowest centrality indices, indicating the poorest performing cities for our research.

As we need geospatial data to find patterns based on the location of the different businesses, we opt for OpenStreetMap (OSM) in favor of Google Maps, because the German community of OSM is much more active and serves as the foundation of high-quality data [19–21]. We extract the different businesses (entities with OSM categories

[1] Data taken from GMA GmbH (2017) and http://www.mb-research.de/.

shop and *amenity*) of highly and poorly ranked cities with an API for OSM1F[2]. For data-cleaning, we unify identical entities found in both *shop* and *amenity* category and remove entities with stopwords (e.g., "wifi," "bench") from our data collection. In sum we extracted 37,955 entities for our 40 selected cities, making it an average of about 1,000 entities per city. Removing entities with stopwords leaves us at 26,384 entities for the following analysis. The remaining entities were classified with different categories for the type of business by the community. However, we still have 386 types of businesses of significantly varying sizes. Therefore, we use a k-means clustering [22] based on word2vec annotations [23] to further group these types of businesses. Word2vec can calculate a multi-dimensional vector from a word to quantify its meaning based on likeliness to other words in a dictionary [23]. We used a pre-trained model2F[3] as our dictionary to calculate the vectors. We input the resulting vectors for each business category into a k-means clustering algorithm, as we then need to cluster the categories into groups. Using an elbow score, we identified $k = 20$ as a suitable number of clusters. Thus, combining these two algorithms yields 20 clusters of business categories with similar meanings.

For our computational analysis, we apply different techniques of machine learning to gather insights from our dataset, i.e., random forests, decision trees, and support vector machines. For each algorithm, we compare the results of analyzing highly-ranked and poorly-ranked cities to discover factors impacting the success of these cities.

4 Results and Discussion

During our analysis, we investigated different geographical features of businesses and their locations inside different city centers. First, the mean number of stores for each category is mostly the same for successful and unsuccessful city centers. This trend only differs for category 13 with a significantly high number of businesses for successful cities ($\varnothing = 115$) compared to unsuccessful cities ($\varnothing = 76$). This category covers gas stations and seaside businesses, comprising, e.g., fishing supply, scuba diving, weighbridges, and loading docks. Gas stations indicate high road traffic from possibly attracted customers to the city center. Thus, we interpret that some of these businesses are present in the city because many people are visiting particular cities, and not that many people are visiting the city for the high number of gas stations. As ports and fisheries are only possible at rivers and seas, the number of seaside businesses is mostly predefined and cannot be improved in many cases.

We analyzed all data we had available and tried to identify possible features significantly influencing the success of city centers. By using different machine learning methods and techniques (cf. Sect. 3), we are able compare different results and confirm the validity of the results. However, our data analyses show that the centrality of the locations of businesses in a city center is the main feature significant for the success of the city center. This was consistent across all applications of different machine learning techniques and methods. Figure 1 shows the average distance of locations to the city

[2] https://developer.mapquest.com/documentation/open/nominatim-search/.
[3] https://code.google.com/archive/p/word2vec/.

center divided by the category of the business. For the highly ranked cities, the mean distance of the locations varies from 1.0 km to 2.7 km depending on businesses' categories. In contrast, the mean distance of the locations from unsuccessful cities to the city center is significantly higher, ranging from 3.0 km to 3.5 km. Placing many shops close to the center of the city and fewer in a further range seems to be a factor drastically influencing the cities success.

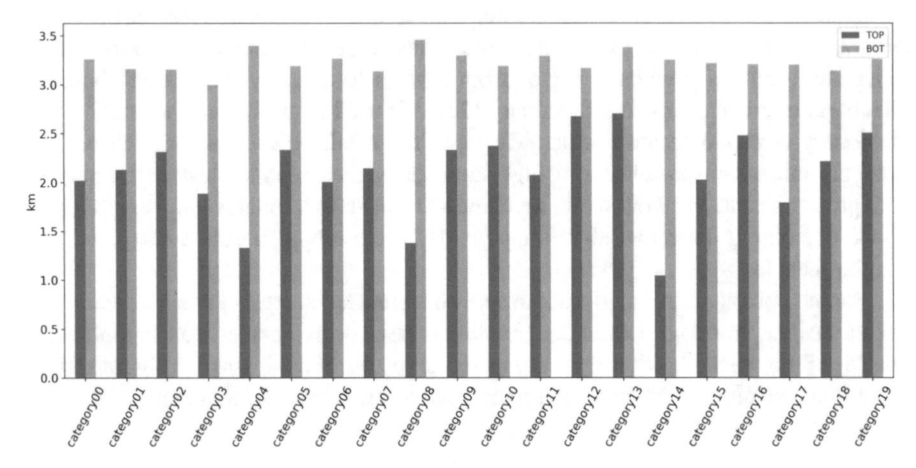

Fig. 1. Average distance from the location to the middle of the city by category

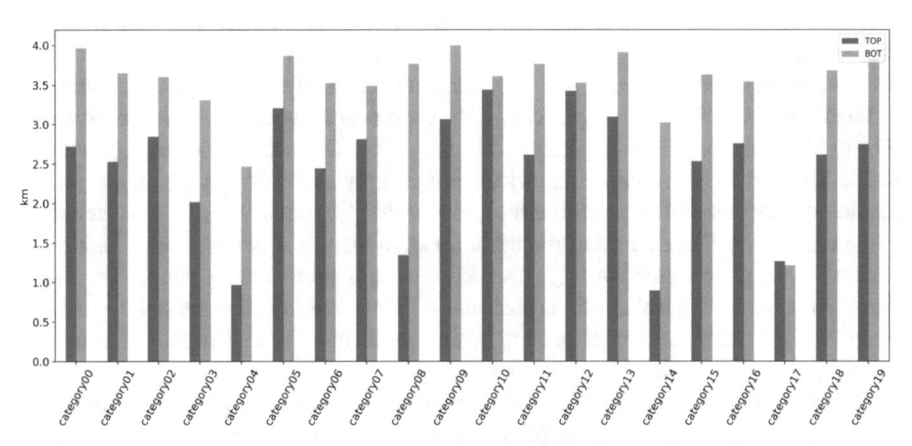

Fig. 2. Average distance between locations of the same category in the same city by category

Similar results can be seen for the average distance between locations of the same category. Figure 2 visualizes these averages for every category of business locations. Again, average distances are smaller for successful city centers than average distances of businesses in less successful cities. Generally, the average distance is lower for better-ranked cities. Our results suggest that centrality is one of the critical features of a successful city center.

With online retail threatening the existence of many retail businesses [3, 4], grouping different retail businesses (independent of their categories) seems to be a foundation for successful retail in city centers. Especially planned shopping areas [24], e.g., shopping malls and outlet centers, excel at pooling retailers on central locations because they do not have to consider natural, private, and governmental hindrances. Further, they are managed centrally in contrast to solitary retailers in organically grown shopping ares. Customers seem to prefer cities with shopping malls or similar structures. Thus, planning shopping areas with a dense presence of retailers could be a focus to improve the attractiveness and success of retail in city centers and to prevent city center retail to perish due to online retail. This does not need to be done in a shopping mall, but can be utilize vacancies in formally organically grown shopping areas. Town center management as a strategic way to improve city center attractiveness [25] can, e.g., benefit from recommending fitting areas to retailers who want to open new business sites in city centers [26].

5 Conclusion

In this paper, we used different methods of supervised machine learning to investigate patterns of retailers' locations in city centers. We discovered that the number of retailer businesses of different types does not influence the city center's success. Still, the centrality of successful cities is much higher, i.e., businesses are geographically closer to businesses of the same category. Our insights are limited by the selection of machine learning methods, the restriction to medium-sized cities in Germany, and by neglecting historical events transforming city centers (e.g., war damage, political agendas).

As our findings on distances between city centers and businesses as well as distances between businesses have to be contextualized, we plan to extend our research for considering further structural attributes, e.g., elevation, courses of roads, and public transportation networks. Our paper serves as an entry point for a detailed analysis of structural attributes in city centers and their influence on the success of retailers. As further analyses have to cope with an increasing volume of data, we consider machine learning techniques to be able to handle such analyses.

References

1. Handelsverband Deutschland e.V. (HDE): Zahlenspiegel 2018, 42 (2018)
2. Handelsverband Deutschland e.V. (HDE): Umsatz im Einzelhandel im engeren Sinne in Deutschland in den Jahren 2000 bis 2019* (in Milliarden Euro). Statista - Das Statistik-Portal (2019)
3. Hagberg, J., Sundstrom, M., Egels-Zandén, N.: The digitalization of retailing: an exploratory framework. Int. J. Retail. Distrib. Mgt. **44**, 694–712 (2016)
4. Verhoef, P.C., Kannan, P.K., Inman, J.J.: From multi-channel retailing to omni-channel retailing. J. Retail. **91**, 174–181 (2015)
5. Verhoef, P.C., Lemon, K.N., Parasuraman, A., Roggeveen, A., Tsiros, M., Schlesinger, L.A.: Customer experience creation: determinants, dynamics and management strategies. J. Retail. **85**, 31–41 (2009)

6. Jordan, M.I., Mitchell, T.M.: Machine learning: trends, perspectives, and prospects. Science (New York, N.Y.) **349**, 255–260 (2015)
7. Keating, W.D.: Linking downtown development to broader community goals: an analysis of linkage policy in three cities. J. Am. Plan. Assoc. **52**, 133–141 (1986)
8. Wegener, M.: Operational urban models state of the art. J. Am. Plann. Assoc. **60**, 17–29 (1994)
9. Stable, E.G.: Die Einzelhandelszentralität westdeutscher Städte : Ein Beitrag zur Methodik der Zentralitätsmessung (Retail centrality of West German urban centres : a contribution to the methodology for measuring centrality). JSTOR **1**, 46–59 (1996)
10. Everling, O., Jahn, O., Kammermeier, E.: Rating von Einzelhandelsimmobilien. Gabler|GWV Fachverlage GmbH, Wiesbaden (2009)
11. Provost, F., Fawcett, T.: Data Science for Business. O'Reilly Media, Inc., Newton (2013)
12. Alpaydin, E.: Introduction to Machine Learning. MIT Press, Cambridge (2009)
13. Swain, P.H., Hauska, H.: Decision tree classifier: design and potential. IEEE Trans. Geosci. Electron. **GE-15**, 142–147 (1977)
14. Rasoul, S., David, L.: A survey of decision tree classifier methodology. IEEE Trans. Syst. Man Cybern. **21**, 660–674 (1991)
15. Breiman, L.: Random forests. Mach. Learn. **45**, 5–32 (2001)
16. Pontil, M., Verri, A.: Support vector machines for 3D object recognition. IEEE Trans. Pattern Anal. Mach. Intell. **20**, 637–646 (1998)
17. Berente, N., Seidel, S., Safadi, H.: Research commentary—data-driven computationally intensive theory development. Inf. Syst. Res. **30**, 50–64 (2019)
18. Müller, O., Junglas, I., Brocke, J., Debortoli, S.: Utilizing big data analytics for information systems research: challenges, promises and guidelines. EJIS **25**(4), 289–302 (2016)
19. Neis, P., Zipf, A.: Analyzing the contributor activity of a volunteered geographic information project — the case of OpenStreetMap. ISPRS Int. J. Geo Inf. **1**, 146–165 (2012)
20. Neis, P., Zielstra, D.: Recent developments and future trends in volunteered geographic information research: the case of OpenStreetMap. Future Internet **6**, 76–106 (2014)
21. Mooney, P., Minghini, M.: A Review of OpenStreetMap Data. In: Foody, G., et al. (eds.) Mapping and the Citizen Sensor, pp. 37–59. Ubiquity Press (2017)
22. Kanungo, T., Mount, D.M., Netanyahu, N.S., Piatko, C., Silverman, R., Wu, A.Y.: An efficient k-means clustering algorithm: analysis and implementation. In: Proceedings of the Sixteenth ACM Symposium on Computational Geometry, pp. 100–109 (2000)
23. Mikolov, T., Chen, K., Corrado, G., Dean, J.: Efficient Estimation of Word Representations in Vector Space, pp. 1–12 (2013)
24. Gilbert, D.: Retail Marketing Management. Financial Times Prentice Hall, Harlow (2002)
25. Coca-Stefaniak, J.A., Parker, C., Quin, S., Rinaldi, R., Byrom, J.: Town centre management models: a European perspective. Cities **26**, 74–80 (2009)
26. zur Heiden, P., Berendes, C.I., Beverungen, D.: Designing city center area recommendation systems. In: Gronau, N., Heine, M., Poustcchi, K., Krasnova, H. (eds.) WI2020 Zentrale Tracks, pp. 506–521. GITO Verlag (2010)

E-Service Touchpoints for Jewelry Retailers: Customers' Perceptions of a Digital Sales Desk

Cara M. Pfabe, Benjamin Barann(✉), Ann-Kristin Cordes, Andreas Hermann, and Torsten Gollhardt

University of Münster, ERCIS, Münster, Germany
c.pfabe@uni-muenster.de, {barann,cordes,hermann, gollhardt}@ercis.de

Abstract. The digitalization of retail also affects the luxury industry. The integration of digital components in local retail stores can be one way to attract customers and stay competitive. One novel in-store technology for jewelry stores could be a digital sales desk intended to support the watch-advisory service. This work proposes a conceptual design for a digital sales desk comprising various e-service touchpoints. It conducts an ex-ante evaluation to investigate the aspects of the digital sales desk that influence customers' perceptions of quality and their re-use intentions toward the digitally enriched advisory service. Therefore, an online survey was conducted. The survey results indicate that some e-service touchpoints are more popular than others. The participants' quality and value perceptions also directly impacted their intentions to re-use the service. The results shed light on the digital sales desk's potentials and provide orientation regarding the most promising e-service touchpoints.

Keywords: Digital transformation · Brick-and-Mortar · Jewelry retail · E-Service · Touchpoint

1 Introduction

The online share for luxury goods has steadily grown and is expected to grow further [1]. This trend is also observable in the watch industry [2]. While the increase of online presence [3], and the use of social media in luxury retailing, can be commonly observed, stationary retailers in the luxury segment have to catch up regarding the adoption of mobile applications and in-store technologies [4]. Interactions with in-store technologies and touchpoints shape customers' experiences [4, 5]. Furthermore, omni-channel experiences in physical stores [6] can drive the shopping intentions of customers [7]. As a result, luxury retailers and brands are searching for technologies to transform their physical stores [8] into an "*experiential place*" [9, p. 47]. However, they need to ensure that an in-store technology "*is relevant for consumers […] and really provides value for them […]*" [10, p. 99] and meets their own and their customers' expectations [9]. When purchasing irregularly purchased goods, customers have different expectations, and they demand, for example, detailed information and knowledgeable sellers [11]. Particularly,

F. Ahlemann et al. (Eds.): WI 2021, LNISO 46, pp. 105–122, 2021.
https://doi.org/10.1007/978-3-030-86790-4_9

luxury customers expect high-quality products and services and are willing to pay for them [12, 13]. Thus, novel in-store technologies for luxury retailers should be designed accordingly.

This article focuses on a novel in-store technology for jewelry stores. In essence, it proposes a touchscreen-enabled digital sales desk (i.e., an IT artifact) supporting watch-advisory services in physical jewelry stores. As behavioral knowledge can support IT artifacts' design [14], this study conducts an artificial, formative, ex-ante evaluation [cf. 15] with potential customers to reduce the uncertainties and risks involved in implementing this retail technology [cf. 15, 16]. Whether customers use a technology depends on their perceptions of quality, value, and satisfaction [17–19]. Thus, this article aims at investigating the aspects of a digital sales desk that affect customers' quality perceptions and their intentions to (re-)use the digitally supported service. An online survey was conducted to reach this objective. The results shed light on a digital sales desk's potentials in jewelry stores and provide practical orientation on its most essential aspects, which need to be considered.

This article's remainder is structured as follows: Sect. 2 proposes the digital sales desk's concept. Section 3 develops the research model and presents the hypotheses. Section 4 elaborates on the research method. Next, the results are presented in Sect. 5 and discussed in Sect. 6. The article concludes with a summary and an outlook.

2 A Digital Sales Desk that Supports the Sale of Watches

Luxury is often associated with excellent quality, exceptional craftsmanship, remarkable beauty, joy, global reputation, exclusivity, and rarity [12, 20, 21]. Next to high material value, luxury products also have an intangible value for the customer, which leads to an increased willingness to pay [4, 21]. In addition, emotions can impact luxury customers' brand attitudes [22]. Their perceptions of excellence value, functional value, experiential values, self-expressive value, social value, and economic value lead to positive brand relationships [12]. In turn, positive brand relationships [12] and affective attitude (e.g., pleasure or enjoyment) [20] can drive behavioral intentions [12] and purchase intentions [20]. Luxury customers often obtain detailed information about the products of interest beforehand [3]. Therefore, they "*expect sophisticated personal service and special treatment*" [12, p. 86]. Furthermore, the merchandising, product offering, store atmosphere, and interior design of the physical servicescape should match the luxury and status expected by customers [23].

"*The Internet plays an important role as an information source on luxury products*" [1, p. 28]. For example, online shops attract customers due to their convenience. Among others, relevant aspects of online shops are extensive product selections, easier product comparison, and access to brand information, product information, product presentations, and reviews [1]. Nevertheless, "*physical stores are still the most relevant source of information on new personal luxury products*" [1, p. 27]. They attract customers due to the physical [1, 9] and direct availability [1] of authentic products [9], personal advice, purchasing experiences, and stores' ambient [1]. However, over the past few years, the online share for luxury goods has steadily grown and is expected to grow further [1]. Now, luxury brands have to become more digital to adapt to this trend. However, they need "*to know the available digital opportunities*" [8, p. 225] to do so.

In-store technologies pose various opportunities for luxury retail stores. For example, they allow bringing personalized and information-intensive experiences or entertaining and pleasurable elements to physical stores [4]. They also enable hybrid customer interactions [24] and generate omni-channel experiences [6], which can drive customers' in-store shopping intentions [7]. In-store technologies offer various customer touchpoints (TPs), which may impact customers' technology acceptance [25]. "*A customer touchpoint is a stimulus fulfilling a specific role within the customer journey. It has an interface, which grants access to the stimulus and is mediated by a human, an analog object, or a technology situated in a physical or digital sphere. When encountering a touchpoint, a message between the customer and the retailer, its brand, or other customers is transmitted. This encounter causes a customer experience*" [26, p. 7]. Brick-and-mortar retailers can complement their stores with in-store technologies and e-service TPs to work toward an omni-channel environment [cf. 9, 25]. "*Service is defined as the application of specialized competences [...], through deeds, processes, and performances for the benefit of another entity or the entity itself*" [27, p. 26]. A brick-and-mortar e-service TP is a customer-directed electronic service (e-service) offering that is mediated by a digital TP interface (e.g., a terminal or smartphone) in the physical servicescape [25].

While some customers perceive digital TP interfaces as more trustworthy and objective than the sales staff [28], consumers in the luxury segment and their emotional involvement with products are influenced by sales assistants [4]. Thus, sales assistants should not be replaced. Indeed, digital and human TP interfaces can complement each other [28]. Heine and Berghaus [8] offer luxury brands some guidance on digital interfaces such as online shops, review sites, or mobile and tablet applications. Their work suggests that e-service TPs should be carefully developed to ensure that they offer customer benefits and reflect the brand's superior luxury and quality. However, prior works provide little guidance on the selection of brick-and-mortar e-service TPs [25].

As stated above, customers have different expectations when buying goods purchased on an irregular basis. This also applies to the purchase of luxury watches. Just as in the luxury retail industry in general, mono-brand stores are losing ground to authorized online retailers and e-boutiques of watch brands [2]. Thus, this article focuses on e-service TPs complementing the employee-mediated watch-advisory service in physical jewelry stores. A sales talk on watches usually comprises five phases [29, p. 145]: Salutation, needs analysis, product presentation, purchase, and conclusion. The majority of these phases take place at a sales desk. Therefore, such a desk can be considered a suitable medium for a digital interface offering e-service TPs.

In a project with the carpentry business *August Kreienbaum GmbH*, which develops and realizes interior designs for jewelers, the authors designed a concept for a touch-sensitive screen embedded in a sales desk in the context of the *Mittelstand 4.0-Kompetenzzentrum Lingen*. This concept is called '*digital sales desk*' in the following. The concept's requirements were defined in discussions between the project partners and interviews with jewelry stores. As stated above, luxury customers have different expectations when buying goods purchased on an irregular basis [11–13]. The interviews reflected these expectations. As a result, several potential e-service TPs were defined (see Table 1) to support jewelers' watch-advisory service.

Table 1. Potential e-service touchpoints for the digital sales desk

Cat	*Touchpoint*	*Description*
General information	Jeweler information	Some customers value the brand of the jeweler itself. Thus, this TP allows the customer to gain insight into the history of the jeweler
	Watch promotion video	When no customer is sitting at the sales desk or the consultation has not yet begun, this TP displays promotional videos of products and manufacturers on the screen
	Watch catalog	To provide an overview of the existing watches, a digitalized product catalog [cf. 30] can be displayed on the digital sales desk
	Brand websites and Apps	Some manufacturers provide (web) applications for concessionaire businesses. These are often accessed via tablets or computers of the jewelers. By granting access to them, this TP should increase their accessibility
Product-specific information	Watch information and Pictures	When a watch with an RFID transponder is placed on the RFID reader or a watch is selected from the catalog, this TP presents essential information about it [e.g., 25]. 3D-images allow customers to see watches in detail [cf. 8, 29, 30]
	Watch part details	This TP presents information on specific watch parts, such as the watch bezel or face, on a separate view to not overload the product information page
	Watch brand information	Many customers are interested in the brand of a product. Information on the brand's history and, if applicable, on characters related to the brand, such as designers, can be conveyed vividly using the screen [31]
Decision support	Watch comparison	If a customer cannot decide between watches, a comparison TP can provide the most important facts about the watches to support the decision-making [e.g., 25, 32]
	Watch configuration	Many watches are available in different materials and designs. The digital sales desk displays these options and enables a simple product configuration

(*continued*)

Table 1. (*continued*)

Cat	*Touchpoint*	*Description*
	Similarity-based Recom	This TP presents products with similar characteristics on the product information page [e.g., 25]
	Customer-based Recom	Many customers trust the opinions of other customers [33]. Thus, this TP presents products that customers with similar preferences have bought
	Purchase-based Recom	Personalization is becoming increasingly important to customers in the luxury segment [34]. Thus, this TP makes suggestions based on customers' prior purchases [e.g., 25]
Purchase	Availability. and Deli. time	This TP provides quick information on the availability of watches in the store. If not available, the digital sales desk also provides information on delivery times [e.g., 25]
	Payment	The purchase is often carried out at the sales desk. Thus, this TP can execute payments and display invoices [29]
	Contact formula	Long-term customer contact management beyond a purchase requires the collection of contact data [29]. Thus, the digital sales desk mediates a contact formula TP

Luxury customers' have various reasons to shop online [33]. Among other things, luxury customers appreciate the availability of product information, customer reviews, exclusive online offers, user-friendliness, brand information, convenient returns, and product presentation when shopping online [1]. The digital sales desk allows retailers to mirror some benefits of e-commerce to the physical servicescape [cf. 25], such as the availability of product and brand information and the digital product presentation. Besides, it offers complimentary entertaining and pleasurable elements [cf. 4] for the watch-advisory service. Thus, the e-service TPs may meet the luxury customers' functional and hedonic needs [cf. 20, 22]. In addition, the provided brand- and watch-specific information conveys individual brands' values [cf. 23]. The seamless integration of brand websites and apps ensures that the brands' superior luxury and qualities are reflected [cf. 8]. Finally, the digital sales desk supports salespersons through quick access to information. Thus, it may support jewelers to meet their customers' expectance for sophisticated personal service [cf. 12].

The concept visualized the e-service TPs with mockups (see example in Fig. 1a). Besides, the *tapdo technologies GmbH* developed a simple hardware prototype (see Fig. 1b) housing a radio-frequency identification (RFID) reader that automatically detects watches equipped with RFID transponders [cf. e.g., 35]. The digital TP interface still needs to be implemented based on its ex-ante evaluation [cf. 15], which is presented in this manuscript.

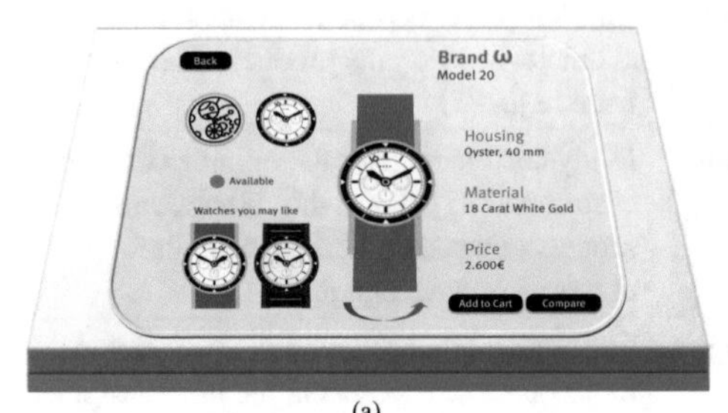

(a)

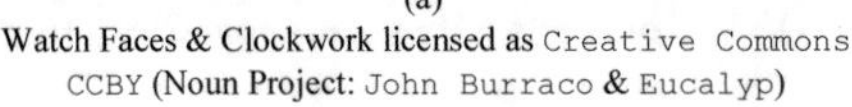
Watch Faces & Clockwork licensed as `Creative Commons CCBY` (Noun Project: `John Burraco` & `Eucalyp`)

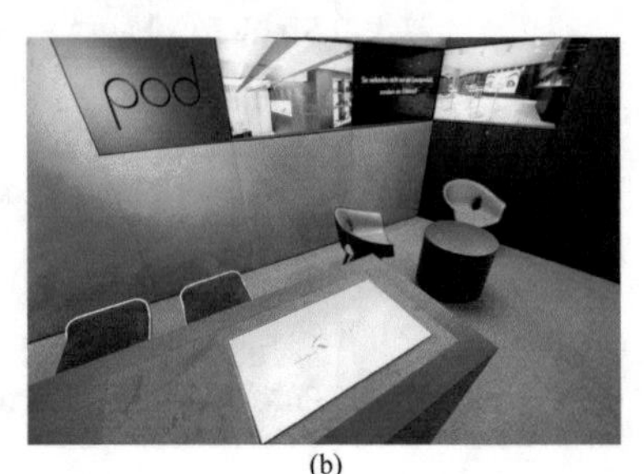

(b)
Picture: *Alexander Polomka*

Fig. 1. (a) Exemplary mockup and (b) Hardware prototype of the digital sales desk

3 Research Model and Hypotheses Development

Luxury customers' quality expectations of the service provided are high [13]. For customers, the quality of service results from comparing their expectations with their perceptions [36]. The aim of a retailer should be to meet or even exceed the expectations of its customers to achieve a high-quality service [cf. 37]. Customers' evaluations of service quality result from the sum of encounters with service TPs [38]. Therefore, retailers must ensure that customers perceive the overall quality of the digitally supported service at the digital sales desk as high. Prior studies have identified relationships between quality, customer value, customer satisfaction, and customers' behavioral intentions [39, 40]. The relationships between the constructs discussed below are congruent with Kettinger et al. [17] and Haddad Rezende et al. [41].

The individually perceived probability that a person will act in a certain way is called the person's behavioral intention [42]. In the digital sales desk's context, retailers need to ensure that customers intend to re-use the digitally supported advisory service in the jeweler's store. According to some prior studies, service quality perceptions directly affect customers' behavioral intentions [40, 43]. In contrast, others have not investigated this theoretical relationship [17, 18] or could not confirm a direct relationship [44]. Thus, the first hypothesis is:

***H1**: Customers' perceptions of the digital sales desk's quality positively impact their intentions to (re-)use a jeweler's digitally supported watch-advisory service.*

The behavioral intentions of customers are influenced by their experiences and impressions. Customers' perceptions of value and their satisfaction positively impact their behaviors [e.g., 39, 45]. Thus, besides the direct effects of quality perceptions on behavioral intentions, prior research also found indirect effects of service quality via customers' perceptions of value and their satisfaction [40, 43].

In the context of products, "*perceived value is the consumer's overall assessment of the utility of a product based on perceptions of what is received and what is given*" [46, p. 14]. Literature also uses this definition in the context of service and shopping values [e.g., 18, 47]. In retailing, costs can be reduced, or benefits can be increased to strengthen customers' value perceptions [48]. The costs for customers in making a purchase not only comprise monetary resources but also include the time, risks, and efforts involved [17, 48]. The customers' benefits include utilitarian (e.g., quality products, personalized offers, or shopping convenience), hedonic, or social values [12, 17, 48]. When introducing new technology, retailers should consider how such an introduction affects value perceptions [48]. Thus, as the digital sales desk aims at supporting and improving the advisory service, the second and third hypotheses are:

***H2**: Customers' perceptions of the digital sales desk's quality positively impact their values perceived from a jeweler's digitally supported watch-advisory service.*
***H3**: Customers' perceptions of a digitally supported watch-advisory service's value positively impact their intentions to (re-)use the service.*

In the context of smart retailing, customers' impressions and evaluations of cumulative experiences with technologies also impact their satisfaction [49, 50]. Customers' satisfaction in general results from their perceptions of service quality [17, 38]. Customers' evaluations of service quality are based on the comparison of their expectations before the purchase with their perceptions after the purchase [18]. Prior research has found that service quality perceptions can increase satisfaction [41, 43]. Furthermore, perceptions of value were shown to drive customers' perceptions of satisfaction [18, 39, 43, 44], and studies have shown that customers' satisfactions influence behavioral and purchase intentions [39, 44, 45, 51]. Satisfied customers are more likely to consider re-consuming or using a service, technology, or system [39, 41, 49, 52]. Thus, the last hypotheses read as follows:

***H4:**Customers' perceptions of the digital sales desk's quality positively impact their perceptions of satisfaction with a jeweler's watch-advisory service.*
***H5**: Customers' perceptions of a digitally supported watch-advisory service's value positively impact their perceptions of satisfaction with the service.*
***H6**: Customers' perceptions of satisfaction with a digitally supported watch-advisory service positively impact their intentions to (re-)use the service.*

4 Method

Measures and Questionnaire: The survey items were adopted from prior research and adapted to the study context. The established *WebQual* (*WQ*) model was chosen to measure customers' *Perceived Quality* of the digital sales desk. *WQ* was developed to assess the quality of websites [53, 54]. As the digital sales desk aims at complementing physical jewelry stores with e-service TPs similar to those known from e-commerce [25], it can be argued that it is appropriate to utilize *WQ* in this context. For this study, the *WQ* measurement items were adapted from Loiacono et al. [53, 54]. *WQ* comprises 36 survey items for 12 reflective first-order constructs, partly determining three formative second-order constructs (see Fig. 2). *Perceived Quality* is a third-order formative construct. *Satisfaction* was measured according to four items adapted from Haddad Rezende et al. [41]. The measurement instruments for the *Value* were adapted from Kettinger et al. [17], who based them on the value categories of Sweeney and Soutar [55]. Besides, the items used by two studies [17, 41] were combined to investigate the customers' *(Re-)Use Intentions* toward the advisory service. Figure 2 shows this study's research model, including its six hypotheses, fifteen first-order constructs, three second-order constructs (i.e., *Usefulness*, *Ease of Use*, *Entertainment*), and one third-order construct (i.e., *Perceived Quality*). Similar to prior studies [25, 56], a single survey item ("*Please indicate how likely you would be to use the following features:*") was added to the survey to measure customers' willingness to use the individual e-service TPs. All survey items were adapted to fit the study's context and translated to German. As the online survey's goal was the artificial, formative, ex-ante evaluation [cf. 15] of the digital sales desk, the items were also transformed into their conjunctive forms.

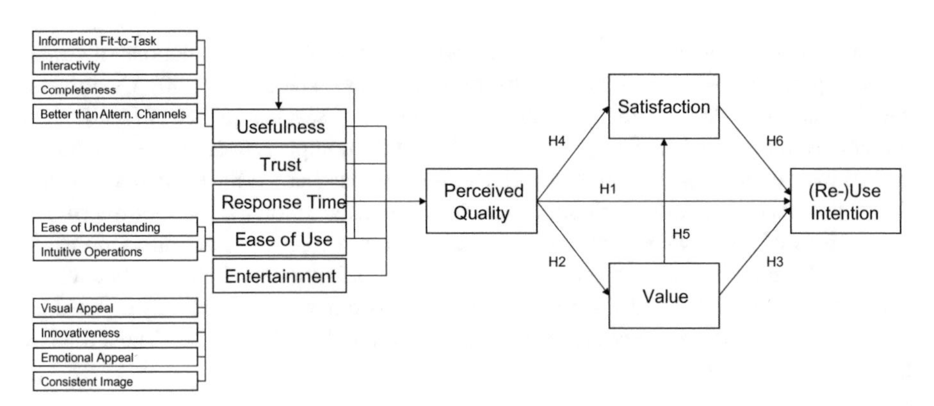

Fig. 2. Research model based on *WebQual*

Data Collection Procedure and Sampling: A quantitative online survey was conducted to assess the digital sales desk's concept. In addition to the possibility of surveying a large sample of people, online surveys ensure that respondents are not influenced by the social interaction that occurs during face-to-face or telephone surveys. Each respondent receives the same questions, which increases the comparability of the results. Also, online surveys facilitate asking complex questions with many possible answers [57]. A seven-point Likert-like scale was employed to record the responses. The use of a Likert scale is particularly suitable for questions that cannot always be answered with "*yes*" or "*no*," but instead with a tendency [57].

The survey started with an introduction to the collaborative project. Based on a textual description and pictures from a jewelry store, participants were asked to put themselves in the situation of a sales conversation. Next, the idea of the digital sales desk was explained in the context of this situation. For further description and clarification, a picture of the prototype and a two-minute animated explanation video (https://youtu.be/pSTK1glTuEI) followed. The participants could review the introductory descriptions at any time. To foster the participants' understanding further, they had to rate the individual e-service TPs at the beginning of the survey. Also, participants could leave comments on the functions in a free-text field. Subsequently, the participants were guided through the *WQ*, *Value*, *Satisfaction*, and *(Re-Use) Intention* items. Finally, several control variables (i.e., an affinity for technology [58], willingness to pay for watches, purchase of a watch in the last two years, age, and gender) concluded the survey. Except for the free-text fields and demographic questions, all questions were mandatory.

The online survey was realized with the tool *LimeSurvey* [59]. In the period from 29.04.2020 to 21.05.2020, participants were invited over personal networks, social networks, and e-mail inquiries. To reach participants interested in luxury watches, profiles, blogs, and groups focusing on watches were directly approached.

Data Analysis: The *Partial Least Squares* (PLS) method was used to carry out the data analysis. It allows making predictions on concrete data points with small sample size and without demands on the data distribution [60]. The PLS and bootstrapping algorithms of *SmartPLS 3* were utilized to drive the evaluation of the measurement model and the subsequent analysis of the data [61, 62]. As *WQ* comprises formative second-order and third-order constructs next to its reflective first-order constructs, the repeated indicator approach was chosen for the final model [63].

5 Results

5.1 Sample Characteristics and E-Service Touchpoint Preferences.

In total, 128 people participated in the survey. 29 of 128 participants started the survey but did not finish it. Consequently, 99 fully completed surveys were considered to evaluate and analyze the data (see Table 2). Disregarding 14 participants that did not state their gender, roughly the same number of females and males participated. The average age of the survey participants was approximately 33 years. Most participants' willingness to pay (WTP) for a watch was up to 500€ and had a moderate technology affinity. Above 50% of the participants had bought a watch in the last two years.

The participants' willingness to use the e-service TPs is shown in Fig. 3. Overall, participants were most willing to use the *Watch Information & Pictures*, *Watch Comparison*, *Watch Configuration*, and *Watch Part Details* TPs. The most unpopular e-service TPs were the *Jeweler Information*, *Watch Brand Websites & Apps*, and *Watch Promotion Video*. The preferences slightly differed for the sub-samples with low and high WTP. For example, the *Watch Brand Information*, *Watch Brand Websites and Apps*, and *Jeweler Information* TPs were more preferred by the high WTP sub-sample. The participants' comments provided further insights into their perceptions of the individual e-service TPs. First, it was noted that the decision to buy a watch is personal. Recommendations based on purchases of other customers were said to be of little help. Second, it was stated that the purchase of a watch is a rare activity. Thus, it would be challenging to create a good customer profile for product recommendations. One participant also noted that the screen would be too large to enter personal data. Four respondents explained that the payment is very important in a high price segment and should not be digitalized

Table 2. Demographic information of the sample and two sub-samples

WTP (Sub-)Sample		*All (n = 99)*		*≤500 (n = 53)*		*>500 (n = 46)*	
Items	*Cat*	*Freq*	*%*	*Freq*	*%*	*Freq*	*%*
Gender	Female	41	41.41%	35	66.04%	6	13.04%
	Male	44	44.44%	14	26.42%	30	65.22%
	N/A	14	14.14%	4	7.55%	10	21.74%
Age	18–30	67	67.68%	39	73.58%	28	60.87%
	31–40	8	8.08%	2	3.77%	6	13.04%
	41–50	9	9.09%	5	9.43%	4	8.70%
	>50	15	15.15%	7	13.21%	8	17.39%
Willingness to Pay (WTP)	≤100	11	11.11%	11	20.75%	0	0.00%
	≤500	42	42.42%	42	79.25%	0	0.00%
	≤800	7	7.07%	0	0.00%	7	15.22%
	≤2400	11	11.11%	0	0.00%	11	23.91%
	≤7000	15	15.15%	0	0.00%	15	32.61%
	≤20000	9	9.09%	0	0.00%	9	19.57%
	>20000	4	4.04%	0	0.00%	4	8.70%
Affinity for Tech. (Ø Over 4 Items; (1 = Low; 7 = High)	[1–3]	5	5.05%	4	7.55%	1	2.17%
	[3–5]	69	69.70%	44	83.02%	25	54.35%
	[5–7]	30	30.30%	9	16.98%	21	45.65%
Bought watch in the last two years	Yes	51	51.52%	27	50.94	24	52.17%
	No	48	48.48%	26	49.06	22	47.83%

too much. Besides, participants argued that information about different brands and the jeweler would not be of much interest and would be, if at all, more relevant before entering the store. It was also stressed that the digital sales desk should not replace essential elements of the physical store—in particular, the sales staff and the opportunity to try on products. Finally, it should fit the store equipment, and the graphical user interface should be clear and scalable such that people with impaired vision can also use it.

5.2 Results Concerning the Measurement and Structural Model

The measurement model's reliability and validity were examined following Hair et al. [62]. As the research model comprises second-order and third-order constructs, a combination of the repeated indicator and the two-stage approach [63] was employed to evaluate the model's formative parts before calculating the final results. For the PLS algorithm, the default path weighting scheme, 500 maximum iterations, and a stop criterion of 10^{-7} were selected. Bootstrapping was performed with 5000 samples [62].

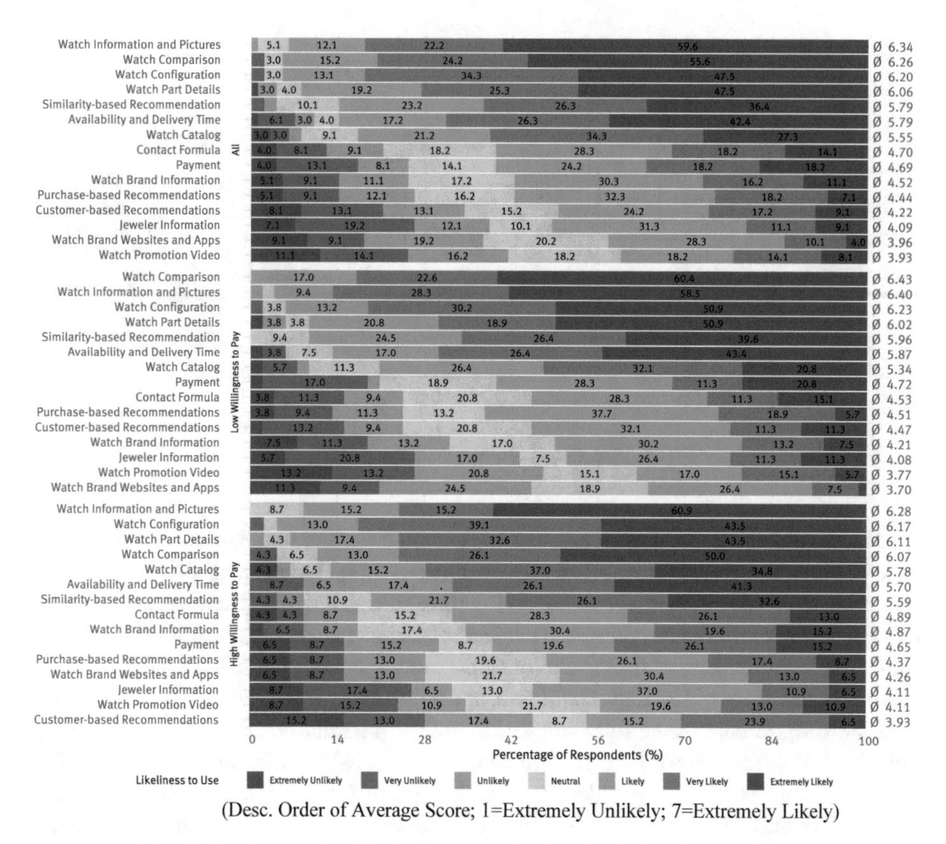

Fig. 3. Participants' willingness to use the jeweler E-Service touchpoint

First, the reflective first-order constructs were evaluated [62]. The evaluation only reported a low *Cronbach's Alpha* for the *Response Time* construct and identified two items with loadings lower than the threshold value of .7 (*Trust #3* and *Response Time #3*). As a result, only *Response Time #3*, which was the inverted attention item, was removed from the model. This removal improved the *Cronbach's Alpha*, the *Composite Reliability*, and the *Average Variance Explained* [62, 64]. The analysis of the *cross-loadings* supported the decision to drop this item. While the *Heterotrait-Monotrait* ratio *(HTMT) Correlation* between *Interactivity* and *Information Fit-to-Task (.938)* exceeded the critical value of .9 [62], the *HTMT Confidence Intervals* did not encompass the value 1 [65]. Therefore, no changes were needed.

Second, the formative second-order and third-order *WQ* constructs were evaluated [62]. When considering the *collinearity*, the *Variance Inflation Factor* did not exceed the critical value of 5 for any of the formative indicators. Concerning the significance and relevance of the formative indicators, insignificant weights for *Intuitive Operations*, *Trust*, *Response Time,* and *Ease of Use* were discovered. Still, whereas *Intuitive Operations, Ease of Use*, and *Response Time* had significant loadings larger than .5, *Trust* had a significant loading slightly below .5 (.462). Thus, the first three can still be considered absolute contributors to their higher-order constructs [62]. As *WQ* is an established research model, the latter formative indicator was retained.

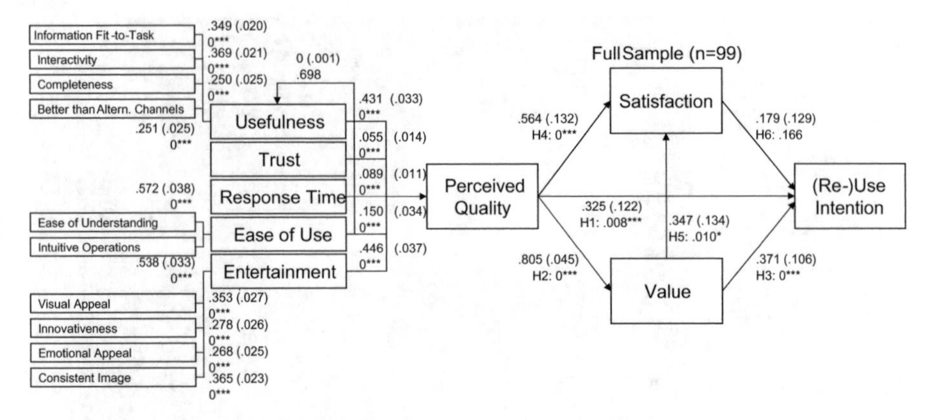

Fig. 4. Structural models with eath coefficients

Hair et al.'s [62] six steps were followed to examine the final structural model (see Fig. 4): First, the *Variance Inflation Factors* are examined to check all driver constructs for *collinearity*. All values were beneath the threshold value of 5. Next, considering the *relevance and significance of the path coefficients*, some path coefficients had low values. Thus, the significances of these relationships were checked. All relationships, besides those between *Ease of Use* and *Usefulness*, and between *Satisfaction* and *(Re-)Use Intention,* were significant in the full sample. Except for the relationship between *Value* and *Satisfaction*, which showed a significance level of 5%, all significant relationships had a significance level of 1%. Besides the relationships of *Ease of Use* and *Usefulness*, and *Satisfaction* and *(Re-)Use Intention*, the confidence intervals did not encompass zero. As a result, only hypothesis *H6* had to be rejected, and the impact of *Ease of Use* on *Usefulness* was insignificant in the full sample. *Entertainment* and *Usefulness*, and their lower-order constructs, *Consistent Image*, *Interactivity*, *Visual Appeal*, and *Information-Fit-to-Task*, had the most substantial mediated *total effects* on *Satisfaction*, *Value*, and *(Re-)Use Intention* and the latter four also on *Perceived Quality*. Next, the *coefficients of determination* (*R^2-values*) were considered and, following Hair et al. [62], all *R^2-values* besides of *Value* (.648) and *(Re-)Use Intention* (.674), which can be considered as moderate, could be regarded as substantial (i.e., larger than .75). When examining the *f^2-effect strength,* according to Hair et al. [62], a strong and significant *effect strength* was only found for the relationship between *Perceived Quality* and *Value*. All other relationships between the exogenous and endogenous constructs had insignificant moderate (i.e., between *Value* and *Satisfaction*) or low effect strengths. Next, the *forecast relevance* was checked by considering the *cross-validated redundancies* of the constructs reported by the blindfolding algorithm. The *Q^2-values* of the endogenous reflective indicators were all above zero, suggesting that all have forecast relevance. Finally, the *q^2-effect strengths* were evaluated. Following Hair et al. [62], *Perceived Quality* had a moderate forecast relevance for *Satisfaction* and a low one for *(Re-)Use Intention*. *Satisfaction* and *Value* had low forecast relevance for each other and *(Re-)Use Intention.*

6 Discussion

The survey suggests that the relationships between *Perceived Quality* and *Satisfaction* (*H4*), *Value* (*H2*), and *(Re-)Use Intention* (*H1*) are significant. Participants' perceptions of *Value* also affected their perceptions of *Satisfaction* (*H5*) and *(Re-)Use Intentions* (*H3*). In contrast, the hypothesis that perceptions of *Satisfaction* lead to *(Re-)Use Intentions* (*H6*) had to be rejected (see Fig. 4). For the low WTP sub-sample (see Fig. 5), *H4* had to be rejected. For the high WTP sub-sample, *H1* and *H3* had to be rejected, but *H6* could be accepted, and the effect of *Value* on *Satisfaction* was stronger (*H4*). The results contribute to the discourse on the direct (*H1*) and indirect relationships (e.g., *H6*) between *Perceived Quality* and *(Re-)Use Intention* [cf. 40, 43, 44].

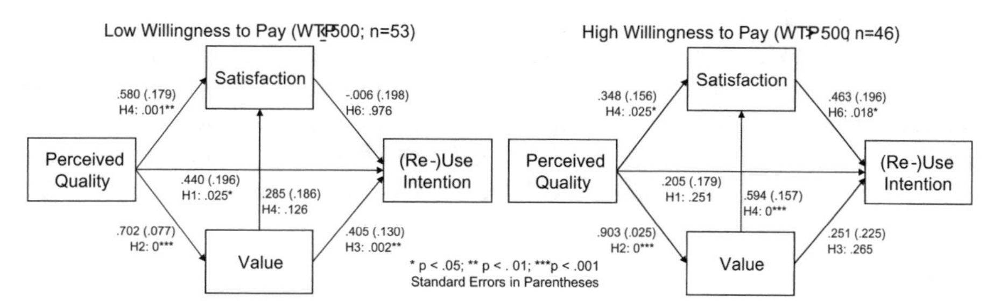

Fig. 5. Hypothesis testing for sub-samples

WQ's [53, 54] first- and second-order constructs can provide clues for interpreting the results and improving the *concept* further. By considering the *total effects* in the structural model, the constructs with the highest (mediated) impact on *Perceived Quality* and *(Re-) Use Intention* could be identified [62]. In the full sample, *Entertainment*, *Usefulness*, *Consistent Image*, *Interactivity*, *Visual Appeal*, *Information Fit-to-Task*, and *Ease of Use* had the strongest effects in descending order. For the low WTP sub-sample, *Visual Appeal* and *Ease of Use* had a stronger effect than *Consistent Image*, *Interactivity*, and *Information Fit-to-Task*. For the high WTP sub-sample, *Usefulness* was more important than *Entertainment*. Besides, *Visual Appeal* and *Ease of Use* were less important for this sub-sample than for the low WTP sub-sample. Overall, the items of *Visual Appeal* had an approval rate of above 70% and, thus, positively contributed to the *Perceived Quality* and *(Re-Use) Intention*. When considering the individual items of *Information Fit-to-task* and *Interactivity*, it is noticeable that over 70% of the participants agreed with all questions except for the question that dealt with whether the digital sales desk is exactly what a customer needs to support the purchase. Similarly, almost 40% of respondents did not agree with the *Completeness* item "*All my business with the jeweler could be completed via the digital sales desk*" [adapted from 53, 54]. Thus, the concept could be further improved concerning these areas for improvement. Still, the optional survey comments and the existing literature suggest that the digital sales desk should support rather than replace the sales assistants [cf. 28]. Consequently, more research is required to determine an optimal set of complementary TPs offered via human and digital interfaces in jewelry stores. Another construct hints at room for improvement is the

Consistent Image. Around 60% of the participants agreed with the questions addressing this topic. Thus, further efforts could concentrate on improving the concept regarding the *Consistent Image*. Also, while only having a slightly lower *total effect*, another area for potential improvement is the *Emotional Appeal*. About 33% of the participants stated that using the digital sales desk would not positively impact their happiness. As brand experience is particularly relevant in luxury retailing [5], customers' emotions should be considered when developing the concept further. Furthermore, even though several participants critically commented on the storage of personal data and the digital support of the payment process, *Trust* had the lowest impact on customers' perceptions of quality and their intentions to (re-)use the service. Still, only 28% of the participants stated that they would not feel secure when carrying out transactions at the sales desk. Thus, future research should focus on the impact of *Trust* on customers' perception of digital interfaces in luxury retail stores.

Overall, e-service TPs increasing the efficiency and effectiveness of the customer journey were most popular (e.g., *Watch Information & Pictures*, *Watch Comparison*, and *Watch Configuration*). In contrast, less popular were the personalized e-service TPs (i.e., the *Purchase-* and *Customer-based Recommendation* TPs). Thus, personalization in the smart servicescape [49] of jewelers should be investigated further.

7 Conclusion

E-commerce retailers have adopted TPs from the physical servicescape and adapted them for e-commerce to substitute for some of brick-and-mortar retail's distinct benefits (e.g., trying on products virtually). To comply with their customers' changing expectations, brick-and-mortar retailers can do the opposite and mirror e-service TPs from e-commerce to the physical servicescape. However, existing research only provides little guidance on the selection of brick-and-mortar e-service TPs. Especially, more research on e-service TPs for brick-and-mortar retailers selling specific product categories is required [25].

This article proposed a digital sales desk offering various potential e-service TPs to support jewelers' watch-advisory services. It also investigates the factors that affect customers' perceptions of the sales desk's quality and their impacts on customers' intentions to (re-)use the digitally supported watch-advisory service. Therefore, customers' willingness to use the proposed e-service TPs and their perceptions of the digital sales desk's quality as a whole were assessed in an online survey. In addition, the digital sales desk's impact on customers' satisfaction with, values derived from, and intentions to (re-)use the digitally supported watch-advisory service were evaluated. The results suggest that the e-service TPs are not equally desired by customers. Furthermore, perceptions of the digital sales desk's quality and the value derived from the advisory service affected the participants' (re-)use intentions toward the service. The results differed for two sub-samples. From a theoretical perspective, this article contributes to the knowledge base on customers' expectations regarding a specific in-store technology in luxury retail [e.g., 4]. From a practical viewpoint, examples of promising e-service TPs are provided, which can be implemented by watch-selling luxury retailers. The results also provide orientation on the aspects of a digital sales desk, which need to consider during its implementation.

This article leaves room for future research. First, most participants were interested in watches costing up to 500€. While the results of the high WTP sub-sample (including 46.46% of the survey participants) provide an idea of a higher paying customer group's perceptions, future research could consider this customer group in more detail. Second, the survey results can now be used to revise the prototype. Subsequently, formative or summative evaluations can be conducted in lab experiments or field studies in cooperation with jewelry stores [cf. 15]. As 84% of the participants agreed with a strong tendency that the digital sales desk would be innovative, it might allow jewelers to gain competitive advantages [4] and meet their customers' changing expectations.

Acknowledgments. This work was created in the context of a project that received funding from the Bundesministerium für Wirtschaft und Energie (BMWi) under the grant agreement 01MF17011D.

References

1. Lüdemann, S.: Luxury Goods Marktreport 2020. Statista (2020)
2. Statista: Zukünftig wichtige Vertriebskanäle von Unternehmen der Uhrenbranche in ausgewählten Ländern weltweit in den Jahren 2015 bis 2017. https://statista.com/statistik/daten/studie/466212/. Accessed 29 Nov 2020
3. Dauriz, L., Remy, N., Sandri, N.: Luxury shopping in the digital age: perspectives on retail and consumer goods. Perspect. Retail Consum. Goods. Summer **3**, 26–31 (2014)
4. Pantano, E., Passavanti, R., Priporas, C.-V., Verteramo, S.: To what extent luxury retailing can be smart? J. Retail. Consum. Serv. **43**, 1–28 (Preprint) (2018)
5. Klein, J.F., Falk, T., Esch, F.-R., Gloukhovtsev, A.: Linking pop-up brand stores to brand experience and word of mouth: the case of luxury retail. J. Bus. Res. **69**, 5761–5767 (2016)
6. Bèzes, C.: What Kind of In-Store smart retailing for an omnichannel real-life experience? Rech. Appl. en Mark. (Engl. Edn.) **34**, 91–112 (2019)
7. Shi, S., Wang, Y., Chen, X., Zhang, Q.: Conceptualization of omnichannel customer experience and its impact on shopping intention: a mixed-method approach. Int. J. Inf. Manage. **50**, 325–336 (2020)
8. Heine, K., Berghaus, B.: Luxury goes digital: how to tackle the digital luxury brand-consumer touchpoints. J. Glob. Fash. Mark. **5**, 223–234 (2014)
9. Aiolfi, S., Sabbadin, E.: Fashion and New luxury digital disruption: the new challenges of fashion between omnichannel and traditional retailing. Int. J. Bus. Manag. **14**, 41–51 (2019)
10. Blázquez, M.: Fashion shopping in multichannel retail: the role of technology in enhancing the customer experience. Int. J. Electron. Commer. **18**, 97–116 (2014)
11. Burke, R.R.: Technology and the customer interface: what consumers want in the physical and virtual store. J. Acad. Mark. Sci. **30**, 411–432 (2002)
12. Choo, H.J., Moon, H., Kim, H., Yoon, N.: Luxury customer value. J. Fash. Mark. Manag. **16**, 81–101 (2012)
13. Türk, B., Scholz, M., Berresheim, P.: Measuring service quality in online luxury goods retailing. J. Electron. Commer. Res. **1**, 88–103 (2012)
14. Patas, J., Milicevic, D., Goeken, M.: Enhancing design science through empirical knowledge: framework and application. In: Jain, H., Sinha, A.P., Vitharana, P. (eds.) DESRIST 2011. LNCS, vol. 6629, pp. 32–46. Springer, Heidelberg (2011). https://doi.org/10.1007/978-3-642-20633-7_3

15. Venable, J., Pries-Heje, J., Baskerville, R.: FEDS: a framework for evaluation in design science research. Eur. J. Inf. Syst. **25**, 77–89 (2016)
16. Pantano, E.: Innovation drivers in retail industry. Int. J. Inf. Manage. **34**, 344–350 (2014)
17. Kettinger, W.J., Park, S.-H., Sunny, S.J.: Understanding the consequences of information systems service quality on is service reuse. Inf. Manag. **46**, 335–341 (2009)
18. Oh, H.: Service quality, customer satisfaction, and customer value: a holistic perspective. Int. J. Hosp. Manag. **18**, 67–82 (1999)
19. Wang, Y.-S.: Assessing E-Commerce systems success: a respecification and validation of the DeLone and McLean model of IS success. Inf. Syst. J. **18**, 529–557 (2008)
20. Bian, Q., Forsythe, S.: Purchase intention for luxury brands: a cross cultural comparison. J. Bus. Res. **65**, 1443–1451 (2012)
21. Kapferer, J.-N., Laurent, G.: Where do consumers think luxury begins? A study of perceived minimum price for 21 luxury goods in 7 countries. J. Bus. Res. **69**, 332–340 (2016)
22. Kim, S., Park, G., Lee, Y., Choi, S.: Customer emotions and their triggers in luxury retail: understanding the effects of customer emotions before and after entering a luxury shop. J. Bus. Res. **69**, 5809–5818 (2016)
23. Dion, D., Borraz, S.: Managing status: how luxury brands shape class subjectivities in the service encounter. J. Mark. **81**, 67–85 (2017)
24. Nüesch, R., Alt, R., Puschmann, T.: Hybrid customer interaction. Bus. Inf. Syst. Eng. **57**(1), 73–78 (2015). https://doi.org/10.1007/s12599-014-0366-9
25. Barann, B., Betzing, J.H., Niemann, M., Hoffmeister, B., Becker, J.: Exploring customers' likeliness to use E-Service touchpoints in brick and mortar retail. Electron. Mark. 1–23 (2020)
26. Barann, B., Hermann, A., Heuchert, M., Becker, J.: Can't touch this? conceptualizing the customer touchpoint in the context of omni-channel retailing. J. Retail. Consum. Serv. **102**, 1–11 (2020)
27. Vargo, S.L., Lusch, R.F.: Why "Service"? J. Acad. Mark. Sci. **36**, 25–38 (2008)
28. Vannucci, V., Pantano, E.: Digital or human touchpoints? Insights from consumer-facing in-store services. Inf. Technol. People. **33**, 296–310 (2019)
29. Duma, F.: Management der persönlichen Interaktion im Verkauf von Luxusgütern: Eine Untersuchung am Beispiel von Schweizer Luxusuhren (2018). https://digitalcollection.zhaw.ch/handle/11475/14672
30. El Azhari, J., Bennett, D.: Omni-Channel customer experience: an investigation into the use of digital technology in physical stores and its impact on the consumer's decision-making process. In: XXIV AEDEM International Conference London, pp. 1–13. London South Bank University, London, UK (2015)
31. Dion, D., Arnould, E.: Retail luxury strategy: assembling charisma through art and magic. J. Retail. **87**, 502–520 (2011)
32. Parise, S., Guinan, P.J., Kafka, R.: Solving the crisis of immediacy: how digital technology can transform the customer experience. Bus. Horiz. **59**, 411–420 (2016)
33. Liu, X., Burns, A.C., Hou, Y.: Comparing online and in-store shopping behavior towards luxury goods. Int. J. Retail Distrib. Manag. **11**(12), 885–900 (2013)
34. Pantano, E., Dennis, C.: Smart Retailing: Technologies and Strategies. Palgrave Pivot, Cham, Switzerland (2019)
35. Hauser, M., Griebel, M., Hanke, J., Thiesse, F.: Empowering smarter fitting rooms with RFID data analytics. In: Proceedings of the 13th International Conference on Wirtschaftsinformatik (WI 2017), pp. 1299–1302, St.Gallen, Switzerland (2017)
36. Parasuraman, A., Zeithaml, V.A., Berry, L.L.: A conceptual model of service quality and its implications for future research. J. Mark. **49**, 41–50 (1985)
37. Parasuraman, A., Berry, L.L., Zeithaml, V.A.: Unterstanding customer expectations of service. Sloan Manage. Rev. **39**, 67(1991)

38. Pantano, E., Viassone, M.: Engaging consumers on new integrated multichannel retail settings: challenges for retailers. J. Retail. Consum. Serv. **25**, 106–114 (2015)
39. Chen, C.-F., Chen, F.-S.: Experience quality, perceived value, satisfaction and behavioral intentions for heritage tourists. Toursim Manag. **31**, 29–35 (2010)
40. Choi, K.-S., Cho, W.-H., Lee, S., Lee, H., Kim, C.: The relationships among quality, value, satisfaction and behavioral intention in health care provider choice. J. Bus. Res. **57**, 913–921 (2004)
41. Haddad Rezende, N.E., Cunha Moura, L.R., Wasner Vasconcelos, F.C., da Silveira Cunha, N.R.: Proposition and test of a quality assessment extension WebQual model in Brazil. Rev. Eur. Stud. **9**, 74–90 (2017)
42. Foroudi, P., Gupta, S., Sivarajah, U., Broderick, A.: Investigating the effects of smart technology on customer dynamics and customer experience. Comput. Human Behav. **80**, 271–282 (2018)
43. Cronin, J.J., Brady, M.K., Hult, G.T.M.: Assessing the effects of quality, value, and customer satisfaction on consumer behavioral intentions in service environments. J. Retail. **76**, 193–218 (2000)
44. Huang, Y.-K.: The effect of airline service quality on passenger's behavioural intentions using SERVQUAL scores: a Taiwan case study. J. East. Asia Soc. Transp. Stud. **8**, 2330–2343 (2010)
45. Cronin, J.J., Taylor, S.A.: Measuring service quality: a reexamination and extension. J. Mark. **56**, 55–68 (1992)
46. Zeithaml, V.A.: Consumer perceptions of price, quality, and value: a means-end model and synthesis of evidence. J. Mark. **52**, 2–22 (1988)
47. Willems, K., Smolders, A., Brengman, M., Luyten, K., Schöning, J.: The path-to-purchase is paved with digital opportunities: an inventory of shopper-oriented retail technologies. Technol. Forecast. Soc. Change. **124**, 228–242 (2017)
48. Inman, J.J., Nikolova, H.: Shopper-Facing retail technology: a retailer adoption decision framework incorporating shopper attitudes and privacy concerns. J. Retail. **93**, 7–28 (2017)
49. Roy, S.K., Balaji, M.S., Sadeque, S., Nguyen, B., Melewar, T.C.: Constituents and consequences of smart customer experience in retailing. Technol. Forecast. Soc. Change. **124**, 257–270 (2017)
50. Homburg, C., Koschate, N., Hoyer, W.D.: The role of cognition and affect in the formation of customer satisfaction: a dynamic perspective. J. Mark. **70**, 21–31 (2006)
51. van Birgelen, M., de Jong, A., de Ruyter, K.: Multi-channel service retailing: the effects of channel performance satisfaction on behavioral intentions. J. Retail. **82**, 367–377 (2006)
52. Pantano, E., Viassone, M.: Demand pull and technology push perspective in technology-based innovations for the points of sale: the retailers evaluation. J. Retail. Consum. Serv. **21**, 43–47 (2014)
53. Loiacono, E.T., Watson, R.T., Goodhue, D.L.: WebQual: a measure of web site quality. Am. Mark. Assoc. **13**, 432–438 (2002)
54. Loiacono, E.T., Watson, R.T., Goodhue, D.L.: WebQual: an instrument for consumer evaluation of web sites. Int. J. Electron. Commer. **11**, 51–87 (2007)
55. Sweeney, J.C., Soutar, G.N.: Consumer perceived value: the development of a multiple item scale. J. Retail. **77**, 203–220 (2001)
56. Lazaris, C., Vrechopoulos, A., Doukidis, G., Fraidaki, K.: Mobile apps for omni channel retailing: revealing the emerging showrooming phenomenon. In: Proceedings of the 9th Mediterranean Conference on Information Systems (MCIS 2015), pp. 1–17, Samos, Greece (2015)
57. Bernard, H.R.: Social Research Methods: Qualitative and Quantitative Methods. Sage Publications, Thousand Oaks (2013)
58. Agarwal, R., Prasad, J.: A conceptual and operational definition of personal innovativeness in the domain of information technology. Inf. Syst. Res. **9**, 204–215 (1998)

59. LimeSurvey: LimeSurvey: An Open Source Survey Tool. https://www.limesurvey.org/. Accessed 29 Nov 2020
60. Huber, F., Herrmann, A., Meyer, F., Vogel, J., Vollhardt, K.: Kausalmodellierung mit Partial Least Squares. Gabler, Wiesbaden, Germany (2007)
61. Ringle, C.M., Wende, S., Becker, J.-M.: SmartPLS3 (2015). http://smartpls.com
62. Hair, J.F., Hult, G.T.M., Ringle, C.M., Sarstedt, M., Richter, N.F., Hauff, S.: Partial Least Squares Strukturgleichungsmodellierung. Franz Vahlen, Munich, Germany (2017)
63. Becker, J.-M., Klein, K., Wetzels, M.: Hierarchical latent variable models in PLS-SEM: guidelines for using reflective-formative type models. Long Range Plan. **45**, 359–394 (2012)
64. Götz, O., Liehr-Gobbers, K.: Analyse von Strukturgleichungsmodellen mit Hilfe der Partial-Least-Squares (PLS)-Methode. Die Betriebswirtschaft. **64**, 714–738 (2004)
65. Henseler, J., Ringle, C.M., Sarstedt, M.: A new criterion for assessing discriminant validity in variance-based structural equation modeling. J. Acad. Mark. Sci. **43**, 115–135 (2015)

Local Retail Under Fire: Local Shopping Platforms Revisited Pre and During the Corona Crisis

Sören Bärsch(✉), Lars Bollweg, Peter Weber, Tim Wittemund, and Valerie Wulfhorst

Fachhochschule Südwestfalen, Soest, Germany
{baersch.soeren,bollweg.lars,weber.peter,Wittemnund.tim, wulfhorst.valerie}@fh-swf.de

Abstract. The digital transformation is threatening the local stationary retail sector. Local Shopping Platforms (LSPs) were considered as a promising approach to support local owner-operated retail outlets (LOOROs) with their digitalization, but they struggled in utilizing the special characteristics, like e.g., the locational advantages of the affiliated retailers. In this study, we assess the current state of LSPs in Germany in 2020 with the help of a structured content analysis and semi-structured telephone interviews, addressing also the impact of the Covid-19 crisis. Our results show that the preferential platform type has changed. The lockdown has significantly boosted the number of Store Locator Platforms as one type of LSP. Furthermore, it turned out that LSPs with a "Strictly Local Approach" introduce more location-based services than LSPs with a "Scaling Local Approach".

Keywords: Local Shopping Platforms · LOOROs · Location-based services · Location-enabled services · Coronavirus (COVID-19/SARS-CoV-2) outbreak

1 Introduction

"The Retail Scenario 2030", as introduced by the Federal Government of North Rhine-Westphalia and conducted by IFH Köln researchers, has predicted significant changes for the retail landscape within the next decade [1]. On the first view pleasing, the study predicts a revenue increase of 134m euros for the entire German retail sector. However, a closer look at the numbers reveals that e-commerce and grocery retailers consume the majority of this growth. Only a small fraction of 1.7m euros is assigned to traditional stationary big box retailers and local owner-operated retail outlets (LOOROs). LOOROs can be characterized as shops with small-sized store areas, a limited number of staff and high owner-involvement in the day-to-day business operations [2]. Accordingly, the study predicts a large number of store closings in German cities - up to 64,000 local retailers are at stake [1]. As bad as this prognosis already is for local retailers, the "Retail Scenario 2030" did not yet include the impact of the coronavirus and the according lockdown in early 2020. In fact, many LOOROs thus need to be considered as threatened in their very existence. The retail sector suffers so bad because of its high share of communication-intensive interactions between the sales personnel and

F. Ahlemann et al. (Eds.): WI 2021, LNISO 46, pp. 123–139, 2021.
https://doi.org/10.1007/978-3-030-86790-4_10

the customers, which became impossible because of the social distancing regulations and lacking use of online channels [3, 4]. In numbers: The outbreak of the coronavirus decreased revenues by 2.8% in March and 6.5% in April 2020 for the whole retail sector. Even though the revenue has recovered by an increase of 13.9% in May 2020, this recovery is mostly driven by e-commerce and the catalog business (+28.7%) [5, 6]. For LOOROs, revenue decreased strongly by 10.1% in March 2020, followed by a recovery of +3.5% in May 2020. However, this increase did not compensate the losses during the lockdown [6]. Despite the support measurements on the European and national levels, like the pan-European guarantee fund for small and medium-sized European companies, many LOOROs face a tense financial situation [3, 7]. This is alarming as studies show that most LOOROs have a very short survival time of only about eight weeks without or with only very low revenues [8]. Furthermore, a high number of store closings negatively affects the attractiveness of the city centers as shopping locations, triggering or intensifying a downward spiral of less shops and less shoppers leading to less attractive highstreets and less tax income for the cities, resulting in less financial resources to support and develop the city centers [9].

LOOROs and cities need to tackle this downward spiral. Therefore, several independent studies recommend LOOROs to reposition their business models, focusing more on convenience and experience as well as local and digital offers for their customers [1, 10, 11]. Despite these recommendations, the reluctance to transform their businesses stays high among LOOROs because of internal and external adoption barriers (e.g., financial constraints or lack of standards) [12–15]. On the other hand, the coronavirus seems to be a game changer, fostering the willingness of LOORO owners to follow e-commerce trends more than ever. Recent studies show that many local retailers started digital services like click & collect, same day delivery, or coupons during the lockdown [16].

To offer these digital services, LOOROs often utilize intermediaries like Local Shopping Platforms (LSPs) as service providers or inter-organizational service hubs [17]. LSPs are based on the three main functions of e-marketplaces plus a local focus [17, 18]. Therefore, research on LSPs has many ties to research on e-marketplaces and e-intermediaries (see Subsect. 2.1). However, many former studies predicted the failure of LSPs [16], criticizing that they do not help LOOROs attracting more customers to their stores, that they do not utilize the locational advantages of LOOROs as a unique selling proposition, and that they do not help generating higher revenues [17, 19].

Anyhow, LSPs are still out there and there is at least one strong argument in favor of them: LSPs help LOOROs to overcome e-commerce adoption barriers and thus support their digital transformation [20, 21]. But it is still questionable if the services offered by LSPs are enough to sustain LOOROs threatened core business, namely, their physical store. Against this background, it is important to assess how LSPs and their service offers have developed over the last years and if LSPs have started to introduce more services that utilize the locational advantages of LOOROs. For instance, LSPs offer services which utilize the locational proximity between LOOROs and their customers with location-enabled services (e.g., click & collect, same-day delivery) or location-based services (e.g., location-based discounts) [22]. Furthermore, it is not yet to say, how the corona crisis has affected the development of LSPs with regard to their service offers and their role in the digital transformation process of local retail. Moreover, in general, LSPs have been neglected by research so far. Therefore, this paper aims to answer the following research question:

Main RQ) ***What is the current state of service & platform type development of LSPs in Germany?***

To answer the stated research question, we have derived three sub questions, which will examine the development of LSPs from different viewpoints.

RQ1) *How did the types of German LSPs develop between 2016 and 2019?*
RQ2) *How did the digital services offered by German LSPs develop between 2016 and 2019?*
RQ3) *How has the corona crisis affected the development of LSPs?*

To answer RQ1 and RQ2, this paper follows up on a sample from 2016 of a preliminary study using a structured content analysis [17]. RQ3 will be answered using answers from structured telephone interviews.

The paper is structured as follows: In Sect. 2, we discuss the existing literature and the theoretical background. In Sect. 3, we introduce the methodological foundation of the two analyses (content analysis and semi-structured telephone interviews). In Sect. 4, the results will be discussed. Section 5 concludes and identifies limitations and discusses future research opportunities.

2 Background: Local Shopping Platforms

Literature on Local Shopping Platforms is scarce. In the following, we introduce the existing literature briefly and build on previous research to derive the necessary theoretical foundations and structures for our analysis.

2.1 Definition of Local Shopping Platforms

Local Shopping Platforms (LSP), which act as intermediaries between LOOROs and their customers, are spreading in German cities. The advent of LSPs has many ties to the long tradition of e-marketplaces, which are described as inter-organizational information systems [23]. Previous studies identified LSPs based on the three main functions of e-marketplaces plus a local focus [17, 18]. Accordingly, an LSP must fulfill at least one of the following main functions of e-marketplaces: 1) They match buyers and sellers; 2) They facilitate the exchange of information; 3) They facilitate transaction and fulfillment services [23, 24]. Additionally, their local focus is a main characteristic of LSPs that distinguishes them from traditional e-marketplaces, like Amazon or Rakuten, where regional or national restrictions blur [23, 25]. Accordingly, LSPs are geographically restricted and they target customers living in a defined region or city [26]. Bärsch et al. (2019) specify this local component of LSPs and introduce a self-restriction criterion as an identifier: *"It is either a limitation to the cooperation with retailers from a certain area, the limitation of just doing business with customers from a certain area, or both."* LOOROs join LSPs to attract customers to their premises and to promote their local advantages. They are usually not interested in targeting people from far away and consider this a waste of their advertising budget [26].

Despite these characteristic objectives of LOOROs, the preliminary study indicated that most LSPs adhere to the self-restriction criterion and strictly address only the local market, while some have started experimenting with addressing a national or even global market [17]. Accordingly, the self-restriction criterion can be extended by a business model view, differentiating between a *"Strictly Local Approach"* and a *"Scaling Local Approach*", with the latter platforms still focusing on local retailers and local customers while at the same time trying to scale to non-local customers [17].

2.2 Types of LSPs

As e-marketplaces, LSPs provide a non-standardized and diverse service landscape. This service landscape ranges from an online business card with just information about store opening hours to a full transaction process with pricing, invoicing and logistics [27]. Following the approach of Peterson et al. (2007) and Bärsch et al. (2019), this diverse landscape enables a typological categorization of LSPs based on their e-marketplace functionalities and their local focus [17, 18] (see Table 1). Bärsch et al. derived the following types: The first function (match of buyers and sellers) allows for the differentiation of two categories of LSPs, *Store Locator Platforms* and *Product Catalog Platforms. Store Locator Platforms* (e.g., "www.like-lippstadt.de") offer only contact information like opening hours and e-mail addresses, whereas *Product Catalog Platforms* (e.g., "www.bummelbu.de") provide an overview of product information (e.g., size, product photos). For the second function (exchange of information), an additional platform category named *Product Enquiry Platforms* (e.g., "www.dein-hsk.de") can be derived. This platform enables customers to request product availability information and product details, like e.g. sizes, colors or prices. Considering the third function (transaction and fulfillment), two more types can be differentiated. First, *Affiliate Transaction Platforms* (e.g., "www.koomio.com") enable the purchase of products, but require the completion of transactions on external "affiliate" websites. Second, *Full Transaction Platforms* (e.g., "www.lozuka.com") offer the full e-marketplace service range for transactions, including payment and logistics services.

Table 1. Local Shopping Platform categories with regards to their e-marketplace functionalities, derived from Peterson et al. (2007)

	Information	Communication	Transaction & Fulfillment
Platform categories	Store locator platforms	Product enquiry platforms	Affiliate transaction platforms
	Product catalog platforms		Full transaction platforms

2.3 Categories of Services on LSPs

In the advent of e-commerce, the location of the retailer seemed to have lost its importance, while it quickly turned out that physical distance still matters, e.g., because of negative effects of growing transportation costs on online sales prices or customer demand for quick delivery [28, 29]. This indicates that the location "is not dead" in the e-commerce age and that it becomes a crucial factor in the rising service competition between pure e-commerce players and stationary retailers [30]. In this context, two categories of digital services can be differentiated, location-dependent and location independent services. Especially location-dependent services (e.g., same-day delivery and click and return) can be considered essential for local retailers to attract and retain customers in multichannel retail environments [31, 32]. They also have a positive impact on the customers' intention, respectively willingness-to-buy on LSPs [22] and they are positively correlated with repurchases and the loyalty of customers [30].

Location-dependent services can be distinguished into location-enabled and location-based services. Location-enabled services are "*services that are feasible if the location of the retailer is close to the households of the customers (Bärsch et al. 2019, p. 606)*". This closeness enables information services (e.g., map with store locations, information about store opening hours or contact data), communication & support services (e.g., loyalty card, customer integration) and fulfilment services with low transportation costs (e.g., same hour, day delivery, click & return). Location-based services on the other hand are *"services that are feasible if the customers are close to the store location (Bärsch et al. 2019, p. 606)"*. Examples again range from information services (e.g., barcode scanner or map with store location), to communication & support services (e.g., price-draws, discounts or support), to navigation services (e.g., in-store navigation, shopping tours or outdoor navigation) and to payment & billing services (e.g., self-checkout).

Location-independent services on the other hand include standard web services, like online recommendations (e.g., further products of the retailer), online communication & support (e.g., service hotline or Facebook communication), or also online payment & billing services (e.g., credit card payment). These services are not bound to a specific location of the customer and accordingly, they are rampant on all national and global e-marketplaces.

3 Analysis

The stated research questions with respect to the development of the LSP market and their services were analyzed in two steps. First, we conducted a content analysis to assess the development of the market and the service offers of LSPs. Second, we assessed the potential impact of the corona crisis on LSPs in an explorative manner, conducting 26 semi-structured telephone interviews with executive managers of selected LSPs (see Subsect. 3.5).

3.1 Development of LSPs: Methodology

In line with previous research, we conducted an extensive content analysis to examine the development of the market and the service offers of LSPs [17]. In order to achieve comparable results to the preliminary study of Bärsch et al. (2019), we followed the guidelines by Krippendorff (1980, 2004) [33, 34] and Mayring (2010) [35]. Accordingly, after defining the research scope and questions, in a first step, we have identified the existing LSPs through an explorative web search. In the second step, we have conducted a pre-test in order to achieve coding consistency. This pre-test was followed by a revision procedure to improve the categorization and to streamline the coding agenda. In the fourth step, three individual coders have conducted a full content analysis. In the fifth step, the verification for the intercoder reliability of the coding results followed. Finally, an expert panel of senior researchers resolved inconsistencies within the coding results (see Fig. 1).

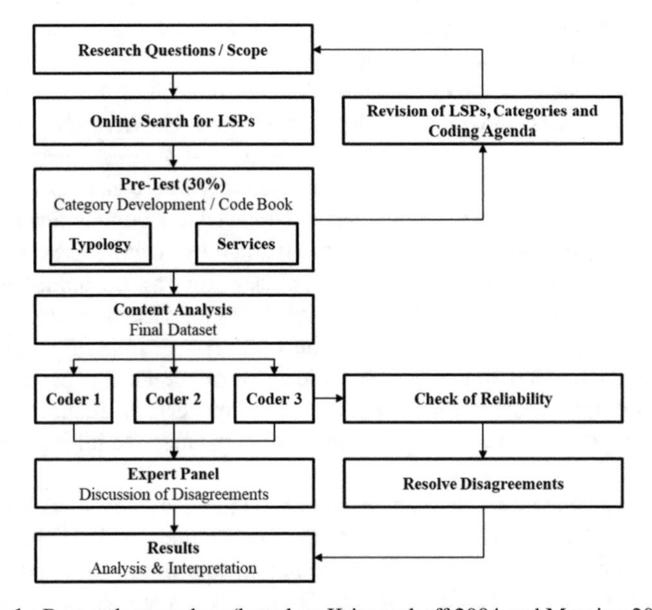

Fig. 1. Research procedure (based on Krippendorff 2004 and Mayring 2010).

3.2 Development of LSPs: Sample of the Content Analysis

For the identification of LSPs in Germany, we used the following keyword combinations for the explorative web search in German: "Local + (E–Marketplace, Shopping Platforms, Shops Online, Vendors Online, Marketplace, Products Online, Retail Online, Online Shop, Retailer Archive, Product Archive, Product Enquiry), Buy Local + City Name". The online search process was conducted via the search engine Google in October 2019. The search process resulted in a first set of 179 candidates for Local Shopping Platforms. However, 77 platforms were excluded for several reasons, e.g., because they were inactive, or addressed business customers rather than consumers. This selection and screening process resulted in a final set of 102 LSPs for the content analysis.

3.3 Development of LSPs: Pre-test and Coding of the Content Analysis

A pre-test (30%) for the categories and the services of LSPs has been conducted to ensure consistent coding. Based on the results of the pre-test, we identified 74 possible items: 5 typological items and 69 service items. Contrary to Bärsch et al. (2019), we changed the location-independent service offerings of two service items due to the pre-test findings. We deleted Google + (the site is down) as a service item for the category communication & support and added "Klarna" (new finding) as a service item for the category payment. For the coding procedure, we created a codebook with a description of each item. Three coders that were different from the ones in the previous study performed the coding and the content analysis between November 1, 2019 and December 22, 2019 [17]. The three coders screened each platform for all 74 possible items, with each item being rated "1" if Yes/Available and "0" if No/Not Available.

3.4 Development of LSPs: Intercoder Reliability of the Content Analysis

The intercoder reliability was verified according to the guidelines of Raupp and Vogelsang (2009) [36] and Tinsley and Weiss [37, 38]. Therefore, the Holsti's Coefficient of Reliability r_H, and Krippendorff's α were calculated to verify the results for the typological items and the service items [34]. With 5 typology items and 102 platforms to screen, each coder judged 510 typology items in total. The three coders achieved a very good intercoder reliability for the Holsti's Coefficient [39] and an acceptable Krippendorff's α [34].

Table 2. Intercoder reliability for typology and service items

	Typology items			Service items		
Coder pair	C1 + C2	C1 + C3	C2 + C3	C1 + C2	C1 + C3	C2 + C3
Coder consensus	948	928	944	13430	13482	13354
Coder differences	72	92	76	646	594	722
r_H Coefficient	0.93	0.91	0.93	0.95	0.96	0.95
Average r_H	0.92			0.95		
Krippendorff's α	0.85			0.80		

Regarding the services in total, each coder had to judge 7038 items. The three coders achieved a very good reliability for Holsti's Coefficient [39] and an acceptable degree of reliability for the Krippendorff's α [34] (see Table 2). Finally, an expert panel of senior researchers with high expertise in the field of e-marketplaces discussed all remaining discrepancies (2202 items) and made the final decisions to harmonize coder inconsistencies.

3.5 Corona-Effects: Methodology and Questionnaire of the Telephone Interviews

The dynamic and complex development since the outbreak of the coronavirus was analyzed with an additional explorative study using semi-structured telephone interviews

[40]. We chose this method because of its efficiency (time and personnel expenditures [41]) and its accordance with the social distancing requirements [42]. The interview guideline contained 11 standard questions to address three main topics: 1) the reasons for the chosen LSP type and the implemented services, 2) the experiences and new developments of the LSP during the corona crisis, and 3) strategies to sustain the LSPs business model after the corona crisis.

To address the dynamics in the development and the potential impact of the lockdown, we added two customized extensions, the first including three questions for LSPs created as a response to the lockdown, and the second including seven questions for LSPs that had been established already before the corona crisis. The questionnaire used two types of questions, one with a dichotomous 5-point Likert scale to capture the intensity of the answers, the other for open questions. We explained both types to the interview partners in order to avoid any biases like the "Response-Order-Effect" [43].

3.6 Corona-Effects: Sample and Documentation of the Telephone Interviews

To examine the current impact of the corona crisis on LSPs, we used the LSP collection provided by the EU-funded research project *"City Lab Südwestfalen"*. The *"City Lab Südwestfalen"* collected the data to offer an overview of existing and new LSPs since the corona crisis from partner municipalities in the region of South Westphalia in Germany [44]. In total, we interviewed 26 LSP providers (9 established LSPs; 17 new LSPs) in June 2020. The average interview lasted for 30 min. We used the "Foot-in-the-Door-Technique", calling two times: In the first call, we introduced the topic, and made an appointment for the actual interview (second call) [41]. We used this approach to decrease the refusal rate and to increase the quality of the data [45]. The responses were collected in an excel sheet during the interviews.

From the interviewed platforms, 21 out of the 26 LSPs represent s *Store Locator Platform* (81%), one a *Product Catalog Platform* (4%), and four a *Full Transaction Platform* (15%).

4 Results

4.1 Results Content Analysis: Development of LSPs Since 2016

To address our first and second sub research question, we discuss our findings of the content analysis and compare them with the findings from 2016 (see Table 3) for 21 German platforms [17]. The findings confirm the derived platform types from 2016 [17], now identifying 65 *Store Locator Platforms*, 3 *Product Catalog Platforms*, 10 *Product Enquiry Platforms*, 2 *Affiliate Transaction Platforms*, and 22 *Full Transaction Platforms*. The current study reveals that the majority of platforms follows the *"Strictly Local Approach"* (89 out of 102) and represents Store Locator Platforms, focusing mostly on information and communication functionality. In contrast to this, the 2016 study identified the majority of LSPs as *Full Transaction Platforms* [17]. Furthermore, platforms which follow a *"Scaling Local Approach"* (2019: 12 *Full Transaction* and one *Affiliate Transaction Platform*) mainly focus on transaction and fulfilment functionality, while neglecting to utilize the locational advantages of LOOROs.

The 102 analyzed platforms still provide most of the same 69 digital services that were identified in the preliminary study from 2016 [17]. Concerning the use of location in the service landscape, of the 69 digital services, 40 are location-independent and 29 are location-dependent services. The 69 services support the different functions of e-marketplaces [23, 24]: Information & recommendation services, communication & support, and payment & fulfillment services. The following tables (see Table 3–7) show the number of offered services by each LSP type for the examination in 2016 and 2019. Reading example: 1) From the sample of 2016, *Store Locator Platforms* have offered 21.88% of the identified location-enabled services. 2) From the sample of 2019, *Store Locator Platforms* have offered on average of 9.88% of the identified services. Calculation example for the services: 65 LSPs *16 location-enabled services = 1040 (e.g., see Table 3).

Table 3. Service landscape offered by store locator platforms

Sample	2016	2019		
Store locator platforms	Total	Total	Strictly local	Scaling local
Number of platforms	2	65		--
Location-enabled services	21.88% (7 of 32)	19.04% (198 of 1040)	19.04% (198 of 1040)	--
Location-based services	2 15.38% (4 of 26)	3.67% (31 of 845)	3.67% (31 of 845)	--
Location-independent services	16.25% (13 of 80)	8.23% (214 of 2600)	8.23% (214 of 2600)	--
Average no. of total services	17.39% (24 of 138)	9.88% (443 of 4485)	9.88% (443 of 4485)	--

For *Store Locator Platforms*, we found a striking increase for location-enabled services, like information (e.g., contact data or the address of LOOROs) or communication & support services (e.g., loyalty cards), location-based services (e.g., outdoor navigation as a navigation service), and location-independent services (e.g., support via E-Mail as a communication & support service) in absolute values. Concerning Product Catalog Platforms, we also found a higher offering of location-enabled services (e.g., information) compared to 2016. This also holds for location-based (e.g., advertisement or discounts) and location-independent services in absolute values (see Table 4). Product Enquiry Platforms provided, in general, a higher level of location-dependent services, especially reserve & collect. Moreover, we found a strong increase in numbers of recommendation services (e.g., product recommendations, further products of the retailers) as location-independent services (see Table 5).

In general, we found a decrease of location-dependent and location-independent services for affiliate platforms. Regarding location-independent services, platforms with a *"Scaling Local Approach"* offer more payment & billing options than platforms with a *"Strictly Local Approach"*. However, platforms with a *"Scaling Local Approach"* offer

Table 4. Service landscape offered by product catalog platforms

Sample	2016	2019		
Product catalog platforms	Total	Total	Strictly local	Scaling local
Number of platforms	2	3		--
Location-enabled services	28.13% (9 of 32)	22.92% (11 of 48)	22.92% (11 of 48)	--
Location-based services	7.69% (2 of 26)	20.51% (8 of 39)	20.51% (8 of 39)	--
Location-independent services	17.50% (14 of 80)	15.00% (18 of 120)	15.00% (18 of 120)	--
Average no. of total services	18.12% (25 of 138)	17.87% (37 of 207)	17.87% (37 of 207)	--

Table 5. Service landscape offered by product enquiry platforms

Sample	2016	2019		
Product enquiry platforms	Total	Total	Strictly local	Scaling local
Number of platforms	5	10		--
Location-enabled services	20.00% (16 of 80)	23.75% (38 of 160)	23.75% (38 of 160)	--
Location-based services	--	2.31% (3 of 130)	2.31% (3 of 130)	--
Location-independent services	17.50% (35 of 200)	13.50% (54 of 400)	13.50% (54 of 400)	--
Average no. of total services	14.48% (51 of 345)	13.77% (95 of 690)	13.77% (95 of 690)	--

slightly more location-based services (see Table 6). This service pattern for the *"Scaling Local Approach"* also holds true for *Full Transaction Platforms* and is in line with their focus on non-local customers who benefit most from such services. Nevertheless, the location-enabled services and location-based services decrease in comparison to 2016 for *Full Transaction Platforms* (see Table 7). In general, the results also confirm that platforms with transaction and fulfillment functionality, e.g., *Affiliate Transaction Platforms* and *Full Transaction Platforms*, offer more services than information and communication focused platforms, like e.g., *Store Locator Platforms*. Concerning the different platform types, the typical platform with a *"Strictly Local Approach"* is a *Store Locator or Product Catalog Platform*, while platforms with a *"Scaling Local Approach"* tend to be *Full Transaction Platforms*.

Table 6. Service landscape offered by affiliation platforms

Sample	2016	2019		
Affiliation platforms	Total	Total	Strictly local	Scaling local
Number of platforms	4	2	1	1
Location-enabled services	34.44% (22 of 64)	40.63% (13 of 32)	43.75% (7 of 16)	37.50% (6 of 16)
Location-based services	11.54% (6 of 52)	11.54% (3 of 26)	15.38% (2 of 13)	7.69% (1 of 13)
Location-independent services	24.38% (39 of 160)	21.25% (17 of 80)	17.50% (7 of 40)	25.00% (10 of 40)
Average no. of total services	24.28% (67 of 276)	23.91% (33 of 138)	23.19% (16 of 69)	24.64% (17 of 69)

Table 7. Service landscape offered by full transaction platforms

Sample	2016	2019		
Full transaction platforms	Total	Total	Strictly local	Scaling local
Number of platforms	8	22	10	12
Location-enabled services	37.50% (48 of 128)	24.72% (87 of 352)	25.00% (40 of 160)	24.48% (47 of 192)
Location-based services	5.77% (6 of 104)	1.05% (3 of 286)	1.54% (2 of 130)	0.64% (1 of 156)
Location-independent services	34.38% (110 of 320)	32.05% (282 of 880)	29.75% (119 of 400)	33.96% (163 of 480)
Average no. of total services	29.71% (164 of 552)	24.51% (372 of 1518)	23.33% (161 of 690)	25.48% (211 of 828)

4.2 Results of the Telephone Interviews: Corona-Effects

The results of the telephone interviews will be discussed along the three defined guiding topics: 1) reasons for the chosen LSP type and the implemented services, 2) experiences and new developments during the corona crisis, and 3) strategies to sustain the LSPs after the corona crisis.

1) **Reasons for the Chosen LSP Type and the Implemented Services**
It turned out that the idea and the implementation of a LSP as a response to the lockdown was spontaneously driven by various actors, mostly city marketing / administration, or also regional business development units. Just five of the contacted LSP providers explained that they had planned the LSP implementation already before the crisis and that the coronavirus only accelerated the process. Contrary, nine interviewees reported that no LSP was in preparation before the lockdown, while six

confirmed that they had some basic ideas before. The institutional background of the platform providers itself also seems to influence the chosen LSP type and the choice of implemented services. For example, city-related actors, like city marketing, apparently focus on supporting their local stationary retailers by providing only rudimentary information on *Store Locator Platforms.* In order to shed more light on their objectives, we asked the interviewees to rate statements on their intentions using a five-point Likert scale (from strongly disagree to strongly agree). Five out of nine providers of the already established platforms, and six out of 17 providers of the newly created LSPs, agreed to the statement *"It is intended to prevent customers from migrating to large online retailers in general"*. Surprisingly, the majority of the providers of the newly created platforms rated this item neutral (eight out of 17). The statement *"It is intended to generate sales (parallel to stationary retailing)"* was only raised towards providers of *Full Transaction Platforms.* Two providers of existing platforms agreed with the statement, while one provider of a new platform rather disagreed, stating that *"revenue via the platform should be understood as a bonus, which exceeds the monthly fee but not as a second income source"*. Other interviewees summarized their intentions as *"improving the digital visibility of their city with its local retailers as a shopping [...] location" or as "[...] supporting local retailers so that customers don't buy on Amazon"*.

The timeframe for implementing the new LSPs ranged from overnight (5 LSPs out of 17) to within two weeks (11 out of 17), except for one *Full Transaction Platform* that was developed in three weeks. In comparison, the already established platforms needed six months up to two years for *Store Locator Platforms* (six out of nine) and two months up to one year for *Full Transaction Platforms.* Regarding problems that occurred during the implementation of the platforms and the digital services, the interviewees reported challenges setting up the payment infrastructure or also missing inventory management systems as a necessary backbone for additional digital services.

2) **Experiences and new developments during the corona crisis**
One major finding is that all existing LSPs extended their services during the corona crisis, e.g., with coupons, more detailed information on delivery options or general information about shopping with corona restrictions in place. During the lockdown, four existing LSPs reported a dynamic increase in numbers of connected retailers, while four existing LSPs reported a regular growth. One platform has extended its area of operation from three to ten regions. Furthermore, it seems that the corona crisis has boosted the attractiveness of LSPs for LOOROs. We asked the participants to evaluate the willingness of LOOROs to join and to actively use the platform or cooperate with the platform providers, e.g., regarding content creation (store and product information) (five-point Likert scale from very easy to very difficult). All interviewees reported that it became easier for them to win new LOOROs for their platforms compared to the pre-coronavirus situation. They further stated that also content creation by the LOOROs themselves and on behalf of them (by the LSP provider) became easier. 15 out of 17 new LSPs (3 out of 9 existing LSPs) rated the content creation by LOOROs as easy, and 14 out of 17 new LSPs (3 out of 9 existing LSPs) rated the content creation on behalf of their LOOROs as easy. According to the providers of *Store Locator Platforms*, one primary reason for the high willingness

of LOOROs to participate and for the perceived ease regarding content creation was the collection of necessary retailer information with a survey or an online document.

3) **Strategies to Sustain the LSPs after the Corona Crisis**
All LSPs reported decreasing interest and decreasing participation of LOOROs since the easing of the coronavirus restrictions. Accordingly, LSP providers now focus on incentivizing active participation on their platforms. As financial incentives to participate, 21 out of 27 interviewed LSP providers do not charge any membership fees from LOOROs. One of the already established LSPs paused the monthly fee until June 2020. Another existing LSP decided to offer free online visibility for new LOOROs, while already participating LOOROs need to pay a fee. Only two existing LSPs did not change their pricing model, and two of the new LSPs offer free participation for a specific period from six months to one year. 15 out of 17 new LSPs agreed to the statement (five-point Likert scale from strongly disagree to strongly agree) that *the platform is designed to ensure the short-term survival of LOOROs during the corona crisis.* 14 out of 17 agreed to the statement that *the LSPs aim to strengthen the online visibility of LOOROs also after the corona crisis.* The majority of the already established platforms (seven out of nine), and also the majority of the new platforms (13 out of 17) intends to improve resp. extend their platform content and also their digital service landscape, e.g., by adding more and better pictures in product and retailer descriptions, or by implementing click & collect functionality.

5 Conclusion

5.1 Discussion

Regarding the first sub research question *"How did the types of German LSPs develop between 2016 and 2019?"*, our results show that the LSP market changed from a majority of *Full Transaction Platforms* to a majority of *Store Locator Platforms.* The majority of LSPs follows a *"Strictly Local Approach"*. This matches other findings from research that state that LOOROs prefer LSPs with a clear focus on local customers over global online platforms with intense price competition [46]. Nevertheless, we found 13 LSPs that have loosened their local self-restrictions to address also non-local customers, now following a *"Scaling Local Approach"*. While this opens new market segments, it also makes the platform less distinguishable from other shopping sites. In contrast to former findings, our results show that LSPs with a *"Scaling Local Approach"* are perceived to act contrarily to the objectives and wishes of their LOORO target group [26]. Furthermore, from the 2016 sample, only eight platforms still exist. Notably, the high number of closedowns of *Full Transaction Platforms* stands out, confirming other studies [46]. Apparently, the business model of a Local Shopping Platform still lacks proof of concept.

Concerning the second sub research question: *"How did the digital services offered by German LSPs develop between 2016 and 2019?"*, we found that LSPs still fall short in providing services that utilize the locational proximity between shops and customers. It seems that LSPs are still not interested in strengthening their locational position and do not support LOOROs to make or sustain profit by attracting customers to their stores [26]. This result indicates that there is no fundamental change in the service landscape compared to 2016 [17]. The implemented services can be considered as one-way communication, providing only general information (e.g., opening hours), instead of facilitating interaction between LOOROs and customers [46].

Finally, with regard to the third sub research question: *"How has the corona crisis affected the development of LSPs?"*, we found that the corona crisis clearly pushed the implementation of LSPs and also reduced the implementation periods drastically. This result shows that the coronavirus is a game changer and that the pandemic is fostering the willingness of LOOROs to follow e-commerce trends. Accordingly, the issue of convincing LOOROs to join the platforms has become much easier. Witt LOOROs focusing on the information-centric platform types, the new platforms provided a quick and easy measure in face of the corona restrictions to stay in business. Former studies confirm the importance of low entry barriers for LOOROs [49]. On the other hand, as LSPs have not substantially further developed there service offers, it needs to be doubted that they will effectively support LOOROs in their digital transformation and help them sustain or even grow their businesses. This is supported by the visibly decreasing interest in the newly created LSPs since the easing of the corona restrictions. LOOROs still seem hesitant and not fully convinced of the positive impact of LSPs.

5.2 Practical Implications

Several lessons can be learned from this study. First, current LSP providers are still not utilizing the locational advantage of their local retailers, although "Location-depended Services" need to be considered as an important success factor [17, 26]. Moreover, platforms with a *"Scaling Local Approach"* loosen their focus on local customers, running the risk of discouraging LOOROs from joining their platforms. LSP providers need to understand that they depend on the existence of LOOROs and that only strong local retail partners can provide a sustainable basis for their platforms [17]. However, LOOROs also need to understand that customers want convenience and that they prefer local shopping malls / agglomerations of local shops over individual online presences [47]. Therefore, LOOROs should also invest in cooperative online initiatives like LSPs. Once connected to a LSP, they should actively improve the visibility of their cooperation through active link-building [48]. Furthermore, LOOROs should learn from the recent lockdown that digitalization is now and not in the far future. They need to overcome their internal adaption barriers and check if their self-perception still matches their actual competitive situation and customer expectations [2].

Second, our study shows that entry barriers matter. LSP providers need to create tools that facilitate and ease the active use of their platforms for LOOROs, this way also reducing entry barriers for them [49].

The lockdown in the context of the spread of the coronavirus lead to an erratic increase of LSPs and moved many new retailers on the platforms. *Store Locator Platforms* with their low level of digital services currently dominate the LSP market in Germany (see RQ1). Forty-four out of 53 platforms from the data sample 2019 with a *"Strictly Local Approach"* turned out to be *Store Locator Platforms,* run by city-related units. Supporting this finding, 10 out of 17 of the new LSPs from the 2020 data sample are run by city-related actors. It is questionable if *Store Locator Platforms* with their currently low service level can substantially contribute to local retail and help to sustain high street shopping. In line with this evaluation, the retailers also expressed their doubts over the ability of *Store Locator Platforms* to help them reach customers [26]. One-way communication on passive, information-centric platforms might not be enough. More services and urban functions need to be implemented on the platforms to attract and keep customers on the platforms [46]. The platform providers should thereby actively make use of the locational proximity between the retailers and customers with the help of "Location-based" and "Location-enabled Services", as this will strengthen and harness their unique selling proposition as against global platforms.

5.3 Limitations and Directions for Future Research

To the best of our knowledge, we found 102 platforms in Germany with the help of the defined keyword list. Future research should extend the regional scope and the keyword list. Thereby, modern technologies like Web Crawlers could help to improve the quality and the completeness of the search process. Secondly, the perspective of retailers needs to be further investigated in a qualitative analysis. Finally, a quantitative, conclusive research approach should follow this first explorative study to validate our findings.

References

1. IFH Köln: Handelsszenario Wachtsumsparadoxen im deutschen Einzelhandel (2030). https://www.ifhkoeln.de/pressemitteilungen/details/handelsszenario-2030-wachstumsparadoxon-im-deutschen-einzelhandel/. Accessed 13 July 2020
2. Bollweg, L., Lackes, R., Siepermann, M., Weber, P.: Digitalization of local owner-operated retail outlets: between customer demand, competitive challenge and business persistence. In: 15 WI 2020, pp. 1004–1018 (2020)
3. Koren, M., Peto, R.: It's retail stores and restaurants, not farms and fisheries that suffer most from social distancing. VoxEU.org (2020). https://voxeu.org/article/it-s-retail-stores-and-restaurants-not-farms-and-fisheries-suffer-most-social-distancing? Accessed 13 July 2020
4. Coyle, D., Nguyen, D.: The impact of Covid-19 on the value of online goods. https://voxeu.org/article/impact-covid-19-value-online-goods. Accessed 24 Aug 2020
5. Statistisches Bundesamt (Destatis): Pressemitteilung Nr. 151 vom 30. April (2020). https://www.destatis.de/DE/Presse/Pressemitteilungen/2020/04/PD20_151_45212.html. Accessed 13 July 2020
6. Statistisches Bundesamt (Destatis): Pressemitteilung Nr. 245 vom 1. July (2020). https://www.destatis.de/DE/Presse/Pressemitteilungen/2020/07/PD20_245_45212.html. Accessed 13 July 2020
7. Bundesfinanzministerium (BMF): Europäische Antwort auf Corona (2020). https://www.bundesfinanzministerium.de/Content/DE/Standardartikel/Themen/Schlaglichter/Corona-Schutzschild/2020-03-27-eurogruppe-rat.html. Accessed 13 July 2020
8. Bosio, E., Djankov, S.: Southern European and emerging market firms are under severe distress. VoxEU.org (2020) https://voxeu.org/article/southern-european-and-emerging-market-firms-are-under-severe-distress. Accessed 13 July 2020
9. Berman, B.: Flatlined: combatting the death of retail stores. Bus. Horiz. **62**(1), 75–82 (2019)
10. Grewal, D., Roggeveen, A.L., Nordfält, J.: The future of retailing. J. Retail. **93**(1), 1–6 (2017)
11. Wiener, M., Hoßbach, N., Saunders, C.: Omnichannel businesses in the publishing and retailing industries: synergies and tensions between coexisting online and offline business models. Decis. Support Syst. **109**, 15–26 (2018)

12. Vize, R., Coughlan, J., Kennedy, A., Ellis-Chadwick, F.: Technology readiness in a b2b online retail context: an examination of antecedents and outcomes. Ind. Market. Manage. **42**(6), 909–918 (2013)
13. Rahayu, R., Day, J.: Determinant factors of e-commerce adoption by SMEs in developing country: evidence from Indonesia. Procd. Soc. Behv. **195**, 142–150 (2015)
14. Kabanda, S., Brown, I.: A structuration analysis of small and medium enterprise (SME) adoption of e-commerce: the case of Tanzania. Telemat. Inform. **34**(4), 118–132 (2017)
15. Kurnia, S., Choudrie, J., Mahbubur, R.M., Alzougool, B.: E-commerce technology adoption: a Malaysian grocery SME retail sector study. J. Bus. Res. **68**(9), 1906–1918 (2015)
16. IFH Köln: Der Handel nach Corona: Digitale Konzepte als Zukunftsperspektive. https://www.ifhkoeln.de/pressemitteilungen/details/der-handel-nach-corona-digitale-konzepte-als-zukunftsperspektive/. Accessed 13 July 2020
17. Bärsch, S., Bollweg, L., Lackes, R., Siepermann, M., Weber, P., Wulfhorst, V.: Local shopping platforms - harnessing locational advantages for the digital transformation of local retail outlets: a content analysis. In: WI 2019, vol. 14, pp. 602–618 (2019)
18. Petersen, K.J., Ogden, J.A., Carter, P.L.: B2B E-marketplaces: a typology by functionality. Int. J. Phys. Distr. Log. **37**(1), 4–18 (2007)
19. Digital pioneers: local commerce: Die sinnlosen Marktplätze von nebenan. https://t3n.de/news/local-commerce-sinnlosen-934455/. Accessed 13 July 2020
20. Sandberg, K.W., Håkansson, F.: Barriers to adapt ecommerce by rural microenterprises in Sweden: a case study. Int. J. Knowl. Res. Manage. E-Commer. **4**(1), 1–7 (2014)
21. Stockdale, R., Standing, C.: benefits and barriers of electronic marketplace participation: an SME perspective. J. Enterp. Inf. Manag. **17**(4), 301–311 (2004)
22. Bollweg, L., Lackes, R., Siepermann, M., Weber, P.: The role of location dependent services for the success of local shopping platforms. In: Abramowicz, W., Corchuelo, R. (eds.) BIS 2019. LNBIP, vol. 373, pp. 366–377. Springer, Cham (2019). https://doi.org/10.1007/978-3-030-36691-9_31
23. Bakos, Y.: The emerging role of electronic marketplaces on the internet. Commun. ACM **41**(8), 35–42 (1998)
24. Standing, S., Standing, C., Love, E.D.: A review of research on E-marketplaces 1997–2008. Decis. Support Syst. **49**(1), 41–51 (2010)
25. Pan, X., Shankar, V., Ratchford, B.T.: Price competition between pure play versus bricks-and-clicks e-tailers. Adv. Appl. Microecon. **11**, 29–61 (2002)
26. Berendes, C.I., zur Heiden, P., Niemann, M., Hoffmeister, B., Becker, J.: Usage of local online platforms in retail: insights from retailers expectations. In: 28th ECIS2020 – A Virtual AIS Conference
27. Zheng, W., Wang, X.: An explorative study of industry influences: on vertical e-marketplaces' adoption of e-procurement auction. Inf. Syst. E-Bus. Manag. **6**(4), 321–340 (2008)
28. Blum, B., Goldfarb, A.: Does the internet defy the law of gravity? J. Int. Econ. **70**(2), 384–405 (2006)
29. Iyer, K.N., Germain, R., Frankwick, G.L.: supply chain b2b e-commerce and time-based delivery performance. Int. J. Distr. Log. **34**(8), 645–661 (2004)
30. Kim, T.Y., Dekker, R., Heij, C.: Cross-border electronic commerce: distance effects and express delivery in European union markets. Int. J. Electron. Commer. **21**(2), 184–218 (2017)
31. Massad, N., Heckman, R., Crowston, K.: Customer satisfaction with electronic service encounters. Int. J. Electron. Commer. **10**(4), 73–104 (2006)
32. Saeed, K.A., Grover, V., Hwang, Y.: The relationship of e-commerce competence to customer value and firm performance: an empirical investigation. J. Manag. Inf. Syst. **22**(1), 223–256 (2005)
33. Krippendorff, K.: Validity in content analysis. In: Mochmann, E. (ed.) Computerstrategien für die Kommunikationsanalyse, pp. 69–112. Campus Verlag, Frankfurt am Main (1980)

34. Krippendorff, K.: Content Analysis: An Introduction to Its Methodology (2nd ed.), p. 237. Sage, Thousand Oaks (2004)
35. Mayring, P.: Qualitative inhaltsanalyse. In: Mey, G., Mruck, K. (eds.) Handbuch qualitative Forschung in der Psychologie, pp. 495–511. Springer, Wiesbaden (2020). https://doi.org/10.1007/978-3-658-26887-9_52
36. Raupp, J., Vogelgesang, J.: Forschungstand, forschungsfragen und begriffsdefinitionen. In: Raupp, J., Vogelgesang, J. (eds.) Medienresonanzanalyse, pp. 119–124. VS Verlag für Sozialwissenschaften, Wiesbaden (2009). https://doi.org/10.1007/978-3-531-91605-7_4
37. Tinsley, H.E., Weiss, D.J.: Interrater reliability and agreement of subjective judgements. J. Couns. Psychol. **22**(4), 358–376 (1975)
38. Tinsley, H.E., Weiss, D.J.: Interrater reliability and agreement. In: Tinsley, H.E.A., Brown, S.D. (eds.) Handbook of Applied Multivariate Statistics and Mathematical Modeling, pp. 95–124. Academic Press, San Diego (2000)
39. Holsti, O.R.: Content Analysis for the Social Sciences and Humanities. pp. 138–141. Addison-Wesley, Boston (1969)
40. Frey, J.H.: Survey Research by Telephone. p. 29, Sage, Beverly Hills (1989).
41. Döring, N., Bortz, J.: Forschungsmethoden und Evaluation in den Sozial-und Humanwissenschaften, pp. 373-375. Springer, Heidelberg (2016)
42. Die Landesregierung Nordrhein-Westfalen Aktuelle FAQ zur Corona-Pandemie (2020). https://www.land.nrw/corona. Accessed 01 June 2020
43. Schumann, H., Presser, S.: Questions and Answers in Attitude Surveys. Sage, New York (1981)
44. City Lab Südwestfalen: Übersicht lokaler Online-Marktplätze der Partnerkommunen. https://www.citylab-swf.de/news/uebersicht-lokaler-online-marktplaetze-der-partnerkommunen/. Accessed 13 May 2020
45. Dillman, D.A., Gallegos, J., Frey, J.H.: Reducing refusal rates for telephone interviews. Pub. Opin. Q. **40**(1), 66–78 (1976)
46. Schade, K., Hübscher, M., Korzer, T.: Smart retail in smart cities: best practice analysis of local online platforms. In: Proceedings of the 15th ICETE, vol. 1, pp. 147–157 (2018)
47. Teller, C., Alexander, A., Floh, A.: The impact of competition and cooperation on the performance of a retail agglomeration and its stores. Ind. Mark. Manag. **52**, 6–17 (2016)
48. Bollweg, L., Lackes, R., Siepermann, M., Weber, P.: The role of e-intermediaries in local retail hyperlink networks: a hyperlink network analysis. In: MKWI (2018)
49. Delgado-de Miguel, J.F., Buil-Lopez Menchero, T., Esteban-Navarro, M.A., Garcia-Madurga, M.A.: Proximity trade and urban sustainability: small retailers' expectations towards local online marketplaces. Sustainability **11**(24), 1–20 (2019)

Towards the Digital Self-renewal of Retail: The Generic Ecosystem of the Retail Industry

Timo Phillip Böttcher(✉), Lukas Rickling, Kristina Gmelch, Jörg Weking, and Helmut Krcmar

Chair for Information Systems and Business Process Management, Technical University of Munich, Garching, Germany
{timo.boettcher,lukas.rickling,kristina.gmelch,joerg.weking, helmut.krcmar}@tum.de

Abstract. E-commerce, digital platforms, and digital transformation (DT) pose major challenges to offline businesses in the retail industry. To offset the benefits of the data available to online businesses, stores must digitalize their stores and rethink their value proposition to customers. In a digitalized world, this value is no longer provided by single companies—leveraging a set of companies in the retail ecosystem to jointly create value is now necessary. Therefore, this research project provides an overview of the roles and value flows in Germany's retail industry in the form of an e^3-value model that can be used by scholars for future research on the digitalization of the retail industry. For practitioners, it provides guidance for forging new partnerships to co-create value in interconnected, digital ecosystems.

Keywords: Retail · Ecosystem · Business model · Digital transformation

1 Introduction

"*You left something in your shopping cart. Check out now and receive a 10% discount on your order!*" Most online shoppers have received similar e-mails after adding something to their cart that they ultimately did not purchase. Even if a shopper does not purchase the item, Google, Facebook, and other online platforms will nonetheless continue advertising similar products to them. The great advantage of doing business online is that such platforms know each individual (potential) customer. They know their interests, past purchases, or, at a minimum, their e-mail address, physical address, age, and gender. Sometimes, they know us so intimately, we might assume these platforms must be surveilling our conversations. Therefore, if your business's point-of-sale is a brick-and-mortar store, you face a major competitive disadvantage.

Driven by recent digital transformation (DT) and changed customer behavior [1], online retailers are currently growing much faster than their store-based counterparts (9.5% compared to 1.5% in 2018 in Germany) [2]. Therefore, the industry is making an effort to close the gap between brick-and-mortar and online stores. For example, Hummel successfully employed an omni-channel sales strategy to connect all relevant players in their retail ecosystem and provide a seamless customer journey both online

F. Ahlemann et al. (Eds.): WI 2021, LNISO 46, pp. 140–146, 2021.
https://doi.org/10.1007/978-3-030-86790-4_11

and offline [3–5]. In their stores, Nike now uses augmented reality to market personalized shoes and encourages customers to use its mobile app to buy outfits by scanning a code on the price tag. Such efforts aim to provide a digital experience to customers even when shopping in brick-and-mortar stores, thereby enabling an online connection to be established through which they can collect invaluable information.

To be successful in these approaches to digitalizing the store-based retail industry, retailers need to rethink their value strategies. In today's complex and highly interconnected world, value is no longer created by linear value chains or by individual companies [6–8]. Today, as digital platforms like Amazon demonstrate, integrating and leveraging a value network in which multiple companies collaborate to create value for the customer is key to retail success [9–11]. Strategy and information systems (IS) research has termed these networks "*ecosystems,*" analogous to nature [7, 12, 13]. In this paper, we define an ecosystem according to the definition by Jacobides, Cennamo and Gawer [14] as a "*set of actors with varying degrees of multilateral, nongeneric complementarities that are not fully hierarchically controlled*" (p. 2264).

Leveraging synergies between actors is imperative for innovating value creation mechanisms. Applying the concept of value paths [15], innovating established connections between companies by leveraging digital resources can be useful in assessing value creation opportunities [16]. Facilitated by digital resources, companies are today able to innovate beyond their integrated supply chain and exploit opportunities through nonhierarchical cooperation with interdependent actors [17]. To leverage this form of complementary cooperation, companies need to recognize the set of actors contributing to their value proposition and creation, the roles these actors fulfill and which values are exchanged between these roles [14, 18, 19]. Therefore, this research applies an ecosystem perspective to Germany's retail industry. We state two research questions: (1) *Which generic roles and value exchanges exist in the German retail ecosystem?* And (2) *How does the German retail ecosystem look like?*

To support practitioners and researchers regarding the DT of retail, this study proposes a model of the retail industry's generic ecosystem. We contribute to IS research by providing an overview of the DT of the retail industry that can be used by scholars for future research. For practitioners, it provides guidance for forging new partnerships to co-create value through interconnected, digital ecosystems.

2 Theoretical Background

Research on the digital transformation in retail has started early with the rise of e-business [20] and consequential e-commerce [21–23]. More recently there is growing interest in business model innovations and the role of digital platforms for retail. The business model of digital platforms has severe implications for the retail industry. They simplify the complex value chain by directly linking customers and producers [7, 13, 24]. The marketplace, e. g. Amazon, is a typical example of such a digital platform that serves as an intermediary and captures value by charging transaction fees – in this case to the seller – or/and by charging for advertising [25]. Rather than simply moving transactions online, digital platforms and e-commerce businesses leverage data analytics to create value from vastly collected data about transactions and consumer behaviors to offer personalized recommendations, competitive prices, and fast delivery to offer a more appealing customer experience [26–29]. Even if the value proposition of department stores is unlikely to be competitive compared to digital platforms, physical presence for specialized brick-and-mortar retail permits physical engagement with products, detailed information, and personal counseling which positively influences customer experience [30]. Augmenting the physical presence with digital technology like tablets, virtual experiences, and combining offline and online channels positively influence sales and customer relations [4, 31–33]. As the ubiquity of digital technology enables consumers to make better-informed decisions [34] and shopping experience in online shops alters expectations for physical shops, consumers transition between the channels easily [31].

Hence, instead of strictly separating e-commerce and physical stores, retailers should emphasize the potentials of interaction between them [35]. Since this applies for both online and offline retailers, research and practice face open questions about revenue generation in physical stores that mainly serve as point of experience rather than point of sale, how do consumers interact with digitally connected sales channels, or how do value propositions change, when the whole retail ecosystem becomes omni-channel [30, 36]. The subsequent challenges require fundamental changes in the organizations, but also in the entire ecosystem. Hence research suggests to openly and actively manage the shifting relationships in the ecosystem [4]. Beyond that, research is asked to regard digitalization in retail not from an *online or offline* perspective, but taking an integrated perspective to analyze how transformations happen and how these impact the entire retail industry [35].

3 Research Approach

To formulate a generic ecosystem model of the retail industry, we follow a three-step research approach based on Riasanow, Galic and Böhm [37]. For this initial research, we focused on the German retail industry. This way, we aimed to consider differences in customer behavior (e.g., willingness to share data), legal regulations (eg., data privacy), and market-specific structures (eg., shopping streets vs. shopping malls). In the first step, we identified the roles and value streams of the ecosystem based on data extracted from Crunchbase (crunchbase.com) on June 9, 2020. The Crunchbase database contains information about existing companies and start-ups, e.g., their value proposition, size, funding rounds, and headquarters location. To delimit the German retail ecosystem, we searched for companies assigned to the industry classifiers "retail" and "retail technology" with headquarters in Germany. The search resulted in an initial sample of 543 German companies. After reviewing all of the companies, we eliminated 83 defunct companies, e. g. the clothing accessories manufacturer VON FLOERKE that filed for insolvency in October 2019. Also, we removed 65 companies not primarily operating in retail, e. g. the telecommunications company Deutsche Telekom. In this sense, the above-mentioned regulatory actors that influence value creation are also not considered, as this study focuses on the digital transformation patterns within the retail industry and the ways in which this value is created, not on its contingency factors. Finally, we analyzed a sample of 395 relevant organizations. Based on this dataset, we conducted a structured content analysis, including inductive category development [38, 39].

Two coders independently coded the sample and identified the 13 distinct roles through constant discussion. The same coders identified the value streams between these roles by combining the Crunchbase data with other publicly available information from company websites and news reports.

In the second step, we visualized the ecosystem, including all identified generic roles and value streams. We selected the e^3-value method for this purpose. We deem this suitable as the e^3-value method aims to elicit, evaluate and identify value creation in ecosystems. It is used to evaluate the economic sustainability of ecosystems by modeling the economic value exchanges of actors [40]. Thereby we built upon the work of [37, 40–42], allowing for inter-ecosystem comparison in later research stages.

In the third step, we will validate our findings using insights from interviews with various retail industry experts and managers regarding our proposed generic ecosystem.

4 Preliminary Results

Table 1. Roles in the retail ecosystem

Role		Description	Examples
Retail	Online retailer	Retailer with online point-of-sale	Otto
	Branch retailer	Brick-and-mortar retailer with different branches	Kaufland
	Multi-channel retailer	Brick-and-mortar retailer with additional online retail channels	Tchibo
Information technology Solution provider		Company providing software systems to retailers or producers	Aifora
Service provider		External service provider offering outsourcing possibilities	Ströer Media
Project/Initiative		Project/Initiative supporting retail	Trusted Shops
Store equipment provider		Company providing in-store fixtures or equipment	Locafox
Producer		Company producing goods, selling to end-customers, or retail	Hugo Boss
Data supplier		Company providing consumer information	Loyalty Partner
Research		Market research institute	Gfk
Logistics		Company transporting goods	Kühne + Nagel
Consumer		Consumers purchase goods, paying with money, data, or both	-

The analysis of the dataset of companies derived from Crunchbase yielded 13 different roles constituting the German retail ecosystem. The identified roles and their corresponding descriptions and examples are listed in Table 1 above. To create a generic ecosystem applicable to all actors involved, we provisionally did not differentiate between business models (BMs) but instead subdivided the *Retail* market segment into three different actors based on their point-of-sale influencing connections with other actors. The value exchange between all actors is characterized by interchanging goods and services for money and data. Combining all analyzed elements, Fig. 1 depicts the e^3-value model of Germany's retail ecosystem.

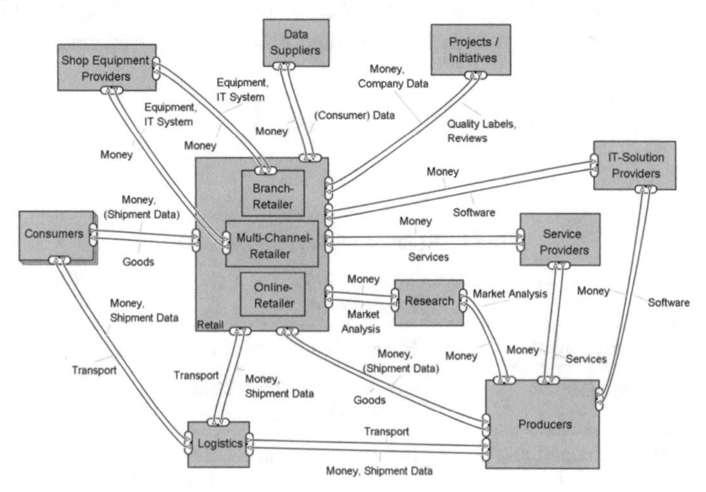

Fig. 1. e^3-value model of the retail ecosystem

5 Contributions and Future Research

This short paper applies an ecosystem perspective to Germany's retail industry. To support practitioners and researchers regarding the DT of retail, this study proposes a model for the retail industry's generic ecosystem. When fully developed and validated by experts, this research will contribute to IS research by providing an overview of the avenues available for digitally transforming store-based retail BMs. It contextualizes existing ecosystem research to the retail industry. The model can then be used by scholars for future research, eg. as a starting-point for in-depth case studies. For practitioners, it supplies initial guidance for forging new partnerships to co-create value in interconnected, digital ecosystems. However, future research is necessary to clearly outline the strategic potentials of value co-creation in the retail ecosystem.

In the next steps, we will enhance our ecosystem model by increasing our dataset and by focusing on BMs that influence omni-channel retailing. We will complete the third step of our methodology by validating the proposed ecosystem with industry experts. Thereby, we will draw from [42], to deeply investigate the value creation process in retail and its implications for the several actors involved and address the limitation of the high level of analysis of e^3-modelling. We aim to propose a model that is useful for both research and practice. Based on our theoretical considerations of the ecosystem perspective's value to retail and identified value exchange, we furthermore seek to contribute strategic implications for the actors involved. Thereby, we consider previous research by [41] and [43] to identify and analyze linkages to other ecosystems.

References

1. Lucas, H., Agarwal, R., Clemons, E., Sawy, O., Weber, B.: Impactful research on transformational information technology: an opportunity to inform new audiences. MIS Q. **37**, 371–382 (2013)
2. Kolf, F.: Der Einzelhandel droht 2019 zum Opfer der Digitalisierung zu werden. Handelsblatt. Handelsblatt GmbH, Düsseldorf (2019)
3. Lemon, K.N., Verhoef, P.C.: Understanding customer experience throughout the customer journey. J. Mark. **80**, 69–96 (2016)
4. Hansen, R., Sia, S.: Hummel's digital transformation toward omnichannel retailing: key lessons learned. MIS Q. Exec. **14**, 51–66 (2015)
5. Böttcher, T., Weking, J.: Identifying antecedents and outcomes of digital business model innovation. In: 28th European Conference on Information Systems, Marrakesh (2020)
6. Benbya, H., Nan, N., Tanriverdi, H., Yoo, Y.: Complexity and information systems research in the emerging digital world. MIS Q. (2020)
7. Hein, A., et al.: Digital platform ecosystems. Electron. Mark. **30**(1), 87–98 (2019). https://doi.org/10.1007/s12525-019-00377-4
8. Hein, A., Weking, J., Schreieck, M., Wiesche, M., Böhm, M., Krcmar, H.: Value co-creation practices in business-to-business platform ecosystems. Electron. Mark. **29**(3), 503–518 (2019). https://doi.org/10.1007/s12525-019-00337-y
9. Ganco, M., Kapoor, R., Lee, G.: From rugged landscapes to rugged ecosystems: structure of interdependencies and firms' innovative search. Acad. Manag. Rev. **45**, 646–674 (2019)
10. Linden, G., Kraemer, K.L., Dedrick, J.: Who captures value in a global innovation network? the case of apple's iPod. Commun. ACM **52**, 140–144 (2009)
11. Hein, A., Böhm, M., Krcmar, H.: Tight and loose coupling in evolving platform ecosystems: the cases of Airbnb and Uber. In: Abramowicz, W., Paschke, A. (eds.) BIS 2018. LNBIP, vol. 320, pp. 295–306. Springer, Cham (2018). https://doi.org/10.1007/978-3-319-93931-5_21
12. Bogers, M., Sims, J., West, J.: What is an ecosystem? incorporating 25 years of ecosystem research. Acad. Manag. Proc. **2019**, 11080 (2019)
13. Moore, J.: Predators and prey: a new ecology of competition. Harv. Bus. Rev. **71**, 75–86 (1993)
14. Jacobides, M.G., Cennamo, C., Gawer, A.: Towards a theory of ecosystems. Strateg. Manag. J. **39**, 2255–2276 (2018)
15. Henfridsson, O., Nandhakumar, J., Scarbrough, H., Panourgias, N.: Recombination in the open-ended value landscape of digital innovation. Inf. Organ. **28**, 89–100 (2018)
16. Nambisan, S.: Architecture vs. ecosystem perspectives: reflections on digital innovation. Inf. Organ. **28**, 104–106 (2018)
17. Enkel, E., Bogers, M., Chesbrough, H.: Exploring open innovation in the digital age: a maturity model and future research directions. R&D Manag. **50**, 161–168 (2020)
18. Shipilov, A., Gawer, A.: Integrating research on inter-organizational networks and ecosystems. Acad. Manag. Ann. **14**, 92–121 (2019)
19. Kapoor, R.: Ecosystems: broadening the locus of value creation. J. Organ. Des. **7**, 12 (2018)
20. Amit, R., Zott, C.: Value creation in e-business. Strateg. Manag. J. **22**, 493–520 (2001)

21. Barua, A., Konana, P., Whinston, A.B., Yin, F.: An empirical investigation of net-enabled business value. MIS Q. **28**, 585–620 (2004)
22. Brynjolfsson, E., Hu, Y., Smith, M.D.: Consumer surplus in the digital economy: estimating the value of increased product variety at online booksellers. Manag. Sci. **49**, 1580–1596 (2003)
23. Zott, C., Amit, R., Donlevy, J.: Strategies for value creation in e-commerce. Eur. Manag. J. **18**, 463–475 (2000)
24. Hänninen, M., Smedlund, A., Mitronen, L.: Digitalization in retailing: multi-sided platforms as drivers of industry transformation. Balt. J. Manag. **13**, 152–168 (2018)
25. Cusumano, M.A., Yoffie, D.B., Gawer, A.: The Future of Platforms. MIT Sloan Management Review, Cambridge (2020)
26. Iansiti, M., Lakhani, K.R.: From disruption to collision: the new competitive dynamics. MIT Sloan Manag. Rev. **61**, 34–39 (2020)
27. Bradlow, E.T., Gangwar, M., Kopalle, P., Voleti, S.: The role of big data and predictive analytics in retailing. J. Retail. **93**, 79–95 (2017)
28. Fichman, R.G., Dos Santos, B.L., Zheng, Z.: Digital innovation as a fundamental and powerful concept in the information systems curriculum. MIS Q. **38**, 329-A315 (2014)
29. Weber, M., Kowalkiewicz, M., Weking, J., Böhm, M., Krcmar, H.: When algorithms go shopping: analyzing business models for highly autonomous consumer buying agents. In: 15th International Conference on Wirtschaftsinformatik, Potsdam (2020)
30. Reinartz, W., Wiegand, N., Imschloss, M.: The Impact of digital transformation on the retailing value chain. Int. J. Res. Mark. **36**, 350–366 (2019)
31. Blom, A., Lange, F., Hess, R.L., Jr.: Omnichannel-based promotions' effects on purchase behavior and brand image. J. Retail. Consum. Serv. **39**, 286–295 (2017)
32. Fuentes, C., Bäckström, K., Svingstedt, A.: Smartphones and the reconfiguration of retailscapes: stores, shopping, and digitalization. J. Retail. Consum. Serv. **39**, 270–278 (2017)
33. Hernant, M., Rosengren, S.: Now what? evaluating the sales effects of introducing an online store. J. Retail. Consum. Serv. **39**, 305–313 (2017)
34. Grewal, D., Roggeveen, A.L., Sisodia, R., Nordfält, J.: Enhancing customer engagement through consciousness. J. Retail. **93**, 55–64 (2017)
35. Hagberg, J., Sundström, M., Nicklas, E.-Z.: The digitalization of retailing: an exploratory framework. Int. J. Retail Distrib. Manag. **44**, 694–712 (2016)
36. Hagberg, J., Jonsson, A., Egels-Zandén, N.: Retail digitalization: implications for physical stores. J. Retail. Consum. Serv. **39**, 264–269 (2017)
37. Riasanow, T., Galic, G., Böhm, M.: Digital transformation in the automotive industry: towards a generic value network. In: 25th European Conference on Information Systems (ECIS), Guimaraes (2017)
38. Miles, M.B., Huberman, A.M.: Qualitative Data Analysis: An Expanded Sourcebook. Sage Publications Inc, Thousand Oaks (1994)
39. Mayring, P.: Qualitative Inhaltsanalyse. VS Verlag für Sozialwissenschaften, Wiesbaden (2010)
40. Gordijn, J., Akkermans, H.: Value-based requirements engineering: exploring innovative e-commerce idea. Requirements Eng. **8**, 114–134 (2003)
41. Riasanow, T., Jäntgen, L., Hermes, S., Böhm, M., Krcmar, H.: Core, intertwined, and ecosystem-specific clusters in platform ecosystems: analyzing similarities in the digital transformation of the automotive, blockchain, financial, insurance and IIoT industry. Electron. Markets **31**, 89–104 (2020)
42. Hermes, S., Riasanow, T., Clemons, E.K., Böhm, M., Krcmar, H.: The digital transformation of the healthcare industry: exploring the rise of emerging platform ecosystems and their influence on the role of patients. Bus. Res. **13**(3), 1033–1069 (2020)
43. Schulz, T., Gewald, H., Böhm, M., Krcmar, H.: Smart mobility: contradictions in value co-creation. Inf. Syst. Front. (2020). https://doi.org/10.1007/s10796-020-10055-y

The Effect of Personality Traits and Gender Roles on Consumer Channel Choices

Dennis Hummel[1] (✉), Tobias Vogel[2], and Alexander Maedche[1]

[1] Institute of Information Systems and Marketing, Karlsruhe Institute of Technology (KIT), Karlsruhe, Germany
{dennis.hummel,alexander.maedche}@kit.edu

[2] Department of Consumer and Economic Psychology, University of Mannheim, Mannheim, Germany
vogel@uni-mannheim.de

Abstract. With the rise of new technologies, consumers have gained new ways of purchasing goods and services through digital channels. A variety of determinants of channel choices have been assessed in previous studies. Still, the role of the individual consumer characteristics (i.e. personality traits and gender roles) in channel choices remains particularly unclear. Yet, better understanding their role would be beneficial to increase the use of digital channels. In this study, we extend an existing decision-making model by adding individual consumer characteristics as antecedents of the model. We test the proposed hypothesis by analyzing data collected in a lab experiment. We find that certain personality traits and gender roles have a significant effect in the extended model of channel choices. Practitioners can use this knowledge to adapt digital channels to their target groups by addressing personality-specific concerns or motivators.

Keywords: Digital channels · Personality · Gender roles · Channel choices

1 Introduction

The rise of new technologies led to the development of new sales channels, such as the online or mobile channel which are collectively referred to as digital channels. The digital channels offer consumers a multitude of options to search, purchase, and use products and services in different channels [1]. Yet, only 7% of the consumers are "online-only shoppers" while the majority (73%) relied on multiple channels during their shopping journey [2]. The remaining 20% were store-only shoppers [2]. An increase in online-only shoppers would reduce free-riding and channel-switching, and lead to substantial monetary savings for channel providers as transactions in physical channels are more expensive [3].

IS and marketing scholars have analyzed multi-channel consumer behavior and detected a variety of channel properties that function as determinants of channel choices. In addition, existing studies assessed demographical factors to analyze individual differences. Yet, demographics alone are not suitable to explain individual differences in

F. Ahlemann et al. (Eds.): WI 2021, LNISO 46, pp. 147–163, 2021.
https://doi.org/10.1007/978-3-030-86790-4_12

channel choices [4, 5]. However, other individual characteristics might be more applicable, such as personality traits and gender roles. They have served as explanatory or moderating variables in other contexts of online behavior before [6–9]. Moreover, the influence of personality traits or gender roles on channel choices has not been covered before as literature reviews on channel choices have shown [10, 11]. Additionally, personality traits and gender roles are well grounded and researched in the psychological literature and thus suitable to derive sound hypotheses.

Personality traits and gender roles can be assessed through different inventories such as the prominent Big Five Inventory (BFI) [12] or the Bem Sex Role Inventory (BSRI) [13]. Personality traits have an influence in various fields of IS Research, e.g. in various forms of decision support [14], to advance the Technology Acceptance Model [15] or the Theory of Acceptance and Use of Technology [6]. The same accounts for gender and gender roles which are used in IS theories, too [8, 9]. Also from a practical point of view, it is important to understand their role in channel choices as companies nowadays are able to assess personality traits based on social media data [16].

Therefore, extending existing decision-making models in the periphery of channel choices with personality traits and gender roles is important to derive insights for the design of digital channels. Among a variety of such decision-making models [17–19], we identified the basic theoretical framework of Kim et al. [18] to be particularly applicable. It examines the influence of perceived risk, consumer trust and perceived benefits on purchase intentions and the purchase behavior, and it has been used or referenced in various similar decision-making studies before. We extend this model in two ways: with personality traits and gender roles by the following research question:

Research Question*: What is the effect of personality traits and gender roles on consumer decision-making processes of channel choices?*

To answer the research question, we conducted a laboratory experiment with 236 participants in a university laboratory using a multi-channel banking context. The participants had to browse a fictitious banking website and to contract a student loan. The data is analyzed using Structural Equation Modeling (SEM).

Our study provides several contributions to the IS literature. First, it highlights the role of personality traits and gender roles in channel choices and extends an existing decision-making model [18]. We find that agreeableness, neuroticism, extraversion, masculinity and femininity are important antecedents of the channel determinants of perceived risk, trust, and perceived benefits. Thereby, we also replicated the original model, which is based on a survey, in an experimental context. Finally, we generate practical knowledge that can be used for the design of digital channels.

2 Related Work and Theoretical Foundations

2.1 Determinants and Models of Channel Choices

Multi-channel behavior of consumers provides the context for our study as using multiple channels has become the standard case for most consumers while only few consumers are "online-only shoppers" [2]. Within this context, several studies have reviewed the determinants of channel choices and categorized them into different dimensions [10, 11, 20].

One study [20] categorizes the determinants into four groups (channel determinants, purchase specifics, external influences, and individual differences), another study [11] identifies the dimensions of context (including channel determinants), consumer and product. According to the literature reviews, particularly channel determinants play a decisive role in the choice of channels. Hence, they are usually integrated into channel choice or decision-making models.

Based on a systematic literature review (SLR) on channel choices, we found at least ten different models of channel choices or intention to use a channel [17, 18, 21, 22]. The SLR used keyword-based search strings such as "multi-channel" AND "consumer behavior", "multi-channel" AND "purchase decisions" OR "multi-channel behavior" or just "channel choice" in the online databases AIS library, ScienceDirect, EBSCOhost and Google Scholar. The full SLR is published in a separate study [11] and we build on those results. Most models have in common that they use a basic set of main constructs that are anteceded by a variety of more context-dependent constructs, such as perceived privacy protection or privacy concerns [18, 23].

One of the most often used and cited models in e-commerce decision-making is presented by Kim et al. [18]. Their core model theorizes that purchase intentions (in our case channel choices) are based upon perceived risk, perceived benefits and consumer trust. For instance, their study shows that trust has a negative impact on perceived risk which, in turn, has a negative impact on consumers' purchasing decisions. This is in line with other studies that show that channel choices are determined by perceived risk, privacy concerns or trust [1, 17], and particularly in a banking context [24, 25]. Our study replicates the main variables of Kim et al. in a services context as the multi-channel behavior in this context is under-researched [11] and as it would be a valuable finding if the results can be repeated in another industry. Thereby, we also build on other studies in a financial services setting [24, 26] which relied on the same framework of Kim et al. [18] before.

We decided to focus on personality traits and gender roles as they have proven to be important in different online behavior contexts before [6, 8], but have been left out as individual differences by the channel choice literature [11, 20]. Moreover, they are well researched in the psychological literature with the Big Five Inventory and the Bem Sex Role Inventory having each several thousand citations. This enables us to derive sound hypotheses and to discuss our results in relation to previous studies which assessed comparable settings [14, 27, 28]. Finally personality traits, once formed in the young ages, remain stable in the following years, and are only subject to change in the old ages again [29]. This makes them perfect to compare different age groups unlike other constructs that are subject to intertemporal changes.

2.2 Personality Traits and Gender Roles

Personality traits can be conceived as a "neuropsychic structure having the capacity to render many stimuli functionally equivalent, and to initiate and guide equivalent (meaningfully consistent) forms of adaptive and expressive behavior" [30]. Several inventories exist to classify personality traits. The most prominent inventory is the Big Five Inventory (BFI) [12], namely extraversion, agreeableness, conscientiousness, neuroticism, and openness to experience. John and Srivastava [31] provided comprehensible definitions for each trait. *Extraversion* "implies an energetic approach toward the social and material world and includes traits such as sociability, activity, assertiveness, and positive emotionality" (p.30). *Agreeableness* "contrasts a prosocial and communal orientation towards others with antagonism and includes traits such as altruism, tender-mindedness, trust, and modesty" (p.30). *Conscientiousness* "describes socially prescribed impulse control that facilitates task- and goal-directed behavior, such as thinking before acting, delaying gratification, following norms and rules, and planning, organizing, and prioritizing tasks" (p.30). *Neuroticism* "contrasts emotional stability and even-temperedness with negative emotionality, such as feeling anxious, nervous, sad, and tense" (p.30). Finally, *openness* "describes the breadth, depth, originality, and complexity of an individual's mental and experiential life" (p.30).

In addition to personality traits, we consider gender roles due to gender differences in personality traits [32, 33]. IS researchers have frequently used gender differences as an explanatory factor in explaining technology acceptance [8, 9]. To account for this stream, we refer to an existing gender role inventory, the Bem Sex Role Inventory [13]. It uses masculine, feminine and neutral characteristics to classify different sex types. The original questionnaire consisted of 20 masculine, 20 feminine and 20 neutral characteristics that can be used to derive different sex-types, especially feminine and masculine. Feminine-typed individuals score high on characteristics like "affectionate", "sensitive to the needs of others" or "loves children" while masculine-typed persons are associated with being "dominant", "forceful" or "willing to take risks" [13]. The inventory has been refined with more up to date characteristics [34, 35] and used and referenced in IS studies in the past [9, 36].

2.3 Personality Traits and Gender Roles in E-Commerce Environments

Personality traits and gender roles have rarely been used in the channel choice literature. However, they were employed outside of the context of channel choices to investigate consumer behavior in e-commerce and online environments in general. Table 1 shows a subset of prior research of personality traits and gender roles in online environments.

Some researchers in the IS domain have studied personality traits and gender roles. Yet, a systematic investigation is missing, and previous research suffers from several shortcomings. Therefore, we see room for differentiation in several dimensions. Firstly, some researchers have performed qualitative studies by conducting interviews [37] or developing a framework [38]. Secondly, some studies [39–41] did not use established inventories of personality traits such as the BFI, which would be helpful in terms of the reliability of constructs, or when different studies want to be compared. Thirdly, it is important to notice that past studies assessed intentions [14, 40, 42] or a different dependent variable [27, 41], such as online impulse buying. The dependent variable is important as it makes a difference whether consumers can choose between different channels or whether they are only asked about their intentions to use one channel. That is, our research aims to clarify the influence of personality traits and gender roles at an early stage of the buying process. Hence, it is important to investigate their role in channel choices and to study their influence as antecedents of the basic theoretical framework [18], which we build upon and extend.

Table 1. Related work using personality traits and gender roles in online environments

Study	Dependent variable	Type of study	Personality trait/gender role	Quantitative results
[39]	Attitude to online shopping	Quantitative - Survey	Openness to experience, risk-taking propensity	Both personality traits significant effect on DV
[42]	Intention to shop online	Quantitative - Survey	Big Five Inventory (BFI)	Neuro., Openness, and Agreeableness with effect on DV
[38]	Channel preferences	Qualitative - Framework	Not specified	n/a as qualitative framework only
[14]	Intention to disclose information	Quantitative - Lab experiment	Big Five Inventory (BFI)	BFI with direct (indirect) effect on privacy concerns (DV)
[40]	Urge to buy impulsively	Quantitative - Survey	Impulsiveness, normative evaluation, instant gratific	All personality traits significant effect on DV
[27]	Online impulse buying	Quantitative - Survey	Big Five Inventory (BFI)	All personality traits significant effect on DV
[41]	Device usage	Quantitative - Survey	Impulsiveness (I.), need for touch (NFT)	I. higher use of mobile devices, NFT prone to online devices

3 Hypothesis Development

3.1 Replication of Basic Theoretical Framework

First, we replicate the basic theoretical model. Therefore, we replace the purchase intention with the channel choice, and we assume that the channel choice is influenced by the perceived risk, trust, and perceived benefits [18]. In addition, perceived risk mediates the relationship of trust and the channel choice [18]. The original study provides a detailed reasoning for each hypothesis which we adopt without any changes.

***H1a**: A consumer's perceived risk negatively affects the choice of the online channel.*
***H1b**: A consumer's perceived benefits positively affects the choice of online channel.*
***H1c**: A consumer's trust negatively affects the consumer's perceived risk.*
***H1d**: A consumer's trust positively affects the choice of the online channel.*

3.2 Personality Traits as Antecedent of the Basic Theoretical Framework

The second hypothesis aims at the relationship of personality traits and the constructs of the basic theoretical framework [18]. Based on previous studies [14, 42], we assume that personality traits are antecedents of perceived risk, trust, and perceived benefits. We assume that the BFI traits are not directed to one integrated construct. Instead, each trait has different relationships with the relevant constructs (similar to [15]).

In particular, neuroticism is associated with anxiety which is illustrated exemplarily by items such as "worries a lot" or "gets nervous easily" [31]. Consequently, neurotic individuals focus on what might go wrong and tend to overlook the benefits of a new technology. Therefore, neuroticism has a positive relationship towards perceived risk and a negative relationship towards perceived benefits, such that highly neurotic participants perceive digital channels as particularly risky and less beneficial. Extraversion is associated being outgoing. Therefore, introverted participants value the anonymity of digital channels and shy away from social interactions. Thus, extraversion may be negatively correlated with the perceived benefits of digital channels. Moreover, extraverted individuals have higher trust [28]. Agreeableness is based on the assumptions of social compatibility, and of a basic trust in the goodness of people. This also influences the trust of individuals with high agreeableness and leads to a positive relationship towards trust [28]. Based on a previous study, conscientiousness is negatively related to perceived risk [43]. Finally, openness antecedes trust. This follows the idea that "more openness leads to more willingness to embrace new concepts and be more careless with respect to new situations and experience" [28].

Similar to other studies [42] and given that personality traits and channel choices are under-researched, it is not possible to derive a relationship for all connections between the BFI and perceived risk, trust, and perceived benefits. Yet, as the BFI is usually measured with all traits, we also estimate the remaining traits and relationships exploratively [44], but which is not reported in detail due to the page limitation.

H2a*: Neuroticism negatively affects the consumer's perceived benefits.*
H2b*: Neuroticism positively affects the consumer's perceived risk.*
H2c*: Extraversion negatively affects consumer's perceived benefits.*
H2d*: Extraversion positively affects consumer's trust.*
H2e*: Agreeableness positively affects consumer's trust.*
H2f*: Conscientiousness negatively affects perceived risk.*
H2g*: Openness to experience positively affects trust* (Fig. 1).

3.3 Gender Roles as Antecedent of the Basic Theoretical Framework.

In addition to personality traits, we suggest adding gender roles to the basic theoretical framework due to gender differences in personality traits [32, 33]. Thereby, we assume that femininity has a negative influence on perceived benefits. This arises from the computer self-efficacy, which is usually lower among feminine individuals [9, 45], and which impacts perceived ease of use and therefore the perceived benefits [9]. When it comes to perceived risk, individuals with feminine traits are more risk-averse [36, 46]

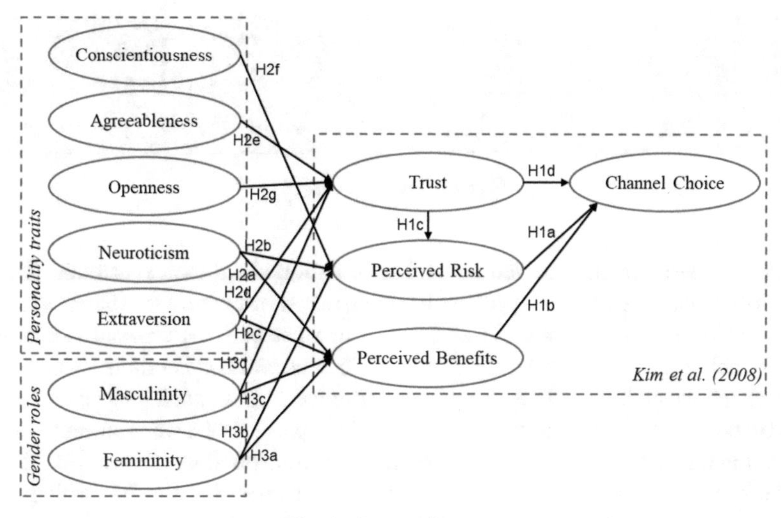

Fig. 1. Research model

which implies a positive relationship of femininity and perceived risk. The hypotheses are supported by the fact that participants with a high score in femininity are socialized to be help-seeking and relationship oriented [9, 47].

In turn, masculinity, which is related to self-efficacy [9, 45], has a positive influence on perceived ease of use and therefore a positive relationship towards perceived benefits [8, 9]. This is also supported by achievement orientation of participants with masculine traits that are usually fulfilled by the benefits of a technology [47]. Further, masculinity has a positive influence on trust as previous studies have shown for an augmented Technology Acceptance Model [8].

H3a*: Femininity negatively affects the consumer's perceived benefits.*
H3b*: Femininity positively affects the consumer's perceived risk.*
H3c*: Masculinity positively affects the consumer's perceived benefits.*
H3d*: Masculinity positively affects the consumer's trust.*

4 Research Methodology

4.1 Experiment Design and Experiment Material

To answer our research question, we conducted an experiment in the KD2Lab (https://www.kd2lab.kit.edu/). Our participants were part of the KD2Lab panel which comprises mainly students studying in Karlsruhe, Germany. In order to become a member of the panel, interested individuals can register themselves. The participants were invited by E-Mail to participate in the study. They received 8€ for their participation. The study consisted of four steps (Fig. 2):

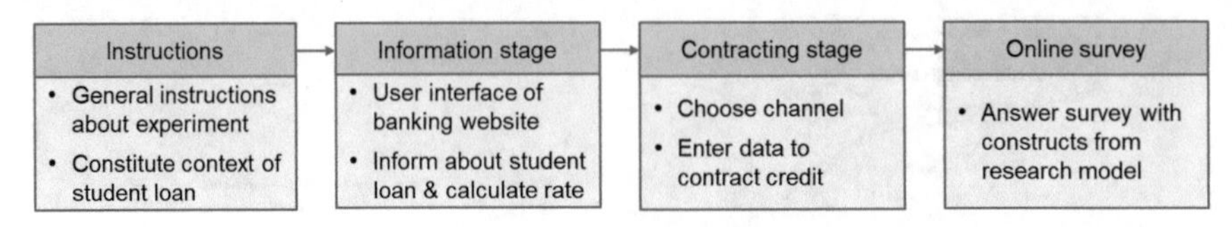

Fig. 2. Research design

First, the participants received general information about the experiment. Thereby, they learned that the experiment covers financial decision-making in a banking context. We have chosen the financial services industry because banking channel structures are currently being reshuffled with major branch closures and considerable investments in digital channels such as online or mobile. Moreover, the financial service of student loans can be contracted online for a few years. Next, participants were presented general information on student loans. These pages have been inspired by the website of a large German bank and made the experiment as realistic as possible for the participants. In the contracting phase, participants had to choose a channel to contract the loan. Next, the participants either had to fill out the loan form on the computer screen or as a paper form. Finally, they completed a survey with the constructs from the research model.

4.2 Measurements

In the experiment, the dependent variable is a channel choice which is operationalized as a binary choice between the online channel and the branch. Additionally, we included a confidence rating asking them how much they inclined towards their decision by presenting this item right after the channel choice in the experiment. For this, we used a seven-point Likert scale ranging from "very weak tendency towards the chosen alternative" to "very strong tendency towards the chosen alternative". For the Structural Equation Modelling (SEM) we used the continuous confidence rating whereas the two seven-point Likert scales (seven-point for branch on the one hand and seven-point for online on the other hand) were scaled-down to one seven-point Likert scale to match the scales of the remaining items.

The constructs of the original model were adapted from the original study. Instead of consumer trust [18], we assessed Internet trust [48] due to the online banking context. The personality traits are based on the BFI using the 42-item questionnaire [31, 49]. Moreover, we measured the BSRI [13] using the 20-item questionnaire [34, 35].

All items were measured using a seven-point Likert scale. As a quality check, we measured further constructs to assess their influence as an alternative explanation for the channel choice. These constructs were personal Internet interest [48], process digitizability [22], information insecurity (new items), and online banking usage [21]. Again, all items, except for online banking usage, were measured using a seven-point Likert scale. Moreover, we asked for age, gender, education, Internet usage, whether and where they contracted a loan in the past, as well as their reasons for the channel choice (open text field). The survey was conducted in German so that some items were forward and backward translated. Several pre-tests of the experiment prototype and the survey were conducted prior to the actual experiment.

4.3 Data Analysis

We used Structural Equation Modelling (SEM) to derive the path estimates. Generally, SEM can be divided into the covariance-based SEM (CB-SEM) and partial least squares SEM (PLS-SEM) which are variance-based [50, 51]. In this study, we used a covariance-based approach. CB-SEM approaches offer a variety of goodness-of-fit indicators and they provide a more reliable evidence for the fit between the theoretical model and the observed empirical data. Moreover, CB-SEM is primarily used for confirmatory research objectives [51]. To do so, we modelled the research model with IBM SPSS Amos 23.0.0 using a maximum likelihood estimation. With a sample size of 236 participants, the experimental study exceeds the threshold of 100, which is suggested for the maximum likelihood estimation in structural equation modelling [52]. We follow the recommendation that the data analysis should comprise the evaluation of the measurement model and the structural model [50, 53]. We used z-scores for the independent variables yielding a consistent threshold value for statistical significance.

5 Results

5.1 Descriptive Analysis

244 participants took part in the laboratory experiment. 8 participants had to be excluded as they failed to answer two test items correctly, or as they showed insufficient language skills in the open text fields. Demographical data showed an age ranging from 16 to 50 years with an average of 24 years. They used the Internet on average 4.8 h per day, and only few participants (12.3%) had contracted a loan before. Hence, pre-knowledge is not a concern. In sum, our sample was more male (59%), younger and higher educated than the German Internet population. Yet, also the original study [18] has a similar age structure and gender distribution with an average age of 22 years and 58% male participants. To replicate and extend their study, we needed a similar sample.

Concerning the channel choices in the experiment, 114 participants (48%) chose the branch, while 122 (52%) participants decided to contract the student loan via the online channel. The online channel was mainly chosen because of its convenience and the speed of closing the transaction. The branch was chosen because of insufficient product knowledge, riskiness of the online channel, and the possibility to clarify open questions.

5.2 Measurement Model, Construct Reliability and Validity

First, the measurement model assessed the reliability, convergent validity as well as the discriminant validity of the relevant constructs. Hence, Cronbach's alpha (Cb. α), the composite reliability (CR), and the average variance extracted (AVE) were estimated.

For Cronbach's alpha, all constructs, except for agreeableness, meet the recommended threshold of 0.70 [54]. Concerning the composite reliability (CR), all constructs, apart from conscientiousness and openness, meet the established cut-off value of 0.70 [55]. Moreover, we calculated the AVE values for each construct as the AVE can be used to estimate the discriminant validity. The AVE values should exceed the threshold of 0.5 [56] which is the case for all constructs except for agreeableness, conscientiousness, openness and masculinity. The implications of the reliability measures will be discussed in the next chapter. The mean values for the personality traits of the BFI are similar to other studies in Germany [49]. Compared with the original study, our sample perceived less risk, had less trust, but slightly higher benefits (Table 2).

Table 2. Measurement model assessment and descriptive statistics

Variable	Construct	Abbr	Cb. α	CR	AVE	Mean	SD
Personality traits	Extraversion	EXT	0.89	0.89	0.51	4.73	1.05
	Agreeableness	AGR	0.64	0.73	0.26	4.72	0.73
	Conscientiousness	CON	0.71	0.31	0.14	4.77	0.77
	Neuroticism	NEU	0.85	0.89	0.53	3.64	1.08
	Openness	OPE	0.72	0.56	0.21	4.84	0.71
Gender roles	Masculinity	MAS	0.88	0.89	0.46	4.72	0.87
	Femininity	FEM	0.89	0.91	0.51	4.88	0.88
Variables original model	Perceived risk	RIS	0.72	0.84	0.64	3.56	1.21
	Trust	TRU	0.70	0.83	0.62	3.91	1.04
	Perceived benefits	BEN	0.79	0.88	0.71	5.80	1.03

In addition, we set up a correlation matrix to be able to compare the inter-construct correlation and the square root of the AVE [56] (see Table 3). The values for the AVE values should exceed the inter-construct correlations for adequate discriminant validity [18, 56]. Note that not all square roots of the AVE exceed the inter-construct correlations, e.g. not for openness and conscientiousness. Again, the implications will be discussed in the next chapter. Overall, the results indicate that the measurement model is appropriate for the research model except for conscientiousness and openness as these constructs fail to meet several criteria. We also estimated the variance inflation factors (VIFs) to control for threats of multicollinearity. However, all VIFs ranged between 1.0 and 1.9, and they were thus below the recommended cutoff value of 5 [50].

The channel choice showed the strongest correlations with perceived risk, perceived benefits and trust which are all constructs from the original model. However, it also shows zero-order correlations with neuroticism, femininity and masculinity. This provides initial support for the predictive value of personality traits and gender roles.

5.3 Structural Model Assessment

Next, following the two-step approach [53], we estimated the structural model. The structural model includes the standardized regression weights for the estimated path coefficients of the model (see Fig. 3 below). Significant paths are presented in bold. The structural model shows that the basic theoretical framework has significant effects between trust, perceived risk, perceived benefits and channel choice. In particular, trust

Table 3. Inter-construct correlation matrix (square root of AVE in bold); CHO = choice

	EXT	AGR	CON	NEU	OPE	MAS	FEM	RIS	BEN	TRU
EXT	**0.71**									
AGR	0.25	**0.51**								
CON	0.28	0.29	**0.37**							
NEU	−0.37	−0.21	−0.25	**0.73**						
OPE	0.31	0.17	0.37	−0.18	**0.46**					
MAS	0.65	0.00	0.35	−0.42	0.38	**0.68**				
FEM	0.25	0.57	0.37	0.01	0.32	0.19	**0.71**			
RIS	−0.06	0.02	−0.03	0.07	0.04	−0.01	0.15	**0.80**		
BEN	0.03	0.04	0.06	−0.25	0.10	0.18	−0.02	−0.16	**0.84**	
TRU	0.04	0.10	−0.03	−0.15	0.02	0.10	0.02	−0.20	0.29	**0.79**
CHO	0.01	−0.04	0.04	−0.17	−0.01	0.14	−0.15	−0.33	0.42	0.34

has a strong negative relationship towards perceived risk while it has a positive relationship towards channel choice. As expected, perceived benefits have a strong positive relationship towards channel choice. The effects have a similar strength compared with the original model. Therefore, hypotheses H1a to H1d are supported.

Concerning the BFI, neuroticism has indeed a strong negative effect on perceived benefits, thus supporting H2a. However, neuroticism does not have a significant positive effect on perceived risk. Hence, H2b is not supported. Similarly, extraversion was expected to negatively affect perceived benefits. The data supports this relationship and thus also H2c is supported. Yet, extraversion shows no significant negative effects on trust. Consequently, H2d is not supported. In turn, agreeableness had a strong positive effect on trust, thus supporting H2e. For the remaining two traits, openness and conscientiousness, we could not find any significant paths. So overall, hypotheses H2a, H2c and H2e are supported, while hypotheses H2b, H2d, H2f, and H2g are not.

Finally, we turn to the BSRI. The relationship of masculinity and trust as well as masculinity and perceived benefits is positive and significant. Thus, hypotheses H3c and H3d are supported. In addition, we predicted a positive relationship of femininity and perceived risk. The data supports this relationship and hence H3b is supported. Only the relationship of femininity and perceived benefits is insignificant. Overall, hypotheses H3b to H3d are supported, but hypothesis H3a is not. We conclude that perceived benefits and trust are significantly anteceded by several personality traits and gender roles. This conclusion still holds true when the model is calculated with all possible combinations between personality traits, gender roles, and the original model.

Finally, we report further results on channel choices using control variables. We could only find marginal differences in the results when controlling for demographics. Thereby, the results do not differ significantly in terms of age, gender, or education.

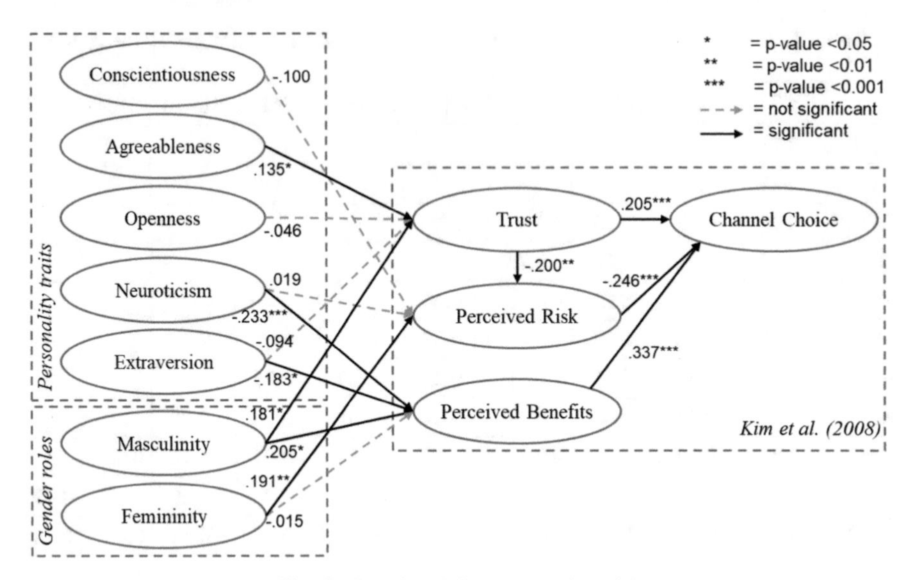

Fig. 3. Results of the structural model

6 Discussion

Overall, we have shown that personality traits and gender roles antecede established constructs of the decision-making model. The results are discussed in three ways:

First, the personality traits generally show an effect on trust and perceived benefits. Let us first have a look at neuroticism which negatively affects online channel choices. Neurotic participants are anxious, focus on the negative aspects, and disvalue the benefits of the online channel. In line with our prediction, neurotic people were less likely to choose the online channel (Table 3). The results of the SEM indicate that this effect is explained by the negative relationship with the perceived benefits of the online channel. Surprisingly, neuroticism did not correlate with perceived risk, nor was this path significant in the SEM (Fig. 3 above) as this would have made sense intuitively.

For extraversion, the data supports the negative relationship towards perceived benefits. An explanation might be that less extraverted (i.e. introverted) consumers value the anonymity of the online channel. We offer an alternative explanation that the items for perceived benefits focus on saving time and convenience [18] while extravert individuals are energetic, active and sociable [12, 31]. Hence, there might be a misfit between convenience and the energy/activity. Complementing this explanation, one study [27] found a positive effect of extraversion on online impulse buying. In turn, we find no effect for extraversion and trust which is in line with a previous study [28].

Agreeableness is the trait complies most with our hypotheses. As agreeableness is positively related to trust, we trace this back to the social compatibility and the basic trust in the goodness of people. This is also in line with the finding that participants with high agreeableness also rated the provider of the online channel as slightly more trustworthy. Again, this is in contrast to Bansal et al. [14], and it might either be attributable to the context, or that their study directed all personality traits towards one construct, and not towards the antecedents of the dependent variable.

Finally, no significant relationships, and no correlation with the dependent variable could be found for conscientiousness and openness. Although this is in line with another study [28], it would be premature to refuse that conscientiousness and openness affect the channel choice. The lack of results in the SEM could reflect the poor reliability of these measures. The validity of conscientiousness and openness to experience cannot be discussed appropriately as the reliability is too low.

How about the direct effects of personality traits on channel choice? Based on our correlation matrix, we see that only neuroticism decreases online channel choice. This result might be due to the insecurity of conducting banking services online. Frequently, banks report security issues related to the online banking which might be considered as more severe by neurotic individuals. Yet, we could not find any effects for the other traits of the BFI, which also lacked a correlation with the dependent variable (Table 3).

Secondly, also gender roles seem to play an important role in channel choices. Except for the relationship of femininity and perceived benefits, all relations are significant. To explain these results, we use the gender schema theory [57] which states that societal beliefs lead to the creation of gender schema in the young ages of individuals. Once established, these gender schemas influence the processing of information and the self-esteem which leads to a behavior that is consistent with the gender schema [57]. Hence, individuals have created gender schema towards what is expected of their gender role in terms of risk-aversion and trust. This leads to their positive/negative association with the predictors of channel choices. E.g. the traditional role of men is to be strong, open and independent, which is reflected in a positive link with trust and perceived benefits, similar to other studies [9]. In turn, there were no direct or moderating effects of biological sex, demonstrating the prime relevance of psychological inter-individual differences for understanding channel choices.

We can only speculate how results would differ with a representative sample. We note some gender differences as women showed a slightly higher perceived risk and a higher conscientiousness. Thus, a less male sample could lead to different results for these constructs and could potentially strengthen the effects that were insignificant in this study. For a more detailed discussion of biological sex and gender roles in online channel choices, we also refer to another of our studies [25].

Third, we replicated the original (survey-based) model in an experimental context. This is important as it has been frequently noticed that replications fail or lead to different results [58]. Our replication in an experimental setting with a financial services context strengthens the basic theoretical framework and its generalizability across various industries. As for the extended model including the personality traits and gender roles it is not yet possible to generalize the results for all industries.

7 Conclusion

To conclude, this study makes several contributions. *Theoretically*, the main finding is the extension of the basic theoretical framework [18] with personality traits and gender roles. These personality traits and gender roles involve especially neuroticism, extraversion, agreeableness, masculinity, and femininity. The study highlights that it is not sufficient to design an information system autarkically but that the individual characteristics of the prospective users always have to be taken into account. In addition, we replicated the original model in an experimental context.

Practitioners are a core target group of IS research. Therefore, especially in financial services companies, they benefit from our work by deriving insights for the design of their channels. Our study provides the basis for matching individual characteristics with channel properties given that companies can assess personality traits based on social media data [16]. Then, the benefits of the digital channel, e.g. broad product spectrum or convenience, should be highlighted particularly to introverted consumers or consumers with low neuroticism. In addition, consumers with feminine traits could be reached with risk-reducing messages, privacy and security seals or other IS artefacts.

Our study also has *societal* implications. As more and more (banking) branches are closed, certain personality traits are systematically excluded from technology-based purchasing opportunities as they avoid using digital channels. From an equality perspective, it would be beneficial to outweigh the disparities in channel choices. This can only be solved by investing in capabilities, such as security features, that attract online-distant personality traits and gender roles. Moreover, consumers themselves could save time and reduce information overload by using individualized channels.

A *limitation* of this study is the somewhat artificial setup of a laboratory experiment. As no financial assets were at stake, the participants might not have felt the anxiety of contracting a real student loan. We tackled this problem by urging them to behave as if real money was involved, and by leaving them in the dark about the intention of the study. In addition, the sample is younger and included more students than the Internet population of Germany, but which is in line with the original study [18]. This limits the generalizability of the results but as we aimed for inter-individual differences unrelated to age, this limitation is of minor relevance. Moreover, two personality traits perform poorly in terms of reliability and no conclusions can be drawn for the BFI as a whole. Finally, a banking service might be different from other retail transactions, future research is to show the generalizability of the results.

Future research could test whether personality traits and channel preferences can be compensated by building decision support systems. Therefore, textual or visual decisional guidance could be implemented using seals or digital nudges [59–62]. Moreover, the decision support could be implemented adaptively by first assessing the characteristics and preferences, and then be adapted in real-time to match them. In addition, the trait of extraversion has produced contradicting results and more research is needed to clarify its role in online environments. Finally, the study should be repeated with a representative sample or with other products and services to be able to generalize the results.

Acknowledgements. This work was supported by the Research Alliance "ForDigital" of the Ministry of Sciences and Arts of the State Baden-Württemberg and Commerzbank Group.

References

1. Verhoef, P.C., Neslin, S.A., Vroomen, B.: Multichannel customer management: understanding the research-shopper phenomenon. Int. J. Res. Mark. **24**, 129–148 (2007)
2. Sopadjieva, E., Dholakia, U.M., Benjamin, B.: A Study of 46,000 Shoppers Shows That Omnichannel Retailing Works. https://hbr.org/2017/01/a-study-of-46000-shoppers-shows-that-omnichannel-retailing-works
3. PwC: Rebooting the branch: reinventing branch banking in a multichannel, global environment (2012)
4. Konus, U., Verhoef, P.C., Neslin, S.A.: Multichannel shopper segments and their covariates. J. Retail. **84**, 398–413 (2008)
5. Cortinas, M., Chocarro, R., Villanueva, M.L.: Understanding multi-channel banking customers. J. Bus. Res. **63**, 1215–1221 (2010)
6. Barnett, T., Pearson, A.W., Pearson, R., Kellermanns, F.W.: Five-factor model personality traits as predictors of perceived and actual usage of technology. Eur. J. Inf. Syst. **24**, 374–390 (2015)
7. Johnston, A.C., Warkentin, M., McBride, M., Carter, L.: Dispositional and situational factors: influences on information security policy violations. Eur. J. Inf. Syst. **25**, 231–251 (2016)
8. Cyr, D., Gefen, D., Walczuch, R.: Exploring the relative impact of biological sex and masculinity–femininity values on information technology use. Behav. Sci. Policy **36**, 178–193 (2017)
9. Venkatesh, V., Morris, M.G.: Why don't men ever stop to ask for directions? Gender, social influence, and their role in technology acceptance and usage behavior. MIS Q. **24**, 115–139 (2000)
10. Neslin, S.A., et al.: Challenges and opportunities in multichannel customer management. J. Serv. Res. **9**, 95–112 (2006)
11. Hummel, D., Schacht, S., Maedche, A.: Determinants of multi-channel behavior: exploring avenues for future research in the services industry. In: ICIS Proceedings, pp. 1–12 (2016)
12. McCrae, R.R., John, O.P.: An introduction to the five-factor model and its applications. J. Pers. **60**, 175–215 (1992)
13. Bem, S.L.: The measurement of psychological androgyny. J. Consult. Clin. Psychol. **42**, 155–162 (1974)
14. Bansal, G., Zahedi, F.M., Gefen, D.: The impact of personal dispositions on information sensitivity, privacy concern and trust in disclosing health information online. Decis. Support Syst. **49**, 138–150 (2010)
15. Svendsen, G.B., Johnsen, J.A.K., Almås-Sørensen, L., Vittersø, J.: Personality and technology acceptance: the influence of personality factors on the core constructs of the Technology Acceptance Model. Behav. Inf. Technol. **32**, 323–334 (2013)
16. Markovikj, D., Gievska, S., Kosinski, M., Stillwell, D.: Mining Facebook data for predictive personality modeling. In: Proceedings of the 7th International AAAI Conference on Weblogs and Social Media (ICWSM), Boston, Massachusetts, USA, pp. 23–26 (2013)
17. Gupta, A., Su, B., Walter, Z.: An empirical study of consumer switching from traditional to electronic channels: a purchase-decision process perspective. Int. J. Electr. Commerce **8**, 131–161 (2004)
18. Kim, D.J., Ferrin, D.L., Rao, H.R.: A trust-based consumer decision-making model in electronic commerce: the role of trust, perceived risk, and their antecedents. Decis. Support Syst. **44**, 544–564 (2008)
19. Chou, S.-Y., Shen, G.C., Chiu, H., Chou, Y.: Multichannel service providers' strategy: understanding customers' switching and free-riding behavior. J. Bus. Res. **69**, 2226–2232 (2016)

20. Trenz, M., Veit, D.: Multichannel integration services: consumer decision making in integrated sales channels. In: ICIS Proceedings, pp. 1–20 (2015)
21. Fang, X., Chan, S., Brzezinski, J., Xu, S.: Moderating effects of task type on wireless technology acceptance. J. Manage. Inf. Syst. **22**, 123–157 (2006)
22. Graupner, E., Maedche, A.: Process digitisation in retail banking: an empirical examination of process virtualization theory. Int. J. Electr. Bus. **12**, 364–379 (2015)
23. Ozdemir, Z.D., Smith, H.J., Benamati, J.H.: Antecedents and outcomes of information privacy concerns in a peer context: an exploratory study. Eur. J. Inf. Syst. **26**, 642–660 (2017)
24. Luo, X., Li, H., Zhang, J., Shim, J.P.: Examining multi-dimensional trust and multi-faceted risk in initial acceptance of emerging technologies: an empirical study of mobile banking services. Decis. Support Syst. **49**, 222–234 (2010)
25. Hummel, D., Herbertz, S., Maedche, A.: Biological sex vs. psychological gender-roles in online channel choices: evidence form two studies in the financial services industry. In: GenderIT Proceedings, pp. 199–208 (2018)
26. Yoon, H.S., Barker Steege, L.M.: Development of a quantitative model of the impact of customers' personality and perceptions on Internet banking use. Comput. Hum. Behav. **29**, 1133–1141 (2013)
27. Turkyilmaz, C.A., Erdem, S., Uslu, A.: The effects of personality traits and website quality on online impulse buying. Proc. Soc. Behav. Sci. **175**, 98–105 (2015)
28. Walczuch, R., Lundgren, H.: Psychological antecedents of institution-based consumer trust in e-retailing. Inf. Manage. **42**, 159–177 (2004)
29. Specht, J., Egloff, B., Schmukle, S.C.: Stability and change of personality across the life course: the impact of age and major life events on mean-level and rank-order stability of the big five. J. Pers. Soc. Psychol. **101**, 862 (2011)
30. Allport, G.W.: Pattern and Growth in Personality. Holt Rinehart and Winston, New York (1961)
31. John, O.P., Srivastava, S.: The big-five trait taxonomy: history, measurement, and theoretical perspectives. In: Pervin, L., John, O.P. (eds.) Handbook of Personality: Theory and Research. Guilford, New York (1999)
32. Weisberg, Y.J., Deyoung, C.G., Hirsh, J.B.: Gender differences in personality across the ten aspects of the Big Five. Front. Psychol. **2**, 1–11 (2011)
33. Giudice, M.D., Booth, T., Irwing, P.: The distance between mars and venus: measuring global sex differences in personality. PLOS ONE **7**, e29265 (2012)
34. Hunt, K., Lewars, H., Emslie, C., Batty, G.D.: Decreased risk of death from coronary heart disease amongst men with higher "femininity" scores: a general population cohort study. Int. J. Epidemiol. **36**, 612–620 (2007)
35. Sieverding, M.: Gender. In: Handbuch der Gesundheitspsychologie und Medizinischen Psychologie, pp. 130–138. Jürgen Bengel und Matthias Jerusalem (2009)
36. Aguirre-Urreta, M.I., Marakas, G.M.: Is it really gender? An empirical investigation into gender effects in technology adoption through the examination of individual differences. Hum. Technol. **6**, 155–190 (2010)
37. Pieterson, W., van Dijk, J.: Channel choice determinants: an exploration of the factors that determine the choice of a service channel in citizen initiated contacts. In: Digital Government Research Proceedings, pp. 173–182 (2007).
38. Florenthal, B., Shoham, A.: Four-mode channel interactivity concept and channel preferences. J. Serv. Mark. **24**, 29–41 (2010)
39. Wang, S., Wang, S., Wang, M.T.: Shopping online or not? Cognition and personality matters. J. Theoret. Appl. Electr. Commerce Res. **1**, 68–80 (2006)
40. Liu, Y., Li, H., Hu, F.: Website attributes in urging online impulse purchase: an empirical investigation on consumer perceptions. Decis. Support Syst. **55**, 829–837 (2013)

41. Rodríguez-Torrico, P., San José Cabezudo, R., San-Martín, S.: Tell me what they are like and I will tell you where they buy. An analysis of omnichannel consumer behavior. Comput. Hum. Behav. **68**, 465–471 (2017)
42. Bosnjak, M., Galesic, M., Tuten, T.: Personality determinants of online shopping: explaining online purchase intentions using a hierarchical approach. J. Bus. Res. **60**, 597–605 (2007)
43. Hampson, S.E., Andrews, J.A., Barckley, M., Lichtenstein, E., Lee, M.E.: Personality traits, perceived risk, and risk-reduction behaviors: a further study on smoking and radon. Health Psychol. **25**, 530–536 (2006)
44. Vogel, T., Hütter, M., Gebauer, J.E.: Is evaluative conditioning moderated by Big Five personality traits? Soc. Psychol. Pers. Sci. **10**, 1–9 (2017)
45. Venkatesh, V., Davis, F.D.: A model of the antecedents of perceived ease of use: development and test. Decision Sci. **27**, 451–481 (1996)
46. Inman, J.J., Shankar, V., Ferraro, R.: The roles of channel-category associations and geodemographics in channel patronage. J. Market. **68**, 51–71 (2004)
47. Diehl, M., Owen, S.K., Youngblade, L.M.: Agency and communion attributes in adults' spontaneous self-representations. Int. J. Behav. Dev. **28**, 1–15 (2004)
48. Dinev, T., Hart, P.: An extended privacy calculus model for E-commerce transactions. Inf. Syst. Res. **17**, 61–80 (2006)
49. Lang, F.R., Lüdtke, O., Asendorpf, J.B.: Testgüte und psychometrische Äquivalenz der deutschen Version des Big Five Inventory (BFI) bei jungen, mittelalten und alten Erwachsenen. Diagnostica **47**, 111–121 (2001)
50. Hair, J.F., Ringle, C.M., Sarstedt, M.: PLS-SEM: indeed a silver bullet. J. Market. Theory Pract. **19**, 139–152 (2011)
51. Hair, J.F., Hult, G.T.M., Ringle, C.M., Sarstedt, M.: A Primer on Partial Least Squares Structural Equation Modeling (PLS-SEM). SAGE Publications Ltd, Los Angeles (2017)
52. Hair, J.F., Anderson, R., Tatham, R., Black, W.: Multivariate Data Analysis. Prentice-Hall, Englewood Cliffs (1998)
53. Anderson, J.C., Gerbing, D.W.: Structural equation modeling in practice: a review and recommended two-step approach. Psychol. Bull. **103**, 411–423 (1988)
54. Bearden, W.O., Nirshleifer, R.G., Mobely, M.F.: Handbook of Marketing Scales: Multi-Item Measures for Marketing and Consumer Behavior Research. Sage Publications, Newbury Park (1993)
55. Nunnally, J.C., Bernstein, I.H.: Psychometric Theory. McGraw-Hill, New York (1994)
56. Fornell, C., Larcker, D.F.: Evaluating structural equation models with unobservable variables and measurement error. J. Mark. Res. **18**, 39 (1981)
57. Bem, S.L.: Gender schema theory: a cognitive account of sex typing. Psychol. Rev. **88**, 354–364 (1981)
58. Erdfelder, E.: Fallstricke statistischer Signifikanz: Wissenschaftliche Fachzeitschriften und die Replikationskrise. Forschung und Lehre **2**, 1–6 (2018)
59. Ingendahl, M., Hummel, D., Maedche, A., Vogel, T.: Who can be nudged? Examining nudging effectiveness in the context of need for cognition and need for uniqueness. J. Consumer Behav. **20**, 324–336 (2020)
60. Hummel, D., Toreini, P., Maedche, A.: Improving digital nudging using attentive user interfaces: theory development and experiment design. In: DESRIST Proceedings, pp. 1–8 (2018)
61. Hummel, D., Schacht, S., Maedche, A.: Designing adaptive nudges for multi-channel choices of digital services: a laboratory experiment design. In: ECIS Proceedings, pp. 1–12 (2017)
62. Hummel, D., Maedche, A.: How effective is nudging? A quantitative review on the effect sizes and limits of empirical nudging studies. J. Behav. Exp. Econ. **80**, 47–58 (2019)

Digital Services and Smart Product-Service Systems

Introduction to the WI2021 Track: Digital Services and Smart Product-Service Systems

Jens Poeppelbuss[1], Susanne Robra-Bissantz[2], and Tilo Böhmann[3]

[1] Ruhr-Universität Bochum, Department of Mechanical Engineering, Bochum, Germany
jens.poeppelbuss@isse.rub.de
[2] TU Braunschweig, Carl-Friedrich-Gauß-Fakultät, Braunschweig, Germany
s.robra-bissantz@tu-bs.de
[3] Universität Hamburg, Department of Informatics, Hamburg, Germany
tilo.boehmann@uni-hamburg.de

1 Track Description

Digital services are becoming increasingly important in business-to-business relationships and our private life. Virtual services complement or replace real services. They can fulfill customer demands more effectively, efficiently or in completely new ways and, hence, can lead to novel value propositions of various kinds. Moreover, through digitalization and the connectivity of so-called smart products, the key idea of product-service systems (PSS) as customer-oriented, integrated bundles of goods and services can now be put into practice better than ever before. Well-known examples of such smart PSS are telematics-supported car insurance, audio and video streaming services or predictive maintenance of industrial machinery and equipment. At the same time, the complexity of initiating, developing and providing digital services as well as smart PSS is increasing because they require the close integration of the resources of multiple actors, including those of customers and partners.

This track includes articles that report important and timely results from studies that investigate the innovation with digital services and smart PSS in a variety of settings. The articles include conceptual, design-oriented as well as qualitative-empirical studies with implications that are meaningful for both academia and practice.

2 Research Articles

The articles of this track cover several topics that refer to the design of digital services and smart PSS. While Häckel et al. take an overarching view by developing a PSS maturity model that can guide capability development in organizations, Richter and Anke as well as Sengewald et al. contribute to making the actual service design process more effective and efficient. Finally, Osterbrink et al. specifically deal with the use of augmented reality technology to support safety-critical services in a harbor.

2.1 Becoming a Product-Service System Provider – A Maturity Model for Manufacturers (Häckel, Huber, Stahl & Stöter)

For manufacturing firms, the digital transformation often goes hand in hand with servitization. They change from being a supplier of physical products to a provider of PSS and, hence, have to advance their organizational capabilities. To guide this organizational transformation process, Häckel et al. present a comprehensive PSS Maturity Model (PSSMM) that is comprised of five focus areas (strategy, culture, structure, practice, and IT), 20 capability dimensions, and capability descriptions along four maturity levels from a pure-product firm to a provider of result-oriented PSS.

2.2 Combining Methods for the Design of Digital Services in Practice: Experiences from a Predictive Costing Service (Richter & Anke)

Although academia has proposed various processes and methods that firms can use to develop innovative digital service and PSS offerings, it appears that practitioners still struggle to adopt and apply them. In their study, Richter and Anke follow an action design research approach to evaluate how existing methods can be applied successfully. For this purpose, they collaborated with a medium-sized firm in a project that aimed at designing a service for predictive costing. They suggest a selection of methods and an overview of their input-output-relationships that can support the systematic design of new digital services in practice.

2.3 A Software Ecosystem for the Development of Digital Service Design Tools: A Conceptual Framework (Sengewald, Jalowski & Schymanietz)

Sengewald et al. deal with the digitization of the service design process itself. Their study is based on the observation that an interoperable set of digital artifacts is still missing that would support the use of service design tools, techniques, and methods (e.g., Personas, Service Blueprinting, Stakeholder Maps). To address this challenge, they suggest a framework that outlines five design objectives and that can provide a foundation for a software ecosystem of digital service design tools.

2.4 Requirements for Augmented Reality Solutions for Safety-Critical Services – The Case of Water Depth Management in a Maritime Logistics Hub (Osterbrink, Bräker, Semmann & Wiesche)

The study by Osterbrink et al. explores the user-centered requirements for augmented reality (AR) solutions in the operations of a large European maritime logistics hub. Based on qualitative data from eleven think-aloud sessions during service delivery, two expert interviews, and two expert workshops, they derived five core requirements for an AR solution in soil sounding, which is the measuring of water depths in a harbor environment. Their study is among the first that investigates the applicability and feasibility of AR solutions in the maritime industry. The identified requirements are expected to impact research on AR use especially in safety-critical environments.

Becoming a Product-Service System Provider – A Maturity Model for Manufacturers

Björn Häckel[1], Rocco Huber[2], Bastian Stahl[1], and Maximilian Stöter[2](✉)

[1] FIM Research Center, Project Group Business & Information Systems Engineering of the Fraunhofer FIT, University of Applied Sciences Augsburg, Augsburg, Germany
{bjoern.haeckel,bastian.stahl}@fim-rc.de

[2] FIM Research Center, Project Group Business & Information Systems Engineering of the Fraunhofer FIT, University of Augsburg, Augsburg, Germany
{rocco.huber,maximilian.stoeter}@fit.fraunhofer.de

Abstract. For the manufacturing industry, exploiting the opportunities of digital transformation often implies the strategic development from being a manufacturer of pure physical products to one providing Product-Service Systems (PSS). In literature, PSS can be distinguished in different types, which differ substantially in their configuration of the underlying business model. However, since distinct PSS types require different organizational capabilities, the transformation toward a PSS provider is a challenge for managers. To provide guidance, scientific and professional literature mostly focuses on selected aspects. Though, a holistic consideration of relevant capabilities for the respective PSS type remains untapped. Against this backdrop, we developed a PSS Maturity Model (PSSMM) to guide organizations in developing appropriate capabilities. To provide an integrated view, the PSSMM refers to 5 focus areas, 20 capability dimensions, and associated capabilities. To develop and evaluate our model, we used the well-known approach of Becker et al. [1].

Keywords: Product-Service Systems · Maturity model · Industry · Digital transformation

1 Introduction

In the context of digital transformation in production, the development of Product-Service Systems (PSS) represents a well-established strategy for manufacturing companies to harness the various opportunities associated with digitalization. To tap new revenue pools and differentiate themselves against competitors, manufacturers are working on enriching their physical products with digital services to increase customer utility [2, 3]. PSS not only enable a higher degree of customization and product quality but also allow for novel value propositions and new data-driven business models (BM) [4]. For instance, models such as Rolls-Royce's "power-by-the-hour" for aircraft engines [5] or Ricoh's "pay per page green" for printing services [6] are examples of successful PSS implementations. Especially for manufacturers, digitalization is a significant driver

F. Ahlemann et al. (Eds.): WI 2021, LNISO 46, pp. 169–184, 2021.
https://doi.org/10.1007/978-3-030-86790-4_13

for PSS [7]. This is demonstrated by the "pay-per-part model" of the German machine manufacturer Trumpf, which provides its customers with laser sheet metal processing without having them to buy or lease equipment [8]. Digital technologies enable novel value propositions and services such as remote and automatic access to machine statuses, proactive detection of failures, and success measurement, facilitating PSS [9]. As physical products often form the core of the existing BM, especially for established companies and market incumbents, these companies are maturing toward more servitization [10].

Hence, along with the increasing degree of servitization, the literature distinguishes three established PSS types: product-, use-, and result-oriented PSS [4, 11, 12]. Challenges arise as the three types of PSS require different capabilities within the organization. The complexity of designing, implementing, and operating these integrated product-service bundles requires holistic guidance on which capabilities need to be developed across organizational departments and levels.

In order to guide organizations in the identification, prioritization, and development of relevant capabilities, Maturity Models (MM) have proven to be a useful management tool [13]. As research on PSS is mature [14], MMs dealing with PSS or service orientation already exist (e.g., Exner et al. [15], Gudergan et al. [16]). Further, MMs in the context of PSS focus on specific issues such as IS support for PSS [17], sustainability through hybrid solutions [18], or for the service development process related to PSS [19]. Nevertheless, existing literature hitherto neglects to bring together the established PSS types with corresponding capabilities. On the one hand, this makes it difficult for organizations to assess their maturity level to meet the desired PSS type. On the other hand, the existing models do not provide a holistic perspective on capabilities for a targeted PSS type.

Since the existing literature does not offer a combined view on PSS types and corresponding capabilities, we raised the following research question (RQ): *What capabilities do organizations need to develop to offer a certain type of PSS?*

To address this research gap, we developed and evaluated the PSS Maturity Model (PSSMM) and followed the well-known procedure model of Becker et al. [1]. The paper is structured as follows, in Sect. 2, we summarize relevant literature on PSS, MMs, and elaborate on related work for PSS-specific MMs. In Sect. 3, our research methodology is outlined, and in Sect. 4, we present essential design decisions and our developed PSSMM. Next, in Sect. 5, we summarize the pre-evaluation with IS scholars. At the end, Sect. 6 concludes this work with our contributions, limitations, and the outlook for further research.

2 Theoretical Background and Related Work

2.1 Product-Service Systems

There are different terms for PSS in literature, e.g., Industrial Hybrid Offerings and Solutions [2], whereby PSS has become the commonly used expression [14]. Also, there are several definitions of PSS in the literature (e.g., Mont [20], Guidat et al. [21]). Yet, PSS are often defined as a type of BM that integrates bundles of products (tangible component) and services (intangible component) aiming at offering more complete solutions and thereby increasing customer utility [3, 12]. Besides, concepts such as *Servitization* and *Hybrid Value Creation* are often named in this context. Servitization describes the transformational process of moving from a product-oriented to a service-oriented BM for offering product-centric system solutions [2, 12]. In contrast, Hybrid Value Creation refers to the process of creating added value through the combination of products and services [22]. To sum up, PSS can be seen as the operational (Hybrid Value Creation) outcome and the transformational process (Servitization).

Also, PSS are often referred to as the trend of servitization in the manufacturing industry [12] and are associated with closer customer contact, more stable revenue streams, and improved resource utilization [22]. Some work on PSS follows the understanding and perspective of *Service(-dominant) Logic* [23] and focus on the co-creation of value between the service provider and customer. Consequently, they define PSS as *Service Systems* [24]. This may especially be true for mature PSS types that are close to a pure service focused BM. However, this definition neglects companies with a product-oriented PSS type. Therefore, we argue that our work's scope mainly addresses manufacturers that are driving forward service provision. The underlying definition of PSS refers to a BM perspective that defines the value proposition through a combination of the product and connected services and whereby the focus on either the product or services shifts with the responding PSS type.

For PSS, three main types are generally admitted in the literature: (a) *product-oriented*, (b) *use-oriented*, and (c) *result-oriented PSS* [10, 25]. These categories have established themselves in the literature (e.g., Raddats et al. [26], Weking et al. [12]), are used in different contexts (e.g., for BM archetypes [27, 28]), and are of importance for this work as we build our maturity levels upon them. For (a) *product-oriented PSS*, the BM is mainly focused on selling products, and only some additional services are added (e.g., maintenance services) [25]. With (b) *use-oriented PSS*, a product's use or availability is sold [10]. An example of use-oriented PSS is Hilti's fleet management offering, a global business partner offering construction tools. Here, Hilti provides a comprehensive bundle of products and complementary services instead of just selling tools. In doing so, Hilti improves fleet transparency, reduces idle time, and simplifies budgeting for customers, while Hilti profits from higher customer loyalty and interaction as a strategic enabler for growth [29]. And with (c) *result-oriented PSS*, the customer and the supplier agree in advance on the result to be delivered, and the customer only pays for that [25]. An example of this PSS-type is the cooperation of Trumpf, a German industrial machine manufacturing company, and Munich RE, a globally operating reinsurance company. The jointly developed 'pay-per-part model' enables customers to use a full-service laser machine without buying or leasing any equipment. Instead, customers pay a previously agreed price for each part in a pre-defined quality, allowing them to avoid massive up-front investments, minimize resources for maintenance tasks, and make their production processes more flexible [8]. Moving from a product- toward a use- or result-oriented PSS, a customer's need is formulated in more abstract terms. It offers new paths for customization [25], which is enabled by developments in digital technologies (e.g., cloud and edge computing), offering a continuous connection to products and customers [20]. Further, the revenue models and pricing strategies in these PSS types are entirely different, changing from single purchases to constant payment models related to the product's use or result [22]. Therefore, the transformation from being a product manufacturer to becoming a PSS provider calls for far-reaching changes within the organization and especially for new capabilities to be developed.

2.2 Organizational Capabilities and Maturity Models

The resource-based view defines organizations as configurations of resources [30]. Competitive advantage and long-term performance enhancement can be accomplished by providing valuable, unique, inimitable, and non-substitute resources [30] that consist of both assets and capabilities [31]. In this paper, we define capabilities as an organizational entity's ability to perform certain activities to achieve a particular outcome [32]. MMs reflect how organizational capabilities develop [33] while assessing and leading the continuous improvement of various organizational capabilities [34], such as technology, practices, or knowledge in a particular domain [13]. Thus, MMs are instruments to assess the maturity in a specific area by conceptually dividing the presumed development of maturity into different phases [33]. Maturity thereby refers to the status of being ready or complete, and the respective maturity level increases with increasing capabilities [1]. In practice, MMs have high relevance and are widely utilized as a management tool [35] that facilitate planning and stepwise capability development [13] and also improve the decision-making regarding organizational development [34]. In the Information Systems (IS) and Information Technology (IT) domain, MMs are often used either as guidance for continuous improvement or as an assessment tool for self- or third-party evaluation [33, 34]. Besides, there are different types of MMs in literature, including descriptive (status quo assessment and potential target state derivation), comparative (benchmarking), and prescriptive *MMs* (enabling roadmap development and suggesting measures for achieving it). Also, combinations of these types exist, as these different model types represent consecutive stages in a MM's evolution [33, 36].

The general structure of MMs is characterized by a sequence of discrete stages [13] reflecting the expected or desired development path from an initial to a potential target state [1]. MMs are usually conceptualized as matrices, including maturity stages on the one and dimensions (e.g., capabilities) on the other axis [36]. To structure capabilities, *focus areas* can be defined, representing domain-specific capability areas that describe different aspects of the corresponding topic [34] and provide more detail by describing specific capabilities as subcategories (i.e., Capability Dimensions). On the other axis, the maturity levels describe the phases of development arranged in sequential order from the lowest stage of maturity to the highest [36]. The number of maturity stages between the initial and target state is not prescribed and varies in existing MMs. However, most MMs use between four to six stages [36]. Also, MM types can furthermore be distinguished into staged, continuous, and focus area MMs [37, 38]. These reflect different ways of assigning capabilities to maturity stages. Thereby, staged MMs require an assignment of capabilities to exactly one maturity stage. Continuous MMs require the specification of capabilities for all maturity stages. In contrast, focus area MMs inductively derive maturity stages per capability area, where each capability area has its number of specific maturity stages.

2.3 Related MMs in the Field of PSS

As the PSS domain is a mature research area and research has been conducted here for over 20 years [14], several MMs already exist in this research field. MMs, with a focus on PSS, address the increasing service orientation in the sense of maturing from traditional product sales to PSS (e.g., Rapaccini et al. [19], Gudergan et al. [16], Karni et al. [39], Exner et al. [15]). Rapaccini et al. [19] created a MM for the new service development process related to PSS. Gudergan et al. [16] introduce their Business Transformation Readiness Assessment – a MM to assess the readiness for PSS. Karni and Kaner [39] present a Process Capability and Enterprise Maturity Model focusing on PSS. Exner et al. [15] developed a PSS capability self-assessment tool for companies named Product-Service-Change. Other MMs in the context of PSS and servitization address more specific issues concerning IS support for PSS [17, 40], service engineering [41], or sustainability through hybrid solutions [18]. There are already several MMs in the research field of PSS. Still, to the best of our knowledge, there is no MM with a holistic perspective on the organization and that combines its maturity levels with the three different types of PSS, including *product-*, *use-*, and *result-oriented PSS*. Thus, existing MMs do not allow conclusions and provide guidance on how the identified capabilities should be developed concerning an aimed, pre-defined PSS type. Our paper aims at filling this gap. Further, our PSSMM provides a multi-dimensional categorization for PSS capabilities and therefore provides guidance for capability development. Therefore, with this work, we propose a continuous MM that can be used for descriptive and prescriptive purposes [33].

3 Research Methodology and Development Process

The approach of Becker et al. [1] for the development of our MM comprises, as presented in Fig. 1, eight steps that are based on design science research principles by Hevner et al. [42]. The first four phases are central to the design and development of the MM, whereas the second four cover the transfer and evaluation. All in all, this work focuses on phases 1 to 4. The other phases will be carried out in future research. In the following, we briefly explain each phase and how we executed it:

Phase 1, *Problem definition*, examines the motivation for the particular MM and derives an appropriate RQ. We address this phase in our *Introduction*, where the topic's relevance and the need for management guidance, like for our PSSMM, are outlined. Thereby, the key problem is that manufacturers face significant challenges in developing toward a PSS provider. While existing MMs for PSS neglect a holistic perspective on the organization, we propose our PSSMM to fill this gap.

Phase 2, *Comparison of existing MMs,* thematizes the relevance of developing a MM by pointing toward the research gap. The lack of existing approaches is initially addressed in the *Introduction* and then outlined at the end of the *Theoretical Background (see* Sect. 2.3*).*

Phase 3 is the *Determination of the development strategy*. Becker et al. [1] differentiate between four strategies, i.e., (1) design of a new model, (2) enhancement of an existing model, (3) combination of models to form a new one, and (4) the transfer of existing models to new application domains. As mentioned in the *Theoretical Background*, there is no MM in the literature that addresses our purpose and RQ. In this

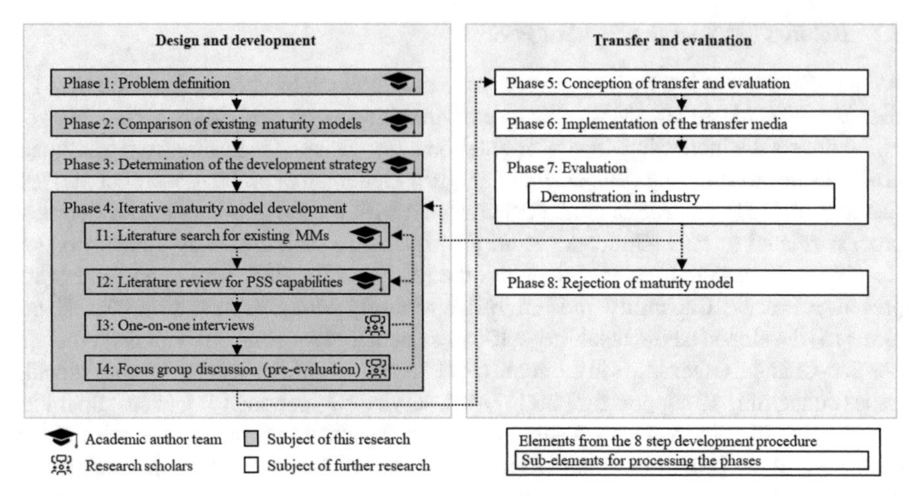

Fig. 1. Applied research approach based on Becker et al. [1]

work, we developed a novel MM (strategy 1) as an artifact based on the insights of existing MMs and additional literature, as neither an existing model was close enough to be enhanced (strategy 2) nor existing models combined (see below) could fulfill the research question.

Within **Phase 4**, the *Iterative MM development*, we – additionally to Becker et al. [1] – considered van Steenbergen et al. [43], as they recommend using a multi-methodological approach for the development of dimension-specific development paths. To assess and integrate different knowledge sources for this manifold topic, we included a literature search and interviews with research scholars [33, 43]. The following figure presents how the development phase of the PSSMM was carried out in four iterations (Fig. 2).

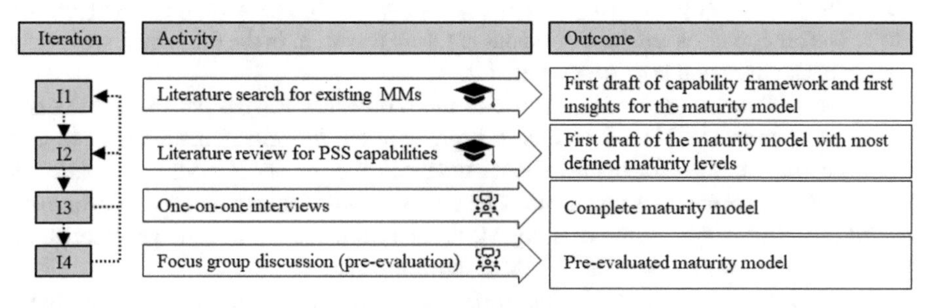

Fig. 2. Applied iterations within the development phase

Within ***Iteration one***, the literature search, we started by identifying existing MMs focused on PSS and related research streams as recommended by Becker et al. [1]. With this iteration, we identified first context-related MMs for PSS and scrutinized those for capabilities and maturity levels related to our research gap. For this, we performed a search on Google Scholar with the following search string: *"product-service system*" OR "PSS" OR "hybrid product*" OR "servitization" OR "hybrid value creation" AND* *"maturity model"*. As a result, we found 15 papers related to MMs for PSS, which came into consideration, e.g., Rapaccini et al. [19], Gudergan et al. [16], Karni and Kaner [39], Exner et al. [15]. To understand and build upon existing work, as recommended by Becker et al. [1], we compared the MMs and partly included them in our MM by identifying relevant capabilities for PSS. Within this bottom-up approach, we identified 180 capabilities for PSS from related MMs. After coding and clustering these capabilities, we came up with 18 capability dimensions within this iteration. We chose this approach because we wanted to develop the MM without being influenced by the different existing MMs on PSS (e.g., on sustainability) and tailor our dimensions toward our research gap, taking a PSS-type specific and holistic view. The interim result here was the first draft of a capability framework with capability dimensions and first insights for the definition of some maturity levels.

Next, with ***Iteration two***, we carried out a literature review for PSS and corresponding capabilities following vom Brocke et al. [44] to ensure that the body of knowledge is covered by existing MMs on PSS but also on recent and domain-specific work. Hence, we applied this by assessing domain-related databases, i.e., ScienceDirect, EBSCOhost, and AISeL, with the following search string: *"product-service system*" OR "PSS" OR "hybrid product*" AND "industrial" AND "capabilit*"*. Thereby, we reviewed 62 articles to identify PSS capabilities. Furthermore, we finished with a forward and backward search to screen the field of research and completed the maturity levels. After carefully reading and screening these publications, we worked out and coded another 72 capabilities from this general PSS literature. Here, 19 capability dimensions were identified. As a result, the first iteration's draft was complemented with the capability dimensions and maturity levels found in literature.

In these first two iterations, all in all, 252 capabilities (= 180 + 72) were found and processed (coded and clustered), which resulted in 37 capability dimensions (18 from existing MMs and 19 from PSS literature). After reducing the duplicates and summarizing similar ones, 20 capability dimensions were finally derived. As we developed a continuous MM, the definition of all maturity levels, including different characteristics, is required to outline each capability dimension's maturation along all stages. We proceeded by using the literature and more specified capabilities.

Iteration three - after developing the second version of the PSSMM and intensively discussing it within the author team, we conducted two interviews with scholars from the IS domain for the understanding and relevance of its focus areas, capability dimensions, as well as each level of maturity. One is specialized in MM development, and the other in digital transformation strategies for manufacturers. The interview partners are summarized in Table 1 (Int 1 and Int 2). Afterward, each proposed model adjustment was critically discussed within the author team and cross-checked with supporting work in literature before including the feedback into the PSSMM.

Iteration four - after reaching consensus among the authors about the maturity of the model, as the interviews brought no significant insights to the MM and instead helped to sharpen the identified capabilities, the MM was pre-evaluated in a focus group discussion with nine domain-specific scholars specialized on PSS and related capabilities (Int 3 in Table 1). Thereby, we used the proposed evaluation criteria of Becker et al. [1], i.e., comprehensiveness, consistency, and problem adequacy. The discussion did not lead to advanced adjustments of the model and underpinned its saturated maturity. This pre-evaluation is addressed in detail in Sect. 5.

Table 1. Interview partner

Interview ID	Type	Expertise	Experience
Int 1	One-on-one interview (n = 1)	Transformation strategies for manufacturers	Junior researcher (1 - 2 years in this field)
Int 2	One-on-one interview (n = 1)	Maturity models and organizational capabilities	Senior researcher (>3 years in this field)
Int 3 (pre-evaluation)	Focus group discussion (n = 9)	Domain focus on Industry 4.0 and PSS BM	PhD students and senior scholars

Phases 5 to 8 are, as mentioned before, not the object of this paper and, thus, the subject of further research. After developing the model, it needs to be tested in a real-world context and evaluated with industry experts for relevance and rigor, including validity and reliability [33]. Also, for guaranteeing broad applicability, the model must be made available in a more general way to investigate its generalizability [1] (phase 5). Next, further evaluations and improvements on wider acceptance are conducted (Phase 6, 7), and finally, a decision on the acceptance or the rejection of the model is made (Phase 8).

4 Product-Service Systems Maturity Model

In the following, we present our PSSMM with its overarching structure by first elaborating on pathbreaking design decisions and afterward outlining each focus area and its associated capability dimensions. At the end of this section, we present the whole PSSMM with its corresponding maturity levels. We developed a continuous MM [33, 37] along the PSS types of Tukker [11, 25]. This design allows reflecting the non-linearity of transformation processes (i.e., being at different maturity stages for different capability dimensions). A certain maturity level thereby describes how a capability in this capability dimension is typically developed within this step (i.e., type of PSS). For the maturity levels, we set the 'pure product' view as the initial stage (1.) that reflects a common starting point of a transformation toward PSS. The three main PSS types [10, 11] represent the remaining maturity levels of our model: product- (2.), use- (3.), and result-oriented PSS (4.). We have arranged the levels 1 to 4 next to each other according to their maturity toward servitization. In doing so, we guide organizations in further developing the needed organizational capabilities (i.e., for service deployment) toward a target type of PSS and do not refer to the commonly used generic maturity levels in existing MMs on PSS (e.g., Rapaccini et al. [19]). As with almost all MMs, the definition of a target state is not primarily dependent on the pursuit of higher levels of maturity, but rather on organization-specific (e.g., customer requirements) as well as economic (e.g., budget) factors. Also, certain PSS types can be skipped or different PSS types can be implemented within the same company, e.g., different markets or customer segments. Further, and in contrast to existing maturity models (e.g., Rapaccini et al. [19], Karni and Kaner [39], Gudergan et al. [16]), our PSSMM aims to demonstrate relevant capabilities for the respective PSS types. Thus, each column offers a detailed specification of the required capabilities for the corresponding PSS type. To take a holistic perspective on the organization and follow Cleven et al. [37], our MM addresses five focus areas: *Strategy*, *Culture*, *Structure*, *Practices*, and *IT*. Those were successfully used for other domain-specific MMs before, e.g., Enterprise Architecture Management [45] or Business Process Management [33]. Table 2 lists the focus areas' definitions based on Cleven et al. [37] and Rosemann and vom Brocke [46] and represent relevant capability areas for organizational capabilities.

Table 2. Five focus areas for capability development in organizations

Focus area	Definition
Strategy	*Strategy* comprises the vision of how an organization creates value and develops toward a defined target state
Culture	*Culture* covers the collective values and behaviors of individuals and teams
Structure	*Structure* comprises the way an organization is shaped and interacts with its environment to achieve its goals
Practices	*Practices* cover key activities, responsibilities, methods, mechanisms, routines, competencies, and processes
IT	*IT* comprises technical solutions that support and enable the operation of the organization but also the design, implementation, execution, and control of activities and objectives

The five focus areas represent action fields for organizations that need to be further specified. This is achieved by assigning our *capability dimensions* to these focus areas. The PSSMM, presented in Table 3, thus provides a holistic overview of relevant capabilities, which we assign to 20 capability dimensions to evolve toward one of the three main types of PSS.

The focus area **Strategy** describes to which extent the organization focuses on enriching its value creation with services until service is at the core of their business model (*Service Focus*) [18]. This strategy shift creates the necessary foundation for an organization to develop and implement a successful PSS. Customer centricity, therefore, becomes an essential part of business strategy and value creation (*Customer Involvement*) [15, 25]. Furthermore, a PSS-driven vision is pursued by allocating human and financial resources (*Resource Allocation for PSS)* [10, 19]. The PSS strategy determines the direction in which an organization should thrive and is, therefore, a signpost for the resulting focus areas.

As a second focus area, **Culture** comprises how employees work together (*Work Culture*) [47, 48] and how the organization's PSS vision is committed by the employees (*Employee-committed PSS Vision*) [16, 17]. This capability dimension is directly enabled by 'Resource Allocation for PSS' from Strategy and underpins that the entire workforce must support the PSS-vision. To successfully master PSS, relevant soft and hard skills need to be developed throughout the organization (*Skill Training*) [49], e.g., data analytics or leadership.

Regarding the organization's **Structure,** PSS require distinct changes in how the product or PSS is marketed and what channels are used to deliver the value (*Channels and Sales*). Here, the product itself becomes a new and essential channel, especially in mature PSS types [50, 51]. Also, through the establishment of new channels, extensive value-added networks, and the deep integration of the product into the customer's processes, the organization's boundaries become blurred as external partners are increasingly integrated into business processes (*Partner Integration*) [10, 15, 20]. As the business model depends less on the sale of the product and focuses on services, the organization must manage the change of its income, changing from one-time product purchases to continuous payments for services (*Capital Management*) [10, 25].

The focus area **Practices** consist of six capability dimensions. The first addresses how an interaction with the customer has to be initialized regarding services (*Customer Interaction and Service Initiative*) [3, 52]. Mature PSS go in line with increasing customer interaction and responsibility for the performance of the product. The next capability dimension addresses how to design and enable high quality of PSS. The specificity of the methods and tools used increases with mature PSS and gains importance for innovation and product management (*PSS Design Methods and Tools*) [53, 54]. As mature PSS have a strong focus on product availability and performance for the customer, feedback on the product and its performance are a crucial factor on the practice level. Therefore, *Product Performance Measurement and Feedback Systems* become increasingly relevant for the provision of additional services or advice, but also regarding the pricing of mature PSS [19, 25]. *Automated Service Offering* is crucial to ensure the product and service availability, especially for mature PSS [55, 56]. In this context, mature PSS also request the ability to develop and offer suitable pricing models and customer-individual prices that are increasingly distinguished by performance-oriented payment structures (*Pricing Mechanism)* [4, 57]. Also, *Life Cycle Management* becomes essential to accompany the customer holistically before, during, and after using the product [25].

IT, at the bottom of our PSSMM, acts as the foundation for enabling the development and operation of PSS. First, the *Role of IT* determines whether IT only supports business or takes over an enabling role regarding the organization's actions and objectives [58]. Due to the increasing collection and exchange of valuable data regarding PSS value chains and business ecosystems, *IT Security and Compliance* activities need to enable holistic IT security concepts across organizational boundaries [59]. Especially result-oriented PSS depend on a continuous connection and data availability for performance measurement or determination of payments [17, 60]. Therefore, *Connectivity and Data Access* were added as an IT-capability. To provide data-driven services, e.g., predictive maintenance, relevant product data needs to be collected (*Data Collection*) [17] and analyzed (*Data Analysis*) [57], so that, e.g., necessary key performance measures can be created that are crucial for offering PSS.

Table 3. The PSSMM

Focus Area	Capability Dimension	Maturity Level: 1. Pure Product	2. Product-oriented PSS	3. Use-oriented PSS	4. Result-oriented PSS
Strategy	Service Focus	Focus on the physical product; no additional services	Limited focus on PSS; additional services like consulting, maintenance, or recycling	Focus on PSS; warranty of the availability of the physical product along with services	Focus on mature PSS as core business model; highly integrated product-service bundles to offer result as a service
	Customer Involvement	No or little involvement to design and evolve the physical product	Growing involvement to design and evolve the product and additional services	Increasing cooperation with and integration of the customer into PSS design processes	Partner-like collaboration and intensive communication for PSS development
	Resource Allocation for PSS	No budget for PSS development and implementation	Little effort for creating additional services to the product; ad hoc investments in organizational changes	Medium effort for creating well-functioning PSS; continuous investments	Great efforts to achieve a high-performance PSS; substantial and continuous investments
Culture	Work Culture	Focus on product-related solutions; independent work or partly in homogenous teams	Focus on product-related solutions and on easy-to-implement services; occasional work in interdisciplinary teams	Solution-oriented in terms of both products and services; usually work in interdisciplinary teams	Solution-oriented for PSS; team-oriented, cross-team, -domain, and -organizational work, continuous exchange with customers and value-added partners
	Employee-committed PSS Vision	Product-oriented way of thinking; working for developing and selling physical products	Product-oriented way of thinking; working for offering complementary services to the product	Thinking in terms of customer usage; working for providing PSS solutions with a higher level of service integration	Thinking in terms of customer results; working for delivering result as a service
	Skill Training	No training or further education regarding PSS skills	Occasional in terms of PSS development, training for product-related consultation	Selective training courses on specific topics for PSS development and implementation	Structured training courses on all relevant PSS topics like development, implementation, sales, customer contact, leadership, and management
Structure	Channels and Sales	Traditional and web-based channels for product sales	Traditional and web-based channels for product and service sales	Traditional and web-based channels or product as point of sale	Traditional and web-based channels and product as point of sale for integrated view on results
	Partner Integration	Only suppliers as value-adding partners; clear organizational boundaries	Additional value-adding partners for service-creation and initial involvement of and cooperation with customer as partner	Blurring of boundaries between company and suppliers as well as service-creation involved partners; close cooperation with customer as partner	Strong collaboration and integration of value-added partners and customer for PSS co-creation; company is deeply integrated into customers' processes and business model
	Capital Management	Bearing all costs until point of sale; management of one-time payments for each product sale	Bearing all costs until point of sale; management of one-time payment for product and demand-driven service provision income	Bearing of production and development costs for products and services until a pre-defined point of time; continuous payments for usage	Bearing all costs for PSS until end of life cycle; continuous and success-related payments for operation of the PSS
Practices	Customer Interaction and Service Initiative	Interaction focuses on product purchase and emerging operation problems; customer is responsible for operations	Interaction is driven by the customer; interactions are pre-defined in the service contract; mostly topic-driven services related to maintenance	PSS provider initiates services and is responsible for ensuring the perpetual availability; planned interactions	Proactive and automated service interaction; connected through pre-defined touch points and processes; result as continuously monitored parameter for service initiative
	PSS Design Methods and Tools	No approach for service or PSS development;	General (management) approaches for product; partial use of PSS methods and tools	Selected approaches and formalized development processes for PSS; appropriate tools for development and implementation	Company-specific and individualized PSS approaches plus fast development cycles and prototyping; continuous improvement and use of methods
	Product Performance Measurement	No need for measuring product performance; only measuring product quality by internal tests	No need for measuring product performance but occasional insights through maintenance services; measuring product quality in order to provide advice and guidance to customers	Measurement of product performance and usage in order to guarantee and optimize product availability	Well-defined measures and feedbacks are systematically used for payments, maintenance, and new service development
	Automated Service Offering	No service provision	Almost no automation; rule-based or instinct-driven service provision	Partly automated or modularized services are provided	Most services with the customer or value-creation partners are automated and/or modularized; optimization toward minimizing human-interaction in the service process
	Pricing Mechanism	Fixed one-time payment (pay for product)	One-time payment for product and situational service fee (pay for product or service order)	Continuous payment like leasing, renting, or sharing (pay on availability)	Customer-specific, result-based payment based on service level agreement (pay on production)
	Life Cycle Management	Development, production, sale, and shipment; no responsibility for operation	Development, production, sale, and shipment; no responsibility for operation but reactive provision of services	Development, production, sale, shipment, maintenance, and usage phase; responsible for guaranteeing the usability of the product	Managing everything until the end of the product life cycle; responsible for delivering results and productivity
IT	Role of IT	IT as supporting function; intra-organizational focus	Supporting function, partly as driver of value creation and change; intra-organizational focus	IT as an enabler and diver for value creation and change; enabler of product-availability; inter-organizational focus	IT as an enabler and driver for value creation and change; enabler of enhanced product-performance, inter-organizational focus
	IT Security and Compliance	Security of highly critical assets; isolated IT security activities	Security of highly critical assets and initially also of external processes	Intra- and inter-organizational IT security activities	Intra- and inter-organizational IT security activities; security by design in product development process
	Connectivity and Data Access	No access to product after point of sale	Indirect, situational data access to customer; possible manual data exchange	Continuous interconnectivity; mainly reading rights; connectivity of the product is a substantial component	Continuous interconnectivity; full access to product; connectivity of the product is a substantial component
	Data Collection	No collection of customer's product data	Reactive and manual collection of data	Partly automated collection of data from the customer	Highly automated collection of data
	Data Analysis	No analysis of product usage or descriptive analysis of internal product testing	Descriptive and diagnostic analysis of product data; initially for service provision	Diagnostic and predictive analysis of product data; focus to keep promise of availability	Predictive and prescriptive analysis; focus on optimization of result

5 Pre-evaluation

As recommended in the development process of Becker et al. [1], we evaluated our PSSMM using proposed evaluation criteria. We conducted a pre-evaluation of the model to anticipate a demonstration and application of the model in practice to first assess the model's quality according to recommended criteria. A comprehensive application and demonstration of the model in practice with industry experts, as proposed by Becker et al. [1], is planned to be subject to further research. Therefore, our theoretical evaluation was carried out through a focus group discussion with domain-specific scholars of the IS discipline. We used the evaluation criteria of Becker et al. [1], which are: (1) *comprehensiveness*, (2) *consistency*, and (3) *problem adequacy.* The focus group comprised nine research scholars with experience in PSS and MM development (see also Table 1 in Sect. 3).

(1) *Comprehensiveness:* Within the focus group, the model was perceived as comprehensive and covering essential PSS aspects. Nevertheless, we enriched several capability dimensions with some details, e.g., IT Security and Compliance with the term 'security by design' in the last maturity level of result-oriented PSS.
(2) *Consistency*: The focus group generally agreed on the overall consistency but objected to a few minor issues. Minor adjustments, such as eliminating non-uniform designations for the same term, e.g., 'teamwork', 'work in teams', and 'collaboration in teams', were made.

(3) Problem adequacy: The focus group discussion led to several iterations of the model, which resulted in an improved specificity for the application context. For example, we have adjusted some generic capabilities for transformational processes and specified them for the intended context of manufacturing companies that aim to offer PSS (e.g., 'project management', 'agility', and 'change management').

6 Conclusion and Outlook

This paper addresses the need for conceptual work to guide manufacturers in becoming PSS providers [61]. It contributes to the interplay between established PSS types and organizational capabilities, which has not yet been sufficiently addressed in literature. To fill this gap, we developed a MM for the transformation into becoming a PSS provider. To structure the MM, we used the well-established PSS types of Tukker et al. [11, 25] – product-, use-, and result-oriented PSS – often applied in literature for distinguishing the different types of BMs and their implications on organization or environment (e.g., Bocken et al. [27], Yang and Evans [28]). For the MM development, we followed Becker et al.'s [1] procedure model. We first searched for existing MMs (e.g., Rapaccini et al. [19], Gudergan et al. [16], Exner et al. [15]) and second conducted a literature review for PSS-specific capabilities. After, we iteratively developed the model by building upon the literature, conducting expert interviews with senior scholars, and pre-evaluated the PSSMM with domain-specific scholars by checking for the proposed evaluation criteria (i.e., comprehensiveness, consistency, problem adequacy) of Becker et al. [1] in a focus group discussion.

Our contribution is relevant for practice and research. For the latter, the PSSMM adds to descriptive and prescriptive knowledge on PSS and supplements the current discussion on PSS (e.g., Exner et al. [15], Pigosso et al. [18]). In particular, our work represents the hitherto missing link between established PSS types and corresponding capabilities. We also contribute by summarizing, structuring, and enriching current PSS literature and providing a foundation for future research on specific PSS capabilities. This work also points out that digitalization is a driver for PSS in the manufacturing industry.

On the one hand, this offers the possibility of differentiation to overcome market pressure at the product level. On the other hand, the developed model reveals at various points how digital technologies may serve as an enabler to offer PSS (e.g., connectivity and data access, customer interaction and service initiative, automated service offering). For practice, the PSSMM guides manufacturers in transforming themselves toward a certain type of PSS. Our model supports this strategic transformation by defining the needed capabilities. For example, management can use the PSSMM to evaluate their status quo and desired target state. This makes it easier for managers to assess the necessary efforts for developing needed capabilities. For the transformation process, additional management tools such as manuals or self-assessment questionnaires are needed to complement the PSSMM [1].

As any research project, this work is beset with limitations, which stimulate future research. Although this paper followed the MM development approach of Becker et al. [1], the development of our PSSMM is limited to phases 1 to 4. To guarantee a high quality of this work, this paper built upon current and PSS-specific literature and was challenged and evaluated by domain experts in IS research. However, an evaluation with industry experts to scrutinize the PSSMM and check its completeness, real-world fidelity, and practical applicability is missing. Also, a demonstration of the PSSMM in a real-world context has not been carried out yet. Both are planned as next steps within the research project. Also, further research could provide an approach for application.

References

1. Becker, J., Knackstedt, R., Pöppelbuß, J.: Developing maturity models for IT management. Bus. Inf. Syst. Eng. **1**, 213–222 (2009)
2. Kowalkowski, C., Gebauer, H., Kamp, B., Parry, G.: Servitization and deservitization: overview, concepts, and definitions. Ind. Mark. Manage. **60**, 4–10 (2017)
3. Boehm, M., Thomas, O.: Looking beyond the rim of one's teacup: a multidisciplinary literature review of product-service systems in information systems, business management, and engineering & design. J. Clean. Prod. **51**, 245–260 (2013)
4. Baines, T., et al.: Towards an operations strategy for product-centric servitization. Int. J. Opt. Prod. Manage. **29**, 494–519 (2009)
5. Mahut, F., Daaboul, J., Bricogne, M., Eynard, B.: Product-service systems for servitization of the automotive idustry: a literature review. Int. J. Prod. Res. **55**, 2102–2120 (2017)
6. Brambila-Macias, S.A., Sakao, T., Kowalkowski, C.: Bridging the gap between engineering design and marketing: insights for research and practice in product/service system design. Des. Sci. **4**, 1 (2018)
7. Lerch, C., Gotsch, M.: Digitalized product-service systems in manufacturing firms: a case study analysis. Res. Technol. Manage. **58**, 45–52 (2015)
8. Munich Re: Pay-per-part: TRUMPF and Munich Re plan new business model for the manufacturing industry. https://www.munichre.com/en/company/media-relations/media-information-and-corporate-news/media-information/2020/2020-10-14-pay-per-part.html
9. Suppatvech, C., Godsell, J., Day, S.: The roles of internet of things technology in enabling servitized business models: a systematic literature review. Ind. Mark. Manage. **82**, 70–86 (2019)
10. Baines, T., et al.: State-of-the-art in product-service systems. Proc. Inst. Mech. Eng. Part B J. Eng. Manuf. **221**, 1543–1552 (2007)
11. Tukker, A., Tischner, U.: New Business for Old Europe: Product-service Development, Competitiveness and Sustainability. Routledge, London (2017)
12. Weking, J., Stöcker, M., Kowalkiewicz, M., Böhm, M., Krcmar, H.: Leveraging Industry 4.0 – a business model pattern framework. Int. J. Prod. Econ. **225**, 107588 (2020)
13. Pöppelbuß, J., Röglinger, M.: What makes a useful maturity model? A framework of general design principles for maturity models and its demonstration in business process management. In: Proceedings of the European Conference on Information Systems (ECIS), vol. 28 (2011)
14. Li, A.Q., Found, P.: Towards sustainability: PSS, digital technology and value co-creation. Procedia CIRP **64**, 79–84 (2017)
15. Exner, K., Balder, J., Stark, R.: A PSS maturity self-assessment tool. Procedia CIRP **73**, 86–90 (2018)
16. Gudergan, G., Buschmeyer, A., Krechting, D., Feige, B.: Evaluating the readiness to transform towards a product-service system provider by a capability maturity modelling approach. Procedia CIRP **30**, 384–389 (2015)
17. Neff, A.A., Hamel, F., Herz, T.P., Uebernickel, F., Brenner, W., vom Brocke, J.: Developing a maturity model for service systems in heavy equipment manufacturing enterprises. Inf. Manage. **51**, 895–911 (2014)

18. Pigosso, D.C.A., McAloone, T.C.: Maturity-based approach for the development of environmentally sustainable product/service-systems. CIRP J. Manuf. Sci. Technol. **15**, 33–41 (2016)
19. Rapaccini, M., Saccani, N., Pezzotta, G., Burger, T., Ganz, W.: Service development in product-service systems: a maturity model. Serv. Ind. J. **33**, 300–319 (2013)
20. Mont, O.K.: Clarifying the concept of product–service system. J. Clean. Prod. **10**, 237–245 (2002)
21. Guidat, T., Barquet, A.P., Widera, H., Rozenfeld, H., Seliger, G.: Guidelines for the definition of innovative industrial product-service systems (PSS) business models for remanufacturing. Procedia CIRP **16**, 193–198 (2014)
22. Velamuri, V.K., Bansemir, B., Neyer, A.-K., Möslein, K.M.: Product service systems as a driver for business model innovation: lessons learned from the manufacturing industry. Int. J. Innov. Manage. **17**, 1–25 (2013)
23. Vargo, S.L., Lusch, R.F.: Institutions and axioms: an extension and update of service-dominant logic. J. Acad. Mark. Sci. **44**, 5–23 (2016)
24. Costa, N., Patrício, L., Morelli, N., Magee, C.L.: Bringing service design to manufacturing companies: integrating PSS and service design approaches. Des. Stud. **55**, 112–145 (2018)
25. Tukker, A.: Eight Types of product–service system: eight ways to sustainability? Exp. SusProNet. Bus. Strat. Env. **13**, 246–260 (2004)
26. Raddats, C., Kowalkowski, C., Benedettini, O., Burton, J., Gebauer, H.: Servitization: a contemporary thematic review of four major research streams. Ind. Mark. Manage. **83**, 207–223 (2019)
27. Bocken, N.M.P., Short, S.W., Rana, P., Evans, S.: A literature and practice review to develop sustainable business model archetypes. J. Clean. Prod. **65**, 42–56 (2014)
28. Yang, M., Evans, S.: Product-service system business model archetypes and sustainability. J. Clean. Prod. **220**, 1156–1166 (2019)
29. vom Brocke, J., Debortoli, S., Müller, O., Reuter, N.: How in-memory technology can create business value: insights from the Hilti case. CAIS **34**, 7 (2014)
30. Barney, J.B.: Resource-based theories of competitive advantage: a ten-year retrospective on the resource-based view. J. Manage. **27**, 643–650 (2001)
31. Wade, M., Hulland, J.: Review: the resource-based view and information systems research: review, extension, and suggestions for future research. MIS Q. **28**, 107–142 (2004)
32. Day, G.S.: The capabilities of market-driven organizations. J. Market. **58**, 37–52 (1994)
33. de Bruin, T., Rosemann, M., Freeze, R., Kaulkarni, U.: Understanding the main phases of developing a maturity assessment model. In: Proceedings of Australasian Conference on Information Systems (ACIS), pp. 8–19 (2005)
34. Mettler, T.: Maturity assessment models: a design science research approach. Int. J. Soc. Syst. Sci. (IJSSS) **3**, 81–98 (2011)
35. Pöppelbuss, J., Niehaves, B., Simons, A., Becker, J.: Maturity models in information systems research: literature search and analysis. Commun. Assoc. Inf. Syst. **29**, 505–532 (2011)
36. Lasrado, L.A., Vatrapu, R., Andersen, K.N.: Maturity models development in is research: a literature review. IRIS Sel. Papers Inf. Syst. Res. Seminar Scandinavia **6**, 1–64 (2015)
37. Cleven, A.K., Winter, R., Wortmann, F., Mettler, T.: Process management in hospitals: an empirically grounded maturity model. Bus. Res. **7**, 191–216 (2014)
38. van Steenbergen, M., van den Berg, M., Brinkkemper, S.: A balanced approach to developing the enterprise architecture practice. In: Filipe, J., Cordeiro, J., Cardoso, J. (eds.) ICEIS 2007. LNBIP, vol. 12, pp. 240–253. Springer, Heidelberg (2008). https://doi.org/10.1007/978-3-540-88710-2_19

39. Karni, R., Kaner, M.: A review of maturity models and their application to PSS: towards a PSS Maturity Model. In: Shimomura, Y., Kimita, K. (eds.) The Philosopher's Stone for Sustainability, pp. 393–398. Springer, Heidelberg (2013). https://doi.org/10.1007/978-3-642-32847-3_66
40. Neff, A.A., Hamel, F., Herz, T.P., Uebernickel, F., Brenner, W.: Fostering efficiency in information systems support for product-service systems in the manufacturing industry. In: Proceedings of the 19th Americas Conference on Information Systems, Chicago, Illinois, pp. 1–9 (2013)
41. Richter, H.M., Tschandl, M.: Service Engineering-Neue Services erfolgreich gestalten und umsetzen. In: Bruhn, M., Hadwich, K. (eds.) Dienstleistungen 4.0, pp. 157–184. Springer, Wiesbaden (2017). https://doi.org/10.1007/978-3-658-17550-4_7
42. Hevner, A.R., March, S.T., Park, J., Ram, S.: Design science in information systems research. MIS Q. **28**, 75–105 (2004)
43. van Steenbergen, M., Bos, R., Brinkkemper, S., van de Weerd, I., Bekkers, W.: The design of focus area maturity models. In: Winter, R., Zhao, J.L., Aier, S. (eds.) DESRIST 2010. LNCS, vol. 6105, pp. 317–332. Springer, Heidelberg (2010). https://doi.org/10.1007/978-3-642-13335-0_22
44. vom Brocke, J., et al.: Reconstructing the giant: on the importance of rigour in documenting the literature search process. In: ECIS Proceedings, vol. 161 (2009)
45. Simon, D., Fischbach, K., Schoder, D.: Enterprise architecture management and its role in corporate strategic management. Inf. Syst. E-Bus. Manage. **12**, 5–42 (2014)
46. Rosemann, M., vom Brocke, J.: The six core elements of business process management. In: vom Brocke, J., Rosemann, M. (eds.) Handbook on Business Process Management 1. IHIS, pp. 105–122. Springer, Heidelberg (2015). https://doi.org/10.1007/978-3-642-45100-3_5
47. Gimpel, H., Hosseini, S., Huber, R., Probst, L., Röglinger, M., Faisst, U.: Structuring digital transformation: a framework of action fields and its application at ZEISS. J. Inf. Technol. Theory Appl. **19**, 31–54 (2018)
48. El Sawy, O.A., Kræmmergaard, P., Amsinck, H., Vinther, A.L.: How LEGO built the foundations and enterprise capabilities for digital leadership. MIS Q. Exec. **15** (2016)
49. Wewior, J.W.: Role-play based assessment of IPS2-specific intellectual capital. Procedia CIRP **30**, 415–420 (2015)
50. Kiel, D., Arnold, C., Voigt, K.-I.: The influence of the industrial internet of things on business models of established manufacturing companies-a business level perspective. Technovation **68**, 4–19 (2017)
51. Fleisch, E., Weinberger, M., Wortmann, F.: Business models and the internet of things (extended abstract). In: Podnar Žarko, I., Pripužić, K., Serrano, M. (eds.) Interoperability and Open-Source Solutions for the Internet of Things. LNCS, vol. 9001, pp. 6–10. Springer, Cham (2015). https://doi.org/10.1007/978-3-319-16546-2_2
52. Oliva, R., Kallenberg, R.: Managing the transition from products to services. Int. J. Serv. Ind. Manage. **14**, 160–172 (2003)
53. Kim, Y.S., Lee, S.W., Kim, S.R., Jeong, H., Kim, J.H.: A product-service systems design method with integration of product elements and service elements using affordances. In: ServDes. 2012 Conference Proceedings Co-Creating Services; The 3rd Service Design and Service Innovation Conference, Espoo, Finland, 8–10 February, pp. 111–119 (2013)
54. Morelli, N.: Designing product/service systems: a methodological exploration. Design Issues **18**, 3–17 (2002)
55. Klötzer, C., Pflaum, A.: Toward the development of a maturity model for digitalization within the manufacturing industry's supply chain. In: Proceedings of the 50th Hawaii International Conference on System Sciences (2017)
56. Müller, J.M., Buliga, O., Voigt, K.-I.: Fortune favors the prepared: how SMEs approach business model innovations in Industry 4.0. Technol. Forecast. Soc. Change **132**, 2–17 (2018)

57. Porter, M.E., Heppelmann, J.E.: How smart, connected products are transforming competition. Harvard Bus. Rev. **92**, 64–88 (2014)
58. Berghaus, S., Back, A.: Disentangling the fuzzy front end of digital transformation: activities and approaches. In: Proceedings of the 38th International Conference on Information Systems (ICIS) (2017)
59. Silva, L., Poleto, T., Moura, J., Paula Costa, A.: An analysis of and perspective on the information security maturity model: a case study of a public and a private sector company. In: Proceedings of the 18th Americas Conference on Information Systems (AMCIS), vol. 11 (2012)
60. Schumacher, A., Nemeth, T., Sihn, W.: Roadmapping towards industrial digitalization based on an Industry 4.0 Maturity model for manufacturing enterprises. Procedia CIRP **79**, 409–414 (2019)
61. Paschou, T., Adrodegari, F., Rapaccini, M., Saccani, N., Perona, M.: Towards Service 4.0: a new framework and research priorities. Procedia CIRP **73**, 148–154 (2018)

Combining Methods for the Design of Digital Services in Practice: Experiences from a Predictive Costing Service

Fabian Richter and Jürgen Anke(✉)

HTW Dresden, Dresden, Germany
{fabian.richter,juergen.anke}@htw-dresden.de

Abstract. Exploiting digital technologies for innovative service offerings as part of the digital transformation has been under discussion for several years. As recent research has shown, practitioners struggle with the systematic design of digital services. Along with the progress in the understanding of digital service systems, academia has proposed various processes and methods which are contributing to a methodology for Service Systems Engineering. However, such methods are rarely applied in practice. In our study, we utilize Action Design Research to evaluate how existing methods can be applied in a project that aims to design a service for predictive costing. Our findings are formalized as a combination of methods and their links. It shows how these methods can be employed to guide the innovation process. Although the generalizability of the results is limited through the single case study approach, the proposed combination of methods provides evidence-based knowledge on Service Systems Engineering, which is relevant for practitioners and researchers alike.

Keywords: Digital services · Service systems engineering · Action Design Research · Methodology · Service innovation

1 Introduction

Applying digital technologies for services enable new value propositions and innovative business models. Such digital or smart services thus represent an interesting source of competitive advantage for many companies. However, companies struggle to design economically sustainable digital service offers [1]. Due to the complexity of such systems and the uncertainty in the innovation process, experts from various disciplines have to be involved [2]. Systematic design and development of digital services are addressed by Service Systems Engineering (SSE). Agile engineering processes for such services have been proposed, e.g. the DIN SPEC 33453 [3] or Recombinant Service Systems Engineering [4]. These process models organize the dynamic aspects, e.g. project phases. Concrete methods can be applied to guide the steps required to create intermediate work products, such as business models, service concepts, or system architectures. A variety of methods that address the specifics of digital service systems has become available as a result of recent research.

F. Ahlemann et al. (Eds.): WI 2021, LNISO 46, pp. 185–202, 2021.
https://doi.org/10.1007/978-3-030-86790-4_14

While the body of knowledge on SSE for digital services is growing, there is little empirical evidence on their suitability and practical application. To inform future research on this topic, we concur with Böhmann et al., who call for evidence-based design knowledge for SSE [5]. As a recent analysis of 14 smart service projects has shown, there is a wide variety of methods employed but in none of the investigated projects, any method specifically design for digital services or smart services was used [2]. At the same time, several established methods are applied for the engineering of Smart Service Systems in practice and appear to be suitable for this task [2]. Against this background, we pose the following research question: *How can existing methods for designing digital service be combined in a real-world scenario?*

We consider this research question as timely and relevant, as it is not required to "re-invent the wheel" but identify existing suitable methods and combine them with new methods specific to digital services. Our research aims to provide insights on both the suitability of different methods for the task but also their combination.

To address the research question, we apply Action Design Research (ADR) as the leading paradigm. It describes the systematic learning from the collaboration between practitioners and researchers in real-world settings to design an artifact. ADR is organized in four stages (1) problem formulation, (2) building, intervention, and evaluation, (3) reflection and learning, and (4) formalization of learning [6]. As previous research has shown, ADR is suitable for transferring knowledge for innovation in the practice [7, 8]. We consider ADR suitable for our research, as it allows us to apply and evaluate methods in a real-world scenario. The intended outcome is organizational knowledge of how digital service innovation can be supported by a set of existing methods. This combination of methods can be considered as the artifact to be designed.

The remainder of this paper is structured as follows: After this introduction, we provide the conceptual foundation, followed by the research approach. The fourth section covers the case study and project organization. This is followed by a discussion of the results. The paper closes with a conclusion and an outlook.

2 Conceptual Foundation

Service Systems are a configuration of people, processes, and technology to co-create value. **Digital Service Systems** utilize digital technologies such as cloud computing, big data, and artificial intelligence as fundamental system elements for the provision of resources, competencies, or value creation. Therefore, value co-creation is mainly based on data [9]. Furthermore, it should be noted that there is a difference between digital and smart services [10]. Smart services are therefore considered as a subset of digital services, as they additionally include the integration of connected objects (smart products). It should be noted that digital services and smart services are often used interchangeably, as the stricter distinction has been proposed only recently.

Service Systems Engineering (SSE) [5] refers to the systematic design of Service Systems and incorporates processes, models, and techniques. Processes for SSE include the DIN SPEC 33453 [3], Recombinant Service Systems Engineering [4], and Smart Service Engineering [11]. They mainly provide a set of phases and activities, which help to structure the overall engineering endeavor. Another set of contributions for SSE consists of concrete methods that guide individual activities through models, e.g. Design Thinking for Industrial Services (DETHIS) [12] or the Smart Service Canvas [13]. To distinguish the four sets of methods, we introduce the categories "digital service specific methods" (DSM), existing "service engineering methods" (SEM), methods regarding "user-centered design" (UCD), and "general-purpose methods" (GPM). These categories represented existing methods and practices, which are applied for different purposes. Methods of the GPM category are the most general ones, e.g. from social research or general management. UCD methods are used within agile projects with innovative character to ensure that the resulting products are accepted by the user. While UCD can be applied to any kind of technical or digital product, service, or process, SE methods are targeted at the engineering of services. Finally, DSM consider the specifics of digital services, such as data, devices, and analytics.

Based on the insight that a single process model will not be suitable for a large variety of project settings, the concept of **Situational Method Engineering** (SME) [14] was proposed. It aims to flexibly combine various methods to adapt to the development process depending on the individual situation at the beginning of the project. However, it requires formal modeling of methods (fragments) and their storage in a method base to flexible combine them at the beginning of a project. A study by Clarke and O'Connor has identified eight groups, 44 factors, and 170 sub-factors that influence the selection of methods [15]. For smart services, there are typically agile approaches employed. They are less formalized, and the choice of methods is not fixed at the beginning of the project. Rather, the agile project team continuously review and adapt their way of working, e.g. during "retrospectives".

3 Preparing the Action Design Research Project

3.1 Problem Formulation

The first step of the ADR approach is problem formulation. Based on the state of the art, we can identify two problems: (1) DSM are unknown in practice, and (2) existing process frameworks for SSE may propose a set of methods but do not provide guidance for their combination. The ADR process can help to solve both aspects of the problem. DSM can be transferred to the project setting through the researcher, which also fulfills ADR principle 2: "Theory-ingrained artifact". For that, a list consisting of 30 methods was created, which serves as the basis for method selection in each iteration (Table 1).

As indicated in Table 1, the method list is largely based on the methods mentioned in the appendix of DIN SPEC 33453. Although the DIN SPEC 33453 is aimed at digital service systems engineering, there were no DSM mentioned. Therefore, we added DSMs that were cited in the 2020 edition of a textbook on data-driven service engineering and management [16] or recently published at information systems conferences. Due to the large number of methods proposed by academia, the list cannot be considered exhaustive. However, as the compiled list contains methods for various purposes in service innovation, we are confident that it is sufficient in a real-world project.

3.2 Introduction of Case

We collaborated with a medium-sized German software company, which we refer to as ALPHA in this paper. It develops solutions for product cost calculation based on a common platform. The products are targeted mainly at car manufacturers and their suppliers. To be competitive in the market, the company aims to expand its product range with a new smart service, known as predictive costing, which supports cost estimation. If a car manufacturer submits a request for an offer to a supplier, they usually have little time to deliver a valid offer in terms of costs to the car manufacturer. The planned service is intended to have a supportive effect on this process. As the innovation project for the predictive costing service is an instance for this class of problems, it fulfills the ADR principle 1 "practice-inspired research". To jointly solve this service innovation problem in a structured way, i.e. use appropriate methods, is the goal of the project.

Table 1. Overview of considered methods

Type	Methods	
GPM	5 Why's [3] 9-P Marketing Mix [3] ABC-Analysis [3] Brainstorming [3] Conjoint-Analysis [3] Environment Analysis [3] Expert Interview [17] How Might We-Questions [3]	Idea-Contest [3] Interview for Empathy [3] MoSCoW- Prioritization [3] Nightmare Competitor [3] Shadowing [3] Stakeholder Analysis [3] Stakeholder Map [3] SWOT-Analysis [3]
UCD	Customer Journey [18] Digital Mock-Up [3] Low-Resolution Prototyping [3] Pains & Gains [3]	Persona [3] Prototyping [3] User Story Mapping [19] Value Proposition Canvas [3]
SEM	Customer Journey Mapping [20] Job Mapping [3]	Minimum Viable Service [3] Service Blueprinting [3]
DSM	Information Service Blueprint [21]	Smart Service Canvas [13]

Long-term support is provided as the partner company is willing to develop a new smart service. One researcher assumes the role of the action researcher, while employees of the company are the practitioners. The development process is led by the action researcher in consultation with the partner company. The selection, application, and evaluation of these methods were discussed with the second researcher to ensure state-of-the-art guidance for the project as well as effective learning and reflection. In conjunction with the knowledge of the practitioners regarding the currently used technologies and their potentials, the ADR principle 4 "Mutually influential roles" is addressed. Additionally, this setup represents an inter-organizational collaboration often found in SSE [22]. Using the set of roles proposed by Anke et al., the company can be characterized by the "Project Sponsor" role, while the university took over the "Digital Innovator" role [22].

3.3 Project Setup and Process Model

As an overall project structure, the basic process of DIN SPEC 33453 was chosen, which describes an agile process with the phases analysis, design, and implementation [3]. These phases are connected by a decision point and can be conducted in any sequence [3]. While other process models for designing Digital Service Systems might be equally suitable, we chose it as we expect it to become more widely known in the future due to its governance by an established standardization body.

The overall project was conducted from April to June 2020. In line with the agile approach of DIN SPEC 33453, it was subdivided into iterations to facilitate feedback and reduce risk. Each iteration begins with the decision on a method that appears appropriate. For its selection, the iteration objective, and the situational factors (conditions) are considered. For example, the "idea generation" activity of the analysis phase is characterized by creativity and cooperative knowledge exchange [3]. Workshops are an organizational format that is suitable for these specific requirements [23] but limits the set of applicable methods, as not every method for generating ideas can be applied in a workshop. For generally applicable methods, it needs to be decided on whether they are suitable for the given context. A qualitative approach is being taken to answer this question. A method is to be considered "suitable" if it creates results that can be used in a subsequent iteration. In the next section, the planning, execution, and results of each iteration will be presented in more detail.

A total of five iterations were conducted to design the predictive costing service. Iterations I and II are part of the analysis phase of the DIN SPEC process model. After that, a decision had to be made on whether the service idea will be further pursued. Following the positive decision, iteration III focused on a more detailed elaboration of customer demands. The decision after that iteration was to pursue activities of the design phase. Iterations IV and V are therefore in the design phase, as the established understanding was used for the development of a service concept. Table 2 provides an overview of the methods and settings for each iteration.

Table 2. Overview of iterations and applied methods

Iteration objective	Applied methods (Type)	Setting
I. Identify Innovation Potentials	- Customer Journey Mapping (SEM)	Workshop (digital)
II. Idea Assessment	- Expert interviews (GPM)	Meetings (digital)
III. Elaborate Customer Assumptions	- Smart Service Canvas (DSM)	Workshop (digital)
IV. Complete the Value Proposition	- Smart Service Canvas (DSM) - How Might We (GPM)	Individual work
V. Design the Service Concept	- Information Service Blueprint (DSM) - Smart Service Canvas (DSM)	Workshop (digital & face-to-face)

Subsequently, details of each iteration are provided based on the following structure. It relates to the "building, intervention, and evaluation" phase of the ADR process:

- What was the initial situation and objective of the iteration?
- Which methods were considered and how were they selected?
- How were they applied and which results did they yield?

Unlike other ADR projects, we did not develop an IT artifact, as a selection and combination of innovation methods is an organizational artifact. Therefore, ADR principle 3 (Reciprocal Shaping) did not apply in our study. To address the ADR the principle 5 "Authentic and concurrent evaluation", we gathered feedback after each workshop. Participants were asked (1) if the applied method or parts of it was known in advance, (2) if the objective were achieved, (3) if the method yielded a meaningful result that could be used further. Additional feedback was collected on potential improvements and positive aspects of the method. This fulfills the ADR principle 6 (guided emergence), as it helps to iteratively design the desired artifact. It also helped us to understand if the introduction of these new methods was rather difficult. After each iteration, the researcher reflects upon the effects of the applied method, which addresses the ADR phase "Reflection and Learning".

4 Application and Evaluation of Methods

4.1 Iteration I: Identify Innovation Potentials

Initial Situation and Objective: The starting point of service development is a rather unclear idea of a predictive costing smart service. The targeted customer segment as well as the outgoing customer process are not sufficiently clear to the practitioners at the beginning of the development. The physical presence of all participants cannot be assumed, which is why methods and technologies must be used that allow execution over the Internet. New service ideas are based on known or assumed customer needs. Within the analysis phase, they can be identified and prioritized [3]. Subsequently, the service concept can be developed from an understanding of customer problems. Possible methods to tackle this objective are e.g. Interview for Empathy, Expert Interview, Job Mapping, Customer Journey Mapping, Shadowing, or the Smart Service Canvas. To speed up the development process, assumptions regarding the customer are made in the first iteration. Subsequently, the service concept is developed incrementally. Its realization as a prototype allows the verification of the assumptions of the customer.

Applied Method and Rationale for Its Selection: A suitable method is *Customer Journey Mapping* (CJM). It helps to describe the service process from a customer point of view and improve the understanding of customer experience during the use of the service. Unlike *service blueprinting* or *multilevel service design*, or *customer experience modeling,* the customer process, ("journey"), is considered holistically in customer *journey mapping.* Instead of using a General Purpose Modeling Language and focusing on a service system or a single service provider, a holistic approach is used here [24]. The chosen organizational setting is a workshop, which has been identified as suitable for the collection and sharing of ideas [23], including CJM [24].

Application of Method and Results: A total of five persons, aged 35–45, from the departments Research & Development (R&D), product management, sales and consulting participated in the workshop. All results were documented by the moderator in "Draw.io" using a shared screen. In the beginning, the participants were instructed on the method and its application. After that, a persona was modeled to represent a typical user of the service. Based on this, the customer journey for the current service process (AS-IS) is modeled. Using a voting scheme, all workshop participants could identify customer touchpoints, which were considered particularly positive or negative on the overall experience, the so-called "moments of truth". Negative touchpoints represent potential sources for innovative ideas that improve the customer experience. In the last step of the workshop, these innovation potentials were jointly identified. After the workshop, identified innovation potentials were evaluated through a first technical analysis and a rough estimation of development cost. The workshop resulted in a definition of a persona with 24 attributes as well as a customer journey with eleven touchpoints and six moments of truth. All the six moments of truth were identified as negative influences on customer experience. Based on that, a potential innovation idea for predictive costing service was identified and documented in the form of a mind map.

Evaluation: The gathered feedback on the iteration was positive, as all participants stated the workshop achieved its objective, and only one participant said that no meaningfully usable result was created. 2 of 5 participants stated they had not known the method used beforehand. Positive feedback was received for structuring the method introduction using an example before each process step. Improvement potential was identified regarding time planning. Especially for the task "Model Customer Journey" participants wanted more time, which was interestingly the part that already took more time than originally allocated for it.

Reflection and Learning: The noted insufficient time for designing the customer journey is most likely attributable to the relatively high level of detail of the produced method artifact. To account for this, it seems reasonable to start with a more general method, e.g. the customer perspective of the Smart Service Canvas.

4.2 Iteration II: Idea Assessment and Follow-Up Decision

Initial Situation and Objective: The second iteration aims to examine whether identified innovation potentials are promising enough to be pursued further or whether new ideas must be searched for. To this end, insights into the related problem "carry-over part analysis", especially the frequency, are to be required. Carry-over parts are elements, which can be used in multiple products with modification. As other vendors in the market are already offering solutions for carry-over part analysis, it is important to understand its relation to the potential new predictive costing service. Generally, suitable methods are e.g. Interview for Empathy or the Expert Interview, "to be" Customer Journey, and Idea Contest.

Applied Method and Rationale for Its Selection: The *expert interview* is a method that is suitable for data collection when the knowledge of the expert to be interviewed appears useful in the design, implementation, or control of problem-solving. The interview attempts to reconstruct (explicit) expert knowledge and to gain useful insight from this. Characteristics of expert interviews are the thematic focus, the use of technical terminology, and the communication of all participants at eye level [17].

Application of Method and Results: In total, three interviews were conducted. Selected experts were two product managers as well as a customer, who is the Head of Cost Engineering and Order Design of an automotive supplier. The duration of the interviews was one hour for each product manager and 30 min for the customer.

The execution is divided into three phases: preparation, interview, and follow-up. The preparation aims to make the actual interview as efficient as possible. Specifically, the interviewer familiarized himself with the topic and elaborated a guideline with relevant questions. Within the preparatory phase, the questions are forwarded to the interviewee, so that they can prepare themselves for the interview, too. The interviews are conducted digitally through the collaboration tool Microsoft Teams. After a short introduction at the beginning of each interview, the questions sent in advance are answered by the expert and recorded in writing by the interviewer. After successfully conducting all three expert interviews, the results are processed and consolidated. Similarities and differences within the answers are identified. This serves as a basis for discussion as to how the developed innovation potential "equal part analysis" should be pursued.

Evaluation and Learnings: The results and the subsequent discussion helped to make an informed decision on the follow-up of the innovation potential. In addition to the decision-making discussion, the expert knowledge collected is useful and valuable for further service development. Due to the intensive preparation of the appointments, it was possible to hold technical and efficient discussions. Expert interviews are suitable for situations in which in-depth knowledge is required and where a common knowledge base and technical language already exist between the participants.

4.3 Iteration III: Elaborate Customer Assumptions

Initial Situation and Objective: According to DIN SPEC 33453, the identification of innovation potentials is followed by the structured elaboration of customer assumptions regarding the innovation potential. In this step, it is important to understand what the customer is doing, what goals he pursues, and which circumstances are inhibiting or promoting, e.g. with Shadowing or the Smart Service Canvas. Ideally, this is done in collaboration with potential customers. Due to external influences, this was not possible for this iteration. The availability of the company's employees, as well as the willingness of customers to spend time on this task, was low due to other priorities (mainly caused by the COVID-19 pandemic). To create high-quality results, this iteration is based on the employees with high customer contact, as they are available for a sufficiently long period. Meetings and workshops could still only be held online.

Applied Method and Rationale for Its Selection: The first workshop shows that a less straightforward and more interactive method should be chosen. A structured yet flexible approach for the analysis, development, and description of smart services is the *Smart Service Canvas* (SSC) [13]. It builds on the Value Proposition Canvas (VPC) [19] and extends it with smart service specific aspects, which classifies it as DSM. The SSC is organized into the value perspective, the customer perspective, the ecosystem perspective, and the fit between these perspectives (see Fig. 1). As one of these perspectives focuses on the customer, this section of the SSC should serve as the basis for the workshop. The customer view is based on the customer profile of the VPC and includes the fields *Customer Routines and Jobs*, *Customer Pains*, and *Customer Gains*. These are supplemented by the fields *Context of Customer Tasks* and *Contextual Things and Data*. A customer view is recommended for each customer segment to be considered [13]. We expect the SSC to support gaining a structured understanding of the customer and elaborate on the service using the other perspectives at a later stage.

Application of Method and Results: To prevent the timing problems that occurred in the first workshop (Iteration 1), the time-boxing technique was applied in this iteration. Time-boxing was originally applied in agile software development to restrict the available amount of time for a task. This should lead to a selection of the most important tasks, which fit in the defined time box and thus lead to an improvement in software quality [25]. In our case, two workshops were planned with three slots of 40 min each to address the modeling of aspects persona, Customer Gains, Customer Routines and Jobs, Customer Pains, Context of Routines and Jobs, Contextual Things and Data. The workshop was conducted using Microsoft Teams and all results were continuously documented in a shared "Draw.io" document. The four participants were aged 35–45 and worked in the departments R&D, product management and sales. The result of the workshop is another persona with 22 attributes. The SSC customer perspective could be filled with 13 entries for Customer Gains, 11 for Customer Jobs, 19 for Customer Pains, 12 for Context of Customer Jobs, and 10 for Contextual Things and Data.

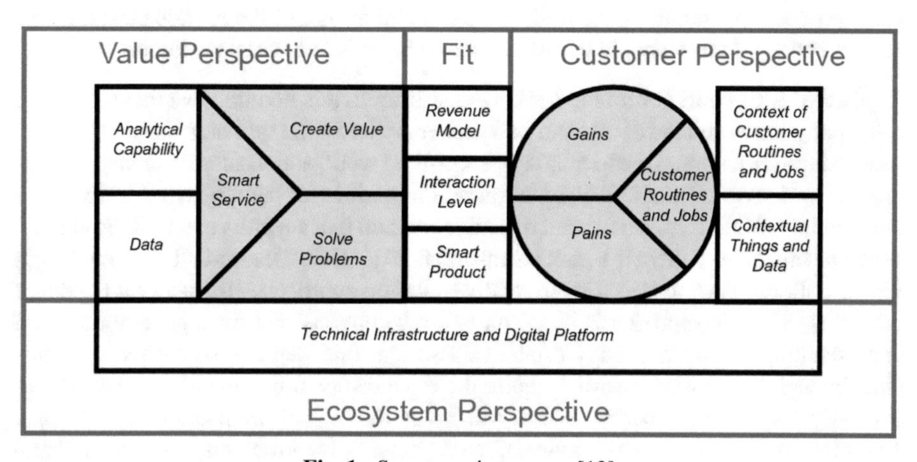

Fig. 1. Smart service canvas [13]

Evaluation and Learnings: The creation of the persona was significantly faster than in the first workshop. According to the principle of time-boxing, the gained time was transferred to the task modeling of Customer Gains. Due to the economic situation of the company, fewer people took part in the second workshop day. This resulted in a lower communication effort, which saved time that was added to the discussion on Contextual Things and Data. The classification of Customer Gains and Jobs/Routines resulting from the literature proved to be difficult and not clear-cut. For this reason, this differentiation was dropped in the second workshop. It was also found that many Customer Gains are mutually dependent. The Contextual Things and Data field received special attention within the workshop, with a focus on the area of data.

The feedback of the workshop participants shows that the method performed was either not known among the participants or was not known in the smart service-specific form. The objective of the workshop has been achieved and the result has been evaluated as reusable. On the positive side, an increase in the participants' understanding was recognized. The structure of the workshop and the time organization was also positively noted. For even more efficient meetings of this kind, a stronger usage of an example scenario was asked for. The customer's perspective of the SSC can be used when an identified customer segment must be investigated. It is important to limit customer activities, which are to be considered within the SSC. Therefore, the method is not suitable for an exploratory approach. However, in the initial phase of service engineering, the open design of the SSC reveals strengths through its flexibility.

4.4 Iteration IV: Complete the Value Proposition

Initial Situation and Objective: The results of the first two workshops in Iteration I and Iteration III were able to provide a comprehensive understanding of the customer. Based on these findings, the first thoughts on the actual service offer are now being made. The goal of this iteration is to formulate the service's value proposition. This value proposition should be the basis for the initial design of the service concept. The service concept in turn should be sufficient as a basis for an initial prototype.

Applied Method and Rationale for Its Selection: In this iteration, we focused on the value perspective and the ecosystem perspective of the SSC. For that, a basic idea of the service is required first. Due to holidays, short-time work, and pandemic-related restrictions, a workshop-format implementation was infeasible for the targeted time frame of this iteration. Therefore, we needed a flexible method that supports creativity in service development. One of them is to ask result-oriented questions, the so-called "How Might We"-questions. They aim to trigger creative solution approaches for relevant customer problems [3]. This approach is based on two assumptions: Firstly, a general common understanding has been already established so that this step can be carried out individually and does not necessarily require the organizational framework of a workshop. Secondly, the value perspective can be filled with the help of result-oriented questions. The relevant fields are Smart Service, Create Value, Solve Problems, Analytical Capabilities, and Data [13]. The ecosystem view describes the digital platform and technical infrastructure that underlies the smart service. The technical infrastructure includes, for example, the necessary hardware for power supply, but also the required network connection. The digital platform encompasses the ecosystem on which the smart service is based [13].

Application of Method and Results: The basis for the creation of the "How Might We"-questions are the customer problems of the SSC's customer perspective. At first, a thematic clustering of the problems is carried out here. Subsequently, the corresponding questions are derived from it. The preparation of the questions is iterative, to ensure that they are neither too broad nor too narrow for the required level of creative freedom. The questions were sent to each participant and answered individually. An individual discussion of the answers takes place after that. The result of this iteration first thoughts on the design of the new smart service. It also provided a reason to discuss the differentiation with the competition. It was also determined that the original service positioning had to be modified: Instead of a general similar part service, the focus shifts towards target price offerings, i.e. a specific form in the preparation of quotations.

Evaluation and Learnings: The method used by the "How Might We"-questions is well suited as a creative solution-oriented introduction. The value perspective of the SSC helped to thematically structure the answers. Individual elaboration seems to be possible if a common understanding of the topic has been established in advance. The integration of an initial definition question ensured that all participants had considered the content of the same topic. This increases the response quality and enables the combination of individual solution proposals. However, the high flexibility must be paid for through high effort in the preparation of the questions, as well as in the follow-up through individual discussions and the evaluation of the answers.

4.5 Iteration V: Design the Service Concept

Initial Situation and Objective: The goal of this iteration is to create a service concept in a structured form. The quality of the result should be sufficient for the creation of an initial simple prototype. Initial considerations from previous iterations are to be incorporated into the concept creation. Based on the results, the value perspective of the SSC is to be refined. To tackle these objectives potential methods are e.g. Job Mapping, Digital Mock-up, Paper Prototyping, and (Information) Service Blueprinting.

Applied Method and Rationale for Its Selection: Service Blueprints are structured visual descriptions of a service delivery process [26]. It allows the separation of tasks performed by the customer and backstage activities. *Information Service Blueprint* (ISB) is a variant of Service Blueprints for Information Intensive Services (IIS) [21]. The ISB is structured in a matrix of layers and phases, to which the individual actions are assigned. The default structure of the ISB comprises the seven rows Customer Action, Information, Information Delivery System (IDS), Information Production System (IPS), and Partners. The IDS and IPS rows are divided into Information and Communication Systems (ICT Systems) and Roles of Employees. This is completed by the horizontal grouping of activities into the seven phases of objective attainment in an IIS process: Define, Prepare, Execute, Monitor, Modify, and Conclude [21]. The first row of the ISB default structure lists the customer's activities, while the second row describes the information content. The rows IDS and IPS shows which roles of the employees, respectively of the ICT systems, participate in the generation and provision of the information. The bottom row represents the partners of the provider network that may be involved in the service process [21]. It is highly recommended to customize the structure of the ISB according to individual needs and the intended scope.

Application of Method and Results: The workshop is carried out on two dates with the partial physical presence of the participants. Two employees of the R&D department and one member of the company's product management department are involved. As a starting point, an overview of the *Service Blueprint* method is given, followed by the ISB. The workshop is organized in three phases according to the ISB design approach: Customization, Blueprinting, and Analysis. In phase one, a customized ISB is created, which is used to design the target service. Depending on the purpose, the default structure of the ISB can be adjusted by deleting, reworking, splitting, consolidating, or extending the rows. The initial step in phase one is to define the scope of service blueprinting. Here, the related customer segment and the participants of the design process are determined. Step two adjusts the rows of the ISB. The IIS is drafted in phase two. All components of the previously defined ISB are traversed row by row. The exact sequence of the rows to be traversed can be varied, provided that the customer-oriented perspective is valued. Finally, for this phase, the ISB is divided into the individual columns that categorize the service process. The third and final phase involves the analysis of the designed IIS. First, the Service Blueprint is thoroughly reviewed to ensure that no important points are missing. The final step is to look for ways to improve the design. If necessary, a further breakdown of customer actions or customer information may also be carried out beyond phase three [21]. The completed ISB for the predictive costing service is shown in Fig. 2. It shows the ISB in the adapted version, as it was used in the workshop. The rows Customer Actions, Information, and ICT Systems were adopted from the default structure. For the optimal mapping of the Predictive Costing process, the rows Algorithm, Data Location, as well as Internal and External Data Provider were introduced. They emphasize the data-heavy nature of the service design developed in this workshop. After the workshop, the existing contents of the SSC value perspective were refined. The discussed findings and the developed service concept from the ISB workshop are incorporated. The result is a further elaborated value proposition of the service.

Evaluation: A structured, comprehensive service design was successfully developed in two workshop appointments. In the beginning, the high degree of abstraction of the method, as well as the high flexibility, was perceived as challenging. However, this was successfully addressed with an iterative approach. Like the CJM method, ISB is particularly suitable for "happy path"-representations. The results of the SSC were a useful basis for the work on this task. By dividing the service process into seven phases, we discovered new customer steps that were not considered before. The ISB helps to discuss specific details of the service, as it shows how individual steps and the various systems interact with each other. Through the discussion within the workshop, also a new customer segment for the service was identified. The first result, classified as a "convincing first draft", can be transferred to a *Paper Prototype* in a further step. It may also be useful for a discussion with customers.

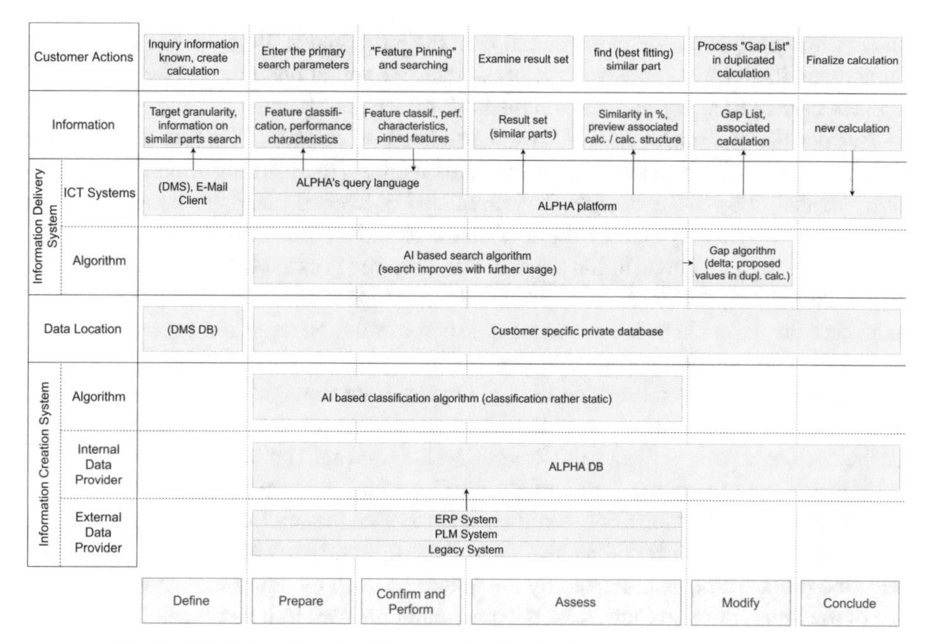

Fig. 2. Workshop Artefact "Information Service Blueprint" (own depiction)

Reflection and Learning: After several iterations, the SSC proves to be a viable tool to keep an overview and consecutively enhance the service while also keeping in check, that the value proposition aligns with the customer needs in the end.

5 Discussion and Formalization of Learning

The overall project can be considered as a success, as a useful service concept was collaboratively developed within the Action Design Research approach. Several artifacts were created, which represent a growing understanding and advancement in the development of a new service. Our research yielded the following **findings**:

1. All identified tasks could be supported with a method from our pre-compiled list, which contained DSM, SEM, UCD, and GPM types of methods.
2. All selected methods were found to be suitable as they created useful results that could be further elaborated and reused in subsequent iterations.
3. The combination of methods is not only possible but also particularly useful. It turned out that they helped to provide structure and guidance for the service innovation project, e.g. through different perspectives and levels of detail.

However, the variety of methods poses a high demand on the competence of project participants. DSM were not known to most practitioners, which underlines the findings by Wolf et al. [1] and Anke et al. [2]. Even more established methods like *Customer*

Journey Mapping required an introduction to the participants. Being aware of a certain method and its purpose, however, is not enough. We found that many details needed to be taken care of to apply the selected methods effectively.

Besides the practically relevant result, the learning regarding the research question must be considered. In phase four of the ADR method, the learning should be formalized. For that, the ADR principle 7 "generalized outcomes" needs to be applied. The main result of our study is a selection of methods and their combination to support the systematic design of a new digital service. For that, we (1) extracted the chosen methods used in the project, (2) identified and labeled the output of each applied method, and (3) connected the methods based on their input-output-relation. A visual representation of the method combination is shown in Fig. 3.

Starting from an initial service idea, the methods on the right-hand side are focused on advancing the understanding of the customer and its problems. These are the input for the customer perspective of the Smart Service Canvas. The link to the value proposition is achieved using the "How might we?"-method. A detailed service concept for the developed value proposition can then be elaborated using the Information Service Blueprint, as shown on the left-hand side of the figure. It has also helped to improve the value proposition, as indicated by the dotted arrow. The figure indicates the central role of the Smart Service Canvas for the innovation process, as it combines the customer view with the value proposition view.

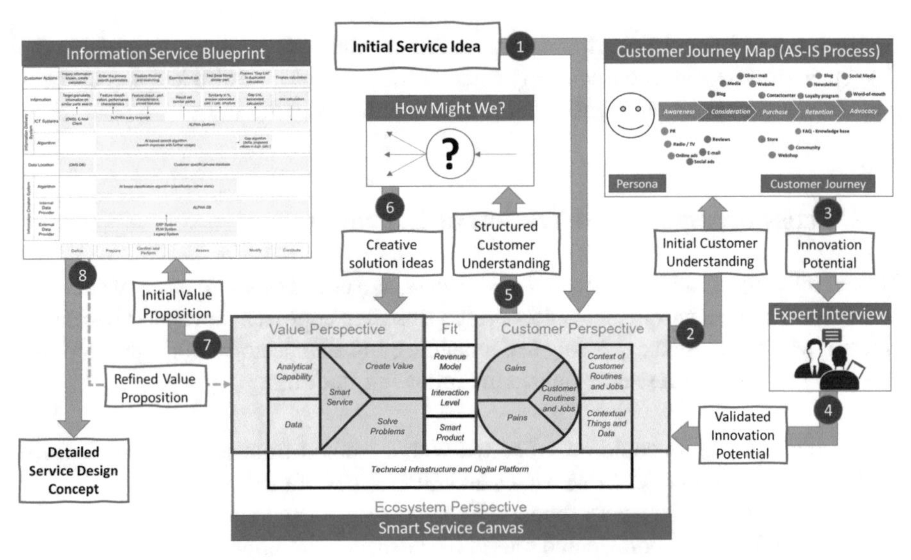

Fig. 3. The proposed combination of methods for iterative service innovation

Concerning the underlying DIN SPEC 33453 reference process model, we found that the first three steps are related to "Analysis" phase activities, while steps 4 and 5 are part of "Design" activities. None of the methods contribute to the "Implementation" phase, as it was not within the scope of the ADR project in this study. However, we would like to highlight that the proposed combination of methods is not limited to projects using the DIN SPEC 33453 process model.

The result shows a combination of existing methods for digital service innovation, which was successfully applied in a real-world project. We assume, that this specific case is a representation of a digital service according to Heuermann, Duin, et al. [27]. It should be noted that the proposed combination is neither claimed to be the best nor the only one. However, we assume that it is applicable to similar innovation projects, as the selected methods are designed for these tasks. Furthermore, the input-output-relationships between the proposed combination of methods are not specific to the concrete case in our study. Practitioners might use it as a starting point, especially if the methodological competence in an organization is low. It might also help to stimulate discussion about method combinations for both practitioners and researchers alike.

The results of our study are subject to **limitations**. ADR, as a research paradigm, is inherently subjective, i.e. a different researcher might have selected different methods and/or applied them slightly differently. Also, the competence and knowledge of methods and their application highly depends on the individual. This is amplified by the application to only a single case. Finally, the underlying list of 30 methods in total was not exhaustive. Other researchers might have known different methods. Due to the many factors that influence the suitability of methods in a concrete situation, our results should be considered as an illustrative yet thoroughly conducted example. Finally, the project took place during the COVID-19 virus pandemic. Therefore, most settings had to be digital rather than face-to-face meetings. This imposed further restrictions on the selection of methods, as not all methods are suitable for digital settings. However, as remote work is a widely used way of collaborating, this is setting is not exceptional.

6 Conclusion

This study sheds light on the application of multiple SSE methods in a real-world project and thus helps to understand how these methods are used together to develop new digital services. It shows how methods are combined and how synergy effects are used. These are DSM, such as *Smart Service Canvas*, and SEM, such as the *Customer Journey Map*, but also GPM such as the *Expert Interview*. The special circumstances of the case study also show that medium-sized companies with scarce resources can successfully develop digital services using new methods. The exchange between science and practice was organized efficiently through the structure provided by ADR, which makes the use of this approach for future innovation projects promising [7].

The **contributions** of this study are as follows: First, we showed how existing methods for SSE can be applied in practice and evaluated their suitability for the task. We provided rationales for the selection of methods, described their application, and created results. Second, we critically reflected on the challenges and pitfalls that occurred during the usage of chosen methods. Third, we showed how the results of the applied method can be used for other methods in a later iteration. The link between inputs and outputs of methods is the basis for a combination of methods in a meaningful way. The work also helped to gain new insights into the methods used, e.g., *Customer Journey Mapping* was carried out in its entirety. Unlike the study by Senderek et al. [11], it was applied to a complex customer process. The *Smart Service Canvas* from Pöppelbuß and Durst [13] proved to be a helpful framework for structuring the development work across multiple iterations. The application of the *Information Service Blueprinting* [9] provides another example of a customized ISB, which can be used as an additional source of inspiration. Finally, our results indicate a set of methods that actors with the "Digital Innovator" role could use to facilitate the creation of new service ideas [22]. From our results in the investigated project, the following **conclusions** can be drawn:

- There was no lack of methods for the tasks at hand, but a lack of awareness for their existence and competence for their application. Hence, the focus should be on the transfer of existing methods to practice, rather than on the development of new ones. This appears to be inconsistent with a study that found that existing methods do not cover all phases and perspectives in SSE for smart services [28]. However, it is not contradictory as they evaluated the suitability of methods regarding smart service characteristics, while we focused on the innovation stage of a single case in practice.
- The combination of methods is helpful to coordinate work in digital service innovation projects, but as of now, there is little guidance on how to combine which methods. Therefore, future research should focus on the potential links between existing methods, e.g. through input/output-relationships.
- High flexibility in selection and combination of methods is needed to cater to different types of tasks, settings, and competencies. Thus, better means for descriptions of such settings are needed, e.g. through taxonomies of services, innovation patterns, and skillsets. Furthermore, there are no criteria to evaluate these combinations, e.g. regarding their suitability to a concrete setting. Some of the concepts from SME might be useful but should probably be less formal.

Overall, the results of this research provide an example for further advancing empirically grounded knowledge on SSE. Due to the high relevance for practice, this topic offers opportunities for collaboration between academics and practitioners.

References

1. Wolf, V., Franke, A., Bartelheimer, C., Beverungen, D.: Establishing smart service systems is a challenge: a case study on pitfalls and implications. In: Gronau, N., Heine, M., Poustcchi, K., Krasnova, H. (eds.) WI2020 Community Tracks, pp. 103–119. GITO Verlag (2020)
2. Anke, J., Ebel, M., Poeppelbuss, J., Alt, R.: How to tame the tiger. exploring the means, ends, and challenges in smart service systems engineering. In: 28th European Conference on Information Systems (2020)
3. Deutsches Institut für Normung e.V.: DIN SPEC 33453:2019-09, Entwicklung digitaler Dienstleistungssysteme. Beuth, Berlin ICS 03.080.01; 35.240.50 (2019)
4. Beverungen, D., Lüttenberg, H., Wolf, V.: Recombinant service systems engineering. Bus. Inf. Syst. Eng. **60**(5), 377–391 (2018). https://doi.org/10.1007/s12599-018-0526-4
5. Böhmann, T., Leimeister, J.M., Möslein, K.: Service systems engineering. Bus Inf. Syst. Eng. **6**, 73–79 (2014)
6. Sein, M.K., Henfridsson, O., Purao, S., Rossi, M., Lindgren, R.: Action design research. MIS Q. **35**, 37 (2011)

7. Becker, F., Meyer, M., Redlich, B., Siemon, D., Lattemann, C.: Open KMU: mit action design research und design thinking gemeinsam innovieren. Eur. J. Mark. **57**, 274–284 (2020)
8. Yang, C.-F., Sung, T.-J.: Service design for social innovation through participatory action research. Int. J. Des. **10**, 21–36 (2016)
9. Lim, C., Kim, K.-H., Kim, M.-J., Heo, J.-Y., Kim, K.-J., Maglio, P.P.: From data to value: a nine-factor framework for data-based value creation in information-intensive services. Int. J. Inform. Manage. **39**, 121–135 (2018)
10. Beverungen, D., Müller, O., Matzner, M., Mendling, J., Vom Brocke, J.: Conceptualizing smart service systems. Elec. Markets **29**, 7–18 (2019)
11. Senderek, R., Ragab, S., Stratmann, L., Krechting, D.: Smart-service-engineering. In: Stich, V., Schumann, J.H., Beverungen, D., Gudergan, G., Jussen, P. (eds.) Digitale Dienstleistungsinnovationen, pp. 3–15. Springer, Heidelberg (2019). https://doi.org/10.1007/978-3-662-59517-6_1
12. Redlich, B., et al.: Das DETHIS-Verfahren. In: Stich, V., Schumann, J.H., Beverungen, D., Gudergan, G., Jussen, P. (eds.) Digitale Dienstleistungsinnovationen, pp. 73–88. Springer, Heidelberg (2019). https://doi.org/10.1007/978-3-662-59517-6_4
13. Poeppelbuss, J., Durst, C.: Smart Service Canvas – a tool for analyzing and designing smart product-service systems. Procedia CIRP **83**, 324–329 (2019)
14. Henderson-Sellers, B., Ralyté, J., Ågerfalk, P.J., Rossi, M.: Situational Method Engineering. Springer, Heidelberg (2014). https://doi.org/10.1007/978-3-642-41467-1
15. Clarke, P., O'Connor, R.V.: The situational factors that affect the software development process: towards a comprehensive reference framework. Inf. Softw. Technol. **54**, 433–447 (2012)
16. Leimeister, J.M.: Dienstleistungsengineering und -management. Data-driven Service Innovation. Springer, Heidelberg (2020)
17. Pfadenhauer, M.: Das Experteninterview. In: Buber, R., Holzmüller, H.H. (eds.) Qualitative Marktforschung, pp. 449–461. Gabler, Wiesbaden (2009)
18. Lemon, K.N., Verhoef, P.C.: Understanding customer experience throughout the customer journey. J. Mark. **80**, 69–96 (2016)
19. Patton, J.: User Story Mapping. O'Reilly Media, Sebastopol (2014)
20. 2019 IEEE 21st Conference on Business Informatics (CBI). IEEE (2019)
21. Lim, C.-H., Kim, K.-J.: Information service blueprint: a service blueprinting framework for information-intensive services. Serv. Sci. **6**, 296–312 (2014)
22. Anke, J., Poeppelbuss, J., Alt, R.: It takes more than two to tango: identifying roles and patterns in multi-actor smart service innovation. Schmalenbach Bus. Rev. **72**(4), 599–634 (2020). https://doi.org/10.1007/s41464-020-00101-2
23. Westhoff, G., Drougas, A.: Content design and methodology of seminars, workshops and congresses (2002)
24. Heuchert, M.: Conceptual modeling meets customer journey mapping: structuring a tool for service innovation. In: 2019 IEEE 21st Conference on Business Informatics (CBI), pp. 531–540. IEEE (2019)
25. Jalote, P., Palit, A., Kurien, P., Peethamber, V.T.: Timeboxing: a process model for iterative software development. J. Syst. Softw. **70**, 117–127 (2004)
26. Lynn Shostack, G.: How to design a service. Eur. J. Mark. **16**, 49–63 (1982)

27. Heuermann, A., Duin, H., Gorldt, C., Thoben, K.-D., Nobel, T.: Reifegradorientierte Konzeption und iterative Implementierung digitaler Dienstleistungen für maritime Logistikprozesse. In: Stich, V., Schumann, J.H., Beverungen, D., Gudergan, G., Jussen, P. (eds.) Digitale Dienstleistungsinnovationen, pp. 17–47. Springer, Heidelberg (2019). https://doi.org/10.1007/978-3-662-59517-6_2
28. Marx, E., Pauli, T., Fielt, E., Matzner, M.: From services to smart services: can service engineering methods get smarter as well? In: 15th International Conference on Wirtschaftsinformatik (2020)

A Software Ecosystem for the Development of Digital Service Design Tools: A Conceptual Framework

Timon Sengewald(✉), Max Jalowski, and Martin Schymanietz

Chair of Information Systems – Innovation and Value Creation, Friedrich-Alexander-Universität Erlangen-Nürnberg (FAU), Nuremberg, Germany
{timon.sengewald,max.jalowski,martin.schymanietz}@fau.de

Abstract. Numerous service design tools, techniques, and methods have been developed in science and practice alike (e.g., *Persona*, *Service Blueprint*, *Stakeholder Map*). Some of these tools build on each other, e.g., different developed *Personas* can be positioned and placed in a broader overall context within a *Stakeholder Map*. Digitisation of the design process can generate significant benefits; for instance, results can be transferred between different digital tools and devices using a common or standardised file format. However, there are few digital tools to support the service design process and most of them are not interoperable. This prevents the design of services using digital technologies from achieving their full benefits. To address this problem, an ecosystem is needed that can foster the development of digital-enabled service design tools. The paper follows a design science approach to create a framework involving five design objectives as necessary steps towards such a software ecosystem.

Keywords: Service design · Digital-enabled service design · Service design tools · Service innovation · Design science research

1 Introduction

For some time now, it has been apparent that the economy is moving from product-based to service-based [1, 2], and Vargo and Lusch's Service-Dominant Logic [3, 4] has influenced business model development from a product-based to a service-based perspective. For researchers and companies alike, the issues of service innovation and service business model innovation have become increasingly central to new forms of competitiveness [5, 6], with calls for a more systematic and structured approach to innovation [7] and service innovation [8]. Service Science addresses this need by advancing the systematic development of services and service systems [2, 9] to make results more predictable [7] and to support creativity during the innovation process [10, 11]. Service design plays an important role in facilitating customer-centred and systematic innovation [12], including a systems perspective that takes account of the extended networks of actors and digital technologies now involved in service provision [13, 14]. This systematic approach is the focus of service systems engineering research [14], and the methods,

F. Ahlemann et al. (Eds.): WI 2021, LNISO 46, pp. 203–218, 2021.
https://doi.org/10.1007/978-3-030-86790-4_15

techniques and tools of service innovation, service design and service systems engineering are extensively reported both in the scientific literature (e.g., *Service Blueprint* [15]; Service *Experience Blueprint* [16]; *Information Service Blueprint* [17]; *TRIGGER* [18]) and in practitioner publications (e.g., *Business Model Generation* [19]; *The digital transformation playbook* [20]; *This is Service Design Doing* [21]; *Sprint* [22]). As well as tools for designing single services or service systems, there are tools for designing the associated business models (e.g., *Service Business Model Canvas* [23]; *SDBM/R* [24]) and for modelling how a company creates, appropriates and captures value by providing a service [25]. As Gilsing et al. [25] have shown, methods can also be developed for evaluating the design of business models.

A systematic approach to innovation is increasingly necessary for a number of reasons, including increased probability of success [7] and mastery of complex systems [8, 14]. This systematic development process can be partly or wholly supported by methods or tools [26, 27]. In many cases, the steps of the process are worked through interactively [28, 29], often involving collaboration with potential customers [30] and other relevant actors [31, 32]. In developing solutions systematically, the design process is also likely to be iterative [28, 29]. Relevant terms, methods, techniques and tools will be more precisely defined in Sect. 2.

Many of the methods, techniques and tools developed by the scientific community to support the service design process have been combined in new ways to create coherent methods (e.g., [18]). For instance, as Li and Peters [33] have shown, the formal structuring and analysis of service systems can also produce service innovations. In relation to the use of digital technologies to support the innovation process, earlier research confirms that IT (especially software) can support user creativity [34, 35] as well as systematic and structured development [10]. For example, because digital objects can be easily duplicated, digital tools make it much easier to create multiple scenarios or variants of a basic design, and the ability to undo or redo actions makes it easier to experiment [10]. Researchers have also investigated the use of digital technologies for collaborative design of business models (e.g., [36–38]).

The advantages of digital solutions for collaborative work extend to support for remote corporate teamworking in crisis situations such as the current COVID-19 pandemic [39]. However, although innovative tools or IT artefacts can make a valuable contribution to the development of service-oriented business models or transformation of existing business models [40], only a few such tools have been developed within service science research and practice. To explore how the development of such tools might be promoted, this paper addresses the following research question:

RQ: What technical standards and prerequisites need to be considered to support the creation of a software ecosystem for the development of digital-enabled service design tools?

We argue that this research is highly relevant as it can help increase the transfer of complex IT artefacts for service design to practice and vice versa. An ecosystem, which interlocks science and practice more closely, can help to apply the quality criteria of research in the development of digital-enabled service design tools in practice and can thus ensure more rigor. The artefacts can then in turn be tested in practice in real-world scenarios and thus transfer knowledge back to science.

The paper is structured as follows. The next section provides an overview of the current state of research on software ecosystems and defines the concept of digital-enabled service design. We go on to describe the artefact by presenting a conceptual framework for a software ecosystem for developing digital-enabled service design. We then discuss how the field of service innovation can benefit from the creation of such a software ecosystem to foster the development of digital-enabled tools and methods for service design research and practice. Finally, we discuss the study's contribution to Information Systems and Service Science, as well as limitations and directions for future research.

2 Theoretical Background

2.1 Digital-Enabled Service Design

In distinguishing between digital and non-digital services [29], the former can be defined as *'a service, which are obtained and/or arranged through a digital transaction (information, software modules, or consumer goods) over Internet Protocol (IP)'* [29, p. 506]. The distinction from a normal service is that the specification of the supply as digital is more restrictive by comparison [29]. The term *digital innovation* has two possible meanings, referring either to digital technologies that support the innovation process itself or to the output of that process [27]. In research contexts, the term *digital service design* commonly refers to the design of digital services as an object of research (e.g., [28]). Equally, however, the term may imply that the design process itself is digital-based. To avoid misinterpretation or ambiguity, the term *digital-enabled service design* is used here to refer to the design of services using digital technologies.

According to Brinkkemper, the terms *method*, *technique* and *tool* are used in the present context [41], but these are not clearly defined in the literature and are used interchangeably [28]. Brinkkemper defines a *method* as *'an approach to perform a systems development project, based on a specific way of thinking, consisting of directions and rules, structured in a systematic way in development activities with corresponding development products'* [41, p. 275 f.] (see also [18, 42]). On the other hand, a *technique* is '*a procedure, possibly with a prescribed notation, to perform a development activity*' [41]. (For an example of a technique, see [43]). Finally, a *tool* is '*a possibly automated means to support a part of a development process*' or to support the entire development cycle [41] (e.g., *Information Service Blueprint* [17])—for instance, a software application, a design template, or a hardware device to support the design process [28]. A tool usually supports one part of a technique [44], although complete mapping of a technique or method is also possible [41]. Based on these distinctions, we understand the term *digital-enabled service design tool* to mean a digital tool that supports the design of services or service systems by representing a design method or technique in full or in part. In this definition, the use of a template in a digital whiteboard tool, as they are common with miro[1], mural[2], or strategyzer[3], would also be understood as a digital-enabled service design tool. This type of tool provides users with a digital whiteboard to which digital post-its can be attached. By providing drawing tools, almost every service design tool that can be displayed on a canvas for a workshop can also be displayed digitally. However, this paper focuses on more complex digital-enabled service design tools - such as ExperienceFellow[4] or smaply[5]. Smaply, for example, is a web service that enables its users to create virtual personas and also offers ready-made avatars, quotes and visualizations [45]. Tools that provide users with ready-made content for exploration can increase users' creativity by providing inspiration [46]. The app ExperienceFellow enables the collection of customer data. Users can capture different types of data (text, video or images) to document emotional experiences at customer touchpoints. These two tools therefore have a very high degree of specificity. These two examples enable two different activities, while the second enables the collection of data, the former directly supports the design process.

2.2 Development of An Software Ecosystem for Digital-Enabled Service Design

A software ecosystem is a system based on a software solution whose functionalities can be extended, for example, by third-party plugins [47]. Software ecosystems have attracted increasing research interest [47–49] and are increasingly used as industry business models [48, 50]. In general, software ecosystems can be defined in business and technical terms [51] or from a social perspective [48]. Scientific definitions differ [e.g., 51–53], but from a business perspective, a software ecosystem can be characterised as *'the set of software solutions that enable, support and automate the activities and transactions by the actors in the associated social or business ecosystem and the organisations that provide these solutions'* [50, p. 2]. Typically, such ecosystems encompass the necessary technology for implementation, the overall project infrastructure (e.g., project repositories, community platform) and the development methodology (e.g., standards, documentation) [52]. The ecosystem is controlled by a central actor or hub, usually the provider of the core software solution [47, 53]. Software ecosystems facilitate the construction of extensive software systems on a central platform, bringing together the components created by internal and external actors [48]. These individuals or organisations have different incentives for participating in the system [54], including increased benefits for existing users, increased attraction of potential new customers, potential for open innovation and reduced total cost of ownership [50]. In defining a set of rules for communication and cooperation among these actors, it is important to adopt a social perspective [48].

Various theories and strategies already exist for the systematic development of software ecosystems [e.g., 47, 50, 52]. Research to date suggests that standardisation can

---

[1] For a more detailed description follow the link: https://miro.com/.

[2] For a more detailed description follow the link: https://www.mural.co.

[3] For a more detailed description follow the link: https://www.strategyzer.com.

[4] For a more detailed description follow the link: https://www.experiencefellow.com.

[5] For a more detailed description follow the link: https://www.smaply.com.

increase innovation capacity [55]—for example, a standardised software architecture or data format [50]. Software architecture can be defined as a *'structure or structures of the system, which comprise software elements, the externally visible properties of those elements, and the relationships among them'* [48, p. 1295]. The software architecture should be designed to be easy for developers to understand, and it should be well documented [52]. The openness of the system and its core components is also crucial [56]—that is, open standards, open formats and open source [47]. Open standards support the development of interchangeable and interoperable components by different actors; open formats are a specific form of open standard that allow the exchange of data, information and knowledge [47]. Open source is the highest form of openness, as enabling access to the source code generates knowledge, modification and re-provision [47]. The ecosystem community and the associated form of organisation is another key factor [48, 52], and within this community or ecosystem, rules for communication and legalities must be clearly defined [52]. A well-formed and integrated community can increase a software ecosystem's robustness [47].

3 Research Design

To address the research question, we adopt a design science research (DSR) approach following Hevner et al. [57]. Within the DSR paradigm, a designer or researcher attempts to solve a problem by designing an innovative artefact [58]. In doing so, this work aims to develop an artefact which can be applied to the real-world and solve the problem [58, 59] of insufficient interoperability of digital-enabled service design tools. The artefact designed to solve the presented problem is a construct, where a construct is understood as a concept or conceptualisation [60, 61]. For artefact development, the six steps of the Design Science Research Methodology (DSRM) by Peffers et al. [62] are applied. These steps are as follows: (1) Problem Identification, (2) Objective Definition, (3) Design & Development, (4) Demonstration, (5) Evaluation and (6) Communication [62]. The methodology follows the Build and Evaluate pattern of Sonnenberg and vom Brocke [63]. This means that we already start the evaluation of the problem and objectives (ex ante evaluation) before we start with the specific design of the artefact. Following step 1, the problem underlying the artefact was treated and explained in the introduction. The design and development of the artefact adopts a conceptual approach, which explores new ideas and new connections between existing theories [64]. As in the case of empirical research methods, there are divergent approaches to conceptual research [65, 66]. In general, these can be divided into theory synthesis, theory adaptation, typology and modelling [65]. To develop the theoretical framework outlined below, we employed a conceptual modelling approach, in which the focal concept [65] is digital-enabled service design and the systematic development of ecosystems. In particular, we explored the factors that promote the formation of an ecosystem for developing digital-enabled service design tools, and to specify a roadmap for creating such an ecosystem—that is, a series of steps or events that achieve the desired output [65], where 'event' means something that causes a certain effect [65] as a mechanism that influences the overall goal. As a framework for theory building, the proposed roadmap takes the form of five design objectives based on previously untested relationships [64] as a foundation for the creation of such an ecosystem. These design objectives are derived from a literature review of existing knowledge about the formation of software ecosystems. The evaluation of the artefact following step 5 is artificial since it is not applied in a real-world scenario [63, 67]. The proposed solution was discussed with a group of researchers from the fields of service innovation and digital technologies. Hence, the artefact was evaluated against the criteria suitability, importance, applicability and novelty [63]. This results in a justified problem statement, a justified research gap and justified design objectives [63]. Step 6 is conducted by this publication and addresses itself primarily to the scholar's community.

4 Conceptual Framework

The five design objectives set out below are prerequisites for an ecosystem for the development of digital-enabled service design tools (cf. Fig. 1).

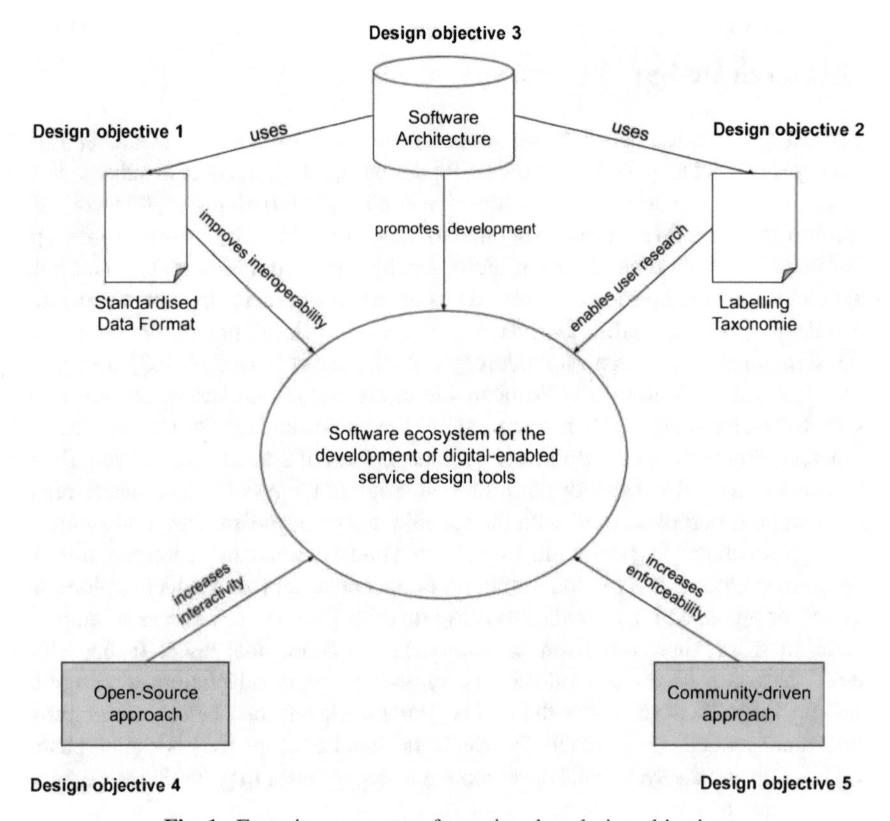

Fig. 1. Fostering ecosystem formation: key design objectives

As mentioned above, many tools build on each other to derive a process or method; others enable a differentiated level of abstraction through mutual use. For example, the *TRIGGER* method developed by Höckmayr and Roth uses four tools for the systematic development of digital-enabled service systems [18]. Another multistage process is classically applied in service design as follows: First, one or more *Personas* are designed, and a *Customer Journey* is then created, depicting each customer's various touchpoints. Based on this, a *Stakeholder Map* can then be drawn for the various actors [21]. Both processes use different tools whose results build on each other, but they also share similar core components. Both the *Job Map* within the *TRIGGER* method from the first example and the *Customer Journey* from the second example map the customer's activities to achieve a specific goal. Both represent a specific sequence of activities, as does the *Service Blueprint* [15], but they differ in terms of the involvement of different actors or the collection of additional information. While the *Customer Journey* records the touchpoints [21], the *Job Map* summarises activities as higher-level universal steps that are necessary to get a specific job done [68]. The tools, therefore, partly have similar structures with different additional information. Using a standardised data format, data can be transferred between different tools within a single design process such as *TRIGGER*.

As another possibility, one or more tools can be used for the design process, and the resulting result can be evaluated using another tool; this also requires the transfer of data or results. In general, digital data can be characterised as unstructured, semi-structured or structured [69]; tools require structured data for processing, and this, in turn, requires a standardised data format to ensure the interoperability of different tools. Digital-enabled service design tools could thus be developed by several actors who can exchange intermediate results via a standardised structured data format. Suppose three different digital-enabled service design tools were developed by three different actors: One to design personas, another one to design customer journeys, and a third one to design stakeholder maps. The output of the first tool can be used directly as input for a second tool via the structured data format and so on. In this way, the structured data format provides a link between otherwise independent digital-enabled service design tools to enable an iterative design process as is common in service design. Referring to the previous examples, one digital-enabled service design tool could help a user to design a persona. Properties of the designed persona can then be exported to a file that conforms to the standardised structured data format. The service designer could then use a second digital-enabled tool, which is specialised in designing a customer journey, to import the persona from this file and design the appropriate customer journey. The third tool could be used independently of tool two and could also process the output data from tool one.

A standardised data format used by a single instrument can also increase the value of the ecosystem, as standards provision generally increases innovation within an ecosystem [47]. For example, it could be used to develop software that digitises the results of an offline workshop and transfers them into an equivalent digital version for further editing. The use of standards enables developers to include functions for saving intermediate results, which supports documentation of the design process. In the case of digital tools, in particular, this capability supports service designers in creating different alternative scenarios and exploring multiple solutions [10]. This results in:

Design Objective 1: A standardised structured data format should be designed to improve the interoperability of digital-enabled service design tools.

Many service design tools require specific knowledge about the customer (e.g., demographic data of a *Persona*), customer goal or job in the *Job Map*. Service designers typically undertake research to acquire knowledge about the customer. Digital technologies can support user research—for example, by enabling customer data collection [e.g., 60]. For instance, the mobile application ExperienceFellow[6]: The app can capture different types of data (text, video or images) to document emotional experiences at customer touchpoints. Digital tools of this kind can also be used to collect customer data at various points in the company or during the product or service life cycle [e.g., 61]; for example, customer support can actively record negative or positive customer experiences for later evaluation or make use of existing data silos either within (e.g., CRM, ERP systems) or outside the company (e.g., social media) [71]. For digital-based business models, in particular, it is useful to collect customer data at various points for further analysis [72], using machine learning and computer algorithms to extract meaningful information for service innovation and service design [73]. Beyond social media and CRM systems, new data sources may be identified in the future [73, p. 36]. A standardised labelling taxonomy can also enhance the development of tools in the ecosystem for digital-enabled service design tools. Standardised labelling facilitates the development of specialised tools for data collection and others for analysing and evaluating those data. This results in:

Design Objective 2: A standardised labelling taxonomy for unstructured data should be designed to facilitate digitisation of user research.

The development of interoperable digital-enabled service design tools can also be enhanced by standardised modular software architecture. In general, the term *software architecture* refers to the core set of design decisions that define the software system itself [49], which is an important determinant of software ecosystem success [48, 52]. This includes, for example, the data formats recommended in *Design objective 1 and* 2. A well-designed architecture enhances the development of digital artefacts; for example, if each digital-enabled service design tool is constructed as a single module within a central software solution, a design method can then be represented as a process that calls individual modules in a specific order and transfers data between them. Therefore, individual design tools such as the *Job Map* or the *Service Blueprint* represent add-ons or modules for this solution. A modular software design can create considerable added value, as it makes it easier to experiment and validate different software components [74]. For instance, a specific service design process may already be well formed and validated, but the corresponding user interface of a digital-enabled service design tool may still have deficiencies. This could particularly occur when existing service design tools are converted into a digital-enabled version. Furthermore, functions necessary for such software, such as saving, undoing and redoing actions [10], can be implemented more easily, as design patterns already exist within the software architecture. However complex the architecture or its purpose, it should be easy to understand, communicate and document [52]. Besides, the architecture should be designed to allow changes, adaptations or new versions to be easily implemented [52]. This results in:

[6] For a more detailed description follow the link: https://www.experiencefellow.com.

Design Objective 3: A standardised modular software architecture should be designed to promote the development of digital-enabled service design tools for both science and industry.

Open source software is often characterised as a private public good produced by a community, involving such contributions as software, hardware, expertise or sponsorship [75] in various forms, which together with free software are referred to as Free/Libre/Open Source Software (FLOSS). FLOSS approaches are now widely used in the software industry to foster ecosystems, as this type of platform meets many of the necessary conditions [52]. It should be emphasised that an open source approach does not preclude partially proprietary use or distribution within the ecosystem; on the contrary, the ecosystem may even benefit from this approach [48, 76]. The content management system WordPress is a good example of an open source project that combines free, libre and proprietary software add-ons and a service ecosystem through its plugin system. Even in cases of partial proprietary use, the scientific community should be granted a free right to use for research purposes, based on a suitable licence (which may have to be developed) [75, 77]. Without appropriate licensing terms, there is no guarantee that researchers will be able to access the source code, which is important, for example, in promoting the further development of service design methods that use different tools in a specific order. An open source approach also has other advantages: As previous research has shown, open source communities can achieve better modularity than projects developed by a single actor [78]. This results in:

Design Objective 4: An ecosystem for digital-enabled service design tools should be designed through an open source approach to increase interactivity among actors.

For complex software systems, the ecosystem approach has proven to be useful [78]. Due to various existing barriers (technical, domain competency etc.), a large number of different stakeholders are usually involved in the design process, which has a positive effect on software development [78]. As mentioned above, this is also very much in the nature of the developing of digital-enabled service design tools. For example, the academic community probably has very high expertise in the domain of service design. However, the technical implementation, maintenance and support might be a barrier here. These in turn may be better provided by private sector actors, who in turn may develop their own business model. The academic community can again benefit from this, as developed IT artefacts may be easier to test in real-world scenarios. By combining the different expertise of these different stakeholders, the value generated for the ecosystem for digital-enabled service design tools can be increased, as research on software ecosystem shows [78]. However, there are also some peculiarities of a community-driven approach, such as software ecosystems are typically driven and controlled by a central actor or hub [47]. To the extent that private sector actor provisions are uncertain, we contend that a community-driven open source approach is essential for creating and enforcing such a system. Although many open source projects are community-driven, the term open source usually refers to software licensing while *community-driven* refers to the perspective of the main driving actor [75]. With reference to the open source software approach advanced in *Design objective 4*, various success factors have already been investigated [79]. In general, an open source software project can be seen as a virtual organisation that bundles competencies to drive development forward [80]. Regarding *Design objective 4*, community suitability and activity are essential for a successful open source project [52]. Similar community-driven approaches already exist in other areas of the scientific community; for example, the Open Science Framework (OSF) platform[7] enables researchers to organise research projects and share research data. It also requires an actor or organisation to act as a catalyst for the ideas proposed. This may include the bundled provision of functions and tracking of activities via a community platform—for example, providing a shared code repository or at least linking relevant works or published artefacts as the platform allows. The OSF platform is also an excellent example of providing guidance (on how to conduct Open Science) and facilitating community networking. The platform can also be used for documentation purposes, fulfilling the requirements of *Design objective 1–3*, as well as enabling subsequent use within the ecosystem of extensions developed by the community [52]. This results in:

Design Objective 5: A community should be designed to increase enforceability of the ecosystem for digital-enabled service design tools.

5 Artefact Evaluation

In an artificial ex ante evaluation – in specific EVAL 1 – following Sonnenberg and vom Brocke [63], the problem statement, the research gap and the design objectives were justified. The proposed theoretical framework was demonstrated to a group of researchers as well as two practitioners and was discussed afterwards. This evaluation is in its nature artificial; however, DSR artefact designs have to be justified and validated before they have been put into use [63]. The goal was to evaluate each *Design objective* against its suitability, importance, applicability and novelty. The artefacts suitability and applicability were confirmed as the proposed design objectives are based on broad fundaments and already sufficiently researched areas of information systems. In contrast, the novelty within the group of researchers was questioned. One of the participants stated that although the proposals were not new, they were applicable to the problem. However, the authors argue that it is not the proposed design objectives that should be seen as novel, but rather their application within the field of service design. For example, one of the practitioners said that networked or interoperable tools are very important as participants in longer workshop sessions often lose interest in transferring intermediate results. The authors conclude from the evaluation results that the proposed design objectives offer a starting point for further research. The evidence will of course have to be further empirically proven within the next evaluation cycles.

6 Discussion

These findings have several implications for service design research and practice. As discussed above, building an ecosystem for the development of digital-enabled service

[7] The platform is accessible at https://osf.io.

design tools affords new opportunities for the evolution of such tools, and the five design objectives advanced here serve as a starting point or roadmap. Although making no claim to completeness, the design objectives are mutually dependent. This does not imply simultaneity; implementation can be modular and linear or non-linear. In terms of simplicity of implementation, *Design objective 1* seems the most reasonable; science and practice should agree on a common standard whose form remains to be further evaluated. *Design objective 3* raises the question of whether a universal architecture is possible—for example, whether the transfer of such software to other platforms should be facilitated [51].

For any realisation in practice, it should be noted that a number of factors can influence the success of implementation, especially concerning *Design objective 4* and *5* [e.g., 68, 69]. These are again intertwined, as *Design objective 5* is an influence variable for *Design objective 4*. A combination of *Design objective 4* and *5*—that is, a community-driven open source project—can help researchers to make IT artefacts more stable and persistent for subsequent use. For example, a faulty code base can be corrected and enhanced by other community members [52, 77]. It should also be mentioned that the ecosystem in question must be designed to provide some incentive for the actors involved [77, 81], who can, in turn, reap certain benefits [77]. For example, science can contribute new ideas [81] or the validation of tools, methods and techniques developed by the community. The community is therefore among the most important factors for long-term ecosystem success [52]. In turn, practitioners can benefit from a greater flow of ideas that can be directly exploited.

7 Conclusion

7.1 Contribution

This paper contributes to the Information Systems knowledge base by arguing the need for an ecosystem for digital-enabled service design tools and by proposing a conceptual framework for this endeavour. As a result, a justified problem statement and a justified research gap, which can serve as a basis for further research. Therefore, the terms *digital service design* and *digital-enabled service design* should be differentiated to distinguish between the different research streams. While the first term refers to research into digital services, the second refers to research into digital technologies for use in service design. To develop a software ecosystem for digital-enabled service design tools, five design objectives were proposed as focus points or roadmap for future research activities. These five design objectives do not claim completeness but represent a snapshot and are subject to modification [82]. The design objectives contribute to the knowledge base in particular as follows. *Design objective 1 to 3* identify essential standardisations within a software ecosystem for the development of digital-enabled service design tools, proposing two data formats and a software architecture construct. One of these standardised data formats would increase tool interoperability, and the other would enable the collection of data for use in service design. A standardised software architecture to increase the reuse of software components is proposed in *Design objective 4,* which addresses the creation of rules or licenses within the ecosystem and recommends an open source approach to promote further development in research and practice. Finally, *Design objective 5* suggests a community-driven approach to building and leading the ecosystem. The *Design objective 1 to 5* were justified [63] for the further design of one or more concrete artefacts, which can be applied to real-world scenarios. A contribution to the knowledge base within the DSR is also seen as a contribution if the presented solution is transferable to other similar problems [59]. Although this paper discusses the application in the field of service design tools, the transfer to similar domains as innovation design is conceivable, so that other researchers could benefit from the presented metamodel.

7.2 Limitations

As our mostly conceptual DSR approach mostly focused on the integration and creation of new relationships between structures without reference to data, the ideas advanced remain to be empirically proven [64]. While *Design objective 1 to 3* are more empirical, *Design objective 4 and 5* seem more difficult to verify, as they are complex and entail a number of potential influencing factors. It should also be mentioned that the logic of the argument essentially represents the researchers' own perspective, and other relevant design objectives may not have been considered here. This is legitimate for conceptual work [64, 83], but there remains an obligation to demonstrate need and utility in practice.

7.3 Directions for Future Research

Future research can draw on various points in this work. For example, the above limitations serve as a starting point for empirical research in relation to utility and feasibility. Equally, the design objectives advanced here offer a starting point for design science research or action research projects. Although the individual design objectives together constitute a framework for building an ecosystem for the development of digital-enabled service design tools, a detailed development plan is also needed. By creating and evaluating new and innovative artefacts [57], design-oriented research can lay the essential foundations for such an ecosystem—for example, in the form of data formats developed from *Design objective 1 and 2* or a software architecture based on *Design objective 3*. Concerning *Design objective 4,* future research can help to create an appropriate licensing model for the software ecosystem that takes account of attractiveness for private sector participation as well as research needs. Action research can extend the relevance of academic research to practical application through intensive exchanges between researchers and practitioners [84], which may help to accelerate ecosystem formation. Furthermore, the implementation of the proposed design objectives could possibly lead to conclusions on how software ecosystems can be created or strengthened.

References

1. Barrett, M., Davidson, E., Fayard, A.-L., Vargo, S.L., Yoo, Y.: Being innovative about service innovation: Service, design and digitalization. In: Thirty Third International Conference on Information Systems (ICIS), Orlando, pp. 1–6 (2012)
2. Chesbrough, H., Spohrer, J.: A research manifesto for service science. Commun. ACM **49**, 35–40 (2006)

3. Vargo, S.L., Lusch, R.F.: Evolving to a new dominant logic for marketing. J. Mark. **68**, 1–17 (2004)
4. Vargo, S.L., Lusch, R.F.: Service-dominant logic: continuing the evolution. J. Acad. Mark. Sci. **36**, 1–10 (2008)
5. Patrício, L., Gustafsson, A., Fisk, R.: Upframing service design and innovation for research impact. J. Serv. Res. **21**, 3–16 (2018)
6. Ostrom, A.L., Parasuraman, A., Bowen, D.E., Patrício, L., Voss, C.A.: Service research priorities in a rapidly changing context. J. Serv. Res. **18**, 127–159 (2015)
7. Ulwick, A.W.: What Customers Want: Using Outcome-Driven Innovation to Create Breakthrough Products and Services. McGraw-Hill Education Ltd, New York (2005)
8. Spohrer, J., Maglio, P.P.: The emergence of service science: toward systematic service innovations to accelerate co-creation of value. Prod. Oper. Manag. **17**, 238–246 (2008)
9. Alter, S.: Metamodel for service design and service innovation: integrating service activities, service systems, and value constellations. In: Thirty Second International Conference on Information Systems (ICIS), Shanghai, pp. 2529–2548 (2011)
10. Shneiderman, B.: Creating creativity: user interfaces for supporting innovation. ACM Trans. Comput. Interact. **7**, 114–138 (2000)
11. Siemon, D., Narani, S.K., Robra-Bissantz, S.: The benefits of creativity support systems for entrepreneurs: an exploratory study. In: Twenty-Third Americas Conference on Information Systems (AMCIS), Boston, pp. 1–10 (2017)
12. Ostrom, A.L., et al.: Moving forward and making a difference: research priorities for the science of service. J. Serv. Res. **13**, 4–36 (2010)
13. Maglio, P.P., Vargo, S.L., Caswell, N., Spohrer, J.: The service system is the basic abstraction of service science. Inf. Syst. E-bus. Manag. **7**, 395–406 (2009)
14. Böhmann, T., Leimeister, J.M., Möslein, K.: Service systems engineering. Bus. Inf. Syst. Eng. **6**, 73–79 (2014)
15. Shostack, G.L.: Designing services that deliver. Harv. Bus. Rev. **62**, 133–139 (1983)
16. Patrício, L., Fisk, R.P., Falcão E Cunha, J.: Designing multi-interface service experiences: the service experience blueprint. J. Serv. Res. **10**, 318–334 (2008)
17. Lim, C.-H., Kim, K.-J.: Information service blueprint : a service blueprinting framework for information-intensive services. Serv. Sci. **6**, 296–312 (2014)
18. Höckmayr, B., Roth, A.: Design of a method for service systems engineering in the digital age. In: Proceedings of the 38th International Conference on Information Systems (ICIS), Seoul, pp. 1–23 (2017)
19. Osterwalder, A.: Business Model Generation: A Handbook for Visionaries, Game Changers, and Challengers. Wiley, Hoboken (2010)
20. Rogers, D.L.: The Digital Transformation Playbook: Rethink Your Business for the Digital Age. Columbia Business School Publishing, New York (2016)
21. Stickdorn, M., Hormess, M.E., Lawrence, A., Schneider, J.: This is Service Design Doing: Applying Service Design Thinking in the Real World. O'Reilly Media Inc, Sebastopol (2018)
22. Knapp, J.: Sprint: How to Solve Big Problems and Test New Ideas in Just Five Days. Simon & Schuster Paperbacks, London (2016)
23. Zolnowski, A., Weiß, C., Böhmann, T.: Representing service business models with the service business model canvas - the case of a mobile payment service in the retail industry. In: Proceedings of the Annual Hawaii International Conference on System Sciences, pp. 718–727 (2014)
24. Turetken, O., Grefen, P.: Designing service-dominant business models. In: Proceedings of the 25th European Conference on Information Systems (ECIS), pp. 2218–2233 (2017)
25. Gilsing, R., Turetken, O., Ozkan, B., Adali, O.E.: A method for qualitative evaluation of service-dominant business models. In: European Conference on Information Systems - ECIS 2020, pp. 1–15. Association for Information Systems (2020)

26. Hund, A., Drechsler, K., Reibenspiess, V.: The current state and future opportunities of digital innovation: a literature review. In: Proceedings of the 27th European Conference on Information Systems (ECIS) (2019)
27. Nambisan, S., Lyytinen, K., Majchrzak, A., Song, M.: Digital innovation management: reinventing innovation management research in a digital world. MIS Q. **41**, 223–238 (2017)
28. Liu, X., Werder, K., Maedche, A.: A taxonomy of design techniques for digital services. In: ICIS 2016 Proceedings, Dublin, pp. 1–12 (2016)
29. Williams, K., Chatterjee, S., Rossi, M.: Design of emerging digital services: a taxonomy. Eur. J. Inf. Syst. **17**, 505–517 (2008)
30. O'Hern, M., Rindfleisch, A.: Customer co-creation: a typology and research agenda. Rev. Mark. Res. **6**, 84–106 (2008)
31. Jonas, J.M., Roth, A., Möslein, K.M.: Stakeholder integration for service innovation in German medium-sized enterprises. Serv. Sci. **8**, 320–332 (2016)
32. Jonas, J.M., Roth, A.: Stakeholder integration in service innovation - an exploratory case study in the healthcare industry. Int. J. Technol. Manag. **73**, 91–113 (2017)
33. Li, M.M., Peters, C.: From service systems engineering to service innovation - a modeling approach. In: Proceedings of the 27th European Conference on Information Systems (ECIS), Stockholm & Uppsala, pp. 1–16 (2019)
34. Seidel, S., Müller-Wienbergen, F., Becker, J.: The concept of creativity in the information systems discipline: past, present, and prospects. Commun. Assoc. Inf. Syst. **27**, 217–242 (2010)
35. Morris, D., Secretan, J.: Computational creativity support: using algorithms and machine learning to help people be more creative. In: CHI 2009 Extended Abstracts on Human Factors in Computing Systems, pp. 4733–4736 (2009)
36. Fritscher, B., Pigneur, Y.: Business model design: an evaluation of paper-based and computer-aided canvases. In: Proceedings of the 4th International Symposium on Business Modeling and Software Design (BMSD), pp. 236–244 (2014)
37. Szopinski, D., Schoormann, T., John, T., Knackstedt, R., Kundisch, D.: Software tools for business model innovation: current state and future challenges. Electron. Mark. (2019)
38. Zec, M., Dürr, P., Schneider, A.W., Matthes, F.: Improving computer-support for collaborative business model design and exploration. In: BMSD 2014 – Proceedings of the 4th International Symposium on Business Modeling and Software Design, pp. 29–37 (2014)
39. Thomas, O., Hagen, S., Frank, U., Recker, J., Wessel, L., Thomas, O.: Global crises and the role of BISE. Bus. Inf. Syst. Eng. (2020)
40. Becker, J., Beverungen, D., Knackstedt, R., Matzner, M., Müller, O., Pöppelbuß, J.: A framework for design research in the service science discipline. In: 15th Americas Conference on Information Systems (AMCIS), pp. 1–9 (2009)
41. Brinkkemper, S.: Method engineering: engineering of information systems development methods and tools. Inf. Softw. Technol. **38**, 275–280 (1996)
42. Poeppelbuss, J., Lubarski, A.: A classification framework for service modularization methods. Enterp. Model. Inf. Syst. Archit. **13**, 11–14 (2018)
43. Chai, K.H., Zhang, J., Tan, K.C.: A TRIZ-based method for new service design. J. Serv. Res. **8**, 48–66 (2005)
44. Palvia, P., Nosek, J.T.: A field examination of system life cycle techniques and methodologies. Inf. Manag. **25**, 73–84 (1993)
45. Chasanidou, D., Gasparini, A., Lee, E.: Design thinking methods and tools for innovation. In: Marcus, A. (ed.) DUXU 2015. LNCS, vol. 9186, pp. 12–23. Springer, Cham (2015). https://doi.org/10.1007/978-3-319-20886-2_2
46. Shneiderman, B.: Creativity support tools: accelerating discovery and innovation (2007)

47. van den Berk, I., Jansen, S., Luinenburg, L.: Software ecosystems: a software ecosystem strategy assessment model. In: Proceedings of the Fourth European Conference on Software Architecture: Companion Volume (ECSA), pp. 127–134. Association for Computing Machinery, Copenhagen (2010)
48. Manikas, K., Hansen, K.M.: Software ecosystems-a systematic literature review. J. Syst. Softw. **86**, 1294–1306 (2013)
49. Medvidovic, N., Taylor, R.N.: Software architecture theory and practice. In: ACM/IEEE 32nd International Conference on Software Engineering (ICSE), pp. 471–472. IEEE, Cape Town (2010)
50. Bosch, J.: From software product lines to software ecosystems. In: 13th International Software Product Line Conference, pp. 111–119 (2009)
51. Jansen, S., Finkelstein, A., Brinkkemper, S.: A sense of community: a research agenda for software ecosystems. In: 31st International Conference on Software Engineering - Companion Volume (ICSE), pp. 187–190 (2009)
52. Kilamo, T., Hammouda, I., Mikkonen, T., Aaltonen, T.: From proprietary to open source - growing an open source ecosystem. J. Syst. Softw. **85**, 1467–1478 (2012)
53. Hanssen, G.K.: A longitudinal case study of an emerging software ecosystem: implications for practice and theory. J. Syst. Softw. **85**, 1455–1466 (2012)
54. Christensen, H.B., Hansen, K.M., Kyng, M., Manikas, K.: Analysis and design of software ecosystem architectures - towards the 4S telemedicine ecosystem. Inf. Softw. Technol. **56**, 1476–1492 (2014)
55. Farrell, J., Garth, S.: Standardization, compatibility, and innovation. RAND J. Econ. **16**, 70–83 (1985)
56. Burkard, C., Widjaja, T., Buxmann, P.: Software ecosystems. Bus. Inf Syst. Eng. **4**, 41–44 (2012)
57. Hevner, A.R., March, S.T., Park, J., Ram, S.: Design science in information systems research. MIS Q. **28**, 75–105 (2004)
58. Hevner, A., Samir, C.: Integrated Series in Information Systems, vol. 28 (2010)
59. Gregor, S., Hevner, A.R.: Positioning and presenting design science types of knowledge in design science research. MIS Q. **37**, 337–355 (2013)
60. March, S.T., Smith, G.F.: Design and natural science research on information technology Salvatore. Decis. Support Syst. **15**, 251–266 (1995)
61. Ostrowski, Ł., Helfert, M., Xie, S.: A conceptual framework to construct an artefact for meta-abstract design knowledge in design science research. In: Proceedings of the Annual Hawaii International Conference on System Sciences, pp. 4074–4081 (2012)
62. Peffers, K., Tuunanen, T., Rothenberger, M.A., Chatterjee, S.: A design science research methodology for information systems research. J. Manag. Inf. Syst. **24**, 45–77 (2007)
63. Sonnenberg, C., vom Brocke, J.: Evaluations in the science of the artificial – reconsidering the build-evaluate pattern in design science research. In: Peffers, K., Rothenberger, M., Kuechler, B. (eds.) DESRIST 2012. LNCS, vol. 7286, pp. 381–397. Springer, Heidelberg (2012). https://doi.org/10.1007/978-3-642-29863-9_28
64. Gilson, L.L., Goldberg, C.B.: Editors' comment: so, what is a conceptual paper? Gr. Organ. Manag. **40**, 127–130 (2015)
65. Jaakkola, E.: Designing conceptual articles: four approaches. AMS Rev. **10**(1–2), 18–26 (2020). https://doi.org/10.1007/s13162-020-00161-0
66. MacInnis, D.J.: A framework for conceptual contributions in marketing. J. Mark. **75**, 136–154 (2011)
67. Prat, N., Comyn-Wattiau, I., Akoka, J.: A taxonomy of evaluation methods for information systems artifacts. J. Manag. Inf. Syst. **32**, 229–267 (2015)
68. Bettencourt, L.A., Ulwick, A.W.: The customer-centered innovation map. Harv. Bus. Rev. **86**, 109–114 (2008)

69. Baars, H., Kemper, H.G.: Management support with structured and unstructured data - an integrated business intelligence framework. Inf. Syst. Manag. **25**, 132–148 (2008)
70. Murthy, D.: Digital ethnography: an examination of the use of new technologies for social research. Sociology **42**, 837–855 (2008)
71. Otto, B., Bärenfänger, R., Steinbuß, S.: Digital business engineering: methodological foundations and first experiences from the field. In: 28th Bled eConference: #eWellbeing – Proceedings, pp. 58–76 (2015)
72. Brenner, W., et al.: User, use & utility research: the digital user as new design perspective in business and information systems engineering. Bus. Inf. Syst. Eng. **6**, 55–61 (2014)
73. Antons, D., Breidbach, C.F.: Big data, big insights? Advancing service innovation and design with machine learning. J. Serv. Res. **21**, 17–39 (2018)
74. Sullivan, K.J., Griswold, W.G., Cai, Y., Hallen, B.: The structure and value of modularity in software design. In: Proceedings of the ACM SIGSOFT Symposium on the Foundations of Software Engineering, pp. 99–108 (2001)
75. O'Mahony, S.: Guarding the commons: how community managed software projects protect their work. Res. Policy. **32**, 1179–1198 (2003)
76. Campbell-Kelly, M., Garcia-Swartz, D.D.: The move to the middle: convergence of the open-source and proprietary software industries. SSRN Electron. J. **17**, 1–39 (2011)
77. Lerner, J., Tirole, J.: The simple economics of open source. SSRN Electron. J. L (2005)
78. Cataldo, M., Herbsleb, J.D.: Architecting in software ecosystems: interface translucence as an enabler for scalable collaboration. In: ACM International Conference Proceeding Series, pp. 65–72 (2010)
79. Radtke, N.P., Janssen, M.A., Collofello, J.S.: What makes free/libre open source software (FLOSS) projects successful? An agent-based model of FLOSS projects. Int. J. Open Source Softw. Process. **1**, 1–13 (2009)
80. Crowston, K., Scozzi, B.: Open source software projects as virtual organisations: competency rallying for software development. IEE Proc. Softw. **149**, 3–17 (2002)
81. Von Krogh, G.: Open-source software development. MIT Sloan Manag. Rev. **44**, 14–18 (2003)
82. Whetten, D.A.: What constitutes a theoretical contribution? The academy of management review what constitutes a theoretical contribution? Source Acad. Manag. Rev. Manag. Rev. **14**, 490–495 (1989)
83. Hirschheim, R.: Editorial Commentary Some Guidelines for the Critical Reviewing of Conceptual Papers (2008)
84. Rose, R., Grosvenor, I.: Action research. Doing Res. Spec. Educ. Ideas into Pract. **42**, 13–17 (2013)

Requirements for Augmented Reality Solutions for Safety-Critical Services – The Case of Water Depth Management in a Maritime Logistics Hub

Anna Osterbrink[1], Julia Bräker[2], Martin Semmann[2(✉)], and Manuel Wiesche[1]

[1] Department of Business and Economics, TU Dortmund University, Dortmund, Germany
{anna.osterbrink,manuel.wiesche}@tu-dortmund.de
[2] Department of Informatics, University of Hamburg, Hamburg, Germany
{julia.braeker,martin.semmann}@uni-hamburg.de

Abstract. Augmented reality (AR) is widely acknowledged to be beneficial for services that have exceptionally high requirements regarding knowledge and simultaneous tasks to be performed and are safety-critical. In such services, AR enables to augment service provision by delivering seamless integration of information in the field of view while enabling hands-free usage in the case of head-mounted displays. This study explores the user-centered requirements for AR solutions in the operations of a large European maritime logistics hub. Specifically, it deals with the process of soil sounding. Based on eleven think-aloud sessions during service delivery, two expert interviews, and two expert workshops, we derived five core requirements for AR in soil sounding. Thus, we present the first study on the applicability and feasibility of AR in the maritime industry and identify requirements that impact further research on AR use in safety-critical environments.

Keywords: Mixed reality · Service engineering · Requirements · Think aloud · Case study

1 Introduction

In various industries, new technologies are becoming increasingly important in the development and improvement of services, and the use of these technologies has gained attention both in service research and in practice [1, 2]. When using new technologies, the IT resources either complement or improve the effects of non-IT resources on the performance of a process or substitute them [3]. Well-known examples of services that were improved by technology are e-tickets in the airline or event business, electronic check-in and check-out systems in hotels, and electronic money transfer in financial services, etc. [4, 5].

As a result, the character of information technology has changed to the extent that it has become the focus of new product and service ideas due to technological developments both in hardware and software [6]. An example of this is the use of augmented reality (AR) head-mounted displays (HMD), through which current challenges, for example,

F. Ahlemann et al. (Eds.): WI 2021, LNISO 46, pp. 219–235, 2021.
https://doi.org/10.1007/978-3-030-86790-4_16

in technical customer services, can be overcome [7]. With the help of HMDs, services can be restructured by enabling information to be displayed directly into the user's field of view under hands-free navigation without media breaks and limited mobility [8]. As a result, HMDs have a high potential to support [9] and improve [10] services such as health care [11], technical customer service [8], and logistics services [12, 13].

While previous studies have largely focused on services in which one task is performed, it is not well understood how AR can support services where two separate tasks are frequently switched. This is the situation in our use case of water depth management where skippers in the service provision of soil sounding simultaneously have to navigate their vessels and measure water depth with high accuracy. Since mistakes or inaccuracies in the performance of the two tasks of the skipper can have serious consequences both directly and indirectly, the use case is a safety-critical service, which can generally be characterized by the fact that a "failure might endanger human life, lead to substantial economic loss, or cause extensive environmental change" [14, p. 547]. Especially, for this reason, effective support and improvement of the process of soil sounding are very important as the resulting information is crucial for vessels to navigate harbor areas. Consequently, soil sounding is a key service to ensure safety for all actors that use the harbor infrastructure as this infrastructure is partially dynamic due to tides and currents. An additive complicating factor for an AR application on a vessel is that, in contrast to the already difficult implementation of AR for cycling or driving a car, there is an additional dimension of motion, namely that of the ground, i.e., the water on which the vessel is moving. Against this background, our research is guided by the questions (RQ1) *How amenable is the service process of soil sounding to be supported by AR?* and (RQ2) *What are the requirements for AR solutions to improve the service process of soil sounding?*

To answer the research questions, the paper is structured as follows: First, we give an overview of the application of AR solutions in different service processes, distinguishing between those with a static setting and those where the environmental setting adapts to the user's motion, such as when driving a car. In Sect. 3, we introduce the methodology, where we conducted a case study with workshop data, expert interviews, and process tracing using video observations and verbal protocols in the form of think-aloud sessions. In Sect. 4, we present the use case of water depth measurement and analyze it firstly with regard to its augmentability (RQ1). In the second part of the analysis, we use the conducted think-aloud sessions to derive the user-centered requirements for an AR solution for the service process of soil sounding (RQ2). The results and their limitations are discussed in Sect. 5, and in Sect. 6, we summarize the main findings and give an outlook on future research issues.

2 Related Work

Innovations in the field of service continue to emerge, with many of the innovations today being digital by integrating resources throughout service systems [15]. In order to apply service innovations and related innovative technologies that can be used to support services, it is important to understand the innovations within the service for which they are to be used, their potential, and the requirements involved [16, 17].

One technology with a very high potential for service innovation is AR. This technology can be used in many different environments that can be distinguished by the degree of dynamics. Environments with little dynamics – here called static environments – can be characterized by the fact that the user's environment does not change because the user does not move in public but is in a limited environment like a room in which objects like machines have a fixed, static place. In those scenarios, there are already insights on applications of AR, such as the design and prototyping of a see-through HMD, which was carried out in the aircraft manufacturing industry to reduce costs and increase efficiency [18]. Increased efficiency was also observed for the use of AR-applied devices in the context of maintenance and repair [19, 20]. In engineering, AR welding guns with cameras to track the exact stud locations were used to support engineering processes [21]. Another AR application that was investigated is the use of smart glasses to support the runtime modeling of services, allowing the process to be documented on-site by the service provider during the execution of his activity [22]. Further applications of AR do exist in the construction industry [23], marketing [24], education [25] as well as healthcare [26, 27].

AR use cases in the context of more dynamic mobile settings, on the other hand, have been hardly the subject of research so far. These environments can be characterized by the fact that they are not limited in space and that objects – in contrast to those in static environments – do not necessarily have fixed positions, but the positions of these objects can change due to movements so that a motion emanates from the user's environment. One example is the process of driving a car, where the motion of other traffic participants influences the own process of driving, e.g., when it is necessary to brake because of the car in front brakes. For applications with relatively little or slow movement, head-mounted AR tools, such as HMDs, or other portable devices used for museum tours can be cited to provide audiovisual enhancements to support the tours [28, 29]. With regard to AR applications in the context of faster movements, the study by Berkemeier et al. [30], in which requirements for an acceptable smart glasses-based information system to support cyclists in cycling training are identified, can be mentioned. The aim of the study is to augment information such as speed or route details, which would otherwise have to be displayed by other devices, into the cyclist's field of view to promote road safety. There are also studies on cars in which head-up displays or head-mounted displays are used to display relevant information in the driver's field of view in order to reduce risks in road traffic [31] or to support driver safety training through simulated dangerous traffic situations [32].

Furthermore, in other safety-critical services, as it is the case in our use case, there are already some investigations on the support potential of AR and how it can be used. For example, the user requirements for an AR-based refinery training tool were determined for an oil refinery in order to develop usable and safe AR applications [33]. Another example is the application of AR in an innovative airport control power, where the aim was to provide the air traffic control operators in the airport control tower with complete head-up information [34, 35].

Theoretical accounts have developed concepts to capture how technologies affect service processes. A well-known theory is the process virtualization theory, which is concerned with explaining and predicting whether a process can be performed virtually [36].

Examples of virtualized processes include e-commerce, online distance learning, or online banking [35, 36]. The theory has been applied and adapted in many different contexts, e.g. [35, 37], and was also examined with regard to augmentation, which led to the idea of the theory of process augmentability [38], that provides the basis for the analysis of the augmentability of our use case of the soil sounding service.

In contrast to the definition of virtualization, augmentation can be defined as the supplement of a synthetic or physical interaction. As a logical consequence, the four main constructs of the process virtualization theory concerning the potential removal of physical interactions from the process cannot be applied to augmentation. Therefore, one main construct – the authenticity requirement, which is based on the essentialist view of authenticity [39] and the authenticity framework of Grayson and Martinec [40] – is proposed to have a positive effect on the dependent variable, namely process augmentability. Process augmentability is described as "how amenable a process is to being conducted in AR environments" [38, p. 5].

Furthermore, three moderating constructs are proposed that are developed from the definition of AR, which is crucial to maintain a sense of hyper-reality [41]. By definition, AR must meet three criteria: combine physical and virtual, be interactive in real-time, and be registered in the real world [38, 42]. According to the definition, Yeo [38] proposed 3D visualization, spatial association, and synchronization as moderating constructs hereafter referred to as characteristics. The proposition of the 3D virtualization characteristic is informed by cognitive load theory [43]. For the characteristic of spatial association, examples were given in [38] of how AR uses the geospatial environments to enrich process experiences [20, 21, 26]. In terms of the synchronization characteristic, most physical processes conducted in the real world tend to be synchronous, and it is therefore important that the physical movement needs to be connected to maintain the sense of immersion [36].

3 Methodology

We conducted a case study [44] to explore the requirements for a user-centered AR solution for safety-critical services in the maritime sector. The use case we investigated was the process of soil sounding, i.e., water depth measurement in a harbor environment, which is carried out during navigation on a vessel.

In order to analyze how amenable the considered use case of the soil sounding process is to be supported by AR (RQ1), we first studied a promotional video of a European harbor operator that provided us with a contextual understanding of the soil sounding process as a foundation for the further analysis. In a second step, we collected data by conducting two semi-structured interviews and two workshops with business and IT experts of the same harbor operator (see Table 1). Both the interviews and the workshops were documented by video recording. In addition, more detailed documents concerning the use case were provided by the participants, and additionally, notes were taken during the interview and workshop sessions. To get the first ideas of requirements for AR solutions for the service process of soil sounding (RQ2), we have briefly discussed them in the last part of the workshops with the experts. Since we wanted to identify user-centric requirements, we collected additional data with three skippers who actually perform the process of soil sounding.

Table 1. Data table of sources

#	Source	Format	Duration (hh:mm)	Focus
1	Harbor TV	Video	00:14	Use case context
2	Head of IT Innovation	Interview	01:00	Overview case strategy
3	Deputy port hydrographer	Interview	01:00	Deeper understanding of the use case context
4	Deputy port hydrographer	Workshop	02:03	Requirements of the use case
5	Project manager R&D	Workshop	00:57	Process steps and requirements of the use case
6	Soil sounding 1	Think aloud	01:27	Soil sounding on a shore
7	Soil sounding 2	Think aloud	01:19	Soil sounding of harbor basin and berths
8	Soil sounding 3	Think aloud	00:19	Follow-up soil sounding in a relatively small area
9	Soil sounding 4	Think aloud	01:16	Soil sounding in a side arm with several bridges and an open lock
10	Soil sounding 5	Think aloud	00:28	Soil sounding of a berth on a quay
11	Soil sounding 6	Think aloud	00:52	Supplementary soil sounding of a berth within a control measurement
12	Soil sounding 7	Think aloud	00:47	Soil sounding of recently dredged fields during heavy traffic
13	Soil sounding 8	Think aloud	00:44	Soil sounding of a dredging field
14	Soil sounding 9	Think aloud	00:55	Soil sounding of a widened shipping channel
15	Soil sounding 10	Think aloud	00:36	Soil sounding of a dredging field

(*continued*)

Table 1. *(continued)*

#	Source	Format	Duration (hh:mm)	Focus
16	Soil sounding 11	Think aloud	00:12	Soil sounding after removal of a ground obstacle as control

In order to gain this central data source, we used the process tracing method [45] of thinking aloud [46], where the skippers were asked to "think aloud" and to explain everything they do while simultaneously engaging in the soil sounding service, in order to analyze which user-centered requirements an AR solution must meet to support the soil sounding process. As the situational features of the service are crucial, we extended the traditional implementation of the method by recording videos from different perspectives. For this purpose, we attached a camera to the skippers' forehead to retrace their field of view and another camera on the monitor to observe the skippers directly. An exact tracking of eye movements of the skippers was not necessary since only the direction of the skippers' view was relevant. With the help of the two recording perspectives and the recorded audio track, we were able to trace the process of soil sounding and derive user-centered requirements for an AR solution. As the service is critical to maintaining harbor operation, only experienced skippers are considered for soil sounding. The think-aloud sessions differ in the type of soil sounding job and its focus as well as the difficulty of the soil sounding, which depends on factors such as the soil sounding environment or traffic volume (see Table 1).

For analyzing the video recordings and verbal protocols of the think-aloud sessions, we used the scanning method, which is one of the four major categories of protocol analysis and the most straightforward one [47]. We did not perform a verbatim transcription of what was said since the observation of the skippers was the primary object of investigation that we used for our analysis. Instead, the statements of the skippers helped to supplement and explain what was observed. For the identified video sequences in which observed behaviors indicated challenges, we transcribed what was said since this often helped to clarify and support the observation. We analyzed the video and audio material with three independent researchers and initially focused on existing challenges and problems in the process of soil sounding. After identifying all difficulties in the process, we derived problem categories by grouping duplicates and similar ones. Based on these problem categories, we finally derived the requirements described subsequently.

4 Use Case of Water Depth Management in a Harbor Environment

In the mobile use cases related to touring, cycling, and driving, two dimensions of motion occur: the motion of the user – which also occurs in static settings – and the motion of the environment. The ground on which the user moves can be described as static because it does not show any motion itself, such as a road. In the case of shipping, however, there is an additional dimension of motion, which is caused by the movement of the water on which the vessel is sailing, e.g., by currents or waves. While already the application of

AR in cases with two dimensions of motion is difficult to implement, the application of AR on a vessel with this additional dimension of motion poses a particular challenge that needs to be investigated.

For our analysis, we chose the service process of water depth management in a European maritime logistics hub. Harbor personnel needs to continuously monitor water depth change due to sedimentation and erosion. In order to ensure the safety of vessel traffic and maintain the infrastructure, water depth management must be ensured by continuous soil sounding as well as finding and recognizing nautically critical obstacles on the water ground (e.g., bikes, cars, or shopping carts). Special soil sounding vessels are used that have the technical equipment to monitor water depth and generate a digital landscape model of the water ground live on board (see Fig. 1).

Fig. 1. Exterior and interior view of a soil sounding vessel

Figure 2 illustrates the measurement depth management cycle to give an overview of the use case context. This states that the measurement of water depths generates knowledge, which in turn causes action, such as deepening a certain area. Since this action causes a change, the changing area must be controlled by measurement.

Fig. 2. Measurement depth management cycle

The task of measuring water depth is particularly challenging: The skippers of soil sounding vessels use echo sounders to measure the water depths in the harbor while simultaneously paying attention to the vessel's traffic and keeping an eye on a variety of information for measurement on monitors so that they have to permanently switch between the monitors and the view out of the window. This leads to limited safety in vessel traffic, extreme exhaustion due to the constant change of view and context, and several health issues. These side effects of the constant shift of perspective can also be observed in other safety-critical services, such as the air traffic control in an airport control tower [34]. In addition to the simultaneous navigation of the vessel and measurement of data, the skipper needs to interact with a measurement engineer, who is accountable for controlling the quality of the measured data. The measurement engineer is either also on the vessel or works from the home office.

4.1 Augmentability of the Use Case

Various attempts have already been made to solve the problem of the exhaustive and safety-critical shift in perspective between the view from the window onto the shipping traffic and the viewing of the data on the monitor. However, for example, the idea of placing the monitor in the windshield at the height of the skipper's eyes so that he no longer has to look down caused the monitor in the windshield to obscure important objects such as other vessels on the water. A further idea to reduce the size of the monitor in the windshield in order to avoid overlaying real objects has, in turn, resulted in the view of the displayed information and data being too small. Since it is important to display information in the skipper's field of view, but a monitor in the windscreen overlays important real objects, the application of AR seems to be a good way to solve the problem. With the help of AR, information can be displayed in the skipper's field of view without completely overlaying real objects. In order to investigate the applicability of AR for the use case, we have analyzed the use case with regard to the four characteristics that – according to the theory of process augmentability [38] – must be present in a process so that an augmentation of the process is appropriate.

Authenticity. The authenticity characteristic is present in the soil sounding service. The skipper requires an authentic experience to be supported in navigating his vessel and measuring data during the actual soil sounding process. This process cannot be virtualized or simulated due to its high complexity and dependence on the actions and decisions of the skipper. Accordingly, the process can only be performed in reality, and the information and support required by the skipper must correspond to this reality and extend it adequately.

3D Visualization. The 3D visualization characteristic is present in the soil sounding process. The skipper requires 3D visualization for an authentic experience because a 2D visualization of obstacles and other ships is too imprecise, making it difficult to estimate sizes and distances, which in turn can affect the quality of the measurement data and traffic safety.

Spatial Association. The spatial association characteristic is present in the soil sounding process. It is very important for the skipper that information, such as water depth and currents, as well as obstacles in the water and other vessels, are displayed with geographical accuracy. The skipper requires the possibility to obtain further information about, e.g., displayed objects through interaction with them. For example, if an obstacle or the water depth is not displayed geographically correct, and the skipper does not have access to important information, the vessel may collide with the obstacle or run aground.

Synchronization. The synchronization characteristic is present in the soil sounding process. The 3D objects to be augmented and the collected measurement data, as well as information about boundary conditions such as currents or the tide, must be continuously synchronized and updated, enabling the skipper to use this information to navigate his vessel safely and detect possible obstacles and measurement gaps or errors.

In summary, the soil sounding service is amenable to be supported by AR based on the analyzed characteristics and identified needs of the skipper involved in the process.

4.2 Requirements for AR Solutions

Based on the challenges and problems that we have observed in the think-aloud sessions and subsequently analyzed, we identified five requirements for designing AR solutions for service processes such as soil sounding, which we specified together with the experts and skippers of the harbor operator. The identified requirements are (1) real-time overlay, (2) variety in displaying information, (3) multi-dimensional tracking, (4) collaboration, and (5) interaction.

Real-Time Overlay Requirement. In all of the think-aloud sessions carried out, it was observed that during soil sounding, the skipper must be aware of a number of factors that may affect navigation and measurement, such as currents, the actual water level in the soil sounding area, in-water obstacles, general traffic and the data quality of the soil sounding. Since some information can only be acquired with the help of sensors and rapidly changing conditions prevail, the visualization of real-time information is an essential requirement to ensure that the skipper can navigate his vessel safely and, for example, is not in danger of running aground or hitting an obstacle.

Fig. 3. Example of the permanent view shift between the sailing window and monitor

During soil sounding on a shore in the first think aloud (soil sounding 1), the skipper explained: "If you like, I'll probably look 80% here on the monitor and maybe a little out the window". Therefore, a further challenge, which can impair traffic safety and even lead to health problems, is the constant shift of the skipper's attention between the sailing window to keep an eye on traffic and his monitors to ensure the quality of the measured data, as seen in Fig. 3. To meet this challenge, the elimination of media breaks by overlaying information directly into the user's field of view is required. For example, overlaying real-time information about other vessels, such as their position or direction of navigation, which is received via the Automatic Identification System (AIS) and currently displayed on different monitors, could help to ensure safety.

The real-time overlay requirement, therefore, arises from the need to display information in real-time and to overlay this display in the skipper's field of view in order to improve vessel traffic safety, prevent health issues, and reduce cognitive load. Additionally, such overlay can drastically improve safety during harsh weather conditions that reduce sight while dependence on digital information increases.

Variety in Displaying Information Requirement. In addition to the frequent shifting of view between the vessel's window and the monitors (see Fig. 3), a variety of sensor information and data about the soil sounding area is displayed on different monitors, resulting in an additional constant shift between the monitors to ensure the quality of the measurement. Thereby the available space of the monitors is not optimally used, and sometimes even redundant information is displayed (see Fig. 4). However, in order to improve usability and thus enable the skipper to execute the measurement efficiently, the skipper requires certain multiple sensor information simultaneously, such as different layers or perspectives of the area of soil sounding, without information and the representation of this information being displayed several times.

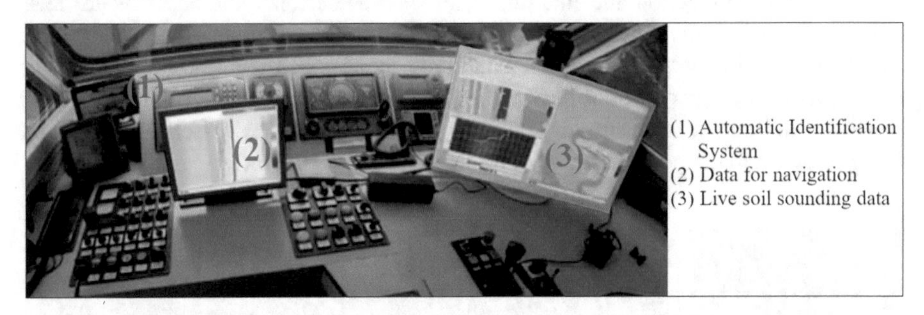

Fig. 4. Variety of information and monitors on a soil sounding vessel

Another difficulty that also leads to the current use of multiple monitors is that information about the water level in general and the measured areas, which include the quality and density of the data, cannot be overlaid in the current IT system but are both required to ensure both traffic safety and measurement quality. Therefore, a further essential requirement regarding the presentation of information is that different views and representation options of the information should be distinguishable. In this context, we found out during the various think-aloud sessions that it is useful, for example, to have different zoom levels for the maps, since the skipper requires more detail to navigate his ship precisely, for instance, when measuring in narrow shore areas, than in wider water areas where he needs a greater overview. In several sessions, we could also observe that the skippers displayed the required information differently. In some measurement situations, for example, displaying the water depths in the measurement area using different color scales was more helpful than displaying this information as exact numerical values, and vice versa.

The variety in displaying information requirement, therefore, arises from the need to be able to choose different representation options of the information to display on demand in order to improve usability and traffic safety as well as ensuring the quality of the measurement.

Multi-dimensional Tracking Requirement. Compared to other means of transport such as bicycles or cars, a vessel has an additional dimension of motion since additional movements emanate from the ground, i.e., the water on which the vessel is sailing, making it even more difficult to track the vessel's exact position. However, it is an essential requirement for the navigation of the vessel during soil sounding to track the exact position of the vessel in relation to the environment. On the one hand, an inaccurate position determination can lead to measurement gaps and, accordingly, to a reduced measurement quality and, on the other hand, traffic safety can be impaired by incorrect positioning, since, for example, distances to obstacles or other vessels can no longer be displayed correctly.

Fig. 5. Direct sunlight and reflections

Tracking of the vessel's position is also made more difficult by the fact that the skipper is inside the ship and perceives the outside world through glass windows, making it difficult to avoid direct sunlight and reflections (see Fig. 5). Although the ships are equipped with sun protection roller shutters, which can attenuate the solar radiation, it is not possible to completely block the sun's rays without restricting the view outside too much by darkening it. Accordingly, the skipper requires tracking that is resistant to sunlight and reflections.

The multi-dimensional tracking requirement, therefore, arises from the fact that the skipper needs an exact positioning of the vessel in order to ensure traffic safety and the quality of the measurement data.

Collaboration Requirement. During soil sounding, the skipper has to communicate a lot with other people to ensure traffic safety and quality of measurement. Both in terms of traffic safety and measurement, the skipper has to communicate with other vessels by radio in some situations. With regard to the quality of measurement, however, the collaboration with the measurement engineer, who is responsible for the technical implementation of the depth measurement, such as the configuration of the echo sounders, is most important. Before and during the measurement, the skipper and measurement engineer must continuously coordinate which areas are to be measured, how and when, and when the measuring devices must be activated or deactivated. They have to do this under consideration of different boundary conditions, e.g., the current water level. If the water level is too low, there is the risk of running aground, and if the water level is too high, it is, for example, no longer possible to pass every bridge. But above all, the constant communication about the observation of the live measured values and the flexible adaption of the course to them is of great importance since areas need to be measured again if the data quality is insufficient. A statement made by a skipper (think-aloud of soil sounding 7) summarizes very well the importance of the collaboration between him and the engineer during soil sounding: "If I don't synchronize with him [the measurement engineer], nothing will work".

To support collaboration, the skipper and the measurement engineer require the same visualization of the measuring areas, with additional highlighting of areas being useful because, especially when the measurement engineer is at the home office, it is not trivial to understand what about the other person is talking. It would also be useful to visualize whether the measurement device is activated and in which area it is currently collecting data. In addition, hands-free communication, i.e., without having to pick up a telephone, is required both with other vessels and with the measurement engineer, enabling the skipper to have his hands free for the navigation of the vessel and thus ensure safety.

The collaboration requirement, therefore, arises from the fact that the skipper has to communicate with other vessels and in particular, has to collaborate a lot with the measurement engineer in order to ensure both traffic safety and the quality of the measurement data.

Interaction Requirement. The requirement of interaction goes along with the above-mentioned variety of displaying information requirement. Currently, information on the monitor cannot be manipulated by the skipper, or in other words, the skipper cannot interact with the system and is only able to consume information. During several think-aloud sessions, we observed that the skipper wanted to change the views on the monitor. Since the skipper is not able to interact with the system himself, he had to explain the necessary changes to the measurement engineer, who could then make the adjustments. It is therefore not possible for the skipper, for example, to show or hide information or to zoom into a map to get a detailed view if he requires it, e.g., to safely avoid obstacles or close measurement gaps. In order to carry out navigation and measurement more safely and efficiently, the skipper requires an appropriate opportunity to interact with the system.

The interaction requirement, therefore, arises from the fact that the skipper requires to show or hide important information or select detailed views to ensure traffic safety and completeness of the measurement data. Furthermore, the way of interaction should be chosen so that the skipper is not distracted from the navigation of the vessel.

5 Discussion

So far, little research on requirements for AR solutions has been done. Since the chosen use case is even more complex than the prior work on application areas of AR, we contribute to the state of research. Prior to investigating what requirements an AR solution must meet to support the service process of soil sounding, we examined the augmentability of the process using the theory of process augmentability [38]. We could determine that all four characteristics – which according to the theory, must be present in a process – are existent in the process of soil sounding so that an augmentation of the process is sensible and could help to facilitate and improve the process. This result is consistent with the taxonomy study by Klinker et al. [48], who investigated for which processes in logistics an AR application is appropriate. As the process of soil sounding is a difficult case from practice, and therefore laboratory conditions are not given, implementing an AR solution is a big challenge, but it should be tackled to support practice.

In sum, we derived five core requirements from the case of soil sounding for the application of AR, namely (1) real-time overlay, (2) variety in displaying information, (3) multi-dimensional tracking, (4) collaboration, and (5) interaction. In addition, three general underlying requirements emerge related to traffic safety, health, and usability, which are included in all five requirement areas. Compared to the requirements for smart glasses-based AR systems for cycling training [30] and to the use of AR in driving situations [31, 32], there are some similarities because in all these cases, an AR solution has to be applied in a mobile environment and the users act in a traffic situation. Both a failure in road traffic and one in the navigation of a vessel in shipping traffic can have serious consequences. In contrast to cycling or driving a car, however, our use case takes place in an environment where there is a further dimension of motion and consequently more degrees of freedom. Therefore, the multi-dimensional tracking requirement poses an even greater challenge to existing AR hardware as it is in the case of road traffic. Especially for soil soundings, where the measurement had to be carried out in a narrow area or where there was a high volume of traffic, exact tracking is essential. This applies not only to soil sounding vessels but to all other types of vessels as well, whereby the failure tolerance decreases as vessels approach narrow or restricted fairways and increasing traffic density [49]. Furthermore, the use case of soil sounding gains in complexity since the user has to perform another task in addition to navigating the vessel, namely the service task of depth measurement in order to ensure harbor infrastructure and thus traffic safety. Moreover, from a methodological point of view, our approach contributes to new standards of research. By underpinning the thinking aloud method with video material from various perspectives, we were able to gain the best possible understanding of the spatial implications and requirements for AR. Thereby the enriched thinking aloud material helps to gain further insights and learnings about the user-centered requirements. Additionally, our approach is beneficial in environments that do not meet the standards of typical scientific interviews by being noisy, weather-dependent, and dirty.

However, our approach is not entirely free of limitations. Since we have only focused on one specific use case, that of soil sounding in water depth management, our results are contextual. Nevertheless, we assume a transferability to other use cases. For this purpose, further use cases in the maritime logistics environment could be considered. One possible case is the dredging industry, which is responsible for adjusting and dredging the water depths. Furthermore, use cases in the field of pilotage in the harbor could be considered. Moreover, a floating drone is used for water depth management and soil sounding. Also, in this case, potentials are recognizable, since with the help of AR, for example, the drone operator could take a first-person view in addition to a third-person view regarding the drone.

6 Conclusion

In summary, we have shown that the soil sounding service is augmentable in general. Knowing the augmentation potential, we derived five user-centered requirements for the soil sounding process, using the results of the thinking aloud sessions as a foundation: (1) real-time overlay, (2) variety in displaying information, (3) multi-dimensional tracking, (4) collaboration, and (5) interaction requirement. The requirements for an AR solution, which we have determined with regard to the navigation task of the skipper, correspond to the results of previous research on AR applications in road traffic. However, never before has such a complex process as that of soil sounding been investigated, so we are contributing to the research at this point. On the one hand, the moving vessel in combination with the moving user inside the vessel poses a great challenge in terms of multidimensional tracking possibilities. On the other hand, it is a knowledge-intense process that requires multitasking, i.e. a constant shift between the navigation of the vessel and the measurement of water depth, and collaboration with the measurement engineer. Furthermore, the process is subject to enormous safety critical requirements, which must be considered additionally.

Besides the above-mentioned tracking, future challenges will be to determine whether supporting the process with AR is beneficial for the skipper from a user perspective and, if so, in what form AR can be used to achieve the greatest possible advantage. For this purpose, a prototypical implementation and evaluation will be initiated in the future to explore the subjective usefulness of AR in the soil sounding context. In this context the requirements should be evaluated more detailed with experts from the maritime industry as well as AR solution developers regarding their technical feasibility, whereby the focus should be on interfaces, data types and data quality. Not least, the transferability to other use cases, e.g. in the harbor environment and general industrial as well as logistic scenarios, remains to be investigated.

Acknowledgements. This research was partly sponsored by the German Federal Ministry for Education and Research and in the project WizARd under the reference 02K18D180 and 02K18D181. Further information can be found under: http://www.wizard.tu-dortmund.de/.

References

1. Ostrom, A.L., Parasuraman, A., Bowen, D.E., Patrício, L., Voss, C.A.: Service research priorities in a rapidly changing context. J. Serv. Res. **18**, 127–159 (2015)
2. Wirtz, J., et al.: Brave new world: service robots in the frontline. J. Serv. Manage. **29**, 907–931 (2018)
3. Jeffers, P.I., Muhanna, W.A., Nault, B.R.: Information technology and process performance: an empirical investigation of the interaction between IT and Non-IT resources. Decis. Sci. **39**, 703–735 (2008)
4. Collier, D.A.: The Service/Quality Solution: Using Service Management to Gain Competitive Advantage. Irwin Professional Publishing, Milwaukee (1994)
5. Haksever, C., Render, B., Russell, R.S., Murdick, R.G.: Service Management and Operations. Prentice-Hall, Upper Saddle River (2000)
6. Böhmann, T., Leimeister, J.M., Möslein, K.: Service systems engineering. Bus. Inf. Syst. Eng. **6**, 73–79 (2014)
7. Niemöller, C., Metzger, D., Berkemeier, L., Zobel, B., Thomas, O.: Mobile service support based on smart glasses. J. Inf. Technol. Theory Appl. **20**, 77–108 (2019)
8. Niemöller, C., Metzger, D., Thomas, O.: Design and evaluation of a smart-glasses-based service support system. In: Proceedings of the 13th International Conference on Wirtschaftsinformatik, pp. 106–120 (2017)
9. Elder, S., Vakaloudis, A.: Towards uniformity for smart glasses devices: an assessment of function as the driver for standardisation. In: 2015 IEEE International Symposium on Technology and Society (ISTAS), pp. 1–7. IEEE, Piscataway (2015)
10. Metzger, D., Niemöller, C., Thomas, O.: Design and demonstration of an engineering method for service support systems. IseB **15**(4), 789–823 (2016). https://doi.org/10.1007/s10257-016-0331-x
11. Klinker, K., Fries, V., Wiesche, M., Krcmar, H.: CatCare: designing a serious game to foster hand hygiene compliance in health care facilities. In: Proceedings of the 12th International Conference on Design Science Research in Information Systems and Technology (DESRIST), pp. 20–28. Karlsruher Institut für Technologie (KIT) (2017)
12. Niemöller, C., et al.: Sind Smart Glasses die Zukunft der Digitalisierung von Arbeitsprozessen? Explorative Fallstudien zukünftiger Einsatzszenarien in der Logistik. In: Proceedings of the 13th International Conference on Wirtschaftsinformatik, pp. 410–424 (2017)
13. Rauschnabel, P.A., Ro, Y.K.: Augmented reality smart glasses: an investigation of technology acceptance drivers. Int. J. Technol. Market. **11**, 123–148 (2016)
14. Knight, J.C.: Safety critical systems. In: Tracz, W., Magee, J., Young, M. (eds.) Proceedings of the 24th International Conference on Software Engineering - ICSE 2002, pp. 547–550. ACM Press, New York (2002)
15. Lusch, R.F., Nambisan, S.: Service innovation: a service-dominant logic perspective. MISQ **39**, 155–175 (2015)
16. Jessen, A., et al.: The playground effect: How augmented reality drives creative customer engagement. J. Bus. Res. **116**, 85–98 (2020)
17. Matijacic, M., Fellmann, M., Özcan, D., Kammler, F., Nüttgens, M., Thomas, O.: Elicitation and consolidation of requirements for mobile technical customer services support systems-a multi-method approach. In: Proceedings of the 34th International Conference on Information Systems (ICIS) (2013)
18. Thomas, P.C., David, W.M.: Augmented reality: an application of heads-up display technology to manual manufacturing processes. In: Proceedings of the 25th Hawaii International Conference on System Sciences (HICCS), pp. 659–669 (1992)

19. Huck-Fries, V., Wiegand, F., Klinker, K., Wiesche, M., Krcmar, H.: Datenbrillen in der Wartung. In: Eibl, M., Gaedke, M. (ed.) INFORMATIK 2017, pp. 1413–1424. Gesellschaft für Informatik, Bonn (2017)
20. Henderson, S., Feiner, S.: Exploring the benefits of augmented reality documentation for maintenance and repair. IEEE Trans. Visual Comput. Graphics **17**, 1355–1368 (2011)
21. Sandor, C., Klinker, G.: A rapid prototyping software infrastructure for user interfaces in ubiquitous augmented reality. Pers. Ubiquit. Comput. **9**, 169–185 (2005)
22. Metzger, D., Niemöller, C., Berkemeier, L., Brenning, L., Thomas, O.: Vom Techniker zum Modellierer – Konzeption und Entwicklung eines Smart Glasses Systems zur Laufzeitmodellierung von Dienstleistungsprozessen. In: Thomas, O., Nüttgens, M., Fellmann, M. (eds.) Smart Service Engineering. Konzepte und Anwendungsszenarien für die digitale Transformation, pp. 193–213. Springer Gabler, Wiesbaden (2017)
23. Dunston, P.S., Wang, X.: Mixed reality-based visualization interfaces for architecture, engineering, and construction industry. J. Constr. Eng. Manage. **131**, 1301–1309 (2005)
24. Yaoyuneyong, G., Foster, J., Johnson, E., Johnson, D.: Augmented reality marketing: consumer preferences and attitudes toward hypermedia print ads. J. Interact. Advert. **16**, 16–30 (2016)
25. Kaufmann, H., Schmalstieg, D.: Mathematics and geometry education with collaborative augmented reality. Comput. Graph. **27**, 339–345 (2003)
26. Sielhorst, T., Feuerstein, M., Navab, N.: Advanced medical displays: a literature review of augmented reality. J. Display Technol. **4**, 451–467 (2008)
27. Klinker, K., Wiesche, M., Krcmar, H.: Digital transformation in health care: augmented reality for hands-free service innovation. Inf. Syst. Front. **22**(6), 1419–1431 (2019). https://doi.org/10.1007/s10796-019-09937-7
28. Sparacino, F.: The Museum Wearable: Real-Time Sensor-Driven Understanding of Visitors' Interests for Personalized Visually-Augmented Museum Experiences (2002)
29. Miyashita, T., et al.: An Augmented Reality museum guide. In: Proceedings of the 7th IEEE/ACM International Symposium on Mixed and Augmented Reality, pp. 103–106 (2008)
30. Berkemeier, L., Menzel, L., Remark, F., Thomas, O.: Acceptance by design: towards an acceptable smart glasses-based information system based on the example of cycling training. In: Multikonferenz Wirtschaftsinformatik (MKWI) (2018)
31. Heymann, M., Degani, A.: Classification and organization of information. In: Shaked, N., Winter, U. (eds.) Design of Multimodal Mobile Interfaces, pp. 195–217 (2016)
32. Regenbrecht, H., Baratoff, G., Wilke, W.: Augmented reality projects in the automotive and aerospace industries. IEEE Comput. Graphics Appl. **25**, 48–56 (2005)
33. Träskbäack, M., Haller, M.: Mixed reality training application for an oil refinery: user requirements. In: Proceedings of the 2004 ACM SIGGRAPH International Conference on Virtual Reality Continuum and its Applications in Industry, pp. 324–327 (2004)
34. Bagassi, S., et al.: Human-in-the-loop evaluation of an augmented reality based interface for the airport control tower. Comput. Ind. **123**, 103291 (2020)
35. Balci, B., Rosenkranz, C.: "Virtual or material, what do you prefer?" A study of process virtualization theory. In: Proceedings of the 22nd European Conference on Information System (ECIS) (2014)
36. Overby, E.: Process virtualization theory and the impact of information technology. Organ. Sci. **19**, 277–291 (2008)
37. Bose, R., Luo, X.: Integrative framework for assessing firms' potential to undertake Green IT initiatives via virtualization – a theoretical perspective. J. Strateg. Inf. Syst. **20**, 38–54 (2011)
38. Yeo, J.: The theory of process augmentability. In: Proceedings of the 38th International Conference on Information Systems (ICIS) (2017)
39. Newman, G.E.: An essentialist account of authenticity. J. Cogn. Cult. **16**, 294–321 (2016)

40. Grayson, K., Martinec, R.: Consumer perceptions of iconicity and indexicality and their influence on assessments of authentic market offerings. J. Consum. Res. **31**, 296–312 (2004)
41. Baudrillard, J.: Simulations. Translated by Paul Foss, Paul Patton and Philip Beitchman. Semiotext (E), New York (1983)
42. Azuma, R.T.: A survey of augmented reality. Presence Teleoperators Virtual Environ. **6**, 355–385 (1997)
43. Huang, W., Eades, P., Hong, S.-H.: Measuring effectiveness of graph visualizations: a cognitive load perspective. Inf. Vis. **8**, 139–152 (2009)
44. Yin, R.K.: Case Study Research: Design and Methods. Sage, Thousand Oaks (2003)
45. Todd, P., Benbasat, I.: Process tracing methods in decision support systems research: exploring the black box. MISQ **11**, 493 (1987)
46. van Someren, M.W., Barnard, Y.F., Sandberg, J.A.C.: The Think Aloud Method: A Practical Approach to Modelling Cognitive. Academic Press, London (1994)
47. Bouwman, M.J.: Human diagnostic reasoning by computer: an illustration from financial analysis. Manage. Sci. **29**, 653–672 (1983)
48. Klinker, K., et al.: Structure for innovations: A use case taxonomy for smart glasses in service processes. In: Multikonferenz Wirtschaftsinformatik (MKWI) (2018)
49. Gardenier, J.S.: Ship navigational failure detection and diagnosis. In: Rasmussen, J., Rouse, W.B. (eds.) Human Detection and Diagnosis of System Failures. NATO Conference Series, vol. 15, pp. 49–74. Springer, Boston (1981). https://doi.org/10.1007/978-1-4615-9230-3_5

Co-creating Value in B2B Platform Ecosystems – Towards a Deeper Understanding of the Emergence and Nature of Actor Engagement

Carina Benz[1(✉)], Lara Riefle[1], and Christopher Schwarz[2]

[1] Karlsruhe Institute of Technology, Karlsruhe, Germany
{carina.benz,lara.riefle}@kit.edu
[2] Celonis SE, Munich, Germany
c.schwarz@celonis.com

Abstract. Digital platforms (e.g., Industrial Internet of Things (IIoT) platforms) are on the rise aiming to foster value co-creation in business-to-business (B2B) ecosystems. However, we often observe actors to only hesitantly engage, and activity levels that fall short of expectations. Arriving at a sound understanding of why and how actors decide to engage in co-creation practices is a crucial first step to further promote and facilitate value co-creation in B2B platform ecosystems. This work builds upon the concept of actor engagement, which offers an actor-centric microlens on the hitherto vague theoretical idea of value co-creation. By pursuing a qualitative approach to theory development based on interviews with platform complementors, we identify factors influencing the formation and extent of actor engagement. Eventually, our research aims to contribute to a refined conception of value co-creation in B2B platform ecosystems by understanding the emergence and nature of actor engagement.

Keywords: Actor engagement · Value co-creation · B2B platform ecosystem

1 Introduction

Along with the introduction of the service-dominant logic (SDL)—proclaiming that value is always co-created, i.e., a result from the interaction and resource integration within service ecosystems [1]—we observe increased efforts in industry to foster co-creation practices. Recently, digital platforms gain ground as means to foster value co-creation in service ecosystems [2, 3]. Also, Lusch and Nambisan [2] acknowledge the role of platforms in facilitating the interaction of actors and easing access to appropriate resource bundles, thus reflecting an instrument to enhance the effectiveness and efficiency of value co-creation. Following impressive success stories of platforms and value co-creation among different actors produced by the business-to-consumer (B2C) sector (e.g., AirBnB, Apple's App Store), the industrial sector is just beginning to tap their potential. One example of such digital platforms in B2B ecosystems are Industrial

F. Ahlemann et al. (Eds.): WI 2021, LNISO 46, pp. 236–242, 2021.
https://doi.org/10.1007/978-3-030-86790-4_17

Internet of Things (IIoT) platforms, which e.g., enable the provision of digital services in the industrial sector based on machine data [4].

Yet, academic knowledge on B2B platform ecosystems is currently still unfolding. Concentrating on the formation of platform ecosystems in industry [5–7], their design, government, and boundary resources [8, 9], or the platform owner's role [10, 11], the majority of current studies is strongly platform-focused. Less considered are actor roles apart from the platform owner. In particular, the perspective of platform complementors—i.e., actors who offer their value proposition (e.g., digital services) via the platform [12]—is still unrepresented, though significantly contributing to the platforms' attractiveness [9, 13, 14]. Equally, a platform's operating phase succeeding the initial launch and joining of actors is less in focus. This, however, is when resources will be shared and integrated, and the co-creation of value will proceed [15]. The same lack of attention can also be observed in practice: B2B platforms are being launched and established, but activity of complementors is limited and collaboration with customers is only approached hesitantly [14]. Hence, academic and practical knowledge on value co-creation in B2B platform ecosystems is still unfolding and requires a deeper understanding of why and how actors in B2B platform ecosystems engage in co-creation practices [16, 17].

The idea of exploring actors' engagement as the lowest observational level of value co-creation in service ecosystems has been recently brought to the discourse by Storbacka et al. [18]. Adopting the theoretical perspective of actor engagement [18] allows bridging the gap between the vague and elusive concept of value co-creation on a macro level and an actor's observable behavior on a micro level [19, 20]. Defined as "both the actor's disposition to engage, and the activity of engaging in an interactive process of resource integration within a service ecosystem" [18, p. 308] actor engagement is recognized as microfoundation for value co-creation and midrange concept in the SDL [21]. However, research on engagement in B2B contexts is only just emerging and knowledge on how engagement advances within service ecosystems of organizational actors is still scarce [22, 23].

With this research, we aim to contribute towards a refined conception of value co-creation in B2B platform ecosystems by understanding the emergence and nature of actor engagement. Specifically, we seek to *explore factors that influence the formation and intensity of actor engagement among complementors in B2B platform ecosystems* [18]. We, therefore, pursue a qualitative and inductive approach to theory development based on interviews with platform complementors. In doing so, we not only provide practical insights on determinants for complementors' motivation to grow, stay and engage in B2B platform ecosystems, but contribute to a refined conceptualization of actor engagement as microfoundation of value co-creation.

The remainder of this paper is structured as follows: Sect. 2 briefly introduces the fundamentals of actor engagement and highlights related work. Section 3 outlines our research approach, while Sect. 4 presents initial findings. Section 5 provides an outlook and summarizes our expected contribution.

2 Fundamentals

Service science is centered on the concept of value co-creation within and among service ecosystems [24]. It builds upon the service-dominant logic (SDL), which declares that value is always co-created, i.e., that value results from the interaction and resource integration of multiple actors for mutual benefit [1]. Yet, scholars agree that the SDL view on value co-creation is still too abstract to be empirically observable [18, 19, 25]. With the concept of *actor engagement,* Storbacka et al. [18] address the need for a more nuanced perspective on value co-creation [19, 26]. Informed by the microfoundation movement [27], actor engagement follows the idea that collective phenomena can only be captured when examining their constituent parts on an actor level [18]. In a three-level model, (1) the abstract idea of value co-creation in service ecosystems on a macro level is broken down into (2) the meso level view of actors and resources that exercise resource integration patterns facilitated by engagement platforms, and (3) the actor engagement on the micro level (Fig. 1). Actor engagement subsumes both, the actor's disposition and engagement properties. *Actor disposition* reflects the actor's willingness to invest resources in their interaction with other actors [28], which is "formed partly by actor specific characteristics and partly by the institutional and organizational arrangements prevalent in the context in which the resource contributions occur" [29, p. 6] (e.g., the willingness to join a platform). *Engagement properties,* in turn, refer to observable engagement activities (e.g., sharing of resources, provisioning of services) [13, 18]. Analogous to the transformation of human intention to behavior in psychology, actor dispositions may translate into observable engagement properties through an action-formation mechanism [18, 30]. The role of an actor generally is generic, hence it can be taken by a single actor (human or machine) as well as a group of actors (collectives or organizations) [22, 29].

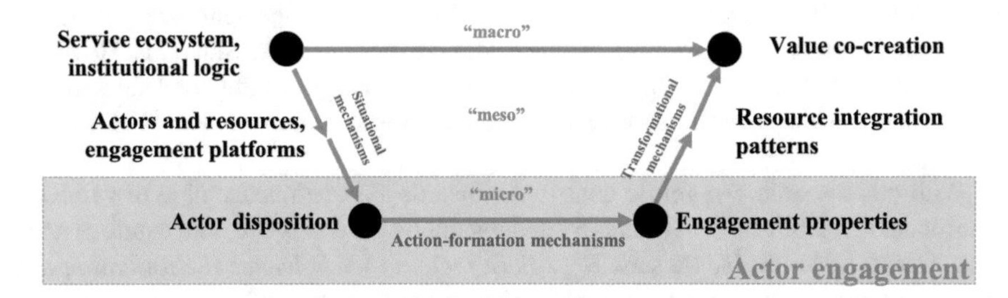

Fig. 1. Actor engagement as microfoundation for value co-creation [18]

Apart from conceptual work, there are empirically driven initiatives to understand value co-creation in B2B platform ecosystems: Hein et al. [15] identify three standard types of co-creation practices in IoT ecosystems: integration of complementary assets, ensuring of platform readiness, and servitization through application enablement. A platform owner's ability to ensure the effective and efficient operation of these co-creation practices is recognized as a prerequisite for platform survival by Blaschke et al. [8]. Also, there is initial research aiming to understand complementors' motivation to join a digital platform ecosystem [7, 9, 14].

3 Research Approach

Our objective is to refine the understanding of actor engagement of complementors in B2B platform ecosystems. To account for the exploratory and inductive nature of our research goal, we adopt a qualitative research approach following Strauss and Corbin [31]. As a starting point, an IIoT platform for the process industry ecosystem hosted by a multinational software corporation serves as a locus for data collection. Data is collected in the form of semi-structured interviews conducted with complementors (e.g., machine manufacturers and service providers) of the IIoT platform. The selection of interview partners follows a theoretical sampling approach, i.e., interview partners are selected based on theoretical relevance assessed through emerging concepts from the analysis of previous interviews [31, 32]. An overview of the interviews conducted so far is provided in Table 1. The interviews are iteratively analyzed in three coding cycles—open, axial, and selective—according to the Straussian approach [31]. After each analysis cycle, the results are discussed by two independent researchers to rule out discrepancies in coding and to collaboratively evolve the emerging concepts [33].

Table 1. Preliminary overview of interviews

Interviewee	Firm	Employees	Industry	Role
Alpha	A	1.000–5.000	Manufacturing	Integrator and User
Beta	B	1.000–5.000	Manufacturing	Integrator and User
Gamma	C	10.000–50.000	Automation	Integrator
Delta	D	1.000–5.000	Industrial Service	Strategic Lead
Epsilon	A	1.000–5.000	Manufacturing	Strategic Lead
Zeta	E	10.000–50.000	Automation	Strategic Lead

4 Initial Findings

With our research endeavor still being in progress, we provide preliminary insights into two concepts in emergence: *partner engagement behavior* and *value realization* (Fig. 2). *Partner engagement behavior* reflects the extent of engagement properties of an actors' potential counterparts for value co-creation. These counterparts can be potential customers or implementation partners, including the platform owner. Interviewee Zeta, whose company has recently scaled down their activities on the platform states: "We have invested a lot of time and money to be ready. But we cannot do more than that [...] if there isn't a single one of our customers [...] to use it productively" (Zeta). In contrast, other actors' effort and commitment in co-implementing new use cases is positively related to the formation of engagement properties: "A requirement is the willingness to work together on concrete topics at eye level—despite a clear difference in size between operators and manufacturers—and the commitment to work on this as partners" (Beta). Our concept of partner engagement behavior is also in line with conceptual research proposing that engagement manifests through behaviors, whereby actors in an ecosystem influence each other's dispositions and behaviors [21, 23].

Value realization refers to the extent of benefits that an actor recognizes to leverage from engaging in the platform ecosystem. We observe the participation in a B2B platform ecosystem to be associated with high expectancies related to access to other actors' data and the provision of novel digital services (Epsilon, Gamma). At the same time, it requires high upfront effort combined with vague benefit prospects, as Epsilon states: "One must recognize the benefits, even if these rather lie in the future" (Epsilon). Hence, noticing that engagement activities are leading to—even small—observable benefits is decisive for continuous engagement. Consequently, engaged interviewees report on a clear potential to realize monetary returns: "This means that the end customer is already willing to pay money for this data. […] We just have to redirect it" (Beta), or internal efficiency improvements: "We also had to work out the benefits ourselves. We were able to find use cases for ourselves, internally; for our own service technicians" (Alpha). This complements previous empirical research in B2C contexts that finds rewards and recognition to encourage customer engagement [34, 35].

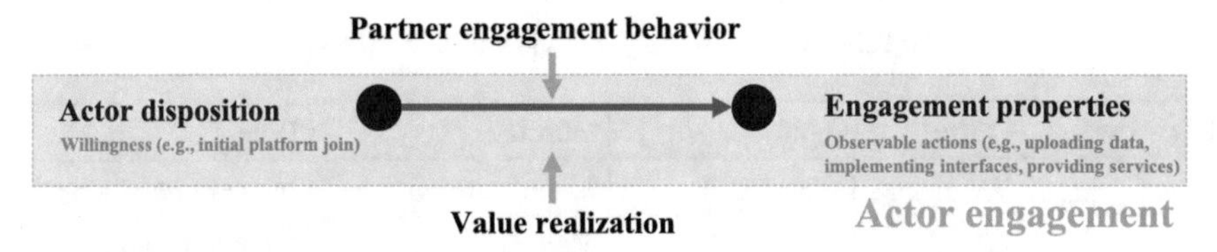

Fig. 2. Partner engagement behavior and value realization as emerging concepts

5 Outlook and Conclusion

Aiming to understand the emergence and nature of actor engagement as micro-foundation for value co-creation in B2B platform ecosystems, we pursue a qualitative approach to theory development. With our sampling strategy being driven by the objective of theoretical saturation, future interviews will be iteratively reassessed, guided by previous findings. As of now, we see the need for subsequent interviews to account for interviewees with above- and below-average engagement and to incorporate companies with different levels of vertical integration.

Upon completion, our results will contribute to research in the field of service science and digital platforms. In the broadest sense, our study will contribute to service theory by following Grönroos and Voimas' [19] call for a theoretically sound foundation for value co-creation. In particular, we adopt the concept of actor engagement [18] to study value co-creation in B2B platform ecosystems on the micro level of an actor's intention and activities. In observing how individual actors assimilate contextual conditions into actions, we refine the understanding of actor engagement and contribute to theory building in this emerging field of research. From the perspective of digital platform research, our contribution arises from offering new insights into the antecedents and evolution of complementors' engagement in B2B platform ecosystems. This knowledge may empower practitioners and platform designers to foster and maintain engagement within their platform ecosystems.

References

1. Vargo, S.L., Lusch, R.F.: Evolving to a new dominant logic for marketing. J. Mark. **68**, 1–17 (2004)
2. Lusch, R.F., Nambisan, S.: Service innovation: a service-dominant logic perspective. MIS Q. **39**, 155–175 (2015)
3. De Reuver, M., Sørensen, C., Basole, R.C.: The digital platform: a research agenda. J. Inf. Technol. **33**, 124–135 (2017)
4. Petrik, D., Herzwurm, G.: iIoT ecosystem development through boundary resources: a Siemens mindsphere case study. In: IWSiB 2019. Tallinn, Estonia (2019)
5. Staykova, K.S.: Managing platform ecosystem evolution through the emergence of micro-strategies and microstructures. In: Proceedings of the 39th International Conference on Information Systems (ICIS). San Francisco, CA, USA (2018)
6. Hein, A., Schreieck, M., Wiesche, M., Böhm, M., Krcmar, H.: The emergence of native multi-sided platforms and their influence on incumbents. Electron. Mark. **29**(4), 631–647 (2019). https://doi.org/10.1007/s12525-019-00350-1
7. Petrik, D., Herzwurm, G.: Towards the iIoT ecosystem development-understanding the stake-holder perspective. In: Proceedings of the 28th European Conference on Information Systems (ECIS). An Online AIS Conference (2020)
8. Blaschke, M., Aier, S., Haki, K., Winter, R.: Capabilities for digital platform survival: Insights from a business-to-business digital platform. In: Proceedings of the 39th International Conference on Information Systems (ICIS). San Francisco, CA, USA (2018)
9. Petrik, D., Herzwurm, G.: Complementor satisfaction with boundary resources in IIoT ecosystems. In: Abramowicz, W., Klein, G. (eds.) BIS 2020. LNBIP, vol. 389, pp. 351–366. Springer, Cham (2020). https://doi.org/10.1007/978-3-030-53337-3_26
10. Mini, T., Widjaja, T.: Tensions in digital platform business models: a literature review. In: Proceedings of the 40th International Conference on Information Systems (ICIS), Munich, Germany (2019)
11. Hein, A., Setzke, D.S., Hermes, S., Weking, J.: The influence of digital affordances and generativity on digital platform leadership. In: Proceedings of the 40th International Conference on Information Systems (ICIS), Munich, Germany (2019)
12. Kapoor, R.: Ecosystems: broadening the locus of value creation. J. Organ. Des. **7**(1), 1–16 (2018). https://doi.org/10.1186/s41469-018-0035-4
13. Hein, A., et al.: Digital platform ecosystems. Electron. Mark. **30**(1), 87–98 (2019). https://doi.org/10.1007/s12525-019-00377-4
14. Pauli, T., Marx, E., Matzner, M.: Leveraging industrial IoT platform ecosystems: insights from the complementors' perspective. In: Twenty-Eighth European Conference on Information Systems (ECIS). An Online AIS Conference (2020)
15. Hein, A., Weking, J., Schreieck, M., Wiesche, M., Böhm, M., Krcmar, H.: Value co-creation practices in business-to-business platform ecosystems. Electron. Mark. **29**(3), 503–518 (2019). https://doi.org/10.1007/s12525-019-00337-y
16. Jonas, J.M., Boha, J., Sörhammar, D., Moeslein, K.M.: Stakeholder engagement in intra- and inter-organizational innovation: exploring antecedents of engagement in service ecosystems. J. Serv. Manag. **29**, 399–421 (2018)
17. Gelhaar, J., Otto, B.: Challenges in the emergence of data ecosystems. In: Proceedings of the 24th Pacific Asia Conference on Information Systems (PACIS), Dubai, UAE (2020)
18. Storbacka, K., Brodie, R.J., Böhmann, T., Maglio, P.P., Nenonen, S.: Actor engagement as a microfoundation for value co-creation. J. Bus. Res. J. **69**, 3008–3017 (2016)
19. Grönroos, C., Voima, P.: Critical service logic: making sense of value creation and co-creation. J. Acad. Mark. Sci. **41**, 133–150 (2013)

20. Grotherr, C., Semmann, M., Böhmann, T.: Using microfoundations of value co-creation to guide service systems design - A multilevel design framework. In: Proceedings of the 39th International Conference on Information Systems (ICIS), San Francisco, CA, USA (2018)
21. Alexander, M.J., Jaakkola, E., Hollebeek, L.D.: Zooming out: actor engagement beyond the dyadic. J. Serv. Manag. **29**, 333–351 (2018)
22. Kleinaltenkamp, M., Karpen, I.O., Plewa, C., Jaakkola, E., Conduit, J.: Collective engagement in organizational settings. Ind. Mark. Manag. **80**, 11–23 (2019)
23. Fehrer, J.A., Conduit, J., Plewa, C., Li, L.P., Jaakkola, E., Alexander, M.: Market shaping dynamics: interplay of actor engagement and institutional work. J. Bus. Ind. Mark. (2020)
24. Vargo, S.L., Akaka, M.A.: Value cocreation and service systems (Re)Formation: a service ecosystems view. Serv. Sci. **4**, 207–217 (2012)
25. Schüritz, R., Farrell, K., Wixom, B., Satzger, G.: Value co-creation in data-driven services: towards a deeper understanding of the joint sphere. In: Proceedings of the 40th International Conference on Information Systems (ICIS), Munich, Germany (2019)
26. Vargo, S.L., Lusch, R.F.: Institutions and axioms: an extension and update of service-dominant logic. J. Acad. Mark. Sci. **44**(1), 5–23 (2015). https://doi.org/10.1007/s11747-015-0456-3
27. Felin, T., Ployhart, R.E.: The microfoundations movement in strategy and organization theory. Acad. Manag. Ann. **9**, 575–632 (2015)
28. Brodie, R.J., Fehrer, J.A., Jaakkola, E., Conduit, J.: Actor engagement in networks: defining the conceptual domain. J. Serv. Res. **22**, 173–188 (2019)
29. Storbacka, K.: Actor engagement, value creation and market innovation. Ind. Mark. Manag. **80**, 4–10 (2019)
30. Ajzen, I.: The theory of planned behavior. Organ. Behav. Hum. Decis. Process. **50**, 179–211 (1991)
31. Corbin, J.M., Strauss, A.L.: Basics of Qualitative Research: Techniques and Procedures for Developing Grounded Theory. Sage, Los Angeles (2015)
32. Halaweh, M., Fidler, C., McRobb, S.: Integrating the grounded theory method and case study research methodology within IS research : a possible ‘road map’. In: Proceedings of the Twenty Ninth International Conference on Information Systems (ICIS), Paris, France (2008)
33. Gioia, D.A., Corley, K.G., Hamilton, A.L.: Seeking qualitative rigor in inductive research: notes on the Gioia methodology. Organ. Res. Methods. **16**, 15–31 (2013)
34. Chan, T.K.H., Zheng, X., Cheung, C.M.K., Lee, M.K.O., Lee, Z.W.Y.: Antecedents and consequences of customer engagement in online brand communities. J. Mark. Anal. **2**, 81–97 (2014)
35. Jaakkola, E., Alexander, M.: The role of customer engagement behavior in value co-creation: a service system perspective. J. Serv. Res. **17**, 247–261 (2014)

Digitisation and Society - Even in Times of Corona

Introduction to the WI2021 Track: Digitalization and Society – Even in Times of Corona

Christian Reuter[1] and Ulrike Lechner[2]

[1] Technical University of Darmstadt, Science and Technology for Peace and Security (PEAESC), Darmstadt, Germany
reuter@peasec.tu-darmstadt.de
[2] Universität der Bundeswehr München, Chair of Information Systems, Neubiberg, Germany
ulrike.lechner@unibw.de

1 Track Description

Information and communication technologies affect all areas of civil society. Digitalization opens up new opportunities to address important social issues. The motor of digitalization can be social necessity, technical feasibility, and also a crisis, as the reaction to the COVID-19 pandemic demonstrates: Out of necessity, ideas are created, systems designed and implemented and the value of digital solutions to society becomes apparent. With the digitalization of everyday working and learning, apps for tracing information chains and containing new infections have potential, but also pose social risks. The current COVID-19 crisis seems to put the role of digitalization in a completely new light. Both, to evaluate the value of digital solutions to society and to identify space for innovation is important in times of intense digitalization efforts.

To meet the societal challenges posed by digitalization, it is particularly important to understand how they arise. The use of digital solutions in safety-critical contexts entails dependencies and the threat of various dangers: Infrastructure disruptions and failures can be caused by criminal acts, terrorist attacks, natural disasters, operational disruptions, and system failures. In addition, there is a concern about data arising from the use of digital solutions. Data protection, data sovereignty, data security, and their social perception must always be closely observed. Furthermore, it is important to ensure that digitalization does not lead to a digital divide. New digital solutions require constant evaluation and assessment of the consequences.

2 Research Articles

This track aims to contribute to this relevant continuous evaluation and assessment of the consequence. Therefore, its focus lies on issues at the intersection of digitalization and society, not only, but also in times of COVID-19, and aims at researchers and practitioners in information systems and related disciplines. Six articles have been selected out of sixteen submissions.

The paper *"The Role of Fear and Trust when Disclosing Personal Data to Promote Public Health in a Pandemic Crisis"* (by Kirsten Hillebrand) investigates citizens' consent to voluntary and legally obliging data disclosure to public authorities and what drives their consent. Results from an online survey during the onset of the crisis in Germany in mid-March show that (1) fear for health increases citizens' consent to voluntary data disclosure, (2) fear increases consent to legally obliging data disclosure directly and indirectly by fostering distrust in others, and (3) trust in the government increases voluntary and legally obliging data disclosure.

The article *"It's not that bad! Perceived Stress of Knowledge Workers During Enforced Working from Home due to COVID-19"* (by Jana Mattern, Simon Lansmann, and Joschka Hüllmann) analyzes whether working from home and in particular "enforced working from home (EWFH)" increases perceived stress due to blurring boundaries between work and private life. The authors suggest psychological detachment and communication overload as explaining variables for the relationship between EWFH and perceived stress.

The contribution *"'Sorry, Museum Facilities are Closed Due to Covid': Towards Online Platforms for Cultural Participation and Education"* (by Kristin Kutzner, Thorsten Schoormann, Claudia Roßkopf, and Ralf Knackstedt) reviews and synthesizes related literature and museum platforms in order to deduce a taxonomy of how online offers leverage cultural participation and education. In doing this, the authors seek to enable platform designers and museum professionals in making informed decisions in terms of how the 'museum experience' can be supported through online platforms.

The study *"Challenges of the Digital Transformation – Comparing Nonprofit and Industry Organizations"* (by Kristin Vogelsang, Sven Packmohr, and Henning Brink) deals with Digital transformation (DT) of various areas: technology-based improvements in business processes, business models, and customer experience. In a grounded theory approach, the authors develop a framework of barriers for two diverse sectors: industry and nonprofit. While in the industry sector, the progress of DT has been slow due to barriers, nonprofit organizations often take the view that they are not in a DT at all. This is due to limited individual and organizational perspectives.

The paper *"Understanding pandemic dashboard development: A multi-level analysis of success factors"* (by Ludger Pöhler, Kevin Kus, and Frank Teuteberg) aims at identifying and understanding success factors of dashboards in crisis situations and more specifically in pandemics. Dashboards refer to graphical user interfaces which often provide at-a-glance views of key performance indicators (KPIs). The paper investigates whether corona dashboards are based on previous helpful crisis dashboards or whether specific success factors of current dashboards can be identified.

The article *"The Impact of Digitizing Social Networks on Refugee Decision Making – The Journey to Germany"* (by Safa'a AbuJarour, Lama Jaghjougha, and Mohammed AbuJarour) reveals four typical streams of utilizing social networks through Social Networking Sites in the context of migration: (1) information gathering, (2) service consumption, (3) understanding the relevant procedures and systems, and (4) content creation and service provisioning. The paper discusses the impact of digitalized social networks on refugees aiming at maximizing the benefits and avoiding possible risks.

The Role of Fear and Trust When Disclosing Personal Data to Promote Public Health in a Pandemic Crisis

Kirsten Hillebrand(✉)

Faculty of Business Studies and Economics, University of Bremen, Bremen, Germany
post@kirstenhillebrand.de

Abstract. During the 2020 pandemic crisis, state surveillance measures violated citizens' privacy rights to track the virus spread. Rather little civic protest resulted—"safety first"? Indeed, many state measures were implemented during the crisis without ever having been discussed in advance of the event of a crisis, which may raise ethical considerations, as individual consent to data disclosure may change while experiencing fear. This paper investigates citizens' consent to voluntary and legally obliging data disclosure to the state and what drives their consent. Results from an online survey conducted with 1,156 respondents during the onset of the crisis in Germany in mid-March show that (1) fear increases consent to voluntary data disclosure, (2) fear increases consent to legally obliging data disclosure directly and indirectly by fostering distrust in others, and (3) trust in the government increases voluntary and legally obliging data disclosure.

Keywords: Data privacy · Fear · Trust · COVID-19 · Data disclosure

1 Introduction

In early 2020 the world started to change in the face of the coronavirus. While in certain regions of China the first mass quarantines and the cancellations of the Chinese New Year celebrations have already been ordered in January [36], many Western nations imposed major restrictions especially in March as a response to the exponentially rising infection numbers: Italy locks its borders and closes all schools and universities [43], France introduces a curfew in which citizens are not allowed to leave their homes without a respective certificate [45]. U.S. President Trump declares a national state of emergency [8] and the Dax faces its highest loss since the September 11 terrorist attacks [20]. Germany, like many other countries, decrees the drastic restriction of social contacts and closes down gastronomy and certain service companies [9]. Spain even closes all "non-essential businesses" [29]. In times of crisis, the state is expected to take action. In most Western democracies, governments restricted basic citizens' rights, though little protest resulted; citizens likely were apt to think that security comes first. In a pandemic crisis, different rules seem to apply—but is this the case even for data protection? Although international politicians have addressed the crisis in various ways, one measure was popular: the use of public information to control the spread of the virus. Some states

F. Ahlemann et al. (Eds.): WI 2021, LNISO 46, pp. 247–262, 2021.
https://doi.org/10.1007/978-3-030-86790-4_18

seem to put safety first and insisted on state supervision of all citizens, whereas others relied on voluntary approaches. In Taiwan, for example, people entering the country were monitored by their mobile data to ensure that they were complying with the quarantine. South Korea had authorities record location data of infected people using GPS tracking and compare their movement with credit card transactions and images from video surveillance. Israel allowed its secret service to analyze mobile phone data of millions of users to track movement flows. In Germany, Deutsche Telekom transmitted a one-time set of mobile data to the Robert Koch Institute (RKI) in mid-May to analyze the spread of the virus [42]. The German Minister of Health recommended continuous tracking of citizens' location data to identify people who came in contact with infected people. However, after criticism from data protectionists and the German Minister of Justice, a draft for a law to this effect was stopped [19]. Similar to Singapore, Germany then followed a voluntary approach [39]. A perquisite for this approach was that users voluntarily disclose their data. At the time this paper was prepared, the discussion in Germany concerned in particular the voluntary sharing of location and health data. The current solution, a Bluetooth-based app without location data, was not considered at that time.

An examination of South Korea, for example, shows that the use of data could indeed have the potential to contain the virus. Although South Korea is democratically governed and, as of this writing, could avoid a lockdown, the spread of the virus is widely controlled. In addition, scientists of the German Academy of Natural Scientists Leopoldina explicitly recommend the use of data [25]. However, despite its apparent potential, the use of data to contain the virus remains internationally controversial from a data protection standpoint. Data protectionists warn that tracking data during the crisis endangers people's privacy far beyond the pandemic crisis period [2]. E.g., location data can serve as a diagnostic measure of sensitive individual attributes such as religious or political views and possible health concerns [15]. The European Union has therefore classified location data as "personal data" in the General Data Protection Regulation. In the course of the 2020 pandemic crisis, it is striking that a majority of governmental data collection measures are discussed ad hoc and implemented in the middle of a global emergency, a time when people may be fearing for their health, the health of loved ones, and consequences for the public. Data protection advocates warn that governments might use the crisis to realize measures of data collection and state surveillance that they may not have been able to enforce outside the exceptional situation [4]. Would protests have been greater if these measures were discussed outside the crisis, considering that preferences change when experiencing fear [26, 27, 46]?

With regard to their safety, citizens face a trade-off: If they make use of the state's voluntary services and thereby disclose their data, the virus can be better controlled without state violation of privacy rights. However, individuals cannot know if a sufficient number of people will comply with these voluntary services to control the virus. Are people willing to take that risk? Or, in times of crisis and fear, do they prefer mandatory data sharing of all citizens to ensure safety? If so, the virus may be better controlled, but the government will violate fundamental privacy rights by surveilling citizens' location without prior individual consent. This paper aims to contribute to a better understanding of what drives preferences of the potentially harmed parties in this trade-off—the citizens.

The study is carried out in the context of the 2020 pandemic crisis with German citizens with regard to location data tracking. In this paper I examine how individuals may prefer data sharing over privacy, and in particular whether German citizens are more likely to agree to voluntary or mandatory data sharing to the state if their goal is to ensure safety. I therefore pose the following research question:

RQ: How do fear and trust influence the willingness to disclose personal data to the state in order to promote public health in a pandemic crisis?

2 Theoretical Background and Research Model

Literature suggests that the individual decision to disclose data is based on a cost–effectiveness analysis, such that data are released if the expected positive outcomes exceed the costs (i.e., the privacy risk). This logic also applies to the disclosure of location data [10]. Researchers have investigated how the willingness to self-disclose location data varies with the nature of the generated benefit. They distinguish between "symbolic" or "hedonic" benefits (e.g., additional values such as better service, personalization of offers) and "utilitarian" benefits (e.g., goods, monetary advantages) [41, 47]. However, extant literature on the disclosure of data based on a privacy calculus neglects crucial particularities of a pandemic crisis. First, the benefit a person gains by voluntary disclosing his or her location is uncertain and delayed. In this situation, whether someone gains an advantage from data disclosure depends on the behavior of others [6]. In this paper's scenario, the spread of the virus can only be controlled without governmental coercion if a sufficient number of people voluntarily disclose their location. Second, the benefit is of varying value for each person in a pandemic crisis. The added value depends on what negative consequences a person anticipates if the spread of the virus cannot be controlled. These particularities reveal a social dilemma: If all citizens voluntarily disclose their location, the spread of the virus can be controlled better, and government coercion is avoided. However, every citizen has an incentive to deviate and to benefit from virus control without restricting his or her privacy. Without control of the virus, people are worse off than if they had cooperated. State surveillance of location data without prior consent of the citizens would solve this dilemma. However, state surveillance also means the government violates citizens' basic privacy rights. This study builds on literature that takes the perspective of a privacy calculus to analyze the decision to disclose data. However, to examine the extent to which citizens prefer their privacy rights to be violated by the state in a pandemic crisis for the sake of safety, the study also focuses on literature on social dilemmas, especially on psychological factors of decisions in "give-some" dilemmas and public good games with imperfect information and uncertainty.

Uncertainty and Trust. Extensive literature has examined interpersonal factors associated with cooperation in public good dilemmas. One factor of consensus is trust. Individuals who trust others show higher rates of cooperation than individuals with low trust in others [7, 23]. Trust is especially relevant in decisions under uncertainty [48]. Respondents in this survey evaluated their consent to state surveillance with imperfect information and under two types of uncertainty: environmental uncertainty (i.e., uncertainty about the situation and conditions for obtaining the public good) and social uncertainty (i.e., uncertainty about the decisions of others) [33]. The current study focuses on social uncertainty. The common favorable outcome will be achieved if the virus spread is better controlled through location tracking without state coercion. Whether control is realized depends on socially uncertain decisions of two groups, fellow citizens and government officials, as it is uncertain whether fellow citizens would consent to voluntary data disclosure and whether government officials would use location data only to actually control the spread of the virus. Considering the role of trust in making decisions under uncertainty, this discussion leads to the following hypotheses about the effect of trust on a citizen's consent to be voluntarily surveilled by the state:

***H_{1a}**: Interpersonal trust (T_{ip}) increases consent to voluntary data disclosure to the state (C_{vd}).*
***H_{1b}**: Trust in the government to actually use the data to control the spread of the virus (T_{gov}) increases consent to voluntary data disclosure to the state (C_{vd}).*

A review of the literature also leads to competing hypotheses about the effect of interpersonal trust on the consent to legally obliging data disclosure. People are often willing to accept personal disadvantages and even prefer institutions that monitor cooperation so that the common good can be promoted [14, 18]. If others are trusted to jointly achieve the control of the virus spread through voluntary cooperation, state coercion becomes obsolete and illegitimate. If others are not trusted, state coercion may be preferred to ensure cooperation and safety.

***H_{2a}**: Interpersonal trust (T_{ip}) decreases consent to legally obliging data disclosure to the state (C_{od}).*
***H_{2b}**: Trust in the government to actually use the data to control the spread of the virus (T_{gov}) increases consent to legally obliging data disclosure to the state (C_{od}).*

Payoff Levels and Group Identity. Research in which experimenters have manipulated payoff levels shows that unequal payoffs influence cooperation [22]. In a pandemic crisis, payoff levels are determined by the real-world situation, in which payoffs are not only uncertain but also unequal. Individuals benefit in varying degrees from a controlled virus spread. Similarly, the negative consequences for individuals vary if the spread of the virus is not controlled. In the context of the current study, survey responses indicate that fear of the consequences of the novel coronavirus determine the perceived payoff level. When making decisions, people's brains are configured to divide people into "us" and "them" [17] and they work in a dual process: fast (i.e., based on gut feeling and intuition) and slow (i.e., analytically and rationally). Judgment based on gut feeling increases intragroup cooperation but leads to an in-group-preferential bias. People especially judge intuitively in situations with imperfect information and under uncertainty, such as the 2020 pandemic crisis [44]. Thus, people may perceive a payoff level differently, depending on which group profits from it. In public good games, too, the willingness to cooperate depends on the group affiliation of the players. If the out-group profits more from a good than its own group, the cooperation rate decreases [6, 34]. The following hypotheses on the influence of unequal payoffs on the consent to surveillance, therefore, differentiate between two groups: the in-group, one's self and closest people, and the out-group, the country's population.

***H_{3a}*:** *Fear (F_{in}/F_{out}) increases consent to voluntary data disclosure to the state (C_{vd}). Fear for self and closest people (F_{in}) has a greater impact than fear for the population (F_{out}).*
***H_{3b}*:** *Fear (F_{in}/F_{out}) increases consent to legally obliging data disclosure to the state (C_{od}). Fear for self and closest people (F_{in}) has a greater impact than fear for the population (F_{out}).*

The Interplay of Fear and Trust. Literature on cooperation shows an interplay of fear and trust. For example, researchers examined high and low trusters' responses to fear in a public good dilemma and found that when fear is present in a game, people with a high level of trust cooperate more than people with a low level of trust [34]. However, fear in this research refers to the possibility of not receiving a payoff despite cooperation. In the context of a pandemic crisis, fear rather is an indicator for the perceived consequences if the virus is not controlled. As described, the negative consequences of the novel coronavirus are not only uncertain but also unequal. To cover this particularity, the current study follows the argumentation of the security dilemma, whose original concept has been further developed for current global security challenges (e.g., the cyber security dilemma) [3, 21]. The security dilemma suggests that states achieve the highest level of security if all states cooperate, but in the real world they do not, because they have incentives to defect. The more a state fears the consequences of defection, (1) the greater the state's incentive to join a larger entity and (2) the greater its distrust in other states. States that can afford a zero payoff have greater trust in others and cooperate more often. In terms of the pandemic crisis, this means that people who greatly fear the consequences of the novel coronavirus can less afford to let the virus spread, and thus can less afford to trust others and are more inclined to consent to regulated surveillance.

***H_{4a}*:** *Fear (F_{in}/F_{out}) indirectly decreases consent to voluntary data disclosure to the state (C_{vd}) by decreasing interpersonal trust (T_{ip}).*
***H_{4b}*:** *Fear (F_{in}/F_{out}) indirectly increases consent to legally obliging data disclosure to the state (C_{od}) by decreasing interpersonal trust (T_{ip}).*

Figure 1 presents a graphic depiction of the research model.

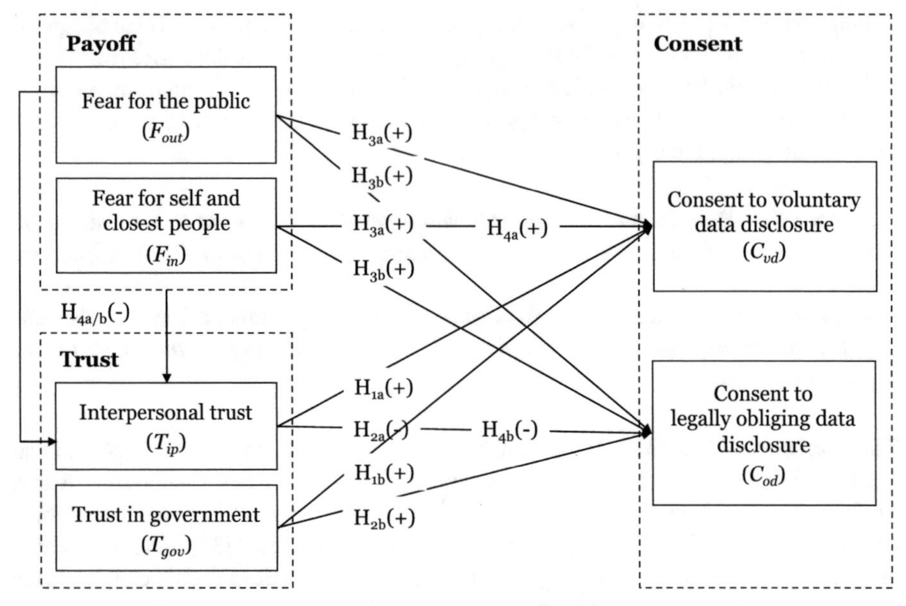

Fig. 1. Research model

3 Method

Data Collection and Sample Description. The data were collected via an online survey in the period from March 18 to March 29, 2020, when the pandemic crisis in Germany intensified such that the increase in infections changed from moderate to exponential. While the first person in Germany died of COVID-19 on March 8, approx. three weeks later, on March 31, there were already 584 reported deaths [38]. Also, the number of new infections per day reached the first wave's peak during the survey period on March 28 with 6,294 newly infected persons [38]. There was heated political and public debate on possible government measures. The German government implemented many actual measures during the course of the survey, such as the drastic restriction of social contacts and the closing of gastronomy and selected service businesses on March 22 [9]. The day before the survey launched, it became public that the German mobile network operator Telekom shared a one-time set of mobile phone data of German citizens with the RKI [42]. At the time of the survey there was no public discussion about the governmental "Corona-Warn-App" as it exists today. The survey period during the crisis outbreak is crucial to the significance of this study's results. During the outbreak, it was still uncertain what measures the state would conclusively introduce and how great the threat of the novel coronavirus really was to the individual; in short, the period was characterized by uncertainty. After the outbreak phase, participants' responses could be influenced by the extent to which the measures implemented up to that point were effective and what damage the virus actually caused to individuals. The advantage of surveying during the outbreak therefore is that the anticipated benefit of location data to contain the virus is less dependent on country-specific government measures and the development of the crisis. The study results are therefore more general and allow for better implications.

Another advantage of surveying during the outbreak is that, due to the increasing state restrictions on civil rights during that period, participants could assume that the government might actually introduce surveillance measures, which contributes to the credibility and realistic nature of the survey content.

The survey respondents were recruited via social media. To obtain a representative sample of the German population, the ad was targeted to all users registered on Facebook and Instagram in Germany. Studies investigating the representativeness of social media samples for the general population provide contradictory results. While Twitter and Facebook users in the UK differ from the general population in terms of age, gender and education, they are representative of values and political behavior [30]. An evaluation of Facebook advertising to generate a representative sample of Canadians for a health survey concludes that the sample is representative of geography, age and income. However, the sample was over-representative of women and higher levels of education [40]. Other scientists compared responses to an online survey on climate change public opinion between two U.S. samples: one was generated with Facebook ads, one based on a high-quality online survey panel. Although the social media sample was not representative of the U.S. population, the responses were mostly identical to those of the high-quality sample [49]. Overall, results suggest that using the Facebook Ad Network to recruit participants, despite a potential lack of representativeness, is suitable for querying population-level public opinion.

The call to participate in the survey appeared in various ad formats such as a "sponsored story" and "sponsored post". The users to whom the ad was displayed were randomly selected. Randomization was implemented by deactivating the Facebook feature of displaying ads optimized for cost efficiency. The survey advertisements were displayed to a total of 40,584 German users (on average 1.15 times per user) on Facebook and Instagram. Of these people, 2,705 clicked on the survey link and were redirected to the survey's introductory text (click rate of 6.67%). 1,253 people have started to actually fill out and 1,156 completed the survey (dropout rate of 7.74%). Participation was voluntary and not compensated. Respondents were randomly assigned to one of two survey versions, which differed only in the dependent variable (C_{vd}/C_{od}). Responses from individuals were excluded from the data set if (1) they answered the survey in less than a minute, (2) answers indicated random clicking (maximum or minimum values selected for all answers), (3) they were under 18 years of age, or (4) they submitted unrealistic answers (e.g., age over 100 years).

In total, 889 participants answered all survey questions without exceptions and irregularities. Data provided by this group serve to test Hypotheses 1–4. The sample consists of 62% female, 29% male, and 1% diverse-gendered respondents, with 9% preferring not to answer. The median age of the respondents is 37 years, with the youngest being 18 years and the oldest 75 years. The majority of the respondents has high vocational training (26%) or a school diploma (21%), followed by a graduate degree (17%). 36% of the respondents, in approximately equal parts (between 6% and 9%), reported attaining less than a high school diploma, having attended college, having a bachelor's degree, or not fitting into any of the answers, and 4% of the participants preferred not to answer. The mean net annual income of the respondents is "15,001€ to 25,000€" (minimum "less than 5,000€", maximum "more than 100,000€"). Respondents indicated their political views on a slider from 1 (“left”) to 20 (“right”). The mean political view is 8, thus skewing slightly more left.

Measures. All independent (T_{ip}, T_{gov}, F_{in}, F_{out}) and dependent (C_{vd}, C_{od}) variables were measured using a 1–20 slider. The language to measure the variables fear, consent, and trust in government is based on Awad et al.’s German question items in the “Moral Machine Experiment” [1]. These items used the wording “To what extent…” on a slider with extreme point labels of “very little” and “very much” and were modified from the original version to fit the context of a pandemic crisis (pretested with five people). The variables on interpersonal trust (T_{ip}) and political views were collected using the original wording of the German socio-economic panel. The control variables for gender, education, net annual income, and age were adopted from Awad et al. [1] without any modifications. To control for possible influences by daily events, timing of participation, coded in 12-h intervals from 1 to 20, serves as an additional control variable. Screenshots of the online questionnaire are available at this link: https://tinyurl.com/yxct485u.

4 Data Analysis and Results

Measurement Model. Ordinary least squares (OLS) regressions were used to test Hypotheses 1–4. Data were checked for various parameters before performing the regressions. None of the regression models have autocorrelation based on values of the Durbin–Watson statistic. Pearson correlation coefficients used to check for possible multicollinearity indicated that all variable correlation coefficients are lower than .7; the highest correlation (.649) manifested between fear for self and loved ones and fear for the population. All other correlations are below .355. Graphical visualization confirmed variance equality and normal distribution of the residuals. Two regression models served to test Hypotheses 1–3: Model 1 uses consent to voluntary data disclosure (C_{vd}), and Model 2 uses consent to state surveillance (C_{od}) as the dependent variable. C is a vector of variables, including age, education, income, political views, gender, and day of measurement as baseline conditions.

$$\boldsymbol{C_{vd}} = \beta_0 + \beta_1 F_{in} + \beta_2 F_{out} + \beta_3 T_{ip} + \beta_4 T_{gov} + \beta_5 C + \varepsilon. \quad \text{(Model 1)}$$

$$\boldsymbol{C_{od}} = \beta_0 + \beta_1 F_{in} + \beta_2 F_{out} + \beta_3 T_{ip} + \beta_4 T_{gov} + \beta_5 C + \varepsilon. \quad \text{(Model 2)}$$

A third set of regression models served as a mediation analysis to test Hypotheses 4_a and 4_b. Mediation is considered present when the following four conditions are met [28]: First, the fear variable (F_{in}/F_{out}) has a significant effect on consent to voluntary data disclosure (C_{vd}) in Eq. 1. Second, the fear variable (F_{in}/F_{out}) has a significant effect on the mediator variable interpersonal trust (T_{ip}) in Eq. 2. Third, in Eq. 3 (identical to Model 1) the mediator variable T_{ip} has a significant effect on C_{vd}, and fourth, the coefficient of β_1 and the coefficient of β_2 must be smaller in absolute terms in Eq. 3 than in Eq. 1. The mediation for consent to state surveillance (C_{od}) is identified analogously (Eq. 3 identical to Model 2).

$$C_{vd} = \beta_0 + \beta_1 \boldsymbol{F_{in}} + \beta_2 \boldsymbol{F_{out}} + \beta_3 T_{gov} + \beta_4 C + \varepsilon. \quad (1)$$

$$T_{ip} = \beta_0 + \beta_1 \boldsymbol{F_{in}} + \beta_2 \boldsymbol{F_{out}} + \beta_3 T_{gov} + \beta_4 C + \varepsilon. \quad (2)$$

$$\boldsymbol{C_{vd}} = \beta_0 + \beta_1 F_{in} + \beta_2 F_{out} + \beta_3 T_{ip} + \beta_4 T_{gov} + \beta_5 C + \varepsilon. \quad (3)$$

Table 1. Results of OLS analyses

	Model 1	**Model 2**	**Set of Models for Mediation Analysis**			
			mediation on *C_vd*		mediation on *C_od*	
			equation 1	*equation 2*	*equation 1*	*equation 2*
	dv: C_vd	*dv: C_od*	*dv: C_vd*	*dv: T_ip*	*dv: C_od*	*dv: T_ip*
Intercept	1.104 (2.115)	1.784 (1.917)	1.208 (2.051)	**7.627***** (1.513)	3.189 (1.850)	**8.802***** (1.411)
F_out	0.135 (0.086)	**0.341***** (0.082)	0.137 (0.085)	**-0.138*** (0.063)	**0,356***** (0.082)	-0.095 (0.062)
F_in	**0.244**** (0.079)	**0.157*** (0.073)	**0.247**** (0.077)	**-0.257***** (0.057)	**0.194**** (0.072)	**-0.232***** (0.055)
T_ip	-0.014 (0.066)	**-0.160**** (0.062)				
T_gov	**0.372***** (0.056)	**0.143***** (0.033)	**0.372***** (0.056)	-0.011 (0.041)	**0.141***** (0.033)	0.017 (0.025)
age	0.033 (0.025)	**0.056*** (0.025)	0.033 (0.025)	-0.032 (0.018)	**0.056*** (0.025)	-0.001 (0.019)
education	0.105 (0.200)	-0.231 (0.178)	0.105 (0.200)	0,010 (0.148)	-0.275 (0.178)	0.277 (0.136)
gender	-0.072 (0.686)	0.134 (0.639)	-0.081 (0.684)	0.652 (0.505)	0.146 (0.643)	-0.074 (0.490)
income	-0.079 (0.176)	-0.129 (0.161)	-0.083 (0.175)	**0.306*** (0.129)	-0.125 (0.162)	-0.022 (0.123)
political view	0.131 (0.081)	0.102 (0.075)	0.132 (0.081)	-0.069 (0.059)	0.107 (0.075)	-0.030 (0.057)
day	-0.068 (0.055)	**-0.119*** (0.055)	-0.067 (0.055)	-0.051 (0.041)	**-1.09*** (0.055)	-0.061 (0.042)

Notes. Unstandardized coefficients and standard deviations are shown. *p*-values are reported as follows: * $p < .05$; ** $p < .01$; *** $p < .001$. Dashed lines indicate no significance. All models are estimated with an OLS linear regression. Model 1 and mediation analysis on C_{vd}: N_1=430, Model 2 and mediation analysis on C_{od}: N_2=459.

Structural Model and Hypotheses Testing. Table 1 summarizes the OLS testing results. H_{1a} predicted a positive relationship of interpersonal trust *(T_{ip})* and consent to voluntary data disclosure. Regression results are not significant; thus, H_{1a} is not supported. By contrast, interpersonal trust and consent to state surveillance show a significant, negative relationship, in support of H_{2a}. Trust in government significantly increases both consent to voluntary data disclosure and consent to state surveillance, in support of H_{1b} and H_{2b}. Fear for self and closest people significantly increases consent to voluntary data disclosure, while fear for the public does not. Although H_{3a} suggested an influence of fear for both the in-group and the out-group, the influence of in-group fear was expected to be stronger. Thus, H_{3a} is considered supported. In line with H_{3b}, fear for self and closest people and fear for the public significantly increase consent to legally obliging data disclosure; however, fear for the public has a higher impact than fear for self and closest people, thus offering only partial support for H_{3b}.

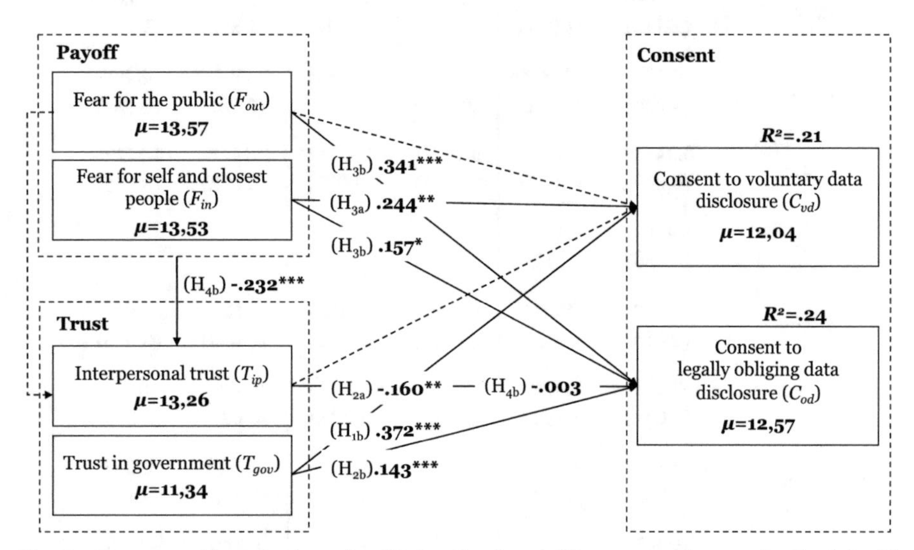

Fig. 2. Summary of hypothesis testing. **Notes**. Goodness of fit, mean, and unstandardized significant coefficients are shown. p-values are reported as follows: $*p < .05$; $**p < .01$; $***\, p < .001$. Dashed lines indicate no significance.

Mediation analyses using several regressions according to MacKinnon et al. [28] offer further results. H_{4a} predicted that fear would indirectly decrease consent to voluntary data disclosure by decreasing interpersonal trust. As interpersonal trust has no significant impact on consent to voluntary data disclosure, mediation according to H_{4a} is not supported. H_{4b} predicted that fear would indirectly increase consent to state surveillance by decreasing interpersonal trust. For fear for self and closest people, all four conditions are met. First, fear (F_{in}) increases consent to state surveillance in Eq. 1 ($\beta_1 = .194, p = .007$). Second, fear (F_{in}) decreases interpersonal trust in Eq. 2 ($\beta_1 = .232, p < .001$). Third, interpersonal trust decreases consent to state surveillance in Eq. 3 ($\beta_1 = .160, p = .010$), and fourth, β_1 is smaller in Equitation 3 (Model 2) than in Equitation 1. Thus, fear (F_{in}) indirectly increases consent to state surveillance by decreasing interpersonal trust. Fear for the public does not indirectly increase consent to state surveillance by decreasing trust, as condition 2 is not met ($\beta_2 = -.095, p = .127$). Therefore, mediation according to H_{4b} is supported for in-group fear. Figure 2 summarizes the significant variable relationships.

5 Discussion

The regression results confirm H_{1b}, H_{2a}, H_{2b}, H_{3a} and partially $H_{3b}$and H_{4b}. In summary, the main testing results are: (1) higher interpersonal trust is associated with less consent to voluntary data disclosure to the state, (2) trust in the government to actually use the data to control the virus spread increases both, consent to voluntary and mandatory data disclosure to the state, (3) fear for self and closest people increases consent to voluntary data disclosure, but fear for the public does not, (4) both, in-group and out-group fear increase consent to legally obliging data disclosure to the state, (5) in-group fear further increases consent to state surveillance indirectly by decreasing interpersonal trust.

Limitations of the results stem from the country-specific survey. Although it is beneficial that data were collected during the outbreak of a crisis, specific daily events in Germany and cultural particularities such as the statutory health insurance system might have influenced the results. Moreover, results would have been more conclusive if the survey had additionally been conducted before the pandemic. This would allow a direct comparison of the fear and trust levels of the two survey dates and would provide clear insights of how consent preferences change while experiencing fear. It may be useful to conduct a repeating survey after the pandemic has abated, but it would remain unclear how responses would be affected by the lasting shock and country-specific measures. In addition, data are based on stated rather than revealed preferences, i.e., there may be discrepancies in the results if people actually had to share their location data. For ethical reasons, it was deliberately avoided to ask individuals to actually disclose their location, as their data would not have actually been used to contain the coronavirus.

Despite those limitations, the findings indicate that the perception of fear affects how people decide on sharing their personal data in a global crisis. It is therefore ethically questionable when people have to make the decision to disclose personal data within a crisis. Governmental officials should initiate the discussion about the handling of personal data in the context of crisis management in advance.

In fact, there have been several stakeholders who have called for a planned approach to handle personal data in crisis management in recent years. International scientists have dealt with the trade-off between security and privacy in crises in various studies. The studies often referred to terrorist crises and disaster control, but the results and political implications can easily be transferred to health crises. For example, Davis and Silver [5] find that a threat to national or personal security contributes significantly to people renouncing their civil rights. The greater the threat, the less people support civil democratic freedom. Pavone and Esposti [35] add that public opinion on surveillance technology is influenced not only by the need for security, but also by the context in which the surveillance technology is implemented. In an exploratory study of the willingness of German citizens to reduce their online privacy in favor of security in times of crisis, Reuter et al. [37] identify a cooperative group that would only do so at certain conditions.

Researchers further suggest that measures concerning security and privacy should be decided with some time lag from the crisis itself. If not, overhasty decisions might unnecessarily restrict the freedom of citizens [16, 33, 37]. Despite varying methods and contexts, existing research results support those of this study. The coronavirus-induced crisis is a special situation in which decisions are potentially made differently than before or after the crisis.

Parts of the political arena have pushed the discussion about the protection of privacy in recent years. For example, the European Union invested billions of euros in security research in the early 2000s [11, 12]. These investments included the research project PRISMS, which ran from 2012 to 2015 and conducted a comprehensive survey of public opinion on the trade-off between privacy and security. The aim of the project was to formulate a decision-support-system to guide the ethical political handling of the trade-off [13]. Nonetheless, there has been no uniform European regulation at the outbreak of the corona crisis. In Germany, too, some politicians recognized the importance of data privacy ahead of the crisis, including Volker Kauder, the parliamentary party leader of the CDU, Stefan Brink, the state data protection commissioner, and Sabine Leutheusser-Schnarrenberger, the federal minister of justice. Also Burkhard Hirsch and Gerhart Baum have been fighting for the protection of basic privacy rights and for a surveillance-free society for many years [e.g., 24]. But in Germany, too, there has been no pre-determined regulation on how personal data may be used to foster security in the event of a crisis – yet the 2007 LÜKEX report has even identified corresponding deficiencies. The report is the result of a nationwide pandemic crisis management audit with the aim of optimizing governmental and public crisis management. The report identifies an extensive need for action in the area of "prevention" and demands a specification of legal provisions and exception regulations. In 2007, the handling of data had not been subject of the report. However, when concretizing prevention measures in response to the report, policymakers could easily have taken the handling of data into account in the following years. It remains ambiguous why the German government not only failed to respond to identified shortcomings, but also kept the report secret for a considerable time.

In contrast to other countries, Germany ultimately refrained from collecting personal data and relied on a voluntary solution based on the "Corona-Warn-App". However, it is a fact that monitoring of location data was at least considered. And indeed, in the middle of the second infection cycle, voices from industry and politics are once again calling for restrictions on data protection in order to make the "Corna-Warn-App" more effective. As Michael Hüther, Director of the Institute of the German Economy, says, "It is difficult to understand that while many basic rights are naturally infringed upon in the fight against the pandemic, data protection becomes a sacred cow" [31]. Other politicians like Dorothee Bär and Dieter Janecek prefer to maintain the population's willingness to cooperate through trust in the government. According to the results of this study, this might be a winning strategy: trusting the government to use the data correctly increases the willingness to share data by using voluntary solutions. If enough people make use of the voluntary offer, the virus spread might be controlled without violating individual privacy. In any case, the resurgent discussion reinforces the importance of the present results.

Overall, exceptional governmental power in a crisis is reasonable in terms of national security measures. A crisis is an extreme situation in which restrictions and violations of personal rights may under certain conditions be appropriate to protect the public. Restrictions may affect economic, cultural and private domains - including the restriction of privacy through the use of personal data. Nevertheless, the results of this study illustrate - in light of relevant studies from other disciplines - that the context in which decisions to restrict privacy are made matters significantly. Decisions in the trade-off of security and privacy must not be forced in the middle of a crisis, both on a political and individual level.

6 Conclusion

This paper examined the role of fear and trust in consenting to disclose data to the state. During the 2020 pandemic crisis many states proposed data collection measures to contain the coronavirus without ever having discussed these measures transparently in advance. The timing of the governmental data collection could imply ethical concerns, as individual consent might change while experiencing fear. I conducted a survey during the outbreak of the 2020 pandemic in Germany in mid-March. Results show that fear indeed correlates with consent: Voluntary data disclosure depends on how anxious people are about themselves and their loved ones. When consenting to legally obliging data disclosure, fear plays an even greater role. Not only does fear for oneself, loved ones, and the public increase the consent to legally obliging data disclosure, but it also promotes consent by fostering distrust in others.

Despite some limitations, the results allow the conclusion that fear for oneself and others, as well as trust in others and in the state, play an important role in a global health crisis when it comes to disclosing personal data. In Germany, location tracking was hotly debated, but ultimately not carried out. The initial discussion, the data collection measures in other countries and the insights of this paper, however, show the need for defining how personal data shall be handled in crisis situations. If not, the state might violate important individual privacy rights. The public should be involved in this discussion in advance, not in the midst of a crisis while experiencing fear. The findings of this paper contribute to a better understanding of the relevance of timing when states collect personal data. Politicians and researchers should take a closer look at the various factors that can influence the citizens' consent to data disclosure in crises so that regulators can handle and collect personal data in the public's best interest.

A follow-up study is currently in progress and will compare the levels of fear, trust and consent to voluntary and mandatory disclosure of personal data during the first and second infection cycle of the coronavirus. The corresponding online experiment has been conducted at the end of October 2020 and contained identical questions as in March 2020 – with one crucial extension: Participants have randomly been primed on content of the recent public debate on how data shall be used in order to control the corona virus spread in Germany. Differences between the experimental groups will allow to draw conclusions as to whether the recent debate has changed citizens' consent to data sharing in the context of a pandemic crisis.

References

1. Awad, E., et al.: The moral machine experiment. Nature **563**(7729), 59–64 (2018)
2. Becker, K.: Mit Apps gegen die Pandemie? Tagesschau. https://www.tagesschau.de/inland/coronavirus-forschung-bab-101.html. Accessed 13 Apr 2020
3. Buchanan, B.: The Cybersecurity Dilemma: Hacking, Trust, and Fear between Nations. Oxford University Press, New York (2016)
4. Chaos Computer Club: Geplante Corona-App ist höchst problematisch. Chaos Computer Club. https://www.ccc.de/system/uploads/300/original/Offener_Brief_Corona_App_BMG.pdf. Accessed 16 Apr 2020
5. Davis, D.W., Silver, B.D.: Civil liberties vs. security: public opinion in the context of the terrorist attacks on America. Am. J. Polit. Sci. **48**(1), 28–46 (2004)
6. Dawes, R.M., McTavish, J., Shaklee, H.: Behavior, communication, and assumptions about other people's behavior in a commons dilemma situation. J. Pers. Soc. Psychol. **35**(1), 1–11 (1977)
7. Deutsch, M.: Trust, trustworthiness, and the F scale. Psychol. Sci. Public Interest **61**(1), 138–140 (1960)
8. Deutsche Presse-Agentur: Donald Trump ruft nationalen Notstand aus. Zeit.de. https://www.zeit.de/politik/ausland/2020-03/coronavirus-donald-trump-verhaengt-nationalen-notstand. Accessed 25 Nov 2020
9. Die Deutsche Bundesregierung: Erweiterung der beschlossenen Leitlinien zur Beschränkung sozialer Kontakte - Besprechung der Bundeskanzlerin mit den Regierungscheffinen und Regierungschefs der Länder. Bundesregierung.de. https://www.bundesregierung.de/breg-de/themen/coronavirus/besprechung-der-bundeskanzlerin-mit-den-regierungschefinnen-und-regierungschefs-der-laender-1733248. Accessed 25 Nov 2020
10. Dinev, T., Hart, P.: An extended privacy calculus model for E-commerce transactions. Inf. Syst. Res. **17**(1), 61–80 (2006)
11. European Commission: On the Implementation of the Preparatory Action on the Enhancement of the European Industrial Potential in the Field of Security Research, Towards a Programme to Advance European Security Through Research and Technology. COM(2004) 72 final. Brussels European Commission (2004)
12. European Commission: Security Research: the next steps. COM(2004) 590 final. Brussels European Commission (2004)
13. European Comission: The PRIvacy and Security MirrorS: "Towards a European framework for integrated decision making". CORDIS Forschungsergebnisse der EU. https://cordis.europa.eu/project/id/285399/de. Accessed 15 Nov 2020
14. Fehr, E., Gächter, S.: Cooperation and punishment in public goods experiments. Am. Econ. Rev. **90**(4), 980–994 (2000)
15. Gambs, S., Heen, O., Potin, C.: A comparative privacy analysis of geosocial networks. In: Proceedings of the 4th ACM SIGSPATIAL International Workshop on Security and Privacy in GIS and LBS, pp. 33–40. ACM (2011)
16. Gethmann, C.F.: Ist die Angst ein schlechter Ratgeber? 5. Essener Forum für psychosoziale Versorgung (1996)
17. Greene, J.: Moral Tribes: Emotion, Reason, and the Gap Between Us and Them. Penguin Books (2013)
18. Gürerk, Ö., Irlenbusch, B., Rockenbach, B.: The competitive advantage of sanctioning institutions. Science **312**(5770), 108–111 (2006)
19. Heberlein, M.: Corona und Handydaten. Mit Tracking zur Bewegungsfreiheit? Tagesschau. https://www.tagesschau.de/inland/corona-handydaten-103.html. Accessed 12 Apr 2020

20. Hock, M.: Die schwärzesten Tage des Dax. Faz.de. https://www.faz.net/aktuell/finanzen/finanzmarkt/traurige-rekorde-die-schwaerzesten-tage-des-dax-16670822.html. Accessed 27 Nov 2020
21. Jervis, R.: Cooperation under the security dilemma. World Polit. **30**(2), 167–214 (1978)
22. Komorita, S.S., Chan, D.K., Parks, C.D.: The effects of reward structure and reciprocity in social dilemmas. J. Exp. Soc. Psychol. **29**, 252–267 (1993)
23. Komorita, S.S., Hilty, J.A., Parks, C.D.: Reciprocity and cooperation in social dilemmas. J. Conflict Resolut. **35**(3), 494–518 (1991)
24. Kurz, C.: Erklärung zur Vorratsdatenspeicherung: Eingriff in die Privatsphäre von Millionen Menschen. Netzpolitik.de. https://netzpolitik.org/2016/erklaerung-zur-vorratsdatenspeicherung-eingriff-in-die-privatsphaere-von-millionen-menschen/. Accessed 23 Nov 2020
25. Leopoldina: Coronavirus-Pandemie – Gesundheitsrelevante Maßnahmen. Leopoldina. https://www.leopoldina.org/uploads/tx_leopublication/2020_04_03_Leopoldina_Stellungnahme_Gesundheitsrelevante_Maßnahmen_Corona.pdf. Accessed 04 Apr 2020
26. Loewenstein, G., Lerner, J.S.: The role of affect in decision making. In: Davidson, R.J., Sherer, K.R., Goldsmith, H.H. (eds.) Handbook of Affective Sciences, pp. 619–642. Oxford University Press, New York (2003)
27. Loewenstein, G., Schkade, D.: Wouldn't it be nice? Predicting future feelings. In: Kahneman, D., Diener, E., Schwarz, N. (eds.) Well-Being: The Foundations of Hedonic Psychology, pp. 85–105. Russell Sage Foundation, New York (1997)
28. MacKinnon, D.P., Fairchild, A.J., Fritz, M.S.: Mediation analysis. Ann. Rev. Psychol. **58**, 593–614 (2007)
29. Mitteldeutscher Rundfunk: Spanien schließt "nicht lebenswichtige Unternehmen" MDR.de. https://www.mdr.de/nachrichten/panorama/ticker-corona-virus-samstag-achtundzwanzigster-maerz-100.html. Accessed 20 Nov 2020
30. Mellon, J., Prosser, C.: Twitter and Facebook are not representative of the general population: political attitudes and demographics of British social media users. Res. Politics **4**(3), 1–9 (2017)
31. Messick, D.M., Allison, S.T., Samuelson, C.D.: Framing and Communication Effects on Group Members' Responses to Environmental and Societal Uncertainty, pp. 677–700. Wheatsheaf Books, Brighton (1988)
32. Neuerer, D., Olk, J., Hoppe, T.: Politiker stellen strengen Datenschutz der Corona-Warn-App infrage. Handelsblatt.de. https://www.handelsblatt.com/politik/deutschland/kampf-gegen-die-pandemie-politiker-stellen-strengen-datenschutz-der-corona-warn-app-infrage/26570478.html?ticket=ST-3222318-FnLZHcl5LYyuavd0R1Vf-ap2. Accessed 29 Nov 2020
33. Orbell, J.M., Van de Kragt, A.J., Dawes, R.M.: Explaining discussion-induced cooperation. J. Pers. Soc. Psychol. **54**(5), 811–819 (1988)
34. Parks, C.D., Hulbert, L.G.: High and low trusters' responses to fear in a payoff matrix. J. Conflict Resolut. **39**(4), 718–730 (1995)
35. Pavone, V., Esposti, S.D.: Public assessment of new surveillance-oriented security technologies: beyond the trade-off between privacy and security. Public Undestanding Sci. **21**, 556–572 (2012)
36. Rabin, R.C.: Coronavirus cases seemed to be leveling off. Not anymore. On Thursday, health officials in China reported more than 14,000 new cases in Hubei Province alone. A change in diagnostic criteria may be the reason. The New York Times. https://www.nytimes.com/2020/02/12/health/coronavirus-cases-china.html. Accessed 27 Nov 2020
37. Reuter, C., Geilen, G., Gellert, R.: Sicherheit vs. Privatsphäre: Zur Akzeptanz von Überwachung in sozialen Medien im Kontext von Terrorkrisen. In: Mayr, H.C., Pinzger, M. (eds.) Informatik 2016. GI-Edition-Lecture Notes in Informatics (LNI). von Menschen für Menschen, Klagenfurt (2016)

38. Robert Koch Institut: Aktueller Lage-/Situationsbericht des RKI zu COVID-19. RKI Archiv. https://www.rki.de/DE/Content/InfAZ/N/Neuartiges_Coronavirus/Situationsberichte/Gesamt.html. Accessed 22 Nov 2020
39. Senzel, H.: Wie Singapur Handydaten nutzt. Tagesschau. https://www.tagesschau.de/ausland/corona-singapur-app-101.html. Accessed 12 Apr 2020
40. Shaver, L.G., et al.: Using Facebook advertising to recruit representative samples: feasibility assessment of a cross-sectional survey. J. Med. Internet Res. **21**, 8 (2019)
41. Sun, Y., Wang, N., Shen, X.-L., Zhang, J.X.: Location information disclosure in location-based social network services: privacy calculus, benefit structure, and gender differences. Comput. Hum. Behav. **52**, 278–292 (2015)
42. Tagesschau: RKI prüft mit Handydaten Mobilität. Tagesschau. https://www.tagesschau.de/inland/corona-handydaten-101.html. Accessed 29 Mar 2020
43. Tagesschau: Italien schließt Schulen und Unis. https://www.tagesschau.de/ausland/corona-italien-schulschliessungen-103.html. Accessed 27 Nov 2020
44. Tversky, A., Kahneman, D.: Judgment under uncertainty: heuristics and biases. Science **185**(4157), 1124–1131 (1974)
45. Wachs, S.: Ausgangssperre in Frankreich. ARD-Studio Paris, Tagesschau. https://www.tagesschau.de/ausland/frankreich-ausgangssperre-101.html. Accessed 25 Nov 2020
46. Weinstein, N.D.: Unrealistic optimism about future life events. J. Pers. Soc. Psychol. **39**(5), 806–820 (1980)
47. Xu, H., Teo, H.-H., Tan, B.C., Agarwal, R.: The role of push-pull technology in privacy calculus: the case of location-based services. J. Manag. Inf. Syst. **26**(3), 135–174 (2009)
48. Yamagishi, T.: Trust: The Evolutionary Game of Mind and Society. Springer, Tokyo (2011). https://doi.org/10.1007/978-4-431-53936-0
49. Zhang, B., Mildenberger, M., Howe, P.D., Marlon, J., Rosenthal, S.A., Leiserowitz, A.: Quota sampling using Facebook advertisements. Polit. Sci. Res. Methods **8**(3), 558–564 (2020)

It's Not that Bad! Perceived Stress of Knowledge Workers During Enforced Working from Home Due to COVID-19

Jana Mattern(✉), Simon Lansmann, and Joschka Hüllmann

Interorganizational Systems Group, University of Muenster, Muenster, Germany
{jana.mattern,simon.lansmann,joschka.huellmann}@uni-muenster.de

Abstract. In March 2020, many organizations requested their employees to work from home to reduce their employees' risk of a COVID-19 infection. Research has suggested that working from home increases perceived stress due to blurring boundaries between work and private life. We examine whether this finding also holds for "enforced working from home" (EWFH) due to COVID-19 based on a four-week diary study in April and May 2020 with 37 participants from a German university. We suggest psychological detachment and communication overload as explaining variables for the relationship between EWFH and perceived stress. Our data show that EWFH leads neither to an inability to detach nor to communication overload. Similarly, EWFH does not increase participants' stress level. The findings show that working from home is a viable option for the future and that specifics of the EWFH setting, such as wide organizational support, can improve the working from home experience.

Keywords: COVID-19 · Working from home · Diary study · Perceived stress · Psychological detachment · Communication overload · Individual focus time

1 Introduction

Information and communication technologies (ICT) have enabled knowledge workers to work anytime and anywhere. Working from locations other than the physical office has been possible since the advent of personal telecommunication technology [1]. While working from home or at clients' sites has been popular among technology and management consultants, other professions have mostly worked from the physical office. In 2014, only 22% of German employees worked at least partly from home [2]. Insufficient technical equipment, companies' concerns about reduced productivity because of less social and informational exchange with colleagues and supervisors, as well as the manager's willingness to allow working from home are among the strongest predictors for the number of employees who work from home [2, 3].

At the beginning of the COVID-19 pandemic, governments mandated social distancing policies. Organizations had to send most of their employees to work from home to reduce the infection risk [4], resulting in "enforced working from home" (EWFH) [5]. One third of all employees in Germany worked from home at the beginning of the

F. Ahlemann et al. (Eds.): WI 2021, LNISO 46, pp. 263–279, 2021.
https://doi.org/10.1007/978-3-030-86790-4_19

pandemic in April 2020 [6]. First survey studies on the impact of EWFH show that this change has provided a welcome acceleration of the digitalization of work as technical equipment [7]. Moreover, policies and routines needed for digital work have been developed in days rather than years [5, 6]. Remarkably, employees feel more productive and less stressed [6, 8]. These initial findings contradict prior literature suggesting that working from locations other than the office increases perceived stress [9] by blurring boundaries between work and private life [10].

Our study contributes to the emerging body of research in information systems studying the behavioral, societal, and organizational aspects of COVID-19 [11]. Our research question is: *How does enforced working from home due to COVID-19 influence knowledge workers' perceived stress?*

To identify factors that explain why employees might experience stress during EWFH, we consult the academic literature for variables that mediate the influence of working from home on perceived stress. We acknowledge that various factors might work as mediators for the relationship between EWFH and perceived stress. However, for the scope of this paper, we focus on psychological detachment [12] and communication overload [13] as explanatory variables for two reasons: (1) EWFH requires increased work-related ICT use, which has been found to result in an extended availability to work [14]_. Due to technology-enabled prolonged working hours, we expect that work spills over to private life, resulting in difficulties to detach from work. (2) Recent studies found an increased volume of electronic communication during EWFH [6, 8]. It has been suggested that employees might compensate the lack of physical visibility by increased electronic communication with colleagues and managers [15]. When the amount of electronic communication exceeds communication needs, employees can suffer communication overload. To account for the differences between EWFH and prior working from home arrangements, we consider additional worries about the COVID-19 pandemic.

To answer our research question, we conduct a mixed method diary study with employees from a German university during the early phase of the country's lockdown in April and May 2020. Our study contributes to the growing body of knowledge that examines the effects of EWFH due to COVID-19 on employees' well-being [6]. In particular, we quantify to which extent the two factors (1) perceived ability to detach from work during non-work hours and (2) communication overload predict the emergence of stress in the COVID-19 situation. Our findings inform the future organization of work that is developing based on the reflections of the pandemic.

The remainder of the paper is as follows: At first, we describe related work regarding (enforced) working from home and perceived stress, psychological detachment, and communication overload. After that, we describe our study design and results. Then, we discuss the findings against the backdrop of recent COVID-19 studies. Before concluding our paper, we consider limitations and avenues for future research.

2 Theoretical Background

2.1 (Enforced) Working From Home and Stress

Working from home is a specific case of telecommuting or telework, which is "a flexible work arrangement that allows employees, usually with the aid of electronic communication devices, to accomplish their work in various locations instead of a fixed, central worksite" ([16], p. 386). This way of working was introduced in the last quarter of the 20th century to decrease real-estate costs and air pollution, and allow for a healthy work-family balance [3]. In the context of working from home, employees do not work from various locations but from their homes. Due to the wide distribution of mobile devices and ICT, working from anywhere is easier than ever before [17]. However, while research on general telework is extensive, the specific context of working from home has been researched only to a limited extent and has been equated with telework (e.g., [5]). Our study examines whether the empirical findings regarding telework hold for the working from home environment and specifically for EWFH due to the COVID-19 pandemic.

Academic research on telework has yielded ambivalent results when examining its effects for employees [18]. Main benefits comprise increased productivity and autonomy, balanced work and private life, reduced commute, reduced overheads for employers, and an increased skill base [19, 20]. Reported problems are, amongst others, social isolation, presenteeism, lack of support, career disadvantages, blurring boundaries between work and private life, and technostress [19, 21].

The negative effects of telework have been complemented by research on ICT-enabled working from home, such as extended availability for work after work hours [22], increased work-life conflict [23, 24], as well as role overload and stress [10, 25]. We expect EWFH to exacerbate these adverse effects as EWFH also impacts employees not having prior experience with working from home. Those employees "have to cope with rapid and fundamental changes in the nature of work environments and they are required to keep pace with technological changes." ([26], p. 141). Therefore, our first hypothesis is:

H1:*EWFH due to COVID-19 increases daily perceived stress.*

2.2 Psychological Detachment

Blurred work-life boundaries because of the increased use of ICT for work explain the negative effects of working from home on employees' health and well-being [21, 25]. Employees are extensively tied to work through work-related ICT [27]. They continuously face the stressors inherent in their work, which impedes their ability to recover [28] and increases their stress level [29]. Recovery research has positioned psychological detachment as a mediating factor for the relationship between work-stressors and employees' stress levels [12]. Psychological detachment means "refraining from job-related activities and mentally disengaging from work during time off the job" ([12], p. 72). The ability to detach has gained importance in modern, distributed work environments, especially in working from home [30]. A collocation of work and private domains renders gaining mental distance from work difficult due to the lack of physical boundaries [25]. While in physical work settings employees can leave work behind by leaving the office and shutting the door, working from home means that work is always present, for example, when seeing the laptop sitting on the kitchen desk. Since ICT allow employees to receive and send messages anywhere and at any time, managers and clients expect an extended availability [31]. Thus, ICT use for work impedes employees' ability to detach, increasing their stress levels [14].

In the situation of EWFH due to COVID-19, employees know that everyone works from home so that strict office times are obsolete. Work is only "one click away" for everyone, blurring the boundaries between work and private life. As clear boundaries cease to exist, employees might be less confident in their ability to detach from work. Accordingly, our second hypothesis is:

H2:*Daily perceived detachment ability mediates the relationship between EWFH and daily perceived stress.*
H2a:*EWFH decreases daily perceived detachment ability.*
H2b:*Daily perceived detachment ability decreases daily perceived stress.*

2.3 Communication Overload

Electronic communication bridges physical distance. It enables collaboration between employees at different locations [32], rendering it necessary while working from home [27]. In general, employees have different needs for communication volumes depending on their role. These needs range from low volumes for "silent workers" to intense volumes for "communicators" [33]. Before the COVID-19 pandemic, employees often worked from home to complete tasks that benefit from uninterrupted work [34]. This specific mode of work has been labeled as "deep work" or, more commonly used, "focus time": episodes of distraction-free individual focus [35].

During EWFH, working from home serves another primary purpose. It is no longer a location designed for the specific mode of individual focus work but the default work location. As EWFH limits physical, in-person communication, we conjecture that employees compensate for this limitation by drawing more intensively on electronic communication. To facilitate electronic communication, organizations use enterprise collaborations platforms, such as Microsoft Teams, more extensively during EWFH [7, 36]. Although the use of such platforms enables seamless collaboration, it can also increase employees' overall communication volumes. When employees spend too much time in communicative episodes and do not have enough time for individual focus work, they experience lower performance and reduced well-being [37]. Research has demonstrated that too much electronic communication increases employees' stress levels [38, 39].

To operationalize being overloaded with electronic messages, we use the construct communication overload [13], which is defined as "a measure of the extent to which, in a given period of time, an organization's member perceives more quantity, complexity, and/or equivocality in the information than an individual desires, needs, or can handle in the process of communication" ([40], p. 8 as cited in [41], p. 2). Hence, our third hypothesis is:

H3:*Daily communication overload mediates the relationship between EWFH and daily perceived stress.*
H3a:*EWFH increases daily communication overload.*
H3b:*Daily communication overload increases daily perceived stress.*

Our research model, including all hypotheses, is illustrated in Fig. 1.

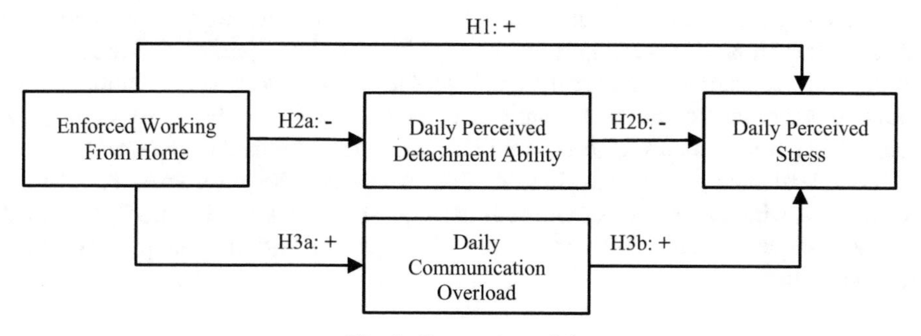

Fig. 1. Research model

3 Method

3.1 Procedure and Participants

We recruited our study participants via a mailing list comprising all staff members of the business and economics faculty at a large German university. Our sample consisted of knowledge workers because most of them worked in research and teaching (see Sect. 4.1), tasks that require a high amount of intellectual work. These employees exert autonomy regarding when and how they work, mainly restricted by external deadlines resulting from projects or publication processes. The university allowed employees to work from home before the COVID-19 pandemic, depending on individual agreements with supervisors. Most of the study participants had the technical equipment required for working from home, such as laptops, before the pandemic. However, 38% had never and only 5% had regularly worked from home before. Their job often required them to collaborate with (international) colleagues so that 70% had used at least one video conferencing tool before the pandemic. Our sample displayed an increased number of meetings in the first weeks of the pandemic. In the first week of our study, 60% reported to have 1–2 additional meetings and 32% reported to have more than 3 additional meetings per week compared to the time before the pandemic. These numbers remained stable throughout our data collection period.

We collected the data between April 28 and May 21, 2020. During this period, the participants worked from home to reduce infection risk. We collected the data via online questionnaires. The first questionnaire included questions regarding demographics, family and living situation, previous working from home experience, and experience with electronic collaboration tools. Furthermore, we included the control variables of Sense of Coherence (SoC) and attitude towards IT. In the end, participants entered their email address in case they wanted to go on with the study.

Participation in the study was voluntary. 55 participants filled out the first questionnaire. We ensured anonymity by developing a personal code in the first questionnaire, which allowed no identification of the email address. A link to the consecutive questionnaires was sent to the participants twice a week (Tuesday and Thursday). The participants were requested to fill out the questionnaire on the respective day at the end of their work. In each questionnaire, participants had to indicate whether their working situation had changed (percentage of working from home, tasks, technical equipment). We chose the diary design to examine whether the employees adapted to working from home. Compared to other diary studies that usually examine one week (e.g., [42, 43]), we chose a long period of four weeks to account for changes in the recommendations and decrees of the federal state government. Indeed, after two weeks, the government relaxed the restrictions, which we captured with additional questions. In total, 37 participants filled out the first questionnaire, and at least five of the eight diaries, which comprises the final sample for our study.

3.2 Measures

The complete questionnaire is available from the authors. All items were in German and answered on a 5-Point Likert-Scale (1 = strongly disagree to 5 = strongly agree).

Enforced Working From Home was measured through the question "What percentage of your work do you work from home in the current situation?" (1 = 0% to 5 = 100%). We controlled for changes in the extent of working from home by asking this question in each diary entry, however, we did not find any significant changes over the four weeks. Therefore, we decided to include the aggregate of entries in the analysis.

Daily Perceived Detachment Ability was measured with two adapted items from the detachment subscale of the Recovery Experiences Questionnaire [44]. We asked our participants to answer the questionnaire after having finished their workday. Therefore, the questions captured the perceived ability to detach in the evening instead of the actual detachment experience, which is usually measured before going to bed. The scale was adjusted for daily measurement and for measuring the confidence regarding detachment (e.g., "I am confident that I will forget about work today in my free time after work."). Cronbach's alpha (α) of the scale varied from .862 to .929, with a mean of .902 over the four weeks.

Daily Communication Overload was measured with four adapted items from the communication overload scale by Cho et al. [13]. The scale was adjusted for daily measurements and addressed all electronic communication means (e.g., "Today, I felt that I had spent too much time on electronic communication (calls, virtual meetings, emails, chats, SMS, etc."). α varied from .856 to .946, with a mean of .905.

Daily Perceived Stress was measured with the four-item-version of the perceived stress scale [45]. The scale was adjusted for daily measurements (e.g., "Today, how often have you felt that things were going your way?"). α varied from .661 to .896, with a mean of .804.

Attitude Towards IT was measured with two items from the personal innovativeness in the IT domain scale by Agarwal and Prasad [46] ($\alpha = .720$).

Sense of Coherence (SoC) was measured with the 13 item version of the Sense of Coherence Scale (SOC-13) [47]. Items were answered on a 5-Point Likert-Scale (1 = never or seldom to 5 = very often) or with the respective anchors (e.g., 1 = under-/overestimate to 5 = estimate correctly) ($\alpha = .784$).

Daily COVID-19 Worries were measured to account for additional stressors while working from home due to the unusual pandemic situation. This self-designed scale comprised health-related worries, technical and financial worries and worries concerning the working situation (e.g., "Today, I was burdened by the spatial situation of my workplace."). Information regarding Principal Component Analysis (PCA) is available from the authors. α varied from .650 to .819 with an average of .715.

Daily Open Reflection was measured by an open text field that asked the participants to reflect on their daily situation ("Please describe how you are feeling today."). In the last questionnaire, we also asked for an overall reflection of the four weeks spanning the study ("If you reflect on the last four weeks in total, what are your take-aways?"). These reflections provided the qualitative data used in our analysis.

3.3 Analysis

Given the repeated measurements were nested within individuals, we specified a two-level random intercept model with a random slope for time. The first level consisted of data at the day level (N = 185–296 study occasions). The second level consisted of individual persons (N = 37). We applied multi-level analysis with SPSS (version 25). Predictor variables at the day level (i.e., perceived psychological detachment ability, communication overload, COVID-19 worries) were centered to the individual mean, while predictor and control variables at the person level (i.e., SoC, prior working from home experience, attitude towards IT) were centered to the grand mean. The control variables attitude towards IT, SoC, and COVID-19 worries had significant correlations with the outcome variable perceived stress and were therefore included in the analysis. Controlling for prior experience with working from home (i.e., "How often did you work from home before the COVID-19 pandemic?") did not yield any significant relationships.

We analyzed the qualitative data according to thematic qualitative text analysis [48] and used MAXQDA for coding. Guided by our theoretical framework and the measures employed in the questionnaire, we developed six initial codes during a first coding cycle: *perceived stress*, *detachment*, *communication overload*, *Corona worries*, *working from office* and *family situation*. The first three codes captured our understanding of the concepts depicted in Sect. 2. We applied the code *Corona worries* for all text passages where the participants expressed feelings regarding the general pandemic situation beyond work topics. We used *working from office* to code all statements where participants described that they chose to work from the office instead of working from home. The code *family situation* indicated participants' accounts concerning family care duties.

The second coding cycle yielded two additional codes: *hardware/software problems* to account for problems with the used equipment including internet access, and the *it's not that bad* code for accounts where EWFH had positive developments and outcomes. Table 1 summarizes the code system and provides examples quotes.

Table 1. Qualitative codes and example quotes

Code	Example quote
Perceived stress	"Today I had a stressful morning with many digital meetings." (ID 7)
Detachment	"Since there is still a busy day ahead of me, I am already looking forward to my evening sports program." (ID 36)
Communication overload	"The 'email flood' is so prevalent that you have to organize yourself very well to keep an eye on everything." (ID 30)
Corona worries	"Corona news really bother me, so I try to avoid this information in my daily routine." (ID 15)
Working from office	"Today, I had a few appointments for which I went to the office instead of WFH, because of a better focus and silence." (ID 7)
Family situation	"WFH is ok if no kids are jumping around." (ID 20)
Hardware/software problems	"Frustrated because Skype is not working and no solution has been found yet." (ID 10)
It's not that bad	"WFH is no longer exhausting, it is just normal." (ID 6)

4 Results

4.1 Descriptive Statistics

The gender of participants was equally distributed with 19 males (51.4%) and 18 females (48.6%). 54.1% of the participants were between 25 and 34 years old, 3% were younger than 25 years old, 35% were between 35 and 54 years old, and 8% were older than 54 years old. 73% worked in research and teaching, 21.6% represented administrative staff, and 5.4% worked in IT. The majority of the participants lived together with another person (51.4%) or with more than two persons (29.7%). 21.6% lived together with at least one child but only 8.1% with a child younger than 3.

Regarding the working situation at home, 32.4% worked in a separate room dedicated for work, 13.5% in a separate room that had been transformed into an office setup (e.g., guest room), 32.4% worked from a desk but not in a separate room (e.g., desk in the living room), and 21.6% worked at a table other than a desk, for example, a kitchen or dining table. Table 2 displays descriptive statistics and bivariate correlations.

4.2 Hypotheses Testing

To test whether EWFH increased daily perceived stress (H1), we compared the multi-level model containing EWFH and the control variables daily COVID-19 worries, SoC, and attitude towards IT to the null model that included only the intercept. The multi-level model showed a significant improvement over the null model ($\Delta - 2x \log = 64.692$, $df = 4$, $p < .001$). The estimate of EWFH was not significant (see Table 3), rejecting hypothesis 1. However, the estimates for the control variables SoC, attitude towards IT, and daily COVID-19 worries were significant.

Since we found no direct relationship between EWFH and daily perceived stress, we rejected hypothesis 2 regarding an indirect effect of EWFH via daily perceived detachment ability on daily perceived stress. However, according to Kenny et al. [49], testing for an indirect effect is still possible when both the predictor and the outcome variable are significantly related to the mediator. Therefore, we tested the multi-level model with EWFH and the significant control variables as predictors of daily perceived detachment ability, which showed a significant improvement over the null model ($\Delta -$ 2x log $= 30.221$, df $= 4$, $p < .001$). However, the estimate of EWFH was not significant (see Table 4), rejecting hypothesis 2a. Only the estimate for daily COVID-19 worries was significant. The multi-level model with daily perceived detachment ability and the control variables predicting perceived stress showed a significant improvement over the null model ($\Delta -$ 2x log $= 70.862$, df $= 4$, $p < .001$). The estimate of daily perceived detachment ability was significant (see Table 3), supporting hypothesis 2b. Since only the mediator-outcome path was significant, hypothesis 2 could not be supported.

Similar to hypothesis 2, we tested whether EWFH and daily perceived stress are significantly related to daily communication overload as a mediator. The multi-level model with EWFH and the significant control variables as predictors for daily communication overload showed no significant improvement over the null model ($\Delta -$ 2x log $= 8.758$, df $= 4$, $p = .067$). The estimate of EWFH was not significant (see Table 5), rejecting hypothesis 3a. The multi-level model with daily communication overload and the control variables as predictors of daily perceived stress showed significant improvement over the null model ($\Delta -$ 2x log $= 63.786$, df $= 4$, $p < .001$.). The estimate of daily communication overload was not significant (see Table 3), thereby rejecting hypothesis 3b. Since both the predictor-mediator and the mediator-outcome path were not significant, hypothesis 3 could not be supported.

Figure 2 depicts an overview of the results regarding each hypothesis.

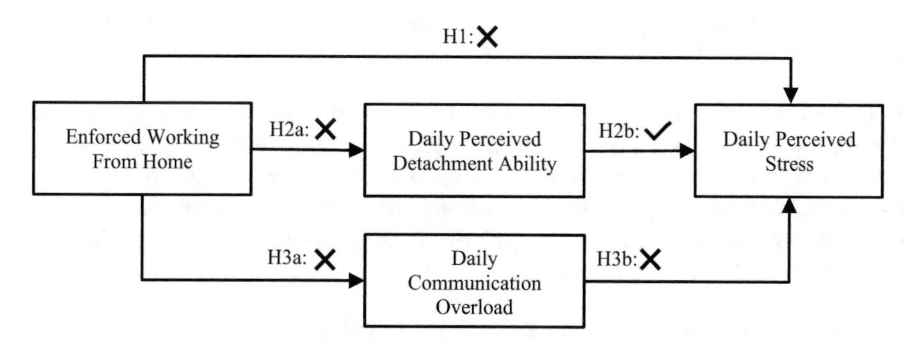

Fig. 2. Research model with results

4.3 Qualitative Analysis

Perceived Stress. Overall, participants described situations as stressful that were related to approaching deadlines and episodes of back-to-back meetings. Except for one participant who described the general work situation as demanding ("*The work situation feels*

Table 2. Descriptive statistics {M = Mean, SD = Standard Deviation, *p < .05, **p < .01, [1]reversed score, [2]based on mean scores across the eight days that the study took place}

	Variable	M	SD	1	2	3	4	5	6	7	8
1	Enforced working from home	4.32	.75	–	.03	.08	.12	−.12	−.15	.21	−.14
2	Daily perceived detachment ability[2]	3.31	.94		–	.00	.03	−.37*	.09	−.01	−.30
3	Daily communication overload[2]	2.24	.82			–	.33*	.12	−.13	.14	.28
4	Daily perceived stress	2.13	.58				–	−.38*	−.52**	−.05	.51**
5	Attitude towards IT	3.34	.91					–	.01	.17	−.10
6	Sense of coherence[1]	3.25	.76						–	−.01	−.35*
7	Working from home experience	1.86	.92							–	−.12
8	Daily COVID-19 worries[2]	2.08	.48								–

like a marathon: the workload remains (too) high." ID 34), we did not find statements providing evidence for a high stress level of our study participants.

Detachment. Problems with detachment were rarely mentioned but present ("*Somehow the work went into the end of the day rather seamlessly [...] at some point I wandered from my desk to the couch (both in the living room), which at least provided a change of location, but the laptop was always with me.*" ID 6). Participants reported that it was easier to stay mentally connected to work due to the possibility to "*quickly look things up*" (ID 30) while working from home.

Communication Overload. Since the majority of our participants worked in research and teaching, their typical work activities comprised reading, writing, or thinking ("*[it is] basically doing a lot of quiet work alone.*" ID 16). The participants did not perceive the decrease of in-person communication and the changes in their volume of electronic communication as problematic. Instead, they were able to engage in individual focus time ("*Today was an almost meeting-free day and the opportunity to concentrate on essays.*" ID 34). Only two participants explicitly named an increased email volume as demanding. Some participants reported the opposite of communication overload. For them, any form of electronic communication, such as team meetings, was a welcome

Table 3. Multi-level results of control variables, enforced working from home (EWFH), daily perceived detachment ability (DetAb), daily communication overload (ComOv) and daily perceived stress (PS) {*p < .05, **p < .01, ***p < .001, [1]reversed score}

Variable	Null model			Predictor model (H1)			Predictor model (H2b)			Predictor model (H3b)		
	Est.	SE	t	Est.	SE	t	Est.	SE	t	Est.	SE	t
Intercept (PS)	2.13	.095	22.318***	2.12	.077	27.571***	2.117	.075	28.251***	2.123	.076	27.946***
Sense of Coherence[1]				−.40	.105	−3.764**	−.40	.101	−3.92***	−.397	.102	−3.879***
Attitude towards IT				−.227	.09	−2.62*	−.234	.084	−2.80**	−.229	.085	−2.700*
COVID-19 Worries				.27	.09	2.88**	.234	.097	2.423*	.274	.097	2.837**
EWFH				.015	.09	.16						
DetAb							−.123	.044	−2.820*			
ComOv										.033	.048	.701
−2x log	460.149			395.457			389.287			396.364		

Table 4. Multi-level results of control variables, enforced working from home (EWFH), and daily perceived detachment ability (DetAb) {*p < .05, [1]reversed score}

Variable	Null model			Predictor model (H2a)		
	Estimate	SE	t	Estimate	SE	t
Intercept (DetAb)	−.001	.041	−.021	−.035	.041	−.855
Sense of coherence[1]				.013	.057	.226
Attitude towards IT				−.033	.045	−.715
COVID-19 worries				−.331	−.135	−2.449*
EWFH				.008	.051	.148
−2x log	563.977			533.756		

social interaction ("*Somehow I'm looking forward to these meetings - no matter what the content is.*" ID 17).

Corona Worries. These worries were mentioned mainly with reference to children and the reduced opportunity to rely on family members, such as grandparents, without increasing the infection risk. Some participants reported that the uncertainty about the future negatively affected their sleep quality ("*I sleep badly and worry about the future.*" ID 4).

Working from Office. For specific work activities, participants perceived a need to work from office since they found it difficult to conduct them at home ("*Today I went to the office, because I had to clarify things in person and sign documents.*" ID 19).

Table 5. Multi-level results of control variables, enforced working from home (EWFH), and daily communication overload (ComOv) {[1]reversed score}

Variable	Null model			Predictor model (H3a)		
	Estimate	SE	t	Estimate	SE	t
Intercept (ComOv)	.002	.037	.043	.008	.040	.198
Sense of coherence[1]				−.016	.056	−.284
Attitude towards IT				.007	.044	.162
COVID-19 worries				.167	.127	1.322
EWFH				−.007	.050	−.118
−2x log	509.911			501.153		

Family Situation. The dominant stressor resulting from EWFH was taking care of children *("[...] this double burden [gnaws] on the nerves, one is stressed and sometimes has the feeling that one is not doing justice to work or family life."* ID 29).

Hardware/Software Problems. Next to taking care of children and the noisy environment at home, participants mentioned hardware/software issues as primary reasons to work from office ("*Today was stressful because I had to drive to the institute due to the poorly performing internet at home.*" ID 2).

It's Not that Bad. Many participants without prior WFH experience reported positive aspects ("*In fact, I like working from home better than I thought beforehand, and a certain amount of anxiety about technologies and how to use them has turned out to be unfounded over time.*" ID 17). Whether or not the home was the preferred work location depended on the task structure ("*I have become more aware that working from home is nothing for me, except for the larger tasks where you have to concentrate on one thing.*" ID 26) as well the spatial and family situation at home; that is, having a separate room for work as well as options for childcare.

5 Discussion

Our study sheds light on how EWFH due to COVID-19 influences the perceived stress level of knowledge workers. We find that, overall, our study participants do not experience more stress while working from home. Although this finding contradicts academic literature on the adverse effects of working from home (e.g., [10]), it supports recent findings on the perceptions of knowledge workers regarding EWFH due to COVID-19 [6]. It seems that employees have adapted swiftly to EWFH. Contrary to our assumptions, we do not find evidence that the blending of work and private life or being overloaded by electronic communication increase the perceived stress level. Instead, general worries about the COVID-19 situation lead to a higher stress level.

5.1 Children at Home and Social Norms at Work

Characteristics of our sample can explain our findings. Working at a public university, our participants do not have to fear financial or even job loss. The majority of our participants live alone or with their partners, and only few have young children. As our qualitative analysis shows that childcare is the predominant stressor in the EWFH setting, it is not surprising that our sample displays a low stress level in the quantitative data. Another reason for the contradiction between our findings and the academic literature is rooted in the specific EWFH setting. EWFH impacts the whole workforce and not only parts of it, as it was the case for prior working from home arrangements. Prior research has reported that employees who often work from home experience power distances compared to their peers who work from the physical office, which results in feelings of social isolation [50] and perceptions of a lack of organizational support [51]. In an EWFH setting, everyone is working from home so that these "marginalizations" [5] do not exist.

Our quantitative data demonstrates that the perceived inability to detach from work during non-work hours leads to an increased stress level, thereby supporting previous literature [14]. However, our sample does not depict problems in detaching from work. Moreover, we do not find a significant relationship between EWFH and perceived ability to detach. This finding contradicts academic literature [24] and current studies stating that EWFH due to COVID-19 impedes the ability to draw the line between work and family life [6]. Apparently, other factors not included in our study account for an inability to detach. Prior research has suggested, for example, that social norms regarding an extended availability for work predict whether employees work beyond their official working hours [24, 52].

5.2 Outeraction and Individual Focus Time

While recent surveys have reported that the goal of EWFH to minimize physical contact increased the overall volume of electronic communication [6, 8], we do not find evidence for an increased volume in our sample. Conversely, both qualitative and quantitative analyses reveal that our sample does not experience stress due to communication overload.

Our qualitative data explains why the number of meetings has not increased: Participants report coordination overhead resulting from the need to schedule each meeting and negotiate availability instead of conducting physical ad-hoc meetings at the desk of a colleague. This overhead has been called "outeraction", as preambles for periods of interaction [53]. These virtual outeractions require more effort than "a tap on the shoulder" in the physical office, reducing the number of meetings, above all of ad-hoc meetings [5].

Furthermore, the need for communication varies for different job roles. Our findings suggest that the task structure of university employees responsible for research and teaching does not require extensive communication and coordination. In contrast, our qualitative data show that they benefit from individual focus time because their work mainly requires solving complex problems and preparing manuscripts or lectures. Others, whose task structure consists of more communication, may have suffered from too much communication in the EWFH situation (cf. [6]).

6 Limitations and Future Research

Although we included questions about the physical and technical equipment in our questionnaire, we did not ask in detail about the characteristics of the individual work setting that could explain differences between prior working from home arrangements and EWFH. As the COVID-19 context provides a specific, enforced work setting, findings should be considered carefully when drawing general conclusions for the working from home literature.

Future studies should examine additional variables, such as ergonomic factors, relationships to members of the household, and the distribution of domestic tasks. As we did not find a relationship between EWFH and the perceived ability to detach, future research is needed that examines which factors of working from home result in particular outcomes. As stated above, social norms present a promising avenue.

We researched a relatively homogenous sample in terms of age and position in the organizational hierarchy. Future research should consider career ambitions, responsibilities, and leadership positions that might result in staying attached to work while working from home. A more heterogeneous sample will allow studying the role of childcare for perceived stress and how differences in task structures lead to different perceptions of working from home.

7 Conclusion

Our study contributes to the academic literature that examines the role of working from home for the perceived stress of knowledge workers by emphasizing that "*it's not that bad*". We apply a unique longitudinal diary study design for researching the impacts of EWFH. We believe that this specific design is beneficial for capturing dynamic changes in the working from home situation resulting from changing lockdown measures. Diary studies capture participants' adaption to the new EWFH setting.

We find that EWFH does not lead to an increased perceived stress level, suggesting (1) that knowledge workers can adapt to the rapid shift from a physical office to the home office, (2) that knowledge workers in an EWFH environment face fewer stressors compared to prior working from home arrangements (e.g., better organizational support, no marginalization of home office workers), and (3) that the benefits of working from home, such as time savings due to less commuting time, outweigh potential negative effects, such as blurred work-life boundaries. Our study, therefore, calls for research taking a deep dive into the specifics of the EWFH environment compared to prior working from home settings as well as into individual coping strategies of employees to explain the effects for employees' well-being. Benefits from the EWFH phase should be kept in a voluntary working from home setting.

Our study further suggests that organizations should consider to allow, or even encourage, employees to continue working from home in the future, at least to a certain extent. We believe that especially job roles that require longer stretches of individual focus work (compared to roles with embedded high communication needs) benefit from working from home.

References

1. Bélanger, F.: Workers' propensity to telecommute: an empirical study. Inf. Manag. **35**, 139–153 (1999)
2. Bitkom Research: Vier von zehn Unternehmen setzen auf Homeoffice. https://www.bitkom.org/Presse/Presseinformation/Vier-von-zehn-Unternehmen-setzen-auf-Homeoffice. Accessed 08 Dec 2020
3. Bailey, D.E., Kurland, N.B.: A review of telework research: findings, new directions, and lessons for the study of modern work. J. Organ. Behav. **23**, 383–400 (2002)
4. Alipour, J.-V., Fadinger, H., Schymik, J.: My home is my castle: the benefits of working from home during a pandemic crisis. Evidence from Germany. ifo working paper 329, pp. 1–48 (2020)
5. Waizenegger, L., McKenna, B., Wenie, C., Taino, B.: An affordance perspective of team collaboration and enforced working from home during COVID-19. Eur. J. Inf. Syst. **29**, 429–442 (2020)
6. DAK-Gesundheit: Digitalisierung und Homeoffice in der Corona-Krise. https://www.dak.de/dak/bundesthemen/sonderanalyse-2295276.html. Accessed 20 July 2020
7. Erdsiek, D.: Unternehmen wollen auch nach der Krise an Homeoffice festhalten. http://ftp.zew.de/pub/zew-docs/brepikt/202002BrepIKT.pdf. Accessed 27 Nov 2020
8. Bockstahler, M., Jurecic, M., Rief, S.: Working from home experience. An empirical study from the user perspective during the Corona pandemic. Office. 21 - Zukunft der Arbeit (2020)
9. Song, Y., Gao, J.: Does telework stress employees out? A study on working at home and subjective well-being for wage/salary workers. J. Happiness Stud. **21**(7), 2649–2668 (2019). https://doi.org/10.1007/s10902-019-00196-6
10. Delanoeije, J., Verbruggen, M., Germeys, L.: Boundary role transitions: a day-to-day approach to explain the effects of home-based telework on work-to-home conflict and home-to-work conflict. Hum. Relat. **72**, 1843–1868 (2019)
11. Agerfalk, P.J., Conboy, K., Myers, M.D.: Information systems in the age of pandemics: COVID-19 and beyond. Eur. J. Inf. Syst. **29**, 203–207 (2020)
12. Sonnentag, S., Fritz, C.: Recovery from job stress: the stressor-detachment model as an integrative framework. J. Organ. Behav. **36**, 72–103 (2015)
13. Cho, J., Ramgolam, D.I., Schaefer, K.M., Sandlin, A.N.: The rate and delay in overload: an investigation of communication overload and channel synchronicity on identification and job satisfaction. J. Appl. Commun. Res. **39**, 38–54 (2011)
14. Büchler, N., ter Hoeven, C.L., van Zoonen, W.: Understanding constant connectivity to work: how and for whom is constant connectivity related to employee well-being? Inf. Organ. **30**, 100302 (2020)
15. Richter, A.: Locked-down digital work. Int. J. Inf. Manage. **55**, 102157 (2020)
16. Leung, L., Zhang, R.: Mapping ICT use at home and telecommuting practices: a perspective from work/family border theory. Telematics Inform. **34**, 385–396 (2017)
17. Boell, S.K., Cecez-Kecmanovic, D., Campbell, J., Cheng, J.E.: Advantages, challenges and contradictions of the transformative nature of telework: a review of the literature. In: Proceedings of the 19th Americas Conference on Information Systems (2013)
18. Di Martino, V., Wirth, L.: Telework: a new way of working and living. Int. Labour Rev. **129**, 529–554 (1990)
19. Mann, S., Holdsworth, L.: The psychological impact of teleworking: stress, emotions and health. New Technol. Work Employ. **18**, 196–211 (2003)
20. Bloom, N., Liang, J., Roberts, J., Ying, Z.J.: Does working from home work? Evidence from a Chinese experiment. Q. J. Econ. **130**, 165–218 (2015)

21. Weinert, C., Maier, C., Laumer, S., Weitzel, T.: Does teleworking negatively influence IT professionals? An empirical analysis of IT personnel's telework-enabled stress. In: Proceedings of the Conference on Computers and People Research (2014)
22. Dettmers, J., Bamberg, E., Seffzek, K.: Characteristics of extended availability for work: the role of demands and resources. Int. J. Stress Manag. **23**, 276–297 (2016)
23. Diaz, I., Chiaburu, D.S., Zimmerman, R.D., Boswell, W.R.: Communication technology: pros and cons of constant connection to work. J. Vocat. Behav. **80**, 500–508 (2012)
24. Fenner, G.H., Renn, R.W.: Technology-assisted supplemental work and work-to-family conflict: the role of instrumentality beliefs, organizational expectations and time management. Hum. Relat. **63**, 63–82 (2010)
25. Golden, T.D.: Altering the effects of work and family conflict on exhaustion: telework during traditional and nontraditional work hours. J. Bus. Psychol. **27**(3), 255–269 (2012). https://doi.org/10.1007/s10869-011-9247-0
26. Suh, A., Lee, J.: Understanding teleworkers' technostress and its influence on job satisfaction. Internet Res. **27**, 140–159 (2017)
27. Messenger, J.C., Gschwind, L.: Three generations of telework: new ICTs and the (r)evolution from home office to virtual office. New Technol. Work Employ. **31**, 195–208 (2016)
28. Meijman, T.F., Mulder, G.: Psychological aspects of workload. In: Drenth, P.J.D., Thierry, H., De Wolff, C.J. (eds.) Handbook of Work and Organizational Psychology, pp. 5–33. Psychology Press, Hove (1998)
29. Lundberg, U., Lindfors, P.: Psychophysiological reactions to telework in female and male white-collar workers. J. Occup. Health Psychol. **7**, 354–364 (2002)
30. Sonnentag, S.: Psychological detachment from work during leisure time: the benefits of mentally disengaging from work. Curr. Dir. Psychol. Sci. **21**, 114–118 (2012)
31. Mazmanian, M., Erickson, I.: The product of availability: understanding the economic underpinnings of constant connectivity. In: Proceedings of the SIGCHI Conference on Human Factors in Computing Systems, pp. 763–772. ACM (2014)
32. Vartiainen, M., et al.: Distributed and mobile work - places, people and technology. Otatieto, Helsinki (2007)
33. Jurecic, M., Rief, S., Stolze, D.: Office analytics - success factors for designing a worktype-based working environment. Fraunhofer IAO, Stuttgart (2018)
34. Weichbrodt, J., Schulze, H.: Homeoffice als Pandemie-Maßnahme - Herausforderungen und Chancen. In: Benoy, C. (ed.) COVID-19: Ein Virus nimmt Einfluss auf unsere Psyche. Einschätzungen und Maßnahmen aus psychologischer Perspektive, pp. 93–101. Kohlhammer, Stuttgart (2020)
35. Newport, C.: Deep Work: Rules for Focused Success in a Distracted World. Grand Central Publishing, New York (2016)
36. Spataro, J.: The future of work - the good, the challenging & the unknown. https://www.microsoft.com/en-us/microsoft-365/blog/2020/07/08/future-work-good-challenging-unknown/. Accessed 26 Nov 2020
37. Lansmann, S., Klein, S.: How much collaboration? Balancing the needs for collaborative and uninterrupted work. In: Proceedings of the 26th European Conference on Information Systems (2018)
38. Barley, S.R., Meyerson, D.E., Grodal, S.: E-mail as a source and symbol of stress. Organ. Sci. **22**, 887–906 (2011)
39. Stephens, K.K., Mandhana, D.M., Kim, J.J., Li, X.: Reconceptualizing communication overload and building a theoretical foundation. Commun. Theory **27**, 269–289 (2017)
40. Chung, C.J., Goldhaber, G.: Measuring communication load: a three-dimensional instrument. In: 41st Meeting of the International Communication Association (1991)
41. Cho, J.: Communication load. In: Scott, C.R., Lewis, L. (eds.) The International Encyclopedia of Organizational Communication, pp. 1–9. Wiley, West Sussex (2017)

42. Derks, D., Bakker, A.B.: Smartphone use, work-home interference, and burnout: a diary study on the role of recovery. Appl. Psychol. **63**, 411–440 (2014)
43. Cambier, R., Derks, D., Vlerick, P.: Detachment from work: a diary study on telepressure, smartphone use and empathy. Psychol. Belg. **59**, 227–245 (2019)
44. Sonnentag, S., Fritz, C.: The Recovery Experience Questionnaire: development and validation of a measure for assessing recuperation and unwinding from work. J. Occup. Health Psychol. **12**, 204–221 (2007)
45. Cohen, S., Kamarck, T., Mermelstein, R.: A global measure of perceived stress. J. Health Soc. Behav. **24**, 385–396 (1983)
46. Agarwal, R., Prasad, J.: A conceptual and operational definition of personal innovativeness in the domain of information technology. Inf. Syst. Res. **9**, 204–215 (1998)
47. Feldt, T., Lintula, H., Suominen, S., Koskenvuo, M., Vahtera, J., Kivimäki, M.: Structural validity and temporal stability of the 13-item sense of coherence scale: prospective evidence from the population-based HeSSup study. Qual. Life Res. **16**(3), 483–493 (2007). https://doi.org/10.1007/s11136-006-9130-z
48. Kuckartz, U.: Qualitative Text Analysis. SAGE Publications, Los Angeles (2014)
49. Kenny, D.A., Kashy, D., Bolger, N.: Data Analysis in Social Psychology. Oxford University Press, New York (1998)
50. Cooper, C.D., Kurland, N.B.: Telecommuting, professional isolation, and employee development in public and private organizations. J. Organ. Behav. **23**, 511–532 (2002)
51. Tietze, S., Nadin, S.: The psychological contract and the transition from office-based to home-based work. Hum. Resour. Manag. J. **21**, 318–334 (2011)
52. Piszczek, M.M.: Boundary control and controlled boundaries: Organizational expectations for technology use at the work–family interface. J. Organ. Behav. **38**, 592–611 (2017)
53. Nardi, B.A., Whittaker, S., Bradner, E.: Interaction and outeraction: instant messaging in action. In: Proceedings of the 2000 ACM Conference on Computer Supported Cooperative Work, pp. 79–88 (2000)

Designing Online Platforms for Cultural Participation and Education: A Taxonomic Approach

Kristin Kutzner[1](✉), Thorsten Schoormann[1], Claudia Roßkopf[2], and Ralf Knackstedt[1]

[1] Institute for Economics and Information Systems, University of Hildesheim, Hildesheim, Germany
{kristin.kutzner,thorsten.schoormann, ralf.knackstedt}@uni-hildesheim.de
[2] Institute for Cultural Policy, University of Hildesheim, Hildesheim, Germany
claudia.rosskopf@uni-hildesheim.de

Abstract. Museums preserve the cultural heritage and aim at providing study and education as well as enjoyment for the general public. In pursuing their missions, museums are increasingly concerned with making these experiences digitally available. Therefore, they start to use online platforms that make cultural objects publicly accessible, and therefore allow discussing cultural issues and provide cultural and educational participation. However, as there is little consolidated knowledge on features of such platforms and limited resources of museums, they face challenges in achieving their missions through a platform. In order to overcome this, we (1) review and synthesize related literature and online platforms and (2) present a taxonomy of how online offers leverage cultural participation and education. In doing this, we seek to enable platform designers and museum professionals in making informed decisions in terms of how the 'museum experience' can be supported/complemented through online platforms.

Keywords: Cultural access · Museum · Society · Digital inclusion · Taxonomy

1 Introduction

According to the International Council of Museums [1], a museum's core mission is to provide study, education, and enjoyment for the general public. By collecting, preserving, exhibiting and interpreting the humanity's heritage, they allow individuals to take part in cultural activities and experiences (i.e., cultural participation) and thus aim to foster social justice and well-being [2]. Along with this, museums allow education for individuals which means reflecting on oneself, others and issues of the world [3] as well as taking critical position towards knowledge, artist experiences and cultural objects [4]. Since museums play a fundamental role in our society, their services should be affordable and equal accessible for everyone. This is however often not the case because of various (individual, social or environmental) obstacles such as time restrictions, geographical distances, financial resources, language barriers, physical handicaps, health reasons, or

F. Ahlemann et al. (Eds.): WI 2021, LNISO 46, pp. 280–296, 2021.
https://doi.org/10.1007/978-3-030-86790-4_20

even global pandemics. One way for museums to cope with these obstacles is given by the use of digital technologies and the Internet, which is in line with the Director of National Museums in Seychelles Beryl Ondiek's statement: "In the mist of chaos, museums break the walls that keep us apart. Museums can use all of the collections and information we have, and transmit our cultural and natural heritage to communities through the Internet to lift spirits and keep everyone connected." Accordingly, museums have started to consider the use of online platforms such as websites, social media, or blogs [5]. This practice enables museums to provide public access to the heritage, leverage cultural participation and mobilization in society as well as allows individuals to engage with and discuss cultural issues [6]—even in cases such as the Covid-19 pandemic that was the trigger for the closure of plenty of museum facilities in 2019/2020 [7].

Despite the great potential of using online platforms for cultural participation and education, their use is far from being fully exploited and museum professionals are usually unfamiliar with digital solutions accompanied by resource restrictions and fragmented know-how [8]. Furthermore, especially small and medium-sized institutions often struggle because of their dependence on public funding and volunteer work [9]. Even though previous research on this topic indicates the importance of digitization, they mostly focus on rather isolated aspects, for instance, the impact of museum websites on users [10] or guidelines for providing access to and presenting museum data [9, 11]. In consequence, we lack knowledge of what platform features should be implemented to best possible support access to cultural participation and education. This lack is problematic as it hinders, for instance, museum professionals—in addition to limited resources and technical know-how—in improving their museum platforms to achieve their educational mission and to attract visitor attention. To bridge this gap, we seek to derive an overview of currently used platform features that act as a foundation for supporting online-based cultural participation and education. Therefore, we formulate the following research question (RQ): *What are the characteristic features of online platforms for providing access to cultural participation and education in society?*

To answer this question, we follow the procedure proposed by [12] and deduce a taxonomy of platform features for access to cultural participation and education. The taxonomy enables, for example, professionals in museums and in further institutions with cultural and educational missions such as theatres, libraries, or heritage centers to (a) be informed within the wide range of platform features to compare, refine and develop their online presence and (b) to make their services publicly accessible and participatory. Furthermore, the taxonomy can help to (c) improve marketing activities [5] and therefore to raise peoples' interest in visiting the institution [13] as well as to increase visitor numbers [14]—despite public sector cuts and financial pressure [14]. From a more societal view, disadvantaged individuals who cannot benefit from local cultural practices are supported in their cultural and educational participation. Based on the taxonomy, potential users (i.e., individuals) can select appropriate platforms for their personal purposes and, in the future, they will benefit from the enhanced landscape of online platforms for cultural participation. For research, the taxonomy can be used, for instance, to explore and advance (social inclusive) online platform designs that enable participating in culture as well as leveraging education.

2 Research Background

The existing Information Systems (IS) research on museum online platforms can be grouped into four areas: (1) Research analyzed the influence of website design features on users. Surveying museum website users, [15] and [10] identified a set of requirements for encouraging enjoyable web experiences and informal online learning for users. In addition, [16] indicated that the use of game-based features led to enjoyment and learning. Furthermore, by examining two sample museum websites, studies discovered a positive influence of website features on users' intention to return to the website and to visit the physical museum [13, 14]. More general conclusions for museum websites are provided, however, the results are limited to the type of online platform. (2) Besides, research investigated guidelines for providing access to and presenting museum data. For example, a conceptual framework for visualizing museum data on mobile applications [9], an IS design theory for the interactive presentation and navigation of digital art collections [11] and a classification of information visualization approaches for digital cultural heritage collections [17] are proposed. These studies examined website features, however, they solely focused on the presentation of data on museum applications. (3) Moreover, research aimed at supporting the development of museum websites by proposing a five-step-procedure [18] and by presenting conceptual guidelines [10]. Nevertheless, both provided general guidance on museum website development without focusing on specific features. (4) In addition, the museums' attitude towards using features of online channels (i.e., social media and museum websites) was investigated which led to the conclusion that online participatory activity among museums was quite uniformed and restrained for technical reasons [5].

Overall, most studies focus on rather isolated aspects, address only a few sample platform features, or provide more general guidance for museums. In consequence, to the best of our knowledge, there is still a need for a comprehensive overview of platform features which allow cultural participation and education. In this study we seek to address this need by developing and evaluating a taxonomy of cultural participation and education in the digital age.

3 Research Design

The development of taxonomies is widely accepted in IS research regarding the design of online platforms/tools [19, 20] and in the context of culture [21–23] to structure, analyze and understand existing and future objects of a domain [12]. Taxonomies, as classified as 'theory for analyzing' [24], are a necessary foundation for developing advanced theories that, for instance, attempt to explain and predict how specific features will leverage the success of engaging in cultural practices. In this study, inspired by a staged approach [19], (Stage 1) we carried out a literature review and (Stage 2) identified relevant objects (i.e., online platforms that provide access to cultural participation and education). Following, based on the findings, (Stage 3) we iteratively built and (Stage 4) evaluated our taxonomy (Fig. 1).

Stage 1: Literature Review. Firstly, we searched for prior literature dealing with museum online platforms based on the rigorous procedure of [25]. On February 12th

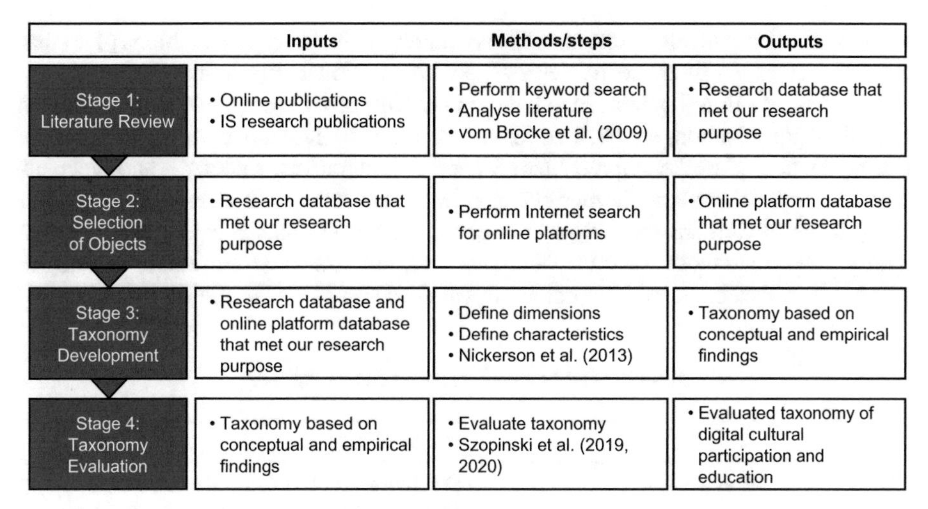

Fig. 1. Research design for developing the taxonomy

2020, to get an overview of research endeavors in the museum context in the IS domain, we searched for literature by using the keyword 'museum' in the AISeL database which covers leading IS outlets as well as publications related to our study's purpose such as with cultural and social media topics [26]. No limitation regarding the year of publication was made. As a result, we found 568 articles. As various studies used the term, however, did not focus on museums itself, we excluded articles that did not contain the term 'museum' in the title, abstract, or keywords. Finally, we obtained 41 articles. Reading each article in detail, we analyzed their research subjects and results. Based on this, we derived four main topics in IS research, appertaining to museum online platforms, namely, (1) the influence of website design features on users, (2) guidelines for providing access to and presenting museum data, (3) guidance for the development of museum websites, and (4) museums' attitude towards using features of online channels (see also Sect. 2, an appendix with details on relevant literature and related features can be made available upon request).

Stage 2: Selection of Objects. Secondly, we performed an Internet search for online platforms that provide access to cultural objects and allow participation. We chose museum websites as objects of investigation because museums, as players of cultural participation and education, make use of them to offer online access to cultural objects. To consider museums with comparable objects and (cultural-) political conditions, we decided to include German-speaking art museums that focus on visual arts and photography and that use digital solutions in particular. We chose this type of museum because art museums recorded particularly declining numbers of visitors in Germany [27] and thus could take advantage of the opportunities offered by digital solutions. Besides, museums expand their activities on rating platforms, for instance, as they present the museum on Google or TripAdvisor, where individuals can communicate and share their opinions or experiences with others. Furthermore, social media sites, such as Facebook and Twitter, are used by museums, to be present in the public, to provide current news, and to enable individuals to rate and discuss cultural objects. Moreover, blogs of art that are also referenced by museum websites, are an additional opportunity for presenting and discussing cultural objects. As all these platforms provide access to cultural objects and allow participation, we decided to include them, to get an overview of platforms. During the taxonomy development (see Stage 3), we iteratively selected additional platforms until there were no further changes in the taxonomy. As a result, we selected ten websites of German-speaking art museums, thirteen German-speaking art museums (partly museums whose websites were analyzed, but also other museums) at Google, TripAdvisor, Facebook, and Twitter as well as seven art blogs (see Table 1).

Table 1. Overview of selected online platforms

Source	Online platforms
10 selected museum websites	Deichtorhallen Hamburg, Kunsthalle Mannheim, Museum der Moderne Salzburg, Kunstpalast Düsseldorf, Österreichische Galerie Belvedere Wien, Die Pinakotheken München, Städel Museum Frankfurt, Sprengel Museum Hannover, Staatliche Kunsthalle Karlsruhe, Staatliche Kunstsammlung Dresden
13 selected museums at Google, TripAdvisor, Facebook and Twitter	C/O Berlin, Helmut Newton Stiftung Berlin, K21 Kunstsammlung Nordrhein-Westfalen Düsseldorf, Kunsthalle Mannheim, Museum für Fotografie Berlin, Museum der Moderne Salzburg, Kunstpalast Düsseldorf, Österreichische Galerie Belvedere Wien, Die Pinakotheken München, Sprengel Museum Hannover, Staatliche Kunsthalle Karlsruhe, Städel Museum Frankfurt, WestLicht. Schauplatz für Fotografie Wien
7 selected art blogs	artblogcologne.com, castor-und-pollux.de, ausstellungskritik.wordpress.com, musermeku.org, kulturundkunst.org, sofrischsogut.com, tanjapraske.de

Stage 3: Taxonomy Development. Thirdly, to develop a taxonomy, we employed the systematic procedure proposed by [12]. As a first step, *meta characteristics* including the target users and purposes need to be specified. Our taxonomy may be potentially used by three target groups: (a) Researchers who are interested in designing online platforms that allow cultural access and participation as well as encourage education; (b) institutions with educational missions and cultural objects like museums, galleries, libraries, heritage centers who want to develop and refine their online platforms; (c) individuals who are interested in cultural participation but cannot participate locally because of individual obstacles and therefore select and use appropriate online platforms for their

personal interest. The purpose is to build an overview of currently used online platform features that provide access to cultural participation and education. Thus, we aim to assist researchers and practitioners with the analysis and future development of cultural online platforms. To do so, the online platform features are particularly relevant, as these features determine the manner of access to cultural objects, and therefore, the possible degree of participation. Thus, we choose 'features of the platforms that are used to provide access to cultural participation and education' as meta-characteristics which must be met by all dimensions and characteristics. Next, to determine when to stop building the taxonomy, we adopted the *objective ending conditions* (i.e., determining when to terminate the taxonomy development) and *subjective ending conditions* (i.e., ensuring high quality while developing the taxonomy) proposed by [12], with one exception: The characteristics of each dimension are not mutually exclusive (i.e., unique) to offer multiple features for one dimension that can be used together on a platform as well as to reduce complexity and to support readability of the taxonomy (see also [28]).

Afterward, we ran through three *empirical-to-conceptual* iterations and one *conceptual-to-empirical* iteration and classified online platforms (Fig. 2). We decided to start with the empirical-to-conceptual iteration because of the emerging openness to use online platforms in the museum context [5] and because of the lack of an overview of available features in research (see Sect. 2). In each empirical-to-conceptual iteration, we adapted the taxonomy by analyzing online platforms with regard to their features. To achieve a robust taxonomy, two researchers (one with an IS background, one from Cultural Policy) independently examined each platform, identified the platform features and constantly consolidated their results in each iteration—uncertain cases were discussed. As a *1st iteration*, five museum websites were investigated and classified by the researchers. The results were consolidated and structured within the initial taxonomy. In the *2nd iteration*, five further platforms (i.e., two rating platforms, one social media platform and two art blogs) were investigated, and the results were consolidated which inserted additional characteristics and adapted descriptions. As a *3rd iteration*, eleven further platforms (i.e., five art blogs, five museum websites and one social media platform) were analyzed. After discussing the results, it turned out that no changes in the taxonomy were necessary. As a *4th iteration* (conceptual-to-empirical), the platform features identified during the literature review have been compared to the current version of the taxonomy (see Sect. 2). Apart from minor wording differences (e.g., linear search instead of user-driven search, non-linear search instead of a presentation of random cultural objects) that have been used for taxonomy description, no further features have been specified in the literature. Finally, the defined objective (o) and subjective (s) ending conditions were fulfilled by the taxonomy. In the following, we justify and contextualize the condition's degree of fulfillment (as suggested by [28]): (o1) A representative sample of objects (i.e., online platforms that allow cultural participation and education) has been examined; (o2) no object was merged or split in the last iteration; (o3) at least one object can be classified under every characteristic; (o4) no additional dimension/characteristic was necessary in the last iteration; (o5) no dimensions/characteristics were merged or split in the last iteration; (o6) there is no dimension duplication; (o7) as stated above, the characteristics are not unique within their dimension to offer features that can be used together on a platform; (o8) each cell is unique; (s1) the taxonomy is concise enough to be easily applied for the purpose of building an overview of currently used platform features that allow cultural participation and education; (s2) the taxonomy provide for differentiation among platform features; (s3) the taxonomy is comprehensive as all sample platforms can be classified; (s4) the taxonomy is easily extendible which allows considering novel platform features in this field; (s5) the current taxonomy sufficiently explains the currently used features for cultural participation and education (see also Sect. 5).

Stage 4: Taxonomy Evaluation. Fourthly, in addition to the development, taxonomies require extensive evaluation. Therefore, we draw on the evaluation framework for taxonomies [29] and follow guidelines for using taxonomy evaluation criteria [28]. We performed two initial evaluation steps, namely (1) illustrating the applicability of our taxonomy, and (2) ensuring the understandability and completeness of the taxonomy by utilizing several expert workshops (for more details see Sect. 5).

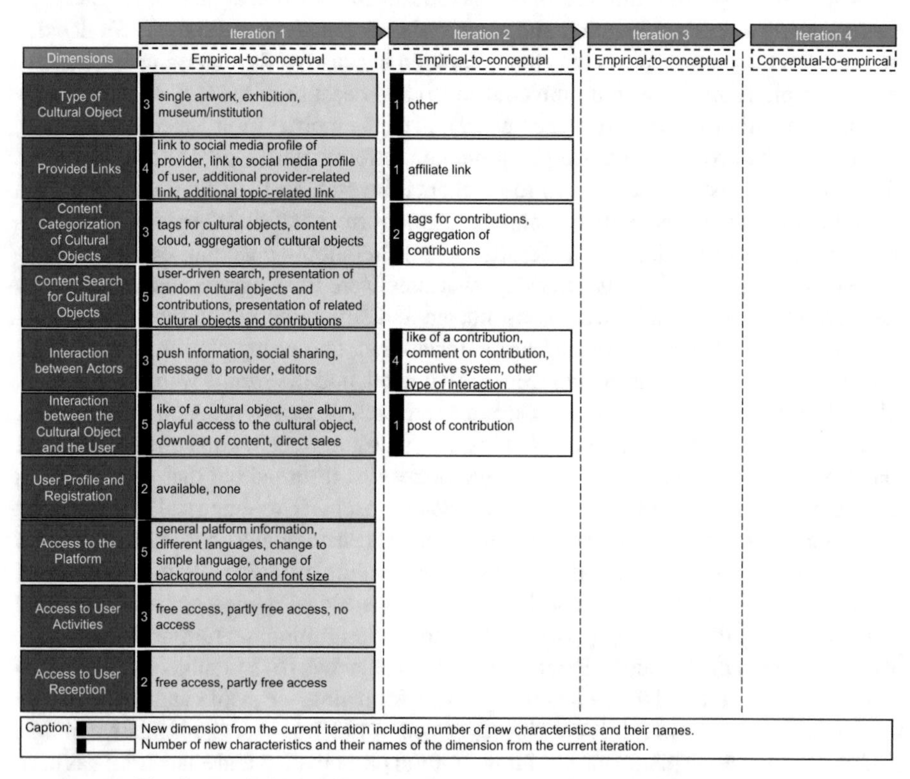

Fig. 2. Evolution of dimensions and characteristics for the taxonomy

4 Taxonomy of Digital Cultural Participation and Education

Our taxonomy of 'Digital Cultural Participation and Education' contains ten dimensions, each with two to seven distinct characteristics (Fig. 3).

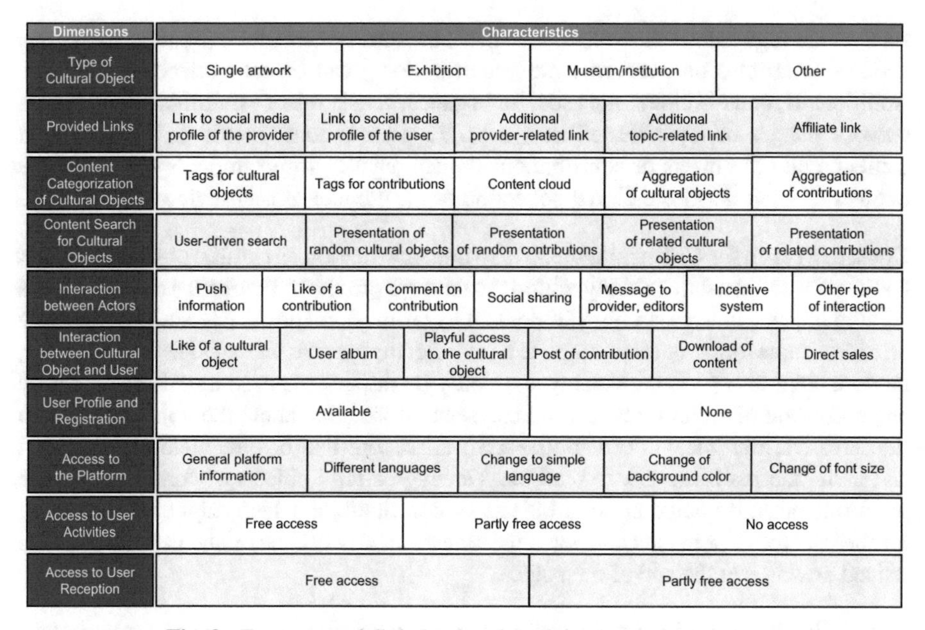

Fig. 3. Taxonomy of digital cultural participation and education

In the following, we explain the taxonomy's dimensions and characteristics in more detail by providing descriptions as well as illustrative examples.

Type of Cultural Object. Online platforms provide access to multiple types of cultural objects for the general public: A single artwork such as a sculpture, a painting, or photography with information about its biographical contextualization, and sometimes detailed artist information are accessible online. Besides, a past, current, or future exhibition of a museum with its curator may be addressed. Moreover, the museum itself is presented with information about its history or current mission supplemented by practical visitor information. Sometimes, other cultural objects such as theatre, literature, or music are provided as well.

Provided Links. Furthermore, for allowing participation in the public and obtaining additional information, the platforms refer to further sources: Social media channels are connected to the platforms. For example, a museum (i.e., the provider of the platform) refers to its social media account. Besides, platform users can utilize their social media accounts, as platforms directly allow sharing artworks or publications via a social media button or they support the platform registration via the user social media accounts. Also, additional provider-related links are offered such as a reference on a museum website to a museum blog or other institutional websites. Furthermore, for providing more informative material, additional topic-related links to wikis, libraries, research databases, external blogs, schools or magazines, and affiliate links are offered.

Content Categorization of Cultural Objects. To provide an abstract view of cultural objects, platforms integrate content categorization: Cultural objects are assigned to tags such as the tags 'motive', 'image elements', or 'atmosphere' for artworks. Also, user reviews or articles on platforms (i.e., contributions) can be categorized by tags too. Additionally, content clouds are used, for instance, consisting of a multitude of miniature artwork images or topic-related keywords. To present some metric of the presented content, cultural objects or contributions are aggregated, for example, by showing the number of artworks of the digital collection or the number of user reviews.

Content Search for Cultural Objects. To find information on cultural objects, different features for information seeking within the data are provided: Platform users can access cultural objects, linear searching for content by terms. Sometimes, the platforms directly provide sample terms, or they complete terms after the user has started to write. Moreover, random cultural objects are displayed, usually on the first page, so that users randomly become aware of cultural objects and can seek information about them in the next step (i.e., creative, non-linear information search). Also, contributions are randomly presented and invite the platform user to read on. Viewing cultural objects or contributions, the platforms present related cultural objects or contributions which might be interesting for the user too. For instance, when a user views an artwork, he or she is provided with related artworks at the end of the page.

Interaction Between Actors. A platform user, a platform provider or editors can potentially act on a platform and are supported to interact with each other, and thus, to participate in the society in several ways: A user may call for push information to receive regular news by registering for a newsletter or by 'liking' content on social media. Besides, actors' contributions can be assessed by a 'like-statement' or commented by actors, and content can be shared by users with others. If a user wants to give feedback to the provider or editors, a contact form or an email address are provided. Whereas some platforms actively ask for messages from their users, for instance, directly under an artwork presentation, others only mention an email address without a further call. To promote interaction between actors, incentive systems are introduced (e.g., a user receives points for activities like writing a review or answering to others and achieves a certain user level). Other types of interaction like a chat function, 'following others', or an offer/search forum are also provided.

Interaction Between the Cultural Object and the User. Platforms not only make cultural objects accessible but also allow a certain degree of interaction between objects and the platform user: A user may assess an object by a 'like-statement' or by writing a contribution such as a review, comment, or the assignment of tags. Besides, users are allowed to build their customized album which contains their favorite cultural objects. Also, playful access to the cultural objects with the use of multimedia is provided: Users can view a series of artworks as a slideshow, they can view an exhibition through a video, they may zoom into an image in very high resolution, or they can take part in a virtual tour of the museum which may include 360° panoramic views and artworks of exhibitions. In addition, users can download content such as high-resolution copies of artworks, exhibition flyers, educative resources, or press material. Besides, direct sales of museum-related items, such as the exhibition catalog, publications, or image templates, are supported.

User Profile and Registration. Some platforms support registration and generation of a user profile so that users can participate on the platform.

Access to the Platform. To get access to the platform at all, general platform information is provided which describes the essential features and tasks of the platform. Moreover, platform users can usually personalize the platform by choosing between different languages, and by changing the font size, the background color or the language into a simpler representation (i.e., use of less and simpler descriptions) via a button.

Access to User Activities. If a platform user is allowed to contribute content on a platform, he or she can either participate without restrictions (i.e., free access) or with some restrictions (i.e., partly free access). For instance, editorial staff checks the user's contribution before publication, or the user has to register before being active on a platform. However, users may have no access and are not allowed to contribute content.

Access to User Reception. Moreover, the public access to the platform content may vary: The platform content can be either completely visible for the general public without constraints (i.e., free access) or partly accessible (i.e., partly free access). Without registration, for example, every user can receive the content. In contrast, some information such as press material is only receivable after registration. Besides in some cases, user activities like a user album or a 'like-statement' on cultural objects are not visible to the public or the users themselves adjust the visibility of their activities.

5 Demonstration and Evaluation

For our preliminary evaluation, we describe two evaluation steps, namely illustrating the taxonomy's applicability as well as evaluating the taxonomy's understandability and completeness in more detail (see also Sect. 3).

Illustrating the Applicability. Applicability is often used as an evaluation criterion for taxonomies and supports investigating whether a taxonomy is applicable in practice which can be carried out, for instance, by classifying objects of the phenomenon of interest [28]. Therefore, two researchers classified two samples of online platforms through the taxonomy: All online platforms that have been used for taxonomy building and five additional art museum websites (i.e., K21 Kunstsammlung Nordrhein-Westfalen, Zentrum für Kunst und Medien Karslruhe, Marta Herford, Schirn Kunsthalle Frankfurt, Kunstmuseum Stuttgart). We thereby explored the distribution of features (i.e., which features are implemented by a platform). The results of the frequency analysis are outlined in Fig. 4 by depicting the percentage of platform types (i.e., museum website, blog, social media, rating platform) that provide a feature.

In doing this, three main observations emerge: Firstly, none of the online platforms provide all of the identified features. Secondly, museums provide access to cultural objects, however, they hardly support the interaction between actors on their websites. They only provide newsletters as push information or allow messages to providers or editors via email. In addition, platform users are not allowed to post contributions such as reviews or comments or mostly cannot assess an object with a 'like-statement'. The discourse on cultural objects is, hence, outsourced to social media sites, blogs of art, and rating platforms. Thirdly, although a broad range of people should be able to get access and participate, only a few platforms support diverse ways of accessibility. Whereas most provide general information or the selection of other languages (e.g., to overcome language barriers), change to 'simple language' or customizing the background color or the font size are only rarely possible, which makes online cultural access problematic for individuals with disabilities. This is surprising, as accessibility is commonly addressed in the local museum policies (e.g., unrestricted access for all).

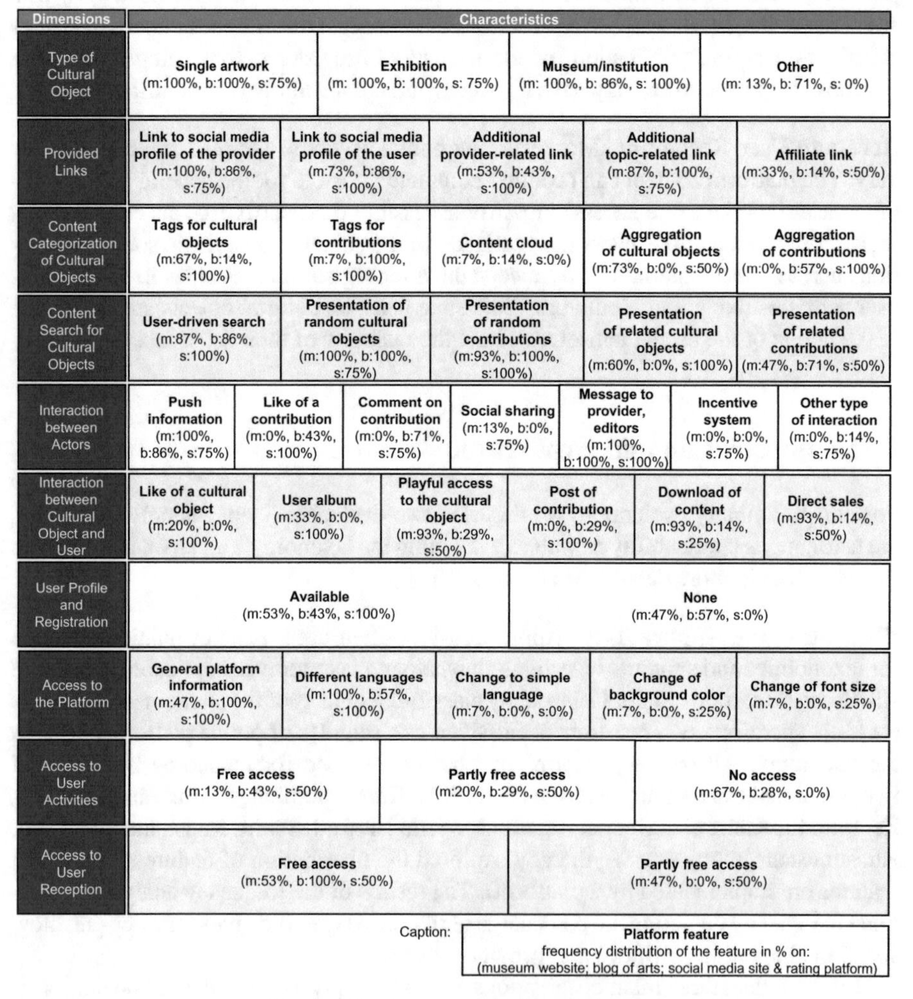

Fig. 4. Distribution of platform features

Evaluating the Understandability and Completeness. To obtain insights in terms of the taxonomy's understandability and completeness for the intended target users and purposes [12, 29], we conducted workshops with three experts. We invited three researchers who were not involved in the taxonomy development process and who have already performed research on online platforms including cultural and educational concerns—i.e., potential target users of the taxonomy (see Sect. 3, Stage 3). As *understandability* is a prerequisite for the correct usage of a taxonomy, a positive answer would be an indication of its usefulness [29]. Therefore, the workshop participants were asked to describe the taxonomy (e.g., what is meant by each element), to assess the taxonomy's understandability and if necessary to make suggestions for improving the taxonomy. The participants stated that most dimensions and characteristics are self-explanatory and only some wording should be adjusted to strengthen the interpretability and understandability of the taxonomy. For example, one participant assessed upper categories (i.e., provision of content, interaction, accessibility) as ambiguous and thus difficult to understand. Another participant suggested to change the term 'findability of content' to 'content search', 'other' to 'additional' for some characteristics of the dimension 'provided links' and 'feedback to editors' to 'message to provider, editors'. Furthermore, the participant recommended changing the order of dimensions. Moreover, the majority of participants we asked to evaluate the *completeness* of the taxonomy, did not see the necessity to add further elements. Only one suggestion included that the characteristic 'accessibility for user with disability' should be split and more differentiated in the next version of the taxonomy. After discussing the results within the author team, we decided to adapt these points and to revise the current version of the taxonomy accordingly.

6 Discussion

Museums play a fundamental role in enabling our society to access, engage with and learn about the cultural heritages but simultaneously face challenges in achieving this mission because of diverse hurdles on an individual but also social and environmental level. Against this backdrop, the booming digitalization [30] provides promising tools such as platforms and social media that can be adapted from museums to develop new strategies for providing cultural participation and education. In attempting to leverage this potential, we sought to explore what are the characteristic features of online platforms providing this participation and education and present a taxonomy of Digital Cultural Participation and Education. Our taxonomy provides an overview of features for such platforms that can be employed to make more informed design decisions in terms of museum platforms as well as lays the ground for future endeavors. We believe that this study is an important step towards how online platforms can improve access to cultural participation and education, which has implications for theory and practice and opens avenues for future research. Next, we discuss four of those avenues.

Enhancing the Possibilities of Interaction on Museum Websites. During the platform analysis, we found that all museums provide access to their cultural objects on their websites, for example, by providing an online collection of multiple artworks with detailed artist information. Furthermore, the majority (93%) allows a playful access to these objects (e.g., users can take part in a virtual tour of the museum or can zoom into an artwork with high resolution). As the use of multimedia and interactive components may lead to enjoyment and informal online learning in the context of museums [10, 16], such a playful access presents potential with participatory and educational relevance. However, museums hardly support their platform users to interact with cultural objects in different ways, users are not allowed to post contributions such as online reviews or comments and mostly cannot assess an object with a 'like-statement' (only 20% of museum websites provides such a feature). Moreover, although establishing social interaction can be seen as a recommended museum website feature [10, 15], we observed that the majority of museum websites only provides newsletter as push information or supports messages to providers/editors and does not allow for interacting with others (e.g., none of them allow liking and commenting contributions). This is in line with [5] who explains that few museums open their websites for users' comments. The discourse on cultural objects and the interaction between users are, hence, outsourced to social media sites, blogs of art, and rating platforms. However, despite the higher level of support for interaction, we observed that such platforms usually arrange the contributions chronologically, placing older contributions far below which might lead to increased search effort for the users. Therefore, as all museums provide access to cultural objects on their websites and thus provide an enormous foundation for consumption and community activities, we would encourage practitioners to pay more attention to these features of interaction, to entirely allow cultural participation and experiences.

Providing Diverse Ways of Accessibility of Cultural Participation. While examining the platforms, we mostly missed different ways of accessibility of cultural participation for a broad range of people (e.g., individuals with visual or cognitive impairments) such as 'change to simple language', 'change of background color' and 'change of font size'. Although such personalization is considered to be an important museum website feature [14], we found that the majority of platforms only implements a feature for selecting different languages. This is surprising, as unrestricted access is commonly addressed in the local museum policies. To advance the challenges of Digital Inclusion [31] and to contribute to the social sustainability of cultural platforms [32], we call for the provision of cultural participation accessible for all individuals.

Investigating Cultural Differences and Integration of Practitioners. Focusing on art museums, we analyzed various online platforms (e.g., museum websites, rating platforms) that provide access to cultural participation. Considering further platforms and research findings, for instance, in the non-German context, platforms of different museum types (e.g., museum of local history or natural history [27]) or platforms of further institutions with cultural and educational missions (e.g., theatre, libraries), may support verifying or extending our results. It might be interesting, for example, to investigate differences in cultural access depending on the region. Moreover, in line with Nickerson's et al. [12] proposal to "query users about their potential use of (a) taxonomy", we plan to conduct a case study with a local museum—i.e., a potential target user of the taxonomy in practice (see Sect. 3, Stage 3). In doing so, we aim to indicate that the taxonomy is useful for its intended purpose, namely, for providing an overview of platform features and for comparing, refining, or developing platforms. In addition, we want to find out to what extent the currently used platform features enable the best possible access to cultural objects as well as the increase of opportunities for cultural participation and education. Case studies "involve intensive research on a phenomenon (a case) within its natural setting (one or more case sites) over a period of time" [33], which, referring to this study, allows exploring how the taxonomy works in a natural environment.

Transferring Existing Knowledge from Cultural Education to Platforms. To promote cultural education through online platforms [34], existing knowledge from education in cultural practices, such as in arts, architecture, or music, may be transferred to the digital space. Doing so, considering best-practices, literature, and theoretical approaches on cultural education can serve as a source of knowledge as it might provide criteria for online platforms and, hence, support in confirming, refining or identifying further platform features. As a valuable source, Marotzki's approach of structural education theory might give insights for the platform design. It undertakes educational processes as transformations of relations to oneself and the world [35] and education itself comprises reflective, problematizing confrontations with (a) oneself, (b) others and things, as well as (c) themes of the world [3]. Referring to the taxonomy, for instance, (a) the building of a user profile is available, which might contribute to statements about the user's identity. Also, (b) sharing opinions and communicating with others is allowed which might influence the user's relationship with others. Moreover, (c) intensively reflecting on cultural objects, forming and changing opinions as well as contextualizing artworks, could change the individuals' relation to the world. These are initial ideas to promote online platforms leveraging cultural education. In this way, one can search for and use a theoretical foundation for deriving/revising features for such online platforms.

In addition, methodical limitations apply to our study. Searching for relevant IS literature, appertaining to museum online platforms, we identified studies that investigated museum websites and platform features. Our literature search is however limited to the selected database, other online databases such as Google Scholar and EBSCO may reveal further data. As another limitation, we primarily collected platform features for providing access to cultural participation and education, thereby did not examine to what extent the features enable the best possible access.

7 Conclusion

Drawing on a literature review and the analysis of museum online platforms we derived and evaluated a taxonomy of Digital Cultural Participation and Education. This taxonomy structures several platform features that provide access to cultural objects, cultural participation as well as education. Overall, the results contribute to research on museum practice in digitization and illustrate a number of museum-specific platform features which are used with varying frequency (see Demonstration). For example, users can build their customized album with their favorite cultural objects, they can take part in a virtual tour of the museum, or they can zoom into an artwork with high resolution. In addition, we found that museums shift the discourse to social media, blogs or rating platforms and, for instance, seldom support diverse ways of accessibility (e.g., change to 'simple language', customizing the background color) to support an unrestricted access for all individuals. These results can be used to derive implications for a new generation of (social inclusive) online platforms that seek to fulfill their mission of cultural and educational participation (e.g., by means of virtual and augmented reality). Moreover, while this study is anchored in the museum context, and therefore, develops knowledge for a specific class of artifacts, it enables further research to understand how a broader class of online platforms need to be adapted for specific contexts. Along with this, it seems fruitful to investigate the applicability of (a subset of) the proposed platform features in further domains.

Ultimately, by shedding light on the importance of accessibility to and participation in cultural information, we hope to boost online access to cultural objects and facilitate cultural participation as well as education—in particular, to face the challenges of the Covid-19 pandemic, leading to the closure of plenty of museum facilities in 2019/20.

Acknowledgements. This research was conducted in the scope of the research project "Rez@Kultur" (01JKD1703), which is funded by the Bundesministerium für Bildung und Forschung (BMBF). We would like to thank them for their support.

References

1. ICOM: ICOM Code of ETHICS for Museums. https://icom.museum/wp-content/uploads/2018/07/ICOM-code-En-web.pdf. Accessed 18 Apr 2020
2. ICOM: Creating a New Museum Definition - The Backbone of ICOM. https://icom.museum/en/resources/standards-guidelines/museum-definition/. Accessed 25 Nov 2020
3. Fuchs, T.: Education and Biography: A Reformulation of Biography Research Oriented on Education Theory [Original: Bildung und Biographie: Eine Reformulierung der bildungstheoretisch orientierten Biographieforschung]. Transcript, Bielefeld (2011)
4. Treptow, R.: Above all, all visitors are equal. Cultural education processes in the museum order [Original: Vor den Dingen sind alle Besucher gleich. Kulturelle Bildungsprozesse in der musealen Ordnung]. Zeitschrift für Pädagogik **51**(6), 797–809 (2005)
5. Lotina, L.: Reviewing museum participation in online channels in Latvia. In: Kristiansen, E. (ed.) Proceedings of the DREAM Conference the Transformative Museum, pp. 188–195. DREAM - Danish Research Center on Education and Advanced Media Materials, Roskilde (2012)
6. Srinivasan, R., Boast, R., Furner, J., Becvar, K.M.: Digital museums and diverse cultural knowledges: moving past the traditional catalog. Inf. Soc. **25**(4), 265–278 (2009)
7. Moon, S.: Effects of COVID-19 on the Entertainment Industry. Int. Digit. Organ. Sci. Res. (IDOSR) J. Exp. Sci. **5**(1), 8–12 (2020)
8. Tim, Y., Pan, S.L., Ouyang, T.: Museum in the age of digital transformation. In: Proceedings of the 22th Pacific Asia Conference on Information Systems, Yokohama, Japan (2018)
9. Baumgärtner, T.: Conceptualizing a mobile app framework for the museum application domain. In: Proceedings of the 27th European Conference on Information Systems (ECIS), Stockholm & Uppsala, Sweden (2019)
10. Lin, A.C.H., Fernandez, W., Gregor, S.: Designing for enjoyment and informal learning: a study in a museum context. In: Proceedings of the Pacific Asia Conference on Information Systems (PACIS), Taipei, Taiwan (2010)

11. Wray, T., Eklund, P., Kautz, K.: Pathways through information landscapes: alternative design criteria for digital art collections. In: Proceedings of the 34th International Conference on Information Systems (ICIS), Milano, Italy (2013)
12. Nickerson, R.C., Varshney, U., Muntermann, J.: A method for taxonomy development and its application in information systems. Eur. J. Inf. Syst. **22**(3), 336–359 (2013). https://doi.org/10.1057/ejis.2012.26
13. Pallud, J., Straub, D.W.: The "love of art" vs. website design: an application of Bourdieu's theory in online environments. In: Proceedings of the 14th Americas Conference on Information Systems (AMCIS), Toronto, Ontario, Canada (2008)
14. García-Madariaga, J., Recuero Virto, N., Blasco López, F.: The Influence of Museums' Websites on Users' Intentions. Esic Market Econ. Bus. J. **48**(2), 369–392 (2017)
15. Lin, A.C.H., Gregor, S.: Designing websites for learning and enjoyment: a study of museum experiences. Int. Rev. Res. Open Distance Learn. **7**(3), 1–22 (2006)
16. Lin, A.C.H., Gregor, S., Huang, J.C.C.: The hedonic experience of enjoyment and its relationship to informal learning: a study of museum websites. In: Proceedings of the 29th International Conference on Information Systems (ICIS), Paris, France (2008)
17. Windhager, F., Federico, P., Mayr, E., Schreder, G., Smuc, M.: A review of information visualization approaches and interfaces to digital cultural heritage collections. In: Aigner, W., Schmiedl, G., Blumenstein, K., Zeppelzauer, M. (eds.) Proceedings of the 9th Forum Media Technology (FMT 2016). St. Pölten University of Applied Sciences, Institute of Creative Media Technologies, St. Pölten (2016)
18. Carugati, A., Hadzilias, E., Demoulin, N.: Setting the framework for developing eGovernment services on cultural heritage. In: Proceedings of the 13th European Conference on Information Systems (ECIS), Regensburg, Germany (2005)
19. Remane, G., Nickerson, R., Hanelt, A., Tesch, J.F., Kolbe, L.M.: A taxonomy of carsharing business models. In: Proceedings of the 37th International Conference on Information Systems (ICIS), Dublin, Ireland (2016)
20. Szopinski, D., Schoormann, T., John, T., Knackstedt, R., Kundisch, D.: Software tools for business model innovation: current state and future challenges. Electron. Markets **30**(3), 469–494 (2019). https://doi.org/10.1007/s12525-018-0326-1
21. Katsma, C., Spil, T.: A taxonomy of digital music services. In: Proceedings of the 16th Americas Conference on Information Systems (AMCIS), Lima, Peru (2010)
22. Kutzner, K., Petzold, K., Knackstedt, R.: Characterising social reading platforms – a taxonomy-based approach to structure the field. In: Proceedings of the 14th International Conference on Wirtschaftsinformatik, Siegen, Germany, pp. 676–690 (2019)
23. Foni, A.E., Papagiannakis, G., Magnenat-Thalmann, N.: A taxonomy of visualization strategies for cultural heritage applications. ACM J. Comput. Cult. Herit. **3**(1), 1–21 (2010)
24. Gregor, S.: The nature of theory in information systems. MIS Q. **30**(3), 611–642 (2006)
25. vom Brocke, J., Simons, A., Niehaves, B., Reimer, K., Plattfaut, R., Cleven, A.: Reconstructing the giant: on the importance of rigour in documenting literature search process. In: Proceedings of the European Conference on Information Systems (ECIS), Verona, Italy (2009)
26. Hu, S., Mou, J.: Impacts of social media usage in cross-cultural social commerce: the roles of cultural intelligence and cultural distance. In: Proceedings of the 19th Wuhan International Conference on E-Business - Cross-Cultural E-Commerce (2020)
27. Institut für Museumsforschung: Statistical Survey of Museums of the Federal Republic of Germany for the Year 2018 [Original: Statistische Gesamterhebung an den Museen der Bundesrepublik Deutschland für das Jahr 2018], Berlin, Germany (2019)
28. Szopinski, D., Schoormann, T., Kundisch, D.: Criteria as a prelude for guiding taxonomy evaluation. In: Proceedings of the 53rd Hawaii International Conference on System Sciences (HICSS) (2020)

29. Szopinski, D., Schoormann, T., Kundisch, D.: Because your taxonomy is worth it: towards a framework for taxonomy evaluation. In: Proceedings of the 27th European Conference on Information Systems (ECIS), Stockholm-Uppsala, Sweden (2019)
30. Kutzner, K., Schoormann, T., Knackstedt, R.: Digital transformation in information systems research: a taxonomy-based approach to structure the field. In: Proceedings of the 26th European Conference on Information Systems (ECIS), Portsmouth, England (2018)
31. Digital Inclusion Team: Digital Inclusion Team [Electronic Version] (2007). http://digitalinclusion.pbwiki.com/. Accessed 24 Nov 2020
32. Schoormann, T., Kutzner, K.: Towards understanding social sustainability: an information systems research-perspective. In: Proceedings of the 41th International Conference on Information Systems (ICIS), Hyderabad, India (2020)
33. Recker, J.: Scientific Research in Information Systems. Springer, Heidelberg (2013). https://doi.org/10.1007/978-3-642-30048-6
34. UNESCO Institute for Statistics: The 2009 UNESCO Framework for Cultural Statistics (FCS), Montreal, Quebec, Canada (2009)
35. Marotzki, W.: Design of a Structural Education Theory: Biography-Theoretical Interpretation of Educational Processes in Highly Complex Societies [Original: Entwurf einer strukturalen Bildungstheorie: biographietheoretische Auslegung von Bildungsprozessen in hochkomplexen Gesellschaften]. Deutscher Studien Verlag, Weinheim (1990)

Challenges of the Digital Transformation – Comparing Nonprofit and Industry Organizations

Kristin Vogelsang[1], Sven Packmohr[2], and Henning Brink[1](✉)

[1] Department of Organization and Information Systems, Osnabrück University, Osnabrück, Germany
{kristin.vogelsang,henning.brink}@uos.de
[2] Department of Data Science and Media Technology (DVMT), Malmö University, Malmö, Sweden
sven.packmohr@mau.se

Abstract. Digital transformation (DT) describes technology-based improvements in business processes, business models, and customer experience. It promises efficiency gains for industrial enterprises. Nonprofit organizations also expect advantages from DT. However, barriers hinder realizing all its possible advantages in both sectors. If decision-makers recognize the potential barriers, they can reflect upon these challenges and take well-coordinated countermeasures. Orienting towards a Straussian grounded theory approach, a framework of barriers is developed with data of two diverse sectors: industry and nonprofit. According to the framework pre-conditions such as profit-orientation and size shape the possibilities to tackle different barriers. In general, the DT process in the industry-sector has been slowed down by barriers. Whereas, nonprofit organizations often take the view that they are not in a DT process at all. This might be due to limited individual and organizational perspectives. Especially, NPOs have to work on their recruitment of skilled volunteers to challenge this view.

Keywords: Barriers · Industry 4.0 · Nonprofit organization · Digital transformation · Qualitative study

1 Introduction

Digital transformation (DT) has massively shaped processes involved in value creation and will continue to do so in the future. This fundamental change has reached almost all areas of life and is by no means uncontroversial in its social effects [1]. It is characterized by the use of new digital technologies to enable significant business improvements [2]. Industry often acts as a role model when it comes to efficiency gains, dealing with realizing other forms of value creation and dealing with the changing nature of work [1]. Especially, advanced manufacturing, which is an important sector in the German economy, is working on its DT and is rather advanced in its journey [3]. DT is also making advances in the social sector. Still, it is lacking behind if looked upon health

F. Ahlemann et al. (Eds.): WI 2021, LNISO 46, pp. 297–312, 2021.
https://doi.org/10.1007/978-3-030-86790-4_21

care or hospitality sectors [3]. However, little information is available about the DT of the nonprofit sector [4]. Nonprofit organizations (NPOs) face increasingly more challenges that are subject to both the principles of the market economy and technology [1]. Competition for support and financial assistance also increases. Therefore, NPOs must think and act more like profit-oriented companies. Digital technologies in NPOs can increase capabilities to build up competitive advantages, such as improved connection to donors to handle requests and the ability to provide more targeted information [5, 6].

Barriers to DT can hinder or stop the successful implementation of DT. Decision-makers in both the manufacturing sector and in NPOs must understand the opportunities and challenges of DT [4, 7]. Only when the nature of the problem is clearly defined can countermeasures be taken to overcome the challenges.

This paper aims to develop a theoretical framework for barriers to DT. It will help to foresee barriers and understand their potential effects. This article compares two sectors that have a vast difference in conditions. The manufacturing industry is used as a benchmark for DT to gain more insights into the relatively under-researched field of DT in NPOs. This scientific work aims to answer the following research questions: What barriers to digital transformation in NPOs and the manufacturing industry exist? What fosters the differences between the two sectors?

This article follows the scientific discussion about the specific challenges of DT [8]. The collected qualitative data provides comprehensive insights into the perception of DT barriers. In this contribution, the nonprofit sector involves the use of digital technologies in an environment that is characterized by social responsibility. The manufacturing industry, on the other hand, embodies the profit-driven actor within the DT. Combining both areas, looking at differences, and enabling mutual inspiration are essential steps towards a more holistic view of DT, which follows Yin's idea of having diverse data [9]. The detailed description of the barriers to DT may act as a basis for future studies on how to overcome them.

The following study is based on the Straussian grounded theory method [10]. Grounded theory permits the generation of theories derived from data to understand the social context [11]. DT influences the social context due to the socio-technical implications of ubiquitous technology use. Therefore, the goal of this study is to develop a theoretical framework that spans and captures this social context. There are five subsequent steps to conduct this research: Literature review and motivation of research questions (1), purposeful sampling (2), data generation (3), coding and side-by-side comparison of results (4), development of a common framework and discussion with literature from the review and further literature (5).

2 Theoretical Foundations

DT empowers innovations that involve the combination of information, computer, communication, and connectivity technologies. The digital possibilities available to companies increasingly alter an enterprises' strategy. Still, DT processes would remain very individualized. In the following, a short overview of actual research on barriers to DT is presented.

A scientific literature search to identify current, reviewed, and academic results regarding barriers to DT was undertaken, focusing English publications in the Scopus database. The search terms from the field of barriers research (barrier OR obstacle OR constraint OR challenge) with terms from the field of DT (digitali* OR "digital transformation") were combined and findings from the subareas of medicine, chemistry, nursing, and other non-topic related fields were excluded. As this research follows a holistic view, "digitali*" was a search term. This term embraces more DT cases than a search for specific technologies. The search was limited to research papers, articles, and conference proceedings and only searched in titles.

In total, 67 articles were identified. The majority was published in 2019. There was no dominating journal or conference. As a second step, the authors went through the titles and abstracts to exclude further articles that were off-topic (4 articles). They dismissed articles that lead too far from the focus of the research, including, for example, country reports, the field of higher education, and digital government (28 in total).

To structure the papers for a better understanding, the authors aligned the articles to different clusters of DT drafted by Morakanyane [12] to give a comprehensive overview of the barriers to DT.

11 publications in the area of business models were found, they range from general industry insights to specific research results in different areas [13–15]. From an epistemological point of view, research has led to research agendas [16], decision support guides [17], and a stepwise model for the implementation of DT [18]. A total of ten articles are devoted to the challenges of transforming operational processes. Some articles deal with obstacles to the introduction of concrete procedures or tools, such as digital supply chain management [19], building information modeling [20], or lean visual planning [21]. Machado et al. [22] and Sjödin [23] present barriers in different maturity stages. A literature review by Kuusisto [24] presents different technology acceptance models and concludes that more profound research on organizational requirements is still needed. Companies have to consider digital change not only at the technological level but also at the socio-technical level [25]. In particular, groups that have little digital know-how, such as elderly employees, need training to be able to adapt to changing requirements [26]. New forms of work, such as digital platforms, will also pose challenges to the legal framework of the employment relationship [27]. One article deals with the challenges of the organizational culture when DT shapes the supplier-buyer relation [28]. In such settings, technical problems, organizational restructuring, and a "not invented here" syndrome may hinder the transformation process.

The cluster infrastructure aggregates nine publications. Here, the articles deal with challenges to the DT of businesses and their structures. The infrastructure does not only include the company's organization but also growth into an inter-organizational network as a result of the increasing vertical integration of the value chain [29]. For this, IT security is an essential factor [30].

One cluster is about recent research topics in the era of DT. Three articles directly address researchers. The findings show a lack of interdisciplinary research [31, 32] and a need to examine organizational frameworks to master the challenges of the DT [32]. A variety of barriers exists when enterprises aim at DT. The DT process alters business processes, organizational structures, and the way people work and communicate. So far, research has only brought up unstructured lists from distinct perspectives, thus showing a clear research gap [33]. A framework that embraces the majority of barriers and sets them into relations is still missing. Furthermore, the existing research concentrates on specific profit-oriented sectors. However, DT is not limited to businesses – it also massively shapes social interaction.

In general, little research exists in the field of NPOs [34] and their DT [4]. The use of modern technologies enhances the value creation and reach of NPOs. Besides, IT gives a competitive advantage by providing quick responses to donor requests and targeted information [5]. NPOs can use IT to improve the efficiency of service delivery and fundraising. Using digital technologies helps to share best practices, enable access to information, raise awareness of community issues, and share information about their activities to gain legitimacy [5]. To facilitate public fundraising, NPOs must take advantage of IT, especially web and social networking technologies, to build and maintain their customer and donor bases. Also, NPOs are under increasing pressure from donors to implement IT to collect and report data for performance evaluation [6].

However, DT's barriers stand in the way of these measures. Some significant obstacles are the lack of a strategic vision, the inability to identify skilled workers, and the increasing complexity of the organizational impact [4]. Innovations are rarely used in NPO to increase financial performance. Decision-makers in NPOs must understand the challenges of DTs [4] and their complexity if they want to handle them successfully [35]. A clear structure of barrier dimensions may help identify the significant obstacles, taking it step-by-step.

3 Method and Research Process

As DT is a complex socio-technical phenomenon, the authors orient towards the Straussian grounded theory approach [10]. To answer the research questions and to not miss out on important concepts during the course of the research, a five-step research approach was conducted.

Recent research about barriers to DT was examined to define the state of the art (step 1, cf. Sect. 2). Due to the lack of a coherent framework, a research gap was deduced. The formulated research gap leads to the research questions of this study.

In step 2, a purposeful sampling method was applied [11]. To come to a carefully selected sample (Table 1) with a clear focus on DT's experience and process, respondents within professional networks were identified. This survey explores the opinions of a representative sample for both sectors. In a first round 30 interviews in industry (related) sectors and 9 interviews in NPOs were conducted. Additional data from 10 industry and 7 NPO participants could be gathered in a second round to proceed the check for the theoretical saturation [36]. In sum, data from 56 interviews was collected.

For the data generation (step 3), a joint interview guideline was used.

(1) Introduction of the interviewee and description of the changes that occurred in the processes of the companies by DT.
(2) A free narration of the current situation of DT in general and DT barriers.
(3) Summary report on three major obstacles to DT.

The interviews had an average length of 37 min and were conducted in German. All the interviews were recorded, transcribed, and translated.

Table 1. The sample

Sector	Area	Case	Role
NPO NPO NPO NPO	Social Health Education Culture & Recreation	NPO_S1–NPO_S7 NPO_H1–NPO_H5 NPO_E1–NPO_E3 NPO_C1	Press Officer, Instructor for national work, Administrative Employee, Pedagogical Management, IT-Management Managing Board, Speaker fundraising, Press Officer, IT Manager Deputy Manager, Managing Director Technical Manager
Ind. Ind. Ind. Ind. Ind.	Automotive Agricultural Engineering Plastics Industry Steel Industry Other Manufacturing	Au1–Au14 AC1–AC9 P1–P5 SI1–SI4 OM1–OM8	Head of R&D, Engineering, Digital Manager Head of Quality Management, Managing Director, IT Management, Operations Management Head of Production, Shift Supervisor, Project Engineer Managing Director, Manager/Head of Production Intelligence Business Development Manager, Deputy Operations Manager

An open coding technique helped to identify specific barrier dimensions and their characteristics in step 4. A team of independent researchers went through the texts and marked sentences, fragments, and passages as codes. In the next step, the axial coding was proceeded. This step results in the identification of the characteristics. For the comparison of the two industries by contrasting the results, the selective coding was applied by taking the codes from the manufacturing industry sample as a basis. A comparative and contrasting approach can lead to mutual learning regarding the perception of barriers. The analytical induction [11] led to a detection of similarities in the codes and allowed to group them into characteristics. To find even more focused dimensions, a third selective coding was applied. These dimensions represent the variables in the grounded theory. In both sectors, the dimensions of barriers are identical but differ in details and preconditions. Relations between the dimensions and their influence on the DT process were developed. Furthermore, variables could be defined that shape these relations (step 5).

4 Presentation of Results

The result of this grounded theory approach is the development of concepts and categories. Due to the different sample sizes, there are no gains by counting the codes or statements. This is why examples of the dimensions' characteristics are given, instead. Further, some key quotations taken from the interviews provide insights. In the following, the dimensions of barriers to DT for the industry and the nonprofit sector are described and defined. Furthermore, the overlapping and differences of the characteristics in the two branches compared are shown.

4.1 Organizational Barriers

One barrier dimension directly affects the organization, for example, when making strategic decisions. Organizational barriers are influenced neither externally nor by single staff members. Furthermore, they embrace the organization as a whole, guided by management. Organizational barriers reflect challenges that arise by the lack of resources and a missing DT vision. "We have no special strategy" (NPO_H4) is a typical statement that indicates the existence of barriers on the organizational level.

The lack of educated staff is a topic that affects both sectors. Industry in particular has a lack of trained specialists who can bring in knowledge at a very high level and thus keep the transformation process going. The focus here is on specific IT knowledge: "Mechanical engineering companies are missing software and IT knowledge" (OM1). Process knowledge is becoming more critical in the industry because DT cannot be successful "if you implement the new technology without questioning your processes," (AC7). While the industry sector moans about missing skills, the NPOs suffer from the severe lack of resources of employees and volunteers: "The social sector often suffers from a shortage of staff" (NPO_S5). The interviewees also attribute this problem to the fact that people who work in social professions rarely have IT training in their education. In the field of voluntary work, many believe that work is limited to services with intense social interaction. The NPOs are asked to show more strongly that administrative support is also sought.

In addition, both sectors do not sense the profits of the DT. In the NPOs, the DT seems to be a kind of black box. Possible benefits cannot be named, so "[...] in the moment the financial resources are only sufficient to maintain our consulting process and finance the ongoing business" (NPO_S3). Thus, those responsible shy away from investing money in the unknown. IT structure when they cannot precisely list the benefits. As a result, there is also a lack of employees able to promote the long-term efficient use and integration of IT: "We have no CDO [Chief Digital Officer]" (NPO_H2). Holding on to traditional roles, principles, or working conditions hinders the DT. This problem occurs in both sectors: "You need the courage to rethink your business model" (Au5). While the resistance of this cultural change is, in industry, based on a kind of inertia, in NPOs, the change resistance is a result of missing IT skills.

4.2 Individual Barriers

Individual barriers are defined as perceptions, assumptions, and feelings about DT and technical innovations. Individual barriers include measures influenced by the individual. In the area of individual barriers, perception in the two sectors continues to diverge. In NPOs, there is a more significant general skepticism towards technical innovations. Here, the employees fear the abuse of data for the social system more than threats concerning their jobs (NPO_E1). The lack of acceptance has two main sources: the structure of the staff with only basic IT skills and the therapeutic as well as social service provided by the NPO, which cannot easily be extended by digital technologies: "What we hardly can get away from is this form of counseling, which we now have" (NPO_H1). The digital goods are supposedly anti-social and therefore do not fit in well with the welfare ideals of the NPO: "If tracking possibilities in the future can be used to determine very accurately individual disease risks, then I fear that this could lead to the undermining of a health insurance system based on solidarity" (NPO_S1).

In the industry, there seems to be less skepticism about new technical innovations in general. However, refusal of certain technologies may occur: "There is a mental hurdle that data stored in the cloud is lost and no longer mine" (OM7). The respondents in the industrial sector also tend to see technology as a personal threat in their area of work: "This implies that we could theoretically check why Colleague A produced more than Colleague B. This is a big problem for our works council" (Au1). The fear is that traceability of performance will lead to increased monitoring of work and more comparability, which will be perceived negatively. Moreover, employees in this sector fear the loss of jobs and the replacement of their services by machines to a greater extent than in the nonprofit sector. However, many respondents believe that in most cases jobs will change rather than be lost: "Automation always means that jobs will change. We try to balance efficiency gains through growth and new products. In the end, these jobs do not disappear, but change" (OM1).

4.3 Technical Barriers

Technical barriers affect the interplay and integration of technical resources. For both groups, the technical barriers show that the use of single technologies is not enough to be successful. Interfaces, as well as seamless integration, are significant issues for both. There is a dependency on other technologies like "mobile data. No matter if this affects the internal infrastructure or the infrastructure outside" (OM5). NPOs also suffer from insufficient network availability, as they often work in remote areas. Moreover, "data security" (OM1, SI3) is mentioned in the industry sample, as companies are worried about hacker attacks (OM2). Hackers could shut down entire factories because the machines are connected via the internet or market relevant information can get into competitors' hands. Especially "security in the meaning of exchanging information with customers and suppliers" (P3) is experienced as a challenge due to the increasing flow of information.

NPO interviewees on the other hand emphasize the technical infrastructure as challenging (NPO_S4). They complain about data quality and interfaces: "So just a big and complex company like ours, where the documentation software has to harmonize with the personnel software and with our basic communication channels. This leads to interface problems that are not trivial" (NPO_S1). In the field of NPOs, there are fewer IT solutions available that fit their needs exactly. NPOs often employ people who are more dependent on help and supporting structures. For them, the digital interface must be as barrier-free as possible. "The reading effort must be as low as possible" (NPO_E3). Those solutions are rare and may trigger the digital divide. Furthermore, the storage of sensitive data challenges the NPOs, by identifying suitable software products. "We are not legally allowed to use this at the moment" (NPO_S6).

Both groups mentioned the current infrastructure and cost of technology as barriers: "Especially, if you have machines that are a bit older, the conversion is not worth it" (AC8). The interviewees from the industry sample report that pilot projects lower the risks. But not every technology introduction can be realized with a pilot project. "For example, I can't just introduce SAP in a single production plant. If I introduce SAP, I must do it completely with one launch" (Au8).

4.4 External Barriers

External barriers are all those that cannot be influenced directly by the company or the individuals in the company. The industrial companies mainly see barriers in the area of missing standards (OM2, OM3, Au5): "We need to agree on standards on how to exchange the information" (Au5). The lack of standards affects interfaces to customers and suppliers, which should support the entire value chain.

Missing laws that guarantee data security and protect data from unauthorized access are of great importance in both sectors [37]: "There are legal problems. Maybe you need the contract processing done by the technologies" (OM2). NPOs often work with sensitive data (for example, in the field of child welfare). The fear of the lack of legal expertise is why the handling and protection of data is an important issue that requires excellent and comprehensive legislation: "You always have to make sure that data protection is adhered to" (NPO_S2). For example cloud-based software solutions have to be carefully reviewed. "We have to look closely at whether the companies are based in the European Union or not" (NPO_H4). NPOs, in contrast to the industry, emphasize almost too many legal constrains. In addition to legal data protection requirements, many NPOs also have to comply with internal data protection guidelines laid down by the parent organization (e.g. church bodies) (NPO_S6). The regulations lead to a higher workload in administration. "In addition to one full-time employee who took care of the people, we needed another full-time employee for the bureaucratic effort" (NPO_E2).

The external barriers of NPOs also tend to show up as a lack of interest or worse as boycott on the part of customers, as many of the services offered cannot be replicated by technical solutions. Often, the problem is due to the customer structure (older people, people in need of protection, children) in which very little customer pull is expected. "It is also again this regional problem. Therefore, these are places where many old people live that you can hardly reach. At least not through the social media or something like that." (NPO_H4) In industry, the customer is often part of the digital value creation chain. Here, external boycott from the customer are rare: "That's the driving force. Less waste, higher customer satisfaction" (AU5). Table 2 gives an overview.

Table 2. Comparison of the characteristics

Dimension	Characteristic	Current topic	NPO	Ind
Organizational	Missing vision	Possible benefits cannot be named	X	X
		Lack of strategy	X	X
		Holding to traditional roles	X	X
	Lack of resources	Absence of employees/volunteers	X	
		Lack of DT budget	X	X
	Lack of IT skills	Lack of IT knowledge	X	
		Lack of deeper IT knowledge		X
		Lack of process knowledge (high level)		X
	Lack of training	No training, the strategic need is unclear	X	
		Lack of training in the enterprise		X
		Missing IT training in education	X	
	Resistance to cultural change	Adhere to established processes	X	X
		Missing knowledge about possibilities	X	
	Lack of new roles	No explicit new roles, e.g., that of a CDO	X	X
Individual	Fear of transparency	Fear of data abuse	X	
		Loss of data control		X
	Lack of technology acceptance	DT regarded as anti-solidary	X	
		Digital products do not fit in the services	X	
		High personal risk aversion		X
	Fear of job loss	In unemployment by computerization		X

(*continued*)

Table 2. (*continued*)

Dimension	Characteristic	Current topic	NPO	Ind
Technical	Technology dependency	Limited mobile data access	X	X
	Current infrastructure	Lack of open interfaces		X
		Cost of technology seems too high compared with the expected value	X	X
		Lack of sector-specific standard programs	X	
	Data Exchange	Data security		X
		Data quality	X	
External	Legal barriers	Too many constraints	X	
		Fear of data theft		X
	Lack of standards	Missing data interfaces		X
	No customer pull	See no need for DT	X	
		Lack of customer technology acceptance	X	

5 Development of the Theoretical Framework and Discussion

The framework aims to contribute to close the research gaps identified in Sect. 2 by 1) structuring the barriers to DT, 2) setting them into relations, and 3) giving first hints on how to overcome the barriers. To support the suggested framework, the findings are linked to related research streams identified in the previous literature review.

The organizational barriers are mostly identical in both areas. The interviewees blame the lack of an IT strategy on a lack of appreciation, combined with a focus on operations. However, the organizational barriers differ slightly: The nonprofit sector suffers from a lack of trained personnel, while the profit-oriented sector emphasizes a lack of specific training on a high IT-knowledge level. Especially, in industrial enterprises there is and has been focus on having connected and transparent supply-chains [29]. SCM concepts are less visible in the NPO sample.

Another dominant problem is the company's willingness to undertake transformation. The lack of transformation readiness is described in its fundamentals in the literature [5, 19, 38]. Although some authors already described the creation of digital services such as consulting [39], the advantages of IT are not yet fully known in both samples. The respondents often claim that their services cannot be digitized. Here, the educational background of the respondents plays an important role. The employees' (IT) experience influences the perception of the DT process.

The absence of an IT strategy [8] is responsible for missing resource allocations [22]. Nevertheless, the creation of a DT vision is not yet a topic among NPOs [4]. This lack exists for NPOs and in the group of industry that works predominantly in the smaller enterprises [40]. A first step towards the introduction of a digital strategy is the development of a social media strategy. Privately funded NPOs are more likely to develop social media strategies. They use social media to recruit donors and to draw attention to their activities [41]. The importance of an IT strategy is recognized in some enterprises, but the problem has not even been solved in the industrial sector [7, 17, 18, 42]. Both industries would benefit if they rise to the challenge and make having a digital strategy a long-term corporate focus [8].

Corresponding roles could promote and accompany the DT holistically [43]. Here, NPOs could learn from profit-oriented companies. There is a link to the role of the education sector, as voluntary work is a critical issue for the interviewees. It may be an issue for industrial countries in particular, but NPOs suffer from both a lack of employees and a massive lack of volunteers [44].

Individual aspects play a crucial role in the effectiveness of NPOs [45], as they often influence the training and professional development of people [25, 46]. Well-trained employees can drive digital change [8, 47], as they have a more positive approach [48]. Older members, a smaller enterprise size, and a low degree of formalization in associations might hamper the DT, but training may help to minimize the imbalance [47]. In the interviews, a less skepticism toward DT was observed when the respondent had an IT-related background. There is a clear need for mutual diffusion between the two sectors. What employees learn in profit-oriented enterprises can probably also find their way into the knowledge of employees in NPOs in the long run. Also, it is down to the NPOs to reconcile the role of digital change with social responsibility. Solutions for the threat of job loss and transparency [27] are rarely mentioned in barriers to DT research so far. However, social sciences show its urgency [1]. There is a lack of social approaches and far-reaching protective provisions [49]. The integration of an agile culture [50] is expected to take away many individual fears. Here, industry can learn from NPOs. Relational job design seems to be a key for establishing a culture of trust [51] through which employee engagement could blossom. If NPOs can attract talented volunteers and employees by providing an agile environment it would help to overcome missing IT skills and become more innovative. In return, this will impact the NPOs' digital capabilities to interact with stakeholders [52].

The results of the interviews show a wide range of fundamental problems at the technical level. Some companies are already making headway in the DT process. Their barriers are concrete and at a very high technical level [53]. However, in other companies, especially NPOs, DT is just beginning. There is a lack of necessary interfaces and knowledge about integration and security possibilities [30]. In this field, there are substantial overlaps to the formulated problem of the missing added value (organizational). The recognition of the DT maturity [54] can be the first hint for future actions that have to be taken in order to foster the DT process, although NPOs do not actively perceive the technical challenge.

The perception of the external barriers differs most. While industry suffers from a lack of laws and an unclear legal structure, NPOs have to cope with rigorous legal requirements. The requirements are based on their clear link to healthcare and welfare, and the topic of uniform legal requirements is discussed in the literature [55]. Nevertheless, there are still uncertainties of ownership rights and the juridical background to be declared. Legal structures shape customer–supplier relations. There exists a customer pull, including new requests for the management to consider [56] and a disaffirmation of digital customer services in the nonprofit sector. Overall, the extent to which external barriers can have an impact appears to be dependent on the enterprises' profit orientation.

Figure 1 shows the theoretical framework of barriers to DT. In both sectors barriers from all dimensions were found. Four dimensions of barriers negatively influence the DT process. The DT process shows the degree of the DT of services and products as well as the DT of processes [54]. The dimensions help to show where the DT barriers occur. The characteristics, described in Sect. 4, express the nature of the barriers. They are useful for the later operationalization of the dimensions to develop a reliable scale for DT barriers.

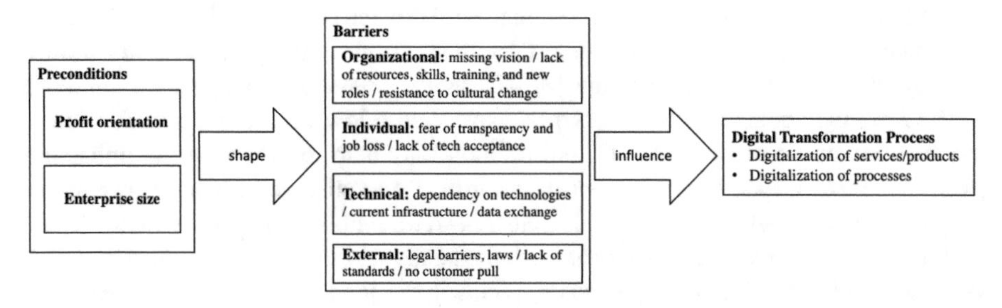

Fig. 1. Theoretical framework

Two dominant preconditions shape the characteristics: profit orientation [57] and enterprise size [58]. These characteristics define the problem-solving paths. There is an apparent practical use. When problems occur in the field of organizational barriers, such as lack of training, the characteristics give a hint as to how the problems can be solved. In smaller enterprises, predominantly in the nonprofit sector, the recruiting of technical experts can be a possible solution. Further, NPOs could recruit younger volunteers to develop social media campaigns. Outsourcing administrative functions like IT management can be a solution for smaller enterprises and NPOs [58]. The NPOs would only have to pay for actual needs and would not have to finance a whole post for IT management.

6 Contributions and Limitations

Our results contribute to the ongoing research discussion on the social effects of DT. This paper shows that barriers, especially at the individual level, are influenced by social implications. In NPOs, services often focus on disadvantaged people. Also, NPOs are dependent on volunteers whose training can be less actively controlled by the company than in profitable companies. NPOs are more likely to encounter the so-called "digital divide" with both their customers and their volunteers [59]. It may foster further digital exclusion for the NPOs if they cannot cope with technological innovations. The framework is useful for researchers, as it gives an idea of how the barriers influence the DT process. For practitioners, the model can be useful to understand which next steps have to be undertaken to minimize the challenges for the DT process. More research with a focus on NPOs, and DT's social responsibility is needed.

The worlds' current situation is changing. The coronavirus forces many organizations into a DT. The organizations had no time to prepare for that change. So we assume a hidden skepticism will remain. There is a fear that some will make steady progress with technology while others are left behind. A social strategy that refers to responsible use is needed, as NPOs take responsibility for societal problems.

Despite the careful approach, this research is not without limitations. A vast number of interviews were conducted with interviewees in the automotive sector compared to the remaining sectors. A wide range of experience in DT characterizes this sector. Further, the sample of NPOs includes organizations with an international reputation. In such global organizations, one would expect a higher level of DT acceptance members from regionally acting groups were often interviewed. Here, a closer look at contrasting impressions from the same organization may be of interest for further study. Furthermore, the IT experience of employers influences the perception of the DT process. These influencing factors may explain why the NPOs often regard themselves as not IN the DT process yet. Qualitative research is useful for developing a theory. At the moment, this theory is not statistically proven. Although, there is a well prepared assessment, a careful operationalization of the dimensions involved is needed.

References

1. Brynjolfsson, E., McAfee, A.: The Second Machine Age: Work, Progress, and Prosperity in a Time of Brilliant Technologies. W. W. Norton & Company, New York (2014)
2. Piccinini, E., Gregory, R.W., Kolbe, L.M.: Changes in the producer-consumer relationship-towards digital transformation. In: Wirtschaftsinformatik, pp. 1634–1648 (2015)
3. Gandhi, P., Khanna, S., Ramaswamy, S.: Which Industries Are the Most Digital (and Why)? (2016). https://hbr.org/2016/04/a-chart-that-shows-which-industries-are-the-most-digital-and-why
4. Nahrkhalaji, S.S., Shafiee, S., Shafiee, M., Hvam, L.: Challenges of digital transformation: the case of the non-profit sector. In: 2018 IEEE International Conference on Industrial Engineering and Engineering Management (IEEM), Bangkok, pp. 1245–1249. IEEE (2018). https://doi.org/10.1109/IEEM.2018.8607762
5. Yoo, S.-C., Drumwright, M.: Nonprofit fundraising with virtual reality. Nonprofit Manag. Leadersh. **29**, 11–27 (2018). https://doi.org/10.1002/nml.21315
6. Zhang, W., Gutierrez, O., Mathieson, K.: Information systems research in the nonprofit context: challenges and opportunities. Commun. Assoc. Inf. Syst. **27**, 1–14 (2010). https://doi.org/10.17705/1CAIS.02701
7. Matt, C., Hess, T., Benlian, A.: Digital transformation strategies. Bus. Inf. Syst. Eng. **57**(5), 339–343 (2015). https://doi.org/10.1007/s12599-015-0401-5
8. Henriette, E., Feki, M., Boughzala, I., et al: Digital transformation challenges. In: Mediterranean Conference on Information Systems (MICS), pp. 1–7 (2016)
9. Yin, R.K.: Case Study Research: Design and Methods. SAGE, Los Angeles (2014)
10. Matavire, R., Brown, I.: Investigating the use of "Grounded Theory" in information systems research. In: Proceedings of the 2008 Annual Research Conference of the South African Institute of Computer Scientists and Information Technologists on IT Research in Developing Countries Riding the Wave of Technology - SAICSIT 2008, pp. 139–147. ACM Press, Wilderness (2008). https://doi.org/10.1145/1456659.1456676

11. Glaser, B.G., Strauss, A.L.: The Discovery of Grounded Theory: Strategies for Qualitative Research. Aldine Publication Company, Chicago (1975)
12. Morakanyane, R., Grace, A., O'Reilly, P.: Conceptualizing digital transformation in business organizations: a systematic review of literature. In: Proceedings of the 30th Bled eConference, pp. 427–443 (2017)
13. Linderoth, H.C.J., Jacobsson, M., Elbanna, A.: Barriers for digital transformation: the role of industry. In: ACIS 2018 - 29th Australasian Conference on Information Systems, pp. 1–11 (2018)
14. Sbarcea, I.R.: Banks digitalization - a challenge for the Romanian banking sector. Stud. Bus. Econ. **14**, 221–230 (2019). https://doi.org/10.2478/sbe-2019-0017
15. Zaharia, S.E., Pietreanu, C.V.: Challenges in airport digital transformation. In: Kazda, A., Smojver, I. (eds.) Transportation Research Procedia, pp. 90–99 (2018). https://doi.org/10.1016/j.trpro.2018.12.016
16. Nambisan, S., Wright, M., Feldman, M.: The digital transformation of innovation and entrepreneurship: progress, challenges and key themes. Res. Policy **48**, 1–9 (2019). https://doi.org/10.1016/j.respol.2019.03.018
17. Heavin, C., Power, D.J.: Challenges for digital transformation–towards a conceptual decision support guide for managers. J. Decis. Syst. **27**, 38–45 (2018). https://doi.org/10.1080/12460125.2018.1468697
18. Parviainen, P., Tihinen, M., Kaariainen, J., Teppola, S.: Tackling the digitalization challenge: how to benefit from digitalization in practice. IJISPM-Int. J. Inf. Syst. Proj. Manag. **5**, 63–77 (2017). https://doi.org/10.12821/ijispm050104
19. Agrawal, P., Narain, R., Ullah, I.: Analysis of barriers in implementation of digital transformation of supply chain using interpretive structural modelling approach. J. Model. Manag. (2019). https://doi.org/10.1108/JM2-03-2019-0066
20. Koseoglu, O., Keskin, B., Ozorhon, B.: Challenges and enablers in BIM-enabled digital transformation in mega projects: the Istanbul new airport project case study. Buildings **9**, 1–24 (2019). https://doi.org/10.3390/buildings9050115
21. Stenholm, D., Bergsjö, D., Catic, A.: Digitalization challenges for lean visual planning in distributed product development teams. In: Bojcetic, N., Marjanovic, D., Pavkovic, N., Storga, M., Skec, S. (eds.) Proceedings of International Design Conference, DESIGN, pp. 1595–1604 (2016)
22. Machado, C.G., Winroth, M., Carlsson, D., Almström, P., Centerholt, V., Hallin, M.: Industry 4.0 readiness in manufacturing companies: challenges and enablers towards increased digitalization. In: Butala, P., Govekar, E., Vrabič, R. (eds.) Procedia CIRP, pp. 1113–1118 (2019). https://doi.org/10.1016/j.procir.2019.03.262
23. Sjödin, D.R., Parida, V., Leksell, M., Petrovic, A.: Smart factory implementation and process innovation: a preliminary maturity model for leveraging digitalization in manufacturing moving to smart factories presents specific challenges that can be addressed through a structured approach focused on people, processes, and technologies. Res. Technol. Manag. **61**, 22–31 (2018). https://doi.org/10.1080/08956308.2018.1471277
24. Kuusisto, M.: Barriers and facilitators of digitalization in organizations. In: Budimac, Z. (ed.) CEUR Workshop Proceedings (2017)
25. Richter, A., Vodanovich, S., Steinhüser, M., Hannola, L.: IT on the shop floor - challenges of the digitalization of manufacturing companies. In: 30th Bled eConference: Digital Transformation - From Connecting Things to Transforming our Lives, BLED 2017, pp. 483–500 (2017). https://doi.org/10.18690/978-961-286-043-1.34

26. Hildebrandt, J., Kluge, J., Ziefle, M.: Work in progress: barriers and concerns of elderly workers towards the digital transformation of work. In: Zhou, J., Salvendy, G. (eds.) Human Aspects of IT for the Aged Population. Design for the Elderly and Technology Acceptance. LNCS, vol. 11592, pp. 158–169. Springer, Cham (2019). https://doi.org/10.1007/978-3-030-22012-9_12
27. Gramano, E.: Digitalisation and work: challenges from the platform-economy. Contemp. Soc. Sci. **15**, 476–488 (2019). https://doi.org/10.1080/21582041.2019.1572919
28. Frick, J.E., Fremont, V.H.J., Åge, L.-J., Osarenkhoe, A.: Digitalization efforts in liminal space – inter-organizational challenges. J. Bus. Ind. Mark. **35**(1), 150–158 (2019). https://doi.org/10.1108/JBIM-12-2018-0392
29. Baraldi, E., Nadin, G.: The challenges in digitalising business relationships. The construction of an IT infrastructure for a textile-related business network. Technovation. 26, 1111–1126 (2006). https://doi.org/10.1016/j.technovation.2005.09.016
30. Mendhurwar, S., Mishra, R.: Integration of social and IoT technologies: architectural framework for digital transformation and cyber security challenges. Enterp. Inf. Syst. **15**(4), 565–584 (2019). https://doi.org/10.1080/17517575.2019.1600041
31. Rana, R., et al.: On the role of cross-disciplinary research and SSE in addressing the challenges of the digitalization of society. In: Babu, M.S.P., Wenzheng, L. (eds.) Proceedings of the IEEE International Conference on Software Engineering and Service Sciences, ICSESS, pp. 1106–1109 (2015). https://doi.org/10.1109/ICSESS.2015.7339245
32. Legner, C., et al.: Digitalization: opportunity and challenge for the business and information systems engineering community. Bus. Inf. Syst. Eng. **59**, 301–308 (2017). https://doi.org/10.1007/s12599-017-0484-2
33. Majchrzak, A., Markus, M.L., Wareham, J.: Designing for digital transformation: lessons for information systems research from the study of ICT and societal challenges. MIS Q. **40**, 267–277 (2016)
34. Huang, H., Umapathy, K.: A preliminary study of information technologies usage in non-profit organizations. In: Twentieth Americas Conference on Information Systems, pp. 1–13 (2015)
35. Hueske, A.-K., Guenther, E.: What hampers innovation? External stakeholders, the organization, groups and individuals: a systematic review of empirical barrier research. Manag. Rev. Q. **65**(2), 113–148 (2015). https://doi.org/10.1007/s11301-014-0109-5
36. Glaser, B.G.: Theoretical Sensitivity: Advances in the Methodology of Grounded Theory. Sociology Press, Mill Valley (1978)
37. Benlian, A., Hilkert, D., Hess, T.: How open is this platform? The meaning and measurement of platform openness from the complementors' perspective. J. Inf. Technol. **30**, 209–228 (2015). https://doi.org/10.1057/jit.2015.6
38. Zhou, H., Ye, S.: Fundraising in the digital era: legitimacy, social network, and political ties matter in China. Voluntas **32**(2), 498–511 (2021). https://doi.org/10.1007/s11266-019-00112-9
39. Filsinger, M., Freitag, M.: Internet use and volunteering: relationships and differences across age and applications. Voluntas **30**(1), 87–97 (2018). https://doi.org/10.1007/s11266-018-0045-4
40. Bollweg, L., Lackes, R., Siepermann, M., Weber, P.: Drivers and barriers of the digitalization of local owner operated retail outlets. J. Small Bus. Entrepreneurship **32**(2), 173–201 (2019). https://doi.org/10.1080/08276331.2019.1616256
41. Guo, C., Saxton, G.D.: Speaking and being heard: how nonprofit advocacy organizations gain attention on social media. Nonprofit Volunt. Sect. Q. **47**, 5–26 (2018). https://doi.org/10.1177/0899764017713724

42. Vogelsang, K., Liere-Netheler, K., Packmohr, S.: Analysis of technology success in times of digital transformation. Presented at the Symposium on Competence-Based Strategic Management SKM Symposium, Berlin (2017)
43. Earley, S.: The evolving role of the CDO. IT Prof. **19**, 64–69 (2017). https://doi.org/10.1109/MITP.2017.4
44. Sundeen, R.A., Raskoff, S.A., Garcia, M.C.: Differences in perceived barriers to volunteering to formal organizations: lack of time versus lack of interest. Nonprofit Manag. Leadersh. **17**, 279–300 (2007). https://doi.org/10.1002/nml.150
45. Mitchell, G.E.: The attributes of effective NGOs and the leadership values associated with a reputation for organizational effectiveness. Nonprofit Manag. Leadersh. **26**, 39–57 (2015). https://doi.org/10.1002/nml.21143
46. Vogelsang, K., Liere-Netheler, K., Packmohr, S., Hoppe, U.: Barriers to digital transformation in manufacturing: development of a research agenda. In: Proceedings of the 52nd Hawaii International Conference on System Sciences, pp. 4937–4946 (2019)
47. Manetti, G., Bellucci, M., Como, E., Bagnoli, L.: Investing in volunteering: measuring social returns of volunteer recruitment, training and management. Voluntas **26**(5), 2104–2129 (2014). https://doi.org/10.1007/s11266-014-9497-3
48. Ngwenyama, O., Nielsen, P.A.: Using organizational influence processes to overcome IS implementation barriers: lessons from a longitudinal case study of SPI implementation. Eur. J. Inform. Syst. **23**, 205–222 (2014). https://doi.org/10.1057/ejis.2012.56
49. Frey, C.B., Osborne, M.A.: The future of employment: how susceptible are jobs to computerization? Technol. Forecast. Soc. Change **114**, 254–280 (2017). https://doi.org/10.1016/j.techfore.2016.08.019
50. Merschbrock, C., Munkvold, B.E.: Effective digital collaboration in the construction industry – a case study of BIM deployment in a hospital construction project. Comput. Ind. **73**, 1–7 (2015). https://doi.org/10.1016/j.compind.2015.07.003
51. Atouba, Y.C., Shumate, M.D.: Meeting the challenge of effectiveness in nonprofit partnerships: examining the roles of partner selection, trust, and communication. Voluntas **31**(2), 301–315 (2019). https://doi.org/10.1007/s11266-019-00143-2
52. Brink, H., Packmohr, S., Vogelsang, K.: Fields of action to advance the digital transformation of NPOs – development of a framework. In: Buchmann, R.A., Polini, A., Johansson, B., Karagiannis, D. (eds.) Perspectives in Business Informatics Research. LNBIP, vol. 398, pp. 82–97. Springer, Cham (2020). https://doi.org/10.1007/978-3-030-61140-8_6
53. Dremel, C.: Barriers to the adoption of big data analytics in the automotive sector. In: Proceedings of the 23rd American Conference on Information Systems (AMCIS), Boston, pp. 1–10 (2017)
54. Klötzer, C., Pflaum, A.: Toward the development of a maturity model for digitalization within the manufacturing industry's supply chain. In: Proceedings of the 50th Hawaii International Conference on System Sciences, pp. 4210–4219 (2017). https://doi.org/10.24251/HICSS.2017.509
55. Calista, D.J., Melitski, J.: Digitized government among countries worldwide from 2003 to 2010: performance discrepancies explained by comparing frameworks. Int. J. Public Adm. **36**, 222–234 (2013). https://doi.org/10.1080/01900692.2012.721246
56. Akram, M.S.: Drivers and barriers to online shopping in a newly digitalized society. TEM J. **7**, 118–127 (2018). https://doi.org/10.18421/TEM71-14
57. Young, D.R.: Complementary, supplementary, or adversarial? Nonprofit-government relations. In: Nonprofits and Government: Collaboration and Conflict, pp. 37–80 (2006)
58. Pope, J.A., Saigal, A., Key, K.A.: Do small nonprofit organizations outsource? A first look. Voluntas **26**(2), 553–573 (2014). https://doi.org/10.1007/s11266-014-9447-0
59. Lameijer, C., Mueller, B., Hage, E.: Towards rethinking the digital divide – recognizing shades of grey in older adults' digital inclusion. In: ICIS 2017 Proceedings (2017)

Understanding Pandemic Dashboard Development: A Multi-level Analysis of Success Factors

Ludger Pöhler(✉), Kevin Kus, and Frank Teuteberg

Accounting and Information Systems, Osnabrueck University, Osnabrueck, Germany
{ludger.poehler,kevin.kus,frank.teuteberg}@uni-osnabrueck.de

Abstract. Although dashboards are already widely used in humanitarian crises, various corporate reports and other fields, the specific success factors for the respective application areas often remain unclear. Especially in the current severe corona pandemic, dashboards are crucial to get an overview of the dynamic infection development. This motivated us to investigate how to successfully design dashboards capable of mitigating crises such as serious pandemics. By means of a systematic literature analysis, we identified scientific success factors of crisis and in specific of pandemic dashboards. Further, we assessed currently used corona dashboards and compared them with our success factors of the literature. In this way, we could discover whether corona dashboards are based on previous crisis dashboards and which specific success factors of current corona dashboards can be worked out for future pandemic dashboard development.

Keywords: Dashboard · Success factors · Pandemic · Corona · COVID-19

1 Introduction

The COVID-19 pandemic is affecting the whole world. To limit the spread and therefore the negative effects of the virus, effective actions need to be undertaken regionally, nationally and internationally. Next to governmental restrictions for the population like lockdowns or the mandatory wearing of face masks, effective information systems about specific outbreaks in local and national regions can help to raise the common knowledge about infection numbers [1]. One outgrowth of these information systems can be found in dashboards. They can be defined as visual presentation forms built upon purposeful chosen data [2]. Apart from pandemics, dashboards are also used in other forms of humanitarian crises like terrorism [3], wars [4] or environmental catastrophes [5, 6]. With occasionally more than one billion clicks per day [7], the COVID-19 dashboard of Johns Hopkins University (JHU) is one of the most widely recognized at present [8]. Beyond the possible advantages like being able to track the outbreak of diseases in order to answer with purposeful measurements, there are challenges to be overcome and success factors to be considered when developing such a dashboard.

Current research analyzing dashboards in general and dashboards in pandemic situations in specific focus either on theoretical information from literature or on practical

F. Ahlemann et al. (Eds.): WI 2021, LNISO 46, pp. 313–330, 2021.
https://doi.org/10.1007/978-3-030-86790-4_22

dashboards [9]. Our study, by contrast, analyzes the success factors in the development of pandemic dashboards by considering both publications on previous pandemics and epidemics (pre-corona dashboards) as well as established, real dashboards used for the COVID-19 pandemic (corona dashboards). In addition, aspects from general crisis dashboards are also included in the literature research, which can be transferred to pandemic dashboards. However, these rather are not specific aspects on the detail level, but mainly design and visualization aspects.

This enables us to compare dashboard-literature from the past with the real-world dashboards of the corona crisis by identifying similarities and differences within these two sources. On this base, we derive implications for effective prospective pandemic dashboard development. With our work, we want to answer the following research questions (RQ):

RQ1: *Which success factors can be identified in the development of dashboards of past pandemics, epidemics and other general crises situations from literature?*
RQ2: *What are the specific success factors of dashboards for the corona pandemic?*

To achieve that, we structure the article as following: In Sect. 2, we present related work dealing with dashboards in the corona crisis. Subsequently, we present the research approach (Sect. 3). In Sect. 4, we analyze the dashboards based on the comparison with identified success factors. Finally, in Sect. 5, we critically discuss our results by referring to the research questions and literature. Additionally, we highlight limitations of our work as well as starting points for future research and practical dashboard development.

2 Related Work

Since the outbreak of the corona virus, the general population or other specific groups have been informed about the development of the pandemic via dashboards. Numerous scientific studies have already been carried out with different foci to conceptualize, create and evaluate such dashboards of the corona crisis.

For example, Grange et al. [10], Bae et al. [11], Verhagen et al. [12] and Reeves et al. [13] describe the data collection and conceptualization of dashboards in hospitals and clinics in different countries, so that these information are specific and less relevant for the general population. Some guidance is provided on how corona dashboards should be designed at national level. Thus, Berry et al. limited their contribution to the conceptual design of a dashboard for Canada [14]. In this context, a publicly accessible, manually updated dashboard is described. Thereby, their focus is on data quality and resources rather than on design. In addition to the numbers of infected, deceased, recovered and tested persons, also specific characteristics such as location, date and travel history are listed for each case. Marivate et al. focus on similar aspects. Their dashboard concept for South Africa allows to capture overall national and more detailed department-specific data at a glance [15]. Other publications rather prioritize the data management behind dashboards and discuss both the necessary multi-resource management [16] and the geoinformatics systems used for location determination [17] in detail. Since it has been discovered that there are extreme deficiencies in the data collection of various known corona dashboards, including the one of World Health Organization (WHO), Ashofteh et al. present an approach for the conceptualization of a dashboard with high data quality [18].

There are also different aspects examined in the publications on dashboards that reflect the global course of the pandemic. For instance, Zavarrone et al. focus on the presentation of socio-economic aspects by using text mining and sentiment analysis to create an overview of social media content in order to identify socially relevant data [19]. Everts et al. describe that corona dashboards also create a feeling of fear in the general population [20]. Approaches and descriptions of how to implement globally accessible dashboards for the entire population are also described. Thus, the basis of the world's most frequently accessed corona dashboard created by the Johns Hopkins University is presented in a short publication by Dong et al. [21]. The basic contents and the structure of the dashboard as well as possible further developments are described. Additional features such as breaking down the information to the local level and comparing pandemic developments in different countries are also offered (c.f. [1, 22]). Tewtia et al. outline how the underlying data can be used to forecast case numbers, which are then compressed and presented in a dashboard [23]. Raghavan et al. are also dedicated to forecasting and its visualization with a focus on Indian population [24].

To the best of our knowledge, in the dynamic development, there is only one publication that compares different worldwide corona dashboards [7]. However, the focus here is strongly on dashboards that use localization technologies such as Global Positioning System (GPS) as well as Artificial Intelligence (AI). Moreover, their investigations are largely limited to Indian dashboards, and the underlying methods are not transparently specified. Thus, a methodological approach should be used to examine the extent to which dashboards in the corona crisis are oriented towards the success factors of dashboards of previous epidemics and pandemics (pre-corona dashboards). In addition, it should be highlighted which further elements in the corona crisis can be identified as success factors for humanitarian crisis dashboards in general and pandemic dashboards in particular.

3 Research Approach

In order to fill the research gap and answer our above questions, we adopted a three-step approach. **Step 1:** By means of a comprehensive literature review according to vom Brocke et al. [25], we systematically identified the success factors of pre-corona dashboards. In the following, we categorized and iteratively determined these by applying a qualitative content analysis according to Mayring [26]. **Step 2:** Through an extensive Google search, we selected an adequately broad sample of current corona dashboards including national and global dashboards as well as dashboards of authorities and public media. **Step 3:** In this step, we defined the extent to which the previously identified success factors are reflected in the corona dashboards. For this purpose, we compared and evaluated the dashboards with the success factors using a matrix. Thus, through the application of this case study, the theoretical findings from the literature could be compared with the characteristics of real existing dashboards. This allowed us to determine to what extent the success factors are still valid or whether additional elements can be mapped in the corona dashboards. Figure 1 summarizes this procedure.

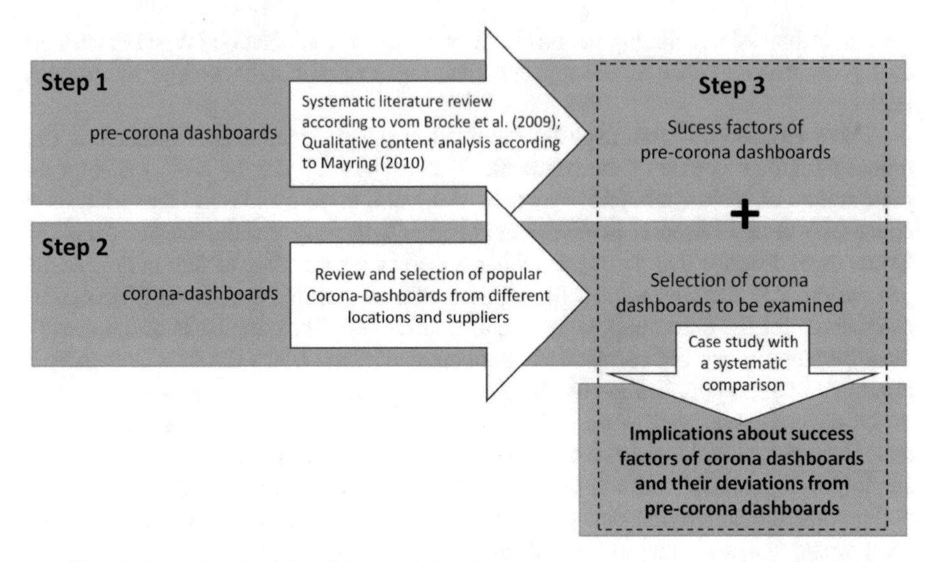

Fig. 1. Procedure for identifying sustainable success factors for pandemic dashboards

The success factors of pre-corona dashboards are mainly a consequence of the requirements and design principles of previous epidemics and pandemics. In order to identify the relevant literature for creating dashboards in such humanitarian crisis situations, a complete literature search was conducted according to vom Brocke et al. [25]. He recommends four basic phases in order to obtain the correct and relevant publications on a specific topic. In the first phase, the depth of the literature analysis should be determined by defining the estimated literature volume. Here, vom Brocke et al. follow the taxonomy proposed by Cooper and define six characteristics with two to four categories for each characteristic [27].

The basic **goal** of the literature analysis was to achieve integration, allowing literature to be compared, summarized and key principles of the dashboard development for epidemics and pandemics to be identified. The **focus** was to gather previous research outcomes on dashboard applications. The subsequent **organization** and classification primarily took place on a conceptual basis with reference to the historical development of some principles. When presenting the identified contributions, we take a neutral and rational **perspective**. Further, the results should be relevant for a broad **audience**, especially for dashboard developers and their clients (practitioners/politicians) as well as for the core target group, the general public. But also, general scholars, who want to make information available to a broad mass in a compressed form, can use the results for future developments. Given the technical progress, we only included sources of the past 15 years and thus chose a representative approach for the **coverage** of the existing literature. Figure 2 summarizes our procedure with regard to Cooper's taxonomy.

In the second phase of step 1 we combined the terms "pandemic", "epidemic", "crisis" or "emergency" with the term "dashboard" in English and German language as well as in singular and plural (search string: (pandemic* OR epidemic* OR cris* OR emergenc*) AND dashboard*). With this search string the literature databases of Scopus,

	Characteristic	Categories			
1	goal	integration	criticism	central issues	
2	focus	research outcomes	research methods	theories	applications
3	organization	historical	conceptual	methodological	
4	perspective	neutral representation	espousal of position		
5	audience	specialized scholars	general scholars	practitioners/ politicians	general public
6	coverage	exhaustive	exhaustive and selective	representative	central/pivotal

Fig. 2. Classification of the literature search according to Cooper [27]

EbscoHost and PubMed were examined in the third phase. We only considered contributions that relate to dashboard structure, design, conception and content in pandemics, epidemics and non-specific crises and address the general population as relevant for our purposes. General visualization and interaction principles in terms of Human-computer interaction (HCI) were not explicitly included. Firstly, including HCI in general would have been too unspecific and secondly, HCI is implicitly covered by the principles of the specific dashboards.

In the fourth phase, we filtered out duplicates (166 excluded) from the search results (891 articles in total). We then selected relevant articles first by their titles (607 excluded) and subsequently by reading the abstracts (61 excluded) and full texts (40 excluded). This resulted in 17 relevant articles. In addition, we carried out an extensive forward (additional three articles) and backward (additional five articles) search. In total, we considered 25 articles relevant for our study (cf. Fig. 3).

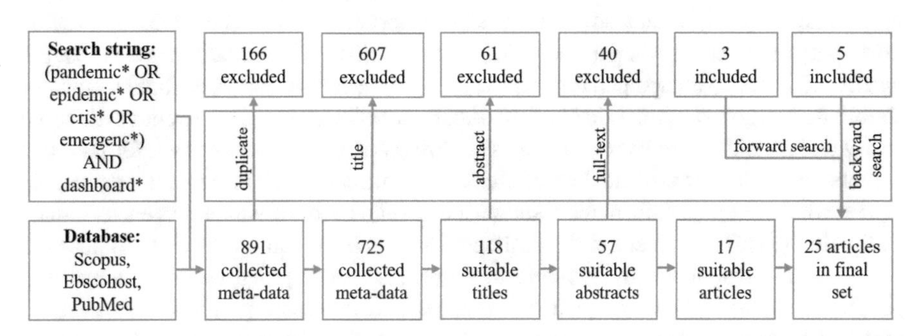

Fig. 3. Literature research for pre-corona dashboards (according to Dyba and Dingsoyr [28])

On the basis of these four phases of literature search, we were able to determine the success factors by using a qualitative content analysis according to Mayring [26]. First of all, it was necessary to form categories to classify the success factors. The inductive category development was used for this purpose. When coding the relevant literature sources, a total of 3 main categories (visualization, functionalities, content) with 3 to 11 success factors each could be identified. A comprehensive Google search for relevant dashboards was then carried out in step 2 of our procedure. We paid particular attention to selecting both global and national dashboards from public institutions as well as private media. In step 3, we applied a case study to investigate the extent to which the previously identified success factors were based on the corona dashboards by using a comparison matrix. We then could investigate whether certain success factors are more sustainable and important than others or whether additional success factors of corona dashboards become evident.

4 Results

4.1 Literature Analysis

Based on the qualitative content analysis according to Mayring [26], we divided the success factors into three categories, which namely are (1) *visualization*, (2) *functionality* and (3) *content*. With regard to our literature analysis, we could find more specific success factors within each category.

While content related success factors aim for the task of choosing the right data, visual success factors deal with the challenge of displaying the right data adequately [29]. Additionally, we analyzed factors regarding functionalities, which deal with an interactive and more comfortable user experience with respect to dashboards. In the following, we explain especially those factors within these categories, which were coded most frequently in our content analysis and are described as important in literature. These success factors are displayed in **bold** in Table 1.

Content: Dashboards must include reliable data [32, 38, 44, 48]. Reliability needs to be proven either manually or by means of new automated techniques such as supervised learning [44]. Another way of validating a certain quality standard of the data included, is to use official sources like governmental databases [48]. According to the literature, the up-to-dateness of the data also constitutes an important factor. It is essential to provide up-to-date information when a user loads the screen [31]. This equally requires that the dashboard needs to be updated constantly, i.e. as soon as new data is available. Updates should be integrated automatically [38]. Apart from that, the data content needs to be easily understandable to its respective users. Provision of only necessary information is essential to avoid overload and loss of important information. To make it understandable to the whole society, information should be displayed on a single screen to reduce navigation [31]. The content of the dashboard should be as self-explanatory as possible [2]. Reducing distraction by avoiding new processes or required learning is essential [2, 39]. In order to gain complete information and minimize probabilities of errors, multiple data sources should be used. Data sources can be situated in local places and in different social networks [30, 37]. Despite the fact that many articles do not explicitly deal with (infectious) diseases, several articles mention specific ratios explaining the current level of disease distribution. These indicators are *number of deaths* [51] and *number of cases* [48, 51, 52], the *mortality rate* [52], *incidence rate* [51, 52], *test numbers* [52] as well as *prevalence rate* [38, 52] or the *distribution of disease subtypes* [38]. Regarding information in visualizations, especially timelines showing cases and rates over time axes are illustrated to show current developments.

Table 1. Success factors based on pre-corona dashboards

	Success factors	Short description	Reference
Visualization	Mixed usage	Combination of visualizations and textual elements	[30]
	Modest visual elements	Avoidance of non-data visual elements like graphics; map reduction to borders	[9, 31]
	Maps	Information about geographical spread; Awareness of regional trends	[30–36]
	Ease and familiarity	Simple visualization interface; Familiar visualizations like graphs; Visual orientation to interfaces of popular institutions	[9, 31, 35, 37–39]
	Colors usage	Moderate use of colors; Black or gray interface	[2, 31]
	Number of visual elements	Avoidance of cognitive overload; Limited number of visual elements	[31, 40, 41]
Functionality	Data sharing option	Knowledge reuse through data sharing; Teamwork function; Messaging function	[37, 42, 43]
	Interactivity	Flexible data filtering; Customization; Drill down functions; Visual interaction; Comments	[2, 31, 34, 37–39, 42, 44–49]

(*continued*)

Table 1. (*continued*)

	Success factors	Short description	Reference
	User-friendliness	Ease of use; Workload reduction; Simple interface; Intuitive navigation	[9, 31, 42, 50]
Content	Data source knowledge	Source identification of data used	[31]
	Reliability	Reliability of used data; Elimination of duplicates and further errors; Usage of official governmental sources	[32, 38, 48]
	High-level-aggregation	Data condensing; Data integration	[31, 48]
	Easy knowledge transfer	Easily understandable information; Only provision of necessary information to avoid cognitive overload	[30, 34, 47]
	Several data sources	Usage of several data sources like social networks, local databases and remote networks	[30, 32, 34]
	(Automated) data currency	Up-to-date information; Illustration of real time activities of infectious diseases; Automated update integration	[31, 32, 36, 38, 39, 43]

(*continued*)

Table 1. (*continued*)

	Success factors	Short description	Reference
	Automated warnings	Alerts when exceeding thresholds; Furthermore, bright colors or general highlighting in case of increasing trends	[2, 43, 46]
	Focus on central information	Provision of important information to avoid overload and consequently loss of important information. User's effort should be reduced both in cognitive and physical way	[31, 41, 47]
	Mainstream usability	Information provision on single screen; Support of correct data interpretation; Self-explaining dashboard; Minimized distraction	[2, 31, 37, 39]
	Key figures	Indicators like mortality rate or prevalence rate; Usage of timelines showing key figures over time periods for development illustration	[2, 34, 35, 51, 52]

Functionalities: Several articles highlight the possibility of flexible data filtering in order to let the user gain more specific data. Exemplarily, users should be able to select specific category groups, data for different time periods or filter data by the type of disease [38]. These filters should be adaptable to the personal needs of the users [2]. Besides, the possibility to select specific geographical characteristics is emphasized [31]. In general, the dashboard needs to be customizable [31]. More concretely, users should be able to choose the style of visual presentation like bar chart, graphs or tables. In order to design an effective dashboard, all relevant information must be made available to all users on one page only, which requires interactive tools such as filters due to the fact that different user groups seek for different information sets. Moreover, navigating through hyperlinks, buttons or going back- and forwards are further ways to interact with the dashboard [42]. Beyond interactivity, user-friendliness was mentioned. Regarding this, the dashboard should reduce the workload for its users [31]. This includes having a simple visualization interface and intuitive, easy navigation methods [32]. Through intuitive use, a cognitive overload is avoided [50]. These aspects are strongly related to a higher ease of use. User-friendliness can also refer to an easy access for all potential users, which includes not only providing an adequate interface for desktop users, but also for mobile devices [30]. Consequently, users can focus on and better understand the content itself without being bound to a specific device.

Visualizations: A map is needed to raise awareness of the general spread of the diseases [31]. GIS-interfaces are considered to be especially important [33]. Maps can display a more detailed view, as users can observe trends within regions [38]. Next to maps in particular, the applied visualization elements should be familiar to users. Those familiar elements like graphs allow rapid customizing [37]. Despite their necessity and benefits, graphical elements should not be used too extensively, but rather rely on the paradigm of minimalism or at least on moderate use. Users should not be overwhelmed by unnecessary and distracting information when provided with graphical elements [46]. This implies both to use only a limited number of graphical elements and to illustrate them in a restrained way. Building on this, colors should be used conservatively, which means working with black or gray for most of the interface [31]. Only specific and important information, like urgent alerts, can be marked in bright colors like red to highlight their relevance [31].

4.2 Dashboard Analysis

In order to compare the above-mentioned success criteria with those of COVID-19 dashboards, an adequate selection of dashboards had to be made first. It was important for us to obtain an overview of the existing dashboards that was as comprehensive as possible. For this purpose, we selected dashboards from general health authorities of governmental organizations (Germany/Robert-Koch-Institute (RKI) [53], USA/Centers for Disease Control and Prevention (CDC) [54], UK [55], India [56], Pakistan [57]), from further public institutions (JHU [7], WHO [58]) as well as dashboards of frequently accessed online newspapers or search engines (New York Times (NYT) [59], Zeit [60], Google [61]). Given that the selected dashboards stem from diverse institutions and mostly focus on different geographical regions, we achieved a higher level of independence between the dashboards. Regarding the granularity level, most of them show more detailed data for their specific geographical areas and thus use different sets of databases. As the dashboard designs differ, we also ensured uniqueness. Figure 4 exemplarily shows the popular JHU dashboard.

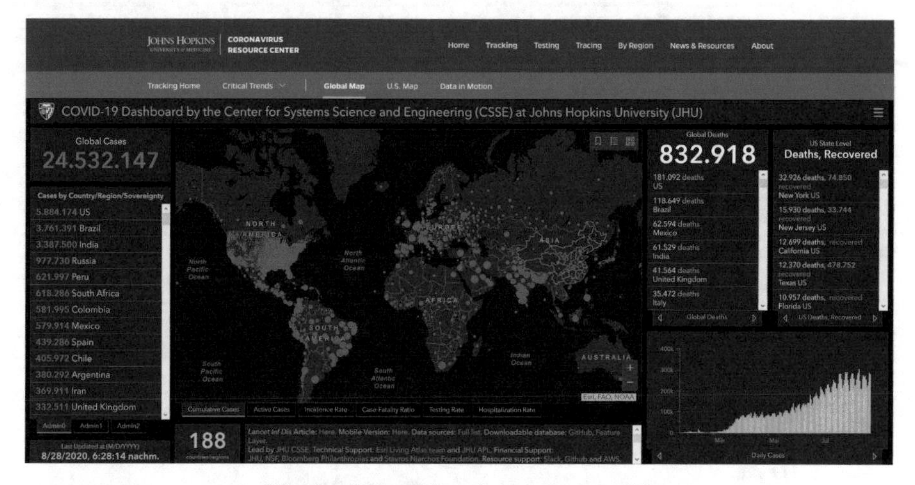

Fig. 4. JHU dashboard central screen [7]

The analyzed dashboards serve as a source of information for a large number of citizens during the pandemic. We have included both dashboards that present the pandemic globally and dashboards that focus on a national overview. For the national dashboards, we concentrated on densely populated countries such as India, the USA, Pakistan, Germany and the UK. Due to the better analyzability of the data, we limited the presentation to dashboards that are available in German or English. In the following parts, we analyzed these dashboards by comparing them with the previously identified success factors as illustrated in Table 1. The evaluation of practical dashboards is presented in Table 2 and shows to what extent the respective dashboard fulfills the success factors. An "x" means, that the respective aspect is fully considered. An "(x)" indicates, that the aspect is either partially fulfilled or not directly visible, because it might be on a subpage. Lastly, a "-" illustrates, that the factor is not included.

Content: We identified a wide range of ratios. All dashboards inform about *overall cases* and *overall deaths* as well as *daily new cases* and *daily new deaths*. In addition to that, *overall recovered cases*, *daily new recovered cases*, *active cases*, *overall tests* as well as the *incidence rates* are given in many dashboards. Other ratios were named less frequently. With regard to this, *new daily tests* or *case numbers with regard to age and gender* need to be mentioned [53, 57]. The UK dashboard also provides the *current number of COVID-19-patients in hospital* and the *number of patients needing artificial ventilation* [55]. Another indicator is the testing rate [7, 56]. Data-currency of the provided information is important, as well. All analyzed dashboards display the

Table 2. Comparison of the corona dashboards with the success factors

	Success factor	JHU	WHO	Google	RKI	UK	IND	PAK	Zeit	CDC	NYT
Visualization	Mixed usage	x	x	x	x	x	x	x	x	x	x
	Modest visual elements	x	x	x	x	x	x	-	x	x	x
	Maps	x	x	x	x	(x)	x	x	x	x	x
	Ease and familiarity	x	x	x	x	x	x	x	x	x	x
	Colors usage	x	(x)	x	(x)	(x)	(x)	-	x	(x)	(x)
	Number of visualizations	8	4	6	9	9	4	17	6	6	7
Functionality	Data sharing option	-	-	-	-	-	-	-	(x)	-	-
	Interactivity	x	x	(x)	x	(x)	x	(x)	(x)	(x)	x
	User-friendliness	x	x	(x)	x	(x)	x	(x)	(x)	(x)	x
Content	Data source knowledge	x	x	(x)	x	x	(x)	(x)	x	x	x
	Reliability	x	x	(x)	x	x	(x)	x	(x)	x	x
	High-level-aggregation	x	x	x	(x)	(x)	(x)	(x)	(x)	(x)	x
	Easy knowledge transfer	(x)	x	x	(x)	(x)	x	(x)	x	(x)	x
	Several data sources	x	x	(x)	x	x	(x)	x	x	x	x
	(Automated) data currency	x	x	x	x	x	x	x	x	(x)	x
	Automated warnings	(x)	(x)	-	-	-	-	-	x	-	-
	Focus on central information	x	x	x	x	(x)	x	(x)	x	(x)	x
	Mainstream usability	x	x	x	(x)	(x)	x	(x)	x	-	x
	Key figures	x	x	x	x	x	x	x	x	x	x

time of the last data update. The majority of dashboards provide data which is not older than 24 h. Several dashboards demonstrate data reliability both by informing the public about the exact and extensive data sources used and by including official governmental sources. In most of the dashboards, the content is presented in an easily understandable way. They display the main information on only one screen and provide only four to nine elements on the screen to avoid cognitive overload. The Pakistani dashboard builds an exception as it deploys 17 elements [57]. Most dashboards offer several subpages to provide further data. In order to explain potentially difficult terms, several dashboards provide an information button [56, 60].

Comparison with Literature: Similar to the findings from the literature, the majority of the analyzed dashboards claims up-to-dateness, the use of several data sources and reliability. Given the severity of the COVID-19 pandemic, this is reasonable, as the potential negative impact of outdated or dubious data is immense and can lead to a significant further spread of the virus. Next to that, we could gain more insights for the used ratios in dashboard design. We know more concretely, which dashboard figures (cases, deaths, increase in cases and deaths, recoveries, active cases etc.) are especially important in pandemics. Contrary to our findings from literature, automated warnings don't play a major role in practical dashboards. This may be reasoned in the fact, that other new technological developments like the "Corona-Warning-App" already focus on such features (like the warning function) more concretely [62].

Functionalities: Interactivity is an essential factor in the analyzed dashboards. Normally, additional information is displayed through simple clicks on links or specific map locations. Filtering is another method to gain more information about chosen time periods, nations or smaller regional areas. The Zeit even allows comment functions [60], which are not available in governmental dashboards. Thus, it can be concluded, that the dashboards provided by media enable more interaction but also are more informal. Data cannot be entered into the dashboards by their users, which is reasonable due to the importance of high data validity. Most of the dashboards achieve user-friendliness through the possibility to use them with mobile devices such as smartphones. FAQs are provided as well [56–58]. Navigating is easy in most dashboards, although it is not always clear which fields can be selected for further filtering. In some cases, user-friendliness was reduced by site loading delays [57], security warnings [57] and the occurrence of downtimes [55]. E-learning possibilities [7], news links [7] or suggested personal behavior [61] are further user-friendly functions.

Comparison with Literature: Given the many different interaction tools in the established COVID-19 dashboards, interactivity seems to be even more important than indicated in the literature. This finding can be attributed to the rapidly advancing technical developments and increasing amount of available data, which nowadays enables higher customization. Higher levels of interaction and customization go along with higher levels of general usability. A potential risk, however, is to confuse users by multiple subpages and information overflows.

Visualizations: All dashboards use maps for illustrating the geographical distribution of COVID-19. Maps are kept in a simple way and mostly do not display detailed geographic characteristics like rivers or mountains. Most of the dashboards combine the map view with the data itself and provide more aggregated data like the respective country's case numbers, but also more granular regional data within the country. Colors often symbolize good or bad information, as, for example, the Indian dashboard displays the numbers of recovered persons in green color, whereas numbers of deaths are illustrated with black and current case numbers with red color [56]. The Zeit highlights the incidence rates shown as bubbles in red, as soon as the critical threshold is exceeded [60]. However, most dashboards are kept in predominantly moderate colors. While several dashboards are kept in grey, black or white background, some like the Pakistani [57] use colors extensively. Beyond the already mentioned maps, timelines are used often to provide current trends of the disease spread. Some of the dashboards like JHU [7], WHO [58] or RKI [53] provide bar charts. Bubble maps, in which the bubble sizes illustrates the incidence rates, are identified as a new development [7, 58, 60]. As recommended in the literature, most of the dashboards do not display more than nine elements on a single screen.

Comparison with Literature: By comparing the analysis results of established dashboards with the literature, it can be stated that the success factors are relatively similar.

Identified salience in the analyzed dashboards lies in the outstanding importance of maps to illustrate regional differences of the virus distribution and timelines to illustrate the current trends of COVID-19. Apart from well-known visualizations, bubble maps play an important role. Further, the position of visual elements follows a certain structure in the analyzed dashboards, as the most important numbers like case and death numbers are displayed on the upper left side of the dashboards mostly. This constitutes a new implication not directly mentioned in literature.

5 Discussion, Limitations and Future Work

Finally, we examined to what extent our research questions could be answered. First, the success factors of the pre-corona dashboards should be determined. These should be based on dashboards of previous pandemics and epidemics. Higher-level aspects of success should also be examined by including general crisis dashboards. A basis for answering the first research question (RQ1) was built by using the literature and content analysis, from which three main categories could be determined. With regard to the category of visualization, the targeted use of color as well as the use of familiar visualization elements such as bar charts plays a major role [31]. Regarding the dimension of functionality, interactive and user-friendly tools should be built in [2, 9, 42]. Special emphasis is placed on interactivity, as it gives the user a feeling of self-determination and a dynamic way of using the dashboard. With regard to the content dimension and given the severity of the topic (the population's health situation and the danger of deaths), it is deemed especially important to use several reliable data sources [30, 37, 48]. Individual important indicators on communicable diseases such as prevalence and mortality rates have also been identified [52].

We also found answers to our second research question (RQ2). Here it should be examined to which scope the previously identified success factors are reflected in the corona dashboards. In the area of visualization, it was recognized that the aspect of maps in the corona dashboards has taken on even a more important role than described in the literature. Furthermore, it was recognized that bubble maps are frequently used in corona dashboards, which allows the user to easily capture how severely a region is affected by the virus. In terms of functionality, the filtering aspect often mentioned in the literature has been further improved in practice. Since higher data transfer rates are possible today, increasingly detailed data can be made available. This allows the user to retrieve an expanding range of regional data. User-friendliness has been frequently mentioned in the literature. By providing the function to use many dashboards as mobile applications, a lot of corona dashboards also meet this requirement. However, at the same time the dashboards lose functionality through the developments of mobile devices. For example, the aspect of warning when thresholds are exceeded is no longer considered to be important. This is due to the fact that efficient corona warning apps take over this function. The user no longer needs to actively obtain the warning and is instead informed via push messages. Considered to be even more important than described in the literature, the aspects "updating" and "reliable data sources" on the content level play an enormous role in the analyzed dashboards. Nearly every dashboard showed the time of the last update which was usually less than 24 h ago. This is due to the high infectivity with the coronavirus, which can lead to drastic changes in the course of infection within a short time.

These results can be relevant for both dashboard creators and clients, like governments or other official authorities. It can be seen that the success factors of pandemic dashboards have changed only to a small extent over time. Most of the functionality of pre-corona dashboards was also used in corona dashboards. It is important to note that functionalities gain in importance as a result of technical progress (e.g. individualization is better possible due to higher data transfer rates) or may even be outsourced to new applications only focusing on a specific function (warning mechanism is executed by other techniques). This demonstrates that technical progress must always be considered when designing dashboards in pandemics in order to create an information tool adapted to the needs and wishes of the users.

There are some limitations in answering our research questions. Only a limited number of databases was included in the search. Thus, there may be other success factors for pandemic dashboards that could not be identified and considered. Likewise, only a limited number of corona dashboards was included in the analysis, so that success factors of other corona dashboards may have been missed. The evaluation of the dashboards depended on the partly subjective examination of the authors of this article. An evaluation of the dashboards by a larger number of reviewers would provide a more objective result. Since the dashboards do not publish their design principles and templates transparently, it can also not be ruled out that they copied from each other during conception. This could neither be proven nor refuted with the available information.

For future work, the same aspects could be examined with the help of a larger number of databases. Likewise, study participants could be questioned on aspects such as usability and information content of corona dashboards with the help of use cases in order to enable a more objective evaluation of the dashboards. Based on this, a best practice for future pandemic dashboards could be developed, which would be available to future governments and dashboard developers as a framework. Mistakes in the development could be avoided and important design aspects could be included. In addition, technical progress in terms of new functionalities must also be considered. Because there is no prediction as to when exactly the next pandemic will come.

References

1. Barone, S., Chakhunashvili, A., Comelli, A.: Building a statistical surveillance dashboard for COVID-19 infection worldwide. Qual. Eng. **32**, 754–763 (2020)
2. Cheng, C.K.Y., Ip, D.K.M., Cowling, B.J., Ho, L.M., Leung, G.M., Lau, E.H.Y.: Digital dashboard design using multiple data streams for disease surveillance with influenza surveillance as an example. J. Med. Internet Res. **13**, e85 (2011)
3. Mansoour, S.: Terrorist watcher: an interactive web based visual analytical tool of terrorist's personal characteristics. Int. J.Data Min. Knowl. Manag. Process. **7**, 1–12 (2017)
4. Sloane, E.B., Rosow, E., Adam, J., Shine, D.: JEDI - an executive dashboard and decision support system for lean global military medical resource and logistics management. In: Proceedings of Annual International Conference of the IEEE Engineering in Medicine and Biology Society, pp. 5440–5443 (2006)

5. Tokgoz, B.E., Gheorghe, A.V.: Resilience quantification and its application to a residential building subject to hurricane winds. Int. J. Disaster Risk Sci. **4**(3), 105–114 (2013). https://doi.org/10.1007/s13753-013-0012-z
6. Toan, N.T., Tam, N.T.: Early bushfire detection with 3D CNN from streams of satellite images (2019)
7. Johns Hopkins Coronavirus Resource Center. https://coronavirus.jhu.edu/map.html. Accessed 27 Aug 2020
8. Devasia, J.T., Lakshminarayanan, S., Kar, S.S.: How modern geographical information systems based mapping and tracking can help to combat severe acute respiratory syndrome coronavirus 2 (SARS-CoV-2) pandemic around the world and India. Int. J. Health Syst. Implement. Res. **4**, 30–54 (2020)
9. Tilley, I., Petit, C.: A dashboard for the unexpected: open data for real-time disaster response. In: Open Cities: Open Data: Collaborative Cities in the Information Era, pp. 265–286. Palgrave Macmillan (2019)
10. Grange, E.S., et al.: Responding to COVID-19: the UW medicine information technology services experience. Appl. Clin. Inform. **11**, 265–275 (2020)
11. Bae, Y.S., et al.: Information technology – based management of clinically healthy COVID-19 patients: lessons from a living and treatment support center operated by Seoul National University Hospital. J. Med. Internet Res. **22**, e19938 (2020)
12. Verhagen, M.D., Brazel, D.M., Dowd, J.B., Kashnitsky, I., Mills, M.C.: Forecasting spatial, socioeconomic and demographic variation in COVID-19 health care demand in England and Wales. BMC Med. **18**, 1–11 (2020)
13. Reeves, J.J., et al.: Rapid response to COVID-19: health informatics support for outbreak management in an academic health system. J. Am. Med. Inform. Assoc. **27**, 853–859 (2020)
14. Berry, I., Soucy, J.-P.R., Tuite, A., Fisman, D.: Open access epidemiologic data and an interactive COVID-19 outbreak in Canada. Can. Med. Assoc. J. **192**, E420 (2020)
15. Marivate, V., Combrink, H.M.: A framework for sharing publicly available data to inform the COVID-19 outbreak in africa: A south african case study. arXiv (2020)
16. Xu, B., et al.: Open access epidemiological data from the COVID-19 outbreak. Lancet Infect. Dis. **20**, 534 (2020)
17. Boulos, M.N.K., Geraghty, E.M.: Geographical tracking and mapping of coronavirus disease COVID - 19/severe acute respiratory syndrome coronavirus 2 (SARS-CoV-2) epidemic and associated events around the world: how 21st century GIS technologies are supporting the global fight against outbreaks and epidemics. Int. J. Health Geogr. **19**, 1–12 (2020)
18. Ashofteh, A., Bravo, J.M.: A study on the quality of Novel Coronavirus (COVID-19) official datasets. Stat. J. IAOS **36**, 959–975 (2020)
19. Zavarrone, E., Grassia, M.G., Marino, M., Cataldo, R., Mazza, R., Canestrari, N.: CO.ME.T.A. – Covid-19 media textual analysis. A dashboard for media monitoring, pp. 1–6 (2020)
20. Everts, J.: The dashboard pandemic. Dialogues Hum. Geogr. **10**, 260–264 (2020)
21. Dong, E., Du, H., Gardner, L.: An interactive web-based dashboard to track COVID-19 in real time. Lancet Infect. Dis. **20**, 533–534 (2020)
22. Wei, X., Wang, M., Kraak, M.-J.: Where we are in fighting against COVID-19. Enviro. Plann. A Econ. Space **52**, 1483–1486 (2020)
23. Tewtia, H.K., Singh, D.: COVID-19 insightful data visualization and forecasting using elasticsearch. In: Raza, K. (ed.) Computational Intelligence Methods in COVID-19: Surveillance, Prevention, Prediction and Diagnosis. SCI, vol. 923, pp. 191–205. Springer, Singapore (2021). https://doi.org/10.1007/978-981-15-8534-0_10
24. Raghavan, M., Sridharan, K.S., Mandayam Rangayyan, Y.: Using epidemic simulators for monitoring an ongoing epidemic. Sci. Rep. **10**, 1–15 (2020)

25. vom Brocke, J., Simons, A., Niehaves, B., Reimer, K., Plattfaut, R., Cleven, A.: Reconstructing the giant: on the importance of rigour in documenting the literature search process. In: ECIS 2009 Proceedings, pp. 2206–2217 (2009)
26. Mayring, P.: Qualitative inhaltsanalyse. In: Mey, G., Mruck, K. (eds.) Handbuch Qualitative Forschung in der Psychologie, pp. 601–613. Springer, Wiesbaden (2010). https://doi.org/10.1007/978-3-531-92052-8_42
27. Cooper, H.M.: Organizing knowledge syntheses: a taxonomy of literature reviews. Knowl. Soc. **1**, 104–126 (1988). https://doi.org/10.1007/BF03177550
28. Dybå, T., Dingsøyr, T.: Empirical studies of agile software development: a systematic review. Inf. Softw. Technol. **50**, 833–859 (2008)
29. Janes, A., Sillitti, A., Succi, G.: Effective dashboard design. Cutter IT J. **26**, 17–24 (2013)
30. Luchetti, G., Mancini, A., Sturari, M., Frontoni, E., Zingaretti, P.: Whistland: an augmented reality crowd-mapping system for civil protection and emergency management. ISPRS Int. J. Geo-Inf. **6**, 41 (2017)
31. Lechner, B., Fruhling, A.: Towards public health dashboard design guidelines. In: Nah, F.-H. (ed.) HCI in Business. LNCS, vol. 8527, pp. 49–59. Springer, Cham (2014). https://doi.org/10.1007/978-3-319-07293-7_5
32. Kostkova, P., Garbin, S., Moser, J., Pan, W.: Integration and visualization public health dashboard: the medi+board pilot project. In: Proceedings of the Companion Publication of the 23rd International Conference on World Wide Web, pp. 657–662 (2014)
33. Rosewell, A., et al.: Health information system strengthening and malaria elimination in Papua New Guinea. Malar. J. **16**, 1–10 (2017). https://doi.org/10.1186/s12936-017-1910-0
34. Marshall, B.D.L., Yedinak, J.L., Goyer, J., Green, T.C., Koziol, J.A., Alexander-Scott, N.: Development of a statewide, publicly accessible drug overdose surveillance and information system. Am. J. Public Health **107**, 1760–1764 (2017)
35. Haddawy, P., et al.: Large scale detailed mapping of dengue vector breeding sites using street view images. PLoS Negl. Trop. Dis. **13**, 1–27 (2019)
36. Domdouzis, K., Andrews, S., Gibson, H., Akhgar, B., Hirsch, L.: Service-oriented design of a command and control intelligence dashboard for crisis management. In: 2014 IEEE/ACM 7th International Conference on Utility and Cloud Computing, pp. 702–707 (2014)
37. Nascimento, B.S., Vivacqua, A.S., Borges, M.R.S.: A flexible architecture for selection and visualization of information in emergency situations. In: 2016 IEEE International Conference on Systems, Man, and Cybernetics, SMC 2016 - Conference Proceedings, pp. 3317–3322. Institute of Electrical and Electronics Engineers Inc. (2017)
38. Campbell, T.C., Mistry, Z.S., Gorelick-Feldman, G.N., Hodanics, C.J., Babin, S.M., Lewis, S.H.: Development of the respiratory disease dashboard for the identification of new and emerging respiratory pathogens. Johns Hopkins APL Tech. Dig. **32**, 726–734 (2014)
39. Kamadjeu, R., Gathenji, C.: Designing and implementing an electronic dashboard for disease outbreaks response - case study of the 2013–2014 Somalia Polio outbreak response dashboard. Pan Afr. Med. J. **27**, 22 (2017)
40. Nogués, A., Valladares, J.: Business Intelligence Tools for Small Companies: A Guide to Free and Low-Cost Solutions. Apress, New York (2017)
41. Zheng, L., et al.: Data mining meets the needs of disaster information management. IEEE Trans. Hum.-Mach. Syst. **43**, 451–464 (2013)
42. Schöffel, S., Weibell, G., Schwank, J.: A novel concept for a collaborative dashboarding framework. In: Nunes, I.L. (ed.) Advances in Human Factors and Systems Interaction, pp. 20–31. Springer International Publishing, Cham (2018). https://doi.org/10.1007/978-3-319-60366-7_3
43. Francalanci, C., Giacomazzi, P.: TORCIA: a decision-support collaborative platform for emergency management. In: DATA 2015, pp. 225–231 (2015)

44. Tsou, M.H., et al.: Social media analytics and research test-bed (SMART dashboard). In: ACM International Conference Proceeding Series, pp. 1–7. Association for Computing Machinery, New York (2015)
45. Hamid, S., Bell, L., Dueger, E.L.: Digital dashboards as tools for regional influenza monitoring. West. Pac. Surveill. Response J. WPSAR. **8**, 1–4 (2017)
46. Mordecai, Y., Kantsepolsky, B.: Intelligent utilization of dashboards in emergency management. In: Proceeding of 15th ISCRAM Conference (2018)
47. Bharosa, N., Janssen, M., Meijer, S., Brave, F.: Designing and evaluating dashboards for multi-agency crisis preparation: a living lab. In: Wimmer, M.A., Chappelet, J.-L., Janssen, M., Scholl, H.J. (eds.) EGOV 2010. LNCS, vol. 6228, pp. 180–191. Springer, Heidelberg (2010). https://doi.org/10.1007/978-3-642-14799-9_16
48. Jamil, J.M., Shaharanee, I.N.M., Yung, V.C.: An innovative data mining and dashboard system for monitoring of Malaysian dengue trends. J. Telecommun. Electron. Comput. Eng. **8**, 9–12 (2016)
49. Bhanumurthy, V., Sharma, V.K.: Integration of multiple technologies in web environment for developing an efficient framework for emergency management. In: Rao, P.J., Rao, K.N., Kubo, S. (eds.) Proceedings of International Conference on Remote Sensing for Disaster Management. SSGG, pp. 159–171. Springer, Cham (2019). https://doi.org/10.1007/978-3-319-77276-9_16
50. Limousin, P., Azzabi, R., Bergé, L.P., Dubois, H., Truptil, S., Le Gall, L.: How to build dashboards for collecting and sharing relevant informations to the strategic level of crisis management: an industrial use case. In: 6th International Conference on Information and Communication Technologies for Disaster Management, ICT-DM 2019. Institute of Electrical and Electronics Engineers Inc. (2019)
51. Ziuzianski, P., Furmankiewicz, M., Sołtysik-Piorunkiewicz, A.: E-health artificial intelligence system implementation: case study of knowledge management dashboard of epidemiological data in Poland. Int. J. Biol. Biomed. Eng. **8**, 164–171 (2014)
52. Joshi, A., Amadi, C., Katz, B., Kulkarni, S., Nash, D.: A Human-Centered Platform for HIV Infection Reduction in New York: Development and Usage Analysis of the Ending the Epidemic (ETE) Dashboard. JMIR Public Health Surveill. **3**, e95 (2017)
53. Robert-Koch-Institute. https://experience.arcgis.com/experience/478220a4c454480e823b17327b2bf1d4. Accessed 27 Aug 2020
54. Centers for Disease Control and Prevention. https://www.cdc.gov/coronavirus/2019-ncov/cases-updates/previouscases.html. Accessed 27 Aug 2020
55. Government of the United Kingdom. https://coronavirus.data.gov.uk/. Accessed 27 Aug 2020
56. Government of India. https://www.covid19india.org/. Accessed 27 Aug 2020
57. Ministry of National Health Services Regulations and Coordination (Pakistan). https://covid.gov.pk/stats/pakistan. Accessed 27 Aug 2020
58. World Health Organization. https://covid19.who.int/. Accessed 27 Aug 2020
59. The New York Times. https://www.nytimes.com/interactive/2020/world/coronavirus-maps.html. Accessed 27 Aug 2020
60. Zeit Online. https://www.zeit.de/wissen/gesundheit/coronavirus-echtzeit-karte-deutschland-landkreise-infektionen-ausbreitung. Accessed 27 Aug 2020
61. Google. https://www.google.com/search?q=coronavirus+dashboard+global&rlz=1C1CHBF_deDE860DE860&sxsrf=ALeKk00U9aio_XVwYKdS1FJgVpQsfS2Dmw:1595849840478&ei=cLweX6LzHNvBmwWe3an4DQ&start=0&sa=N&ved=2ahUKEwii6-z2q-3qAhXb4KYKHZ5uCt84ChDy0wN6BAgLEC8&biw=1920&bih=975. Accessed 27 Aug 2020
62. German Government. https://www.bundesregierung.de/breg-de/themen/corona-warn-app/unterstuetzt-uns-im-kampf-gegen-corona-1754756. Accessed 27 Aug 2020

The Impact of Digitizing Social Networks on Refugee Decision Making – The Journey to Germany

Safa'a AbuJarour[1](✉), Lama Jaghjougha[2], and Mohammed AbuJarour[3]

[1] Business Informatics, University of Potsdam, Potsdam, Germany
safaa.abujarour@uni-potsdam.de
[2] International Migration, University of Kent, Brussels, Belgium
lj299@kent.ac.uk
[3] Coding and Software Engineering, XU University of Applied Sciences, Potsdam, Germany
m.abujarour@xu-university.de

Abstract. The high reliance of refugees on digital tools has been the motor of digitization, which includes not only mobile applications, but also digitization of human aspects, namely, social capital (networks). Refugees tend to rely on their social capital (networks) to make well-informed decisions, especially related to the migration journey. An ideal supporting tool here has been Social Networking Sites (SNS). To investigate this topic, we have followed a qualitative approach and conducted 15 interviews with Syrian refugees in Germany. The analysis of our interviews has revealed four typical streams of utilizing social networks through SNS in the context of migration: (1) information gathering, (2) service consumption, (3) understanding the relevant procedures and systems, and (4) content creation and service provisioning. Our goal is to discuss the impact of digitized social networks on refugees aiming at maximizing the benefits, e.g., information gathering, and avoiding the risks, e.g., frauds.

Keywords: Digitization · Social networks · ICT · Refugees · SNS · Social capital

1 Introduction: Refugee Social Networks

The recent migration waves, especially from the Middle East, raise the need to study the new migration processes and the changes that have occurred in migration in light of the recent technological development. Since 2011, more than 5.6 million people have fled Syria searching for safe places [1]. Most of the Syrian refugees went to neighboring countries: Turkey, Lebanon, Jordan, Iraq and Egypt and others. Yet, other refugees decided to make their way to Europe. In 2015, around one million refugees arrived to Europe [1]. According to the International Organization for Migration (IOM), more than 970 thousand refugees arrived Europe by sea and about 34 thousand refugees arrived Europe by land in 2015 [2]. This situation has created a challenge among the European Union countries concerning the best strategy to resettle people, especially after the long

F. Ahlemann et al. (Eds.): WI 2021, LNISO 46, pp. 331–345, 2021.
https://doi.org/10.1007/978-3-030-86790-4_23

and risky journey to the hosting countries. Decision makers had to propose a fair, feasible, and fast strategy to handle this 'crisis'.

Yet, the more complex decision-making process lies on the side of the refugees seeking asylum in Europe. The decision by migrants to make this journey and to move to Europe is a tough one to make. During the migration journey, the experience of migrants and the decisions they make are complex processes, where searching for a safe place in which they can build a better life is a priority [3]. There are several factors that make this process a complex one: Risk, cost, legal constraints, and trust issues. Because of the complexity and criticality of this process, refugees tend to rely on their social capital (networks) to support their decision making. Social capital is a measure of the amount of networks person has built [4]. Therefore, we use the term social networks to capture the social capital of people.

Social networks represent trustful and reliable environments for refugees, to which they can refer for support whenever needed. Those networks typically consist of family members, relatives, and friends. The larger and more diverse one's network is, the more reliable that network is. In this context, the decision to migrate or where to migrate is not primarily based on economic and rational thinking only, but also on the information gathered about the availability of people who can support the migrant financially and psychologically during all stages of the migration journey and after reaching the final destination as assumed by the network theory of migration [3]. Social networks help in establishing "migration networks", which help in establishing social ties between the refugees in the country of destination and the prospective refugees who are still waiting to start their migration journey. In fact, every migrant provides opportunities for people from their social network to help them migrate as well.

Because the size and diversity of refugee social networks have a direct impact on their migration journeys, it is typically important for refugees to expand their social networks. For instance, refugees tend to consider the friends of their friends as part of their own social networks. This concept of "friends of friends" resembles very well with the core concepts of modern Social Networking Sites (SNSs). Therefore, it is not surprising that refugees rely largely on SNSs to digitize and expand their social networks.

Social Networking Sites are no longer simple personal tools used for entertainment, but they have rather evolved into a key source of information. Previous research has shown that this observation holds in particular true for refugees before and during their migration journeys [5]. Their reliance on SNSs and other Information and Communication Technologies (ICTs) has increased due to factors related to the forced migration from conflict zones, the need to communicate with their (geographically dispersed) families and friends, to collect information, and seek assistance during their migration journeys.

In this paper, we investigate the impact of digitizing refugee social networks by means of SNSs on their complex decision-making processes. Towards this goal, we used a qualitative approach where we interviewed 15 Syrian refugees in Germany. Our analysis has revealed four main categories of using SNSs for refugee decision-making: (1) information gathering, (2) service consumption, (3) understanding the relevant procedures and systems, and (4) content creation and service provisioning.

The rest of this paper is organized as follows. In Sect. 2, we introduce related work on the social capital to support migration decision making and ICT-enabled tools to support the migration journey. In Sect. 3, we introduce our methodology and then we show our empirical evidence on how ICT solutions support migration decision making in Sect. 4. We discuss further topics related to our paper in Sect. 5. And summarize our paper in Sect. 6.

2 Related Work

2.1 Social Capital to Support Migration Decision Making

The social and economic dimensions affect the decisions that migrants, refugees, and asylum seekers make throughout their journeys to the destination countries. This makes the migration process complex; due to wars and conflicts, the dangerous flee journey, and finally to the resettlement after arriving at the host country [6, 7]. Recently, researchers have been interested in uncovering the effects of social capital on the increasing international migration, especially considering that migrant networks are a form of social capital that people can rely on to access opportunities in the destination country [3]. This form of social capital consists of networks of connections of potential migrants that can be relied on to reach the destination country. Thus, the migrant networks of personal relationships that are formed by the connections between migrants and non-migrants can increase the possibility of international migration, affect the perpetuation of migration, and change the nature of migration patterns [3]. Moreover, social ties might lead as well to increasing in international migration because they provide financial assistance, psychological support, help with migration costs, and reduce risks until migrants reach the country of destination [8, 9].

In general, social capital supports the decision making of migrants to pursue the migration journey for individuals who have strong relationships with members of their social networks due to two factors; declining costs and declining risks. Migrants who have strong ties to their social network and expand their social networks in the home- and destination-countries with reliable people can rely on them to help the migrants reduce the costs of the trip by providing advice and reliable information, including among others, the cheapest means of transportation, the most reliable roads to reach the destination, hotels, transportations, etc. [3, 10].

On the other hand, declining risks is also related to reducing the risks of migration by providing a sense of security, support, and confidence in the presence of an auxiliary person during all stages of the migration journey [3]. Therefore, migrants often travel in groups from the same region or city of origin to reduce the risk and make them feel reassured in their journey toward reaching safe countries. This requires building trust networks with strong relationships of migrant networks that link current migrants, former migrants, potential migrants, and non-migrants in the countries of origin and the destination countries [11, 12].

Despite the acknowledgement of the importance of ICTs in migration-related studies on a large scale, social sciences are still striving to integrate their convergence theoretically within the "network society" [13]. Permanent and constant development of ICT requires the establishment of continuous empirical studies to discuss updates in migration which are evolving with the continuous development of ICT. Therefore, scientific interest in migrants and refugees using ICT to communicate with their networks during the migration stages has increased; examining their journey in the country of origin, requiring assistance during the migration journey, and after their arrival in the destination country (e.g. [14]).

Research shows that the use of SNSs influences migration decisions, where SNS is now considered one of the most important communication channels that make migrants more aware of the possibilities and methods of migration and the directions of stability that suit them [14]. Technology plays an important role in the social networks of migrants as it positively affects social capital by strengthening connections between people and allowing them to expand their social networks [15]. ICT-enabled tools by migrants has been helping them in creating and maintaining social ties between destination countries and countries of origin. According to [16] several studies have addressed the impact of ICTs on migration processes [17, 18]. In the next section, we introduce related studies to using ICT-enabled tools and solutions to support migrants in their migration journey to the destination countries.

2.2 ICT as a Medium to Support the Migration Journey

Most refugees suddenly had to leave their homes carrying only their smartphones and little money – often just enough to reach their host countries. In cases of forced migration, ICT-enabled tools and solutions are vital to assist people on their journeys, for instance by enabling the communication with their social networks, locating and requesting help, and for general safety during the risky journey to the country of destination [19]. In some cases, the lack of mobile phone coverage could lead to dangerous threats, as migrants depend on their smartphones for asking for help and rescue, according to Lesvos Solidarity[1]. In addition, staying connected with migrants who have preceded and knowing the route to Europe is a crucial part of the must-have information for the migration journey [20].

For nowadays' migrants, charging their smartphones is more important than having food and water, as they consider it the only tool that will help them move to the destination country, as described by [21]. One of the main ICT usages by migrants during their journey to the country of destination is using SNS, as it is an important source of information in the migration decision-making process and to keep abreast of the latest changes in the roads leading to Europe. Moreover, SNS is a primary means for refugees to communicate with their families and access services such as translation, guidance, and navigation facilitation, and to learn about legal and organizational structures in the host country [22, 23].

Refugees use ICTs in specific and simple ways that are easy for all of them to understand and share. For instance, Fig. 1 shows the migration map "The Road to Germany – الطريق الى المانيا" that many refugees circulated via WhatsApp during their journey to Europe [10]. It shows the route and geographical stations that refugees can take from Izmir in Turkey to reach Germany, the total cost of the journey, the cost of each phase, the currency to be used, and the parts that refugees need to make on foot [10]. Additionally, ICT-enabled communication tools and social networking sites also enable

[1] https://lesvossolidarity.org/en/.

establishing relationships between migrants and smuggling networks that may include (travel agents, lawyers, employment offices, translators, housing agents, and drivers to transfer them to collection points), which makes it a multilateral process [23, 24]. These networks are crucial to make the migration journey to the country of destination possible. Besides, "virtual migration network" has been created on SNSs, where migrants' participants report about their migration journeys, the routes, transportation, risks, and helpful advice [20]. All that can help future migrants in their journey to the destination countries. As a result, these social networks have contributed to the decision making and choices of the country of destination, based on the information of the experiences of previous refugees who arrive at the host countries [10, 20, 25]. For instance, this information includes the duration of asylum procedures in each country of destination, details on obtaining a residence permit, and information about family reunification duration and procedures.

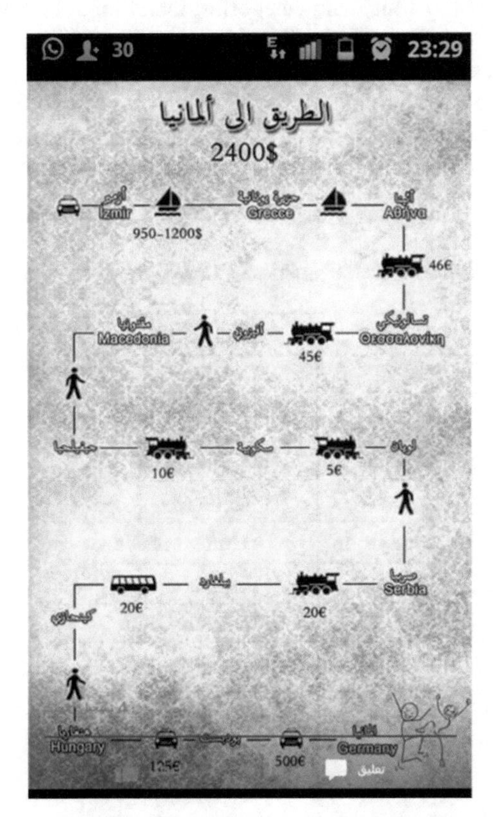

Fig. 1. The road to Germany - الطريق الى المانيا [10]

3 Methodology

Germany received the largest number of asylum applications among its European neighbors in 2015 with more than 476,000 asylum seekers [1]. Therefore, it is interesting to investigate how the refugees who arrived Germany during the latest refugee wave in 2015 used digital tools to achieve their goal of reaching Germany.

In this study, we followed a qualitative approach and conducted 15 semi-structured, face-to-face interviews with Syrian refugees in Germany. The goal is to collect more relevant insights about their stories to reach Germany and how ICT and their social networks helped them before and during the migration journey. All interviewees were recruited and conducted by the first author following a snowball sample. We asked our respondents questions related to the usage of their social networks to facilitate their journey to Germany. We specifically looked for themes reflecting the use of digitized social networks by our respondents and in which way these networks have been contributing to the success of their journey to Germany and to their integration into the society upon arrival. All interviews were initially conducted in Arabic, audio-recorded, transcribed, and then carefully translated into English. After iterative coding of the interviews using Atlas.ti, we could identify four main categories, including: (1) information gathering, (2) service consumption, (3) understanding the relevant procedures and systems, and (4) content creation and service provisioning.

Table 1 shows the demographics of our respondents. It is worth mentioning that the proportion of male/female is representative. As shown by [26], over two thirds (69.2%) of asylum applicants in Germany from the principal countries of origin in 2015 were male.

Table 1. Demographics of 15 refugee interviews

Gender		Education	
Female	6	High school or lower	8
Male	9	Bachelor or above	7
Age group		**Current residency**	
18–24	4	Apartment	6
25–30	3	Shelter/Camp	5
31–39	6	Temporary residence	4
Above 40	2		

4 Empirical Insights: The Benefits of Digitized Social Networks

“There are many specialized Facebook pages that collect the experiences of asylum seekers during their journeys including all details. [...] They alert us about police operations. They also report about the smugglers they had dealt with. [...] Although we come from another country, we knew the smugglers before meeting them, through the information on Facebook. When I arrived Greece, I had in mind taking the land path. Then,

I changed the plan because I knew from others on Facebook that it was too difficult and that path was dangerous and not safe, especially, in Macedonia, Hungary, and Serbia. All of that was posted on Facebook. Right now, I can tell you that more than 95% of people who left used [advice from people on] SNS." – an interview quote.

Based on our review of related work and the collected insights from Syrian refugees in Germany, we have been able to reveal four main streams, where digitizing social networks through ICT (mainly SNSs) supported the complex refugee decision making processes. These streams are: (1) Information gathering (mainly before the migration journey), (2) service consumption (during the journey), (3) understanding the relevant procedures and system (mainly upon arriving the country of destination), and (4) content creation and service provisioning. Each of these streams has its own specialties that affect the decision-making processes. Yet, the four streams have one aspect in common, namely, the reliance on social networks to make efficient decisions.

4.1 Information Gathering

It is important to understand that preparing to escape to Europe (or somewhere else) could be a dangerous step to make while being in Syria. Each party of the conflict needs people to support their actions, and therefore, they do not allow people simply to leave. On the contrary, trying to escape might be considered as a 'crime' that is punishable. In these circumstances, collecting the required information and taking the necessary preparatory steps to escape should be done within a circle of trust to avoid any further complications. During this phase, there are two key questions to be answered: (1) where to seek asylum and (2) how to prepare for the journey.

Where to Seek Asylum: Refugees start searching for information about the potential countries of destination before starting their asylum-seeking journeys. This simple task is not straightforward for them due to several challenges. First, there is too much information available describing the situations and processes at several potential countries of destination, yet the majority of this information is misleading. This information includes out-of-context information, rumors, out-of-dated information, incomplete information, and fake news. One of our interviewees described this stating: *"[...] this information [on Facebook Pages] is not reviewed or approved. It is a matter of luck; the information might be correct or wrong."* Second, there is too little information provided by official websites, which forces migrants and asylum seekers to collect the required information from other sources. Third, there are language barriers. Even the too little official information is not typically provided in the mother language of the asylum seekers making it less useful for them. One respondent stated: *"This Turkish smuggler speaks Arabic, as well. His Facebook page is well-known and the largest one on Facebook. All the information posted on this page is most probably 95% accurate."* As a result, asylum seekers tend to rely on information provided by members of their social networks.

Utilizing refugee social networks to collect information about potential counties of destination is mainly done using SNSs. Our respondents reported various types of information that can be obtained through SNSs, such as planning the best route to Europe, gaining knowledge about how to get there, and choosing the most suitable destination country. Finally, staying in contact with their social networks in the country of origin and who have preceded them to the destination country. One interviewee expressed this clearly: *"I used my smartphone mainly during the preparation for our trip to read the latest updates on Facebook about the stories of the refugees travelling from Turkey to Europe, such as the page 'Refugees to Europe'"*. SNSs were used prior to the migration journey to stay up-to-date: *"I used to ask them about the best way to leave Syria and reach Germany. People used to inform me through social networking sites, and the result is that I am in Germany now."* One of our respondents explained how he used Facebook to obtain and share information while planning the migration journey: *"Before travelling to Europe, I had subscribed to many Facebook pages that I could find and provide information about travelling to Europe."*

Preparation for the Journey: Because arranging the escaping journey is complex and might be dangerous, it is important that refugees consider each step in details. Typically, failing to escape is even more dangerous, because their intention to leave becomes public and reaches local authorities. Therefore, it is essential to secure all the required resources and information to ensure reaching at least the borders of Europe. One participant described this stating: *"As soon as I had the intention of leaving my country, I started using Facebook. Up to now, it is the largest source of information with respect to crossing the way from Turkey to Greece."* One interviewee revealed examples on how Facebook groups helped them to gather information about the logistics of the journey from their social networks: *"I communicated with some people who left before me through Facebook groups, such as 'Refugees to Europe' group. And with people who tried several paths and experience in identifying the safe path at the right times."*

Because the journey is dangerous and complex, migrants tend to pay attention to all details and collect as much information and stories as possible. One respondent mentioned: *"We benefited from reading the stories of those who left before us to Germany via Facebook so that we learn from their experience and gather information about the road and avoid the mistakes that others had faced and find out the equipment and stuff needed for this journey and risks."* Along the same line, another participant stated: *"Without smartphones during the entire journey, it would have been too difficult. Our predecessors used to share the best practices with us; TODOs, Not TODOs, etc. This was a huge relieve for us during the journey."*

Our research clearly shows that migrants seekers consider SNSs as the primary source of information, especially information based on personal experiences. Furthermore, SNSs enable users to communicate directly with the user who created the content and follow-up further if needed. One of our interviewees stated: *"When I was in Syria, I was following the people who left before us to Germany and Europe and I was in touch with them through the Internet, through social networking sites, through Viber, and through WhatsApp."*

4.2 Service Consumption on the Move

The migration journeys that refugees had to go through are unique. They are expensive, tedious, and dangerous. Furthermore, they face many legal constraints. Therefore, migrants rely to a large extent on their social networks to survive their journeys.

"We have relied mostly on Facebook during our journey" reported on respondent. Our analysis shows three typical usages of social networks during the migration journeys: (1) communicate with facilitators, (2) obtain real-time directions, and (3) survive emergency situations.

Find and Communicate with Trusted Facilitators: Our interviews showed the importance of using refugee social networks through SNSs during their migration journeys to find trusted smugglers, who facilitated their journeys. One respondent reported: *"I knew the smugglers from Turkey to Greece through Facebook. Simply by visiting the [Facebook] group 'Immigration to Europe and Smuggling Routes'"*. Moreover, it was important to be able to communicate with smugglers via SNSs applications, because they function across borders. Another respondent stated: *"We communicated with the smugglers through Facebook and WhatsApp."* One crucial issue in this context is trust. Migrants typically do not know those smugglers and because this step is risky and involves large amounts of money, migrants tend to ensure they deal with a trusted smuggler. Using SNSs, previous migrants and refugees give "reviews" to smugglers they have dealt with. This information is then used by later migrants to determine with which smuggler they want to deal. One interviewee mentioned: *"We used to communicate with other asylum seekers who had experience with smugglers, to avoid bad smugglers (fraudsters or those who sell human organs). This way, we avoided harmful facilitators."*. Another factor that helped migrants select trusted smugglers is direct recommendation from members of their social networks. One respondent stated: *"I was introduced to the smugglers who helped me to leave Turkey through friends and acquaintances."*

Obtain Real-Time and Contextual Directions: Due to the unique nature of their journeys, migrants need real-time and context-relevant directions. Followed paths are typically dynamic, therefore, it is important for migrants to receive real-time information about the path they have to follow. Also, it is typical that some rules apply to families and not to individuals. Thus, what might apply for some migrants might not apply to others. Our analysis shows that migrants consider SNSs as the primary source of information about routes, especially information based on personal experiences. For instance, one interviewee noted: *"Along the road, we were in contact with several groups on Facebook to ask about the next steps and ask for advice and directions."* Our analysis shows an interesting setup of combining both GPS (standard services) and social networks input (through SNSs). One respondent described this setup stating: *"When we were crossing countries, we used GPS and we were in touch with others who went before us, through WhatsApp and Facebook, to know which roads were safe. We used to do the same with the people behind us."*

Emergency: One of the vital benefits of utilizing social networks of refugees during their migration journeys is asking for help during emergency situations. The majority of our participants confirmed that the use of a smartphone saved them on the journey to Europe due to the possibility of seeking help and being rescued during their dangerous migration journeys. One of our respondents expressed the reliance on their social networks through SNS: *"I used the smartphone in the middle of the sea when the engine of our boat was damaged. I called the smuggler and we called our families, and as we* *had an Internet connection, we posted what happened with us on Facebook and asked for help.*" Furthermore, volunteers have created specialized SNSs channels to provide direct support for refugees during their sea trips through virtual rescue groups. One respondent described this stating: "*One example is the rescue group on Facebook that is used to track the refugees on their way. Before leaving, we used to inform them that we're leaving so that they call the police or coast guards in case of emergency.*"

4.3 Understanding Relevant Procedures and Systems

Every migrant provides opportunities for people from their social network to help them migrate as well. Having a trusted member of their social networks in the new home plays an important role for migrants, asylum seekers, and refugees to be ready to start the integration process. A successful integration process requires completing the asylum-seeking process, and understanding the important legislations and regulations. During this stage, our analysis shows three benefits of social networks upon arriving the country of destination: (1) Complete the asylum-seeking procedures, and (2) understand important legislations and system.

Complete the Asylum-Seeking Procedures: It is important to understand that the asylum-seeking procedures are typically complex. Obviously, the entire procedures use the local language (e.g., German), which represents a considerable barrier for newcomers. Here comes an important benefit of social networks, where previous asylum seekers guide newcomers during the complex procedures. They even provide hints from their own experience. Our interviews show that refugees and asylum seekers tend to share their personal experiences to help similar cases with respect to various stages of the asylum-seeking process: "*I don't personally know the people on the Facebook pages. They share their experiences about what happened with them; such as who arrived here, who went to the immigration office, whether Berlin is the best city to apply for asylum or it is better to apply anywhere else. You find answers to all questions that might come to one's mind, just like a dictionary that you use to search for any term.*"

Relying on the experience of previous refugees and asylum seekers through SNSs to complete one's procedures has been emphasized by several respondents. For instance, "*Through SNSs, we knew that we had to apply for asylum at the police station in the Greek island.*" and "*Upon our arrival to Greece, I contacted the people who left before us through WhatsApp, Viber, and Facebook to figure out what we had to do next.*"

Understand Important Legislations and System: One of the key challenges for asylum seekers upon their arrival to the new home is to learn a new system that is widely different from what they had been used to. They have to pick up important legislations to avoid unnecessary penalties. Because previous refugees and asylum seekers are familiar with the background of the newcomers, it is easy for them to quickly 'onboard' these newcomers without overwhelming them with regulations that are not relevant for them. A prime example of propagating this knowledge is the high number of SNS channels created by previous refugees and asylum seekers to provide this knowledge to newcomers in their mother language. For instance, "كراجات المشنططين"(translated to Station of

People on the Move), with more than 300,000 members. One interviewee stated: *"The majority of this Facebook Group live already in Germany since 2013 or 2014. They have their own experiences."*

4.4 Content Creation and Service Provisioning

One of the important benefits of SNSs in the context of facilitating the complex decision making processes for migrants is the ability to create content and provide services based on own's experience and knowledge. Given the lack of comprehensive information from trusted official content providers, the large portion of misleading information about asylum-seeking, and trust issues, migrants tend to rely on content created by other fellow migrants based on their own experiences that had qualified them to be domain experts in asylum-seeking. *"I share information about my journey on Facebook to help others just like we had used similar help."* – an interview quote.

Furthermore, refugees and asylum seekers are the best to identify missing services in the context of asylum-seeking process. A prime example is the process of applying for family reunification. One of our interviewees explained how his own struggle through this process motivated him to provide this service for free for other fellow asylum seekers, who might lack the required skills to do this process on their own: *"I spent a lot of time struggling to book an appointment for my family in the German Embassy (in Lebanon or Turkey). Therefore, I have created a Facebook group through which I help people to book appointments for family reunification in the German Embassy in Turkey or Lebanon for free."*

Refugees know that they are the main content providers in this context and therefore they spend time and effort to create relevant and up-to-date content for prospective migrants and asylum seekers. One respondent stated: *"I learnt a lot from the experiences that I got from the people, who left before me. I shared my experience with the people who came after me. This is how such information and experiences keep propagating from one to another."* Another interviewee echoed the same message emphasizing the role of SNSs in this context: *"Through SNSs, we publish all what we have passed through and all our experiences so that others benefit from it just like we have done."* As mentioned earlier, SNSs enable users to communicate with the content creator to clarify further details. For instance, one respondent mentioned: *"When I arrived Germany, many people, who wanted to leave Syria, communicated with me and asked me many questions [about my journey]. They asked me to give them the name of a smuggler either in Macedonia, Turkey, or Hungary."*

Another important insight is the ability of bridging the language barriers by providing the initial support from migrants from previous waves who share the same language of the current asylum seekers. For instance, the Arab community in Turkey played an important role to reduce the number of dangerous accidents while crossing the sea to Greece. One interviewee mentioned: *"The admins of this group are Arabs in Turkey, who decided to establish this group to help [asylum seekers] traveling to Europe and reduce the deaths on the way. I knew this group through other Facebook groups and some Facebook friends."*

5 Discussion

The considerable reliance of migrants on using their smartphones to access SNSs has been one of the main characteristics of the recent refugee wave. It has been necessary for refugees not only to keep in touch with family and friends, but also to receive advice from members of their social networks, and to communicate with facilitators while crossing the borders of ten to twelve countries to reach the destination country. It is interesting to observe how migrants had been exchanging information and experiences from their journeys through SNSs, in order to provide meaningful information, reduce risks, and save the cost of the journey for fellow migrants. The main asset for migrants is trusted and meaningful information about the journey and the migration process.

This meaningful information represents the fuel of the migration decision-making process. Migration networks through SNSs have enabled creating and sharing the necessary information about safe routes, procedures at destination countries, and further details relevant to asylum-seeking process. Migrants and refugees tend to form "virtual" social networks on SNSs to exchange information, and rely mainly on trusted social ties and personal experiences from those who preceded them a few months, days, or even hours prior, and believe that this method protects them from fraud and misleading information. Therefore, many migrants are keen to stay online by connecting to Wi-Fi hotspots or buying SIM phone cards in every country they cross to receive advice from their social networks and to be informed about the latest developments related to the route to destination.

Due to the intensive usage of smartphones by migrants and refugees, they prefer to use SNSs to communicate with and obtain information from their social networks that are known and trusted for them. They look to the different experiences of members of their social networks (e.g., friends or families), where these experiences are largely embraced and considered as a trusted source [20]. Trust plays an essential role in this context, therefore, migrants used to compare information from different channels to evaluate their quality. One interviewee mentioned: *"When I used to ask about a specific route through different SNSs and get several answers, I was comparing the answers I got through Facebook, Viber, and WhatsApp, and I took the common answer among the different sources."* This is one of common techniques that refugees typically use to avoid getting trapped by fake news, rumors or misinformation. This kind of false information might lead to bad decisions during the migration journey. Another technique that refugees tend to use to avoid the obvious risks associated with the use of digital SNS, such as, fraud, or attacks by anti-migration groups is engaging in closed groups where strict rules are followed by group admins to filter anti-migration content and users.

It is worth mentioning that information needs have special requirements in this context. This information is critical to human lives, has direct impact on financial cost, and has a dynamic nature. Additionally, there are legal constraints that apply to this situation, trust issues that affect the creditability of the information, and language barriers to make the information digestible. Therefore, personal experiences and direct social connections play a crucial role. One respondent stated *"When I told a friend of mine in Syria that I was planning to come to Germany, he told me that one of his relatives had recently left to Germany. He connected us together so that I can learn from his experience."*

Social networks of migrants, as part of their social capital, positively affect not only their migration journeys, but also their integration process in the new homes. For instance, by facilitating their entrance to the job market and providing information on job opportunities in the host countries [27, 28, 29] In this context, researchers have found that almost half of Germany's migrant population relied on interpersonal contacts to obtain job opportunities [27]. Moreover, refugees and migrants with strong relations to the local social networks have better opportunities to access cultural knowledge that contributes to facilitating their integration into social environments and provides the opportunity to participate in the civil society [30, 31].

Our analysis reveals useful implications for several stakeholders and target audiences relevant to refugee topic. These include:

1. Governments and decision makers, to apply and support e-government solutions in reaching refugees to inform them about the rules and regulations, and possible integration opportunities.
2. NGOs and the local community, to inform them about possible usages of ICT to foster the integration process between them and refugees by providing online means to exchange skills on culture, language, etc.
3. Researchers and academics, who are interested in researching topics related to digitalization, social capital, social networks, crowdsourcing with respect to vulnerable groups, in particular migrants and refugees.

6 Summary

The complex decision-making processes that migrants and refugees have to perform are typically exacerbated by lacking meaningful information from trusted sources. Therefore, they rely on their social networks to acquire the required information and to seek support along their migration journeys. Because larger and more diverse social networks mean higher chances of succeeding the migration process at low cost and low risk, migrants expand their social networks before starting their journeys. An ideal supporting tool here has been Social Networking Sites (SNSs), e.g., due to the concept of "friends of friends", the ability to contact content creators directly for further clarifications, and the crowd impact.

Migrants and refugees rely on their social networks, especially through SNSs, that enable them to maximize the benefits of their social networks. In this context, we had identified four streams of utilizing social networks through SNSs by migrants, namely, information gathering (mainly before the migration journey), service consumption (during the journey), understanding the relevant procedures and system (mainly upon arriving the country of destination), and content creation and service provisioning. Social networks of migrants and refugees, as part of their social capital, have a positive impact not only on their migration journeys, but also on their integration process in the new societies, which is an important goal of local authorities, organizations, locals, and all members of the societies.

References

1. UNHCR: Persons of concern (2020). http://popstats.unhcr.org/en/persons_of_concern
2. IOM: Irregular Migrant, Refugee Arrivals in Europe Top One Million in 2015. IOM (2015). https://www.iom.int/news/irregular-migrant-refugee-arrivals-europe-top-one-million-2015-iom
3. Massey, D.S., Arango, J., Hugo, G., Kouaouci, A., Pellegrino, A., Taylor, J.E.: Theories of international migration: a review and appraisal. Popul. Dev. Rev. (1993)
4. Paldam, M.: Social capital: one or many? Definition and measurement. J. Econ. Surv. **14**(5), 629–653 (2000)
5. Abujarour, S., Krasnova, H.: Understanding the role of ICTs in promoting social inclusion: the case of Syrian refugees in Germany. In: European Conference on Information Systems Guimarães, Portugal (2017)
6. Koser, K.: Asylum policies, trafficking and vulnerability. Int. Migr. **38**(3), 91–111 (2000)
7. Doornbos, N., Kuijpers, A.M., Shalmashi, K.: Refugees on Their Way to a Safe Country. Centre for Migration Law, University of Nijmegen, The Netherlands (2001)
8. Massey, D.S., Durand, J., Malone, N.J.: Principles of operation: theories of international migration. In: The New Immigration. An Interdisciplinary Reader, pp. 21–33 (2005)
9. Haug, S.: Migration networks and migration decision-making. J. Ethnic Migr. Stud. **34**(4), 585–605 (2008)
10. Gillespie, M., et al.: Mapping refugee media journeys: smartphones and social media networks (2016)
11. Brettell, C.B., Hollifield, J.F. (eds.): Migration Theory: Talking Across Disciplines. Routledge, New York (2014)
12. Granovetter, M.S.: Economic action and social structure: the problem of embeddedness. Am. J. Sociol. **91**(3), 481–510 (1985)
13. Borkert, M., Cingolani, P., Premazzi, V.: The State of the Art of Research in the EU on the Take up and Use of ICT by Immigrants and Ethnic Minorities. Office for Official Publications of the European Communities, Luxembourg (2009)
14. Dekker, R., Engbersen, G., Faber, M.: The use of online media in migration networks. Popul. Space Place **22**, 539–551 (2016)
15. Alam, K., Imran, S.: The digital divide and social inclusion among refugee migrants. Inf. Technol. People (2015)
16. Kozachenko, I.: Horizon Scanning Report: ICT and Migration. Working Papers of the Communities & Culture Network+, 2 (2013)
17. Hiller, H.H., Franz, T.M.: New ties, old ties and lost ties: the use of the internet in diaspora. New Media Soc. **6**(6), 731 (2004)
18. Parham, A.A.: Diaspora, community and communication: internet use in transnational Haiti. Global Netw. **4**(2), 199–217 (2004)
19. Gillespie, M., Osseiran, S., Cheesman, M.: Syrian refugees and the digital passage to Europe: smartphone infrastructures and affordances. Soc. Media Soc. **4**(1), 2056305118764440 (2018)
20. Dekker, R., Engbersen, G., Klaver, J., Vonk, H.: Smart refugees: how Syrian asylum migrants use social media information in migration decision-making. Soc. Media Soc. **4**(1), 2056305118764439 (2018)
21. Brunwasser, M.: Migrant essentials extend to smartphone'. International New York Times (2015). https://www.nytimes.com/2015/08/26/world/europe/a-21st-century-migrants-checklist-water-shelter-smartphone.html
22. AbuJarour, S., Krasnova, H., Hoffmeier, F.: ICT as an enabler: understanding the role of online communication in the social inclusion of Syrian refugees in Germany. In: European Conference on Information Systems, Portsmouth, UK (2018)

23. Schreieck, M., Zitzelsberger, J., Siepe, S., Wiesche, M., Krcmar, H.: Supporting refugees in everyday life- intercultural design evaluation of an application for local information. In: PACIS 2017 Proceedings (2017)
24. Alkousaa, R., Popp, M.: European Purgatory: Migrant Smugglers Helping Refugees Return to Turkey. SPIEGEL ONLINE (2016). http://www.spiegel.de/international/europe/why-refugees-in-greece-are-trying-to-go-back-to-turkey-a-1100452.html
25. Dekker, R., Engbersen, G.: How social media transform migrant networks and facilitate migration. Global Netw. **14**(4), 401–418 (2014)
26. Juran, S., Broer, P.N.: A profile of germany's refugee populations. Popul. Dev. Rev. **43**, 149–157 (2017). https://doi.org/10.1111/padr.12042
27. Drever, A.I., Hoffmeister, O.: Immigrants and social networks in a job-scarce environment: the case of Germany. Int. Migr. Rev. **42**(2), 425–448 (2008)
28. Lancee, B.: The economic returns of immigrants' bonding and bridging social capital: the case of the Netherlands. Int. Migr. Rev. **44**, 202–226 (2010)
29. Lancee, B.: The negative side effects of vocational education: a cross-national analysis of the relative unemployment risk of young non-western immigrants in Europe. Am. Behav. Sci. **60**(5–6), 659–679 (2016)
30. Cederberg, M.: Embodied cultural capital and the study of ethnic inequalities. In: Ryan, L., Erel, U., D'Angelo, A. (eds.) Migrant Capital: Networks, Identities and Strategies. Migration, Diasporas and Citizenship, pp. 33–47. Palgrave Macmillan, Basingstoke (2015)
31. Elliott, S., Yusuf, I.: 'Yes, we can; but together': social capital and refugee resettlement. Kotuitui New Zealand J. Soc. Sci. Online **9**(2), 101–110 (2014)
32. Gelb, S., Krishnan, A: Technology, migration and the 2030 Agenda for Sustainable Development (2018)

Smart City and E-Government

Introduction to the WI2021 Track: Smart City and E-Government

Moreen Heine[1] and Bettina Distel[2]

[1] University of Lübeck, Institute for Multimedia and Interactive Systems, Lübeck, Germany
heine@imis.uni-luebeck.de
[2] University of Münster, Department for Information Systems, Münster, Germany
bettina.distel@ercis.uni-muenster.de

1 Track Description

With societal and technological changes taking place with an ever-increasing pace, today's public administrations face many challenges. The digital transformation is one of them and is – at the same time – considered as a solution for others. The continuing pandemic illustrates the weak spots in e-government progress in a particularly impressive way and posed many challenges, for example, to the public work force and public organisations that were not prepared for a major shift of work to the home office. Yet at the same time, the crisis acts as the catalyst that has been sought for years. In Germany in particular, the crisis has accelerated the digital transformation of public administrations by using data-driven policy making approaches, unlocking budgets for digitalizing public service, and showing the potential of innovative and open source/open government initiatives [1]. The crisis is also intensifying the debate on Smart Cities and Data-Driven Governance. Monitoring, analysis and decision-making are based on extensive, integrated data from a wide range of sources. The cooperation of different actors – both local and cross-divisional – is a prerequisite for rapid e-government progress.

This track contains several articles dealing with these issues and sheds light onto current debates in our field. The articles cover a range of topics, covering both the technical dimensions and social dimensions of e-government and smart cities. The first three articles in this track focus on smart cities and city development, emphasising several aspects surrounding the future-oriented development and decision-making in modern cities. Two articles focus on the potential of new technological concepts (blockchain technology, artificial intelligence) for public administrations and the delivery of public services, whereas the last article focusses on the social dimension of the digital transformation and sheds light onto changing competence requirements in public administrations.

2 Research Articles

The first article *How Could Smart Cities Use Data? – Towards a Taxonomy of Data-Driven Smart City Projects* by Babett Kühne & Kai Heidel deals with concepts for data-driven smart city projects. In particular, it aims at establishing a taxonomy of data-driven smart city projects in order to enable the structuring of this nascent research field and to support the derivation of design theories for data-driven smart city projects. The authors arrive at a taxonomy with 11 dimensions, such as usage of data, user of solutions, and data ownership, that is evaluated with a total of 45 existing smart city projects. In *Towards Sustainable Transport: A Strategic Decision Support System for urban Logistics Operations* Maximilian Heumann, Richard Pump, Michael H. Breitner, Arne Koschel, and Volker Ahlers develop the prototype for a decision-support system that enables the evaluation of logistic-based concepts in (smart) cities. The system enables public administrations and other stakeholders to arrive at city logistic decisions more efficiently. Anja Schulte, Tim Wittemund, Peter Weber, and Alexander Fink (*Preparing for an Uncertain Future: South Westphalia City Scenarios 2030*) use a multi-stakeholder participatory approach to develop future scenarios for cities in more rural areas. Cities outside of metropolitan areas are faced with challenges in particular and, thus, need tailored approaches to address these challenges. The presented approach and resulting scenarios may help decision makers to navigate the challenges posed through digital transformation.

The article *What Do We Really Need? A Systematic Literature Review of the Requirements for Blockchain-based E-government Services* (Julia Ahmend, Julian Kaiser, Lucas Uhlig, Nils Urbach, Fabiane Völter) presents a category system for specific requirements for blockchain systems in the public sector that provides guidance for both researchers and practitioners. In this way, a systematic approach to the requirements is opened up, which prevents relevant requirements from being neglected in the context of specific use cases.

In the public sector, the explainability of AI systems and their behaviour plays a central role, as only comprehensible decisions can be evaluated and safely integrated into administrative processes. Nijat Mehdiyev, Constantin Houy, Oliver Gutermuth, Lea Mayer and Peter Fettke describe in their article *Explainable Artificial Intelligence (XAI) Supporting Public Administration Processes – On the Potential of XAI in Tax Audit Processes* the potential of different XAI approaches for tax authority processes. The paper also provides XAI usage guidelines for the public sector.

Julian Christ, Gunnar Auth, Frank Bensberg discuss in *Competence Requirements for the digitalisation of public administrations: An empirical analysis based on job advertisements* necessary skill sets for public sector digitalization. The focus is on the side of the authorities. The study presents which competences are currently in demand. More than 20,000 job advertisements were examined in order to arrive at a comprehensive set of required e-skills.

Reference

1. Meijer, A., Webster, C. William R.: The COVID-19-crisis and the information polity: an overview of responses and discussions in twenty-one countries from six continents. Inf. Polity **25**(3), 243–274 (2020)

How Could Smart Cities Use Data? – Towards a Taxonomy of Data-Driven Smart City Projects

Babett Kühne(✉) and Kai Heidel

Department of Informatics, University of Hamburg, Hamburg, Germany
{babett.kuehne,kai.heidel}@uni-hamburg.de

Abstract. The process of urbanization has caused a huge growth in cities all over the world. This development makes the organization and infrastructure of an individual city increasingly important. In this context, the idea of a smart city is growing and smart city projects are beginning to appear. As the amount of data is growing with connected technologies, such projects rely on data as a key resource. However, current research does not provide an overview on these projects and which constructs are involved in data-driven smart city projects. Therefore, this research begins the building of a taxonomy on such projects through the establishment of a common language among researchers in this new field through eleven dimensions. Additionally, it develops a concrete conceptualization of data-driven smart city projects for practitioners as an initial guidance for the field of smart cities.

Keywords: Smart cities · Taxonomy · Data-driven smart city · Smart city projects

1 Introduction

A study from the United Nations Organization shows that 64,8% of the world population will live in urban regions by 2050 [1]. This lead to a 13.1% increase in the population of urban regions as compared to 2018 [1]. Most of these projected increases will take place on the African and Asian continents while a growth of 9.8% is expected in Europe [1]. Comparing the urbanization rates in Europe show huge growth in the coming years: 0.22% from 1990–2018, 0.33% from 2018–2030, and 0.38% from 2030–2050 [1]. It is clear that urbanization process will challenge cities all over the world.

This urbanization could be seen as the biggest change in the infrastructure and rebuilding processes of humanity [2]. Furthermore, the daily routine in an urban city becoming more digital and more increasingly inclusive of factors such as smartphones or sensors [3]. This digitalization could help to solve the challenges that are occurring due to urban growth. In doing so, information and communication technology (ICT) could be used to improve living conditions and quality of life as well as enable environmental protection [4]. Such ICT enables the city to become a smart city and improve the lives of citizens with the help of technology [5].

F. Ahlemann et al. (Eds.): WI 2021, LNISO 46, pp. 351–366, 2021.
https://doi.org/10.1007/978-3-030-86790-4_24

In order to use the data of ICT and inventory data in smart cities, data needs to be acquired, stored somewhere in some data structure, analyzed, and proceeded. Using these data analysis processes could generate new insights which could provide a new value proposition [6] for citizens. The usage of data in such a context is called data-driven [7]. Such data-driven smart city projects could be in the areas of industry, tourism, logistics, buildings, public transport and many others [8]. This research focuses on data-driven smart city projects that contain one use case in order to build a taxonomy.

As there are so many different use cases for data-driven smart city projects, current research does not provide an overview of the possibilities in this field. Perboli et al. provide three dimensions for a smart city: description, business model, and purpose [9]. These three dimensions are focused on a private versus public view. Furthermore, the taxonomy does not focus the data-driven aspect of a smart city and only differentiates between potential tools of a smart city. Niaros provide a taxonomy of smart cities in two dimensions: local versus global and capital versus commons [10]. This taxonomy is focusing on a more strategic view of a smart city project and does not integrate all possible smart city components. Additionally, the data-driven aspect is missing in this research. Thus, to the best of the current knowledge, there is no taxonomy of data-driven smart city projects available in research yet. However, the development of such data-driven smart city projects is growing but the theoretical understanding of such projects is lacking in knowledge, yet. In order to understand such projects more detailed and create methods and tools for the development of such initiatives, the knowledge of the constructs and characteristics of data-driven smart city projects needs to be increased. As a consequence, this research focuses on developing such a taxonomy by using the methodology of Nickerson et al. [11] with the goal of answering the following research question:

RQ: What are the empirically validated and conceptually grounded characteristics that describe data-driven smart city projects?

This taxonomy participates to the present body of knowledge in the field of smart cities by establishing a joint understanding of data-driven smart city projects. Such a shared knowledge contributes to the structuring of this field of research by supporting researchers as they position their work in this field. Furthermore, the shared understanding resulting from this taxonomy allows for the materialization of ideas and considerations that will lead to the development of design theories in the field of smart cities. However, the taxonomy could also support practitioners and offer initial guidance for assessing the chances and opportunities of a data-driven smart city project in order to analyze how this project could be implemented.

In order to do so, the paper is structured as follows. First, it provides an overview of the related research of smart cities. Second, the general approach of developing the taxonomy is described. Third, the development stages of the taxonomy for data-driven smart cities are presented, a detailed overview of the taxonomy itself is provided, and the evaluation is described. The paper closes by discussing the implications of the research, reflecting its limitations and describing possible next steps.

2 Related Work

2.1 Smart Cities

The study of smart cities (SCs) is a new field in research. Several cities have started projects with the goal of improving their citizens' quality of life and rely on ICT as key drivers [12], and so data from this technology plays an important role in this context.

Due to contextual changes in the public sector, an unbundling of services from production processes appeared [13], cities are experiencing a shift in value creation from offering products to providing services to citizens [14]. SC services are therefore predominantly designed from the service-dominant logic's perspective [14, 15]. Another contextual change has occurred due to the increasing presence of digital technologies [13] and connection of cities [16]. An exponential growth in data, leveraged by connected technologies such as Internet of Things (IoT), currently characterizes cities. The data that these connected technologies produce, as well as that gathered from citizens' interaction with the connected technologies, can be used to stimulate innovation and to develop new projects aimed at contributing to the citizens quality of life [14, 17].

In general, the definition of a SC is inherently connected to the idea of a digital city (DC) [4]. These two are often used as synonyms although there is a difference between the two terms [5]. The idea of a DC developed during the 1900s. By contrast, SC started appearing regularly in research in the 2010s [5]. Both terms address the citizen and have the following goals regarding improving quality of life: improving electronic services, promoting social inclusion, supporting economic and political efficiency, and facilitating urban development [5]. However, there is a key difference between a SC and DC. A SC is limited by the city boundaries. By contrast, a DC is not limited by such boundaries and has only virtual boundaries [4]. In terms of infrastructure, a DC is only represented by its ICT while a SC includes all infrastructure, such as, streets, buildings, railways, and ICT. The idea of a citizen is also different in these two concepts. Each citizen of the city can profit from and enable services in a SC, even if they are not able to use ICT. In a DC, citizens are enablers and receivers that can profit from the DC only if they are able to use ICT. In summary, SC and DC differentiate from each other in some parts but share the goal of improving quality of life for citizens [5].

As the research field of SCs is relatively new, there is no definition that is well accepted in research yet [5]. All in all, a SC is characterized by its intercultural and social capital, the citizens' government, the smart strategic planning of the city, and ICT [5, 18]. The component 'smart' in this context can be defined in a city that is innovative, integrative, connected, efficient, effective, adaptive and attractive [19].

2.2 Dimensions of Smart Cities

Current research show dimensions of SCs from different viewpoints. As the research goal of this study is to develop a taxonomy, this section introduces all existing taxonomies and dimensions of SCs in detail.

In order to analyze which data is being used in a SC, we take a look onto the different applications in a SC. Lombardi et al. developed a schema to model the performance of a SC. After an extensive literature review, they identified the following dimensions of a

SC: Smart Economy, Smart Mobility, Smart Environment, Smart People, Smart Living, and Smart Governance. The dimension Smart People is seen in a demographical context [20]. Other research takes a private economy perspective and developed the following dimensions: Smart Building, Smart Mobility, Smart Energy, Smart Infrastructure, Smart Technology, Smart Governance, Smart Citizen, and Smart Healthcare. The dimension Smart Citizen is seen in a demographical context, for example, usage of green mobility [21]. Lim and Maglio build the following dimensions based on 1234 news articles: Smart Device, Smart Environment, Smart Home, Smart Energy, Smart Building, Smart Transportation, Smart Logistics, Smart Farming, Smart Security, Smart Health, Smart Hospitality, and Smart Education [22]. They also introduce a hierarchical structure, meaning that the customer, provider or things could provide services like Smart Logistics through a linkage to Smart Devices and Smart Environments [22]. They provide five principles of smart services that a SC should have: (1) connection between humans and things, (2) processing of the data in the cloud, (3) wireless communication, (4) collection of data with context awareness, and (5) co-creation of value. If the first four principles are met, a co-creation of value between the customer and provider is possible [22]. All in all, these authors show different dimensions of SCs that somewhat overlap; Smart Mobility and Smart Transportation, for example, could be the same. However, these dimensions give the first indication of the context in which smart services in SCs appear.

In addition to these dimensions, Bischof et al. analyzed which data could be used in a SC. They structured the data according to the update frequency: static, semi-dynamic, and dynamic. Static data is leveraged at one time and could only be updated manually. Semi-periodic data is updated periodically. Dynamic data is updated all the time (every time new data appears) [23]. They developed the following data categories for SCs: transport, air quality, traffic, events of the city, services of the city, citizen data, and health data. The data is generated from different sources, which offers a challenge due to the homogenization of data. Such a homogenization is necessary in order to utilize the whole potential of a SC [23], but a centralization of the data could be helpful in order to make data usage easily assessable [24].

In order to identify all existing taxonomies in the field of SCs, a structured literature review is performed here[25] by searching for the combination of "taxonomy" and "Smart City" in different databases such as Science Direct, IEEE, ACM, and Google Scholar. After analyzing all titles, analyzing abstracts if necessary, and conducting a backward and forward search [25], two taxonomies were identified in the field of SCs. The selection criteria for identifying relevant papers were: (1) the paper offers dimensions for smart city projects and (2) these dimensions are specified by characteristics for smart city projects.

The first taxonomy shows three dimensions of a SC [9]. The dimensions are split into categories and these categories into major fields. According to Nickerson a taxonomy has only the elements, dimension, and characteristics [11]. The dimension 'description' in this taxonomy describes the main project features of the SC (context and components) divided into objectives, tools, project imitators, and stakeholders. The dimension 'business model' shows the actions that need to be performed to introduce a new business model into an SC. This dimension has the following categories: management, infrastructure financing, and financial resources. The last dimension 'purpose' indicates the final goal of a SC and is characterized by the categories: client, product, and geographical target [9]. Besides the category 'tools', no data-driven specific characteristics were indicated in this taxonomy. The components are not very detailed, including things such as 'data base'. Thus, the origin of the data is not clear; there were other data specific characteristics [23] that also could not be identified in this taxonomy. Thus, we argue that this taxonomy could give an overview of SC initiatives but does not meet data-driven goals that are the focus of this study.

The second taxonomy [10] involves differentiating the SC projects according to local versus global and capital versus commons projects. The projects could therefore be identified in four quadrants: corporate SC, commons-based SC, sponsored SC, and resilient SC [10]. As a consequence, the taxonomy is puts SC projects into these categories, which does not reflect the data-driven aspect of a SC. Thus, it does not answer the research question of this study.

3 Methodology

This study aimed to show the empirically validated and conceptually grounded characteristics that describe data-driven smart city projects and develop a taxonomy. In terms of taxonomy development, the methods of Nickerson et al. [11] were followed and their approach was adapted to this research context. This methodology seemed to be appropriate this study's purpose as several information systems studies have successfully used this method in different study contexts [26–28], suggesting its robustness in developing taxonomies. The evaluation illustrates use cases, a common method for evaluating taxonomies [29].

The taxonomy development method suggested by Nickerson et al. [11] constitutes an iterative approach which allows researchers to build taxonomies conceptually, based on literature, and empirically.

In order to build a taxonomy using the method of Nickerson et al. [11], the following steps need to be performed: (1) Meta-characteristics that all dimensions and characteristics following in the methodology will be a logical consequence of are defined by the researcher. (2) The researcher defines ending conditions that need to be fulfilled entirely for the taxonomy development process to end. These conditions could be objective or subjective. An objective criterion is characterized by the condition that each dimension of the taxonomy contain characteristics that are exclusive and complete. The dimension also needs to be unique but in the last iteration it is not possible to split or summarize objects and characteristics of the taxonomy. Additionally, one object needs to be assigned to a dimension and the last iteration should not add any dimensions or characteristics. The subjective conditions to end the process are achieved if the taxonomy is succinct, robust, complete, expendable and explainable [11].

(3) The third step is differentiated between an empirical to conceptual, or conceptional to empirical approach. The first one is qualified if there is a lot of data available about the research object and not a lot of domain understanding. The second is qualified if there is a lot of domain understanding but not a lot of available data on the research object. If the domain understanding and the available data of the research object are at the same level, the researcher could decide which approach should be chosen [11].

Due to the huge data set and some extant literature in the field of data-driven SC projects, a mix was chosen here – the study starts with the conceptual to empirical approach in the first iteration and moves on to the empirical to conceptual approach for the following iterations. A detailed description of the development stages can be found in Sect. 4.1.

In the conceptual to empirical approach, the researcher starts to build up knowledge about the dimensions and characteristics that are a logical consequence of the meta characteristics. Afterwards, the researcher examines the existence of each object that fulfills each characteristic of each dimension and decides which dimensions can be verified [11].

In the empirical to conceptual approach, a subset is first identified, which then needs to be classified. This subset is known to the researcher due to a literature review. Subsequently, common characteristics of these objects are identified as a logical consequence of the meta characteristics. If there is a characteristic that fits all objects it should be seen as useless as characteristics should be assigned to one dimension [11].

After performing one iteration, the researcher checks if the subjective and objective end conditions are fulfilled. If this is not the case, a subsequent iteration would be started until no new object could be identified and the subjective and objective end conditions are fulfilled [11].

4 Taxonomy

4.1 Development Stages

Step 1: Following the research design by Nickerson et al. [11], we start to define meta characteristics. The goal of the taxonomy is to show possible use cases and characteristics of data in a SC. As a consequence, the meta characteristics of the taxonomy are data and its usage in a SC.

Step 2: We adopted the subjective and objective criteria from Nickerson et al. [11]. However, the criterion of excluding mutual characteristics was not adopted because overlapping is possible in this context. A characteristic 'mixed' could avoid such overlapping but this would not be precise enough and would not meet the subjective criteria. All in all, we selected the following objective criteria: (1) each dimension contains characteristics which are complete, (2) each dimension is unique, (3) each characteristic of a dimension contains at least one object, (4) there are no added dimensions and characteristics in the last iteration, and (5) no dimension, characteristics or objects were summarized in the last iteration. The subjective criteria indicate that the taxonomy is: (1) precise, (2) robust, (3) complete, (4) expendable, and (5) explainable.

After the first two steps, the iterations to develop the taxonomy start. All dimensions and characteristics of the taxonomy will be described in detail in the next section.

Step 3.1: The first iteration starts with a conceptual to empirical approach. Thus, the literature review was performed to build up the findings (see Sect. 2.2). The first dimensions identified and examined with additional literature were: user of the solution [22, 30, 31], connection to the user [22], domain of the application [20, 21, 32], and periodicity of the data [23]. If a dimension was identified as not exclusive and more than one characteristic can be identified for a data-driven SC project, it was marked with the additional note 'NEX' (not exclusive). After the first iteration, the following taxonomy was developed:

T = { D_1 user of the solution | D_1 = {things; customer; provider} {NEX}
D_2 connection to the user | D_2 = {smart devices; smart environment} {NEX}
D_3 domain of the application | D_3 = {governance; environment; mobility; infrastructure; technology; citizen; services}
D_4 periodicity of the data | D_4 = {static; semi-dynamic; dynamic}}

Step 3.2: This iteration switches to an empirical to conceptual approach. The database of the EU Smart Cities Information System was used in order to gather empirical information [33]. This platform opens information about SC projects in order to encourage the exchange know-how and collaboration between citizens, developers, cities, industry, experts, and research centers. The data quality of this platform is sometimes expandable and sometimes a clear definition of a SC is missing. As a consequence, a large number of the projects in the database are not SC projects (e.g. an energetic reconstruction of buildings). However, GrowSmarter, Triangulum, and Smarter Together were established as projects with detailed data. All projects have the goal to improve the quality of life of the citizens and the ecological footprint of the city. All the projects also contain different subprojects. Thus, these provide a good database to further develop the taxonomy. These projects were analyzed by two independent researchers with a structured content analysis using an open coding system [34]. These two independent coding systems were compared and synchronized afterwards. After analyzing the projects, dimensions and characteristics were added to the taxonomy which are listed as follows:

T = { D_1 user of the solution | D_1 = {things; customer; companies, cities} {NEX}
D_2 connection to the user | D_2 = {smart devices; smart environment, smart data platforms} {NEX}
D_3 domain of the application | D_3 = {governance; environment; mobility; infrastructure; technology; citizen; services}
D_4 periodicity of the data | D_4 = {static; semi-dynamic; dynamic}
D_5 data ownership | D_5 = {citizen; company; city} {NEX}
D_6 data storage location | D_6 = {company server; cloud server; city server; open data platform; end device} {NEX}
D_7 data processing | D_7 = {manually; automatically; part-automatically}
D_8 data quality | D_8 = {reviewed; review necessary; no review}
D_9 data type | D_9 = {numeric measuring data; numeric data; geographic data; textual data; machine recognizable data} {NEX}
D_{10} usage of the data | D_{10} = {evaluation; analysis; monitoring; user application; open data portal} {NEX}
D_{11} data user | D_{11} = {citizen; company; city; journalist} }

Step 3.3: The empirical to conceptual approach is applied here as well. Empirical data was added from the database Nominet [35], which is mainly a provider for the registration of domains but also offers additional services. Nominet provided information about 150 projects. After filtering the projects according to SC characteristics and skipping projects analyzed in the second iteration, we analyzed 54 SC projects in total. These projects were analyzed by two independent researchers with a structured content analysis using an open coding system [34]. These two independent coding systems were compared and synchronized afterwards. This analysis led to the further development of the taxonomy as follows:

T = { D_1 user of the solution | D_1 = {things; citizen; companies; cities; journalists; researcher; developer} {NEX}
D_2 connection to the user | D_2 = {smart devices; smart environment; smart data platforms} {NEX}
D_3 domain of the application | D_3 = {governance; environment; economy; mobility; infrastructure; technology; citizen; services}
D_4 periodicity of the data | D_4 = {static; semi-dynamic; dynamic}
D_5 data ownership | D_5 = {citizen; company; city} {NEX}
D_6 data storage location | D_6 = {company server; cloud server; city server; open data platform; end device}
D_7 data processing | D_7 = {manually; automatically; part-automatically}
D_8 data quality | D_8 = {reviewed; review necessary; no review}
D_9 data type | D_9 = {numeric measuring data; numeric data; geographic data; textual data; video data; machine recognizable data} {NEX}
D_{10} usage of the data | D_{10} = {evaluation; analysis; monitoring; practical application; open data portal; atomization} {NEX}
D_{11} interaction with the data | D_{11} = {synchronic; asynchronous; no interaction}}

Step 3.4: The empirical to conceptual approach was applied again in the last iteration. In order to expand the number of SC projects, another database called Bable [8] was analyzed. This database is a spin-off of the Frauenhofer IAO. It provides an overview of realized SC projects and provides a platform to gather objects in this field. As many SC projects had already been analyzed, only ten more projects came from this database. Thus, a free search on Google was performed to find additional projects; eight additional ones were found [30, 32]. After analyzing these 18 SC projects, no new dimensions or characteristics could be identified. Additionally, the characteristics are complete, the dimensions are unique, and they each contain only one object. In terms of the guidelines from the methodology section, all objective end criteria were fulfilled at this point. Additionally, the taxonomy is succinct, robust, complete, expendable, and explainable. Thus, the subjective end criteria are also fulfilled. The taxonomy is presented in detail in the next section.

4.2 Taxonomy for Data-Driven Smart City Projects

Our final taxonomy for data-driven SC projects can be found in Table 1. The dimensions and characteristics of the taxonomy are as follows: (1) The dimension *'domain of application'* summarizes all areas of use in a SC project [20–22]. This dimension summarizes similar domains such as demographic, health, and education. The characteristics of these dimension are governance, environment, economy, mobility, infrastructure, technology, citizen, and services [20–22]. Measurement of the air quality can be seen as an environment characteristic [32]. (2) The second dimension is '*usage of the data'* dimension. This dimension contains qualitative and quantitative evaluation and analyzes of the data [36]. Monitoring of the data and its practical application as well as open data portals were identified [37]. An automatic control with the data was also identified as one characteristic of this dimension [38]. The characteristics of this dimension are not exclusive because the data could be used in different use cases at the same time, such as analysis and practical application [36]. (3) The third dimension is about the '*user of the solution*' in a SC [39]. Users could be citizens, companies, cities, or journalists [36, 39]. Another potential user of the solution could be a thing, such as a streetlight that could use data to control themselves automatically [38]. Researchers and developers were also identified as data users of the solution [40]. This dimension is not exclusive because users could use the solution simultaneously; the city and companies could use the solution at the same time, for example [36]. (4) A fourth dimension was identified as the '*connection of the user'* [22]. This dimension could include smart devices and smart environments [22]; smart data platforms were also identified as a connector in this dimension [41]. The characteristics of this dimension are not exclusive because different users could participate a smart system or solution at the same time and through different connection possibilities [22]. (5) '*Data ownership*' was identified as a fifth dimension [36]. This could be citizens, companies, public authorities respectively public facilities – summarized as cities – or mixed forms [36]. As mixed forms are possible, this dimension is not exclusive. (6) The next identified dimension was the '*data storage location*'. Data is mostly stored on a company's own server, in cloud solutions, in open data platforms, and on servers belonging to the city [36, 42]. These data storage locations are mainly used by the creators of the data, while end users are more likely to save the data on their end device or to open the data via app or website [24]. As the data needs to be saved on one platform in order to analyze it but it is possible to transfer the data from different platforms, this dimension is not exclusive. However, it is possible to gather the data from many different storage locations. (7) Another identified dimension was '*data processing*' which includes the data creation and processing. The creation and processing can be done manually, automatically, or partly automatically, meaning that some parts are processed automatically and some input needs to be processed manually [36]. As the last characteristic is a combination of both first ones, this dimension is exclusive.

(8) The next dimension of the taxonomy is '*data quality*'. This can vary depending on whether the data could be pre-checked by the data supplier or not. A review of the data quality is necessary in the latter case [36]. Thus, the data could be reviewed, not reviewed or partly reviewed. As the last characteristic is a combination of both first ones, this dimension is exclusive. (9) As data can be structured differently, the dimension '*data type'* was identified. This could be numeric measuring data, numeric other data, geographical data, and textual data [36]. Numeric measuring data is an extra characteristic although this data type is a subtype of numerical data as the empirical study identified an accumulation of numeric measuring data. Further, we could identify the characteristic video data which is used in smart car parking systems for instance [30]. If the data is meant to be processed automatically, it needs to be in a structure of machine

Table 1. Taxonomy of data-driven smart city projects

Dimension	Characteristics								exclusive
Domain of application	Governance	Environment	Economy	Mobility	Infrastructure	Technology	Citizen	Services	yes
Usage of the data	Evaluation	Analysis	Monitoring	Practical application	Open data portal	Automatization			no
User of the solution	Things	Companies	Cities	Citizen	Journalists	Researcher	Developer		no
Connection to the user	Smart devices	Smart environments	Smart Data platform						no
Data ownership	Citizen	Company	City						no
Data storage location	Company server	Cloud server	City server	Open data platform	End device				no
Data processing	manually	automatically	Part-automatically						yes
Data quality	reviewed	review necessary	No review						yes
Data type	Numeric measuring data	Numeric data	Geographical data	Textual data	Video data	Machine-recognizable data			no
Interaction with the data	synchronic	asynchronous	No interaction						yes
Periodicity of the data	static	semi-dynamic	dynamic						yes

recognizable data [24]. This characteristic was therefore added to the dimension. All in all, it is possible for data to be available in different data types at the same time; data can be both, numerical data and machine recognizable data, for example. As a consequence, this dimension is not exclusive in the taxonomy. (10) As a subsequent dimension, '*interaction with the data*' was identified [31]. For example, a citizen could use a smart traffic light system that enables them to receive a green light at every intersection on their way [31]. In this case, the characteristic is synchronic. More examples show that there could be also no communication with the user resulting in everything being automatically controlled, e.g. smart lighting in the city [38]. Additionally, an asynchronous interaction is also possible, such as if the user is receiving messages under certain data circumstances [43]. This dimension is exclusive because we do not indicate a combination of these three characteristics. (11) The last dimension of the taxonomy is '*periodicity of the data*' which could be static, dynamic, or semi-dynamic [23]. As the last characteristic is a combination of the two previous ones, this dimension is exclusive.

4.3 Evaluation

As mentioned by Szopinski et al., researchers use often use cases to evaluate their taxonomy [29]. Thus, we decided to use this method in order to evaluate our data-driven SC projects taxonomy.

Table 2. Use cases for evaluation

Category	Use cases	Examples
Internet of Things	18	Toyotas Woven City, Smart Road in Hamburg, Train Station Berlin Südkreuz, VTG Connect
Online Services	6	Smart Networks for Citizens Participation, Windcloud 4.0, ELEVATE Delta
Smart Grids	5	Grow Smarter Cologne, Sync Fuel
Robotics	7	Robotic Vessels as a Service, Powder Buddy
Big Data	5	Port Monitor Harbor Hamburg, NUNAV
Network technologies	1	My SMARTLife electricity
Artificial Intelligence	2	Project HEAT, Forum 4.0
Augmented Reality	1	Speicherstadt Digital

As many different projects from many databases had already been analyzed, other databases that could offer use cases that reflect data-driven SC projects were sought out. A SC project was found in the database 'Smart City Compass' [44]. This database contains 45 different smart city projects (excluding projects which are doubled in the database) in Germany. The different categories used by the database can be found in Table 2. The evaluation of the taxonomy occurs through its implementation across all 45 cases in the database by two independent researchers. If there was not enough data about the project available in the database, more available information was sought out on the internet. Neither of the researchers could identify a case that did not fit into the taxonomy or had characteristics that needed to be added into the taxonomy of data-driven smart city projects. How often each characteristic was selected during the evaluation of the 45 use cases can be seen in Fig. 1.

Dimension	Characteristics								exclusive
Domain of application	Governance (3)	Environment (4)	Economy (5)	Mobility (9)	Infrastructure (4)	Technology (3)	Citizen (9)	Services (8)	yes
Usage of the data	Evaluation (12)	Analysis (34)	Monitoring (10)	Practical application (15)	Open data portal (21)	Automatization (32)			no
User of the solution	Things (18)	Companies (22)	Cities (37)	Citizen (35)	Journalists (6)	Researcher (11)	Developer (13)		no
Connection to the user	Smart devices (34)	Smart environments (16)	Smart Data platform (17)						no
Data ownership	Citizen (8)	Company (32)	City (36)						no
Data storage location	Company server (17)	Cloud server (32)	City server (13)	Open data platform (18)	End device (7)				no
Data processing	Manually (8)	Automatically (15)	Part-automatically (22)						yes
Data quality	Reviewed (14)	review necessary (23)	No review (8)						yes
Data type	Numeric measuring data (23)	Numeric data (18)	Geographical data (17)	Textual data (5)	Video data (7)	Machine-recognizable data (45)			no
Interaction with the data	Synchronic (18)	Asynchronous (22)	No interaction (5)						yes
Periodicity of the data	Static (9)	semi-dynamic (21)	Dynamic (15)						yes

Fig. 1. Evaluation of the taxonomy

In order to illustrate the evaluation, one use case out of the 45 use cases was selected to be described and illustrated in the next paragraphs. The selected use case is called ELEVATE Delta. This is a SC initiative which aims to improve the lives of wheelchair users. ELEVATE Delta is an app which shows all elevators in the city with real time data of their functionality. Therefore, a wheelchair user can plan their trip from A to B in the city with this app with the advantage of knowing where elevators are located, and real time information regarding whether the elevator is disabled and cannot be used [44]. This case is a data-driven SC project because (1) it improves the lives of wheelchair users and (2) the data of the elevators is an essential key resource of the app. Thus, this project is a suitable use case to evaluate this study's data-driven SC project taxonomy.

As seen in Fig. 2, the taxonomy could be used to identify the characteristics of the use case. All exclusive dimensions reflect only one characteristic of this dimension in the given use case. As the project improves the mobility of wheelchair users, the characteristic of the dimension '*domain of application*' is mobility. The data is used in different ways in this case. The first way is in the monitoring of the elevators. Secondly, the data is available in an open data portal. Thirdly, the data has a practical application because it supports the wheelchair users. Fourthly, the data evaluates the functionality of the elevators. These are the four characteristics of the dimension '*usage of the data*'. As the '*users of the solution*' are citizens with wheelchairs, the characteristic in this dimension

Dimension	Characteristics								exclusive
Domain of application	Governance	Environment	Economy	Mobility	Infrastructure	Technology	Citizen	Services	yes
Usage of the data	Evaluation	Analysis	Monitoring	Practical application	Open data portal	Automatization			no
User of the solution	Things	Companies	Cities	Citizen	Journalists	Researcher	Developer		no
Connection to the user	Smart devices	Smart environments	Smart Data platform						no
Data ownership	Citizen	Company	City						no
Data storage location	Company server	Cloud server	City server	Open data platform	End device				no
Data processing	manually	automatically	Part-automatically						yes
Data quality	reviewed	review necessary	No review						yes
Data type	Numeric measuring data	Numeric data	Geographical data	Textual data	Video data	Machine-recognizable data			no
Interaction with the data	synchronic	asynchronous	No interaction						yes
Periodicity of the data	static	semi-dynamic	dynamic						yes

Fig. 2. Evaluation example of the taxonomy

is citizen. The *'connection to the user'* takes place via smartphone, smart devices, and the app - a smart data platform. As the project was initiated by a company, the *'data ownership'* lies with them. Due to the small size of the company, they use a cloud server for the *'data storage location'*. As the data on the elevators is partly processed automatically and party manually, the dimension *'data processing'* is reflected by a part-automatically processing. The *'data quality'* dimension is reviewed because by the quality department of the company. The dimension *'data type'* is reflected by the three data types: geographical data (location of the elevator), textual data (information about the elevator), and machine recognizable data (automatic processing of the data). The *'interaction with the data'* is synchronic because it is real time data. Lastly, the *'periodicity of the data'* is semi-dynamic because of the mix of automatically and manually processed data.

5 Discussion and Conclusion

Constructing on a well-established methodology from information systems literature introduced by Nickerson et al. [11], a taxonomy of data-driven SC projects was developed in this study. Overall, four iterations were conducted, one being conceptually based on a literature review of current SC literature and three being empirically grounded in a heterogeneous set of SC projects. The taxonomy of data-driven SC projects consists of eleven dimensions, each represented through a distinct set of characteristics and all providing a means to conceptualize data-driven SC projects as a phenomenon. The evaluation of the taxonomy indicates its reliability in terms of classifying and distinguishing cases of data-driven SC projects different studies. Thus, the taxonomy was proven to be useful and it meets its purpose by providing empirically validated and conceptually grounded characteristics of data-driven SC projects.

Introducing a thoroughly developed, reliable taxonomy of data-driven SC projects offers immediate implications for research and practice. The taxonomy offers an effectual way to indicate the characteristics of data-driven SC projects – effectual because the taxonomy allows researchers to describe data-driven SC projects in a consistent approach and to distinguish them from each other. Thus, the taxonomy contributes to the existing body of knowledge on data-driven SC projects, resulting in a shared language that has been missing up to this point. In particular, the added descriptive knowledge helps to build a better understanding of the key dimensions and the characteristics they entail. A common knwodege based on this taxonomy highlights the materialization of SC project ideas and understanding among scholars that will lead towards the development of a deeper theorizing process on data-driven SC projects. All of this leads to the creation of new ideas according to data-driven smart city projects and researchers can better position their work in the SC field based on this taxonomy. A common understanding of data-driven SC projects also gives rise to implications for organizations. Despite the taxonomy's simplicity, it may prove to be highly effective in identifying the chances and opportunities for data-driven SC projects. This could be due to the different characteristics in the taxonomy, such as the opportunity of cloud computing, was not taken into account at the beginning of the data-driven SC project initiative. Therefore, the application of the taxonomy allows for strategic differentiation of SC initiatives. Practitioners may also benefit from the taxonomy as it could provide them with initial guidance in terms of the materialization of ideas and considerations regarding new SC projects.

Nevertheless, this research has some boundaries and limitations that open up the potential for future research. The methodology of the taxonomy follows a design science approach building an effective solution in order to solve identified problem [45]. However, it is not given that it provides an optimal solution and other independent studies may generate different results. The results from our evaluation are also limited in their generalization because all the use cases which are taken into consideration were from Germany. Applying the taxonomy to a set of use cases with global origins would help better evaluate the concept; future research should re-evaluate and adjust the taxonomy accordingly. Common databases in this field were used to collect the dataset of SC projects. It appeared that this study captured a sufficient set of diverse SC projects from different contexts and regions. Yet, there are still more use cases that have not been realized which may lead to increased diversity in the dataset.

There is also potential for this taxonomy to serve future research as it lays the foundation for a deeper process to theorize the nature of data-driven SC projects. With a reliable taxonomy at hand future research may focus on collecting more use cases of SC initiatives, leading to high-order constructs such as data-driven SC projects archetypes. Such archetypes could help to further theorize how data can be further used in the SC context. Overall, this research lays the foundation for future developments in the field of data-driven SC projects and initiatives.

References

1. United Nations. https://www.un.org/development/desa/publications/2018-revision-of-world-urbanization-prospects.html. Accessed 10 July 2019

2. Sankhe, S., et al.: India's urban awakening: building inclusive cities, sustaining economic growth. McKinsey Global Institute (2010)
3. Barreto, L., Amaral, A., Baltazar, S.: Urban mobility digitalization: towards mobility as a service (MaaS). In: 2018 International Conference on Intelligent Systems (IS), pp. 850–855. IEEE (2018)
4. Dameri, R.P.: Smart city implementation. Progress in IS; Springer: Genoa, Italy (2017)
5. Dameri, R.P., Cocchia, A.: Smart city and digital city: twenty years of terminology evolution. In: X Conference of the Italian Chapter of AIS, ITAIS, pp. 1–8 (2011)
6. Hartmann, P.M., Zaki, M., Feldmann, N., Neely, A.: Big data for big business? A taxonomy of data-driven business models used by start-up firms. In: University of Cambridge, Cambridge Service Alliance, pp. 1–30 (2014)
7. Kühne, B., Böhmann, T.: Data-driven business models - building the bridge between data and value. 27th European Conference on Information SystemsStockholm, Sweden, pp. 1–16 (2019)
8. Bable. https://www.bable-smartcities.eu/explore/use-cases/?L=0. Accessed 24 April 2020
9. Perboli, G., De Marco, A., Perfetti, F., Marone, M.: A new taxonomy of smart city projects. Transp. Res. Procedia **3**, 470–478 (2014)
10. Niaros, V.: Introducing a taxonomy of the "smart city": towards a commons-oriented approach? tripleC: communication, capitalism & critique. Open Access J. Global Sustain. Inf. Soc. **14**, 51–61 (2016)
11. Nickerson, R.C., Varshney, U., Muntermann, J.: A method for taxonomy development and its application in information systems. Eur. J. Inf. Syst. **22**, 336–359 (2013)
12. Chourabi, H., et al.: Understanding smart cities: an integrative framework. In: 45th Hawaii International Conference on System Sciences, pp. 2289–2297 (2012)
13. Anttiroiko, A.-V., Valkama, P., Bailey, S.J.: Smart cities in the new service economy: building platforms for smart services. AI Soc. **29**, 323–334 (2014)
14. Giourka, P., et al.: The smart city business model canvas—a smart city business modeling framework and practical tool. Energies **12**, 4798 (2019)
15. Vargo, S.L., Lusch, R.F.: Evolving to a new dominant logic for marketing. J. Market. **68**, 1–17 (2004)
16. Cheng, B., Longo, S., Cirillo, F., Bauer, M., Kovacs, E.: Building a big data platform for smart cities: experience and lessons from santander. In: 2015 IEEE International Congress on Big Data, pp. 592–599. IEEE (2015)
17. Bifulco, F., Tregua, M.: Service innovation and smart cities: linking the perspectives. In: Russo-Spena, T., Mele, C., Nuutinen, M. (eds.) Innovating in Practice, pp. 261–287. Springer, Cham (2017). https://doi.org/10.1007/978-3-319-43380-6_12
18. Albino, V., Berardi, U., Dangelico, R.M.: Smart cities: definitions, dimensions, performance, and initiatives. J. Urban Technol. **22**, 3–21 (2015)
19. Su, K., Li, J., Fu, H.: Smart city and the applications. In: 2011 International Conference on Electronics, Communications and Control (ICECC), pp. 1028–1031. IEEE (2011)
20. Lombardi, P., Giordano, S., Farouh, H., Yousef, W.: Modelling the smart city performance. Innovation. Eur. J. Soc. Sci. Res. **25**, 137–149 (2012)
21. Sillivan, F.: https://ww2.frost.com/wp-content/uploads/2019/01/SmartCities.pdf. Accessed 18 Jan 2019
22. Lim, C., Maglio, P.P.: Data-driven understanding of smart service systems through text mining. Serv. Sci. **10**, 154–180 (2018)
23. Bischof, S., Karapantelakis, A., Nechifor, C.-S., Sheth, A.P., Mileo, A., Barnaghi, P.: Semantic modelling of smart city data. In: Wright State University CORE Scholar Conference, pp. 1–5 (2014)

24. Tcholtchev, N., Farid, L., Marienfeld, F., Schieferdecker, I., Dittwald, B., Lapi, E.: On the interplay of open data, cloud services and network providers towards electric mobility in smart cities. In: 37th Annual IEEE Conference on Local Computer Networks-Workshops, pp. 860–867. IEEE (2012)
25. Webster, J., Watson, R.T.: Analyzing the past to prepare for the future: writing a literature review. MIS Q. **26**, xiii–xxiii (2002)
26. Paukstadt, U., Gollhardt, T., Blarr, M., Chasin, F., Becker, J.: A taxonomy of consumer-oriented smart energy business models. In: Proceedings of the 27th European Conference on Information Systems, pp. 1–17 (2019)
27. Nagel, E., Kranz, J., Sandner, P., Hopf, S.: How blockchain facilitates smart city applications–development of a multi-layer taxonomy. In: Proceedings of the 27th European Conference on Information Systems, pp. 1–17 (2019)
28. Heinrich, K., Roth, A., Zschech, P.: Everything counts: a taxonomy of deep learning approaches for object counting. In: Proceedings of the 27th European Conference on Information Systems, pp. 1–16 (2019)
29. Szopinski, D., Schoormann, T., Kundisch, D.: Because your taxonomy is worth it: Towards a framework for taxonomy evaluation. In: Proceedings of the 27th European Conference on Information Systems, pp. 1–19 (2019)
30. Smart Parking. https://www.smartparking.com/smartpark-system/anpr. Accessed 21 Apr 2020
31. Cardwell, D.: Copenhagen lighting the way to greener, more efficient cities. New York Times 8 (2014)
32. iCity Project, http://icityproject.eu/information-systems-map. Accessed 13 Apr 2020
33. EU SCIS, https://smartcities-infosystem.eu/content/about-smart-cities-information-system-scis. Accessed 10 Apr 2020
34. Mayring, P.: On generalization in qualitatively oriented research. In: Forum Qualitative Sozialforschung/Forum: Qualitative Social Research (2007)
35. Nominet, https://www.nominet.uk/about. Accessed 19 Apr 2020
36. Enarson, L.: Data management plan for GrowSmarter. City of Stockholm, Stockholm (2017)
37. Stoppel, V., Klassen, B.: Smart City Munich Lighthouse Project - Documentation of activities and achievments. München: Stadt München D4.1.3 (2019)
38. Tviligth. https://www.tvilight.com/case-studies. Accessed 21 Apr 2020
39. Schieferdecker, I., Tcholtchev, N., Lämmel, P., Scholz, R., Lapi, E.: Towards an open data based ICT reference architecture for smart cities. In: 2017 Conference for E-Democracy and Open Government (CeDEM), pp. 184–193. IEEE (2017)
40. Greater LondonAutority. https://data.london.gov.uk. Accessed 25 Apr 2020
41. VMZ Berlin. https://www.smarter-together.eu/file-download/download/public/1257. Accessed 07 May 2019
42. Rolando, D., Palm, B., Claesson, J., Nilsson, A., Robert, M., Shahrokni, H.: https://grow-smarter.eu/fileadmin/editor-upload/reports/growsmarter_validation.pdf. Accessed 08 May 2019
43. Bigbelly. https://bigbelly.com/platform. Accessed 24 Apr 2020
44. ThiS. https://www.smartcity-kompass.de/smartcity/elevate-delta/. Accessed 15 July 2020
45. Hevner, A.R., March, S.T., Park, J., Ram, S.: Design science in information systems research. MIS Q. 75–105 (2004)

Towards Sustainable Transport: A Strategic Decision Support System for Urban Logistics Operations

Maximilian Heumann[1(✉)], Richard Pump[2], Michael H. Breitner[1], Arne Koschel[2], and Volker Ahlers[2]

[1] Information Systems and Management Institute, Leibniz University Hannover, Hannover, Germany
{heumann,breitner}@iwi.uni-hannover.de
[2] Department of Computer Science, University of Applied Sciences and Arts Hannover, Hannover, Germany
{richard.pump,arne.koschel,volker.ahlers}@hs-hannover.de

Abstract. Global urbanization for decades has led to unprecedented levels and growing demands for urban logistics. Thus, problems such as congestion, environmental noise, and urban sprawl are growing. As a result, many cities face problems of optimal decision-making regarding green and sustainable smart transportation systems and infrastructures. However, various possible measures and logistics concepts are available to improve urban logistics, while effects are unclear and difficult to predict. To meet the growing need for future-oriented decisions by city authorities, we developed a decision support system prototype that allows a strategic simulation-based evaluation of different logistics concepts regarding defined targets, e.g., pollutant emissions, traffic flow, space requirements, or economic efficiency on a city district level. An expert system for the strategic evaluation of logistics concepts on a city district level is integrated to achieve transferability and scalability.

Keywords: Urban logistics · Liveable city · Data-driven government · Decision support system · Expert system

1 Introduction

The world's urban population is growing rapidly and already accounts for 55% of the total population, a share that the UN expects to rise to 68% by 2050 [1]. Together with the continuous growth of e-commerce, urbanization is leading to a rising transport demand in cities. The ongoing digital transformation and emerging digital business models in urban food, beverage, and parcel delivery are causing an increasingly dynamic transport demand characterized by time-critical services. The recent global COVID-19 pandemic has further changed the logistics industry's landscape and strongly intensified this already growing parcel delivery demand [2, 3]. As a result, many cities face growing challenges to their transport systems and infrastructure that affect the urban population's health and

F. Ahlemann et al. (Eds.): WI 2021, LNISO 46, pp. 367–381, 2021.
https://doi.org/10.1007/978-3-030-86790-4_25

quality of life, such as congestion, environmental noise, CO_2 emissions, accidents, and urban sprawl. The future transport system, the cityscape, and the cities' quality of life will depend on city authorities' actions regarding the urban transport landscape.

One way city authorities can influence the future transport and mobility system of a city is to promote innovative logistics concepts. Since the most cost-intensive part of the supply chain in parcel delivery is urban "last mile" delivery [4], logistics providers also have an interest in urban transport and try to optimize their business through various innovative concepts. The call for sustainable and future-oriented decisions by city authorities is therefore pushed by various possible measures and logistics concept developments of service providers to improve urban transport. It is then necessary for decision-makers to ex-ante assess on a strategic level which of the available logistics concepts are likely to achieve the best effects depending on the requirements. Since the impact of a logistics concept depends not only on the concept itself but also on the distinctive attributes of a city or district, this is a complex issue of uncertain effects, which must be considered in each specific case. The impacts of a logistics concept may vary in districts with different populations or built environments.

Furthermore, testing logistics concepts within a city district by implementing small-scale pilot projects is neither cost-efficient nor useful. The uncertainty concerning suitable logistics concepts for a more sustainable future is growing. Especially with the rising number of delivery companies, the need for decision support regarding the strategic planning of logistics initiatives in urban areas is increasing from an Information Systems (IS) perspective [5, 6]. The described challenges lead us to our research question:

How can an IS support decision-makers in the strategic planning of urban logistic concepts while assessing its economic and environmental impacts?

We investigate this question following a Design Science Research (DSR) approach and develop a technological artifact that integrates three components into a holistic decision support system (DSS): prototype: (1) a simulation-based micro- and macro-scale database for scenarios of urban logistics concepts; (2) an integral expert system (ES) to provide scalability and transferability enabling individual problem specifications; and (3) a user-oriented web application to assess the impact of logistics concepts on traffic, economic as well as environmental objectives and to map the decision making of economic actors.

The focus of this article is on the technical design of these components and their integration. We instantiate the artifact as a DSS prototype and apply it in a case study based on real-world data to enable a proof of concept. Also, expert assessments are included in the evaluation [7, 8].

First, related scientific work is described in Sect. 2. Afterward, Sect. 3 presents the applied research design. Subsequently, the DSS prototype development with database development, integral ES and the web-based platform is introduced in Sect. 4. Section 5 demonstrates the applicability of the DSS prototype and serves to evaluate our artifact. After elaborating limitations and future research perspectives in Sect. 6, we complete our article with a conclusion in Sect. 7.

2 Related Work

Relevant related work includes research on urban logistics, DSS, and ES for urban logistics. The majority of literature in the area deals with optimizing existing technologies and traditional urban freight operations. Lagorio et al. identify focus areas in urban logistics to suggest the best possible directions for future research [6]. They conclude that municipal administrations' decision support receives growing attention in current research as reasonable decisions in urban development are increasingly relevant and urgent [6, 9]. However, research in this area is still underrepresented and ex-ante approaches need to be addressed more intensively.

In a more recent review, Dolati et al. further emphasize the importance of decision support for city authorities in the context of urban logistics and point out the relevance of stakeholder involvement [10]. The initiative "Urban Transport Roadmaps" funded by the European Commission, developed a web-based DSS for urban transport. The project group implemented an informative platform for city authorities to evaluate future mobility scenarios in urban areas in a time horizon up to 2030, allowing the comparison of different urban structures and a selection of measures for urban transport. The quantified effects of various measures (e.g. car sharing, prioritized public transport) are based on modeling future macroeconomic trends. The project parties do not consider any microscale traffic effects of logistics concepts in city districts. The portfolio of measures is limited to regulatory actions and mobility services. Their web-tool thereby aims at a different use-case, showing detailed traffic development predictions for entire cities instead of predicted impacts of novel logistics concepts on traffic on a city district scale [11].

With a decision support framework for simulation-based ex-ante assessment of regulatory measures for urban logistics, Bozzo et al. suggest a more disaggregated approach. However, the authors remain with a theoretical framework without an actual application. The approach does not specify any logistics concepts and is moderately scalable; in any case, very resource-intensive simulations are necessary for an assessment. The developed model did not lead to an application [12].

Sarra et al. also highlight a lack of applicable simulation-based DSS approaches in a literature review. The sensitivity of existing models on urban commercial vehicle flows is limited when evaluating individually tailored measures in urban districts [5, 13–15]. These models focus on individual vehicle movements and neglect logistic and traveler behavior underlying these movements [5, 16].

While DSS are well established in urban logistics, ES are less common. ES are computer-based IS, designed to represent expert domain knowledge to provide solutions to problems that generally require a large scope of expert knowledge [8, 17]. Against this background, despite complex information and knowledge in urban logistics, we only identified one article that directly addresses an ES in the field of urban logistics. Schröder et al. [16] conceive a conceptual framework for an ES to analyze smart policies for urban courier-express-parcel (CEP) transport but remain with a conceptual framework, without application. Besides, urban logistics also combines other sectors, such as food deliveries, shopping and service trips, or trips by tradespeople and medical care services, and as such is much more complex than stand-alone CEP transport.

In summary, although the relevant literature provides substantial preliminary studies, there is a lack of practical solutions for user-oriented strategic decision support for city authorities in planning sustainable urban logistics at the micro-scale level, despite growing relevance. In both, literature streams and the expert opinions of conducted interviews, decision support implementation based on spatially disaggregated information is considered promising. However, designing an applicable DSS is challenging, requiring further research on practical solutions [5, 6, 10–12].

3 Research Approach

We tackle this research gap from an IS perspective by creating a technological artifact following the DSR approach of Peffers et al. [18]. The introduction to our research is considered problem-centered according to the DSR approach. Our research motivation results from a real-world problem as part of a collaborative project, namely the support of strategic decisions for system integration of logistics concepts to improve urban transport.

To define our problem-solving objectives, we analyzed the scientific literature on research streams on urban logistics. We conducted expert interviews and workshops with urban transport planners, from which we derive our core requirements. We use modeling elements for the optimal design of logistics concept scenarios from the literature on decision support for sustainable logistics concepts. These modeled scenarios serve as the basis for the conducted simulations. Knowledge about relevant decision target values resulted from the expert interviews and periodical workshops. From the literature on the development of application-oriented ES and DSS, we used the knowledge of system design elements to create a scalable and transferable architecture that is easy to implement. With our technological artifact, we investigate a possible approach for strategic decision support for district-specific logistics while remaining flexible concerning different innovative logistics concepts.

To demonstrate the use of the designed artifact, we instantiated the technical back- and front-end of a DSS prototype. We conducted a case study based on real-world data in Hannover, Germany. To evaluate our DSS prototype, we compared our case study results with the effects expected by experts in Hannover. Involved practitioners and experts work in the automotive industry, the CEP delivery sector, logistics, transport, and urban planning. The experts based their conclusions on their experience and the evaluation of the simulations carried out. We evaluated the congruence of the results with the experts' expectations and considered different cases. Two cases concern districts for which the concepts were simulated, i.e., data are available in the database. In two other cases, we analyzed a district similar to the representative pilot districts and a district that differs significantly from our representative districts' structural parameters, for which no data are available and the ES is triggered.

4 DSS Prototype for Urban Logistics

The pursued DSR approach provides improvements for both the rigor and the relevance of DSS research. However, DSS artifacts are often criticized for their lack of relevance to practice and for neglecting configurability and contextual dynamics [19, 20]. To counteract this lack, we oriented our DSS prototype development towards essential DSS design elements [21]. We worked towards the highest possible practical relevance, configurability and contextual dynamics [19]. Practitioners and experts from the fields of transport planning and logistics were involved throughout the development process to achieve a high relevance to practice. The architecture of the DSS prototype with its main components is illustrated in Fig. 1. By applying our DSS prototype, users are presented with general impact tendencies of defined concepts on eight key performance indicators (KPIs): pollutant emissions, traffic flow, space requirements, economic efficiency, costs, innovative substance, technology acceptance and ecological efficiency, which have been identified in expert interviews and workshops as most significant and relevant for city authorities.

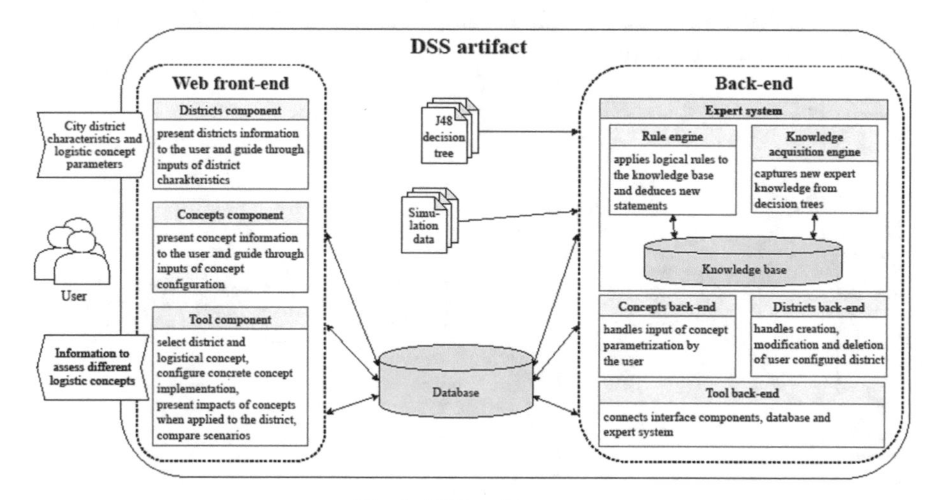

Fig. 1. DSS architecture.

To evaluate the logistics concepts' effects, users choose from a selection of representative district types and preset logistics concepts, or individually configure both the district parameters and the desired concepts. The districts' inputs are mainly structural parameters and statistical features such as population density, the share of individual population groups, registered cars, living space per inhabitant. Concept parameters include specific characteristics such as hub capacities, degree of supply fleet electrification, percentage of the participating population. By using the tool component, concepts can then be compared and examined for their effects and impacts.

If the desired scenario corresponds to a simulated scenario, the simulation database provides the information for the evaluation. If individual scenarios are to be examined, the ES and knowledge database in the backend is used to check the fact inputs and infer effects. To provide an efficient and easily scalable solution, we implemented an upload function that allows extending the knowledge base with human-readable decision trees, which are then automatically processed and implemented in the rules engine. Moreover, the database can be extended by uploading new simulation results.

In the following sections, the development process regarding (1) the database, (2) the development of the integral ES, and (3) the development of the user interface of our web-based DSS, with all functionalities for input, output, and presentation of decision-related data, is explained.

4.1 Creating the Database

The first step in creating the DSS was creating a database containing the KPI impacts of logistics concepts on the representative district types. To create the database, three steps were executed within the collaborative project USEfUL: (1) the identification of projects and concepts for sustainable urban logistics, (2) the definition of simulated logistics concepts and scenarios and (3) the acqusisition of domain knowledge through expert assisted simulations. The process was supported by experts from the automotive sector, parcel delivery services, and urban transport planning. Figure 2 shows the process from data collection to results analysis.

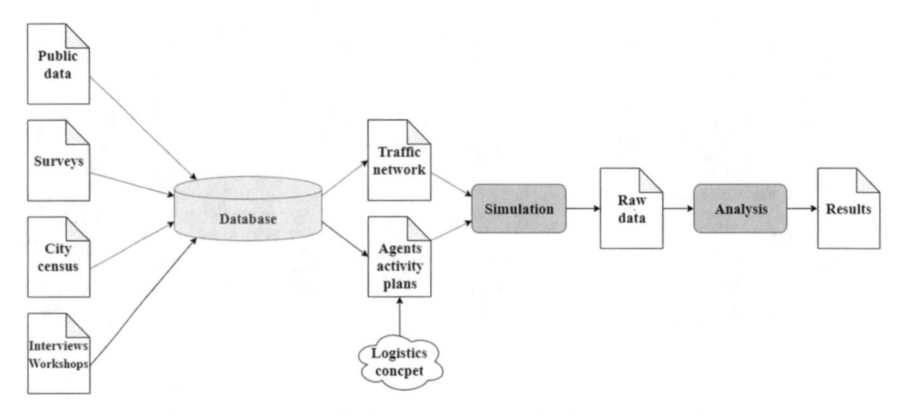

Fig. 2. Process of logistics concept and scenario simulations

First, necessary data regarding urban logistics and citizen behavior were collected from different sources like public data repositories, surveys, expert interviews and workshops. Sources include *OpenStreetMap*, General Transit Feed Specification (GTFS) data [22], the latest German mobility study "Mobilität in Deutschland" (MiD) [23], and the survey of German Mobility Panel (MOP) [24]. Independent surveys and interviews supplement the data. All data were collected in a database to generate a model of the current traffic in Hannover's city. The spatially disaggregated database is crucial for decision support on the level of city districts. The detailed process of model creation and simulation process can be found in [25] and [26]. Starting from a basic scenario, which represents the current transport and mobility landscape in Hannover, different logistics scenarios like e-grocery, parcel pickup stations, Smart City Loop and others were modelled and simulated. For the logistics concepts' individual scenarios, literature reviews, surveys, and statistics were conducted, evaluated, and integrated into the models. The macro- and micro-scale simulations are carried out using *MATSim* framework and *AnyLogic* software. The raw output data produced by the simulations consist of large event files (essentially a record file of the simulation) and extensive statistics that need to be analyzed before results can be presented. Using data mining tools for event file analysis and models for cost and emission calculation, the impacts of the logistics concepts on the city districts were evaluated to produce a foundation upon which the DSS could be built.

4.2 Integral Expert System

The presented ES corresponds to a rule-based system and thus primarily consists of a knowledge base (consisting of rules) and the inference engine, to process corresponding knowledge and interpret fact inputs. Following Waterman's established guidelines, the development process of our ES includes the steps of identification, conceptualization, formalization, implementation, and testing [27]. As it is flexible, robust, and offers a practical approach for data analytics, we further adapted and applied the cross-industry standard process for data mining (CRISP-DM) methodology for our data and rules mining purposes [28]. Figure 3 presents the schematic development process in line with our DSR approach.

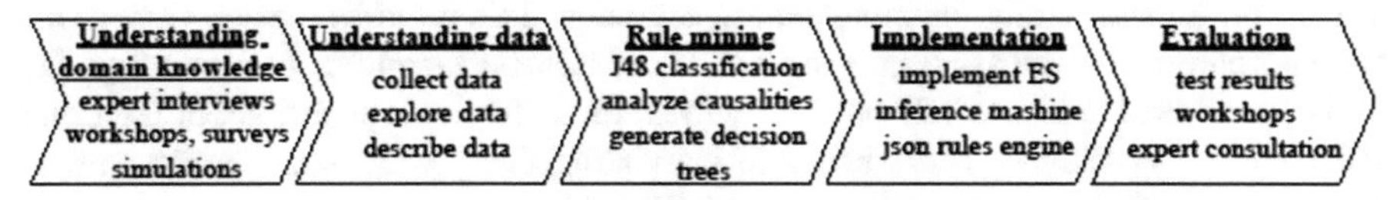

Fig. 3. Process of ES development.

To develop the ES, an understanding of the domain knowledge in urban logistics, traffic, and city planning was initially established. We elaborated the problem, possible solutions, target values, and other decision factors in cooperation with experts. Moreover, we carried out a requirements analysis for the ES. All findings then lead to the simulations described in Sect. 4.1. The simulation results provide the data basis for all further steps.

To process the results more efficiently and better understand the outputs, all numerical continuous output values were classified into ordinal data. The data were processed using the *WEKA* data mining tool and the *J48* classification algorithm to derive decision trees. The human-readable decision trees can then be transferred to the knowledge base through an automated interface. The interface translates the decision trees into rules for the inference engine. For the implementation of the integral ES as part of the DSS, appropriate interfaces were implemented within the backend to check user input and for the inference of results.

The algorithm used for rule mining, *J48*, is an open-source Java implementation of the *C4.5* statistical classification algorithm [29]. The algorithm is widely used and is considered best practice in data mining [30–32]. It offers a very efficient implementation and results that are easy to understand by the end user. A comprehensible human readable and interpretable rule base is necessary to achieve a hybrid intelligence of experts and computer systems.

The results of the rule mining classification are decision trees for each concept and effect. Each decision tree reflects the input parameters for which causal relationships were identified in the rule mining process. These facts can be both district-specific characteristics and concept parameters. The rules are used to derive positive, negative, or constant effects on local exhaust emissions for the specific concept.

After the rule base was created, the ES was implemented using the JavaScript-based json-rules-engine. The rules consist of simple *JSON* structures, making them human-readable and easy to persist.

The functionality of the ES is illustrated in the architecture in Fig. 1. Core components of the ES are the knowledge base consisting of the *J48* decision trees based on simulation results and expert knowledge, the rule engine for inferring results from input facts, and the facility to extend the knowledge base by uploading new decision trees. The ES implementation enables the user to create his or her configurations of districts and concept scenarios. The users' fact input is checked based on the rule base and causal effects are inferred and presented in a comprehensible way, similar to the output shown in Fig. 4.

4.3 The Web-Based DSS Prototype

The proper presentation of the collected evaluations and inferred data is paramount to their usefulness in city planning's daily activities. This requires a clear view of the system's purpose as well as primary users and use cases. Furthermore, the product quality of the web-based DSS needs to be closely monitored. To create an artifact of high user satisfaction, the design process needs to work extensively with future product users. Therefore, the first step of developing the DSS is identifying key users, and analyzing the use cases, describing system interactions. Main user groups of the DSS are city planners and urban decision-makers, like local politicians. During requirement analysis, we again used interviews and workshops to identify the main user groups' needs. With an ever-increasing amount of different logistics concepts and uncertain effects, keeping an overview becomes more challenging. City planners and politicians need a solution providing at-a-glance decision support.

During our interviews, we identified five major use cases for the DSS: (1) Collect information about logistics concepts, (2) collect information about predefined representative city districts, (3) configure an own individual district, (4) evaluate effects of logistics concepts in a district, (5) export evaluation results.

The main goal of the DSS needs to be the presentation of information, as users want to collect information and analyze connections between concrete implementations of logistics concepts and properties of city districts. The DSS needs to explain the processes involved in logistics concepts and parameters that define concrete implementations on a level that is quickly understood, preferably by using simple pictures. Similar to logistics concepts, the predefined representative city districts need to be presented with all characteristics relevant to city planning. Again, a graphical representation is preferred. Furthermore, users want to input own scenarios of own city districts if the representative districts do not cover preferences. While the representative districts aim to be representative of many other urban areas, not all possible districts can be covered with simulation data within the project's timeframe. Since therefore no data are available for user-configured districts, the application needs to infer information using the ES described in Sect. 4.2. The essential function of the DSS is the presentation of the effects of logistics concepts within a given city district, e.g. the emission effects of using micro hubs for parcel delivery in urban area [33].

To expand user groups to the general public, enabling participation of citizens, the decision was made to provide the DSS as a web-based tool, instead of a standard desktop application or a smartphone app. In this way, not only political and administrative decision-makers are involved in logistics initiatives of the city, but also residents can use the platform to inform themselves about new logistics concepts. This allows us to provide an easy-to-use solution that does not require installation and can be used from many different devices.

Lastly, an export of the information is implemented to allow users to take the results, integrate them into presentations, and use them without access to the application. Since functional requirements are covered through the definition of use cases, quality requirements and technical restrictions need to be examined. A major quality requirement is a high degree of usability as defined by *ISO25010* [34]. The projected user groups of city planners and decision makers are not technical specialists and do not necessarily have the time or motivation to learn the usage of a complex software system.

The technical restrictions were rather loose, as the city of Hannover already uses a wide range of web-servers and databases in their current operation. Therefore, modern technologies can easily be used without putting unnecessary strain on the IT-department.

Building on the defined vision of the DSS, the technical components can be designed. For most of the functionality, a simple database combined with an attractive front end suffices. Only the creation of own districts and the inference of new information requires more sophisticated elements of the ES. Figure 1 shows the rough architecture of the web-based DSS. Within the web–interface, three central components are implemented. The Districts and Concepts components will present the districts and concepts to users by accessing the information stored in the Database. In combination with its backend components, they further handle the creation, modification, and deletion of user configured districts and concept scenarios. The component Tool presents the main functionality, which uses the other two interface components, the Database, and the Rule Engine. Through the interface provided by the web-tool users can select a district and a logistics concept, configure the concrete concept implementation and is presented the impact of the concept when applied to the district. While all known combinations are loaded from the database, unknown combinations (i.e., selecting a user created district) query the rule engine for the rule-based inference of results.

Figure 4 shows a screenshot of the finished prototype. Since the DSS addresses German users from the public, political, and administrative milieu, the website is designed in German. The user first selects a city district and a logistics concept. After configuring the concrete implementation of the logistics concept, the user is presented the general tendencies on KPIs like emissions and costs. This process requires few interactions for a rough overview and presents results in an easily understandable way, achieving our initial design goals. Furthermore, a more in-depth inspection of concepts can be achieved by changing the concept parameters and creating own districts, which is not shown in the presented screenshot. The prototype also provides functionalities to inform about the innovative logistics concepts, the representative city districts and to compare different concepts in terms of their impact.

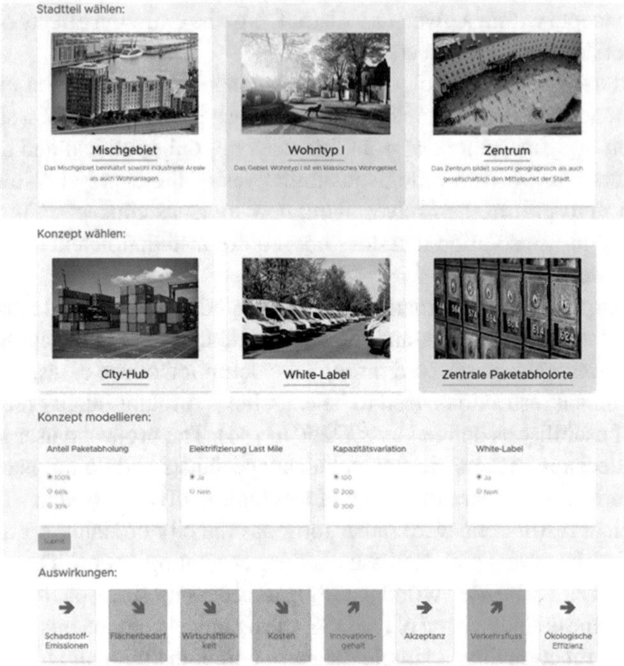

Fig. 4. Screenshot from the web-based DSS prototype.

5 Case Study and Discussion

To demonstrate the applicability and evaluation of our DSS prototype as part of our DSR approach, we conducted a case study. We choose a use case in which the evaluation of a micro hub concept is performed in different environments. On the one hand, the performed simulations substantiate the validity of our DSS prototype, on the other hand all results were reviewed and evaluated by domain experts throughout the case study in focus group discussions.

For the applicability check, two Hannover districts were considered [35], which were simulated as two of the predefined representative districts. In terms of transferability, one structurally similar, and one strongly different district were also considered. The similar case is the district Dresden Neustadt [36] that is similar to the Hannover district Oststadt. The structurally different area is the district Hohenstein in Wolfsburg [37]. For the case study it was necessary to enter structural data of the four study areas. This includes values such as population (absolute and relative as a proportion of total cities population), area (absolute and relative as a proportion of total city area), population density, number of private households and commercial establishments, average population per household, number of registered cars and commercial vehicles, number of social security employees, unemployment rate, and more. In addition, the concepts to be investigated can be assessed by input on the degree of delivery penetration in the district, the capacity of the micro hubs in packages, the selection of optimized or non-optimized locations, or the white-label (WL) or conventional delivery. As requested by the experts, results are presented in roughly classified trends (see Fig. 5).

		pollutant emissions	traffic flow	space requirements	economic efficiency	costs	innovative substance	ecological efficiency
Micro-Hub scenario 1	**Hannover List**	→	→	↓	↑	↓	↓	→
20% share of total deliveries	**Hannover Groß-Buchholz**	↓	→	↓	↑	↓	↓	→
300 p. capacity	**Dresden Neustadt**	↓	→	↓	↑	↓	↓	→
non-optimized, conventional	**Wolfsburg Hohenstein**	↓	→	↓	↑	↓	↓	→
Micro-Hub scenario 2	**Hannover List**	↑	→	↓	→	↓	↑	→
80% share of total deliveries	**Hannover Groß-Buchholz**	↑	→	↓	→	↓	↑	→
800 p. capacity	**Dresden Neustadt**	↑	→	↓	→	↓	↑	→
non-optimized, white-label	**Wolfsburg Hohenstein**	↑	→	↓	→	↓	↑	→
Micro-Hub scenario 3	**Hannover List**	↑	↑	↓	↑	↓	↑	→
80% share of total deliveries	**Hannover Groß-Buchholz**	↑	→	↓	↑	↓	↑	→
800 p. capacity	**Dresden Neustadt**	↑	↑	↓	↑	↓	↑	→
optimized, white-label	**Wolfsburg Hohenstein**	↑	→	↓	↑	↓	↓	→

Fig. 5. Case study results for different concept scenarios and city districts.

It is apparent that the DSS prototype for each scenario can show a trend for all of the defined KPIs in an ordinal scale of three levels. Involved domain experts were able to judge all of the outputs as valid. Despite the very different scenarios, the district structures have little effect on the impact. The three different concepts are more likely to have the most significant impact. The results also show that a standalone WL delivery does not necessarily positively affect traffic flow. Rather, in addition to the WL delivery, an optimized infrastructure of hub locations is required to utilize all operating CEP transport providers' capacities optimally. The KPIs of costs and space requirements seem to be increasing regardless of any variation. However, given the cost-intensive micro-hub concept with high capital commitment, the consulted experts believe this is a realistic effect [33]. The experts also point out that for the third concept scenario, it is striking that the positive changes in traffic flow depending on the similarity of districts testify to the DSS prototype's validity. The similar districts Dresden Neustadt and Hannover List show a positive effect, whereas the more suburban-like districts Wolfsburg Hohenstein and Hannover Groß-Buchholz show no positive effect. According to the experts, the case study allows to confirm that the application meets the requirements set. Our DSS prototype allows realistic statements about logistics concepts in known and unknown districts through the presented tendencies. This confirms the basic transferability of the application. However, it must also be pointed out that the inferred statements about unknown districts cannot be validated by a simulation basis because they are only given on the foundation of derived causalities by the ES.

Consequently, effects in transferred city districts are plausible but not validated. According to experts in urban planning, the results are sufficiently explicit for strategic decision support and at the same time, adequately fuzzy to be suitable for public use. According to the requirement, the results are understandable for political decision-makers and city dwellers without expert knowledge.

However, it is noted that the results in the implemented classification rather address all stakeholders on a political level for first assessments of different logistics concepts. Regarding our requirement for a scalable DSS, our upload function offers a way for expanding the database with new districts and logistics concepts, thus providing an efficient and easy-to-use solution. In the course of conducting the case study, we received further positive feedback on the user-friendliness of the system with regard to the objectives of our artifact. Transparent user workflows and easy navigation throughout the entire websites received particular emphasis. The suggestions for improvement of the DSS prototype included the expansion of the database and the integration of further structural traffic parameters primarily.

6 Limitations and Future Research

This study has several limitations that must be addressed. In the presented case study, only seven of the eight identified KPIs can be depicted yet. For the eighth value of technology acceptance, we are currently surveying to add results after completion. As the system is self-contained, the knowledge base can easily be expanded with the new knowledge from the completed study.

Beyond that, all of the presented results base on simulations and expert knowledge referring to our four selected representative pilot districts in Hannover. As the case study and focus group discussions indicated, further simulations are necessary to expand the database and the knowledge base for a seamless validation of logistics scenarios even in unknown districts or city types and structures. Experts also state that other key figures on individual districts' transport infrastructure can be decisive and show certain relations with the effects of logistics concepts.

However, no infrastructural peculiarities such as rotary traffic or road types were in our work due to the selection of the four representative pilot districts. Another limitation concerning the representative pilot districts in Hannover became apparent since all districts are similar in their structure. Therefore, the inclusion of traffic infrastructure metrics and a more diverse and broader selection of city districts for simulations and data acquisition are recommended, specifically with regard to the rule mining process.

Although our results are based on simulations resulting in continuous numeric output values, only three scaled tendencies should be shown to the end-user to be understandable to a wide range of different knowledge backgrounds. Showing general tendencies only, the application can be opened to the public, presenting information not only to strategic city planners but also to interested citizens possibly affected by decisions made using the DSS. Since the effects of individual concepts in specific urban districts can be perceived as threatening and can worry affected citizens, continuous numerical values were not desired, and the ordinal scale was required to be limited to three categories. In doing so, we contribute to our objective of the involvement of stakeholders. This requirement leads to the limitation of a rather vague three-level output of the DSS. To provide a more detailed assessment for application experts, user authorization and administration could be included in the system to provide separate expert functions.

Regarding the latest COVID-19 pandemic, another limitation arises, as we did not consider the changing mobility and transport behavior and other effects of such a pandemic and the resulting correlations related to logistics concepts [2]. Given the ongoing situation and a growing risk of similar pandemics and catastrophes in the future, such effects should be investigated and included in further research. Future research can also focus on accompanying the implementation of pilot projects of logistics concepts in cities with the presented DSS's help. For this purpose, field studies could be carried out together with experts and the effects predicted by the DSS could be compared with real data from logistical pilot projects.

7 Conclusions

In this paper, we presented our developed DSS providing IS-based strategic decision support for urban logistics. For a well-founded development process based on existing literature on DSS in urban logistics and related disciplines, we used a DSR approach. The developed DSS artifact shows significant progress compared to existing approaches [5, 6, 9, 10]. The DSS provides transferable and scalable strategic decision support for political and administrative decision-makers and involves other stakeholders, such as the public. The insights result from the expert knowledge of practitioners in the fields of traffic models and simulations as well as from scientific literature. A case study and focus group discussion served to test the practicability of the model.

The DSS is a useful and enriching tool for the strategic planning of urban logistics concept initiatives, and funding, towards a liveable city. It serves as decision support and information platform for political and administrative authorities and the public, who can evaluate existing transport structures for the effects of innovative logistics concepts to assess and classify the feasibility of such concepts and resulting benefits. The DSS draws on a comprehensive simulation and knowledge database and uses an integral ES to derive unknown city district structures' effects. Expert interviews have shown that these elements have a great potential to support strategic decision making, especially on a level of political processes.

The simulation and knowledge database should be extended to further urban structures and metrics, and data should be condensed in future work. The provided ordinal scale of results should also be extended from three to five or seven levels based on the condensed data for more precise assessments beyond the strategic dimension.

Acknowledgement. This work is funded by the German Federal Ministry of Education and Research project "USEfUL" (grant ID 03SF0547). The authors cordially thank all USEfUL partners, too.

References

1. United Nations Department of Economic and Social Affairs (UN-DESA): World Urbanization Prospects: The 2018 Revision (2018)

2. Choi, T.M.: Innovative "bring-service-near-your-home" operations under Corona-virus (COVID-19/SARS-CoV-2) outbreak: can logistics become the messiah?. Transp. Res. Part E Logis. Transp. Rev. **140**, 101961 (2020)
3. Singh, S., Kumar, R., Panchal, R., Tiwari, M.K.: Impact of COVID-19 on logistics systems and disruptions in food supply chain. Int. J. Prod. Res. 1–16 (2020)
4. Gevaers, R., Van de Voorde, E., Vanelslander, T.: Characteristics of innovations in last-mile logistics-using best practices, case studies and making the link with green and sustainable logistics. Association for European Transport and contributors (2009)
5. Jlassi, S., Tamayo, S., Gaudron, A.: Simulation applied to urban logistics: a state of the art. In: 10th International Conference on City Logistics, Phuket (2017)
6. Lagorio, A., Pinto, R., Golini, R.: Research in urban logistics: a systematic literature review. Int. J. Phys. Distrib. Logist. Manage. (2016)
7. Nunamaker, J.F., Briggs, R.O., Derrick, D.C., Schwabe, G.: The last research mile: achieving both rigor and relevance in information systems research. J. Manage. Inf. Syst. **32**(3), 10–47 (2015)
8. Miah, S.J., Genemo, H.: A design science research methodology for expert systems development. Aust. J. Inf. Syst. **20** (2016)
9. Karakikes, I., Nathanail, E., Savrasovs, M.: Techniques for smart urban logistics solutions' simulation: a systematic review. In: Kabashkin, I., Yatskiv (Jackiva), I., Prentkovskis, O. (eds.) RelStat. LNNS, vol. 68, pp. 551–561. Springer, Cham (2019). https://doi.org/10.1007/978-3-030-12450-2_53
10. Dolati Neghabadi, P., Evrard Samuel, K., Espinouse, M.L.: Systematic literature review on city logistics: overview, classification and analysis. Int. J. Prod. Res. **5**(3), 865–887 (2019)
11. Kollamthodi, S., Hitchcock, G., Fiorello, D., DeStasio, C.: Development of a Web-Based Tool to Support the Development of City-Level Urban Transport Roadmaps to 2030, no. 16-5913 (2016)
12. Bozzo, R., Conca, A., Marangon, F.: Decision support system for city logistics: literature review, and guidelines for an ex-ante model. Transp. Res. Procedia **3**, 518–527 (2014)
13. Hunt, J.D., Stefan, K.J.: Tour-based microsimulation of urban commercial movements. Transp. Res. Part B Methodol. **41**(9), 981–1013 (2007)
14. Joubert, J.W., Fourie, P.J., Axhausen, K.W.: Large-scale agent-based combined traffic simulation of private cars and commercial vehicles. Transp. Res. Rec. **2168**(1), 24–32 (2010)
15. Soares, G., Kokkinogenis, Z., Macedo, J.L., Rossetti, R.J.F.: Agent-based traffic simulation using sumo and jade: an integrated platform for artificial transportation systems. In: Behrisch, M., Krajzewicz, D., Weber, M. (eds.) SUMO 2013. LNCS, vol. 8594, pp. 44–61. Springer, Heidelberg (2014). https://doi.org/10.1007/978-3-662-45079-6_4
16. Schröder, S., Dabidian, P., Liedtke, G.: A conceptual proposal for an expert system to analyze smart policy options for urban CEP transports. In: 2015 Smart Cities Symposium Prague (SCSP), pp. 1–6. IEEE (2015)
17. Silva, W.T.P.D., Souza, M.A.A.D.: Expert system for selecting and prioritizing projects for handling urban water supply crises. Urban Water J. **15**(6), 561–567 (2018)
18. Peffers, K., Tuunanen, T., Rothenberger, M.A., Chatterjee, S.: A design science research methodology for information systems research. J. Manage. Inf. Syst. **24**(3), 45–77 (2007)
19. Miah, S.J., Gammack, J.G., McKay, J.: A Metadesign theory for Tailorable decision support. J. Assoc. Inf. Syst. **20**(5), 4 (2019)
20. Arnott, D., Pervan, G.: Design science in decision support systems research: an assessment using the Hevner, March, Park, and Ram Guidelines. J. Assoc. Inf. Syst. **13**(11), 1 (2012)
21. Holsapple, C.W.: DSS architecture and types. In: Handbook on Decision Support Systems, vol. 1, pp. 163–189. Springer, Heidelberg (2008). https://doi.org/10.1007/978-3-540-48713-5_9
22. Connect Fahrplanauskunft GmbH: Connect-OpenData-Pool (2019)

23. Bundesministerium für Verkehr und digitale Infrastruktur: Mobilität in Deutschland (MiD) 2017 (2018)
24. Bundesministerium für Verkehr und digitale Infrastruktur: Deutsches Mobilitätspanel 2015/2016 (MOP), Dataset (2016)
25. Bienzeisler, L., Lelke, T., Wage, O., Thiel, F., Friedrich, B.: Development of an agent-based transport model for the city of hanover using empirical mobility data and data fusion. Transp. Res. Procedia **47**, 99–106 (2020)
26. Auf der Landwehr, M., Trott, M., von Viebahn, C.: E-Grocery in Terms of Sustainability – Simulating the Environmental Impact of Grocery Shopping for an Urban Area in Hanover. Simulation in Produktion und Logistik 2019, Matthias Putz & Andreas Schlegel (eds.), Wissenschaftliche Scripten, Auerbach (2019)
27. Waterman, D. A.: A Guide to Expert Systems: Reading. Addison-Wesley, UK (1986)
28. Shearer, C.: The CRISP-DM model: the new blueprint for data mining. J. Data Warehousing **5**(4), 13–22 (2000)
29. Quinlan, J.R.: C4. 5: Programs for Machine Learning. Morgan Kaufmann, San Francisco (1993)
30. Wu, X., et al.: Top 10 algorithms in data mining. Knowl. Inf. Syst. **14**(1), 1–37 (2008)
31. Witten, I. H., Frank, E., Hall, M. A.: Data Mining, ser. Practical, Machine Learning Tools and Techniques. Morgan Kaufmann, San Francisco (2011)
32. Kapoor, P., Rani, R.: Efficient decision tree algorithm using J48 and reduced error pruning. Int. J. Eng. Res. General Sci. **3**(3), 1613–1621 (2015)
33. Ninnemann, J., Hölter, A.K., Beecken, W., Thyssen, R., Tesch, T.: Last-Mile-Logistic Hamburg–Innerstädtische Zustelllogistik. Studie im Auftrag der Behörde für Wirtschaft, Verkehr und Innovation der Freien und Hansestadt Hamburg. Hamburg: HSBA Hamburg School of Business Administration (2017)
34. Iso, I.S.O.: Iec25010: 2011 systems and software engineering–systems and software quality requirements and evaluation (square)–system and software quality models. International Organization for Standardization, vol. 34, p. 2910 (2011)
35. Landeshauptstadt Hannover: Strukturdaten der Stadtteile und Stadtbezirke. Statistikstelle der Landeshauptstadt Hannover (2018)
36. Landeshauptstadt Dresden: Stadtteilkatalog 2018. Kommunale Statistikstelle, Dresden (2018)
37. Stadt Wolfsburg: Statistisches Jahrbuch 2018, Wolfsburg (2018)

Preparing for an Uncertain Future: South Westphalia City Scenarios 2030

Anja Schulte[1(✉)], Tim Wittemund[1], Peter Weber[1], and Alexander Fink[2]

[1] Fachhochschule Südwestfalen, Soest, Germany
{schulte.anja,wittemund.tim,weber.peter}@fh-swf.de
[2] Scenario Management International ScMI AG, Paderborn, Germany
fink@scmi.de

Abstract. For example, because of the demographic change, the fast pace of technological advance, and changing citizen habits (e.g. in buying behavior), cities face fundamental challenges and lack orientation in approaching their (digital) transformation. Especially cities in rural areas struggle in this situation which makes it necessary to reconsider predominant structures in city management. The use of scenario management can support decision-making processes by broadening the perspective through thinking in future scenarios. This paper elaborates on a scenario planning project that was conducted with 25 cities from South Westphalia (Germany) in 2020. Eight scenarios have been developed in a multi-stakeholder process with participants from different city domains. Both, the process of scenario planning and the developed city scenarios for 2030, aim to support city managers and other city stakeholders expand their focus, triggering a future-oriented examination of cities.

Keywords: Scenario management · Action design research · City centers in rural areas · Smart city

1 Introduction

Urbanization is a much cited challenge in smart city publications – too many citizens for the existing infrastructure. Despite an increase in city residents, the vitality of city centers seems to decline. This paradox deserves attention: on the one hand, an increasing number of people moves into the cities, prospectively 70% of the population until 2050, while on the other hand, a decreasing number of people visits the actual city centers [1]. As a consequence of declining city visitors, stationary retail is at stake [2]. The concept of a smart city suggests answers to the major city challenges by using modern information technologies to improve the planning of the cities and to reach sustainable economic growth and a high quality of life [3, 4]. It is a holistic concept that aims to implement improvements in six city-related areas (environment, living, people, economy, mobility and government), connecting the stakeholders in order to co-create accepted solutions [5]. Thereby, a citizen-centric focus shall ensure especially the acceptance by citizens, harnessing also new forms of political participation [6].

F. Ahlemann et al. (Eds.): WI 2021, LNISO 46, pp. 382–397, 2021.
https://doi.org/10.1007/978-3-030-86790-4_26

To help the cities tackle their challenges and maintain their vitality, the EU-funded project *City Lab Südwestfalen* aims to support proactive city transformation. In order to provide orientation and to create a more robust basis for strategic decisions, a scenario process was initiated, involving a broad range of city stakeholders.

Against the background of curfews and COVID-19 restrictions, the Association of German Cities and Towns warns against the death of city centers making the discussion of city transformation and smart city concepts even more relevant [7]. Despite respective funding programs of the federal government, the complexity of the topic and the uncertainty about future developments hampers planning in many cities. The predominant uncertainties demand for a methodological approach to support systematic decision-making. Scenario planning can help to reduce the complexity of an unknown future by building different scenarios that could occur in a defined timespan. Both, the process of scenario planning and the resulting scenarios, support city managers and other city stakeholders expand their focus, triggering a future-open examination of the cities.

2 Problem and Research Questions

In April 2019, the Federal Ministry of the Interior, Building and Community (German: BMI) announced to fund the digital change of cities throughout the upcoming decade with 750 million euros [8]. The Ministry called for 50 smart city pilot projects aiming at the creation and maintenance of modern, technology-supported cities worth living. A proclaimed goal is the strategic implementation of digitalization by the cities. However, a study by the German Association of Towns and Municipalities (German: DStGB) reveals that only half of the 538 queried cities currently have a defined digitalization strategy [9]. Due to the multitude of tasks and the fast pace of technological change, cities lack orientation to answer the questions what is to do, and when, how and in which order to approach the challenge of digitalization. This leads to the threat of isolated, uncoordinated efforts and bad investments. In order to face this problem, this paper addresses the following research questions (RQs):

RQ1: How can a multi-city scenario planning process be accomplished to help the cities in South Westphalia prepare for an uncertain future?
RQ2: What are possible future scenarios of South Westphalian city centers in 2030?

These questions were examined as part of the EFRE-Project *City Lab Südwestfalen*, involving 25 (out of 59) cities in South Westphalia (North-Rhine Westphalia, Germany). While the scenario process itself can be transferred also to other regions and cities, it does not lead to turnkey solutions. Every city needs to assess and work with the scenarios individually, considering its own initial situation, development path, and objectives.

3 Theoretical Grounding

3.1 Scenario Development

In order to work out profound concepts to apply for the offered funding programs and to align digitalization projects in a future-oriented way, cities need to deal with potential future developments systematically. Scenario planning as a method of future research presents a strategic instrument for this.

A scenario is "a description of a future situation and the development of the path that leads from the present to the future" [10]. Scenarios enable individuals, companies or other organizations to consider possible future developments in their decisions today. The scenario method is a planning technique to develop a set of heterogeneous but internally consistent scenarios [10].

Literature offers a variety of scenario methods. A comparison by Mietzner (2009) reviews five selected model-based methods (methods using algorithms) and three intuitive methods [11], helping us to choose the most appropriate approach. As part of the model-based approaches, von Reibnitz (1992) proposes a systematic and transparent eight-step process named scenario technique [10]. Anyhow, as in her approach the number of scenarios is originally limited to three (best-case, worst-case, trend), it can lead to a black-and-white manner of thinking. Addressing this issue, the scenario management approach by Fink/Siebe (2016) which is closely related to the scenario technique, aims at the development of four up to ten scenarios instead [12]. Burmeister et al. (2004) regard scenarios as one component of a complex toolbox for strategic foresight [13]. Since their method includes a more dedicated trend monitoring and offers less process definitions, it does not match with our intentions. While Godet et al.'s (2001) integrated "La Prospective" approach is focused on deriving strategic implications, it is criticized for being highly complex [11, 14]. The probability theories by Helmer/Gordon (1994) also do not match, considering the given uncertainty and complexity of the cities' future, as this prevents from assessing probabilities in a reliable manner [15]. Finally, we also decided against the intuitive approaches (Schwartz (1996), van der Heijden (2002), Schoemaker (2002), Ramirez/Wilkinson (2016), Cairns/Wright (2018)), as they lack detailed descriptions of the scenario development process while containing many elements similar to the model-based approaches [11, 16–20].

For a well-founded choice of the appropriate methodology, we also reviewed existing city related scenario projects from literature. In order to avoid a mere technology focus in smart city projects, Eschenauer et al. (2017) examine three methods of scenario development (formative, intuitive, delphi), involving three different stakeholder groups to answer the question, how scenario development can support smart city transformations [21]. As opposed to their approach, we ensured a balanced choice of participants by means of a stakeholder map and recommendations of city representatives. On the other hand, we considered their recommendations to create a catalogue of influence factors and to include a partner with scenario planning experience. Ronay and Egger (2014) examine the role of smart city stakeholders and Near Field Communication technology within tourism industry based smart city concepts [22]. The authors use scenario planning to discuss the plausibility of respective future scenarios. The underlying methodology relates to von Reibnitz (1987) and Gausemeier et al. (1996), but the approach is strongly industry-specific, making it hard to be used in a holistic smart city context [10, 23].

In conclusion, we therefore decided to work with the scenario management approach as suggested by Fink/Siebe (2016) based on von Reibnitz (1992) and Gausemeier et al. (1996), which will be outlined in the following section before we cover its specific application and the developed scenarios as part of Action Design Research (ADR) [10, 12, 23].

For a balanced methodological review, also points of criticism regarding the scenario technique need to be addressed. Complexity reduction as an inherent part of the method can be considered ambivalently. On the one hand, it is required to approach a complex topic; on the other hand, important details may be neglected. In this respect, also the low prediction accuracy is criticised. Considering the complex environment of future cities and the fact that the value of scenarios is rather awareness than prediction accuracy, these downsides seem acceptable to a certain degree [24].

A commonly stated point of criticism is the high dependency of results on the participants and their level of expertise, their ability for connected thinking and their willingness for active participation [24]. In the presented case, appropriate expertise was ensured by working with an experienced moderator and by the careful selection of scenario team members. In fact, the city representatives as experts themselves were asked to suggest local experts from a predefined set of domains. The challenging task to ensure active participation was tackled with regular communication but also the online format of workshops made it easier to take part. Further points of criticism are acceptance problems of people who have not taken part in the process and the lack of intuitive instructions for result-based problem solving [25]. To address the acceptance problem, not only target-oriented communication and process transparency but also professional management of expectations is vital. Accordingly, the results need to be presented as a tool to be used in strategic planning, not as a solution itself. Apart from this, the lack of theoretical grounding for the use of scenarios is criticised [26].

Literature confirms the need for a holistic approach to smartness concerning city governance and policy decision making to avoid a mere technological, fast-paced but uncoordinated smart city development. In line with a call for suitable instruments that serve as a compass on the way to a smarter future, Scenario Management is suggested to be used as a strategic tool [27].

3.2 Scenario Management

The scenario management process consists of three phases: 1) preparation, 2) development and 3) interpretation of future scenarios. The **preparation phase** covers formal issues of the project and the organizational setup. Formalities comprise the definition of the subject matter, goals, the definition of the future horizon and the regional scope of the scenario process [12]. Furthermore, it contains the composition of a heterogeneous scenario team, the distribution of roles and the coordination of a collaboration pattern and format.

The **development** of scenarios is carried out in three sub-phases, 1) Scenario Field Analysis, 2) Scenario Prognostics, and 3) Scenario Development.

Sub-Phase 1: Scenario Field Analysis. In the Scenario Field Analysis, a set of key factors needs to be identified that describes the scenario field. To reach this goal, four steps have to be followed [12]:

- Step 1: Structuring the scenario field.
- Step 2: Identifying influence factors.
- Step 3: Analyzing the influence factors.
- Step 4: Selecting key factors.

In the first step, the scenario field is structured by subdividing it into system levels (e.g. the general environment, the regional environment, citizens, etc.) and influence areas (e.g. technology, living, work, etc.). The system picture visually summarizes the scenario field and guides the further process (see Fig. 2). In the second step, a catalogue is developed to collect and describe influence factors for each of the influence areas. At this point, the number of factors is still unrestricted, and factors can be identified e.g. by surveying the relevant stakeholders, by reviewing literature, or by assessing existing influence factors from similar studies [12]. In the third step, the collected influence factors are then analyzed by assessing their importance, uncertainty and potential influence with the help of a questionnaire (questionnaire 1) and/or by examining their relationship with each other in an influence matrix. Visualizations of the influence matrix, like e.g. in a system grid, provide hints for suitable key factors by revealing their influence on each other (see Fig. 3 and 4) [12]. This allows for the selection of approximately 20 key factors in step four.

Sub-Phase 2: Scenario Prognostics. Scenario Prognostics systematically identifies possible future developments (also known as projections) for each key factor. Therefore, a second questionnaire (questionnaire 2) is used to ask the participants about questions, trends and insecurities regarding every key factor's future. First, two characteristic projections per factor are defined. Second, the derived projections are opposed in a matrix to identify a maximum of five projections per key factor (see Fig. 5) [12]. Each key factor is dealt with separately, so that no conclusions can be drawn from this step regarding the coherence of the factors and projections. Furthermore, also explanations and possible implications of the defined projections did not matter at this point [12].

Sub-Phase 3: Scenario Development. In the Scenario Development phase, so-called 'draft scenarios' as a cluster of consistent bundles of future projections are derived. The consistency of the projections is assessed by using a consistency matrix, before a software determines plausible projection bundles. An iterative cluster analysis then groups similar projection bundles to a reasonable number of draft scenarios. The projection bundles are visualized in a 'future map' by means of multidimensional scaling (see Fig. 7) [12]. An overview matrix displays all scenarios (columns), key factors (rows) and projections (cells), and serves as a base to formulate the scenarios.

The **interpretation** includes the communication and the assessment of the developed scenarios, as well as the analysis of their implications. For an effective communication, scenarios need to be verbalized in condensed form considering the language and the interests of the target group. The assessment usually involves a questionnaire (questionnaire 3), asking the scenario team members to assess the propinquity of the scenarios to the present, the expected, and the desired future. In a final step, implications in terms of chances and risks are assessed for each scenario [12].

3.3 Action Design Research Framework

After reviewing the seven Design Science Research (DSR) guidelines by Hevner et al. [28] and the differentiation between different DSR genres by Peffers [29], we chose ADR as described by Sein et al. [29] as the appropriate research design. The applied research process complies with the four characteristics as outlined by Peffers [29]. Hence, the focus of the paper is to develop a problem-solving artifact in form of future scenarios of cities in South Westphalia, triggered by the difficulties in planning of smart city projects in view of an unknown future and in a setup of 25 participating municipalities. The class of problems addressed is systematic smart city development in today's complex and dynamic world. The participation of stakeholders and end-users in the scenario team ensured learning from intervention by collaboration through questionnaires in parallel to the work of the internal core scenario team. The evolving artifact is ingrained in scenario planning theory, stipulating a sequential development process. Moreover, a continuous evaluation of the artifact was conducted through the inquiry of stakeholders in every phase of the scenario process. The four stages of ADR have been mapped with the described scenario process in Fig. 1, serving as the framework for our study.

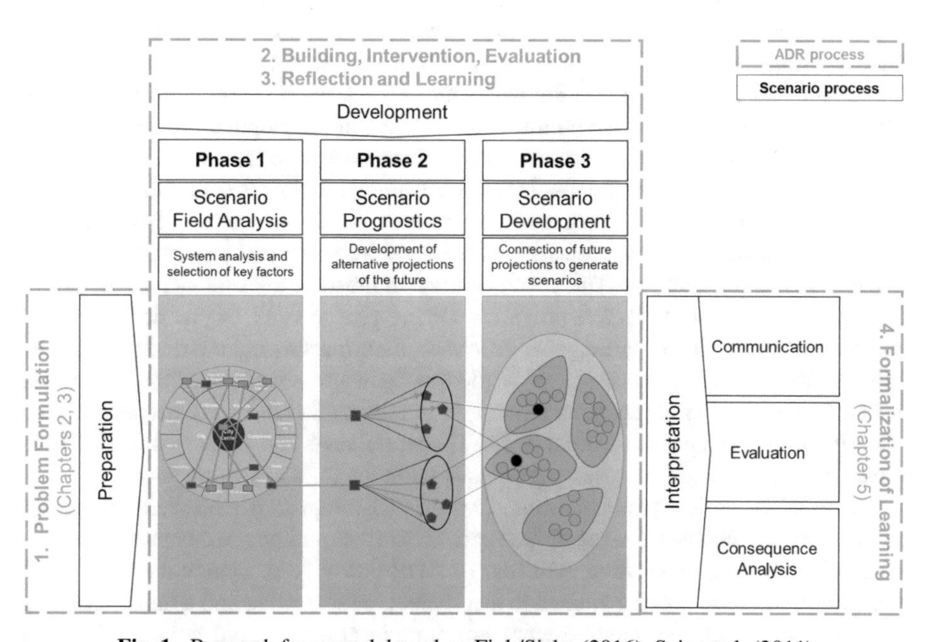

Fig. 1. Research framework based on Fink/Siebe (2016), Sein et al. (2011)

The core outline of Fig. 1 stems from the original work by Fink and Siebe (2016), however, the graphical elements are marginally adapted, translated and integrated into the surrounding ADR process (Sein et al. 2011) with references to the respective chapter of this paper in which the process step is performed. The four ADR stages also represent the respective seven ADR principles and exhibit clear parallels to the scenario process. For instance, principle 3 (reciprocal shaping) is inherent in the iterative scenario development process including workshops and the consideration of feedback in the final scenarios, i.e. the artifact. Furthermore, principle 4 (mutually influential roles) is reflected in the heterogeneity of the team that ensures mutual learning of researcher and practitioners.

4 South Westphalia City Scenarios 2030

4.1 Process Preparation

The scenario process aims to develop scenarios that describe possible futures of city centers in South Westphalia in 2030. With the help of the developed scenarios, the project team behind the *City Lab Südwestfalen*, consisting of three academic partners and two chambers of industry and commerce (IHKs), aims to support the participating cities (resp. city stakeholders) in making more robust decisions and to initiate sustainable measures for increasing their city's attractiveness.

The project context guaranteed organizational commitment of the participants. By signing a Letter of Intent, the participating cities manifested their motivation while Scenario Management International (ScMI) AG from Paderborn (Germany) was commissioned as a service provider to moderate the process. Two teams were established: The core scenario team consisted of three members of one of the academic partners and two members of the service provider. The core team was responsible for preparing, moderating and following up on the workshops. The scenario team, consisting of the core team members plus twelve representatives of the participating cities, was involved in the scenario workshops and participated in three questionnaires. The heterogeneity of the team was ensured by systematically requesting participants from different stakeholder fields in all 25 cities as proposed in literature [31, 32]. As a result, representatives from retail, services, politics, tourism, startups, architecture and city marketing from nine different cities took part. The use and outline of the three questionnaires was part of the general process of the service providers and has proven as a best practice method to systematically include the participants' feedback. Each questionnaire is designed specifically for the respective process step. While questionnaire 1 was provided as an Excel sheet prepared for the participants input, questionnaires 2 and 3 were dispatched as a PowerPoint file with prepared input fields. The participants had about two weeks' time to send back their feedback which was discussed in the followed workshop.

In the initial project plan two scenario team workshops in person were scheduled, one to cover the first two phases of the scenario process and one to cover the interpretation which reflects stages two until four of ADR (see Fig. 1). Due to the COVID-19 restrictions, the format was switched to a complete online setting and a third workshop was added to reduce the required workshop time in order to avoid fatigue. Since the participants had to assess factors like health care or gastronomy offerings, questions came up if and how the new situation should be considered in view of the upcoming COVID-19 pandemic. Since, at this time, nobody could foresee the extend, duration and effects of the crisis, the participants were asked to consider the current situation including the pandemic as far as it was assessable at this time.

4.2 Phase 1 – Scenario Field Analysis

In order to prepare for the next steps, the core team defined a system picture, as depicted in Fig. 2. It consists of seven different system levels including 21 influence areas in total. The groundwork for the system picture was developed during a kick-off meeting of the *City Lab Südwestfalen* together with 46 city representatives. In a world café setup, typical roles of city centers and important factors that have turned cities into what they are today were discussed, providing a starting point to identify the system levels and influence areas.

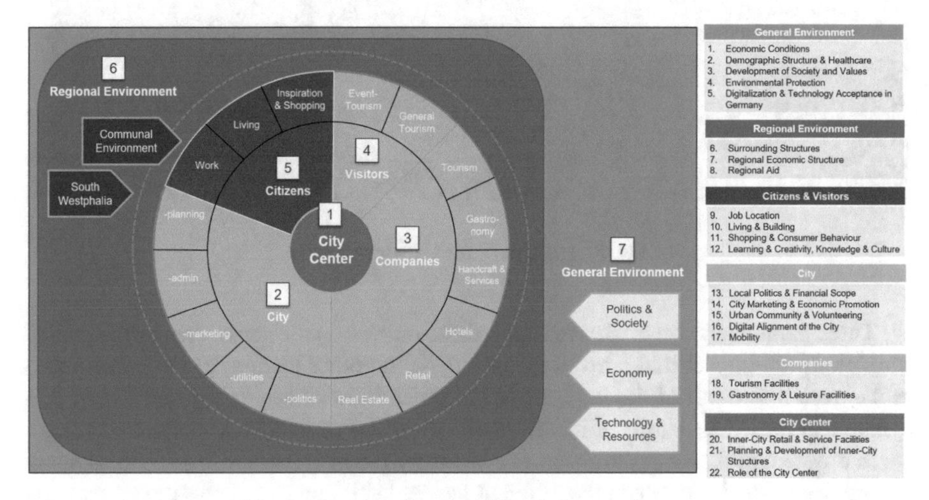

Fig. 2. System picture and key influence factors

Based on the system picture, 63 influence factors have been identified by the core team. This set of influence factors was suggested to the scenario team by sending out a questionnaire, asking for feedback and missing factors. The scenario team members were asked to evaluate every single influence factor on a 5-point Likert scale regarding its:

- **Importance:** How important is this factor for the development of city centers in South Westphalia?
- **Uncertainty:** How predictable is the future development of this factor?
- **Designability:** To what degree can the future development of this factor be influenced by city stakeholders?

In total, questionnaire 1 was dispatched to 71 respondents in 24 different partner cities. We received back 25 questionnaires from 16 cities, resulting in a response rate of 17.75%.

At the same time, the members of the core team created the influence matrix depicted in Fig. 3. In this matrix, the impact that the 63 influence factors have on each other is assessed by rating it using a scale from 0 (no impact) to 3 (strong and direct impact) [12].

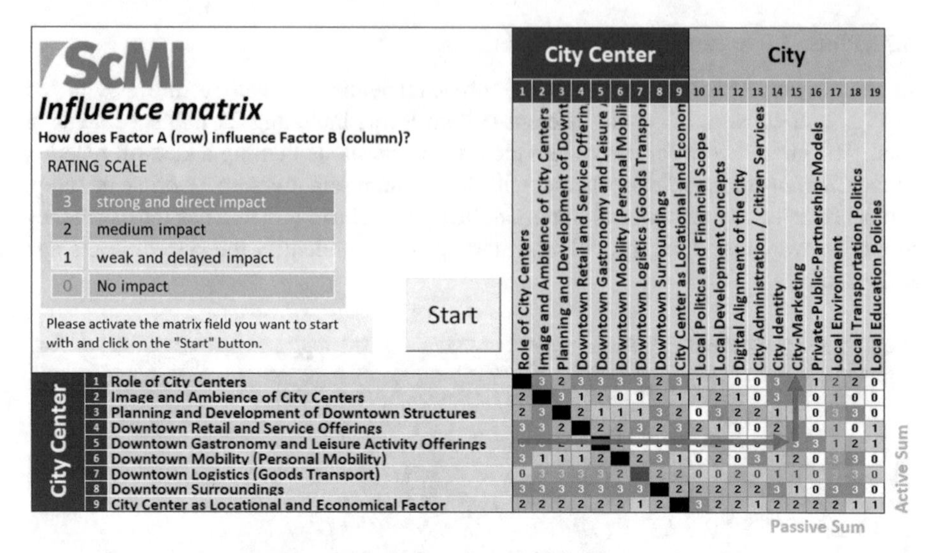

Fig. 3. Excerpt of the influence matrix

Three parameters can be derived from these ratings: 1) the active sum as the overall strength of the impact that a given factor has the other factors; 2) the passive sum as the overall strength of the impact that the other factors have on a given factor; 3) a dynamic index as the degree of inclusion of a given factor in the entire system [12].

In a system grid, these parameters can be visualized in order to recognize the dynamics and dependencies between the different factors [12]. Figure 4 shows the system grid as a result of the influence matrix. The activity of a factor is applied on the y-axis, whereas the passivity is applied on the x-axis. Four different areas are distinguished: **leverage factors** with a wide influence on the whole system (upper left corner), **system knots** with a high connectivity with other factors (upper right corner), **system indicators** that are strongly influenced by other factors (bottom right corner), and **independent factors** with a low influence on the system (bottom left corner) [12].

These two steps, the influence matrix and the scenario team questionnaire 1, were used to identify the key factors that could be considered in the further process while keeping the scenario process manageable [12].

Once the suggested key factors were identified by the core team, they were extensively discussed in a first (online) scenario workshop with all members from the scenario team, leading to a final set of 22 key factors to proceed with (see Fig. 2). This step represented the alpha cycle of the ADR approach with an evaluation of the key factors to refine them as a first outcome of the artifact [30].

4.3 Phase 2 – Scenario Prognostics

Within this process step, alternative projections for all key factors were generated, in order to prepare for the scenarios as internally consistent projection bundles [12]. The process step started with questionnaire 2, addressing the scenario team. The scenario team members were asked to report all questions that came to their mind regarding each

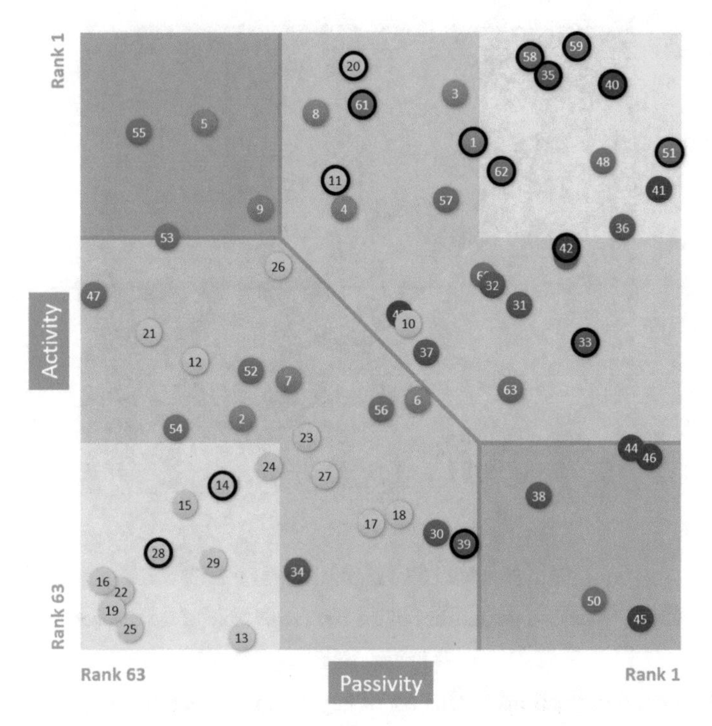

Fig. 4. System grid

key factor's future development. Based on these questions, the core team developed the different future projections. During a second workshop with the scenario team, the projections for all key factors were presented and discussed, leading to 108 projections for the 22 key factors. As an example, Fig. 5 shows the projections for the key factor "Role of the City Center". This factor draws on the function the city center fulfils and regards it either as a place to go for shopping (marketplace) or as a place to visit as a pastime, like a theme park (world of experience).

In the next step, not only the scenario team members, but also a set of further city representatives that had been involved in the *City Lab Südwestfalen* before, were approached with questionnaire 3 to evaluate the projections from their individual city's perspective. Later, after the scenarios had been compiled, these evaluations allowed the core team to provide individual feedback to the cities regarding what scenario (as a consistent set of projections) is most similar to the current situation of each city, and what scenarios are the most expected and the most favored ones. For this, the respondents rated each projection regarding its match with the presence, its likelihood, and its desirability on a Likert scale from 1 (lowest) to 5 (highest). Questionnaire 3 was dispatched to 38 participants from 24 partner cities and resulted in a response rate of 71% (27 responses).

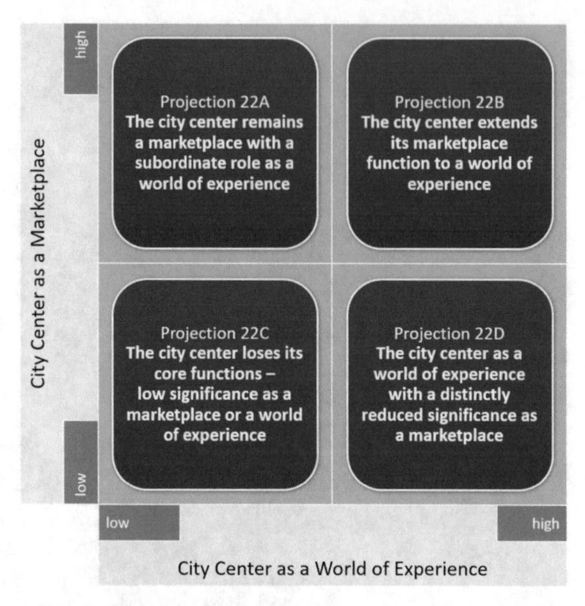

Fig. 5. Scenario prognostics of the key factor 'role of the city center'

The developed projections for the set of key factors reflect the beta evaluation cycle described in the ADR research framework [30].

4.4 Phase 3 – Scenario Development

After agreeing on the projections and after collecting the evaluations from the extended scenario team, the scenarios were compiled with the help of a software-driven consistency analysis [12]. Using ScMI's scenario software, the projections were set into relation with each other by assessing their plausibility [12]. Especially when dealing with a high number of factors and projections, the software, being a proprietary development of ScMI, is a useful tool to ensure reliable results and save time. This software-supported approach led to a set of eight draft scenarios, which were visualized by means of multidimensional scaling in a so-called 'future space mapping'[1] (Fig. 7). In this mapping, four core dimensions could be identified, which fundamentally differentiate the scenarios: (A) Economic development and digitization, (B) Quality of life and participation, (C) Sustainability and regionality and (D) Retail and marketplace function. This tool-based process was followed by a core team discussion, in which the scenarios were selected and a first draft of the 'map of the future' was derived.

[1] *For details on future space mapping, see* [12], *p. 111ff.*

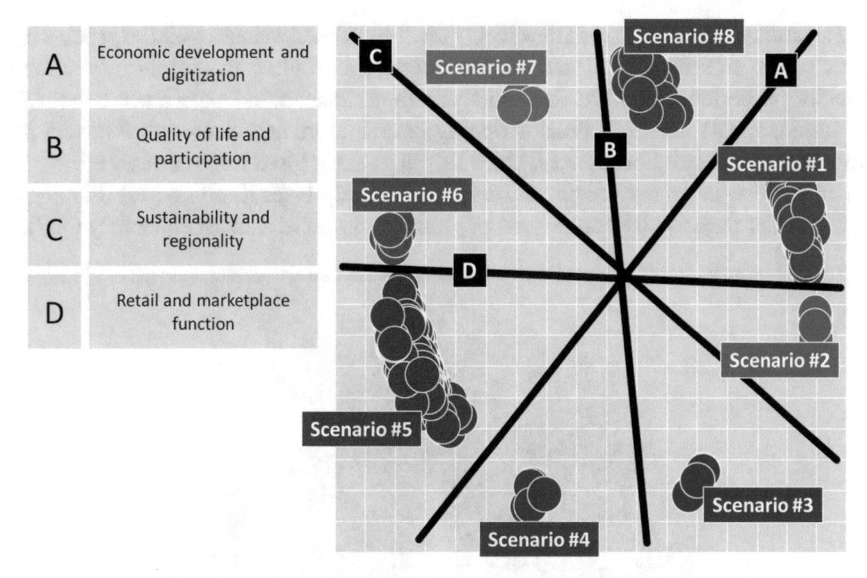

Fig. 6. Draft scenarios and core dimensions in a multi-dimensional scaling

5 Interpretation of Results

5.1 Scenario Communication

The scenario development process resulted in the eight draft scenarios depicted in Fig. 6. This rather technical visualization was then schematized and transformed into a simpler form of a 'map of the future' (Fig. 7). Each of the scenarios was verbalized in a story, covering its most characterizing projections. In the following, each scenario is outlined in brief, before one scenario is described in more detail.

Scenario #1 ('Regional Marketplace') describes a promising future where the city center has turned into a magnet for local shoppers and tourists. **Scenario #2 ('Experience Instead of Shopping')** pictures a city center that has developed from a marketplace into an entertainment area, mostly because of digitalization and a changed buying behaviors. As a result of social distancing and service orientation, **Scenario #3 ('Service Shapes Reinvention')** outlines a city center with displaced retailers, which is mainly visited for services. Presenting the first outlook to a rather negative future, **scenario #4 ('Abandonment of the City')** sketches a web-focused smart city, which is attractive online, but mostly neglected in physical life. While in **scenario #5 ('Desertification of the City')**, the city center loses any of its functions with today's players having disappeared, **in scenario #6 ('Chains Shape the Shopping City')**, the importance of the marketplace function remains. However, in this scenario chain stores prevail over local owner operated retail outlets. **Scenario #7 ('Back to the old City')** describes the city center in its traditional form, in which the smart city concept did not have any profound impact. Eventually, **scenario #8 ('City Center as an Anchor')** tells the story of a city center that has developed into the focal point of social life, with a flourishing gastronomy and distinct citizen participation.

Regarding the future role of the city center, the outlined scenarios can be grouped into four clusters: In scenarios #1 and #8, city centers extent their marketplace function by providing experience opportunities. In scenario #2 instead, the experience-factor takes the dominant role and high street shopping loses importance. Scenarios #3 to #5 pose a threat to current city businesses, since the city center loses its current core functions and either focuses on service provision (#3) or entirely loses its allure (#5). Finally, the fourth cluster depicts city centers that predominantly serve as marketplaces (#6/#7).

Fig. 7. Map of the future for city centers in South Westphalia until 2030

As an example, the story of scenario #4 is provided in the following: The prospering economy supports a digital Germany with innovation grants for cities. Digitalization has made the society more independent and has led to less physical contacts. As opposed to the far-reaching digital advancements, the physical infrastructures and existing businesses are neglected. Unsatisfactory local facilities for healthcare, education and work make it hard for the city to provide a high quality of life in its city center. To reduce the need for commuting, the city tries to attract new businesses by highlighting its digital image with the support of city marketing promoting its online facilities. Unfortunately, the city missed out on integrating the physical city center into its smart city concept. Despite sufficient financial means, political activities regarding the city center are rather passive. Citizens have lost their identification with the city center and turned into online shoppers. Without incentives and reasons to visit, citizens rarely go downtown and gastronomes lose ground. In this dark scenario, the city fails to clearly position itself either as a marketplace, as a world of experience, or as both. It forfeits its attractiveness in a self-reinforcing downward spiral.

5.2 Scenario Assessment

After the scenarios have been finalized, the individual evaluations of the projections from Phase 2 allowed the core team to analyze 1) which scenario matches the current situation in each city best, 2) which scenario the city expects, and 3) which scenario it favors. It turned out that most cities hope for scenarios #1, 2 or 8. At the same time, the majority of the participating cities also expect one of these scenarios to become true. As compared to the current situation, scenario #8 was rated the most fitting. While these overall results might leave the impression of strong starting points and optimistic perspectives, it needs to be pointed out that these evaluations are nothing more than subjective appraisals and that several of the cities also show different results. It is important to mention, that the scenarios need to be considered as strategic tools to work with and not as reliable guidelines.

The scenarios and the evaluations have been communicated on the final online workshop not only to the scenario team but also to further representatives of the participating cities. After all scenarios had been presented in brief, the audience was split into five online meeting rooms in order to discuss appropriate measures in accordance with the characteristics and the implications of one specific scenario. Following these split-sessions, the ideas were presented to the entire audience again, in order to point out how the scenarios could be utilized in decision-making and in strategic planning.

As a final step and following up on the completed process, a report will now be created with a detailed documentation of the scenario project, the developed scenarios and the city-specific evaluations.

6 Conclusion

The EFRE-project *City Lab Südwestfalen* aims to strengthen the attractiveness of city centers in rural areas like South Westphalia. For this, it is highly important to ascertain the challenges and uncertainties that the cities are faced with today and in the future. In such complex and uncertain situations, scenario management can facilitate more robust decision-making, better strategic alignment, smarter investments, future-oriented thinking, and also attentive monitoring [11].

This paper describes a complete scenario process that was accomplished between 02.2020 and 07.2020 to address the two research questions of how city centers in South Westphalia can prepare themselves for an unknown future (RQ 1) and how they could look like in 2030 (RQ 2). For this purpose, a combination of ADR and scenario management was used as a framework to develop scenarios in a multi-stakeholder process. A better understanding of needs and problems that city stakeholders in rural areas are faced with could be obtained through the collaboration with diverse city stakeholders in a heterogeneous scenario team.

Through this structured and participatory process, eight scenarios were developed, which, first of all, describe possible future developments of cities in South Westphalia. In principle, the results can be transferred to other regions with similar conditions. These scenarios point out the different developments and roles that cities might take in the future, answering RQ 2. The overall scenario process that we ended up with and that lead the way to the derived scenarios answers RQ 1.

The scenarios that have been worked out gain a special value because they can be evaluated separately for individual cities. In this way, individual needs and wishes for change can be identified. In addition, a repeated evaluation makes it possible to monitor current and future perspectives.

With regard to the COVID-19 pandemic which came up at the very beginning of the process, initially it was unclear how well the process will work in a purely online format, since situational factors of participation, engagement and group dynamics play an essential role in the workshops. Although incomparable to a physical workshop, many intensive discussions came up and no technical issues hampered the process. Moreover, the online workshops caused less organizational effort for both the participants and the moderators. An examination of differences between the online and offline format in the process flow and results leave room for future research. As intended, the COVID-19 pandemic had an influence on the results, e.g. to be noted in the inclusion of 'social distancing' in scenario #3.

Future research should also assess if and in what way the scenario process and the developed scenarios have been and could be embedded in future-robust decision-making and strategic planning in the participating cities.

References

1. United Nations Department for Economic and Social Affairs: World Urbanization Prospects 2018. Highlights (ST/ESA/SER.A/421). United Nations, New York (2019)
2. Ministerium für Wirtschaft, Innovation, Digitalisierung und Energie des Landes Nordrhein-Westfalen: Handelsszenarien Nordrhein-Westfalen 2030 (2019)
3. ISO/IEC JTC1: Smart cities - Preliminary report. Information Technology (2015)
4. Caragliu, A., del Bo, C., Nijkamp, P.: Smart cities in Europe. J. Urban Technol. 18 (2009)
5. Giffinger, R., Fertner, C., Kalasek, R., Pichler-Milanovic, N.: Smart cities - ranking of European medium-sized cities. Vienna University of Technology (2007)
6. Gassmann, O., Böhm, J., Palmié, M.: Smart Cities - Introducing Digital Innovation to Cities. Emerald Publishing Limited, Bingley (2019)
7. ZDFheute: Städtetag warnt vor Innenstadt-Sterben. https://www.zdf.de/nachrichten/wirtschaft/coronavirus-innenstaedte-102.html. Accessed 23 July 2020
8. Bundesministerium des Innern, für Bau und Heimat: Neuer Zuschuss für Stadtentwicklung und Digitalisierung: Modellprojekte Smart Cities. https://www.bmi.bund.de/SharedDocs/pressemitteilungen/DE/2019/04/smart-cities-modellprojekte.html. Accessed 14 July 2020
9. Hornbostel, L., Nerger, M., Tillack, D., Wittpahl, V., Handschuh, A., Salden, J.: Zukunftsradar Digitale Kommune. Ergebnisbericht zur Umfrage 2019 (2019)
10. Reibnitz, U.: Szenario-Technik Instrumente für die unternehmerische und persönliche Erfolgsplanung. Gabler Verlag, Wiesbaden (1992)
11. Mietzner, D.: Strategische Vorausschau und Szenarioanalysen Methodenevaluation und neue Ansätze. Gabler Verlag / GWV Fachverlage GmbH Wiesbaden, Wiesbaden (2009)
12. Fink, A., Siebe, A.: Szenario-Management Von strategischem Vorausdenken zu zukunftsrobusten Entscheidungen. Campus Verlag, Frankfurt, New York (2016)
13. Burmeister, K.G., Neef, A., Beyers, B.: Corporate Foresight. Unternehmen gestalten Zukunft. Murmann, Hamburg (2004)
14. Godet, M.: Creating futures Scenario planning as a strategic management tool. Economica, London (2001)

15. Gordon, T.J.: Trend Impact Analysis. AC/UNU Millennium Project. Futures Research Methodology (1994)
16. Schwartz, P.: The Art of the Long View. Paths to strategic insight for yourself and your company. Bantam Doubleday Dell Pub. Group, New York (1996)
17. van der Heijden, K., Bradfield, R., Burt, G., Cairns, G., Wright, G.: The Sixth Sense. Accelerating Organizational Learning with Scenarios. John Wiley & Sons Ltd, Hoboken (2002)
18. Schoemaker, P.: Profiting from uncertainty Strategies for succeeding no matter what the future brings. Atria Books, New York (2002)
19. Ramirez, R., Wilkinson, A.: Strategic Reframing The Oxford Scenario Planning Approach. Oxford University Press, Oxford (2016)
20. Cairns, G., Wright, G.: Scenario Thinking. Preparing Your Organization for the Future in an Unpredictable World. 2nd edn. Palgrave/Macmillan, Basingstoke (2018)
21. Eschenauer, U., et al.: Smart City in Theorie und Praxis. Szenarien, Strategien und Umsetzungsbeispiele (2017)
22. Ronay, E., Egger, R.: NFC Smart City: Cities of the Future A Scenario Technique Application (2014)
23. Gausemeier, J., Fink, A., Schlake, O.: Szenario-Management: Planen und Führen mit Szenarien. 2nd edn. Hanser, München (1996)
24. Schönauer, D.: Nutzen der Szenario-Technik für die Personalentwicklung bei Mercedes-Benz. Diplomica Verlag, Norderstedt (1999)
25. Dönitz, E.: Effizientere Szenariotechnik durch teilautomatisiche Generierung von Konsistenzmatrizen. Gabler, Wiesbaden (2008)
26. Neuhaus, C.: Zukunft im Management Orientierung für das Management von Ungewissheit in strategischen Prozessen. Carl-Auer-Verlag, Heidelberg (2006)
27. Castelnovo, W., Misuraca, G., Savoldelli, A.: Smart cities governance: the need for a holistic approach to assessing urban participatory policy making. Soc. Sci. Comput. Rev. **34**(6), 724–739 (2016)
28. Hevner, A.R., March, S.T., Park, J., Ram, S.: Design science in information systems research. MIS Q. **28**, 75–105 (2004)
29. Peffers, K., Tuunanen, T., Niehaves, B.: Design science research genres: introduction to the special issue on exemplars and criteria for applicable design science research. Eur. J. Inf. Syst. **27**, 129–139 (2018)
30. Sein, M.K., Henfridsson, O., Purao, S., Rossi, M., Lindgren, R.: Action design research. MIS Q. **35**, 1–20 (2011)
31. Gassmann, O., Böhm, J., Palmié, M.: Smart City. Innovationen für die vernetzte Stadt - Geschäftsmodelle und Management. Hanser, München (2018)
32. Schlake, O.: Verfahren zur kooperativen Szenario-Erstellung in Industrieunternehmen. HNI-Verlagsschriftenreihe, Band 67, Paderborn (2000)

What Do We Really Need? A Systematic Literature Review of the Requirements for Blockchain-Based E-government Services

Julia Amend[1], Julian Kaiser[2], Lucas Uhlig[2], Nils Urbach[3,4], and Fabiane Völter[1](✉)

[1] Project Group Business and Information Systems Engineering of the Fraunhofer FIT, University of Bayreuth, Bayreuth, Germany
{julia.amend,fabiane.volter}@fit.fraunhofer.de
[2] University of Bayreuth, Bayreuth, Germany
{julian.kaiser,lucas.uhlig}@uni-bayreuth.de
[3] FIM Research Center, Frankfurt University of Applied Sciences, Frankfurt, Germany
nils.urbach@fim-rc.de
[4] Project Group Business and Information Systems Engineering of the Fraunhofer FIT, Bayreuth, Germany

Abstract. Information Systems research acknowledges the importance of identifying requirements to ensure the artifact's relevance. However, many research articles addressing blockchain technology for e-government capture the requirements that need to be fulfilled only implicitly by defining system objectives or evaluation criteria. Furthermore, focusing on specific use-cases encompasses the risk of overlooking those requirements, which are not as obvious but equally important. This procedure causes uncertainty regarding the requirements a blockchain-based e-government service needs to fulfill. Therefore, we conducted a systematic literature review on blockchain-based government-to-citizen (G2C) e-government services. On this basis, we categorized the requirements as we find that they address either the data of the system, the user, or the system itself. Our categorization provides a structured overview supporting researchers in conducting research on blockchain technology in the public sector and giving practitioners input to develop, test, and evaluate new blockchain-based G2C e-government services.

Keywords: e-government · Blockchain · Requirements · Literature review · Public service

1 Introduction

E-government describes the use of information technologies to improve access to governmental information and services to citizens, businesses, or other governmental agencies [1, 2]. By using (digital) technology to make interactions more convenient, e-government aims to improve the relationship between governmental agencies and the public [1, 3]. The relation may be between a government and its citizens (Government-to-Citizen, G2C), other public institutions (Government-to-Government, G2G), or businesses (Government-to-Business, G2B) [4]. Despite recent advancements in the field of

F. Ahlemann et al. (Eds.): WI 2021, LNISO 46, pp. 398–412, 2021.
https://doi.org/10.1007/978-3-030-86790-4_27

e-government, Norris [4] emphasizes the unsatisfying development of activities in this domain as "e-government has not produced either e-democracy or e-governance, nor is it likely to do so any time in the foreseeable future" (p. 339). However, the advent of new emergent technology may help fulfill this aim, as governments and public sector bodies are increasingly assessing their potential for delivering services [5]. As such, researchers and practitioners consider blockchain technology to enhance the efficiency of government operations by increasing trust in public sector bodies and improving the delivery of public services [6]. They attribute this potential to the technology's characteristics. Blockchain enables peer-to-peer transactions without an advocate in a tamperproof, transparent, and trustless manner.

Researchers and practitioners developed multiple use cases for blockchain technology in e-government, most of those focusing on G2C applications. For example, blockchain technology may facilitate electronically held election processes, in short called e-voting [7], or taxation services [8], and may serve as an underlying technology for creating digital identities [9]. Most research articles propose applying blockchain technology to specific contexts [10]. Thus, they capture requirements for the solution in a very use case-specific context while some articles capture requirements even only implicitly. Accordingly, blockchain-based G2C e-government services are still immature and mostly lack empirical evidence as well as requirements-driven solution approaches [10]. This observation may also be caused by terminological ambiguities and conceptual fuzziness when it comes to blockchain technology [11]. As a result, it remains unclear which requirements blockchain-based G2C e-government services have to fulfill independent from a specific use case. However, the process of defining requirements is specifically important as it records the specifications of the system's stakeholders. Also, practitioners do not only need to understand the application domain, but also the constraints, functionalities, and essential system characteristics [12]. As a result, capturing the requirements ensures that the proposed solution meets the goals and expectations of potential users [12]. Batubara et al. [11] also stress "the need for a proper design solution at the architecture level in accordance with the specific requirements from e-government processes" (p. 7). For this reason, our research aims to answer the following research question:

Which requirements do blockchain-based G2C e-government services need to fulfill?
To answer the research question, we conducted a literature review on blockchain-based G2C e-government services. This approach allowed us to provide a structured overview of the use case-independent requirements which a blockchain-based G2C service needs to fulfill. Furthermore, we grouped these requirements around the three core categories "data", "user", and "system", which provides further structure for researchers and practitioners during the development and evaluation of new blockchain-based solutions. Answering this research question does not only imply supporting the design and evaluation of artifacts. We also contribute to the academic discourse by supporting rigorous design science research in the blockchain domain.

The remainder of this paper is structured as follows: Sect. 2 introduces e-government services and blockchain technology. Section 3 describes the methodology applied. In Sect. 4, we present the results of our literature review and provide an overview of the resulting requirements. Finally, we reflect on our findings concerning the requirements of blockchain-based G2C e-government services in Sect. 5 as well as on limitations and future research opportunities in Sect. 8.

2 E-government and Blockchain Technology

A central motivation for providing e-government services is to increase accountability, enhance transparency, and increase stakeholder participation [13, 14]. The latter depends on achieving higher efficiency, quality, and effectiveness in the management of public state institutions [15, 16]. E-government initiatives not only provide faster services to citizens while being more cost-effective [17], but also reduce the administrative burden and other bureaucratic hurdles for government employees [18]. Furthermore, initiatives have tried to provide public services in a more direct way, tailored to the needs of citizens [19]. However, better cooperation with partners of all kinds will be required [20] to exploit the potential of e-government services fully. In summary, Moon [2] characterizes the provision of e-government services with four aspects: First, service delivery is based on the web, and second, e-commerce is suitable for conducting transactions. Third, digitalization may reinforce democratic structures, as it enhances the transparent accountability of governments. Lastly, fourth, a secure government intranet and central database increase the efficiency and cooperation between different governmental agencies. However, observing the characteristics of blockchain technology, the latter aspect may be challenged, as blockchain allows inter-organizational collaboration in a decentralized manner [5].

In contrast to a centralized database, blockchain technology is a distributed data structure used to store transactions in a tamper-resistant, decentral, and transparent manner in a peer-to-peer network [21]. The transactions are recorded in chronologically ordered blocks, which are linked using cryptographic hashes, ensuring high tamper-proofness of information and thereby creating a chain of blocks. Accordingly, by design, blockchain encompasses specific characteristics. Among those are *transparency* [5, 22–24], *integrity* [5, 22, 24], *redundancy* [23, 24], *immutability* [5, 22] and *privacy* [24, 25]. The consolidated definitions for each of these characteristics can be observed in Table 1. However, no consensus exists regarding the distinction between the characteristics encompassed by design and further properties of the technology, which can be derived from the latter. For example, while some authors mention auditability as a fundamental characteristic [24], one may also argue that auditability is caused by the underlying characteristics *transparency* and *immutability*. Similarly, Wüst and Gervais [24] state that "*transparency* [..] is a requirement for verifiability" (p. 46), while some authors categorize verifiability as a fundamental characteristic of the technology [23]. Due to those reasons, we identified the characteristics of *transparency*, *integrity*, *redundancy*, *immutability*, and *privacy* as the fundamental characteristics of blockchain technology. Since the invention of blockchain technology in 2008, researchers and practitioners have addressed a considerably high amount of attention to the exploration of the technology. As a result, use cases and application domains of the technology have expanded immensely. Therefore, blockchain-based solutions have gained visibility in the context of supply chains, healthcare, the Internet of Things, data management, and governmental services [26, 27]. Also, public institutions increasingly acknowledge the enormous potential of blockchain technology for governmental services as they address current challenges by strategically identifying promising use cases of the technology [27]. Thereby, use cases are not only evaluated on a conceptual level but also in pilot projects [28]. For example, an advanced use case for digital identities exists in Estonia using the e-Identity ID card on a blockchain [9].

The potential attributed to the technology in the area of e-government is based primarily on its ability to provide an incorruptible system, to make processes more transparent, and to eliminate the need to entrust in specific institutions or individuals [30]. Furthermore, blockchain technology enables inter-organizational cooperation on a neutral platform [5]. For those reasons, various use cases have been proposed and discussed in the academic literature. Among the most popular G2C use cases are blockchain-based electronic voting processes and the creation of digital identities using blockchain technology as the underlying infrastructure. Furthermore, researchers propose blockchain-based handling of taxes to prevent tax fraud and enhance tax payments transparency [8, 31]. Researchers also attribute the potential to blockchain-based land and property management. Accordingly, the transparent and accountable recording of land titles on a blockchain is more reliable and trustworthy than a paper-based process, especially in developing countries [32, 33]. Also, blockchain-based smart city solutions are addressed. Other G2C use cases include the tracking of funds to prevent misusage due to corruption [34]. Concerning the detection and combat of such misbehavior, blockchain technology may create significant value [32, 35]. Besides, blockchain technology can be very beneficial in sharing data for e-government applications, especially for the citizens' privacy and data reliability [36, 37]. Depending on those use cases, blockchain applications' design and governance may differ. Practitioners may choose between a public and private [38] as well as permissionless and permissioned [5] infrastructure. For the public sector, Shahaab [39] identified "private" and "permissioned" configurations as widely-spread design patterns.

3 Method

We conducted a systematic literature review following Kitchenham and Charters [40] to identify the requirements for blockchain-based G2C e-government services. As literature sources, we chose databases complementary to the ones that Batubara et al. [10] selected to extend existing literature reviews. As a result, we included the databases WebofScience, Business Source Premier, ACM Digital Library, and IEEE Explore Digital Library also to consider the academic discourse in the Computer Science domain. We derived our search string from the main keywords of our research question and complemented them with synonyms and similar terms: ("blockchain" OR "block chain" OR "distributed ledger") AND ("e-government" OR "government" OR "public service" OR "public sector"). We set the search period to the beginning of 2008 since blockchain was firstly proposed in that year [41]. We searched all databases until the 7th of August, 2020, which revealed 1,051 articles in total.

In the next step, we included all articles that met our inclusion criteria (IC). Regarding the publication type, we only included peer-reviewed research articles and conference proceeding papers. Furthermore, only articles published in the English language were considered. After we applied the said inclusion criteria, our article set included 853 articles in total.

For selecting relevant studies, we also defined exclusion criteria (EC) based on our research question. First, we excluded duplicate articles (EC1). Second, we omitted articles from our study that were incomplete, e.g., that had no conclusion (EC2). Third, also the research domain served as an exclusion criterion (EC3). Articles that neither addressed e-government nor blockchain technology were excluded. Furthermore, this criterion also addressed that the paper's use case needs to address the relation of G2C. Applying the exclusion criteria, we reduced the total amount of 853 to 160 articles for full-text reading. In the next step, we reviewed these articles against defined quality criteria to ensure that the study results were relevant for our research. We discarded articles that mainly describe technical details of a construct, do not address the public sector, or only provide a general overview of e-government applications instead of addressing a specific use case. Besides, we excluded articles addressing only the regulatory aspects of e-government. After this quality assessment, the article set ultimately contains 89 articles. Figure 1 depicts the data collection process.

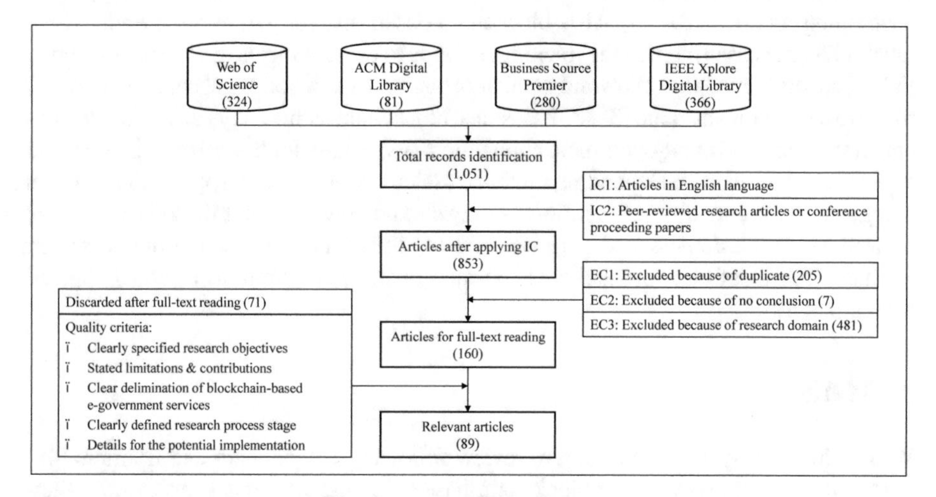

Fig. 1. Data collection process

During the data extraction phase, we extracted the following information: use case, research question or objectives, evidence, validity of the study, research challenges, and limitations. In the subsequent data synthesis phase, we analyzed the results of the selected studies considering the publication year and type, use case, research process stage, and the requirements imposed on a blockchain-based e-government solution. For the classification of the research process stage, we used the categorization of system development research proposed by Nunamaker [42]. Those stages are: (1) conceptualization, (2) system architecture, (3) system design, (4) prototype, and (5) evaluation. Following the data extraction phase, we consolidated the identified requirements by analyzing the definitions of the requirements. Thereby, we found that they are addressing either the data, the system itself, or the user. For this reason, we chose to classify the requirements in the three categories “user”, “data”, “system”. Furthermore, we consolidated overlapping requirements, which addressed the same aspect but used synonyms.

4 Results

4.1 Descriptive Findings of Selected Articles

The number of publications and the variety of use cases show that the academic literature on blockchain-based G2C e-government services develops rapidly. Our article set contained 89 scientific articles that have analyzed or taken up blockchain-based G2C e-government services after we applied our defined inclusion and exclusion criteria. Of these, 75 articles are published in conference proceedings, and 14 articles appeared in scientific journals. A total of 80 articles have been published within the last 2,5 years, which indicates a growing research interest. Furthermore, the research stage has progressed since Batubara et al.'s [10] literature review as the number of publications focusing on evaluating solutions has increased. In particular, the research stages are distributed according to Nunamaker et al. [42] as follows: (1) conceptualization (20 articles), (2) system architecture (19 articles), (3) system design (12 articles), (4) prototype (9 articles), and (5) evaluation (29 articles). The range of discussed use cases is broad. While Batubara et al. [10] found a predominant focus on healthcare, education, and smart cities, we found immense attention on **e-voting** (51 out of 89). Also, articles propose blockchain technology for supporting **land & property management** (12 out of 89) and **smart city** (7 out of 89) solutions. Besides, researchers discuss using blockchain technology as the underlying technology for creating **digital identities** (7 out of 89). However, this use case may address varying aspects [9, 43]. It ranges from government-issued digital identities [9] to using blockchain as a foundation for self-sovereign identities [44]. The idea of using blockchain technology in the domain of **education** (6 out of 89) also becomes more popular. Moreover, researchers discussed blockchain-solutions for **fund tracking** (2 out of 89) and **taxation** (4 out of 89). Most researchers observe the latter use case from the government's perspective [8, 30] rather than from the citizen's perspective.

4.2 Requirements of Blockchain-Based G2C E-Government Services

As we identified that the extracted requirements address either the user interacting with the blockchain-based solution, the data to be recorded, or the system itself, we used the three categories “data”, “user”, and “system” to categorize the identified requirements. Additionally, we consolidated requirements addressing the same aspect but using synonymous terminology. For example, some authors used the term *privacy* [43] while others used anonymity [45] or secrecy [46]. Similarly, authors used the term usability [47] as a synonym for *ease of use* [8], accuracy [48], and correctness [49] for *integrity* [50], credibility [51] and trustworthiness [52] for *reliability* [53]. Also, the definitions of *auditability* [50] with traceability [54] coincide as well as of *instant information* [48] with real-time information [55]. Another overlap exists for *affordability* [56] with low-cost [57] and cost-efficiency [58]. Lastly, *accessibility* [47] represents the same aspect as availability [57].

We found interesting gaps in requirements for some use cases, e.g., all use cases require system-related *interoperability*, except for e-voting applications. In our opinion, this finding is not due to the fact that *interoperability* is not an essential requirement for e-voting applications, as all created services need to be integrated into the existing process and system landscapes. Also, only articles addressing the taxation use cases mention *reversibility*. However, we claim that it is equally important for other use cases, such as land & property management, to correct or delete false transactions. This finding highlights the importance of an integrative observation beyond each use case. Observing a use case in isolation would entail that important but less obvious requirements are potentially missed. Another notable finding impacts the requirement data-related *redundancy*. From our perspective, this requirement should not only focus on "data", as *redundancy* is crucial to reduce the impact of system downtime. Nevertheless, the authors addressed only data-related *redundancy*. However, to create secure and reliable systems, researchers should also assess redundancy from a systems perspective. Table 1 provides an overview of these requirements with their different terminologies, their definitions, and their frequency.

Table 1. List of requirements and their definitions

	Requirement *(synonyms)*	Definition	Freq.
User	Privacy *(anonymity, secrecy, confidentiality)*	The data may not be associated with a user	61
	Verifiability	Anyone may verify the correctness regarding the system state, including its transactions and results	56
	Trust	The user must trust in the system itself	59
	Authenticity *(identifiability)*	Users are who they claim to be	74
	Integrity *(eligibility)*	Users fulfill specific prerequisites to use the system	43
	Ease of use *(user-friendly, usability)*	The system is convenient to use, and users can easily add transactions	30
Data	Transparency	Process information and data are generally visible for users, but in case of necessity, this visibility can also be limited	75
	Integrity *(accuracy, correctness)*	The data may not be altered, such that the resulting evaluation of the data (e.g., election result) is accurate	68
	Reliability *(credibility, trustworthiness)*	The credibility of the data and transactions can be trusted	53
	Immutability	No data is lost or deleted	43
	Auditability *(traceability)*	The transaction history may be shared in a traceable and reliable manner	43

(continued)

Table 1. (*continued*)

	Requirement *(synonyms)*	Definition	Freq.
	Confidentiality	The contents of transactions are hidden or unreadable	27
	Instant Information	Data is exchanged instantly	21
	No double spending	Every transaction is executed only once	25
	Reversibility	Conflicting edits or errors can be managed by counter-transactions	1
	Redundancy	Data is kept redundantly	3
System	Security	The system is resistant to errors and attacks	86
	Scalability	The system can handle a growing number of transactions	30
	Affordability *(low cost, cost-efficient, financial viability)*	The implementation and maintenance of the system should be affordable and, in the best case, also be less expensive than analog alternatives	37
	Accessibility *(availability)*	Users can remotely access the system to participate regardless of their physical location at any time	34
	Robustness	The system is not only resistant to attacks but is also scalable and resource-efficient	32
	Interoperability	The system is integrable with existing systems and processes	12
	Ease of maintenance	Services are separated to guarantee efficient maintenance	7

Based on the analysis of various definitions, we are able to form a categorization of all requirements and their inter-relation with general blockchain characteristics, which we described in Sect. 2. Accordingly, analyzing the definitions of the found requirements allowed us to categorize the identified requirements either as a characteristic embedded in blockchain technology or as further feature. However, this differentiation between "characteristics" and "features" is not unambiguous in all cases. For example, researchers on blockchain technology often refer to user-related *trust* as one of the underlying characteristics of blockchain technology [25]. However, we follow the argumentation of Ostern [59] and Marella [60] that users' trust is not inherent to blockchain technology itself. Instead, other underlying characteristics and requirements like integrity and immutability of the data stimulate *trust*. For this reason, we categorize *trust* as a user-related feature rather than as a blockchain characteristic.

Similarly, some authors refer to the data-related *auditability* requirement as an underlying characteristic [5]. However, *auditability* is defined as the ability to examine records. Accordingly, we argue that data-related *transparency, redundancy,* and *immutability* create this ability for the said examination. Thus, we categorized *auditability* as a feature. Resultingly, we positioned *transparency*, *integrity*, *immutability, redundancy,* and *privacy* as characteristics, which, however, also serve as requirements for blockchain-based G2C e-government services. Figure 2 provides an overview of the relation between characteristics and features as identified requirements.

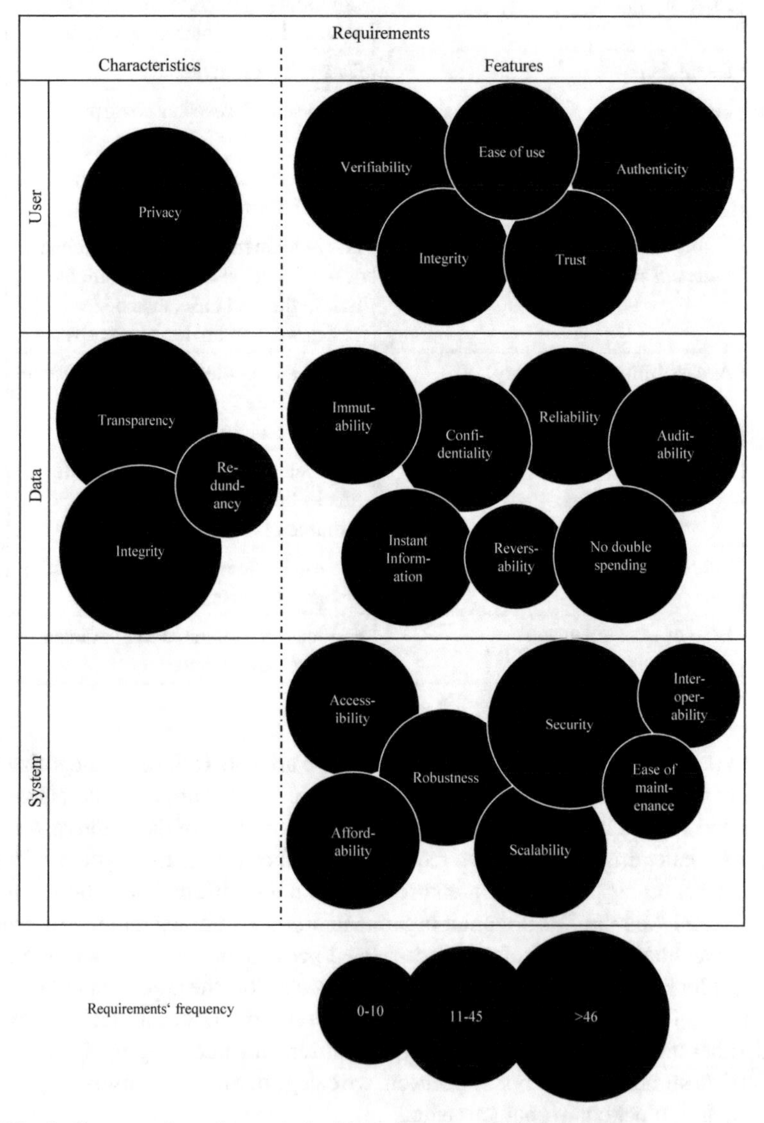

Fig. 2. Structured requirements for blockchain-based G2C e-government services

5 Discussion

The current literature on blockchain-based e-government does not provide practitioners and researchers with a precise specification of the requirements that blockchain-based G2C e-government services must fulfill. For this reason, we present a structuring and categorizing overview of requirements as a basis for the development, testing, and evaluation of such services. Our analysis revealed that the requirements user-related *privacy*, data-related *transparency,* and system-related *security* are mentioned particularly frequent. This finding may indicate an extraordinary importance of those mentioned requirements. Considering that we observe the public sector, this finding is not surprising, as those three requirements are particularly relevant for service delivery in the highly sensitive public sector. Firstly, *privacy* plays an important role in the public sector as it is crucial to prevent discrimination, which most states are committed to eradicating. Secondly, *transparency* is essential for citizens to trace whether the state represents their interests and manages their financial resources to a satisfactory degree. Finally, *security* must be guaranteed within a system, as an attack, for example during an election, would have an immense impact on the country's stability due to the great number of people affected. Against this backdrop, researchers and practitioners should consider the requirements *privacy, transparency,* and *security* when developing, testing, and evaluating blockchain-based G2C e-government services.

However, an alternative explanation for their frequency is that they are rather apparent requirements. Thus, researchers and practitioners should also be aware of the less frequently mentioned requirements, as they might be equally important. For example, *reversibility* was mentioned in total only once as a requirement for the use case taxation. However, we argue that reversibility of the data is not only essential for blockchain-based taxation services, but also for other use cases like land and property management. A mistaken assignment of a property to an individual, which lasts perpetually, would have immense consequences and may even discredit the proposed solution. This finding might even imply that blockchain, which was originally designed to immutably record unchangeable transactions, may not be the ideal solution. However, workarounds for this problem prevail [28]. In any case, the configuration and design of blockchain-based solutions must be considered very carefully and in light of alternative solutions. Furthermore, we found this requirement only once while we consider it equally important for other use cases. This gap highlights the importance of an integrative observation of all use cases to prevent missing out on some less obvious but still vital requirements.

In fact, our analysis shows that compliance with specific requirements is crucial for blockchain-based services in the public sector. Consequently, our results offer a guideline for practitioners and researchers for the development and testing as well as the evaluation of such services. In the following, we demonstrate how this can be accomplished by defining user stories. Using the taxation services use case as an example, we show how the three requirements *privacy*, *transparency, security,* and *reversibility* can be specified further. A user story addressing *privacy* might be that firstly, "as a user, my personal and financial information shall remain anonymous for the public", but secondly, "be accessible for authorized individuals such as authorized public officials". The latter is also addressed under the requirement of *transparency*: "As an authorized person, such as a public official, I may see personal and financial data of a set of specific persons". Furthermore, "as a citizen, I am able to see the aggregated sum of collected taxes transparently". Regarding its *security,* a taxation system needs to be protected against cyberattacks such as a denial-of-service attack. Moreover, practitioners could specify the requirement *reversibility* as "transactions of tax payments, which are mistakenly associated with the wrong individual, are reversible based on a substantial justification". While we exemplarily used the use case taxation services for the specification of potential user stories, we propose that our requirements can be used as a basis for all use cases targeting the relation of G2C. Furthermore, our requirements can serve as an input for evaluation. In specific, we suggest the definition of key performance indicators based on the requirements and user stories for an evaluation of the developed services.

6 Conclusion

Regarding our theoretical contribution, our comprehensive literature review as well as the organizational and technical requirements identified lay the foundation for a successful application of blockchain-based G2C in the public sector. While we present a snapshot of the current research on blockchain-based G2C e-government services, the identified requirements may also function as a basis for an evaluation encompassing acceptance criteria. Regarding our managerial contribution, we offer a guideline for researchers and practitioners in developing, testing, and evaluating their solutions. By categorizing the identified requirements, we contribute to a harmonized and integrated view on requirements, which a blockchain-based G2C e-government service needs to fulfill. We captured requirements independently from its use case, which has two implications. On the one hand, we showed that many use cases demand similar requirements. As a result, our overarching requirements are valid for all investigated use cases. On the other hand, this approach allowed us to identify those requirements, which are not as obvious, but important, nevertheless. Hence, we support researchers and practitioners in preventing to overlook the latter.

Although having pursued a rigorous research approach, we acknowledge three limitations of our study, which may stimulate further research opportunities. Firstly, we only included peer-reviewed research articles to ensure that our results are based on high-quality research. However, grey literature may deliver even further, recent aspects. Secondly, we also observed conflicts with terminological determinism according to Ostern [11], which represents a significant problem for meaningful empirical research. Thus, the current literature on blockchain technology does not provide a clear overview of the characteristics inherent to the underlying technology and further features. By proposing a delimitation on those characteristics and features, we aim to stimulate the academic discourse on blockchain terminology. Lastly, we exclusively addressed blockchain-based G2C e-government services. In our opinion, the assessment of the relations G2G or G2B would be a promising future research opportunity, as currently no conclusion can be made whether our structured requirements in the context of G2C can also be applied to the relations of G2G and G2B.

In conclusion, our research, despite limitations, provides a structured overview of requirements, which blockchain-based G2C e-government services need to fulfill. As we showed that many requirements are rather obvious, whilst some are at risk of being overlooked, our created overview serves as a important input for the development, testing, and evaluation of such services.

References

1. Layne, K., Lee, J.: Developing fully functional e-government: a four stage model. Gov. Inf. Q. **18**, 122–136 (2001)
2. Moon, M.J.: The evolution of e-government among municipalities: rhetoric or reality? Public Adm. Rev. **62**, 424–433 (2002)
3. Janowski, T.: Digital government evolution: from transformation to contextualization. Gov. Inf. Q. **32**, 221–236 (2015)
4. Norris, D.F.: e-government… not e-governance… not e-democracy not now! In: Proceedings of the 4th International Conference on Theory and Practice of Electronic Governance, pp. 339–346. ACM (2010)
5. Fridgen, G., Radszuwill, S., Urbach, N., Utz, L.: Cross-organizational workflow management using blockchain technology-towards applicability, auditability, and automation. In: Proceedings of the 51st Hawaii International Conference on System Sciences (HICSS), pp. 3507–3516 (2018)
6. Konashevych, O.: The concept of the blockchain-based governing: Current issues and general vision. In: Proceedings of the European Conference on e-Government, ECEG, pp. 79–85 (2017)
7. Khan, K.M., Arshad, J., Khan, M.M.: Investigating performance constraints for blockchain based secure e-voting system. Future Gener. Comput. Syst. **105**, 13–26 (2020)
8. Hyvärinen, H., Risius, M., Friis, G.: A blockchain-based approach towards overcoming financial fraud in public sector services. Bus. Inf. Syst. Eng. **59**, 441–456 (2017)
9. Kuperberg, M., Kemper, S., Durak, C.: Blockchain usage for government-issued electronic IDs: a survey. In: Proper, H., Stirna, J. (eds.) Advanced Information Systems Engineering Workshops CAiSE 2019 International Workshops, vol. 349, pp. 155–167. Springer Cham (2019). https://doi.org/10.1007/978-3-030-20948-3_14
10. Batubara, F.R., Ubacht, J., Janssen, M.: Challenges of blockchain technology adoption for e-government. In: Proceedings of the 19th Annual International Conference on Digital Government Research Governance in the Data Age, pp. 1–9. ACM Press, New York (2018)
11. Ostern, N.K.: Blockchain in the IS research discipline: a discussion of terminology and concepts. Electron. Markets **30**(2), 195–210 (2019). https://doi.org/10.1007/s12525-019-00387-2
12. Sommerville, I.: Integrated requirements engineering: a tutorial. IEEE Softw. **22**, 16–23 (2005)
13. Gaventa, J., McGee, R.: The impact of transparency and accountability initiatives. Dev. Pol. Rev. **31**, 3–28 (2013)
14. Kosack, S., Fung, A.: Does transparency improve governance? Ann. Rev. Polit. Sci. **17**, 65–87 (2014)
15. Mensah, I.K., Vera, P., Mi, J.: Factors determining the use of e-government services: an empirical study on Russian students in China. Int. J. E-Adoption (IJEA) **10**, 1–19 (2018)
16. Scholl, H.J., Klischewski, R.: E-government integration and interoperability: framing the research agenda. Int. J. Public Adm. **30**, 889–920 (2007)
17. Carter, L., Weerakkody, V., Phillips, B., Dwivedi, Y.K.: Citizen adoption of e-government services: exploring citizen perceptions of online services in the United States and United Kingdom. Inf. Syst. Manage. **33**, 124–140 (2016)

18. Zawaideh, F.: Acceptance of e-government services among Jordanian citizen. Int. J. Recent Adv. Multi. Res. **4**, 2348–2351 (2016)
19. Molnar, A., Janssen, M., Weerakkody, V.: E-government theories and challenges: findings from a plenary expert panel. In: Proceedings of the 16th Annual International Conference on Digital Government Research, pp. 160–166. ACM Press, New York (2015)
20. Abu-Shanab, E.A.: Reengineering the open government concept: an empirical support for a proposed model. Gov. Inf. Q. **32**, 453–463 (2015)
21. Glaser, F.: Pervasive decentralisation of digital infrastructures: a framework for blockchain enabled system and use case analysis. In: Proceedings of the 50th Hawaii International Conference on System Sciences (2017). Hawaii International Conference on System Sciences (2017)
22. Xu, X., et al.: A taxonomy of blockchain-based systems for architecture design. In: IEEE International Conference on Software Architecture (ICSA), pp. 243–252. IEEE (2017)
23. Fridgen, G., Schlatt, V., Urbach, N., Schweizer, A.: Unchaining social businesses–blockchain as the basic technology of a crowdlending platform. In: Proceedings of the 38th International Conference on Information Systems (ICIS) (2017)
24. Wüst, K., Gervais, A.: Do you need a blockchain? In: Crypto Valley Conference on Blockchain Technology (CVCBT), pp. 45–54. IEEE (2018)
25. Zheng, Z., Xie, S., Dai, H., Chen, X., Wang, H.: An overview of blockchain technology: architecture, consensus, and future trends. In: IEEE International Congress on Big Data (BigData Congress), pp. 557–564. IEEE (2017)
26. Casino, F., Dasaklis, T.K., Patsakis, C.: A systematic literature review of blockchain-based applications: current status, classification and open issues. Telematics Inform. **36**, 55–81 (2019)
27. Alketbi, A., Nasir, Q., Talib, M.A.: Blockchain for government services — use cases, security benefits and challenges. In: 15th Learning and Technology Conference, Piscataway, NJ, pp. 112–119. IEEE (2018)
28. Guggenmos, F., Lockl, J., Rieger, A., Wenninger, A., Fridgen, G.: How to develop a GDPR-compliant blockchain solution for cross-organizational workflow management: evidence from the German asylum procedure. In: Proceedings of the 53rd Hawaii International Conference on System Sciences (HICSS), pp. 4023–4032 (2020)
29. Lacity, M.C.: Adressing key challenges to making enterprise blockchain applications a reality. MIS Q. Executive 201–222 (2018)
30. Avital, M., Beck, R., King, J., Rossi, M., Teigland, R.: Jumping on the blockchain bandwagon: lessons of the past and outlook to the future. In: Thirty Seventh International Conference on Information Systems (2016)
31. Hoffman, M.R.: Can blockchains and linked data advance taxation. In: Companion Proceedings of the the Web Conference, pp. 1179–1182. ACM, New York (2018)
32. Natarén, C., Herran, A.: Restoring trust in mexican government. Preliminary assessment of DLT implementation. In: Proceedings of the 2019 International Conference on Blockchain Technology, New York, pp. 24–29. ACM, New York (2019)
33. Yapa, I., Heanthenna, S., Bandara, N., Prasad, I., Mallawarachchi, Y.: Decentralized ledger for land and property transactions in Sri Lanka acresense. In: 2018 IEEE Region 10 Humanitarian Technology Conference (R10-HTC), New York, NY, USA. IEEE (2018)
34. Sanka, A.I., Cheung, R.C.: Blockchain: panacea for corrupt practices in developing countries. In: 2019 2nd International Conference of the IEEE Nigeria Computer Chapter (NigeriaComputConf), pp. 1–7. IEEE (2019)
35. Mohite, A., Acharya, A.: Blockchain for government fund tracking using Hyperledger. In: Proceedings of the 2018 International Conference on Computational Techniques, Electronics and Mechanical Systems (CTMES), New York, NY, USA, pp. 231–234. IEEE (2018)

36. Liu, L., Piao, C., Jiang, X., Zheng, L.: Research on governmental data sharing based on local differential privacy approach. In: 2018 IEEE 15th International Conference on E-Business Engineering (ICEBE), Los Alamitos, CA, USA, pp. 39–45. IEEE (2018)
37. Fan, L., et al.: Sharing big data using blockchain technologies in local governments: some technical, organizational and policy considerations. Inf. Polity **24**, 419–435 (2019)
38. Beck, R., Müller-Bloch, C.: Blockchain as radical innovation: a framework for engaging with distributed ledgers as incumbent organization. In: Proceedings of the 50th Hawaii International Conference on System Sciences (HICSS), pp. 5390–5399 (2017)
39. Shahaab, A., Lidgey, B., Hewage, C., Khan, I.: Applicability and appropriateness of distributed ledgers consensus protocols in public and private sectors: a systematic review. IEEE Access **7**, 43622–43636 (2019)
40. Kitchenham, B., Charters, S.: Guidelines for performing Systematic Literature reviews in Software Engineering Version 2.3. Engineering (2007)
41. Nakamoto, S.: Bitcoin: A peer-to-peer electronic cash system (2008)
42. Nunamaker, J.F., Chen, M., Purdin, T.D.: Systems development in information systems research. J. Manage. Inf. Syst. **7**, 89–106 (1990)
43. Fu, M.-H.: Ballot mechanism design based on blockchain methodologies. In: Proceedings of the 2nd International Conference on Computing and Big Data, pp. 91–93. ACM, New York (2019)
44. Rotuna, C., Gheorghita, A., Zamifiroiu, A., Smada, D.-M.: Smart city ecosystem using blockchain technology. Informatica Economica **23**, 41–50 (2019)
45. Hossain, S.S., Arani, S.A., Rahman, M.T., Bhuiyan, T., Alam, D., Zaman, M.: E-voting system using blockchain technology. In: Proceedings of the 2019 2nd International Conference on Blockchain Technology and Applications, pp. 113–117. ACM, New York (2019)
46. Akbari, E., Wu, Q., Zhao, W., Arabnia, H.R., Yang, M.Q.: From blockchain to internet-based voting. In: 2017 International Conference on Computational Science and Computational Intelligence (CSCI), pp. 218–221. IEEE (2017)
47. Perez, A.J., Ceesay, E.N.: Improving end-to-end verifiable voting systems with blockchain technologies. In: 2018 IEEE International Conference on Internet of Things (iThings) and IEEE Green Computing and Communications (GreenCom) and IEEE Cyber, Physical and Social Computing (CPSCom) and IEEE Smart Data (SmartData), pp. 1108–1115. IEEE (2018)
48. Singh, A., Chatterjee, K.: SecEVS : Secure electronic voting system using blockchain technology. In: 2018 International Conference on Computing, Power and Communication Technologies (GUCON), pp. 863–867. IEEE (2018)
49. Murtaza, M.H., Alizai, Z.A., Iqbal, Z.: Blockchain based anonymous voting system using zkSNARKs. In: 2019 International Conference on Applied and Engineering Mathematics (ICAEM), pp. 209–214. IEEE (2019)
50. Sheer Hardwick, F., Gioulis, A., Naeem Akram, R., Markantonakis, K.: E-voting with blockchain: an e-voting protocol with decentralisation and voter privacy. In: 2018 IEEE International Conference on Internet of Things (iThings) and IEEE Green Computing and Communications (GreenCom) and IEEE Cyber, Physical and Social Computing (CPSCom) and IEEE Smart Data (SmartData), pp. 1561–1567. IEEE (2018)
51. Khan, K.M., Arshad, J., Khan, M.M.: Secure digital voting system based on blockchain technology. Int. J. Electron. Gov. Res. **14**, 53–62 (2018)
52. Wibowo, S., Sandikapura, T.: Improving data security, interoperability, and veracity using blockchain for one data governance, case study of local tax big data. In: 2019 International Conference on ICT for Smart Society (ICISS), pp. 1–6. IEEE (2019)
53. Cooley, R., Wolf, S., Borowczak, M.: Blockchain-based election infrastructures. In: 2018 IEEE International Smart Cities Conference (ISC2), Piscataway, NJ, pp. 1–4. IEEE (2018)

54. Nguyen, N.-H., Nguyen, B.M., Dao, T.-C., Do, B.-L.: Towards blockchainizing land valuation certificate management procedures in Vietnam. In: 2020 RIVF International Conference on Computing and Communication Technologies (RIVF), pp. 1–6. IEEE (2020)
55. Alam, A., Zia Ur Rashid, S.M., Abdus Salam, M., Islam, A.: Towards blockchain-based e-voting system. In: 2018 International Conference on Innovations in Science, Engineering and Technology (ICISET), Piscataway, NJ, pp. 351–354. IEEE (2018)
56. Fatrah, A., El Kafhali, S., Haqiq, A., Salah, K.: Proof of concept blockchain-based voting system. In: Proceedings of the 4th International Conference on Big Data and Internet of Things, pp. 1–5. ACM, New York (2019)
57. Garg, K., Saraswat, P., Bisht, Aggarwal, S.K., Kothuri, S.K., Gupta, S.: A comparitive analysis on e-voting system using blockchain. In: 2019 4th International Conference on Internet of Things: Smart Innovation and Usages (IoT-SIU), pp. 1–4 (2019)
58. Zaghloul, E., Li, T., Ren, J.: Anonymous and coercion-resistant distributed electronic voting. In: 2020 International Conference on Computing, Networking and Communications (ICNC), pp. 389–393. IEEE (2020)

Explainable Artificial Intelligence (XAI) Supporting Public Administration Processes – On the Potential of XAI in Tax Audit Processes

Nijat Mehdiyev(✉), Constantin Houy, Oliver Gutermuth, Lea Mayer, and Peter Fettke

Germany Research Center for Artificial Intelligence (DFKI), Saarland University, Saarbrücken, Germany
{nijat.mehdiyev,constantin.houy,oliver.gutermuth,lea.mayer, peter.fettke}@dfki.de

Abstract. Artificial Intelligence (AI) can offer significant potential for public administrations which – in Germany – are likely to face considerable skills shortages in the next few years. AI systems can especially support the automation of processes and thus disburden administrative staff. As transparency and fairness play a major role in administrative processes, explainable AI (XAI) approaches are expected to enable a proper usage of AI in public administration. In this article, we investigate the potential of XAI for the support of tax authority processes, especially the selection of tax audit target organizations. We illustrate relevant tax audit scenarios and present the potential of different XAI techniques which we currently develop in these scenarios. It shows that XAI can significantly support tax audit preparations resulting in more efficient processes and a better performance of tax authorities concerning their main responsibilities. A further contribution of this article lies in the exemplary application of XAI usage guidelines in the public administration context.

Keywords: Explainable Artificial Intelligence · XAI · Public administration · Tax audit

1 Introduction

Public administrations in Germany will likely face significant skills shortages in the coming years according to a current PwC study [1]. In order to keep up the needed public services and to provide them timely and in a good service quality, more and more public administrations consider taking advantage of the potential of artificial intelligence (AI) to support public administration processes [2]. However, while AI applications generally need to be reliable, trustworthy and need to provide good results, e.g. correct predictions of events, AI solutions for public administrations especially must be transparent, fair, and non-discriminatory in their results. In this context, it is important that the outcomes delivered by an AI system, e.g. using machine learning (ML), and the way how these

F. Ahlemann et al. (Eds.): WI 2021, LNISO 46, pp. 413–428, 2021.
https://doi.org/10.1007/978-3-030-86790-4_28

results came into existence are explainable. It is, e.g. important that human users can understand and follow the results which have been produced by an ML technique, even if the approach is a "black box". Explainable AI (XAI) approaches aim at providing and supporting the needed transparency of delivered outcomes by AI systems. While the potential of XAI methods has been broadly acknowledged for industrial scenarios, their potential for the support of public administration processes has not been intensely investigated, so far, and only little research exists in this field.

This article aims at contributing to the current state of research with an in-depth illustration of XAI potential for supporting public administration processes with a special focus on the tasks and duties of the German tax authorities. The methodical approach of this work is based on literature analysis and an in-depth case examination. The *main contribution* of this article is twofold. First, we define and describe various innovative AI-based use-cases for tax audit processes especially by following the key propositions recommended in the conceptual framework proposed by [3] for developing XAI solutions. By using this XAI design and deployment guideline in the context of public administration we were able to define and introduce the motivation and objectives for using generated explanations, the expected outcome and the context of explanation situation, the target audience and their expectations, preferences and requirements which impact the choice and implementation of the relevant XAI methods in public administration. Second, this study illustrates the applicability of XAI approaches by presenting the prototypically developed explanation solutions by using the semi-synthetically generated data based on the relevant variables identified by [4] which investigated similar processes in Austria by using conventional rule-based models. Our proposed solutions are presumed to support the proper selection of target organizations for tax audit as well, but by generating explanations on top of the applied black-box models. For the examined *process prediction* problem, it was of interest to examine two different use-cases and consequently to investigate two families of post-hoc explanation methods which support various user groups in their specific decision making objectives. On one hand, we applied three widely accepted local post-hoc explanations such as Shapley Values [5, 6], LIME [7] and Individual Conditional Expectation (ICE) plots [8] which facilitate the auditors in justifying each individual decision provided by the black-box model. On the other hand, the global post-hoc explanation approaches such as feature importance, model tree-based regression surrogate model and Partial Dependence Plots (PDP) [9] were adopted which enable the management level decision makers or process owners to make more strategic decisions such as enhancing the business processes [10].

The article structure is as follows: after this introduction, Sect. 2 presents conceptual foundations and related work. Section 3 introduces the tax audit context and motivates the tax audit scenario on which we focus in our in-depth case analysis as well as the description of the XAI potential and the discussion including our developed solution approaches. Section 4 discusses the findings before Sect. 5 concludes the paper.

2 Conceptual Foundations and Related Work

2.1 Artificial Intelligence and Public Administrations

AI pursues the goal of developing technical systems that can solve problems for which a human being requires intelligence. Investigating the potential of AI in public administrations has been a trending topic in recent years. In their landscaping analysis for examining and classifying the AI implementations in public services [11], Misuraca et al. identify more than 85 AI application projects in the chosen European countries. In his study [12], Etscheid develops a framework for evaluating the opportunities of public administration processes which can be partially or fully automated through AI techniques. In [2], Djeffal analyzes and describes interesting application opportunities of AI in public administration while focusing on legal issues and the necessary free space for experimenting to tap its full potential for the improvement of public services. In this context, first normative guidelines for AI in public administrations have been discussed from different perspectives [13]. In [14], Wirtz et al. propose an integrated AI governance framework after examining the AI challenges and different AI regulation approaches for public administration. In their proposed assessment framework [15], van Noordt and Misuraca discuss the effects of AI in the government context by examining drivers impacting the adoption of AI and by analyzing the need for organizational changes. Other related work illustrates further interesting potential of AI in public administration processes or in the public sector. e.g. in the following concrete use-cases [16–18]:

1. Tax audit scenarios, especially the selection of tax audit target organizations: this case will be examined in detail in Sect. 3.
2. AI-based traffic engineering and traffic management systems (TMS): AI can be used in complex Smart City environments to manage traffic based on current situational data, such as available capacities, the utilization status of certain routes or current sensor values, e.g. concerning air pollution etc.
3. Social welfare procedures: AI techniques from the field of natural language processing (NLP) and image recognition can support administrative back office procedures in the context of social welfare, e.g. the social integration assistance procedure or the assessment of personal handicap situations. In this context application forms and provided documents, e.g. medical reports, can be automatically analyzed, and decisions can be automatically prepared and suggested to the administrative staff based on this analysis.
4. AI-based application assessment for monetary support, e.g. for small and medium-sized enterprises (SME) and businesses in times of the Covid-19 pandemic: in the context of the current pandemic situation, German SMEs had the possibility to apply for monetary support. In this context, a sheer flood of applications was filed and could only be handled by random assessments while most of the applications were approved without a proper assessment because of staff shortage in the administrations. AI could provide more intense examinations of all applications filed in such situations, which would be politically necessary as many cases of fraud have been identified in the meanwhile.

In such scenarios when using ML-based AI approaches, the developed results, e.g. predictive statements, provided decision support or automated decision making typically remain non-transparent, as the underlying ML approaches mostly function like "black boxes" and often provide no explanation why a certain conclusion has been drawn or why a certain decision has been proposed. However, this can be a severe showstopper for AI in public administration in Germany, because of the rigorous requirements concerning the transparency and fairness of decisions made by public administrations. In this context, decisions made and communicated to applicants should be "bulletproof", as a large amount of decisions made by public administrations in Germany are challenged in court. If public administrations want to use AI to gain reliable and "bulletproof" support, the explainability of AI results and thus reliable XAI approaches gain more and more importance, which will be discussed in more detail in the following section.

2.2 XAI and Its Necessity in Public Administration

To utilize the benefits of AI in the public administration while mitigating its risks, it is crucial to ensure the trustworthiness of the underlying systems. According to ethical guidelines drafted by a high level expert group on AI set up by the European Commission, three aspects should be considered throughout the entire lifecycle of intelligent systems in harmony to achieve the trustworthy AI [19]. These systems should comply with all laws and regulations (lawful), follow ethical principles and values (ethical) and should be technically and societally robust. A recent study proposes different recommendations at three different level (team, organization and industry) for building reliable, safe and trustworthy human-centered AI systems [20]. Another study suggests that various categories of trustworthiness approaches for AI such as fairness, explainability, auditability and safety should be considered when designing and implementing AI-based solutions [21]. In this context, apart from ensuring consideration of various requirements such as diversity, non-discrimination and fairness, technical robustness, privacy and data governance, societal and environmental well-being, etc. it is also essential to make the underlying AI-based systems accountable, responsible and transparent.

XAI methods have recently reemerged as crucial technical approaches to address these issues by making black-box AI systems more comprehensible, interpretable, and accountable [22]. The history of the research on making intelligent systems reaches back to more than three decades, where the initial studies concentrated mainly on making expert systems explainable [23, 24]. The recent proliferation of advanced black-box machine learning systems has triggered a new generation of explainable artificial intelligence [25]. An overview of taxonomies of modern explanation methods, required quality desiderata, various evaluation mechanisms, types and tools and other relevant aspects and dimensions can be found in [10, 22, 26, 27]. In the light of recent studies on application of XAI methods in different research and application domains such as healthcare, transportation, security, production, finance etc., we can observe the potential of explanations on top of underlying advanced machine learning approaches for enhancing the decision making processes [28–30]. Considering the practical implications of explanatory systems in operationalizing the data-driven artificial advice givers and the lack of relevant research in the public administration domain, this study is a first attempt to introduce an approach that defines what prerequisites to consider and how to develop

XAI solutions by examining tax audit processes. Furthermore, this study introduces and visualizes the outcomes of prominent XAI approaches for tax audit cases for illustration purposes.

3 On the Potential of XAI in Tax Audit Processes

3.1 Motivation and Case Context

In general, the key task of tax authorities is to make sure that taxes are paid properly, e.g. regarding the correctness of paid amounts, the equal and fair treatment of every person and organization who must pay taxes. Hence, this relates to both companies and private individuals. However, performing tax audits in companies are a much bigger challenge for tax authorities, since the amount of relevant information needed to do a proper tax audit is larger and more complex in companies. Furthermore, tax audits in companies can generate considerable additional tax revenues for states, which makes this task particularly important for tax authorities [16].

In Germany, tax audits are regulated by law, especially by §§ 193–207 of the German Fiscal Code (Abgabenordnung, AO). Possible types of audits are, e.g. tax audits, wage tax audits, special turnover tax audits, the abbreviated tax audit as defined in § 203 AO, as well as other audits such as standard rate audits. According to § 194 AO tax audits serve for the determination of the taxable person's tax circumstances and can comprise one or more tax types and taxation periods. The admissibility of a tax audit is regulated in § 193 AO in which is determined who may be subject to a tax audit. Within the scope of corporate tax audits, e.g. trade taxes, income taxes, corporate taxes, sales taxes, and other tax charges are among the factors that may be considered.

The data used by tax authorities for tax audits usually stem from financial accounting, asset accounting and payroll accounting. While these data provide tax authorities with a wide range of information for comprehensive analyses, the scope and depth of this audit information also imply considerable efforts and expenses. Although these efforts can be reduced by using IT systems, a complete analysis of all eligible companies or organizations is still challenging. Therefore, and for capacity reasons, companies and organizations that shall be audited are selected instead of deeply examining every single case [16].

The German tax audit regulations (Betriebsprüfungsordnung, BPO) are the basis for tax audits of the federal states' fiscal authorities and the Federal Central Tax Office (§ 1 BPO). The determination and evaluation of the tax-relevant facts must take place to ensure the equality of taxation (§§ 85, 199 AO). In legislative terms, this addresses the accurate determination and assessment of tax-relevant facts and does not aim at additional taxes [31]. At first, companies are classified according to their size: large companies, medium-sized companies, small companies, or micro-entities. The classification of size is determined by the Federal Ministry of Finance (§ 3 BPO). According to § 4 BPO, large companies are audited without any gaps, the audit period directly follows the preceding audit period. Organizations in other size classes are often audited at irregular intervals [32]. The empirical outcomes of a recent study which used the real world data for analyzing tax audit processes in Austria have revealed that a segmentation of the firms in terms of various criteria including their size has significant implications on the performance of the applied machine learning models for identifying suspicious firms [4]. Such a classification increases the predictive strength of the underlying local models which is an important prerequisite for generating plausible explanations for auditors to justify the appropriateness of recommendations delivered by the data-driven intelligent systems. The following additional criteria can e.g. also be included in the selection: random audits, audit requests at the instigation of corporate tax offices, evaluation of operating data, sector audits, indicative rate audits, risk groups or evaluation of control material [31]. An important objective of tax authorities is to make the audit as efficient as possible while considering insufficient staffing and the principle of equal burden. Furthermore, organizations can apply for an audit because there is e.g., a special interest in a timely tax audit due to the sale of a business. This must also be considered in the context of discretionary selection [33].

For the tax audit selection, typical indications in a company's data are analyzed in more detail. The more suspicious aspects, inconsistencies, or potential violations against existing rules are found in one case, the more likely an in-depth analysis will be suggested [16]. It should be noted that, in addition to rule-based approaches and purely statistical procedures, the selection of audit cases can also be based on the auditors' experience in combination with indications in the data. In addition, other exogenous events such as applications of external auditors can also influence the selection of target organizations to be tested [33].

3.2 Issues

The tax audit which is referred to as a conclusive and retrospective review of the individual cases with regard to certain types of taxes and taxation periods is an essential tool for the corresponding authorities to accomplish their task of assessing and collecting taxes in accordance with the law. According to the reports of the Federal Ministry of Finance in Germany, 13,525 auditors were employed nationwide in the tax audits of the federal states in 2018 who were able to audit 188,973 enterprises out of the 7,816,301 firms registered in the business register of the tax offices [34]. These numbers suggest the audit coverage was just 2.4% which resulted in additional tax claims of 13.9 Billion Euros. A further analysis suggests that 10.9 Billion Euros additional taxes are claimed from large enterprises for which the audit coverage was 21.6%. From more than 5.5 Million of small enterprises only 1.1% were audited. These numbers especially related to the personnel shortage reveal the necessity of intelligent decision support to overcome the complications in enhancing the underlying processes. It is very important to emphasize that the identification of firms for examination is not sample-based and the processes behind a solid audit are very knowledge-intensive. The auditors are therefore obliged to analyze potential cases over several years and provide a thorough justification for their choices. This time-consuming and mentally exhausting process is also affected by the heuristics and biases that prevent rational decision making.

Recent advancements in various branches of AI, particularly regarding ML, offer possibilities to enable such data-driven decision making for the identification of relevant cases for tax audit. Adoption of relevant machine learning approaches facilitates to develop intelligent systems that are capable to automate the tax audit processes fully or act as decision support systems to enhance the processes which cannot be automated due to legal, economic and technical factors. Moreover, due to the variety, volume, and veracity of the underlying data in the tax audit use-case, more complicated ML approaches with non-linear data processing mechanisms are expected to provide superior results compared to conventional statistical approaches. The recent AI democratization attempts that aim at the wider adoption in daily work practices and making the participation of interdisciplinary communities possible have reduced the barriers to the accessibility of such innovative and advanced machine learning frameworks, methods, and applications. Therefore, the complexity in the current use-case does not solely lie in the adoption of advanced AI methods for public administration scenarios, but rather in their operationalization by incorporating them into business processes. Nevertheless, due to their black-box character, such advanced ML techniques including deep learning methods, suffer especially from the inability to provide appropriate explanations for their actions. Consequently, the lack of mechanisms which are required to verify the validity and robustness of models and to justify individual model assessments complicates the process of establishing human trust in developed intelligent systems.

3.3 Solution: XAI-Driven Intelligent Decision Support Systems

3.3.1 Machine Learning for Tax Audits with Strong Predictive Capabilities

Like other public administration processes in the tax audit use-case there is a need for intelligent decision support systems that can alleviate inefficiencies regarding the personnel shortage and due to the exhaustive nature of the problem. This, in turn, requires in the first step a systematic approach to structure the relevant machine learning projects and productionize the AI-based intelligent systems by making them explainable. To carry out a thorough, consistent, diligent and comprehensive predictive analytics and development project, it is of utmost importance to follow well established scientific [35] or industrial frameworks [36]. According to these guidelines it is crucial to understand the AI project requirements and functionalities for the tax audit processes both from business and technical perspectives, collect and prepare the required data, choose the appropriate modelling approaches and deploy them robustly after an evaluation phase.

In [4], Setnicka has examined the applicability of predictive analytics for the identification of the tax audit cases in Austria which is equivalent to the purpose of this study. His study has investigated a data-driven identification of cases for subsequent claims and determination of fraudulent cases with the purpose to evaluate the quality of case selection and the audit process in general. After performing segmentation in terms of different criteria such as branches or the total amount of claims, various features such as turnover before taxes, operating expenses, assets in the balance sheet, total liabilities, the results of previous inspections, internal and external personnel costs, the amount of input taxes, travel expenses, maintenance costs etc. are collected. Although this path-breaking study has already addressed various important aspects and issues related to the tax audit, it adopted a comprehensible but less performant machine learning model, decision trees. Considering the imbalanced structure of the data and the non-linear relationships among the input features in the tax audit use-case and our previous experience from other public administration projects, it is conceivable to suggest that more advanced ML approaches such as deep learning or ensemble methods would provide more precise results. However, to enable collaboration among these ML techniques and the users in the tax audit scenario it is important to develop explanation solutions.

3.3.2 A Guideline for Structuring XAI Scenarios and Activities in Tax Audit

It is important to grasp that XAI is not a monolithic concept and the adoption of universal one-fits-all solutions for public administration is not necessarily reasonable [3]. Indeed, the sufficiency and relevance of the explanations are determined by the properties of the decision making environment, including but not limited to the user characteristics, the objectives of the explanation mechanisms, the nature of the underlying processes, the credibility and quality of predictions generated by adopted artificial intelligent systems [37]. Therefore, for developing solutions to generate relevant explanations for public administration processes, it is important to identify and describe the elements of these various factors and examine their interdependencies. For this purpose, this study uses a conceptual framework proposed in [3] by describing the key elements for designing an XAI solution in the tax audit use-case. This approach can also be used as a guideline for carrying out XAI projects in other public administration use-cases.

According to this concept it is crucial first to examine the characteristics of the stakeholders. Auditors, managers, data subjects (the firms), supervisory/regulatory authorities and AI developers are some of the stakeholders in the underlying tax audit use-case. These users who have different interests in using the XAI systems can be further classified in terms of their AI background (knowledge engineers vs. domain experts) or regarding their previous experiences (novice users vs. experienced users). The studies on explanations for intelligent systems suggest that the novice users prefer terminological explanations and may benefit from learning using the insights delivered by systems, whereas more experienced users opt for verifying the model knowledge [38, 39]. These users demand explanations for different objectives, e.g. verification of a reasoning trace in the adopted AI methods, justification/ratification of the reliability in the generated system outcomes, debugging the underlying AI models for improving accuracy and computational efficiency, learning from the system especially in the absence of domain knowledge, improving effectiveness or efficiency for making good decisions fast etc. By using these explanations tailored to their preferences, not only trust in the AI system is established but the users can also analyze the technical robustness of the model by checking its consistency, stability and representativeness or examine the reasons if the algorithmic fairness is violated. Various XAI approaches are proposed to address these requirements. These approaches can be model-specific which imply that they explain only particular models or model-agnostic which are independent of the adopted ML models. Furthermore, the scope of the explanations can be global or local depending whether a single outcome or the whole model behavior for the total population is explained. Finally, explanations can be generated before training models (pre-model), during the model training (in-model) and after obtaining the results from trained models (post-model).

After examining the characteristics of the process stakeholders and interdependencies among various process specific and decision making environment-related aspects, this study identifies various scenarios for the tax audit use-case for which different XAI solutions should be developed (see Fig. 1 on the next page). We would like to note that the introduced four scenarios are chosen to demonstrate how diversified the explanation solutions can be within a single use-case, tax audit. The list of potential scenarios can be easily extended by addressing the requirements of different stakeholders, their multifaceted explanation objectives, or the context of the predictions. In the first scenario, the proposed XAI solution is assumed to facilitate the tax auditors to ratify the data-driven recommendations. These users are responsible for making decisions for identifying suspicious firms and have interest to justify individual model decisions. They pursue mainly the purpose whether the provided AI decisions regarding the proposed audit cases are reliable and reasonable. Thus, for this audience it is appropriate to develop local post-hoc explanation approaches such as ICE Plots, Shapley values, LIME or other alternative local surrogate models, case-based explanations, counterfactual explanations etc.

On another side, the management is concerned with making strategic decisions to enhance the underlying processes by identifying process bottlenecks in relation to the identification of the cases for audit and developing measures to boost the effectiveness and efficiency of case handling by understanding the implications of the underlying AI models. Thus for this XAI scenario 2, the global post-hoc explanation approaches such as PDP, global surrogate models, Shapley dependent plots, Shapley Summary Plots, Accumulated Local Effects (ALE) Plots etc. are more suitable since they allow the decision-makers to examine all decisions made by the model globally [40]. In the third scenario, the supervisory/regulatory authorities may have an interest in carefully identifying samples for testing or verifying the availability of discrimination elements. Since they also lack in-depth technical AI knowledge like the first two stakeholders, post-hoc explanations are also relevant here. The scope of interpretability depends on their objective of examination. Finally, the AI developers are more interested in validating the inner

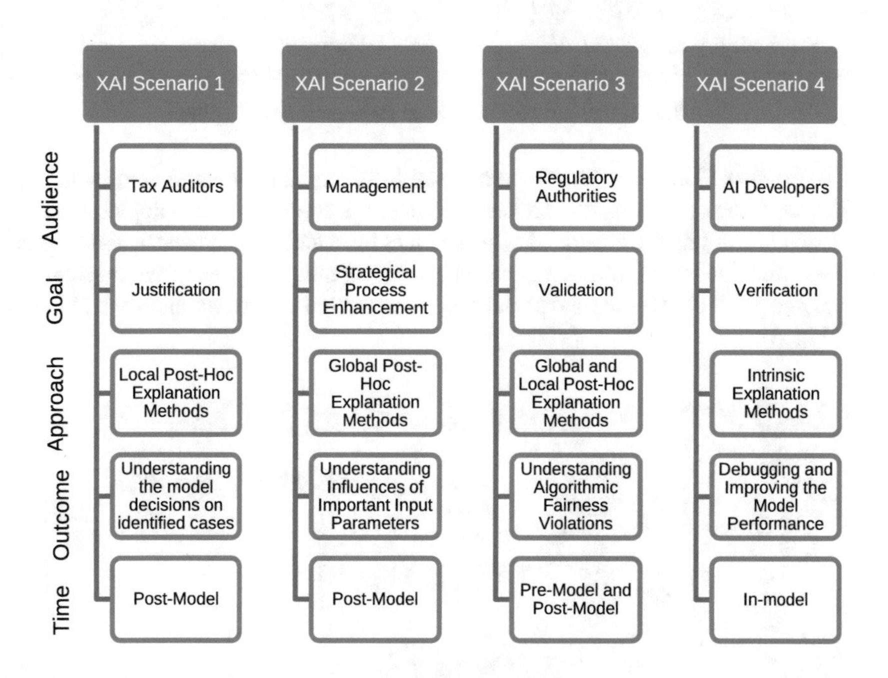

Fig. 1. XAI scenarios for tax audit

working mechanism and reasoning trace of black-box AI approaches. By using e.g., the explanations generated by intrinsic model-specific approaches, they can debug models by understanding the problematic areas.

3.3.3 Demonstration of Chosen XAI Methods for Tax Audit

For illustrative purposes, we have implemented various local and global post-hoc explanation approaches on top of the applied gradient boosting machine (GBM) model for the binary classification problem and visualized the obtained explanations by using synthetic data based on the variables identified by [4]. The main idea of ICE is examining the influence of individual variables by analyzing each feature separately (see Fig. 2). After choosing the variable of interest, the new data instances are created by making marginal changes to it through the identified grid of values and by keeping the values of other variables constant for the examined instance. The created data instances are scored by the black-box model and prediction scores on these value changes are then visualized.

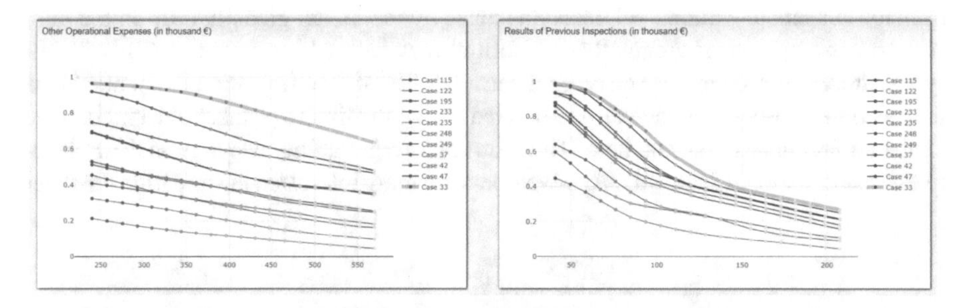

Fig. 2. Individual Conditional Expectation (ICE) plots

The steps of LIME, a perturbation-based local explanation approach, include perturbation of the dataset for the chosen instance, the scoring by the adopted black-box approach, weighting the generated new instances by calculating the distances to the original examined instance, fitting a comprehensible technique by using the original input values and prediction scores and presenting the extracted feature weights as explanations (see Fig. 3).

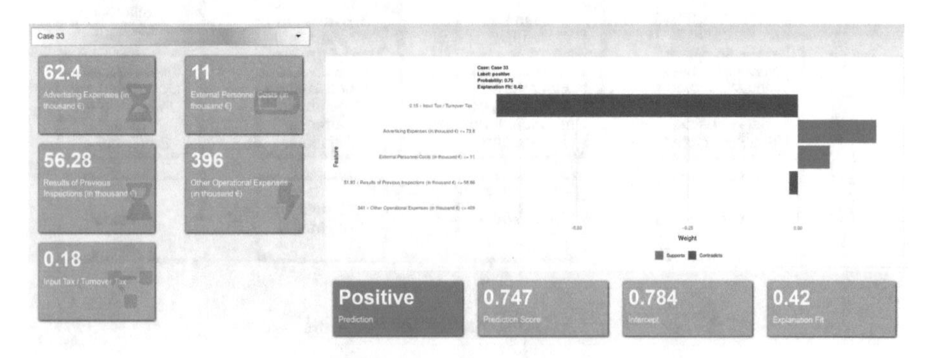

Fig. 3. LIME explanations

Shapley values is another feature attribution-based explanation method which stems from cooperative game theory. For the machine learning explanation situation, the input variable values of the examined observations are considered as cooperative game players and the model predictions are the respective payoffs. The sum of the obtained Shapley values illustrates and explains the contribution of each variable to the deviation between obtained prediction for the observation and average model prediction for the examined dataset (see Fig. 4).

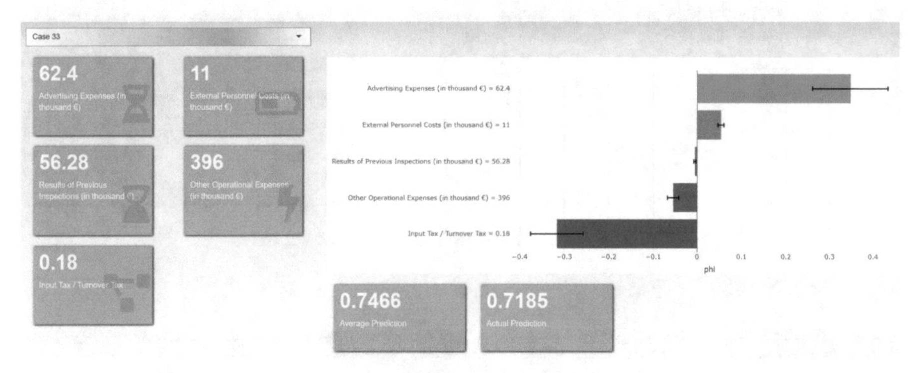

Fig. 4. Shapley values

Figure 5, 6 and 7 present the global post-hoc explanations from our dashboard namely, the surrogate regression model tree, PDP and the model-specific feature importance graph respectively. The main objective of global surrogate models is making the black-box model understandable by approximating its decisions. In our use-case we score the validation dataset by using the adopted black-box model, gradient boosting machine. Once the prediction scores are available, a white-box model of choice is fitted by using the original feature values as input data and prediction scores as output data. An overview of the comprehensible models that can be used as surrogate models can be found in [41]. In our use-case we implemented M5 regression model trees that combine the decision trees and linear models. The learned representations are then used as explanations (see Fig. 5).

PDP is a widely recognized model-agnostic approach that examines the effects of marginal changes of chosen variables to the response of the black-box predictors (see Fig. 6). It can be seen as the average of ICE plots described earlier; however, it provides a global interpretation. In [42], Zhao and Hastie suggest that under specific circumstances the PDP can be used to generate causal explanations.

Finally, the feature importance graph reveals what features are seen as important by the model when making the decisions. In our study, we use the model-specific approach for neural networks (see Fig. 7). Alternatively, the model agnostic approaches can be adopted. The practical applications and findings also suggest that using the explanation generated by different XAI methods together can generate more value since it allows the users to examine the model outcomes from different perspectives. For this purpose, it is essential to ensure harmonic transitions among different explanations by avoiding the confusions for users.

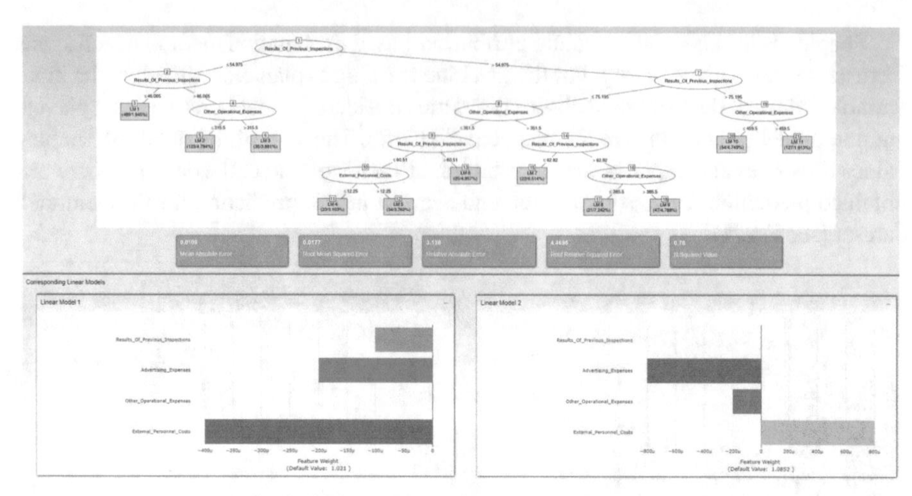

Fig. 5. Global surrogate regression model tree

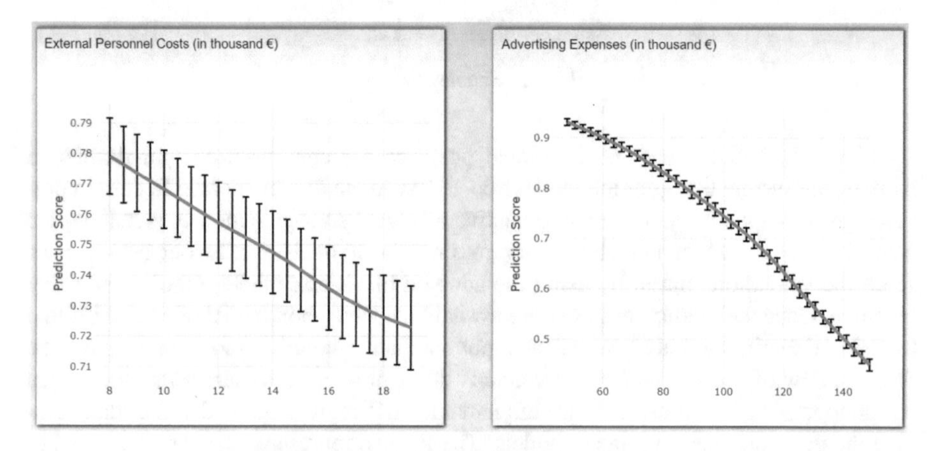

Fig. 6. Partial Dependence Plots (PDP)

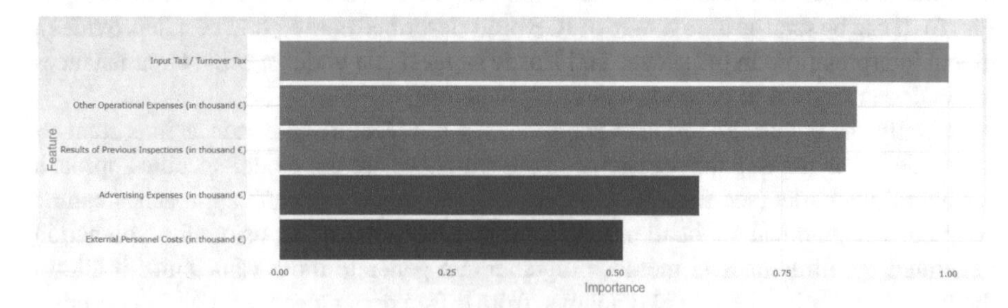

Fig. 7. Feature importance

4 Discussion

Public sector can benefit from AI projects that are expected to enhance the public good [43]. At the same time, such projects should not restrict themselves to increasing the efficiency or reducing costs only but generate added value for different stakeholders with various, sometimes conflicting objectives [44]. Various requirements such as transparency, safety, reliability, trustworthiness and fairness for designing, developing and deploying intelligent systems for supporting the decision making processes pose challenges by increasing the complexity of AI projects in public administration [45]. Furthermore, in difference to private sector projects, public sector projects often face scrutiny and oversight which increases the demand for explainability [45].

A well performed machine learning model and generated relevant explanations play a crucial role for establishing a data-driven culture in the public administration which is an essential aspect of a digital transformation. By bringing the people, processes, and technology together, this culture has great implications for enhancing the processes and improving "business models" in public administration that result in great advancements in provided services. Therefore, it is crucial to reduce the barriers between human users and data-driven intelligent systems and enable the human-in-the-loop concept. In this regard, this study aims to explore the potential of XAI for decision making processes in public administration particularly by examining the decision support structures for tax audit processes. Considering the research gap regarding the development and application of the explanation methods and corresponding interfaces in the public administration context, this study is one of the first attempts to present an approach to structuring the relevant XAI activities in this domain. Since the requirements of the users and the context of the explanation situation significantly influence the appropriateness of the generated explanations, such a holistic approach is required to mitigate the risks that can lead to the prospective failures.

Generating explanations for black-box machine learning methods with high quality and conveying them to the relevant stakeholders in a suitable and robust manner also facilitates creating added value by productionizing the intelligent systems. Some of the benefits offered by explanations for the tax audit use-case are (i) effectiveness: the explanations enable the auditors to identify the potential audit cases more precisely by making good decisions, (ii) efficiency: the explanations facilitate the auditors to make decision more quickly, (iii) persuasiveness: considering the bureaucratic and legal complexities it is hard to convince the users to use machine learning decisions and relevant explanations can help to overcome this challenge, (iv) education: by using consistent and robust explanations especially the novel users can learn from the intelligent system about the relationships among various factors, (v) trust: explanations are sought to increase the auditors trust in the artificial advice givers [46].

For illustration purposes the chosen prominent XAI approaches from global and local post-hoc explanation families are presented in this study as well by discussing their suitability for various use-cases in tax audit domain. However, it is important to note that these solutions were developed based on the semi-synthetically generated data and have mostly informative character for the corresponding research community. In the future work, we aim to develop the XAI solutions by examining the processes with corresponding authorities, to integrate the relevant explanation approaches by considering various desiderata for explanations and finally to perform a thorough evaluation by using the relevant measures and mechanisms.

5 Conclusion

In this paper we have examined the potential which XAI can offer for supporting public administration processes with a focus on the tasks and duties of German tax authorities. We concentrated on the process of preparing tax audits by supporting advantageous selections of target organizations for tax audits. We have, furthermore, presented according XAI solutions which we are currently developing, e.g. the XAI-based information dashboard supporting the selection of target organizations by providing an in-depth explanation of the major influencing factors which lead to the selection suggestions of the AI system. Responsibility, fairness, transparency, and the avoidance of discrimination are some of the key values of public administration. XAI methods can significantly contribute to the realization and implementation of these key values when using AI to support public administration processes. We have demonstrated this in our in-depth case description. However, the current efforts for further developing these approaches are definitely needed to provide a better acceptance and trust into AI systems, which is particularly necessary in the context of public administrations.

References

1. Detemple, P., Höhn, A.: Fachkräftemangel im öffentlichen Dienst. Prognose und Handlungsstrategien bis 2030. Stud. der PricewaterhouseCoopers (2018)
2. Djeffal, C.: Künstliche Intelligenz in der öffentlichen Verwaltung (Artificial Intelligence in Public Administration). Berichte des NEGZ 3 (2018)
3. Mehdiyev, N., Fettke, P.: Explainable artificial intelligence for process mining: a general overview and application of a novel local explanation approach for predictive process monitoring. arXiv Prepr. arXiv:2009.02098 (2020)
4. Setnicka, M.: Predictive Analytics in der österreichischen Finanzverwaltung. Informatik (2016)
5. Štrumbelj, E., Kononenko, I.: Explaining prediction models and individual predictions with feature contributions. Knowl. Inf. Syst. **41**(3), 647–665 (2013). https://doi.org/10.1007/s10115-013-0679-x
6. Lundberg, S.M., Lee, S.-I.: A unified approach to interpreting model predictions. In: 31st Conference on Neural Information Processing Systems, Long Beach, CA, USA, pp. 4765–4774 (2017)
7. Ribeiro, M.T., Singh, S., Guestrin, C.: Why should I trust you? Explaining the predictions of any classifier. In: Proceedings of the 22nd ACM SIGKDD International Conference on Knowledge Discovery and Data Mining, pp. 1135–1144. ACM Press, New York (2016)
8. Goldstein, A., Kapelner, A., Bleich, J., Pitkin, E.: Peeking inside the black box: visualizing statistical learning with plots of individual conditional expectation. J. Comput. Graph. Stat. **24**, 44–65 (2015)
9. Friedman, J.H.: Greedy function approximation: a gradient boosting machine. Ann. Stat., 1189–1232 (2001)
10. Lipton, Z.C.: The mythos of model interpretability. Queue **16**, 31–57 (2018)

11. Misuraca, G., van Noordt, C., Boukli, A.: The use of AI in public services: results from a preliminary mapping across the EU. In: Proceedings of the 13th International Conference on Theory and Practice of Electronic Governance, pp. 90–99. ACM Press (2020)
12. Etscheid, J.: Artificial intelligence in public administration. In: Lindgren, I., et al. (eds.) EGOV 2019. LNCS, vol. 11685, pp. 248–261. Springer, Cham (2019). https://doi.org/10.1007/978-3-030-27325-5_19
13. Djeffal, C.: Artificial intelligence and public governance: normative guidelines for artificial intelligence in government and public administration. In: Wischmeyer, T., Rademacher, T. (eds.) Regulating Artificial Intelligence, pp. 277–293. Springer, Cham (2020). https://doi.org/10.1007/978-3-030-32361-5_12
14. Wirtz, B.W., Weyerer, J.C., Sturm, B.J.: The dark sides of artificial intelligence: an integrated AI governance framework for public administration. Int. J. Public Adm. **43**, 818–829 (2020)
15. van Noordt, C., Misuraca, G.: Evaluating the impact of artificial intelligence technologies in public services: towards an assessment framework. In: Proceedings of the 13th International Conference on Theory and Practice of Electronic Governance, Athens, pp. 8–16 (2020)
16. Fettke, P.: Digitale Betriebsprüfung. In: Klenk, T., Nullmeier, F., Wewer, G. (eds.) Handbuch Digitalisierung in Staat und Verwaltung, pp. 553–563. Springer, Wiesbaden (2020). https://doi.org/10.1007/978-3-658-23668-7_51
17. Bauer, W., Riedel, O., Braun, S., Etscheid, J., Von Lucke, J., Stroh, F.: Künstliche Intelligenz in der Öffentlichen Verwaltung - Anwendungsfelder und Szenarien. Fraunhofer-Institut für Arbeitswirtschaft und Organ (2020)
18. Houy, C., Gutermuth, O., Fettke, P., Loos, P.: Potentiale künstlicher Intelligenz zur Unterstützung von Sachbearbeitsungsprozessen im Sozialwesen. Berichte des NEGZ **8**, 1–32 (2020)
19. Ethics Guidelines for Trustworthy AI. Report, European Commission (2019)
20. Shneiderman, B.: Bridging the gap between ethics and practice: guidelines for reliable, safe, and trustworthy human-centered AI systems. ACM Trans. Interact. Intell. Syst. **10**, 1–31 (2020)
21. Toreini, E., Aitken, M., Coopamootoo, K., Elliott, K., Zelaya, C.G., van Moorsel, A.: The relationship between trust in AI and trustworthy machine learning technologies. In: Proceedings of the 2020 Conference on Fairness, Accountability, and Transparency, pp. 272–283 (2020)
22. Doshi-Velez, F., Kim, B.: Towards a rigorous science of interpretable machine learning. arXiv Prepr. arXiv:1702.08608 (2017)
23. Swartout, W.R., Moore, J.D.: Explanation in second generation expert systems. In: David, J.M., Krivine, J.P., Simmons, R. (eds.) Second Generation Expert Systems, pp. 543–585. Springer, Heidelberg (1993). https://doi.org/10.1007/978-3-642-77927-5_24
24. Wick, M.R., Thompson, W.B.: Reconstructive expert system explanation. Artif. Intell. **54**, 33–70 (1992)
25. Gunning, D., Aha, D.W.: DARPA's explainable artificial intelligence program. AI Mag. **40**, 44–58 (2019)
26. Guidotti, R., Monreale, A., Ruggieri, S., Turini, F., Pedreschi, D., Giannotti, F.: A survey of methods for explaining black box models. ACM Comput. Surv. **51**(5), 1–42 (2018)
27. Miller, T.: Explanation in artificial intelligence: insights from the social sciences. Artif. Intell. **267**, 1–38 (2019)
28. Tjoa, E., Guan, C.: A survey on explainable artificial intelligence (XAI): towards medical XAI. arXiv Prepr. arXiv:1907.07374 (2019)
29. Arrieta, A.B., et al.: Explainable Artificial Intelligence (XAI): concepts, taxonomies, opportunities and challenges toward responsible AI. Inf. Fusion **58**, 82–115 (2020)

30. Rehse, J.-R., Mehdiyev, N., Fettke, P.: Towards explainable process predictions for Industry 4.0 in the DFKI-smart-lego-factory. KI Künstliche Intelligenz **33**(2), 181–187 (2019). https://doi.org/10.1007/s13218-019-00586-1
31. Buck, R., Klopfer, M.: Betriebsprüfung. Springer, Wiesbaden (2011)
32. Waschbusch, G., Zieger, G.L.: Die steuerliche Betriebsprüfung als wichtigste Form der Außenprüfung - Grundlagen und Ablauf einer Betriebsprüfung (Teil I). Der Steuerberater, pp. 329–225 (2016)
33. Mösbauer, H.: Steuerliche Außenprüfung: (Betriebsprüfung) - Steuerfahndung - Steueraufsicht. Oldenbourg Verlag, München (2005)
34. Bundesfinanzministerium: Ergebnisse der steuerlichen Betriebsprüfung 2018. Monatsbericht des BMF (2019)
35. Shmueli, G., Koppius, O.R.: Predictive analytics in information systems. MIS Q. **35**, 553–572 (2011)
36. Chapman, P., et al.: CRISP-DM 1.0: Step-by-step data mining guide. SPSS Inc. **9**, 13 (2000)
37. Mehdiyev, N., Fettke, P.: Prescriptive process analytics with deep learning and explainable artificial intelligence. In: European Conference on Information Systems (ECIS) (2020)
38. Gregor, S., Benbasat, I.: Explanations from intelligent systems: theoretical foundations and implications for practice. MIS Q. **23**, 497–530 (1999)
39. Ji-Ye Mao, I.B.: The use of explanations in knowledge-based systems: cognitive perspectives and a process-tracing analysis. J. Manag. Inf. Syst. **17**, 153–179 (2000)
40. Adadi, A., Berrada, M.: Peeking inside the black-box: a survey on Explainable Artificial Intelligence (XAI). IEEE Access **6**, 52138–52160 (2018)
41. Freitas, A.A.: Comprehensible classification models. ACM SIGKDD Explor. Newsl. **15**(1), 1–10 (2014)
42. Zhao, Q., Hastie, T.: Causal interpretations of black-box models. J. Bus. Econ. Stat., 1–19 (2019)
43. Cath, C., Wachter, S., Mittelstadt, B., Taddeo, M., Floridi, L.: Artificial intelligence and the 'good society': the US, EU, and UK approach. Sci. Eng. Ethics. **24**(2), 505–528 (2018)
44. Crawford, K.: Can an algorithm be agonistic? Ten scenes from life in calculated publics. Sci. Technol. Hum. Values. **41**(1), 77–92 (2016)
45. Desouza, K.C., Dawson, G.S., Chenok, D.: Designing, developing, and deploying artificial intelligence systems: lessons from and for the public sector. Bus. Horiz. **63**(2), 205–213 (2020)
46. Nunes, I., Jannach, D.: A systematic review and taxonomy of explanations in decision support and recommender systems. User Model. User-Adap. Inter. **27**(3–5), 393–444 (2017). https://doi.org/10.1007/s11257-017-9195-0

General Track - Innovative, Emerging and Interdisciplinary Topics

Introduction to the WI2021 Track: General Track – Innovative, Emerging and Interdisciplinary Topics

Sara Hofmann[1], Maximilian Röglinger[2], and Jan vom Brocke[2]

[1] University of Agder, Department of Information Systems, Kristiansand, Norway
sara.hofmann@uia.no
[2] University of Bayreuth, FIM Research Center Finance and Information Management, Bayreuth, Germany
maximilian.roeglinger@uni-bayreuth.de
[3] University of Liechtenstein, Institute of Information Systems, Vaduz, Liechtenstein
jan.vom.brocke@uni.li

1 Track Description

The WI2021 General Track bundles innovative and interdisciplinary contributions that go beyond the regular track structure. We have welcomed a variety of topics related to the conference theme: "Innovation through information systems – WI as a trend-setting science" as well as a wide range of research methods. We have particularly encouraged contributions that leave well-trodden paths and stimulate discussion through emerging topics, technologies and theories as well as unconventional research designs. The General Track therefore has offered an additional degree of freedom and broadens the spectrum of the conference in terms of topics and methods.

Articles in this track investigate phenomena of the design, use and impact of information technology. They shed light on socio-technical aspects and in particular take the dynamic interplay between task, technology and people into account. In doing so, they contribute to the advancement of Information Systems as a discipline and to developing solutions for problems relevant to practice and society.

2 Research Articles

The general track comprises five full research as well as two short papers. The full research papers cover the topics of developing a comprehensive taxonomy for data strategy tools and methodologies, analyzing the role of 3D models in the product development process for both physical and virtual consumer goods, developing design principles for an adaptive empathy learning tool that helps students to develop their ability to react to other people's experiences, unpacking critical success factors for designing initiatives to disseminate a realistic and attractive image of BI among upper secondary school students for study programs in BI, as well as exploring what influence organizational culture exerts on the implementation of idea platforms.

The two short papers are research-in-progress. While one is concerned with developing a decision support tool that provides the designers of plastic products with important information and supports design decisions based on ecological, but also economical and functional criteria, the other one proposes a research methodology for building a tool that acts as middleware between sensors and systems, translating standards while maintaining their respective advantages.

Many Hands Make Light Work: The Influence of Organizational Culture on Idea Platform Implementation

Timo Koppe(✉) and Peter Buxmann

Technical University of Darmstadt, Software and Digital Business, Darmstadt, Germany
{koppe,buxmann}@is.tu-darmstadt.de

Abstract. Recent years have seen an increasing emphasis on IT-enabled crowdsourcing for innovation in organizations. However, information systems literature has so far paid little attention to the role of information systems in idea crowdsourcing, including its relation to organizational culture. To address this research gap, we conducted a quantitative study with IT and innovation managers from various organizations (N = 81) to explore whether culture influences the implementation of idea platforms. Our key findings show that idea platform implementation is facilitated by a culture that emphasizes policies, procedures, as well as information management (hierarchical culture). Although a culture of creativity should be stimulated in the front-end of innovation, the results indicate that idea platforms are predominantly used in conjunction with a strong internal focus and set of values.

Keywords: Crowdsourcing · Organizational culture · Idea platform · Innovation · Quantitative study

1 Introduction

The emergence and diffusion of digital technologies confront organizations with significant pressure to innovate and renew themselves. For this purpose, organizations are exploring new ways to identify promising opportunities and examine how their organizational knowledge can lead to the introduction of innovation [1, 2], especially since innovation processes are becoming more distributed and open [3]. In this regard, organizations can leverage a multitude of methods and measures of innovation management that have been established in recent years. They use open innovation, co-creation, and crowdsourcing to break out of their traditional innovation process [4].

Especially crowdsourcing has increased popularity as a method for gathering ideas and innovation [5, 6]. Simultaneously, the rapid development of social information technologies and platforms provide new ways to enable crowdsourcing. These technologies facilitate cooperation and collaboration between users, exchange of insights and experiences, build social networks [7], connect intelligence, and thus access to the "wisdom of the crowds" [8]. In this paper, we refer to idea platforms as specific crowdsourcing IT

F. Ahlemann et al. (Eds.): WI 2021, LNISO 46, pp. 433–447, 2021.
https://doi.org/10.1007/978-3-030-86790-4_29

tools for collecting, discussing, enhancing, and evaluating ideas [5]. Thereby, information systems (IS) play a huge role in enabling and shaping crowdsourcing for innovation and will become more relevant in the future since, e.g., ideas are valuable data [6]. However, IS literature has so far paid little attention to the role of IS in idea crowdsourcing [5, 9]. Instead, prior management research has largely dealt with the optimal design of idea competitions, i.e., the motivation of employees [10, 11], characteristics of idea authors [12, 13], and the role of community functions [14, 15]. Still, many IT-based idea competitions fail to achieve active participation [16]. Simula and Vuori [6] state that organizational culture (OC) can be seen as an issue when motivating participants to submit their ideas to IT platforms. At the same time, internal idea crowdsourcing can also support OC [6]. Prior research indicates that IT tools, i.e., idea platforms, must be in line with complementary non-IT resources, like culture, to leverage value for the business [17]. For example, idea competitions need to emphasize a climate of cooperation and competition at the same time [18]. Against this background, we examine the influence of OC on the current status of idea platform implementation. For this purpose, we use the competing values framework (CVF) to measure OC, which is common and frequently used in this context [19–22]. Our research question is: *How do the organizational culture dimensions influence idea platform implementation?* To answer the research question, we conducted a quantitative study with IT and innovation managers from various organizations (N = 81). In this context, we also examined the planned versus the actual implementation of idea platforms in an additional part to inspire theory building [23]. Our research goal is to indicate further criteria that influence the value contribution of idea platforms in organizations.

The remainder of this paper is structured as follows. After describing on the theoretical background and research design, we analyze the relationship between organizational culture and idea platform as well as differences in the planning and actual implementation of idea platforms. Finally, we discuss theoretical and practical implications as well as limitations and further research based on the findings of the empirical analysis.

2 Theoretical Background

2.1 IT-Enabled Crowdsourcing for Innovation

The first phase of an organization's innovation process comprises the activities of generating and selecting ideas. This phase is referred to as the *front-end of innovation* or as the "fuzzy" front-end. It is described as informal, knowledge-intensive, and irregular [24]. These characteristics make it particularly difficult to manage this phase. This is also due to the fact that innovation management faces the challenge of creating a balance between a context of supporting and stimulating as well as orientation and focus [25]. Support and stimulation refer to creating a culture of creativity that enables employees and external users to increase the number and novelty of ideas. Simultaneously, the number of ideas is supposed to be reduced through orientation and focus to enhance quality and strategic direction [24]. Relevant ideas do not only emerge within the organization but can also be developed with the concept *open innovation.* This approach enables knowledge across organization boundaries and identifies and captures external knowledge to support the internal innovation process [26]. The inclusion of external sources of innovation has several advantages, e.g., it gives organizations access to distant knowledge that is far from an organization's current knowledge base [27]. A popular mechanism of gaining access to little explored and a richly heterogeneous pool of knowledge through online infrastructure is called *crowdsourcing* [28]. Crowdsourcing refers to the outsourcing of a variety of tasks [29]. In crowdsourcing, an open call is used to address a "crowd" and, thus, a group of individuals. Afuah and Tucci [27] distinguish two forms of crowdsourcing. First, in the competition-based approach, each individual chooses to work on their own solution to the problem. The best solution is selected as the winning solution. Second, in the collaboration-based approach, members of the crowd decide whether they want to collaborate on solving the problem. The result is a common solution of the crowd.

Idea crowdsourcing can be implemented in different formats and is often named differently: Idea competitions, challenges, contests, and tournaments. Members of the crowd can be, e.g., customers, partners, or employees [30]. Beyond that a distinction is made between design dimensions, such as task/topic specificity, target group, contest period, reward/motivation, or evaluation [31]. In this context, the task of an IT-enabled idea platform is to support the various formats and processes through its functionalities. Due to the diversity and the different naming conventions, we broadly refer to idea platforms as an online IT tool for collecting, discussing, enhancing, and evaluating ideas.

2.2 Organizational Culture

According to Hofstede and Hofstede [32], *organizational culture* is "the collective programming of the mind which distinguishes the members of one group or category of people from another." OC affects all areas of a company and has far-reaching consequences [33]. In particular, it influences the attitude of employees, e.g., job satisfaction [34], the operational performance of organizations, e.g., innovative strength [35], and the financial performance of organizations, e.g., profitability [36]. At the same time, the OC has an integration function for the employees of a company by conveying cohesion and a common identity. Recognized behavior patterns influence the behavior of employees and, thus, also their innovative behavior [37].

Although the OC is difficult to influence, management can still actively influence it and create the conditions for an innovation-friendly culture. By consistently participating in innovation projects and supporting employees, organizations can ensure that all employees have a positive experience with innovation. According to the basic assumptions of the OC, these experiences are condensed into a common, fundamental innovation image among the employees [37]. To achieve the goal of an innovation-conscious company, Hauschildt et al. [37] recommends to break down bureaucracy and to use innovation-promoting elements. This includes, among other things, promoting cooperation between different business functions and, in some cases, different business units [38].

An understanding of OC is also essential for IS research, as it can influence the successful implementation and use of IS. For example, culture plays a role in management processes that directly or indirectly impacts information technology [39]. Furthermore, introducing IT often encounters cultural resistance [40]. For these reasons, extensive literature on the relationship between IT and culture was produced, which Leidner and Kayworth [39] examined and synthesized. They identified two relevant topics in IT cultural research:

1. Culture and IS Development - The core of this topic is how culture influences the design of IS. It has been shown that in a culture where uncertainty is avoided, project risks are perceived differently and are more likely to be abandoned. It is also advantageous if the values of the OC match the values of the information system to be developed.
2. Culture, IT Adoption, and Diffusion - The core of this topic is whether culture influences the adoption and diffusion of IT. The dominant idea is that uncertainty avoidance plays a significant role in deciding how groups adopt and disseminate information and communication technologies. Most studies conclude that those who avoid uncertainty tend to adapt more slowly to new information technologies.

3 Research Model

To investigate the cultural factors affecting the implementation of an IT-enabled idea platform, we have oriented to the procedure of Ruppel and Harrington [41], which contributes to the topic 'Culture, IT Adoption, and Diffusion'. In their study, they examined the relationship between OC and intranet implementation in organizations. As a result, the acceptance of intranets is much more likely if there is a development culture. Ruppel and Harrington's study is based on the Competing Values Framework (CVF) [20] and was extended by them to include the ethical dimension. In research, the CVF is widely used to conceptualize OC [19, 20] and to investigate the relationships and effects of OC [21, 22]. The CVF distinguishes four types of OC based on two dimensions. The first dimension represents the degree to which the company's focus is internal or external. The internal focus emphasizes the integration and maintenance of the socio-technical system, while the external focus is on competition and interaction with the organizational environment. The second dimension refers to the differences between change and stability, with change focused on flexibility and spontaneity, while stability focuses on control, continuity and, order [20]. The resulting four types of OC are called group, development, rational, and hierarchical culture [19].

3.1 Hypothesis Development

Organizations with a developmental culture value flexibility and have an external focus. They are therefore not oriented towards their own company, but towards the market and the company's environment. The core of the development culture refers to growth, creativity, and continuous adaptation to external requirements, which are strongly market- and environment-related. Management believes in survival and growth through innovation [42, 43]. Hence, it can be assumed that organizations with this culture know the advantages of idea platforms and are prepared to use them for themselves to remain competitive: *H1 - There is a positive correlation between development culture and the implementation of idea platforms.*

A company with a rational culture has a strong external focus and a focus on control. The main management activities are focused on maximizing profit through planning, control, and goal setting. By emphasizing order and stability, control structures with varying degrees of formalization and centralization are created to deal with contextual factors such as company size and environmental uncertainty [41]. Organizations with this culture focus primarily on competition and the optimization of their operations. We can assume that organizations with a rational culture will quickly become aware of the introduction of idea platforms through their external focus, but that the desire for order can stifle innovation. Since these effects are likely to balance each other out, we do not expect any significant influence of rational culture on the implementation of idea platforms: *H2 - There is no correlation between rational culture and the implementation of idea platforms.*

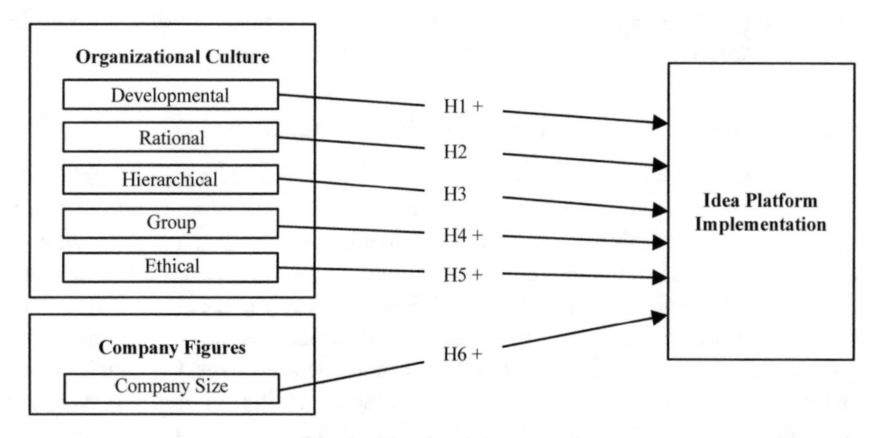

Fig. 1. The theoretical model

In a hierarchical culture, the corporate environment is not seen as an essential factor. Management's interest focuses on measurement, documentation, and information management. The focus of these organizations is on control. Idea platforms can support an internal use in defined user groups as well as the implementation of clear processes for the idea process [44]. Idea platforms can also support the collection of ideas for continuous improvements and suggestions. However, the success of an idea platform in the innovation Front-end is supported by a creative and encouraging culture [18, 37]. In contrast, a hierarchical culture focuses on internal orientation and order. Therefore, we assume that the effects are likely to balance each other out: *H3 - There is no correlation between hierarchical culture and the implementation of idea platforms.*

In a group culture, maintaining the company and its human resources is critical, with a focus on cohesive relationships, individual engagement and participation. While this culture is internally focused, it also values flexibility. Managers encourage dialogue, participation, and training of employees to achieve this goal. As they value employee participation, we believe idea platforms are an appropriate tool for organizations with a strong group culture. Idea platforms collect ideas by single employees as well as by groups, respectively [45]. Besides, idea platforms can support various social and community functions, which make idea competitions even more successful [14, 46, 47]. *H4 - There is a positive correlation between group culture and the implementation of idea platforms.*

Ethical culture reflects trust and an ethical working environment. Ruppel and Harrington expend the Competing Values Framework by this dimension since the CVF does not include specific measures for trust and an ethical work environment. Following them, there is no exchange of knowledge without a climate of trust [48, 49]. Therefore, our assumption is *H5 - There is a positive correlation between ethical culture and the implementation of idea platforms.*

Finally, we believe that idea platforms are used independently of corporate industries because, the overall pressure to innovate in the economy has increased. However, we also believe the challenge to manage ideation initiatives increases with the company size. This would confirm other studies that report that web-based ideation systems are used especially within large organizations [15, 44, 50]. *H6 - There is a positive correlation between company size and the implementation of idea platforms.*

3.2 Data Collection, Research Design and Measurements

We chose an online survey as the instrument for collecting the data for our study. Prior studies on organizational culture indicate that questionnaires are a reliable and well-established method for this kind of study [41]. In addition, the degree of anonymity in online questionnaires is perceived as very high, which tends to lead to greater openness and less often to social desirability bias [51]. When selecting participants for the study via social business networks, we considered three criteria. First of all, we address participants from various organizations in different industries and sizes. Our ambition is to reach a broad cross-section of organizations to compare the impact of different cultural types on the implementation of idea platforms between these organizations. Secondly, we restricted the job profiles during our search for participants. Following Ruppel and Harrington [41], IT managers are argued to be an appropriate source of evaluation of the overall culture and the extent of IT implementation. Since our focus is on the implementation of idea platforms, we filtered for IT managers as well as managers working in the area of innovation. We believe they are best placed to assess the company's innovation process and tools because they shape it or are at least directly involved in it. Before we sent the survey by e-mail, we tested the survey in a pre-test with five other researchers as well as two external managers in the field of innovation management. After our test and revision, we sent e-mails to our recipient list, introducing the project. The participants were informed which profile they should bring along so that they fit as a participant. We distributed the online survey to participants during August and November 2019. Our participant profiles in Table 1 shows that our participant selection was successful and matches our participant profile.

At the very beginning of the online survey, we informed the participants on the welcome page that there are no wrong answers, that they should answer honestly, and we ensured that all answers are processed anonymously. In addition, we have included information on processing time, target group specifications, and the topic without mentioning the term idea platforms. This was done to avoid the participants to be subject of a common method bias as well as a social desirability bias [52, 53].

Table 1. Profiles of responding organizations and individuals (N = 81)

Organization profiles				Individual profiles			
Business area *(multiple selection possible)*	%	Organization size *(in persons)*	%	Professional field of activity	%	Management responsibility	%
Chemistry/Pharma	24,7	Less than 10	2,5	Communication	1,2	Management level (no staff responsibility)	19,8
Communication	3,7	10 to 49	6,2	Finance & Controlling	1,2		
Consumer goods (e.g., food)	4,9	50 to 249	8,6	Human resources	1,2		
Electrics/Electronics	9,9	250 to 499	25,9	IT	43,2	Lower management level (e.g., team leader, group leader)	14,8
Finance/Insurance	13,6	500 to 999	34,6	Manufacturing & Production	0		
Human health	11,1	1,000 to 4,999	8,6	Marketing	3,7		
IT	19,8	5,000 to 19,999	7,4	Purchase & Sales	1,2	Middle management (e.g., department-, division heads)	42,0
Mechanical engineering	8,6	20,000 to 99,999	1,2	Research & Development	25,9		
Service	7,4	100,000 or more	4,9	Other activity	22,2		
Transport	1,2					Upper management level (e.g., executive board)	23,5
Vehicle construction	2,5						
Others	25,9						

We adapted the items (including reverse items) and overall questionnaire structure from Ruppel and Harrington [41] to measure the OC. The construct name/culture type was not mentioned to avoid influencing the respondents. Since the questions have already proven to be reliable, we did not expect a ceiling or floor effect for the items. We furthermore included an attention check [54]. All OC items were measured using a five-point Likert scale. After the questionnaire part on OC, we provided our definition of idea platforms to create a common understanding of the following questions. When asked about the progress of the introduction of an idea platform, the participant could select between the following options: "An idea platform: (a) has not yet been relevant and is, therefore, not in use (b) was evaluated, but we consciously decided against a deployment at this point (c) is being planned and evaluated (d) is currently being introduced (e) is in use (f) was used and abolished again".

Later, we grouped the options a), b) & f) as (1) "no use", options c) & d) as (2) "planning" and option e) as (3) "in use". This categorical measure is preferable to a dichotomous use/non-use variable. It allows the variables to be analyzed in terms of the progress of the idea platform implementation [41].

Since there are not many comparable studies on the implementation of idea platforms focusing on the software component, we surveyed additional variables on the actual or planned design of idea platforms. For group (1) "no use", we asked for reasons for the decision against the implementation of an idea platform as an open question, as well as whether the participant was involved in the decision. For group (2) "planning" and (3) "in use", we surveyed the type of use, the associated objectives, and the frequency of use. The questions of group (3) correspond in content to the questions of group (2) and differ only in the tense of the question. These additional measurement instruments were developed by us for this study. We validated these questions with two experts in the field of consulting and software solutions for idea and innovation management solutions.

3.3 Data Analysis

We used SmartPLS software (v.3.2.8) for structural equation modeling and analysis of the organizational culture constructs as well as idea platform implementation. This software was also used together with the bootstrap resampling method to determine the significance of the paths within the structural model. This method is especially appropriate to handle small sample sizes [55].

Table 2. Cronbach's α, composite reliability, AVE, HTMT (*single item constructs)

Construct	Reliability and validity			Heterotrait-Monotrait ratio (HTMT) of correlations					
	Cr. α	CR	AVE	DC	EC	GC	HC	IIP	RC
Develop. Culture (DC)	0.810	0.884	0.795						
Ethical Culture (EC)	0.701	0.818	0.603	0.446					
Group Culture (GC)	0.660	0.823	0.705	0.662	0.651				
Hierarch Culture (HC)	0.731	0.875	0.779	0.191	0.212	0.249			
Implementation (IIP)*	1.00*	1.00*	1.000	0.124	0.135	0.214	0.320		
Rational Culture (RC)	0.667	0.821	0.607	0.362	0.480	0.537	0.136	0.062	
Company Size (CS)*	1.00*	1.00*	1.000	0.018	0.082	0.113	0.168	0.267	0.089

Before running the analysis in SmartPLS, we inverted the reversed items and removed 7 participants who did not pass our attention check. Furthermore, we searched for straight-liner and racer in our data, which did not appear. The remaining sample size was 81. Then, we performed a Partial Least Squares Regression (PLS Regression). Factor analysis following the procedure of Hair Jr et al. (2016) led to the removal of two items: one from rational culture and one from ethical culture. Afterward, we successfully checked the loading of each item on the respective construct, which needs to be greater than the cross-loadings to all other constructs [56], which could be confirmed. The reliabilities of measures were tested using Cronbach's α, Composite Reliability (CR), AVE and, HTMT, as shown in Table 2. All Cr. α values are above 0.6 as a threshold for internal consistency reliability. Furthermore, AVE values are above 0.5 and CR values above 0,8 [55]. Since the Fornell-Larcker criterion is considered less reliable for discriminant validity in variance-based structural equation models [57], such as the present one, the HTMT was used and showed good results with all values below the more conservative threshold of 0.85. Therefore, we can assume that the resulting measures had good internal reliability and validity. Lastly, we tested for multicollinearity between the constructs by calculating the related variance inflation factors (VIF). With a maximum VIF of 1.754, all values are well below the cutoff criterion of 5 [55].

Next, we analyzed our additional variables for the actual or planned design of idea platforms. Thereby, we mainly carried out group comparisons between the two groups (2) "planning" and (3) "in use". First, we isolated the data of the two groups from the first group. When capturing the type of implementation and objectives of the platform through our items, we allowed clicking the option "I can't judge". The removal of incomplete data records brought us to a sample size of 45 for our group comparison. This was to ensure that only participants who were able to assess the design criteria of the idea platform were evaluated.

To test if the proportions in group 2 and group 3 are not equal (H_0: $P_1 = P_2$), we used the chi-square test of homogeneity [58]. Therefore, we reviewed four assumptions that are necessary to perform this test. First, our independent variable group was measured at the dichotomous level. All other dependent variables, which were tested individually, were also dichotomous variables. Second, by having different participants in each group, we could confirm that our observations have independence, which means there is no relationship between the observations in each group or between the groups themselves. Third, in our study design, we did purposive sampling through the characteristic of implementation of an idea platform. Lastly, our minimum sample size was greater than five for each expected frequency [59]. We were able to confirm all the requirements for this test.

4 Results

Our analysis was performed by a bootstrapping algorithm with 5,000 subsamples within SmartPLS software. In total, 21,3% of the variance in idea platform implementation is explained by the organizational culture and company size ($R^2 = 0.213$).

Only hypothesis H2 of the OC dimensions was supported since there is no significant relationship between a rational culture and idea platform implementation. Surprisingly, we found a positive correlation between the hierarchical culture orientation and idea platform implementation: the more hierarchical a culture is perceived, the more likely an idea platform is implemented ($p = 0.004$, $f^2 = 0{,}107$). The f^2 effect size can be interpreted as a small to medium effect size [55].

The group culture ($p = 0.089$, $f^2 = 0.055$) had a weak f^2 effect size and was not significant at a significance level of 5%. It was, however, marginally significant ($p < 0.1$), which is worth mentioning due to an explorative character of the study, where a significant level of 10% is often assumed in research [55]. The other cultures did not exhibit any significant association with idea platform.

Lastly, H6 could be confirmed ($p = 0.013$, $f^2 = 0{,}069$), having a weak f^2 effect size. Thereby, it could be confirmed that the company size has a significant positive influence on the introduction of an idea platform.

In the second part of the study, we analyzed whether the two groups (2) 'in planning' and (3) 'in use' pursue different objectives when implementing idea platforms. For this purpose, we defined seven objectives in advance, referred to as O1–O7, which are described in this section, along with their results. The difference between the two implementation groups was not statistically significant ($p > .05$) for the following objectives: 'Finding ideas for new innovations in the core business (**O2**)', 'Finding ideas for new innovations in new business areas (**O3**)', 'Creating knowledge exchange, communication and awareness for strategic topics (**O4**)' and 'Building an innovation culture (**O7**)'. Therefore, we fail to reject the null hypothesis (H_0: $P_1 = P_2$) and can assume that there are non-statistically significant differences in proportions.

The two goals 'Continuous improvement of business processes (**O1**)' and 'Search for solutions to known and concrete problems (problem-oriented) (**O6**)' were statistically significantly different ($p < .05$). Fourteen participants (73,7%) plan to implement problem-oriented initiatives on the idea platform compared to 10 participants (38,5%) who actually implement problem-oriented initiatives, a statistically significant difference in proportions of .352, $p = .019$. Even greater is the difference with 'Continuous improvement of business processes'. Here, 7 participants (36,8%) plan to implement idea platforms for continuous improvement compared to 21 participants (80,8%), a statistically significant difference in proportions of .44, $p = .003$.

Less strong is the difference with 'Breaking down silos and bringing together employees from different expertise and functions (**O5**)'. Here, 12 participants (63,2%) planned to explicitly pursue this goal with the implementation of the idea platform compared to 9 participants (34,6%) who actually pursue this goal with the deployment, a difference in proportions of .286, $p = .058$.

Furthermore, we also used the test of two proportions to analyze the differences between three different usage types: 'submit ideas on any topic at any time', 'participate in targeted and time-limited campaigns of a specific user group', and 'take part in company-wide idea challenges'. None of the differences were significant. Besides, none of the other control variables were significant.

5 Discussion

Commencing with the theoretical implications, the results of our study confirm that the OC as a whole influence the current status of idea platform implementation. Our analysis shows that 15.9% of the implementation status can be attributed to the organizational culture (21.3%, including company size). Hence we can conclude that idea platforms are not only used to transform OC [30] but that a corresponding OC makes the implementation of idea platforms more likely. Thereby, we contribute to the research stream 'Culture, IT Adoption, and Diffusion' [39]. Against our assumption, we show that idea platform implementation is facilitated by a hierarchical culture that emphasizes policies, procedures, and information management. A possible explanation for this could be that internal idea competitions harmonize better with the internal focus of the hierarchical culture than, e.g., an open innovation platform would have done. Idea platforms, as software tools, can support to structure their ideation process [44] and, thus, the management in its efforts for internal order. This effect is reinforced by the fact that a large proportion of idea platforms are used to collect continuous improvements in operational improvement, which is characterized by a very formal and regulated process. The results also show that a stronger group culture has a (marginally significant) positive effect on the level of idea platform implementation, as hypothesized. Organizations fostering a group culture emphasize employee involvement, which may be realized through idea platforms [45]. Alongside employee participation the group culture also embraces personal dialogue [41]. When managers promote ideation techniques through dialogue, this may weaken the additional benefit from idea competitions for them and, thus, limiting the significant influence in our model. Next, as hypothesized, a stronger rational culture was not related to idea platform implementation. Organizations with a rational culture may be familiar with idea platforms and their potential for open innovation through their external focus but have no preference for or against their use. The benefit of using idea platforms is not only derived from the ideas themselves. Other advantages can arise, such as the identification of key individuals, which is also interesting from the point of view of the promoter theory in innovation management [60]. However, these kinds of advantages are usually difficult to measure, which is not in line with a strong rational culture since it values objective-based measures. If crowdsourced and open innovation can provide more objective measures in the future, we imagine that a rational culture will have a positive impact on the implementation of idea platforms. Then, there was no positive correlation between development culture and the implementation of an idea platform. Organizations with a development culture are focused on growth and innovation. However, it does not appear that idea platforms are currently used in practice to promote innovation nor open innovation. Lastly, our hypothesis about a positive correlation between ethical culture and the implementation of idea platforms could not be confirmed either. Our survey measures on objectives indicate that using an idea platform to facilitate knowledge exchange is the least pursued objective between our participants. Against this background, ethical culture may have less influence on the design of the platform in terms of knowledge exchange.

Overall, we believe that the significant relationship between organizations with a strong group and hierarchical cultures and idea platforms can be explained by the way the idea platform is designed. In the past, idea platforms were initially intended for internal use. This internal focus was also shaped by the culture in which idea platforms were used since both significant cultures share this orientation in the CVF. In recent years, organizations have begun to open up their innovation processes and diffuse them more widely [4]. However, especially in B2B [6], idea platforms that open up to involve larger crowds may not encounter a culture that promotes innovation and creativity and therefore may not achieve active participation or expected results [16]. This fact reinforces the current discussion about the uncertain overall value of crowdsourced ideation initiatives [31].

Moving beyond theoretical implications, our study also has practical implications for idea platform provider, innovation managers, and organizations implementing idea platforms. Our study highlights the importance of taking OC into account when introducing a new technology or process that may be incompatible with the existing culture. Our analysis of planned versus the actual implementation objectives further indicates that idea platform usage will shift towards crowdsourced idea generation with a higher degree of innovation (e.g., less continuous improvement and more problem-oriented usage). Furthermore, culture also influences the design of idea platforms as well as the adoption and influence of IT Tools [39], as with idea platforms. As a result, organizations must be aware of their existing organizational culture when implementing and designing idea platforms to meet their expectations. Adoption is more likely when the values of a group match the values of information technology [39] as well as the design of idea platform needs to be in line with complementary factors of strategy and structure [17].

6 Limitations and Future Research

Certainly, this study also has its limitations. First, we only used a 5-step Likert scale in order not to overwhelm the respondents. In combination with the low number of items per construct, the lower gradation leads to a worse differentiation of persons, organizations, and cultures. The significance of the results is, therefore, weakened. Furthermore, we sent the survey to unknown contacts and busy managers. This resulted in a low response rate (around 8%). Because of this, the generalizability of these findings is somewhat in question. Since we defined idea platforms very broadly in our study, we have not been able to measure the impact of culture on specific deployment forms. However, this was not intended and opens up the field for further research.

Further research could focus on specific applications of idea platforms as open innovation, specific idea competition formats, or similar. It is particularly interesting to see whether an OC that promotes the implementation of idea platforms also increases their chances of success and user satisfaction. Moreover, it would be particularly relevant in practice to know whether OC can also provide negative effects. This would enable organizations to decide more quickly whether i.e. idea competitions are a suitable method for them.

Further research is necessary to see the influence of the idea platform on the culture. In particular, we could imagine that certain designs of idea platforms could even reinforce some cultures. Next, further research is needed to identify the advantages and role of an idea platform as a digital platform. The influence of the properties of digital goods, in particular network effects, on idea platforms can be investigated. Finally, more research is required to explore the advantages of idea platforms, taking into account the promoter theory, in connection with areas of social network analysis, the identification of key persons for the success of idea platforms, and innovation in general.

References

1. Kohli, R., Melville, N.P.: Digital innovation: a review and synthesis. Inf. Syst. J. **29**, 200–223 (2019)
2. Gregory, R., Wagner, H.-T., Tumbas, S., Drechsler, K.: At the crossroads between digital innovation and digital transformation. In: ICIS 2019 Proceedings (2019)

3. Bogers, M., West, J.: Managing distributed innovation: strategic utilization of open and user innovation. Creat. Innovat. Manag. **21**, 61–75 (2012)
4. Ili, S., Albers, A., Miller, S.: Open innovation in the automotive industry. R&D Manag. **40**, 246–255 (2010)
5. Zuchowski, O., Posegga, O., Schlagwein, D., Fischbach, K.: Internal crowdsourcing: conceptual framework, structured review, and research agenda. J. Inf. Technol. **31**, 166–184 (2016)
6. Simula, H., Vuori, M.: Benefits and barriers of crowdsourcing in B2B firms: generating ideas with internal and external crowds. Int. J. Innov. Manag. **16**, 1240011 (2012)
7. Yoo, Y., Boland, R.J., Lyytinen, K., Majchrzak, A.: Organizing for innovation in the digitized world. Organ. Sci. **23**, 1398–1408 (2012)
8. Surowiecki, J.: The Wisdom of Crowds: Why the Many Are Smarter Than the Few and How Collective Wisdom Shapes Business, Economies, Societies, and Nations. Doubleday, New York (2004)
9. Majchrzak, A., Malhotra, A.: Towards an information systems perspective and research agenda on crowdsourcing for innovation. J. Strateg. Inf. Syst. **22**, 257–268 (2013)
10. Nov, O.: What motivates Wikipedians? Commun. ACM **50**, 60–64 (2007)
11. Wasko, M.M., Faraj, S.: Why should I share?: Examining social capital and knowledge contribution in electronic networks of practice. MIS Q. **29**, 35–57 (2005)
12. Poetz, M.K., Schreier, M.: The value of crowdsourcing: can users really compete with professionals in generating new product ideas? J. Prod. Innovat. Manag. **29**, 245–256 (2012)
13. Schemmann, B., Herrmann, A.M., Chappin, M.M.H., Heimeriks, G.J.: Crowdsourcing ideas: involving ordinary users in the ideation phase of new product development. Res. Policy **45**, 1145–1154 (2016)
14. Bullinger, A.C., Möslein, K.M.: Innovation contests-where are we? In: AMCIS, pp. 28–35 (2010)
15. Zhu, H., Kock, A., Wentker, M., Leker, J.: How does online interaction affect idea quality?: The effect of feedback in firm-internal idea competitions. J. Prod. Innovat. Manag. **36**, 24–40 (2019)
16. Leimeister, J.M., Huber, M., Bretschneider, U., Krcmar, H.: Leveraging crowdsourcing: activation-supporting components for it-based ideas competition. J. Manag. Inf. Syst. **26**, 197–224 (2014)
17. Kohli, R., Grover, V.: Business value of IT: an essay on expanding research directions to keep up with the times. J. Assoc. Inf. Syst. **9**, 23–39 (2008)
18. Hutter, K., Hautz, J., Füller, J., Mueller, J., Matzler, K.: Communitition: the tension between competition and collaboration in community-based design contests. Creat. Innovat. Manag. **20**, 3–21 (2011)
19. Denison, D.R., Spreitzer, G.M.: Others: organizational culture and organizational development: a competing values approach. Res. Organ. Chang. Dev. **5**, 1–21 (1991)
20. Quinn, R.E., Rohrbaugh, J.: A spatial model of effectiveness criteria: towards a competing values approach to organizational analysis. Manage. Sci. **29**, 363–377 (1983)
21. Iivari, J., Huisman, M.: The relationship between organizational culture and the deployment of systems development methodologies. MIS Q. **31**, 35–58 (2007)
22. McDermott, C.M., Stock, G.N.: Organizational culture and advanced manufacturing technology implementation. J. Oper. Manag. **17**, 521–533 (1999)
23. Malhotra, M.K., Grover, V.: An assessment of survey research in POM: from constructs to theory. J. Oper. Manag. **16**, 407–425 (1998)
24. van den Ende, J., Frederiksen, L., Prencipe, A.: The front end of innovation: organizing search for Ideas. J. Prod. Innovat. Manag. **32**, 482–487 (2015)
25. Birkinshaw, J., Gibson, C.B.: Building Ambidexterity into an Organization. MIT Sloan Manag. Rev. 47–55 (2004)

26. Chesbrough, H.W.: Open Innovation: The New Imperative for Creating and Profiting from Technology. Harvard Business Press, Boston (2003)
27. Afuah, A., Tucci, C.L.: Crowdsourcing as a solution to distant search. Acad. Manag. Rev. **37**, 355–375 (2012)
28. Allen, B.J., Chandrasekaran, D., Basuroy, S.: Design crowdsourcing: the impact on new product performance of sourcing design solutions from the "Crowd." J. Market. **82**, 106–123 (2018)
29. West, J., Bogers, M.: Leveraging external sources of innovation: a review of research on open innovation. J. Prod. Innovat. Manag. **31**, 814–831 (2014)
30. Ebner, W., Leimeister, J.M., Krcmar, H.: Community engineering for innovations: the ideas competition as a method to nurture a virtual community for innovations. R&D Manag. **39**, 342–356 (2009)
31. Mortara, L., Ford, S.J., Jaeger, M.: Idea Competitions under scrutiny: acquisition, intelligence or public relations mechanism? Technol. Forecast. Soc. Chang. **80**, 1563–1578 (2013)
32. Hofstede, G., Hofstede, G.J.: Cultures and Organizations: Software of the Mind: Intercultural Cooperation and Its Importance for Survival. McGraw-Hill, New York (2005)
33. Schein, E.H.: Organizational Culture, vol. 45, pp. 109–119. American Psychological Association (1990)
34. Kirkman, B.L., Shapiro, D.L.: The impact of cultural values on job satisfaction and organizational commitment in self-managing work teams: the mediating role of employee resistance. Acad. Manag. J. **44**, 557–569 (2001)
35. Naranjo-Valencia, J.C., Jiménez-Jiménez, D., Sanz-Valle, R.: Innovation or imitation?: The role of organizational culture. Manag. Decis. **49**, 55–72 (2011)
36. Narver, J.C., Slater, S.F.: The effect of a market orientation on business profitability. J Market. **54**, 20–35 (1990)
37. Hauschildt, J., Kock, A., Salomo, S., Schultz, C.: Innovationsmanagement. Verlag Franz Vahlen, München (2016)
38. Grote, M., Herstatt, C., Gemünden, H.G.: Cross-divisional innovation in the large corporation: thoughts and evidence on its value and the role of the early stages of innovation. Creat. Innovat. Manag. **21**, 361–375 (2012)
39. Leidner, D.E., Kayworth, T.: Review: a review of culture in information systems research: toward a theory of information technology culture conflict. MIS Q. **30**, 357–399 (2006)
40. Coombs, R., Knights, D., Willmott, H.C.: Culture, control and competition; towards a conceptual framework for the study of information technology in organizations. Organ. Stud. **13**, 051–072 (2016)
41. Ruppel, C.P., Harrington, S.J.: Sharing knowledge through intranets: a study of organizational culture and intranet implementation. IEEE Trans. Prof. Commun. **44**, 37–52 (2001)
42. Cooper, R.B.: The inertial impact of culture on IT implementation. Inf. Manag. **27**, 17–31 (1994)
43. Cooper, R.B., Quinn, R.E.: Implications of the competing values framework for management information systems. Hum. Resour. Manage. **32**, 175–201 (1993)
44. Elerud-Tryde, A., Hooge, S.: Beyond the generation of ideas: virtual idea campaigns to spur creativity and innovation. Creat. Innovat. Manag. **23**, 290–302 (2014)
45. Björk, J., Magnusson, M.: Where do good innovation ideas come from?: Exploring the influence of network connectivity on innovation idea quality. J. Prod. Innovat. Manag. **26**, 662–670 (2009)
46. Blohm, I., Bretschneider, U., Leimeister, J.M., Krcmar, H.: Does collaboration among participants lead to better ideas in IT-based idea competitions?: An empirical investigation. Int. J. Netw. Virtual Organ. **9**, 106–122 (2011)
47. Björk, J., Di Vincenzo, F., Magnusson, M., Mascia, D.: The impact of social capital on ideation. Ind. Innov. **18**, 631–647 (2011)

48. Brown, R.B., Woodland, M.J.: Managing knowledge wisely: a case study in organisational behaviour. J. Appl. Manag. Stud. **8**, 175–198 (1999)
49. Curry, A., Stancich, L.: The intranet — an intrinsic component of strategic information management? Int. J. Inf. Manage. **20**, 249–268 (2000)
50. Beretta, M., Björk, J., Magnusson, M.: Moderating ideation in web-enabled ideation systems. J. Prod. Innovat. Manag. **35**, 389–409 (2018)
51. Scholl, A.: Die Befragung. UVK Verlagsgesellschaft mbH UVK/Lucius, Konstanz; München (2018)
52. Podsakoff, P.M., MacKenzie, S.B., Lee, J.-Y., Podsakoff, N.P.: Common method biases in behavioral research: a critical review of the literature and recommended remedies. J. Appl. Psychol. **88**, 879–903 (2003)
53. Mummendey, H.D., Grau, I.: Die Fragebogen-Methode: Grundlagen und Anwendung in Persönlichkeits-. Einstellungs-und Selbstkonzeptforschung. Hogrefe Verlag, Göttingen (2008)
54. Meade, A.W., Craig, S.B.: Identifying careless responses in survey data. Psychol. Methods **17**, 437 (2012)
55. Hair Jr., J.F., Hult, G.T.M., Ringle, C., Sarstedt, M.: A Primer on Partial Least Squares Structural Equation Modeling (PLS-SEM). Sage Publications, Thousand Oaks (2016)
56. Bagozzi, R.P., Yi, Y.: Specification, evaluation, and interpretation of structural equation models. J. Acad. Market Sci. **40**, 8–34 (2012)
57. Henseler, J., Ringle, C.M., Sarstedt, M.: A new criterion for assessing discriminant validity in variance-based structural equation modeling. J. Acad. Mark. Sci. **43**(1), 115–135 (2014). https://doi.org/10.1007/s11747-014-0403-8
58. Marascuilo, L.A., MacSweeney, M.: Nonparametric and distribution-free methods for the social sciences. Brooks/Cole, Monterey, Calif. (1977)
59. Hollander, M., Wolfe, D.A., Chicken, E.: Nonparametric Statistical Methods. John Wiley & Sons, Hoboken (2013)
60. Witte, E.: Power and innovation: a two-center theory. Int. Stud. Manag. Organ. **7**, 47–70 (1977)

Data Strategy Development: A Taxonomy for Data Strategy Tools and Methodologies in the Economy

Inan Gür[1(✉)], Markus Spiekermann[1], Michael Arbter[1], and Boris Otto[1,2]

[1] Fraunhofer Institute for Software and Systems Engineering, Dortmund, Germany
{Inan.Guer,Markus.Spiekermann,Michael.Arbter, Boris.Otto}@isst.fraunhofer.de, Boris.Otto@tu-dortmund.de
[2] Chair for Industrial Information Management, TU Dortmund, Dortmund, Germany

Abstract. Data are a key driver of the digital era. They shift the strategic landscape of organizations and change how companies approach their business. Nevertheless, existing approaches on data strategies vary vastly and little common ground is visible. Therefore, we develop a comprehensive taxonomy for data strategy tools and methodologies in order to identify characteristics and relevant properties of data strategy. We derived the taxonomy inductively by analyzing existing data strategy tools and methodologies offered in the current economy and deductively by conducting a structured literature review on the existing body of knowledge in the scientific literature. It serves as a scientific instrument to profoundly assess and create data strategies and work towards a consensus in the respective research field.

Keywords: Data strategy · Digital strategy · IT-strategy · Taxonomy

1 Introduction

In the digital era, in which organizations need to improve their response to ever changing and faster markets [1], companies need a strategy to react to the forces and influences of the surrounding environment. To respond to internal and external dynamics as well as to reduce uncertainty, companies form strategies and create a shared understanding of goals within the entire organization [2, 3] claimed that the field of strategic management needed more than one definition for the concept of strategy, since the term is being used in various ways. In that regard, he gave five definitions: strategy as plan – a consciously intended course of action and guideline to deal with a situation -, strategy as ploy – a specific maneuver intended to outwit an opponent or competitor -, strategy as a pattern – a stream of actions -, strategy as position – means of locating an organization in an environment – and strategy as perspective – an ingrained way of perceiving the world by the pursuer [3]. In any manner, strategy, while being complex, has to provide guidance [4] on how to achieve competitive advantage [5]. It is the essence of what a business does different or better than competitors in order to gain sustainable advantage and achieve its declared objectives [6].

F. Ahlemann et al. (Eds.): WI 2021, LNISO 46, pp. 448–461, 2021.
https://doi.org/10.1007/978-3-030-86790-4_30

For crucial competitive innovations and advantages, nowadays data lay the foundation and are the driver of the digital economy [7]. With the advances of data generation and collection technologies, vast amounts of data are available and accessible [8, 9]. Data enable organizations to make rational and resourceful use of information and therefore empower them to better decision-making processes and better realization of their strategic objectives [10]. Hence, using data strategically and creating a unique organization-wide data strategy is indispensable. Nevertheless, surveys e.g. the on from [11], which was conducted within 189 companies and published in the Harvard Business Review in 2018, indicate, that still today many companies struggle in proper implementation and execution of profound and well-defined data strategies, even though data itself or the amount of data sources do not pose a problem [12]. The benefits of strategic data usage are widely known [13].

In that regard, more and more organizations publish their own understanding of data strategy and offer data strategy methodologies or tools e.g. [14–16]. These methodologies and tools serve as an endeavor to define a data strategy approach and develop a distinctive data strategy perspective. Similar methodologies on data strategy can be found in academic literature as elaborated by [17]. Nevertheless, to the best of our knowledge, there is little scientific work towards a consensus for data strategy in the current economy. Practitioners would benefit from better elaboration, since they would profit from a comprehensively acknowledged understanding of data strategy and its properties to develop an appropriate data strategy on their own. Researchers would benefit from a structured analysis of data strategies both in the economy and in academic environments. The goal of this study is to create a unifying perception on data strategy by consolidating scientific and economic knowledge on data strategy. Therefore, our research question reads as follows:

Research Question: What are the characteristics and relevant properties of data strategy tools and methodologies offered in the current economy and academic literature?

To answer this research question, we follow the approach for taxonomy development by Nickerson [18]. We chose the artifact of a taxonomy, since taxonomies reveal valuable insights and analyze, structure and conceptualize complex entities [19]. We decided on this development procedure, since Nickerson's approach allows a deductive iteration on relevant objects from the targeted area as well as an inductive iteration on the existing body of knowledge in academic literature for data strategy.

On that regard, our work is structured as follows: After the introduction we set the theoretical foundation by defining data strategy research in the field of Information Systems (IS) and circumventing the concepts from other terms. In the following, we elaborate the given research design by outlining, presenting and discussing our course of action and procedural method concerning the taxonomy process and structured literature review. In chapter four we present our final taxonomy and elaborate the results. Finally, in the last sections we discuss our implications, limitations of the research and future research.

2 Theoretical Foundation

Derived from business strategy there are variations, which differ in the level of abstraction while addressing strategical considerations in specific business areas or organizational functions.

In order to comply with scientific rigor it is important to get an overview of the strategical perspective that is related to the data strategy, which we discuss in the paper. During our Structured Literature Review (SLR), which is described in the following section, we identified digital strategy as well as IT-strategy as related derivations. By comparing the three, one can better understand the addressed dimensions they have in common and the ones that characterize the specific approaches.

2.1 Data Strategy

Data are creating a new generation of decision support data management [20] and disruptively changes the way business can be strategically approached [21]. That applies not only on a functional level but also on a corporate level to a point that it shifts the strategic landscape and how companies approach and evaluate their business models [9]. Generating value from data has reached a broad notion, that a well-organized data management can only be achieved with a coherent strategy for organizing, governing, analyzing and deploying the organization's data assets [22]. In that regard, developing a data strategy on how to extract value from data is crucial for today's organizations [12]. A data strategy can be defined as a "blueprint that requires the establishment of goals, identification of data sources and the use of analysis" [23] in order to "find the right questions […] from strategic thinking in collaboration with technological savviness" [24] to create "additional value for internal and external stakeholders" [2]. The data strategy sets a clear direction for data value generation, ensures that all stakeholders work towards the same objective and is linked to the business unit level strategy on a functional level [2]. Several authors pick up on Davenports conception of data strategy as the most important step of data initiatives [25] as it describes the objectives, scope and advantages on a fundamental basis for data value generation [6 p.3].

2.2 Digital Strategy

Digital Strategy can be seen as the most extensive focus, since it represents the first level of the fusion of IT and business strategy by tactfully incorporating digital technologies in the business strategy [21, 26]. The definition of digital business strategy is given as an "…organizational strategy formulated and executed by leveraging digital resources to create differential value" [27] and assesses the changes of how business is conducted due to digital technologies [28, 29]. Out of new capabilities enabled by these technologies, companies can create new value propositions by combining them with already existing capabilities. This encompass strategic, technological, human capital, and organizational culture considerations within the company and defining a strategy for its digital transformation [30]. This does not necessarily replace any former strategies, but most likely will need to be aligned with them [26]. This could be either done by common targets in customer-centricity or based on companies' digitized solutions. While the first aims at higher engagement and building trust and creating loyalty, the second focuses on the transformation of the business model towards digitized products and value-added services to create recurring revenue [31, 32]. Both approaches have in common, that the most important aspect are the *business capabilities* enabled by these strategies to build efficiency and technical reliability, agility and innovation [29]. A digital strategy is inherently multi-functional [27]. Alignment requires the simultaneous development and reinvention of business resources, especially IT and data resources, across multiple organization processes [33].

2.3 IT-Strategy

The crucial roles of IT and IT strategy are to support and enable the business [27, 34, 35]. An IT strategy is described as the "…planning and transformation of strategic IT goals into IT governance structures, IT processes, applications and infrastructure by adjusting them to the business" [35]. The implementation leads to improved control of investments, deployments and usage of IT, which leads to higher efficiency, productivity and revenues in the business [36, 37]. Due to the importance of IT for the business, alignment of IT and business is an essential component of IT strategies. Consequently, the boundaries between the IT strategy as a functional strategy and the business strategy are becoming increasingly fuzzy, resulting in new strategy development streams (digital business strategy). Therefore, the development of the IT strategy can be an integrated part of the digital business strategy or can be derived from the business strategy [27, 35, 38]. Considering IT as a functional strategy, three sub-strategies are relevant in addition to the IT mission and vision: Information Systems (IS-Strategy), Information Management (IM-Strategy) and the Information and Communication Technology (ICT-Strategy). All three sub-strategies are related and influence each other. They define which requirements are mandatory (IS-Strategy), how the IT organization is aligned (IM-Strategy) and which infrastructure complies with the requirements (ICT-Strategy) [39, 40]. However, often times the successful instantiation of an IT strategy lacks detailed concepts for implementation and continuous alignment [35, 41].

3 Research Design

3.1 Methodology by Nickerson

For this research, we decided to follow the taxonomy development method by Nickerson et al. [18] as it is a frequently used method in IS research publications e.g. [42–45]. This method is consistent with the design science research guidelines of Hevner et al. [46] and consists of seven steps (see Fig. 1). The first step is the identification of the meta-characteristic which derives from the purpose of the taxonomy and its expected use. Since this method is an iterative process, the second step is to define ending conditions which "determine when to terminate" [18]. This research follows the eight objective and five subjective ending conditions given out by Nickerson et al. [18]. The next step requires the selection of one of two approaches to identify the characteristics and dimensions of the taxonomy. The user of the method can either chose a conceptual-to-empirical approach, which follows a deductive procedure to derive characteristics and dimensions from the theory, or an empirical-to-conceptual approach can be chosen, in which results are derived inductively from a particular set of objects. The method is executed for as long as ending conditions are not met, which would terminate the iterative design process.

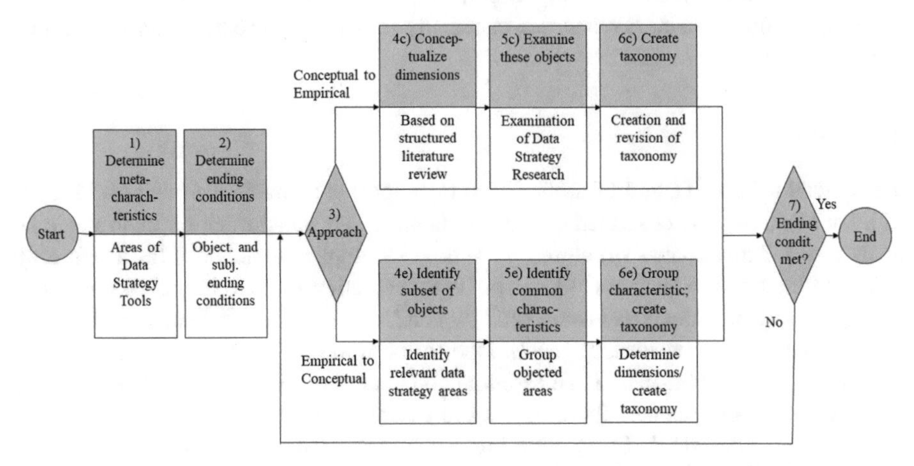

Fig. 1. Taxonomy development method according to Nickerson et al. [18]

3.2 Taxonomy Development Process

Meta-characteristics: The meta-characteristic is "based on the purpose of the taxonomy" [18]. The purpose of the taxonomy is defined by the target group and intended future use. In regard to this, we set the meta-characteristic following the research question as "characteristics and areas of data strategy tools".

1st Iteration (Empirical-to-Conceptual): For the first iteration we chose an empirical-to-conceptual inductive approach. In this context, we conducted an analysis of data strategy tools and methodologies in the economy following the descriptive review process in IS research elaborated by King [47] and Pare [48]. The descriptive review intents to reveal the body of empirical studies in a specific research area and therefore involves a systematic search of as many relevant objects in the investigated area as possible, while collecting, coding and analyzing the results concerning a certain interest from each study [47, 48]. To ensure the rigor in the conducted systematic search, we followed the guidelines for literature reviews proposed by vom Brocke et al. [49].

The first step of the procedure was the search process involving the keywords, database, backward and forward search and the evaluation of sources [49]. To systematically identify relevant objects, we used the Google search engine to secure a heuristic search without domain or industry boundaries. We set the keywords to ("Data Strategy" AND (Tool OR Framework)) and stretched the search up to first 150 results. We scanned for data strategy methodologies published by organizations through whitepapers, insights and reports, because these publications offer further information and application indications on the respective tools. We only included publicly available results, which provided thorough information and were written in English. We conducted a backward and forward search to see if the organizations offered more recent objects or referred to other data strategy methodologies. Our search yielded 16 objects, from which 10 met the criteria. They cover a variety of different domains and are extracted from organizations ranging from 11 employees up to +10000, including start-ups and established companies.

The next step of this iteration was the analysis of the research objects. We decided to conduct the investigation by three researchers individually and independently to prevent bias. The three researchers analyzed the methodologies and tools concerning relevant characteristics, targeted areas and functions. The results were discussed in a one day workshop, including the fourth researcher as a "devil's advocate" to ensure critical distance and a broad discussion to identify relevant dimensions and characteristics for the taxonomy.

2nd Iteration (Conceptual-to-Empirical): In order to meet the proposed ending conditions, we additionally performed a conceptual-to-empirical deductive iteration. Therefore, we conducted a SLR as a "systematic, explicit and reproducible method for identifying, evaluating and synthesizing the body of completed and recorded work by researchers, scientists and practitioners" [50]. In order to meet the quality requirements of appropriate research breadth, rigor, consistency, clarity and brevity [51], we followed the approach of Webster and Watson [52] and vom Brocke et al. [49, 53].

The scope of this research can be allocated in the scientific domain of Information Systems (IS). We selected the four literature databases, "Scopus", "Emerald Insight", "Aisel" and "IEEE Xplore", since these databases include relevant IS research journals and scientific conferences. We determined three search terms, namely "Data Strategy", "Digital Strategy" and "IT Strategy" to cover the research field and ensure the traceability, repeatability and transparency of the search. The search yielded 3613 results in total. After the first filter process, based on the title, 103 publications remained. A second filter process based on the abstract and content reduced the findings to 49. Thereafter, duplicates have been filtered and a forward and backward search has been conducted, after which the literature basis for the analysis resulted in 48 scientific publications (see Table 1). These 48 publications were analyzed concerning key characteristics and crucial elements of data strategy development in organizations.

Table 1. Structured literature review results

	Scopus	Emeral	Aisel	IEEE	Relevant
"Data Strategy"	483	175	25	51	16
"Digital Strategy"	481	394	64	37	9
"IT Strategy"	789	387	571	156	24
				Duplicates filtered	−5
				F. and B. Search	4
				Literature Basis	48

Ending Conditions: We used the eight objective and five subjective ending conditions elaborated by Nickerson to determine the ending of the iteration process. After the first iteration, seven of the 13 ending conditions were met. Since the results from the first iteration were not sufficient to fulfill every ending condition acceptably, we conducted the second conceptual-to-empirical approach in the form of a structured literature review. After the elaborated meeting to discuss the results, the identified dimensions and characteristics for the taxonomy indeed met the required conditions. These results and the final taxonomy will be presented and discussed in the next section.

4 Results

4.1 Dimensions and Characteristics

The resulting taxonomy consists of 9 dimensions (D_x) with 30 corresponding characteristics (c_{xy}). To showcase the application of the taxonomy, we implemented the 10 objects that formed the basis for the empirical-to-conceptual iteration (see Table 2). In the following, we explain our findings along the dimensions and characterizations.

The first two dimensions were derived by Etsiwah and Hilbig [17]. The dimension **Purpose (D_1)** "describes the objective of a data strategy within an organization" [17]. This dimension consists of three corresponding characteristics. The characteristic *Product Development* (c_{11}) is on hand when the data strategy is designed to create new products or innovate existing products. In this case the data strategy helps to identify use cases for data analytics and plans the implementation in product development [2]. Such a data strategy is especially crucial for the development and improvement of connected, digital or smart products [12]. The characteristic *Business Dev.* (c_{12}) describes the cases in which the data strategy generates changes on a business model level. Data enables disruptive innovations that change the way a business can be approached and business decisions can be made more strategically [21]. A data strategy shifts the strategic landscape and further promotes the evolution of existing business models [9]. The characteristic *Strategy Development* (c_{13}) is on hand when the strategy is set to design a strategy based and solemnly on data [17] separated from other business functions.

The second dimension **Level (D_2)** "provides a link to traditional classifications of strategy in strategic management literature as it describes the scope of a given data strategy" [17 p.5]. It provides a co-evolutionary strategy alignment with other strategies within an organization [54]. The data strategy can be on a *functional* (c_{21}) level, aligned with e.g. product development or marketing. Furthermore, the data strategy can be on a *business* (c_{22}) level, linked to business units and deciding which on markets the business competes or the data strategy can be on a *corporate* (c_{23}) level, setting the objectives and direction of a company [2].

The third dimension **Practice** (D_3) describes in which form the organizations offer their data strategy tool or methodologies. The analysis of the different objects showed, that the data strategy tools are generally set out as a *method* (c_{31}), defining certain steps to derive a data strategy, or as a *model* (c_{32}), giving logical and objective representations of empirical objects. Objects that could not be assigned to one of the two characteristics fall under the third characteristic *general framework* (c_{33}).

The fourth dimension **Data Asset** (D_4) describes on what data the data strategy methodology focusses. The iterative analysis yielded four predominant data types. The characteristic *master data* (c_{41}) is on hand when the data strategy focusses on the core data entities of an enterprise [55]. *Customer data* (c_{42}) involves data from and around stakeholders on a customer level, including retailers and end customers [56] and transactional data from business documents [57]. *Process Data* (c_{43}) describes all data from the value generation process like the operation of machines or processing units that provide valuable information about value generation processes [19]. *Big data* (c_{44}) is characterized by the key attributes of great variety, high velocity and high volume [10] measuring tens of terabytes demanding big data analytic methods [58].

The fifth dimension is **Data Source** (D_5). It describes where the focused data of the data strategy originates and is acquired. This dimension can be divided into *internal* (c_{51}) data sources and the combination of *internal and external* (c_{52}) data sources [45]. Internal data sources can be self-generated data from the organization's assets like machine sensor data [43]. External data can be obtained from outside the organization in various ways e.g. like free data or acquired data from providers like data marketplaces [44].

The sixth dimension shows to what extend the data strategy requires a **Strategic Statement** (D_6). Strategy, thoroughly discussed in literature and commonly used in business, generally defines the purpose and objectives of an organization to reduce uncertainty provide direction for decisions [2]. This dimension is divided into the three characteristics, namely *vision* (c_{61}), *mission* (c_{62}) and objectives (c_{63}). The vision is the definition of the "end-state towards which the organization strives" [56], whereas the mission defines the primary activities to reach the vision [56]. Fundamental for strategy development is a clear set of objectives [6, 59].

The seventh dimension describes the **Business IT Alignment** (D_7). This dimension defines the continuous fit between IT applications and infrastructure on one hand and business strategy and processes on the other [33, 39]. The alignment is a key process to maintain business value as it models business and IT together in a common organizational framework to define the future state [56]. It is a dynamic and continuous process that adjusts and synchronizes business and IT [40] and enables data initiatives [33]. The analysis yielded four characterizations that are most relevant within a data strategy initiative, namely the alignment of *objectives* (c_{71}), *architecture* (c_{72}), *people* (c_{73}) and *communication* (c_{74}) in terms of canals and processes.

Strategy Implementation (D_8) is the eighth dimension as it is a primary success factor in strategy development [60], offering clear benefits when conducted successfully [24]. It is defined by three dominant characteristics, namely *road map* (c_{81}), *roles* (c_{82}) and *resource allocation* (c_{83}). The creation of a road map is a crucial task in the implementation of data strategy, as it describes the timeline for the implementation process including different use cases and required tasks of the involved stakeholders [2]. Furthermore, the implementation sets out specific roles like chief data officers or data-management functions [22] to effectively execute the data strategy. The resource allocation defines the resources required to implement and achieve the data strategy and considers whether the resources are allocated internally or externally [61].

The ninth dimension concretizes the **Service and Support** (D_9) the applicant of the data strategy tool receives. As stated in the beginning of this paper, there are several sustainable advantages of conducting a data strategy [10]. The analyzed objects focus on four specific benefits and offer service and support in that regard: *use case derivation* (c_{91}), *data management optimization* (c_{92}), *analytics improvement* (c_{93}) and *strategic management improvement* (c_{94}). The first characterization focusses on data strategy development, which supports the identification of use cases for e.g. data analytics or data strategy implementation [2]. The second characterization is on hand, when the respective data strategy tool aims to develop a data strategy primary to enable superior data management capabilities [22]. The third characterization focusses on obstacles and barriers in organization [13], which constrain the data analytics capabilities, since these challenges are often of organizational and strategic nature [60]. The fourth characterization is on hand for data strategy tools focusing on improving the general strategic management of the organization by implementing a data strategy to e.g. timing of and general decision-making [21].

4.2 Application of the Data Strategy Tool Taxonomy

Table 2 shows the final taxonomy including the application on the ten data strategy tools and methodologies yielded from the first iteration. The classification of empirical objects verifies the usefulness of our taxonomy using the ten examples [18]. As explained in our empirical-to-conceptional iteration, the tools originate from organizations out of a variety of different branches, industries and sizes, showcasing the generality and applicability of our taxonomy.

Table 2. Taxonomy of data strategy tools and methodologies

Dimensions	Characteristics	Data strategy tools and methodologies									
		Booz Allen H. [62]	CDQ [63]	Measurelab [64]	BCG [65]	Keller [66]	Global data strat. [67]	IBM [68]	Breakthrough [69]	Equifax [70]	Big Data Framework [71]
Purpose	Strategy dev				•		•		•		
	Business dev	•	•	•		•		•			•
	Product dev									•	
Level	Functional	•		•						•	
	Business		•			•	•	•	•		•
	Corporate				•						
Practice	Method	•				•					•
	Model				•			•			
	General framework		•	•			•		•	•	

(continued)

Table 2. (*continued*)

Dimensions	Characteristics	Data strategy tools and methodologies									
		Booz Allen H. [62]	CDQ [63]	Measurelab [64]	BCG [65]	Keller [66]	Global data strat. [67]	IBM [68]	Breakthrough [69]	Equifax [70]	Big Data Framework [71]
Data assets	Master data				•		•				
	Customer data			•					•	•	
	Process data	•				•	•	•	•		
	Big data		•	•	•	•	•	•			•
Data source	Internal		•		•	•		•			•
	Internal and external	•		•			•		•	•	
Strategic statement	Mission	•	•						•		
	Vision	•	•		•						
	Objectives	•	•		•	•	•	•	•	•	•
Business IT alignment	Objectives	•	•	•	•	•	•	•	•	•	•
	Architecture	•			•	•	•				•
	People		•	•				•			
	Communication	•	•	•							
Strategy implementation	Road map	•	•	•		•	•	•	•		•
	Roles		•		•		•	•			
	Resource allocation	•		•		•	•			•	•
Service and support	Use case derivation				•	•			•	•	
	Data management optimization	•	•		•	•	•	•	•		•
	Analytics improve	•		•	•	•	•	•			
	Strat. management improve	•		•		•	•	•	•	•	•

5 Discussion, Implications and Further Research

Our research created a taxonomy for data strategy tools and methodologies using a structured literature review and the method by [18]. The design and application of the taxonomy answers the main research question of this research paper.

From our research, we can deviate several managerial and scientific implications. In terms of **managerial implications**, this taxonomy serves as a tool for organizations to create new or assess existing data strategy tools and methodologies in order to draw conclusions for their individual data strategy approach and derivation. Our findings emphasize the holistic range of the strategic approach on data as a data strategy can impact an organization from a functional to a corporate level. In that regard, a comprehensive understanding of data strategy, its tools and methodologies is a prerequisite to draw implications for a unique, organization-wide data strategy and our taxonomy supports such a comprehensive understanding. The implementation or concretization of a data strategy requires significant insights in order to incorporate a sustainable organization-wide conception of data-driven value generation, which is supported by our taxonomy, as it systematically disaggregates data strategy interpretations.

As for the **scientific implications**, our research created a resolute and profound analysis of data strategy tools and methodologies. Our analysis had both a deductive as well as an inductive approach to derive our results theoretically and verify them empirically in order to generate a common understanding of data strategy. Our aim was to improve the body of knowledge on data strategy tools and methodologies and to support future researches by systematizing and classifying different data strategy comprehensions. Our taxonomy serves as a tool to profoundly describe and distinguish data strategy tools from one another to emphasize the differences and commonalities. We hope to diminish the gap between the scientific field and economics as well between different researchers.

Naturally, our research has **limitations**. Since the derivation of a data strategy involves a variety of stakeholders [2] and creates specific use cases [24], it is an ever-evolving and unique endeavor. Therefore, our taxonomy requires critical updating and questioning in the shadow of technological, economical and societal changes in order to stay relevant and up to date. Furthermore, limitations arise from subjectivity, as other researchers might value or derive other dimensions and characterizations differently. With our research method, we tried to secure objectivity and impede bias as much as possible. Lastly, limitations arise from the fact that the scientific field of data strategy and its respective tools are relatively new and therefore subject to change and updates.

Future research in this field could incorporate the derivation of archetypical patterns, as it is a common instance in IS taxonomy research [72]. Besides, further research could include a structural analysis for data strategy and its tools for a specific area and perform a scientific comparison to derive sectoral differences of data strategy.

References

1. Wong, T.Y.T., Peko, G., Sundaram, D., Piramuthu, S.: Mobile environments and innovation co-creation processes & ecosystems. Inf. Manag. **53**, 336–344 (2016)
2. Wilberg, J., Triep, I., Hollauer, C., Omer, M.: Big data in product development: need for a data strategy. In: Proceedings of PICMET 2017 (2017)
3. Mintzberg, H.: The strategy concept I: five PS for strategy. Calif. Manag. Rev. (1987)
4. Sull, D., Turconi, S., Sull, C., Yoder, J.: Turning strategy into results. MIT Sloan Manag. Rev. (2017)
5. Altamony, H., Alshurideh, M.T., Masa'deh, R., Obeidat, B.: Information systems for competitive advantage: implementation of an organisational strategic management process. In: Innovation and Sustainable Competitive Advantage: From Regional Development to World Economies (2012)
6. Collis, D.J., Rukstad, M.G.: Can you say what your strategy is? Harvard Bus. Rev. (2008)
7. Otto, B., Österle, H.: Corporate Data Quality, Springer, Berlin (2016). https://doi.org/10.1007/978-3-662-46806-7
8. Lim, C., Kim, K.-H., Kim, M.-J., Heo, J.-Y., Kim, K.-J., Maglio, P.P.: From data to value: a nine-factor framework for data-based value creation in information-intensive services. Int. J. Inf. Manage. **39**, 121–135 (2018)

9. Mazzei, M.J., Noble, D.: Big data dreams: a framework for corporate strategy. Bus. Horiz. **60**, 405–414 (2017)
10. Ebner, K., Buhnen, T., Urbach, N.: Think big with big data: identifying suitable big data strategies in corporate environments. In: 2014 47th Hawaii International Conference on System Sciences, pp. 3748–3757. IEEE (2014)
11. Hurley, J.: Why your data strategy is your B2B growth strategy. Harvard Bus. Rev. (2018)
12. Wilberg, J., Kalla, T., Fetscher, M., Rimböck, F., Hollauer, C., Omer, M.: Managing technological entrepreneurship: the engine for economic growth. In: Portland International Conference on Management of Engineering and Technology (PICMET '2018). (2018)
13. Posavec, A.B., Krajnovic, S.: Challenges in adopting big data strategies and plans in organizations. In: 2016 39th International Convention on Information and Communication Technology, Electronics and Microelectronics (MIPRO), pp. 1229–1234. IEEE (2016)
14. SAS: 5-essential-components-of-data-strategy- (2019)
15. Barton, D., Court, D.: Three Keys to Building a Data Driven Strategy. Mckinsey & Company Q. (2013)
16. Gurevich, A., Dey, S.: Defining a data strategy (2018)
17. Etsiwah, B., Hilbig, R.: What is data strategy? An analysis of an ambiguous concept. In: ISPIM Innovation Conference, Florence (2019)
18. Nickerson, R.C., Varshney, U., Muntermann, J.: A method for taxonomy development and its application in information systems. Eur. J. Inf. Syst. **22**, 336–359 (2013)
19. Azkan, C., Iggena, L., Gür, I., Möller, F., Otto, B.: A taxonomy for data driven services in manufacturing industries. In: Twenty-Fourth Pacific Asia Conference on Information Systems. Dubai (2020)
20. Valdez, A., et al.: Big data strategy. IJACSA 10 (2019)
21. Lakoju, M., Serrano, A.: Saving costs with a big data strategy framework. In: IEEE International Conference on Big Data (BIGDATA) (2017)
22. DalleMulle, L., Davenport, T.: What's your data strategy - DalleMule. Harvard Bus. Rev. (2017)
23. Hochhauser, R.: Data strategy: a critical component of marketing success. Handbook Bus. Strat. **5**, 227–232 (2004)
24. Lakoju, M., Serrano, A.: Framework for aligning big-data strategy with organizational goals. In: Twenty-third Americas Conference on Information Systems. Boston (2017)
25. Feinleib, D.: Big data at work. In: Big Data Bootcamp, pp. 49–62. Apress, Berkeley, CA (2014). https://doi.org/10.1007/978-1-4842-0040-7_4
26. Chanias, S., Myers, M.D., Hess, T.: Digital transformation strategy making in pre-digital organizations: the case of a financial services provider. J. Strateg. Inf. Syst. **28**, 17–33 (2019)
27. Bharadway, A., El Sawy, O.A., Pavlou, P.A., Venkatraman, N.: Digital business strategy: toward a next generation of insights. Mis Quart. (2013)
28. Ross, J.W., Beath, C., Moloney, K.G., Sebastian, I.M., Mocker, M., Fonstad, N.O.: Designing and executing digital strategies. In: ICIS, Dublin (2016)
29. Sebastian, I.M., Ross, J.W., Beath, C., Mocker, M., Moloney, K.G., Fonstad, N.O.: How big old companies navigate digital transformation. Mis. Quart. (2017)
30. Gurbaxani, V., Dunkle, D.: Gearing up for successful digital transformation. MISQE **18**, 209–220 (2019)
31. Porter, M.E., Heppelmann, J.E.: How smart, connected products are transforming competition. Harv. Bus. Rev. **92**, 64–88 (2014)
32. Porter, M., Heppelmann, J.: how smart, connected products are transforming companies. Harv. Bus. Rev. (2015)
33. Yeow, A., Soh, C., Hansen, R.: Aligning with new digital strategy: a dynamic capabilities approach. J. Strateg. Inf. Syst. **27**, 43–58 (2018)

34. Henderson, J.C., Venkatraman, N.: Strategic alignment: leveraging information technology for transforming organizations. IBM Syst. J. (1999)
35. Bartenschlager, J., Goeken, M.: Designing artifacts of IT strategy for achieving business/IT alignment. In: Americas Conference on Information Systems (2009)
36. Chen, D., Mocker, M., Preston, D., Teubner, A.: Information systems strategy: reconceptualization and implications. MISQ **2010**, 233–259 (2010)
37. Mithas, S., Rust, R.T.: How information technology strategy and investments influence firm performance- conjecture and empirical evidence. Mis Quart. (2016)
38. Holotiuk, F., Beimborn, D.: Critical success factors of digital business strategy. In: 13th International Conference on Wirtschaftsinformatik (2017)
39. Drechsler, A., Weißschädel, S.: An IT strategy development framework for small and medium enterprises. Inf. Syst. E-Bus. Manage. **16**(1), 93–124 (2017). https://doi.org/10.1007/s10257-017-0342-2
40. Cuenca, L., Boza, A., Ortiz, A., Trienekens, J.J.M.: Business-IT alignment and service oriented architecture - a proposal of a service-oriented strategic alignment model. In: Proceedings of the 16th International Conference on Enterprise Information Systems, pp. 490–495. SCITEPRESS - Science and Technology Publications (2014)
41. Ball, N., Adams, C., Xu, W.: Overcoming the elusive problem of IS/IT alignment: conceptual and methodological considerations. In: Americas Conference on Information Systems (2003)
42. Möller, F., Stachon, M., Hoffmann, C., Bauhaus, H., Otto, B.: Data-driven business models in logistics: a taxonomy of optimization and visibility services. In: Proceedings of the 53rd Hawaii International Conference on System Sciences, pp. 5379–5388 (2020)
43. Paukstadt, U., Strobel, G., Eicker, S.: understanding services in the era of the internet of things: a smart service taxonomy. In: ECIS 2019 (2019)
44. Hunke, F., Engel, C., Schüritz, R., Ebel, P.: Understanding the anatomy of analytics-based services - a taxonomy to conceptualize the use of data and analytics in services. In: ECIS 2019 (2019)
45. Hartmann, P.M., Zaki, M., Feldmann, N., Neely, A.: Capturing value from big data – a taxonomy of data-driven business models used by start-up firms. IJPEM **36**, 1382–1406 (2016)
46. Hevner, A.R., March, S.T., Park, J., Ram, S.: Design science in information systems research. Mis Quart. **28**, 75–105 (2004)
47. King, W.R., He, J.: Understanding the role and methods of meta-analysis in IS research. In: CAIS 16 (2005)
48. Paré, G., Trudel, M.-C., Jaana, M., Kitsiou, S.: Synthesizing information systems knowledge: a typology of literature reviews. Information & Management **52**, 183–199 (2015)
49. Vom Brocke, J., Simons, A., Niehaves, B., Reimer, K., Plattfaut, R., Cleven, A.: Reconstructing the giant: on the importance of rigour in documenting the literature search process. In: Proceedings of the 17th European Conference on Information Systems. AIS, Verona, Italy (2009)
50. Fink, A.: Conducting Research Literature Reviews. From the Internet to Paper. Sage, Los Angeles (2014)
51. Levy, Y., Ellis, T.J.: A systems approach to conduct an effective literature review in support of information systems research. Inf. Sci. Int. J. Emerg.Transdiscip. **9**, 181–212 (2006)
52. Webster, J., Watson, R.T.: Analyzing the past to prepare for the future: writing a literature review. Mis Quart. **26**, xiii–xxiii (2002)
53. Vom Brocke, J., Simons, A., Riemer, K., Niehaves, B., Plattfaut, R., Cleven, A.: Standing on the shoulders of giants: challenges and recommendations of literature search in information systems research. CAIS **37**, 205–224 (2015)

54. Lakoju, M., Serrano, A.: A strategic approach for visualizing the value of big data (SAVV-BIGD) framework. In: 2016 IEEE International Conference on Big Data (Big Data), pp. 1334–1339. IEEE (2016)
55. Vayghan, J., Garfinkle, S., Walenta, C., Healy, D., Valentin, Z.: The internal information transformation of IBM. IBM Syst. J. 669–683 (2007)
56. Cuenca, L., Boza, A., Ortiz, A.: An enterprise engineering approach for the alignment of business and information technology strategy. Int. J. Comput. Integr. Manuf. **24**, 974–992 (2011)
57. Otto, B.: Quality and value of the data resource in large enterprises. Inf. Syst. Manag. **32**, 234–251 (2015)
58. Bakhtiani, R., Gandhi, M., Churi, P., Gupta, P.: Big data strategies – a review and survey. In: 4th International Conference on Applied and Theoretical Computing and Communication Technology (iCATccT) (2018)
59. Falge, C.: Methode zur Strategieentwicklung für unternehmensweites Datenqualitätsmanagement in globalen Konzernen. St.Gallen (2015)
60. Wilberg, J., Fetscher, M., Rimböck, F., Hollauer, C., Omer, M.: Development of a use phase data strategy for connected products: a case study in industry. In: Proceedings of PICMET 2018 (2018)
61. Adner, R.: Match your innovation strategy to your innovation ecosystem. Harvard Bus. Rev. **84**, 98–107, 148 (2006)
62. Booz Allen Hamilton: Booz Allen Hamilton Data Strategy Framework. https://www.boozallen.com/s/insight/thought-leadership/a-framework-to-guide-your-data-strategy.html
63. CDQ: Data Strategy Canvas. https://www.cc-cdq.ch/request-publications#16
64. Measurelab: Measurelab Data Strategy Canvas. https://www.measurelab.co.uk/blog/what-is-a-data-strategy-and-do-i-need-one/
65. Boston Consulting Group: BCG Data Strategy Transformation Model. https://www.bcg.com/publications/2017/digital-transformation-transformation-data-driven-transformation
66. Keller Schroeder: Data Strategy Framework. https://www.kellerschroeder.com/data-strategy-framework/
67. Global Data Strategy: Data Strategy Framework. https://globaldatastrategy.com/our-services/data-strategy/
68. IBM: IBM Big Data Maturity Model. https://www.ibmbigdatahub.com/blog/big-data-analytics-maturity-model
69. Breakthrough Strategy: Breakthrough Data Strategy Canvas (2019)
70. Equifax: Data Strategy Framework. https://www.dataversity.net/developing-and-executing-a-global-data-strategy/
71. Big Data Framework: Big Data Strategy Framework. https://www.bigdataframework.org/formulating-a-big-data-strategy/
72. Glass, R.L., Vessey, I.: Contemporary application-domain taxonomies. IEEE Softw. **12**, 63–76 (1995)

Designing an Adaptive Empathy Learning Tool

Thiemo Wambsganss[1(✉)], Florian Weber[2], and Matthias Söllner[2]

[1] Institute of Information Management, University of St. Gallen (HSG), St.Gallen, Switzerland
thiemo.wambsganss@unisg.ch

[2] University of Kassel, Information Systems and Systems Engineering, Kassel, Germany
{weber,soellner}@uni-kassel.de

Abstract. Empathy is a fundamental competency for daily communication, interaction, and teamwork, and thus most relevant for future jobs. Nevertheless, educational organizations are limited in providing the necessary conditions for students to develop empathy skills, due to traditional large-scale and distance-learning scenarios. In this paper, we present insights on how to design an adaptive learning tool that helps students to develop their ability to react to other people's observed experiences through individual feedback independent of an instructor, time and location. Based on theoretical insights of 110 papers and 28 user interviews, we propose preliminary design principles for an adaptive empathy learning tool. Moreover, we evaluate the design principles as an instantiated prototype in a proof-of-concept evaluation with 25 students. The results indicate that an empathy learning tool based on the presented design knowledge seems to be a promising approach to help students to improve their empathy skills in different learning scenarios.

Keywords: Empathy learning · Adaptive skill learning · Cognitive dissonance theory · Design science research

1 Introduction

> *"The biggest deficit we have in our society, and in the world right now, is an empathy deficit. We are in great need of people being able to stand in somebody else 's shoes and see the world through their eyes"*
>
> *Barack Obama in 2009, talking to Students in Istanbul.*

As *Barack Obama, former president of the United States*, stated, empathy is not only an elementary skill for our society and daily interaction but also for professional communication as well as successful teamwork and thus elementary for educational curricula (i.e., *Learning Framework 2030* [1]. It is the "*ability to simply understand the other person's perspective […] and to react to the observed experiences of another" (Davis* [2], *p.1),* which is defined as *empathy*[1]. Empathy skills not only pave the foundation for successful interaction in digital companies, e.g., in agile work environments

[1] Being aware that empathy is a multidimensional construct, in this study we focus on *the emotional and cognitive empathy* [2, 25].

F. Ahlemann et al. (Eds.): WI 2021, LNISO 46, pp. 462–476, 2021.
https://doi.org/10.1007/978-3-030-86790-4_31

[3], but they are also one of the key abilities in the future that distinguish human work force and artificial intelligence agents [4]. However, besides the growing importance of empathy, research has shown that empathy skills of US college students have decreased from 1979 to 2009 by more than thirty percent and even more rapidly from 2000 to 2009 [5]. On these grounds, the *Organization for Economic Cooperation and Development* (OECD) claims that training empathy skills should receive a more prominent role in today's higher education [1]. To train empathy to students, educational institutions traditionally rely on experiential learning scenarios, such as shadowing, communication skills training or role-playing, e.g., in medical education [6]. Individual empathy training is therefore only available for a limited number of students, since individual tutoring through a student's learning journey is often hindered due to traditional large-scale lectures or the growing field of distance learning scenarios such as Massive Open Online Classes (MOOCs, [7]). However, to develop skills such as empathy, it is of great importance for the individual student to receive continuous feedback throughout their learning journey [8, 9]. In fact, educational institutions are limited in providing these individual learning conditions especially for empathy skill training.

A promising way to support students to train the ability to react to other people's observed experiences [2] and enable teachers to convey it to classes of large sizes and independent from location might be the usage of adaptive technology-based applications in a pedagogical scenario for a student's learning journey (e.g., as done for other metacognition skills [10, 11]). Researchers especially from the field of *Educational Technology* have designed pedagogical scenarios to train the empathy skills of students through *virtual reality role-playing* for social work education [12], *virtual agents* to simulate patient treatments for nurses (e.g., [6]) or adaptive *empathy text feedback* on computer-mediated communication platforms to foster empathy for company–client and employee–customer relationships [13].

However, novel technological-enhanced pedagogical scenarios based on recent advances of *Natural Language Processing* (NLP) or *Machine Learning* (ML) to design new forms of *human–computer interaction* for learners to train empathetic interaction through adaptive tutoring fall rather short in literature [14, 15]. A possibility to provide adaptive empathy feedback on natural language bears the field of empathy detection form *Computational Linguistics* [16]. Empathy detection has been a growing research approach to identify and model empathetic structures and phrases of a given text in real-time, which could be leveraged to provide students with individual feedback, e.g., on peer reviews on business models or team conversation logs [13, 16]. However, despite the vast amount of studies, current literature falls short of providing an approach with principles and proof on how to design an adaptive and intelligent learning tool to help students learn *how to react to other students' perspectives* with intelligent feedback on natural language. Thus, we aim to contribute to the field of technology-enhanced empathy learning by answering the following research question (**RQ**):

***RQ**: What are design principles for an adaptive learning tool that helps students to improve their empathy skill in large-scale or distance learning scenarios?*

To answer our research question, we follow the *design science research approach* (DSR) by Hevner [17]. As stated above, there is a lack of design knowledge for technology-enhanced tools to convey empathy skills. We intend to iteratively design and evaluate an IT learning artifact on the baseline of existing theory (*cognitive dissonance* based on Festinger [18]) informing the artifact design [19]. We believe *cognitive dissonance theory* could explain why formative text feedback on a student's empathy skills will motivate the student to be more aware and sensitive towards empathetic behavior. The theory has been widely applied in HCI and Information Systems (IS) research before, e.g., for adaptive argumentation skill learning (e.g., [11, 20]). To the best of our knowledge, there is no study that rigorously derives requirements from both scientific literature and potential users to develop an adaptive IT learning tool for helping IS students learn *how to react to other students' perspectives* based on this theory. With adaptive learning tool, we mean a tool which provides *individual and real-time feedback on the emotional and cognitive empathy level to students* on a given text, e.g., a chat conversation, and provides suggestions on how to write more empathetically, e.g., when writing peer reviews on business ideas. In this paper, we present our preliminary design principles we derive from literature and user interviews. Moreover, we provide a proof-of-concept evaluation of the instantiated design principles with 25 students. Our results indicate, that an adaptive empathy learning tool based on our design principles might be a promising approach to assist lecturer and educational organizations in helping students to receive empathy feedback on natural language input

In the following, we will first introduce the reader to the necessary theoretical background. Afterwards, we present our methodological approach for developing the artifact following the three cycle view of Hevner [17]. We present our preliminary results, followed by a proof-of-concept evaluation. Finally, we discuss the results and close with a conclusion.

2 Theoretical Background

2.1 Empathy Learning

The ability to perceive the feelings of another person and to react to their emotions in the right way requires empathy – the ability *"of one individual to react to the observed experiences of another"* (Davis [2], p.1). Empathy plays an essential role in daily life in many practical situations, such as client communication, leadership or agile teamwork. Therefore, especially business schools today are increasingly trying to focus on fostering empathy skills [21] to provide students with the right skill set to meet future job profiles [22]. The importance of empathy and other metacognition skills has been manifested by the *OECD*, which included them as a major element of their *Learning Framework 2030* [1]. Despite the interdisciplinary research interest, the term *empathy* is defined from multiple perspectives in terms of its dimensions or components [23].

Being aware that there are multiple perspectives on empathy, in this paper we focus on the *cognitive and emotional components* of empathy as defined by Davis (1983) and Spreng et al. [2, 24]. Therefore, we follow the *"Toronto Empathy Scale"* [25] as a synthesis of instruments for measuring and validating empathy. Empathy refers to the "*ability to simply understand the other person's perspective [...] and to react to the observed experiences of another" (Davis* [2], *p.1),* where empathy consists of both *emotional and cognitive components* [25]. While emotional empathy lets us perceive what other people feel, cognitive empathy is the human ability to recognize and understand other individuals [24].

Besides the importance of empathy in daily life, studies have shown that empathy skills of US college students have decreased from 1979 to 2009 by more than thirty percent and even more rapidly in the last period from 2000 to 2009 [5]. Possible explanations are given by the growing amount of digital communication in our society [5]. Scientists therefore urge that training empathy skills should receive a more prominent role in today's higher education (e.g., [1, 12]). In fact, individual support of empathy learning is missing in most learning scenarios. In some domains training programs are designed to increase empathy skills through role plays, films, literature or video games (e.g., [21]). Since social professions, in particular, are characterized by interactions, similar training programs that promote empathy or empathetic forms of expression have so far also been successfully implemented for social workers [27], doctors and nurses [28]. In business education, empathy is usually trained through communication scenarios, classroom exercises, role plays or experiential learning (e.g., [21]). In fact, empathy is often regarded as a subcomponent of social competence [29], corresponding support measures often take place in extensive programs to promote social development.

However, in order to train skills such as empathy, it is essential for the individual student to receive continuous feedback, also called formative feedback, throughout the learning process [8]. According to Sadler [30], the result of feedback is specific information about the learning task or process that fills a gap between what is understood and what should be understood. Even in areas where empathy is part of the curriculum, such as health or social work, the ability of a teacher to provide tutoring is naturally limited by time and availability constraints. Especially in more frequent large lectures and distance learning scenarios, the ability to individually support a student's empathy ability is hampered because it is becoming increasingly difficult for educators to provide continuous and individual feedback to a single student.

2.2 Technology-Based Learning Systems for Empathy Skills

Many researchers, especially from the fields of *Educational Technology*, have analyzed how technology-based systems in sociotechnical scenarios can address this gap and enhance students' learning of empathy. The application of information technology in education bears several advantages, such as consistency, scalability, perceived fairness, widespread use and better availability compared to human teachers, and thus technology-enhanced empathy learning systems can help to relieve some of the burden on teachers to convey empathy by supporting learners with adaptive empathy feedback.

Scientist have successfully embedded *computer-assisted instruction (CAI)* in the form of *virtual reality* (*VR*) learning tools in pedagogical scenarios to enable students to directly dive into the perspective of a peer, e.g., a client or patient (e.g., [28]). Moreover, *intelligent tutoring systems (ITS)* are used in the form of virtual agents built into online tools, e.g., to enable interaction with emotional avatars (e.g., [31]). Lastly, *computer-supported collaborative learning (CSCL)* tools are implemented to enhance empathy in the text communication of learners [13]. In their approach, Santos et al. [13] use a simple library of messengers based on neurolinguistics, psychometrics and text mining techniques to promote empathy among students' interaction, based on identification and text matching suggestions [13]. The combination of ITS and CSCL to design adaptive empathy learning tools is scarcely investigated in literature [13]. The aim is to provide pedagogical feedback on a learner's actions and solutions, hints and recommendations to encourage and guide future activities in the writing processes or automated evaluation to indicate whether a *student's reaction to another person's perspective is emotionally appropriate.* The design and implementation of ITS and CSCL to build adaptive learning tools is a rather complex endeavor that must rely on expertise from the fields of *computer science* (i.e., development of feedback algorithms), *human–computer interaction* (i.e., design of the interface) and *educational technology* (i.e., integration into the learning process).

Therefore, we aim to address this research gap and aim to contribute with rigorous design knowledge for an empathy learning tool based on educational theory through the application of recent developments in NLP and ML, in which empathy detection has been a growing research approach to identify and model empathetic structures of a given text in real-time [13, 16]. The potential of empathy detection has been investigated in different domains but not leveraged for individual tutoring or feedback in a student's learning progress [16].

2.3 Cognitive Dissonance as a Kernel Theory for Individual Learning

We believe that *Cognitive Dissonance Theory* supports our underlying hypothesis that individual and personal feedback on a student's ability to react to other people's perspectives in an emotionally appropriate manner motivates the student to improve their skill level. Cognitive dissonance refers to the uncomfortable feeling that occurs when there is a conflict between one's existing knowledge or beliefs and contradicting presented information [18]. This unsatisfying internal state results in a high motivation to solve this inconsistency. According to Festinger's theory, an individual experiencing this dissonance has three possible ways to resolve it: change the behavior, change the belief or rationalize the behavior. Especially for students in a learning process, dissonance is a highly motivating factor to gain and acquire knowledge to actively resolve the dissonance [32]. It can be an initial trigger for a student's learning process and thus the construing of new knowledge structures [33]. However, the right portion of cognitive dissonance is very important for the motivation to solve it. According to Festinger, individuals might not be motivated enough to resolve it if the dissonance is too obvious, whereas a high level of dissonance might lead to frustration. Therefore, we believe that the right level of feedback on a student skill, such as empathy skills, could lead to cognitive dissonance and thus to motivation to change the behavior, belief or knowledge to learn how to react to other people's perspectives in an appropriate manner.

3 Research Methodology

Our research project is guided by the *DSR approach* [17]. Figure 1 shows the steps that are being carried out. We followed a theory-driven design approach by grounding our research on the cognitive dissonance theory [18].

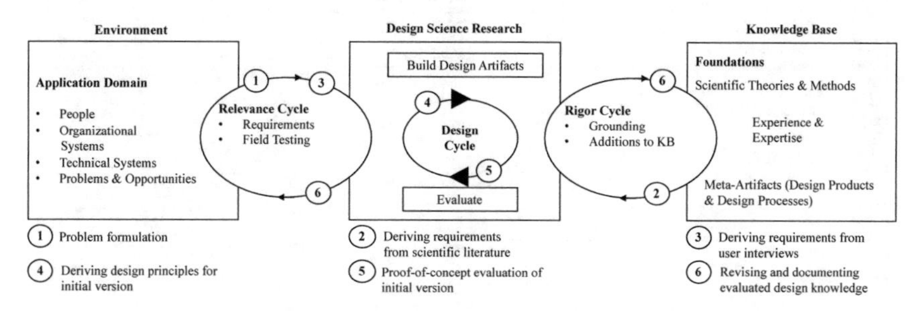

Fig. 1. Three cycle design science process according to [17]

The *first step* of the DSR cycle includes the problem formulation. We therefore described the relevance of the practical problem in the introduction of this work. As the *second step*, we derived a set of *meta-requirements* (**MRs**) from the current state of scientific literature for the design of an empathy learning tool. Based on those insights, we conducted *28 semi-structured interviews* with master students, using the expert interview method by Gläser and Laudel [34] and gathered *user stories* (**USs**) and u*ser requirements* (**URs**) for the design of an a*daptive empathy learning tool* based on those interviews. In the *fourth step,* we derived *five preliminary design principles* (**DPs**) addressing the **MRs** and **URs** using the structure suggested by Gregor et al. [35] and designed an initial version as a first instantiation of these **DPs**. In the *fifth step,* we conducted a proof-of-concept evaluation based on evaluation criteria proposed by Venable et al. [36]. Based on the design principles, we created a mock-up prototype, where students were able to receive an empathy feedback based on chosen pre-defined answers. The goal of this evaluation was to see how the students perceive the value of our instantiated design principles, to note change requests and to gather additional design principles. We conducted an experiment with 25 students to achieve our goal. The students had a short interaction with the prototype and received an adaptive empathy feedback based on chosen answers. Afterwards we captured their perception with a post-survey. In *step six*, we close with a short discussion thereby documenting the design knowledge.

4 Designing the Artifact

In this section, we will describe and discuss how we gathered the preliminary requirements, derived the preliminary **DPs** and evaluated them in an instantiated initial version. The problem formulation (*step one*), described in the introduction, serves as the foundation for the derivation of the requirements. The main insights are illustrated in Fig. 2.

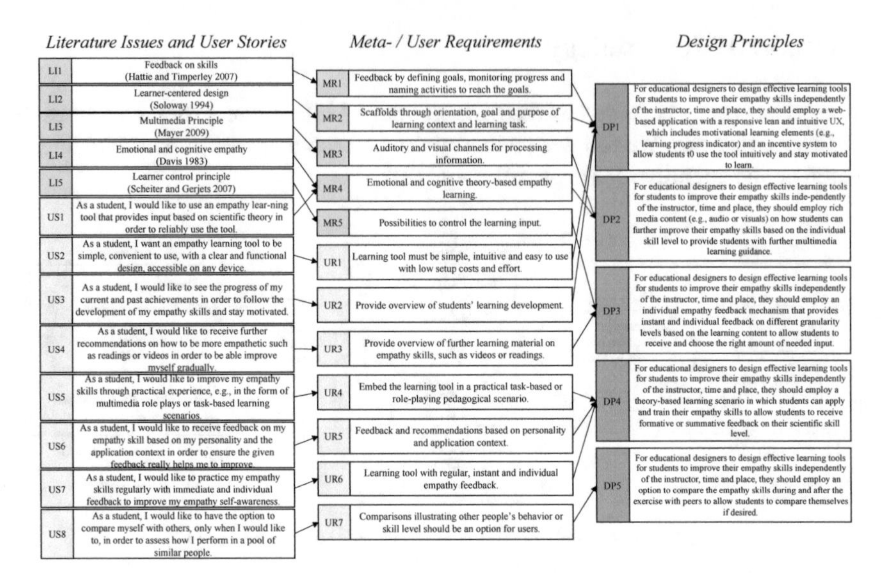

Fig. 2. Overview of the derived design principles according to [35]

Step 2: Deriving Meta-requirements from Scientific Literature

To derive requirements from scientific literature, a systematic literature search was conducted using the methodological approaches of Cooper [37] and vom Brocke et al. [38]. We initially focused our research on studies that demonstrate the successful implementation of learning tools for empathy skills. Two broad areas for deriving requirements were identified: *educational technology* and *learning theories*. Since the creation of a learning tool for empathy skills is a complex project that is studied by psychologists, pedagogues and computer scientists with different methods, we first concentrated on these literature streams. We only included literature that deals with or contributes to a kind of learning tool in the field of empathy learning, such as an established learning theory.

On this basis, we selected 110 papers for more intensive analysis. We have summarized similar topics of these contributions as *literature issues* (**LIs**) and formed five clusters from them. Individual formative feedback is essential for the learning of skills such as empathy (**LI1,** i.e., [8]). Hence, it is crucial to define goals, monitor the progress towards the goals and name activities to reach the goals for the learner (**MR1**). Following their *theory of learner-centered design* (**LI2**), [39] named the concept of scaffolds with a specific goal, purpose and learning guidance as a central component of learning software when the purpose is to complete constructive activities such as writing empathetic texts (**MR2**). In his *cognitive theory of multimedia learning*, Mayer (2007) [40] named the "multimedia principles" (**LI3**), which states that "*people learn more deeply from words and pictures than from words alone*" (p.47, Mayer 2009). Therefore, to guide learners, the tool needs to incorporate both words and images to reduce the load for a single processing channel (**MR3**). Moreover, we follow the empathy construct of Davis [2] (**LI4**), which guides our empathy learning tool with the structure of *emotional and cognitive* *empathy tutoring* (**MR4**). Lastly, the *learners' control principle* (**LI5**) is of special significance for learning skills, since it aims to enable learners to adjust the information needed for their personal learning process (**MR5**) [41].

Step 3: Deriving Requirements from User Interviews
Based on the derived **LIs** and **MRs**, we conducted *28 semi-structured interviews* according to Gläser and Laudel [34]. The interview guideline consists of 30 questions and each interview lasted mean = 40.91 min (SD = 15.9 min). The interviewees were a subset of students at our university who are all potential users of an empathy learning tool.

The participants were asked about the following topics: *experience with technology-based learning systems, importance of skills in university education, requirements for a system that supports learning metacognition skills* (e.g., functionalities, design) and *requirements for a system that supports learning empathy* (e.g., functionalities, design). In order to gain impressions resulting from many years of learning experience, only master students were recruited for the interviews. The interviewed students had a mean age of 24.82 years (*SD = 1.98)* and all students were studying economics, law or psychology; 15 were male, 13 were female. After a more precise transcription, the interviews were evaluated using a qualitative content analysis. The interviews were coded, and abstract categories were formed. The coding was performed using open coding to form a uniform coding system. Based on these results, we gathered *269 user stories* (**USs**) and identified seven user *requirements* (**URs**) following Cohn (2004) [42].

For all interviewees, it was very important that an empathy learning tool relies on a scientific theory to reliably use the tool (**US1**), which is reflected in **MR4**. All students mentioned that the learning tool must be simple, convenient to use, with a clear and functional design and accessible on any device (**US2**), which we incorporated in **UR1**. Moreover, all students stated that they would like to continuously use an empathy learning tool for practical experience, e.g., in the form of multimedia role plays or task-based learning scenarios (**US5, UR4**), and therefore would like to see the progress of their learning development for current and past activities to stay motivated (**US3, UR2**). On top of that, a majority clearly mentioned that they would like to receive immediate and individual empathy feedback (**US7, UR6**) based on their personality and the context of the application scenario to ensure that the feedback is valuable for them (**US6, UR5**). The interviewed students also mentioned that they would like to receive direct recommendations on how to be more empathetic in a certain scenario and further learning material (e.g., readings or videos) to gradually improve themselves (**US4, UR3**). Regarding social comparison, we received differentiated feedback resulting that students would like to have an option to compare their individual empathy feedback with peers. The comparison function should not be directly shown without the user selecting it (**US8, UR7**).

Step 4: Deriving Design Principles and Instantiating an Initial Version
We have identified five **LIs,** eight **USs** and formulated five preliminary **MRs** and seven preliminary **URs**. Based on these findings, we derived *five preliminary DPs* following the structure of Gregor et al. [35] for an adaptive learning tool for empathy skills as a special class of learning tools for metacognition skills. The design principles are depicted in Fig. 2.

Design principle 1 (**DP1**) states that the artifact should be developed as a web-based application with a responsive, lean, and adaptable user interface. The learning tool should also contain learning elements that motivate the students during the application. Therefore, we instantiated a lean and adaptive learning process with an intuitive learning experience and a dialogue-oriented interface. Furthermore, the student can learn with an individual empathy learning dashboard. The dashboard provides users with an intuitive overview of the learning content and empathy theory. Furthermore, feedback on the empathy task is displayed in different granularity levels, and further learning options are offered (e.g., comparison with other students). The dashboard also leads the user to a progress bar, which gives the student an overview of his learning progress, which underlines the motivating character of **DP1**. Besides, the learning tool is equipped with audio or visual material to provide the students with further multimedia learning support (**DP2**).

In **DP4**, we propose to use a learning-based scenario to train empathy. Therefore, the empathy learning tool should be embedded in a proven teaching-learning scenario that is easy to set up and domain-agnostically applicable. We used student peer reviews, as students can apply and train their empathy skills by giving feedback on a peer's business model [39]. The potential of student peer reviews and training of metacognition skills has already been successfully demonstrated for other NLP-based skill training, such as argumentation skills [40]. **DP5** includes the possibility for students to compare their empathy levels with other students. One way to do this could be a progress bar, which allows students to compare themselves optionally.

Next, **DP3** emphasizes the need for individual feedback to learn skills such as empathy. Students should receive feedback on the pre-defined response options that have been selected beforehand. Therefore, we have introduced a direct and individual feedback mechanism to help students train their empathy skills. We also set up a mechanism to provide students with further learning material. The advanced learning material consists of videos and literature. These materials will help students to learn more about the different dimensions of empathy.

To instantiate and evaluate the design principles above, we created a mock-up-based prototype by using the tool *marvel*[2]. Our prototype (Fig. 3) guides students through providing a peer review on another student's business model through a conversational interface and an empathy learning dashboard. Our **DPs** were formulated based on the analysis of current issues related to the theory of learning and teaching metacognition skills and needs and requirements of users based on cognitive dissonance theory [18]. We argue that a learning tool for empathy skills (and possibly other metacognition skills) that instantiates our **DPs** should increase the motivation of students to learn how to apply the certain skills, for example, learn how to appropriately react to another person's perspective and thus improve the learning outcome. For example, an empathy learning tool that provides instant and individual feedback and gives students the flexibility to control their learning input and provides further learning material should increase the students' motivation to resolve dissonance and therefore construct new knowledge.

[2] marvelapp.com

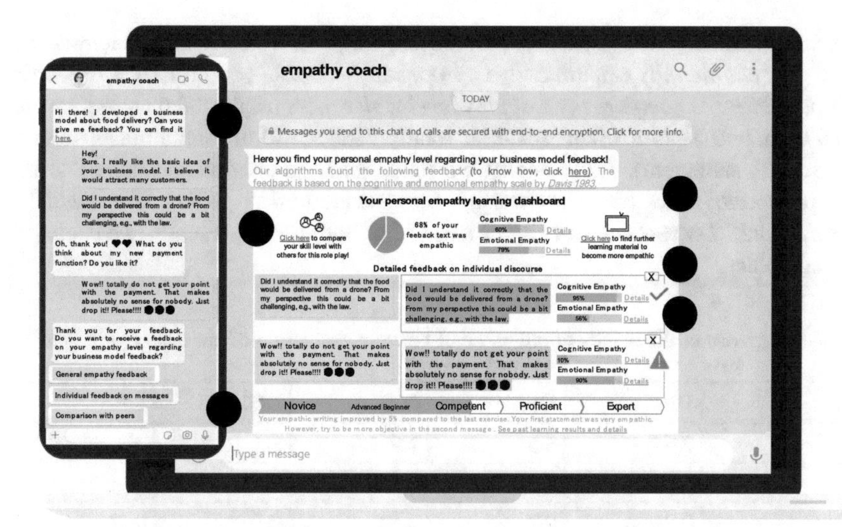

Fig. 3. Empathy learning tool based on the preliminary design principles (DP 1–5)

5 Proof-of-Concept Evaluation of Initial Version

In this section, we describe the proof-of-concept evaluation of the initial version of our empathy learning tool. Based on the gathered requirements and design principles, we designed a clickable mock-up displaying a conversational learning interface which provides empathy feedback based on pre-defined answers (without implementing trained chat intents in the back end). For the evaluation, we followed an *ex ante* evaluation using an *artificial* evaluation setup as proposed by Venable et al. (2016) [36]. The purpose of the evaluation is to check whether the design principles are useful for learners, in order to incorporate any change requests. The design principles were specifically examined based on the criteria of usefulness and usability and evaluated by means of various questions. Therefore, a questionnaire with 14 items was created with specific questions about the **DP**, e.g., we asked questions about the perception of the empathy learning input, the usability and usefulness of the adaptive empathy functions and the concept of the adaptive learning tool as a whole.

To do so, we designed an experiment in which participants were asked to provide a peer review based on a provided business model essay. The participants were using our initial version for providing a business model review to an imaginary peer (see Fig. 3). After the review task, they received adaptive feedback on their cognitive and their emotional empathy level based on Davis [2]. Afterwards, we asked specific question to evaluate the design principles. Thus, we gave participants items addressing the instantiated principles: For evaluating **DP1,** „*The learning journey would give me an overview of my learning process and thus motivate me.*"; for **DP2,** "*I would find the information about learning empathy helpful.*"; for **DP3,** "*The rating of my messages reflects my actual empathy.*", "*The tool has accurately rated my empathy*" and "*The feedback I received from the tool was an accurate rating of my empathy*".; for **DP4,** "*I assume that the learning tool would help me improve my ability to give empathically* *appropriate feedback."* and *"I assume that the learning tool would help me improve my ability to give emotionally empathically appropriate feedback.*"; and for **DP5,** "*I would find the possibility to compare my empathy level with others useful."* All answers were captured on a 1-to 5-point Likert scale (1: totally disagree to 5: totally agree, with 3 being a neutral statement). Additionally, we asked three qualitative questions: *"What did you particularly like about the use of the empathy tool?"*, *"What else could be improved?"* and *"Do you have any other ideas?"* to both groups. Finally, we captured the demographics.

Table 1. Overview of the results of the proof-of-concept evaluation of our design principles

$n = 25$	DP1	DP2	DP3	DP4	DP 5
Mean	3.64	3.5	2.9	3.5	3.8
SD	0.86	0.87	0.73	0.88	0.76
Normalized	0.72	0.7	0.58	0.7	0.76

In total, we received 25 completed answers. 17 were from males, 8 from females. The mean age was 25.12 years (SD = 2.78). Our evaluation confirmed that **DP1**, **DP2**, **DP4** and **DP5** are mostly positively perceived by the participants (see Table 1). The mean values for the **DPs** are promising when comparing the results to the midpoints of the scale. The results for **DP1**, **DP2**, **DP4** and **DP5** are better than the neutral value of 3 and all normalized values are equal or greater than 0.7. Only the rating of **DP3** is less positive with a neutral value of 2.9 (see Table 1).

We also included open questions in the survey to get students' impressions of how they perceived their interaction with our initial version and further evaluate **DP**. The respondents were asked to indicate what they liked, what weaknesses they see, and whether they had any ideas for improving the tool. The general attitude towards interaction with our tool was very positive. Data analysis confirms that students are interested in using a learning tool for empathy skills and would be motivated to work with it. A learning tool that evaluates empathy is perceived as "*very useful*". Participants emphasized, however, that "*the tool was easy to use. The fun factor was also present, and it was fun to write with the bot*" (**DP1**). They also expressed their confidence in the instrument and praised the theoretically well-founded background, which "*explains the different types of empathy in more detail*" (**DP2**). The direct and individual feedback and the resulting potential for improvement for users were mentioned by many participants (**DP3**), e.g.: "*The tool obviously and objectively evaluates a skill that previously seemed subjective to me. This helps to improve oneself better and to identify possible improvement potentials*". The qualitative evaluation also revealed some interesting and relevant suggestions for improvement. The participants asked for more pre-defined response options for the business model feedback in order to be able to give specific answers. Also, the pre-defined response options should be more differentiated. Many also mentioned that they would like to write the feedback themselves in natural text, e.g. the Toll should be equipped with an "*extended answer function*" to get "*more individual feedback*" on the answers (**DP3**).

6 Discussion and Conclusion

In this paper, we derived a set of five preliminary design principles on how to design an adaptive empathy learning tool. Therefore, we discussed five literature issues based on *110 scientific papers and* presented five preliminary **MRs** and seven **URs** from *28 interviews*. We built an initial version as an instantiation of these design principles, evaluated the principles through our initial version in a *proof-of-concept evaluation* [36] and captured the perception of students.

Therefore, our work makes several contributions to research. To the best of our knowledge, we provide the first study with evaluated design principles for the design of an empathy learning tool. Our **DPs** were formulated based on the analysis of current issues related to theories of learning and teaching metacognition skills and needs and requirements of users based on cognitive dissonance theory [18]. We argue that a learning tool for empathy skills (and possibly other metacognition skills) that instantiates our **DPs** should increase the motivation of students to learn how to apply certain skills, for example, learn how to appropriately react to another person's perspective and thus improve the learning outcome. For example, an empathy learning tool that provides instant and individual feedback and gives students the flexibility to control their learning input and provides further learning material should increase the students' motivation to resolve dissonance and therefore construct new knowledge. We argue that lecturers and educational institutions can use these design principles to create their own empathy learning tools to improve their individual pedagogical scenarios. Our evaluation showed that the initial design principles are promising for students to use such a learning tool. Only **DP3** falls short on expectations in our data analysis. However, we believe, that the relatively low ratting of the items is related to the mock-up version of our prototype with only predefined response options. Since the answer options do not reflect the students' individual empathy level, the feedback from the students is not seen as corresponding to their personal empathy level. By extending the tool with a function that allows users to write personal answers, we think we might be able to resolve the discrepancy in the evaluation of **DP3**.

A number of limitations have to be considered with respect to our study. First, we gathered requirements from a certain theoretical perspective and a specific user group. It might be possible that other areas of literature and user groups might have led to different results. Moreover, we were not yet able to fully implement our empathy learning tool with a fully functional automatic feedback algorithm based on NLP and ML in the back end (reflected in responses towards **DP3**). In fact, we are creating a new annotation scheme (such as [43] for argumentation skills) to capture emotional and cognitive empathy structures in student peer feedbacks with the aim to train a predictive model to provide students with individual skill feedback based on deep and transfer learning [15, 44]. Therefore, we aim to analyze the impact of the instantiated learning tool on students' learning performance in a large-scale lecture experiment in the future. The trained model could be also embedded in a conversational tutoring system, e.g., to enhance user satisfaction in education such as [14, 45, 46]. We expect our overall research project to contribute a nascent design theory [47] to the artifact class of IT learning tools for metacognition skills and thus contribute to the OECD Learning framework 2030 towards a metacognition-skill-based education.

References

1. OECD: The Future of Education and Skills - Education 2030 (2018). 2018-06-15
2. Davis, M.H.: Measuring individual differences in empathy: evidence for a multidimensional approach. J. Pers. Soc. Psychol. **44**, 113–126 (1983). https://doi.org/10.1037//0022-3514.44.1.113
3. Luca, J., Tarricone, P.: Does emotional intelligence affect successful teamwork? In: Proceedings of the 8th Annual Conference on Australian Society for Computers in Learning in Tertiary Education, pp. 367–376 (2001)
4. Poser, M., Bittner, E.A.C.: Hybrid teamwork: consideration of teamwork concepts to reach naturalistic interaction between humans and conversational agents. In: WI2020. GITO Verlag (2020). https://doi.org/10.30844/wi_2020_a6-poser
5. Konrath, S.H., O'Brien, E.H., Hsing, C.: Changes in dispositional empathy in American college students over time: a meta-analysis. Personal. Soc. Psychol. Rev. **15**, 180–198 (2011). https://doi.org/10.1177/1088868310377395
6. Lok, B., Foster, A.E.: Can virtual humans teach empathy? In: Foster, A.E., Yaseen, Z.S. (eds.) Teaching Empathy in Healthcare, pp. 143–163. Springer, Cham (2019). https://doi.org/10.1007/978-3-030-29876-0_9
7. Seaman, J.E., Allen, I.E., Seaman, J.: Higher Education Reports - Babson Survey Research Group (2018)
8. Hattie, J., Timperley, H.: The power of Feedback. Rev. Educ. Res. **77**, 81–112 (2007). https://doi.org/10.3102/003465430298487
9. Vygotsky, L.S.: Mind in Society: The Development of Higher Psychological Processes. Harvard University Press, Cambridge (1980)
10. Wambsganss, T., Söllner, M., Leimeister, J.M.: Design and evaluation of an adaptive dialog-based tutoring system for argumentation skills. In: International Conference on Information Systems (ICIS), Hyderabad, India (2020)
11. Wambsganss, T., Rietsche, R.: Towards designing an adaptive argumentation learning tool. In: 40th International Conference on Information Systems (ICIS 2019), pp. 1–9. Munich (2020)
12. Gerdes, K.E., Segal, E.A., Jackson, K.F., Mullins, J.L.: Teaching empathy: a framework rooted in social cognitive neuroscience and social justice. J. Soc. Work Educ. **47**, 109–131 (2011). https://doi.org/10.5175/JSWE.2011.200900085
13. Santos, B.S., Junior, M.C., De Souza, J.G.: An experimental evaluation of the neuromessenger: a collaborative tool to improve the empathy of text interactions. In: Proceedings. 10th IEEE Symposium on Computers and Communications, 2018 June, pp. 573–579 (2018). https://doi.org/10.1109/ISCC.2018.8538442
14. Zierau, N., Wambsganss, T., Janson, A., Schöbel, S., Leimeister, J.M.: The anatomy of user experience with conversational agents : a taxonomy and propositions of service clues. In: International Conference on Information Systems (ICIS), pp. 1–17 (2020)
15. Landolt, S., Wambsganss, T., Matthias, S.: A taxonomy for deep learning in natural language processing. In: Hawaii International Conference on System Sciences (HICSS) (2021)
16. Buechel, S., Buffone, A., Slaff, B., Ungar, L., Sedoc, J.: Modeling empathy and distress in reaction to news stories. In: Proceedings of the Conference on Empirical Methods in Natural Language Processing (EMNLP 2018), pp. 4758–4765 (2018). https://doi.org/10.18653/v1/d18-1507
17. Hevner, A.R.: A three cycle view of design science research. Scand. J. Inf. Syst. **19**, 1–6 (2007)
18. Festinger, L.: Cognitive dissonance. Sci. Am. **207**, 93–106 (1962). https://doi.org/10.1038/scientificamerican1062-93

19. Hevner, A.R., March, S.T., Park, J., Ram, S.: Design science in information systems research. Des. Sci. IS Res. MIS Q. **28**, 75 (2004)
20. Wambsganss, T., et al.: An adaptive learning support system for argumentation skills. In: ACM CHI Conference on Human Factors in Computing Systems, pp. 1–14 (2020)
21. Peterson, R.T., Limbu, Y.: The convergence of mirroring and empathy: communications training in business-to-business personal selling persuasion efforts. J. Bus.-to-bus. Mark. **16**, 193–219 (2009). https://doi.org/10.1080/10517120802484551
22. vom Brocke, J., Maaß, W., Buxmann, P., Maedche, A., Leimeister, J.M., Pecht, G.: Future work and enterprise systems. Bus. Inf. Syst. Eng. **60**(4), 357–366 (2018). https://doi.org/10.1007/s12599-018-0544-2
23. Decety, J., Jackson, P.L.: The functional architecture of human empathy (2004). https://doi.org/10.1177/1534582304267187
24. Lawrence, E.J., Shaw, P., Baker, D., Baron-Cohen, S., David, A.S.: Measuring empathy: reliability and validity of the empathy quotient. Psychol. Med. **34**, 911–919 (2004). https://doi.org/10.1017/S0033291703001624
25. Spreng, R.N., McKinnon, M.C., Mar, R.A., Levine, B.: The Toronto empathy questionnaire: scale development and initial validation of a factor-analytic solution to multiple empathy measures. J. Pers. Assess. **91**, 62–71 (2009). https://doi.org/10.1080/00223890802484381
26. Bell, H.: Creative interventions for teaching empathy in the counseling classroom. J. Creat. Ment. Heal. **13**, 106–120 (2018). https://doi.org/10.1080/15401383.2017.1328295
27. Hen, M., Goroshit, M.: Emotional competencies in the education of mental health professionals. Soc. Work Educ. **30**, 811–829 (2011). https://doi.org/10.1080/02615479.2010.515680
28. Bailenson, J.N., Yee, N., Blascovich, J., Beall, A.C., Lundblad, N., Jin, M.: The use of immersive virtual reality in the learning sciences: digital transformations of teachers, students, and social context. J. Learn. Sci. 7, 102–141 (2008). https://doi.org/10.1080/10508400701793141
29. Weis, S., Süß, H.-M.: Social intelligence—a review and critical discussion of measurement concepts. In: Schulze, R., Roberts, R.D. (eds.) Emotional Intelligence. An International Handbook, pp. 203–230. Gottingen, Hogrefe (2005)
30. Sadler, D.R.: Formative assessment and the design of instructional systems. Instr. Sci. **18**, 119–144 (1989). https://doi.org/10.1007/BF00117714
31. Kralicek, D., Von Rabenau, L., Shelar, S., Blikstein, P.: Inside out: teaching empathy and social-emotional skills. In: IDC 2018 - Proceedings of the 2018 ACM Conference on Interaction Design and Children, pp. 525–528. Association for Computing Machinery, Inc., New York (2018). https://doi.org/10.1145/3202185.3213525
32. Elliot, A.J., Devine, P.G.: On the motivational nature of cognitive dissonance: dissonance as psychological discomfort. J. Pers. Soc. Psychol. **67**, 382–394 (1994). https://doi.org/10.1037/0022-3514.67.3.382
33. Piaget, J., Brown, T., Thampy, K.J.: The equilibration of cognitive structures: the central problem of intellectual development. Am. J. Educ. **94**, 574–577 (1986). https://doi.org/10.1086/443876
34. Gläser, J., Laudel, G.: Experteninterviews und qualitative Inhaltsanalyse : als Instrumente rekonstruierender Untersuchungen. VS Verlag für Sozialwiss (2010)
35. Gregor, S., Chandra Kruse, L., Seidel, S.: The anatomy of a design principle. J. Assoc. Inf. Syst. (Forthcoming, 2020)
36. Venable, J., Pries-Heje, J., Baskerville, R.: FEDS: a framework for evaluation in design science research. Eur. J. Inf. Syst. **25**, 77–89 (2016). https://doi.org/10.1057/ejis.2014.36
37. Cooper, H.M.: Organizing knowledge syntheses: a taxonomy of literature reviews. Knowl. Soc. **1**, 104–126 (1988). https://doi.org/10.1007/BF03177550

38. vom Brocke, J., Simons, A., Riemer, K., Niehaves, B., Plattfaut, R., Cleven, A.: Standing on the shoulders of giants: challenges and recommendations of literature search in information systems research. Commun. Assoc. Inf. Syst. **37**, 205–224 (2015). https://doi.org/10.17705/1cais.03709
39. Soloway, E., Guzdial, M., Hay, K.E.: Learner-centered design: the challenge for HCI in the 21st century. Interactions **1**, 36–48 (1994). https://doi.org/10.1145/174809.174813
40. Mayer, R.E.: Multimedia Learning. Cambridge University Press, Cambridge (2009). https://doi.org/10.1017/CBO9780511811678
41. Scheiter, K., Gerjets, P.: Learner control in hypermedia environments. Educ. Psychol. Rev. **19**, 285–307 (2007). https://doi.org/10.1007/s10648-007-9046-3
42. Cohn, M.: User Stories Applied For Agile Software Development (2004)
43. Wambsganss, T., Niklaus, C., Söllner, M., Handschuh, S., Leimeister, J.M.: A corpus for argumentative writing support in German. In: 28th International Conference on Computational Linguistics (Coling) (2020)
44. Wambsganss, T., Molyndris, N., Söllner, M.: Unlocking transfer learning in argumentation mining: a domain-independent modelling approach. In: 15th International Conference on Wirtschaftsinformatik. , Potsdam, Germany (2020). https://doi.org/10.30844/wi_2020_c9-wambsganss
45. Wambsganss, T., Winkler, R., Schmid, P., Söllner, M.: Unleashing the potential of conversational agents for course evaluations: empirical insights from a comparison with web surveys. In: Twenty-Eighth European Conference on Information Systems (ECIS2020), pp. 1–18. , Marrakesh, Morocco (2020)
46. Wambsganss, T., Winkler, R., Schmid, P., Söllner, M.: Designing a conversational agent as a formative course evaluation tool. In: 15th International Conference on Wirtschaftsinformatik, Potsdam, Germany (2020)
47. Gregor, S., Hevner, A.R.: Positioning and presenting design science research for maximum impact. MIS Q. **37**(2), 337–355 (2013)

Opening the Minds of Upper Secondary School Students for Business Informatics: An Exploratory Study and an Outline for a Dedicated Teaching Program

Carola Schauer[1(✉)] and Hanno Schauer[2]

[1] Institute for Computer Science and Business Information Systems, Research Group for Information Systems and Enterprise Modelling, University Duisburg-Essen, Essen, Germany
carola.schauer@uni-due.de
[2] Mons-Tabor-Gymnasium, Montabaur, Germany
hanno.schauer@mtg-mt.de

Abstract. Graduates of Business Informatics (BI) have excellent job perspectives. The ongoing digital transformation entails the fascinating opportunity for our students to participate in designing future organizations. At the same time, enrollment statistics for German universities indicate relatively low first-year-student numbers in BI bachelor's degree programs. Personal experience additionally suggests that many first-year-students have no clear idea about BI and their future role in practice. Hence, we assume that the perception of BI by secondary schools students is already biased by substantial misconceptions. This paper intends to contribute to the debate on how to raise the awareness of upper secondary school students for study programs in BI. Based on an exploratory survey and practical experience through a case study teaching program employed by "school ambassadors", we propose critical success factors for designing initiatives to disseminate a realistic and attractive image of BI and the professional perspectives it enables.

Keywords: Business informatics · Student perceptions · Secondary schools

1 Motivation and Objectives

In virtually all industries, business enterprises are exploring ways to deal with the challenges and opportunities that arise from a continued increase in digitalization. Designing information systems for businesses and organizations using digital technologies has for decades been the subject of research of the field of Business Informatics (BI)[1] ("Wirtschaftsinformatik") in the German speaking countries (e.g. [1, 2]).

[1] In this paper we use "Business Informatics" as a literal translation of "Wirtschaftsinformatik", because we find this to be better suited to translate our research activities, which have been conducted in German with students at schools in Germany. Information Systems is commonly known as the international equivalent of the discipline "Wirtschaftsinformatik" in German speaking countries.

F. Ahlemann et al. (Eds.): WI 2021, LNISO 46, pp. 477–491, 2021.
https://doi.org/10.1007/978-3-030-86790-4_32

University study programs in BI prepare students for acting as mediators between the different stakeholders participating in and affected by IT innovation projects. For years there has been a continually high demand for BI graduates in German speaking countries [3]. Respective study programs seek first-year students, who show sufficient interest and capacity for successfully completing their studies. As members of a BI Institute at a large University in North-Rhine-Westphalia (NRW), Germany, we have the impression, that many of our first-year students choose our study program with inadequate assumptions about the field in mind. Additionally, we feel that there is a great potential among the secondary school students that is currently not realized. Thus, being aware of a constantly high demand for BI graduates on the job market and a successful and application oriented academic field of BI, we ask ourselves why first-year-student numbers and students' conceptions about their field of study are unsatisfactory.

Secondary schools are in their current state likely not capable of fulfilling the requirements necessary to solve this problem (see Sect. 2). The shortage of students creates a threat to research in BI, because it is likely to lead to an insufficient number of graduates, who are interested in pursuing a PhD. Research addressing the specific challenges of the field of BI to attract adequate first-year-students is rare (see Sect. 3). Thus, it seems advisable, in the discipline's own interest, that the academic field directs more attention to this situation and starts to explore approaches to foster the field's perception among secondary school students.

The intention of this paper is to serve as a starting point to improve the perception of BI among prospective university students by (1) exploring how secondary II level students perceive the university study program BI and (2) formulating requirements for initiatives on how to better address the field's characteristics and relevance at schools.

While this article is based on experience with students in Germany and the specific situation of BI, it addresses a gap also perceived in international Information Systems study programs (e.g. [4–6]). Albeit, the rapid decline in enrollments that struck Management Information Systems programs after 2000 [7], has not as much affected the more application oriented BI programs in German speaking countries (cf. [2]).

This paper is structured as follows: In order to derive an initial hypothesis and research questions Sect. 2 looks at the status of school curricula and evaluates first-year-student numbers in Germany. Section 3 provides an overview of related work on existing initiatives for informing students about BI or Information Systems study programs. In Sect. 4 we report on results of an exploratory survey of secondary II level students to inquire their perceptions about the field of BI. Section 5 presents a case based teaching program for secondary II level classes and reports on practical experience at schools. In the final section, we formulate conclusions and propose requirements for future initiatives based on our exploratory study results and practical experience (Sect. 6).

2 Current Status: Secondary School Subjects and First-Year-Student Numbers

Various factors can influence the choice of a study program, including parents or friends and informative events at schools or universities. In the best case, insights about a prospective future study program can be gained in a structured manner, when a school subject is taught that relates to the corresponding academic field. For the field of BI, possibly corresponding school subjects are Business Administration ("Wirtschaft"), Computer Science ("Informatik"), and Business Informatics ("Wirtschaftsinformatik").

In Germany, federal states are responsible for educational policy. We focus on NRW and its secondary school system. In NRW Business Administration and BI are mandatory subjects at "Wirtschaftsgymnasien" and vocational schools [8]. Both subjects are not part of the current curriculum at general secondary schools. For many years, Computer Science has been an elective subject at secondary schools. Thus, only a relatively small fraction of each age group actually attends Computer Science classes [9]. In several states in Germany, including NRW, compulsory Computer Science courses have recently been or will in short time be introduced to lower secondary school grades.

There have been recent curriculum changes beyond Computer Science classes: In NRW curricula of various school subjects have been adjusted to include topics on digitalization [10]. Remarkably, all respective changes to the curriculum relate to lower secondary classes only. Furthermore, the curricula changes to these non-computing subjects primarily address issues pertaining to the use of information technology devices and applications, but not to their design. Hence, despite all recent curriculum initiatives in NRW to better prepare students for the digital world, there is still a considerable lack of dedicated support for, in particular, upper secondary students to learn about the challenges and opportunities of the increasing digitalization.

Against this background and based on anecdotal evidence we assume that **the discipline of BI is either not known or is connected with misleading ideas by secondary II level students in Germany** (hypothesis I). We derive two research questions that will be addressed in the following sections:

RQ 1: What are the perceptions of secondary II level students towards BI?
RQ 2: To what extent do the perceptions vary between students who have attended Computer Science classes at school and those who have not?

Assuming that first-year student numbers are an indicator for secondary school graduates' interest in the field, we analyzed statistical data provided by the German census bureau for the most recent study year (2018). Analysis results indicate – compared to Business Administration and Computer Science – relatively low numbers of first-year students, particularly in university study programs for BI.

Figure 1 differentiates the available data on first-year-students according to different education institution types: universities with traditional on campus classes, distance universities, Fachhochschulen (Universities of Applied Sciences) with full-time study programs as well as other Fachhochschulen who offer study programs that do not require full-time studying (e.g. distance, dual or on the job, part-time).

Compared to universities there have been twice as many first-year students starting a BI bachelor's degree at Fachhochschulen in 2018. These results affirm the conclusions of Hachmeister, who analyzed data from 2017 on Informatics study programs in Germany [11]: Compared to all other Informatics related study programs, BI has the highest rate of "dual", part-time, and distance study programs offered by Fachhochschulen which are frequently pursued while doing a full-time job ([11], p. 21).

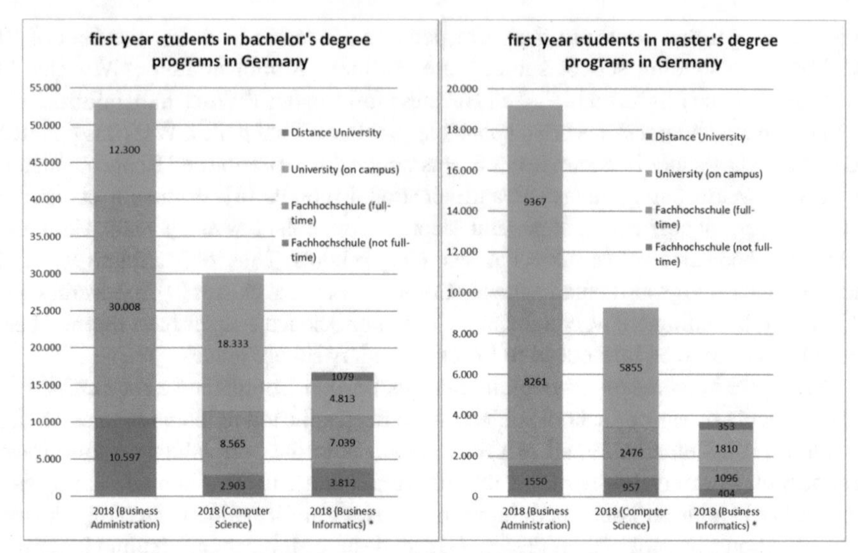

* With respect to BI ("Wirtschaftsinformatik"), the census data are incomplete: there are six universities with BI programs that are not included. Therefore, 510 University first-year-students in bachelor's programs and 135 first-year-students in university master's programs have been added to the census data (based on CHE data for study year 2019 [13]).

Fig. 1. Comparison of first-year-student numbers per field enrolled at Fachhochschulen and universities in Germany (source: Statistisches Bundesamt)

Even when only considering full-time BI degree programs, Fachhochschulen are apparently outnumbering universities in terms of first-year-student numbers at undergraduate level. Conversely, on master's level there are about twice as many first-year-students enrolled at university BI programs compared to Fachhochschulen. The statistics on student numbers indicate that universities are experiencing a tough competition with Fachhochschulen in particular on the bachelor's level (cf. [12]).

Hence, the question remains, what can be done to attract more students to BI university programs? Assuming that students' perceptions are currently biased by severe misconceptions about BI, we intend to develop a dedicated teaching program. To this end we formulate the third research question:

(RQ 3): What are the requirements for a successful teaching program to inform secondary II level students about academic BI study programs at universities?

3 Related Work

An intensive Internet and literature search revealed one documented initiative specifically aimed at informing secondary school students about the characteristics of BI study programs: A coalition of Fachhochschulen developed the "WI case", a collection of teaching materials and games related to BI for secondary school students. A paper describing the development and the objectives was published in 2016 [14]. Further initiatives driven by individual BI institutions might exist, but have – according to our knowledge – not yet been publicly reported.

Several initiatives aimed at attracting new students are documented for the German Computer Science discipline (see proceedings of the biannual conference HDI "Hochschuldidaktik der Informatik", e.g. [15]). In 2013 an article was published describing the concept of "Informatics ambassadors", i.e. graduates who visit schools to inform about the study program "Informatics", implemented at the HTW Berlin College [15]. So far, no more recent publication could be found discussing experience of applying the approach.

In 2008 Thonabauer and Mayr published an article reflecting gender issues in the German BI field. They see a need for initiatives, e.g. certain topics and female role models in order to make BI a more attractive study choice for female students [16].

At secondary schools in Germany, there have been many projects and initiatives to acquaint female students with the MINT[2] areas. Several studies revealed that role models can be an effective means to attract female students [17]. Reports about successful female role model initiatives include projects targeted at Informatics or BI [18].

Anderson et al. provide an overview of various initiatives at universities in the US to encourage more female undergraduates to major in Information Systems. Experimental teaching settings as part of an introductory Information Systems (IS) class aimed at convincing more female students to choose IS as a major. However, the initiatives' results are rather disillusioning: "none were effective in encouraging more female students to consider majoring in IS" [19].

Vainionpää et al. recently published a literature review analyzing existing studies on the low number of women in IT related study programs and jobs [6]. They summarize, that "despite all good work of different actors to entice young women to consider the IT field as a welcoming career choice, the situation seems to be going to even worse direction as the decreasing number of women working in the IT field shows." ([6], p. 13). They conclude that in order to arouse children's interest for the field of IT/IS we need to better "link our efforts to children's life worlds" ([6], p. 13).

4 Exploratory Study: Perceptions and Misperceptions About BI

We developed a survey for secondary II level students intended as a means to get a clearer idea of their perception concerning the academic field of BI by exploring research question RQ 1 and RQ 2.

The survey instrument was tested in March 2018 by two secondary II level students using a preliminary paper based questionnaire. Necessary adjustments were made for higher clarity and understandability of the terms used in the questions. The survey was subsequently implemented and pilot tested by two bachelor's students using LimeSurvey. The questions considered in this article are part of the online questionnaire that takes about 10 to 15 min to complete.

We deliberately chose open questions in order to allow the participants to use their own words when describing their perceptions [20]. The questions asked were: "What is

[2] The acronym MINT (Mathematik, Informatik, Naturwissenschaften, Technik) is the German counterpart to STEM (Science, Technology, Engineering, Mathematics) in English speaking countries.

your current perception of the study subject of BI?" and "According to your impression: how good are the job perspectives of BI university graduates?"

The results interpreted in this article are based on 331 questionnaires completed between November 2018 and March 2020. All survey participants were secondary II level students at 18 different schools in NRW, who were later visited by our school ambassadors (see Sect. 5).

Of the 331 participants 40% (134) are female and 56% (187) male (10 chose to provide no answer to gender). The majority of the participating students (79%) stated to have attended a Computer Science class. 70 participants (21%) stated to have never been in a Computer Science class before.

4.1 Classification of Answer Statements

In the spirit of an exploratory study, we deliberately did not pursue the answer analysis with a pre-structured classification scheme in mind. In order to evaluate the answers, we performed a hermeneutic text analysis and successively identified groups of similar answers. After reading all statements on the participants' current perception about BI, sixteen first level categories were identified as appropriate to classify all given statements (see Table 1). In a second step, the first level categories were grouped to six higher-level categories. Figure 2 depicts the shares of each higher-level category.

The largest group of the participants (42%) stated not to have any idea about the field BI (red). The red colored area also includes the answers that only vaguely describe that the field is somehow about "Business" ("Wirtschaft") and "Informatics" ("Informatik") (13%).

We assessed 13% of the answers as positive (light green), because they include statements that express either interest in the field, assess it as challenging and/or effortful, or describe a relevant topic (incl. digitalization in businesses, intermediator role of the field, business software systems). Additionally, 6% of the statements are classified as acceptable (green), because they entail appropriate statements about a selected area in the field, but are rather one-sided. For example, this category includes 17 statements expressing that BI focuses on the analysis of economic data.

We see varying statements concerning the role of programming or Computer Science in the field (orange): while a few state that Informatics plays only a minor role (7), a greater number of participants expresses that programming and Computer Science plays a major role in the field (23). 14% of the statements entail only a brief, rather negative statement (dark grey), such as "a lot mathematics/computers/theory". 6% of the participants expressed, that they are not interested in the field.

When we focus on the statements made by students who have never attended a Computer Science class at school, we see even more clearly the lack of knowledge about the field. Almost 60% of those students state to have "no idea" about the field. Only 3% of the statements in this group include an acceptable assessment of the field's characteristics. There is, however, a number of students (10%) who name a specific selected topic in our field (such as analysis of economic or business data).

The majority of the participating students formulate positive statements when asked for the job perspectives of future university graduates in the BI field: 62% wrote "good" or "very good". However, even among those who have attended Computer Science classes

Table 1. Derived groups of categories for answer statements

Summarized categories	# of stmts.	Summarized categories	# of stmts.
Informatics is less important, more business/economics	7	Specific: data analysis using IT (economic data)	17
Primarily Programming/Computers, less business	23	Specific: software sales/marketing/consulting	4
A lot mathematics	9	Interesting	9
A lot computers	11	Challenging, effortful	10
A lot theory	6	Specific: digitization in businesses, process orientation	11
Not interesting for me	21	Intermediator between business and IT	3
No idea	137	Business software systems	10
"Business" and "Informatics"	44		
Other (incl. comparison to school subject "Business Informatics")	9		

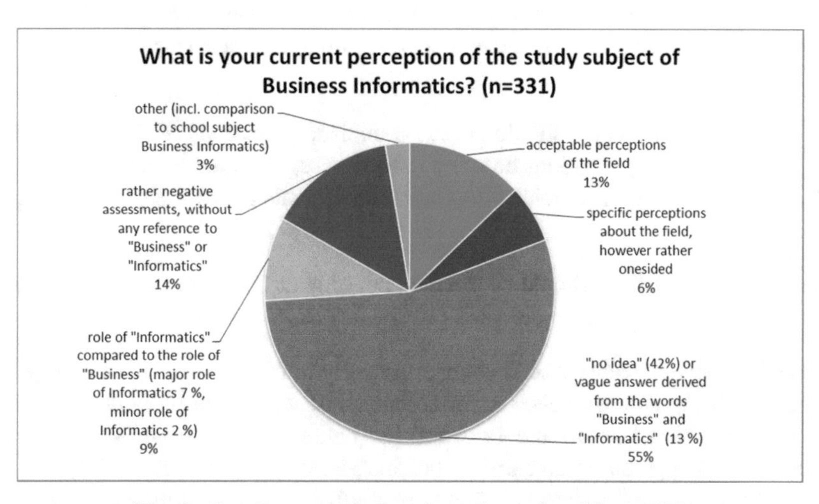

Fig. 2. Results on perception about the study subject of BI

at school, 24% expressed to have "no idea" about the job perspective of BI graduates. This rate is even higher (33%) in the group of those students who have not attended a Computer Science class at school.

4.2 Discussion of Survey Results and Requirements for a Teaching Program

The results of the interpretative text analysis support hypothesis I. While this is not surprising at first, we could also identify various aspects with regard to RQ 1 and RQ 2:

- A large proportion (40%) of the surveyed students states to not have any idea about the field; in the group of those who have not attended a Computer Science class, the proportion is even higher (60%). Hence, we can constitute a severe perception or knowledge gap concerning the field BI even among those who attended Computer Science classes at schools.
- Many answers stay vague, just repeating the words "Business" and "Informatics". Few answers indicate an understanding of the role of IT in organizations. Only about one fifth of all survey participants formulate a perception of the field's characteristics using appropriate terms.
- Notwithstanding the omnipresent digitalization topic, about one third of the surveyed students describe BI job perspectives with "not so good" or "no idea".

In consequence, we argue for the need of efforts in the BI field aimed at addressing the misconceptions and knowledge gaps among secondary students. We acknowledge that this includes not only a teaching program but also pertinent changes in educational policy.

Our survey results and the analysis of prior studies (see Sect. 3) lead us to the following requirements for a dedicated teaching program for upper secondary classes (RQ 3):

Subject: Teaching concepts should convey a realistic picture (1) of the important role of digitalization in organizations now and in the future, (2) of the field of BI in business practice, and (3) of the specific qualities and requirements of university study programs in BI.

***Target Group*:** Initiatives should be directed not only at Computer Science classes but also at students, who have not attended Informatics related classes.

***Means*:** Teaching concepts should connect properly to the students' life world [6]. We suggest that using **role models**, i.e. former students, who share life and school experience with the target group, can be helpful to better connect to students. Secondary school students apparently have difficulties imagining the role of IT and digital innovations for society and industry. Using **case studies** in combination with **narratives** seems a promising approach to help students overcome their current limited perception concerning our field and allow for imagining the possible worlds that can be created with IT innovations [21, 22].

5 A Case Study Based Teaching Approach

We developed a case study based teaching program for upper secondary school classes. The program was designed and tested in school practice by the authors. Reflecting the challenge of getting access to the target group in a way that is perceived as authentic and interesting, we decided to set up and test a school ambassador program: undergraduate and graduate university students of BI volunteered and were specifically trained as school ambassadors to employ the case study with learners at their former schools.

Using the case study method, the ambassadors address not only those who are interested in a particular study program but all learners: The case study is directed at enhancing their competencies of critically reflecting and analyzing the challenges and opportunities in the digital world. Hence, this case study based teaching concept is also an explorative approach to address the lack of teaching digitalization issues in upper secondary classes in NRW (see Sect. 2).

The teaching concept pursues three major **learning objectives**, adhering to a design-oriented constructive view on digitalization typical for the German BI discipline (cf. [33–35]). The learners are to be enabled to understand the following three aspects:

1. **Multiplicity of perspectives**: the perspectives of various stakeholders should be taken into account when analyzing the potential benefits and costs of IT innovations in organizations.
2. **Central role of structuring**: in order to analyze opportunities and challenges of IT in organizations, it is basal to identify appropriate technical concepts or terms of the domain to structure the analysis.
3. **IT affects action systems**: introducing new IT in an organization does not only change the technology available for the different stakeholders but also allows new creative ways to design actions, workflows and processes, hence the organization itself.

The case study is embedded in a sequence of presentations tailored to a 90-min class. During the opening phase, the ambassadors briefly describe their own educational background. After the completion of the case study, the ambassadors present the specifics of the bachelor's study program and explain differences to neighboring fields (Business Administration, Computer Science) and to Fachhochschulen.

5.1 Role of the Case Method in Teaching and Requirements for Success

On university level, case based teaching has early been applied in medicine and law courses, and, later, in business graduate schools. Its practical application in business classes at Harvard School is documented by Jackson [23]. Many cases have been developed, published and applied in classes since the early twentieth century ([24], p. 15). Case study based teaching methods are nowadays commonly applied in business school graduate courses (see e.g. [24, 25]). More recent publications document their use in undergraduate business classes [26]. Meanwhile, computing disciplines have adopted case based teaching approaches as well (e.g. [27–29]). At secondary school level, the case study ("Fallstudie" in German) is known as a didactical method allowing learners to develop self-contained problem solving abilities (e.g. [30] p. 36 ff; [31] p. 257 ff).

In his early accounts on the practice of the case method at Harvard University Jackson explains that a case gives insights into the procedure or method applied to tackle a problem by a certain role in the organization ([23], p. 110). Burgoyne and Mumford extend this early account by emphasizing the role of group work and learner discussions on an initially presented situation that should be further developed ([24], p. 14).

Specifically, the case-study based teaching approach allows the learners.

- to analyze complex real-life problems from multiple viewpoints (see e.g. [26], p. 343), thus explicitly supporting learning objective 1,
- to identify and apply useful structures and terms in group discussions and presentations, thus supporting learning objective 2, and
- to reflect upon certain roles, their activities and methods (see e.g. [31]), thus addressing learning objective 3 as well.

Understanding the opportunities and possible effects of digitalization in organizations is a challenging task in particular for learners who have little knowledge in business and/or computing. A case based approach with an introductory narrative, therefore, seems a promising instrument to help learners to reflect on existing and imagine future digital innovations in organizations.

5.2 Case Study Teaching Program: "Digitalization in classes at Konrad-Adenauer-Gymnasium"

So far, at general-education schools in NRW there is no subject on business economics. Hence, knowledge related to roles and processes in private businesses cannot be assumed as given. Secondary school students are, however, usually familiar with the different roles and processes at their own school. Moreover, investment decisions in the schools' information technology infrastructure have been a current topic at every school in Germany, starting in 2019 because of the federal "DigitalPakt" funding program for schools [32]. Hence, a case study on digitalization at an exemplary school is an up-to-date and highly relevant topic in the students' life world, that we expect learners as well as school teachers to connect to easily. Therefore, we chose a general public school, the fictitious Konrad Adenauer Gymnasium (KAG), as object of our case study.

The case study teaching concept comprises several steps (see Table 2): an introduction of the case situation, a structured analysis phase, and a final discussion in a simulated teachers' meeting. Depending on the prior knowledge of the participating learners as well as class size, the teaching concept is planned to take between 45 and 60 min.

5.3 Preliminary Evaluation through Practical Experience

Between November 2018 and March 2020 twelve of our students volunteered as ambassadors and employed the case study in 22 lessons with upper secondary learners. The ambassadors reached 491 students at 18 different schools in NRW. About 30% of the participating learners were female.

Up to two classes participated in each lesson during the regular school hours with two visiting ambassadors acting as lecturers. In most cases the teacher, who scheduled the ambassadors' visit at his or her school, was a former teacher of one of the visiting ambassadors. 50% of the participating courses were Computer Science classes. Several other subject teachers had shown interest in the program as well. Hence, the classes

Table 2. Main steps of the case study including roles and didactical means.

#	Who (role)	What (learning content)	How (didact. means)
1	Ambassador as school principal	**Introduction** of the case at KAG, consulting task: "Analyze potential benefits and costs of enhancing IT in classes."	Presentation (2 min)
2	Ambassador as leading consultant, students as consultants	**Analysis I:** identify interest groups **Analysis II:** substantiate the term *information technology*	Discussion (5–8 min)
3	Ambassador as leading consultant	**Analysis III:** • Basic structure of application areas for digitization in classes	presentation and class discussion (5 min)
4	Students as consultants	• Analyze digitization areas from the viewpoint of your assigned interest group	Discussion in groups, group presentations (25–35 min)
5	Ambassador as critical school principal,students as consultants	**Teachers' meeting:** a critical statement is given, students are asked to provide a well-grounded and justified answer	Discussion (5–10 min)

visited include Mathematics, Natural Science, Social Science and Business Informatics classes (at a "Wirtschaftsgymnasium").

For evaluation purposes the ambassadors were asked to provide a personal account of each visit (as a voice message or a brief text) assessing the students participation and the success of the case study in class. The following brief evaluation is based on the ambassadors' reports as well as on the authors' own experience in classes.

For all lessons performed at the different schools, the ambassadors expressed that the case study could be completed successfully: the analysis steps, the group work, and presentations were carried out by the learners and learning objectives were addressed by the learners themselves or the ambassadors. Several teachers actively participated in the case study apparently out of personal interest in the case. Several teachers positively acknowledged the high student activity in the teaching concept.

Our school ambassadors are not professionally educated teachers, but specifically trained and highly motivated (under-)graduate BI students. However, the special role of the ambassadors as school alumni and role models for the learners apparently facilitated a fruitful learning atmosphere in most classes – an important requirement for achieving good learning results with case studies [25, 26].

In our experience, the participation of learners in class discussions does not depend on the course subject. The ambassadors reported fruitful class discussions and differentiated analysis results in Computer Science Classes and in other classes as well. However, we perceived that attentive teachers in class positively affected the learning atmosphere as well as the learners' participation in several classes.

While the participating teachers from non-Computing subjects have shown general interest in the case study, the learners in three of these six courses showed rather disparate levels of contribution to class discussion. Therefore, we are planning to extend the case study to include special analysis questions and teaching material for different subjects aimed at increasing the learners' perceived relevance of the case study.

6 Conclusions and Future Work

Digitalization in businesses and organizations are the core of the BI discipline in German speaking countries. Our explorative study suggests a considerable lack of understanding and misperceptions about the field of BI among secondary II level students (hypothesis I, RQ 1, RQ 2). We developed a case study based teaching approach in order to address the identified need to open and change the mind of prospective students. Founded on educational principals and requirements we chose an explorative way through practical experience in secondary school classes to assess the adequacy of the chosen approach (RQ 3).

Although the effectiveness of our case study based teaching program has not yet been formally evaluated, based on practical lessons learned we suggest several requirements and potential success factors. These should be understood as preliminary propositions intended to serve as a basis for designing future initiatives for informing secondary school students about the field of BI:

Case study teaching concepts are promising, but should be flexible to adapt to different levels of discourse and take into account student knowledge conveyed by different school subjects. For example, a class discussion should be on a relatively high level of abstraction for Social Science classes with routine in critical discourse while more structuring is advisable in a Computer Science class with little experience in presentations and discussions.

Narratives can serve as a vivid means to connect to secondary school students and attract attention. A colorful narrative to introduce the case study and simulate a teachers' conference motivates students to participate more actively, because it helps to better understand the problem situation and tasks at hand. Ambassadors acting as role models can embed stories about their own experience. These narratives are helpful for the learners to get a feeling for the yet unknown situation of being a BI university student.

Schools are generally willing to cooperate and invite ambassadors. Out of 20 schools that were offered a visit, 17 accepted the offer, leading to an acceptance rate of 85%. The majority of schools visited is looking forward to organizing annual or biannual ambassador visits.

Motivated BI students, who already understand their future role as mediators, are promising role models. In our experience, many students are motivated to act voluntarily as ambassadors at their own school and at other schools as well.

Authenticity in class, however, requires a prior critical reflection of personal decisions and assessments. A differentiated understanding of the specifics of BI is a prerequisite for ambassadors to authentically lead the discussion and adequately react to the learners' arguments.

Testing the teaching concept with the target group and implementing an ambassadors' training concept is crucial in order to enable the ambassadors to apply it successfully in practice. Perceived effective visits are an important factor to retain ambassadors and motivate them for further visits.

The proposed teaching program requires considerable efforts for developing teaching material, training ambassadors and scheduling regular visits to schools. Its reach in terms of visited schools and students is rather limited for a single institution. Hence, it seems advisable to strive for a coordinated project in the BI community to take advantage of synergy effects. A respective draft should take into account the competitive situation of individual institutions.

Since digitalization is increasingly affecting the planning and practice of businesses and organizations across all industries, preparing all secondary II level students as critical (future) designers and planners of digitalization seems an important objective of future research in BI (cf. [6]). Thus, we view our contribution in this paper not only as a practical report about an initiative to attract new BI-students, but also as a first step towards BI teaching concepts for upper secondary school classes.

References

1. Legner, C., et al.: Digitalization: opportunity and challenge for the business and information systems engineering community. Bus. Inf. Syst. Eng. **59**(4), 301–308 (2017). https://doi.org/10.1007/s12599-017-0484-2
2. Frank, U., Schauer, C., Wigand, R.T.: Different paths of development of two information systems communities: a comparative study based on peer interviews. In: Communications of the Association for Information Systems, vol. 22 (2008)
3. Schauer, C., Frank, U.: Wirtschaftsinformatik und Information Systems. In: Lehner, F., Zelewski, S. (eds.) Wissenschaftstheoretische Fundierung und wissenschaftliche Orientierung der Wirtschaftsinformatik, pp. 121–154. GITO-Verl, Berlin (2007)
4. Iivari, N., Molin-Juustila, T., Kinnula, M.: The future digital innovators: empowering the young generation with digital fabrication and making. In: ICIS 2016 Proceedings (2016)
5. Elder, K.L., Goette, T., MacKinnon, R.: A method to increase is enrollments. Issues Inf. Syst. **20**(4), 137–146 (2019)
6. Vainionpää, F., Kinnula, M., Iivari, N., Molin-Juustila, T.: Girls' Choice - Why Won't They Pick It? Research Papers (2019)
7. Saunders, G., lLockridge, T.: Maurice: declining MIS enrollment: the death of the MIS degree? Contemp. Issu. Educ. Res. **4**, 15–26 (2011)
8. Schauer, C., Frank, U.: Wirtschaftsinformatik an Schulen. Duisburg-Essen Publications Online, University of Duisburg-Essen, Germany, DuEPublico (2018)
9. Schauer, C., Schauer, H.: IT an allgemeinbildenden Schulen: Bildungsgegenstand und -infrastruktur. ICB Research Reports (2019)
10. Ministerium für Schule und Bildung, NRW: Ministerin Gebauer: Landesregierung bringt Einführung der Fächer Wirtschaft und Informatik für alle Schulformen auf den Weg (2019)
11. Hachmeister, C.-D.: Frauen in Informatik: Detaillierte Ergebnisse der Strukturanalyse. Gütersloh (2018)

12. Loos, P., Clarner, R., Hermann, F., Hess, T., Gadatsch, A., Sinz, E.: Business and information systems engineering programs at Universities and Fachhochschulen – convergence or differentiation? Bus. Inf. Syst. Eng. **5**, 281–286 (2013)
13. CHE Hochschulranking: Ranking für Wirtschaftsinformatik, https://ranking.zeit.de/che/de/
14. Ketterer, N., Kuhn, E., Meister, V.G., Röckle, H.: Marketing Für Ein Wirtschaftsinformatik-Studium Mit Hilfe Des "Wi-KofferS"Anwendungen und Konzepte der Wirtschaftsinformatik 1–8 (2016)
15. Göttel, T.: Schnupperveranstaltungen Informatik in der Hochschullandschaft. In: Forbrig, P., Rick, D., Schmolitzky, A. (eds.) HDI 2012 – Informatik für eine nachhaltige Zukunft. 5. Fachtagung Hochschuldidaktik der Informatik, 06–07 November 2012, Universität Hamburg, pp. 45–55. Univ.-Verl. Potsdam, Potsdam (2013)
16. Thonabauer, C., Mayr, D.: Gender Mainstreaming in der Wirtschaftsinformatik HMD **45**, 105–115 (2008)
17. Augustin-Dittmann, S., Gotzmann, H. (eds.): MINT gewinnt Schülerinnen. Springer, Wiesbaden (2015). https://doi.org/10.1007/978-3-658-03110-7
18. Battistini, M.: Ganz normale Exotinnen. In: Augustin-Dittmann, S., Gotzmann, H. (eds.) MINT gewinnt Schülerinnen, pp. 93–110. Springer, Wiesbaden (2015). https://doi.org/10.1007/978-3-658-03110-7_6
19. Anderson, L., Edberg, D., Reed, A., Simkin, M.G., Stiver, D.: How can universities best encourage women to major in information systems? CAIS **41**, 734–758 (2017)
20. Fink, A.: How to Ask Survey Questions. Sage, Thousand Oaks (2003)
21. Alvarez, R., Urla, J.: Tell me a good story. SIGMIS Database **33**, 38 (2002)
22. Frank, U.: Theories in the light of contingency and change: possible future worlds and well-grounded hope as a supplement to truth. In: Hawaii International Conference on System Sciences (HICSS-50 2017). January 4–7, 2017, Waikoloa Village, Hawaii. AIS Electronic Library (AISeL), Erscheinungsort nicht ermittelbar (2017)
23. Jackson, H.J.: The case method. Account. Rev. **1**, 108–111 (1926)
24. Burgoyne, J., Mumford, A.: Learning from the case method department of management learning, Lancaster University Management School, A report to the European Case clearing house (2001)
25. Bruner, R.F., Gup, B.E., Nunnally, Jr., B.H., Pettit, L.C.: Teaching with Cases to Graduate and Undergraduate Students. Fin. Pract. Educ. **9**, 111–119 (1999)
26. Trejo-Pech, C.J.O., White, S.: The use of case studies in undergraduate business administration. Rev. Admin. Empress. **57**, 342–356 (2017)
27. Harper, J.S., Lamb, S.W., Buffington, J.R.: Effective use of case studies in the MIS capstone course through semi-formal collaborative teaching. J. Inf. Syst. Educ. **19**, 411–418 (2008)
28. Varma, V., Garg, K.: Case studies: the potential teaching instruments for software engineering education. In: Fifth International Conference on Quality Software (QSIC 2005), pp. 279–284 (2005)
29. Daun, M., Salmon, A., Weyer, T., Pohl, K., Tenbergen, B.: Project-based learning with examples from industry in university courses: an experience report from an undergraduate requirements engineering course. In: Proceedings of IEEE 29th International Conference on Software Engineering Education and Training (CSEET), pp. 184–193 (2016)
30. Zendler, A.: Unterrichtsmethoden: Steckbriefe, Prozessmodelle und Beispiele. In: Zendler, A. (ed.) Unterrichtsmethoden für MINT-Fächer, pp. 21–78. Springer, Wiesbaden (2018). https://doi.org/10.1007/978-3-658-22513-1_2
31. Frey, K., Frey-Eiling, A.: Ausgewählte Methoden der Didaktik. vdf Hochsch.-Verl. an der ETH, Zürich (2010)
32. Verwaltungsvereinbarung: DigitalPakt Schule 2019 bis 2024 (2019)

33. Frank, U.: Die Konstruktion möglicher Welten als Chance und Herausforderung der Wirtschaftsinformatik. In: Wissenschaftstheorie und gestaltungsorientierte Wirtschaftsinformatik, pp. 161–173. Physica-Verlag HD, Heidelberg (2009)
34. Österle, H., Becker, J., Frank, U., Hess, T., Karagiannis, D., Krcmar, H., Loos, P., Mertens, P., Oberweis, A., Sinz, E.J.: Memorandum on design-oriented information systems research. Eur. J. Inf. Syst. **20**, 7–10 (2011)
35. Bergener, K., Räckers, M., Stein, A.: The art of structuring. Bridging the Gap Between Information Systems Research and Practice, 536 p. Springer, Cham (2019). https://doi.org/10.1007/978-3-030-06234-7

Creating the Virtual: The Role of 3D Models in the Product Development Process for Physical and Virtual Consumer Goods

Jakob J. Korbel(✉)

Chair of Information and Communication Management,
Technische Universität Berlin, Berlin, Germany
jakob.j.korbel@tu-berlin.de

Abstract. The role of 3D models has substantially changed for companies that focus on the creation of consumer goods. For manufacturing and retail firms, virtual objects are today the predominant medium for product development and customization while virtual world and game developers not only build their entire products based on 3D models but found that selling virtual goods in games and virtual worlds can be more lucrative than selling the actual virtual environment. The objective of this study is to emphasize the role of 3D models in the product development processes and to identify similarities and differences between both domains based on a literature review. The results imply that 3D models are today prevalent in the entire value chain of both domains, while non-functional attributes of 3D models are of increasing value. A commonality is the growing importance of the user as source of knowledge for and creator of 3D models.

Keywords: Virtual product · Virtual good · Product development · User creation

1 Introduction

3D models are to date indispensable across a variety of industries and already being used in numerous fields of application, such as digital entertainment, cultural heritage, medical modelling, and architecture [1–5]. While companies in these industries utilize 3D models mainly as a mean to an end during the product development process or create products and goods for business customers, two domains rely on 3D models throughout the entire value chain for the creation of end consumer goods: manufacturing and retail firms and virtual world and game developers. Modern manufacturing and retail firms today draw on virtual products throughout their entire value chain, from sketching and manufacturing to resale and visualization [6]. For virtual world and game developers, however, 3D models are the essence to create their environments and gain revenue through virtual goods. Even though both domains thus heavily depend on 3D models, companies in these domains have long been considered to have only few points of contact, given that collaborations were mostly limited to branding and marketing efforts, e.g., in [7].

F. Ahlemann et al. (Eds.): WI 2021, LNISO 46, pp. 492–507, 2021.
https://doi.org/10.1007/978-3-030-86790-4_33

But both domains are facing trends which might bring them closer together: For virtual world and game developers, the steadily increasing dominance of the free-to-play model [8] forces the providers of virtual environments to offer incentives and put mechanisms in place which induce the players to purchase virtual goods. Since the sale of the environment does not generate revenue, the free-to-play business model relies on the monetization through the items within the environment [9]. These in-game sales, although in most cases based on micropayment to make the player believe that s/he is not paying that much for a single transaction [10], to date established a multi-billion-dollar revenue market [11]. Market consumer goods to customers, however, is the core discipline of manufacturing and retail firms. Manufacturing and retail firms on the other hand identified virtual (VR) and augmented reality (AR) technologies as an opportunity to provide customers in online retail with the possibility to experience and customize their product in an enhanced and enjoyable manner [12] and leverage the technology for inhouse product development (e.g., [13, 14]). Vice versa, creating enjoyable interactive environments for users and virtual environments with complex dependencies and collaboration are core disciplines of virtual world and game developers.

Hence, the aim of this study is to investigate how the role of 3D models in the product development process changed in both domains due to these emerging trends and whether the processes show similarities and differences which in turn offer the opportunity for collaboration and exchange of knowledge and methods. To achieve these objectives, this study synthesizes literature from both domains in relation to the usage of 3D models in the creation process for goods and products based on the literature review methodology (Sect. 2). The findings from the literature review are illustrated in Sect. 3 and discussed in Sect. 4, leading to a preliminary model of the product development stages and intermediate 3D models. Lastly, limitations and future research are described in Sect. 5.

2 Methodology

A systematic literature review is conducted to identify, synthesize, and discuss publications in the manufacturing and retail firm and the virtual world and game developer domain regarding the application of 3D models in the product development process. To ensure the integrity of the results, the literature review process includes all required steps recommended by Webster and Watson [15]. The search and inclusion process is illustrated in Fig. 1.

2.1 Search

First, a pre-screening of literature in relation to the creation of digital 3D models were conducted to identify eligible keywords for the search process. Since the objective of the study is to identify literature on end consumer goods, the selected terms should represent 3D models that either are consumer goods or used for the creation of consumer goods. For the manufacturing and retail domain, the commonly used term for the development of consumer goods is "virtual product", while virtual world and game developers refer to the goods created for and sold in virtual environments as "virtual good", "virtual item" or "virtual asset". Furthermore, the study focusses on the creation and development of end consumer goods. Hence, the terms were searched in combination with the words "creat*" and "develop*" in the title, abstract and keywords of publications, resulting in the search string: *("virtual product*" OR "virtual good*" OR "virtual item*) AND ("creat*" OR "develop*")*. Second, the databases Web of Science, ScienceDirect and IEEExplore were identified as eligible for the search due to their high reputation in the research field. The preliminary search process in the three databases resulted in 545 articles (Web of Science: 323 | Science Direct: 93|IEEExplore: 129). Third, duplicates were removed from the sample (98), as well as false entries, retractions and publications that were not available (32). Finally, to ensure a high quality of literature, both keynotes and book chapters (8) as well as conference proceedings (198) were excluded.

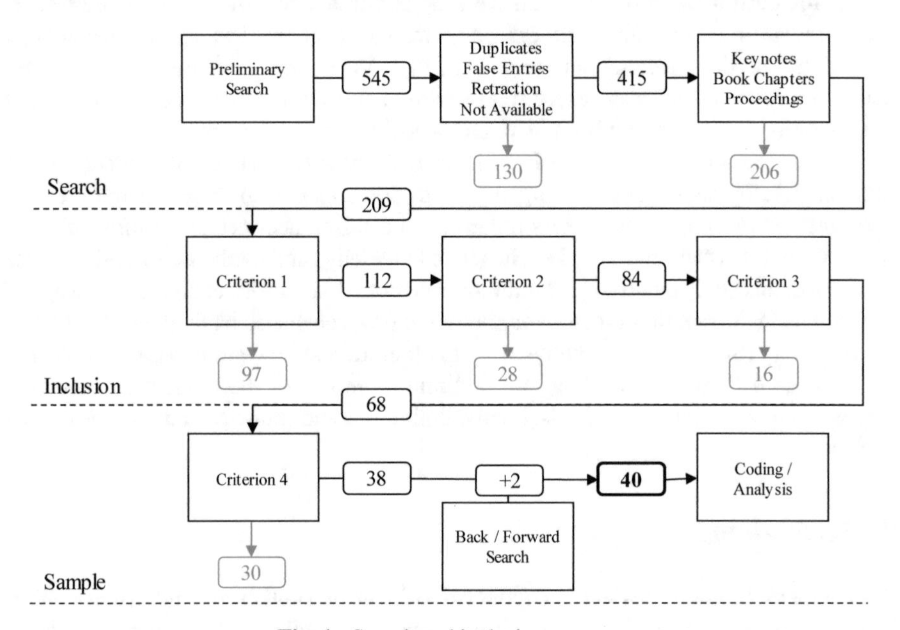

Fig. 1. Search and inclusion process

2.2 Inclusion Criteria

The titles and abstracts of the remaining 209 publications were read and evaluated regarding their suitability for the research objective. Since the study focusses on digital 3D models, publications that use the term "virtual" in relation to digital goods (e.g., eBooks) and the virtualization of hardware components (e.g., virtual server) were excluded (criterion 1). In addition, other domains, and industries, such as architecture or digital entertainment, rely on 3D models for their processes but are not in the scope of the study. Thus, 28 publications were removed from the sample because they did not focus on either of the two domains in scope (criteria 2). In a last step, the full-text of the remaining publications was read. In this process, publications regarding the distribution of goods and products were removed from the sample if the papers did not contain contributions or implications for the creation of the good (criteria 3). Finally, 30 publications addressed the creation of tools that facilitate creation processes (e.g., Computer-Aided-Design software) rather than the actual development process of a good or product and were thus excluded from the sample (criteria 4). Subsequently, a back and forward search was conducted [15] which lead to the inclusion of 2 publications. Hence, the final sample consists of 40 studies (Table 1).

Table 1. Coding of literature

Manufacturer and retail firms	Prototyping	Virtual prototyping	[13, 14, 16–23]
		Virtual collaboration	[24–28]
	Production		
		Virtual fabrication	[29–31]
	Distribution	Virtual product experience	[12, 32–35]
		Virtual customer integration	[36–43]
Virtual world and game developers	Prototyping	Virtual prototyping	[45, 46]
	Production	Virtual production	[9, 10, 47, 48]
	Distribution	Virtual entrepreneurship	[49, 50]
		Virtual customer integration	[49, 51]

2.3 Coding

The studies in the final sample were analyzed and coded in relation to generic product development processes and the approaches in the publications to use or integrate 3D models in the development process (Table 1). The identified generic processes are *prototyping, production* and *distribution.* The two domains manufacturing and retail firms and virtual worlds and game developers were preliminary set. In the manufacturing and retail firm domain, most publications focus on concepts of how to use 3D models to allow for spatial sketching, haptic interaction with a prototype, an enhanced immersion with the product and an evaluation of the design. Since these processes are needed for the creation and evaluation of prototypes, these publications refer to the concept of *virtual prototyping.* A small proportion of literature focus on the constraints between components of product which often requires the collaboration of multiple designers. The tool and platforms developed for this purpose are therefore summarized in the concept of *virtual collaboration.* Furthermore, two publications describe the actual use of 3D models for the virtual simulation of the production process (*virtual fabrication*). In addition, publications examine how the user can experience the product before and after the purchase or how customers can be integrated both in the creation and customization process of the products. Hence, the approaches for the former are referred to as *virtual product experience* and for the latter as *virtual customer integration.* In the virtual world and game developer domain, only two publications mention how virtual goods can designed prior to the distribution of the good (*virtual prototyping*). Furthermore, four publications focus on attributes that virtual goods may possess to be purchased by the user. Although the papers concern virtual consumptions, the implications in the studies affect how virtual goods should be designed and integrated in the virtual environment and are therefore assigned to the concept of *virtual production* in this study. Lastly, studies examine how users can be integrated in the product development process or create and sell their own virtual goods in virtual environments. Consequently, these studies belong to the concepts of *virtual customer integration* and *virtual entrepreneurship.*

3 Results

The results of the study are aligned to the outcome of the coding process in Sect. 3. First, literature regarding the usage of 3D models in the manufacturing and retail firm domain is reviewed, followed by the analysis of publications in the virtual world and game developer domain. Reviewing literature from both domains reveals that publications in the manufacturing and retail firm domain mostly focus on the in-house prototyping (10 publications) and virtual collaboration (5 publications) while studies on the actual creation of virtual goods are sparse in the virtual world and game developer domain (2 publications). Publications rather focus on the virtual markets, i.e., the consumption and distribution of virtual goods which have implications on the virtual production of the virtual goods (4 publications). Both consider the user as integrational part of the development process, either as entrepreneur (2 publications), contributor (10 publications) or consumer (5 publications).

3.1 Manufacturing and Retail Firms

Virtual Prototyping. Today, virtual prototyping is a common practice for manufacturers to create first product drafts because the use of virtual instead of physical objects is associated with less costs and allow an easy configurability, variant support, the possibility to run several simulations on the same object [16]. Thereby, 3D models can already be used in the sketching phase. In [17], 2D and 3D sketching is compared in a virtual reality (VR) environment. The results show that users perceive 3D sketching to be superior to 2D sketching due to a better spatial thinking and inspiration. VR based approaches are also examined in the subsequent steps of virtual prototyping. To enhance the immersion with the 3D models, i.e. the desired product, VR allows the designer not only to develop but to interact with the product and other participants in the virtual environment, leading to higher success rates in the development process [13, 14]. In [18], the VR environment is further enhanced by semantic schemes which enable even unexperienced users to quickly adjust to the VR development interface. The resulting prototypes can also be assessed and evaluated in these VR environments which is found to be superior compared to 2D screen or even real prototypes [19]. While these studies provide impressive results for using exclusively virtual environments to enhance the virtual prototyping process, other approaches integrate 3D models into the reality. Since human interactions with products are difficult to simulate, haptic sensors can facilitate the virtual integration of human behavior. The sensors can capture the human movements during the physical interaction which provides valuable feedback on the usage behavior that can be integrated in the 3D model simulation [16]. In addition, haptics lead to more realism and interactivity with the 3D object in the prototyping process [20]. Given that the presence of the 3D model in the real environment is expedient, developers can shift to AR instead of VR applications. In [21], the authors utilize AR technology to place 3D models of the virtual product directly in the hand of the user. With the help of a marker attached to the user's hand, the product developer can manipulate the 3D model in the real environment which leads to an enhanced user experience and performance in the product evaluation process. Apart from the ability to interact with the 3D models, the dependencies of product components constitute a challenge in virtual prototyping. Due to the complexity of virtual products, systems have been developed which allow to handle these assembly dependencies and facilitate a collaborative product development process. Considering these assembly constraints in the prototyping phase is essential and has determined effects on the overall product performance and component alignment. Setting and testing the assembly features virtually bears the potential to identify difficulties in the interplay of components beforehand and thereby enhancing production efficiency [22]. In case that the assembly modelling is not well conducted, uncertainties occur that can lead to the failure of the overall product, for example in its function or size [23].

Virtual Collaboration. Often, several designers are included in the development of the same product, especially in the assembly of a product. Thus, concepts and tools are required to facilitate collaborative development. In [24], the authors describe basic characteristics for virtual collaboration environments: First, all assemblies should be designed as independent components, so that every developer can manipulate the object. Second, to avoid conflicts in the collaborative process, session manager systems are required that clarify which developer can access the model in which session. To extent this process not only to one developer team but to teams at different stages throughout the entire lifecycle of the product, the file format of the 3D model is essential [25] as well as creating an IT infrastructure that is able to communicate information about the 3D model [26, 27]. The file format must be accessible and modifiable by all involved parties and allow the transfer of the data. In turn, the comparability of file formats and the ability of data exchange between systems is tremendously important for the concept of virtual twins. The concept of the virtual twin goes beyond the initial product development process and aims on including the subsequent stages of the product lifecycle. Thereby, the product can be customized and modified after purchase. Often, the term virtual twin is used in combination with the term smart product which refers to the ability of the product to communicate its condition and other relevant information [28]. This allows for modifications of the product in use. However, these reconfiguration options are currently mainly limited to IT services since they can be added to existing hardware components by wireless connections and do not require a transportation of the product to a facility [28].

Virtual Fabrication. The 3D models designed in the collaborative virtual prototyping process are the basis to retrieve important information, such as the bill of materials or component functions, and to create repositories that provide these information for the fabrication of the product [29]. The production process can also be pretested in a virtual manner, i.e., by virtual fabrication. In [30], the virtual fabrication process is enhanced based on VR and AR technology. The technologies allow the users to work collaboratively on the 3D models meant for the production process and conduct a 3D model validation and verification directly at the shop floor. But 3D models are not only a medium to enhance the fabrication process of major firms. Today, the development in additive manufacturing systems enables even individual businesses and start-ups to manufacture their products based on a 3D design [31].

Virtual Product Experience. Apart from the ability to prototype and fabricate products based on 3D models, virtual objects can be the basis for product visualization and customization [32]. Based on software tools, users can change the design of a product, for example the color of a car, hence adjusting the product to their specific needs. However, the requirements for a 3D model used as a representation of the product, for example in an online shop, differ from the requirements of a 3D model used for in-house purposes. 3D models with the purpose of visualization and customization must be user friendly, provide design attributes and a high level of enjoyment [12]. A consideration of these characteristics leads to a positive attitude towards the website and presented product [12] and in turn towards the manufacturer or retailer offering the product. The virtual product experience is often divided in visual and functional control, while both have a positive effect on the perceived diagnostic and flow of consumers using online shopping environments [33]. In turn, the visual and functional control can be increased by AR. Seeing the virtual product in the real environment supports the user to make the right purchase decisions [34]. Recent VR based approaches even allow the developers to directly interact with the customer supported by sensory data to find perfectly fitting garments [35].

Virtual Customer Integration. But users can not only be considered as consumers but as an essential asset for the product creation process itself. Working with users to co-invent and innovate new products have become an established mechanism for manufacturing companies. The user can be included in all phases of the development process [36]. In early phases, the user mostly functions as a feedback mechanism for the design of the product. To facilitate the integrations of the user in the product development process, virtual interaction tools help users to articulate their product needs and transfer these information to the product development team [37, 38]. 3D Models are used in this stage as a less cost and time consuming alternative to show potential users a prototype of the product, to evaluate the functionality and usability of the product and to gather knowledge about the customers' purchase intention [39]. For the product assessment, user control and media richness are drivers for the immersion with the product [40]. Since VR can increase both factors, the technology is applied in user integration processes. In [41], VR is used in combination with physiological measurements, allowing the developers to capture the users emotional assessment of the virtual product design. In the same vein, [42] use VR to measure the user impressions of different design variants. However, relying on 3D models in this early stage is considered risky because even slight changes in the final product may affect the initial impression [39]. Apart from integrating the user for product testing, companies rely on online communities to gather new ideas for product design [43], or let the user customize and evaluate variants of the product [36].

3.2 Virtual World and Game Developers

Virtual Prototyping. Literature on the virtual good development processes of virtual world and game developers is sparse. Virtual goods are intangible, mostly 3D models, and only exist and have value in the virtual environment they have been created for or in [8, 44]. Thus, they cannot be transferred and used in other virtual worlds or games. Most research on virtual goods do not focus on the creation of the virtual good but rather on the purchase and consumption of even such or the occurrence and role of different types of virtual goods. However, two publications describe the creation process of virtual assets that can be used as virtual goods. In [45], the authors adapted the quality function deployment (QFD) method, mainly used in manufacturing for the development of new products, to derive a QFD suitable for the development of virtual items which can match the user needs with the characteristics of the virtual good. In [46], the creation process of virtual goods is described from a user perspective, i.e. the user as the creator of the good: The virtual world Second Life allows users to create and assembly products and object parameters. Apart from shape, color, and texture, the user can write scripts that define the functionality of the virtual good.

Virtual Production. Despite these two publications, most studies do not focus on the creation of the virtual good but rather on determinants that influence the purchase of the good, i.e., how the good must be produced to be consumed by the users. However, one's conclusion could be drawn from the implications of these studies. Amongst others, user engagement, both behavioral and psychological (such as game satisfaction, game customization, and social interaction), is identified as a key criterion that leads to increasing virtual good purchase [47]. In turn, game developers are advised to maintain engagement at a high level when they intend to gain significant revenue. This is in direct contradiction to how game developers often design their games based on the freemium business model: creating weak user experience to force the user to access additional content [10]. Besides user engagement, social aspects are one of the main drivers for in-game consumption. Virtual world and games are self-contained environments that bear social hierarchies which are to some extend comparable to reality from a consumption perspective. As for physical possession, having premium accounts and specific valuable virtual goods can lead both to social distinction and discrimination against users which have neither [48]. This can be intensively observed for cosmetic, or non-functional virtual goods which do not provide the player with a competitive advantage. Even though non-functional items have no competitive advantages, user express themselves through these goods, for example by decorating their virtual rooms or dressing their avatars [48]. These non-functional attributes gained relevance in the past years because cosmetic goods can today be considered as the main revenue stream for most free-to-play games [9].

Virtual Entrepreneurship and Customer Integration. The role of the user as creator or contributor to virtual good creation differs in virtual worlds and games. In virtual worlds, the user has the possibility to not only create both functional and non-functional virtual goods, but act as a virtual entrepreneur and sell the created goods directly to other participants in the virtual world. In most game environment, this is not the case. The approaches are defined in [49] as bazaar versus cathedral standard. The former facilitates the ability of the user not only to be involved in the creation but distribution process of the virtual goods, for example in Second Life, while the latter exclude the user from these processes, leading to markets governed by the provider, for example World of Warcraft. Based upon these results, the authors explicitly examine "virtual entrepreneurship" in the virtual worlds [50]: In virtual worlds, self-accomplishment or reputation and social features are the main drivers for a user to become a virtual entrepreneur. In addition, virtual entrepreneurship spurs the virtual economy in virtual worlds. In turn, the growing virtual economy is recognized by other users and lead to further endeavors to create own businesses in the environment. While the user thus can be the actual creator of a virtual good, the integration of the user in the creation process, is examined in [51]. In this study, user co-creation is the user's willingness to contribute to product development by sharing game experience in forums or cooperate with others, not by explicitly designing virtual objects themselves for the game environment. From the authors' perspective, the role of users shift from "passive consumers to active collaborators" ([51], p. 247).

4 Discussion and Implications

In this section, the findings from the literature review are synthesized and discussed, resulting in a preliminary model of product development processes and intermediate 3D models illustrated in Fig. 2. Three major findings can be derived from the discussion of the results: the holistic integration of 3D models in the product development process in the form of virtual assets, the gaining importance of the non-functional attributes of 3D models, and the increasing user involvement in the creation process.

4.1 Virtual Assets

First, literature suggests that 3D models are prevalent in the entire value chain of manufacturer and retail firms and virtual world and game developers. In the manufacturer and retail firm domain, concepts have been developed that allow for an entirely virtual product development process, from sketching to testing, evaluation and fabrication [6, 17, 21, 30]. Especially VR and AR based applications are utilized in the prototyping and fabrication phase to enhance the interaction with and the spatial perception of the product in development. The sketches and models from the prototyping and fabrication phase are thereby stored and exchanged based on digital platforms [26]. Hence, while the virtual sketches are the basis for the creation of virtual products (Fig. 2, M2), both virtual sketches and products can be considered as *virtual assets* [52] that can be used and adapted in different phases of the product development process (Fig. 2, M1, M3). Although no publication in the virtual world and game domain explicitly focusses on the prototyping process for virtual goods, the study on user created designs in virtual worlds provides insight in the creation process from a prosumer perspective [46]: As for manufacturers, virtual sketches and models are designed that can be considered as a virtual asset and adopted in subsequent steps of the prototyping and virtual production process (Fig. 2, V1, V3). But essentially, the virtual sketches are the basis for the creation of virtual objects that in turn can become virtual goods when they are integrated in the dedicated virtual environment (Fig. 2, V2, V4). By using VR and AR environments, manufacturers implicitly shift their product development to virtual environments, where the core competences of virtual worlds and game developers are essential: interactivity, usability, and user engagement [12]. Hence, a collaboration with virtual world and game developers or an adoption of product development methods from virtual world and game developers may foster the advantages that result from the application of the VR and AR in the manufacturers' product development processes. Vice versa, virtual worlds and game developers may adopt product development methods from manufacturers, as already examined in [45].

4.2 Non-functional Attributes

Second, both virtual products and virtual goods consist of non-functional (design) and functional (function) attributes that determine the production of the good, either in form of a physical process (Fig. 2, M4) or an integration of the good in a specific virtual environment (Fig. 2, V4). In both domains, the appearance, thus the non-functional attributes of the 3D model, is of increasing relevance. While virtual world and game developers concentrated on functional attribute for virtual goods to provide the player with a competitive advantage, gaining advantages by paying money is not welcomed by the majorities of players [8]. Hence, most virtual world and game developers today generate revenues by selling non-functional goods to address consumption mechanisms inherent to physical goods, for example social distinction and hedonic motivation [48]. While manufacturing and retail firms draw on established methods to foster the consumption of their products, their need for non-functional attributes occurs due to the complexity of their virtual products. Since virtual products include complex components and material attributes to allow the simulation, testing or virtual fabrication of the physical product, virtual products are mostly not of use for virtual environments or virtual product experiences. The 3D models must be down-sampled by neglecting specific components of the model or displaying them in a simplified way with adjusted functionalities (e.g., as in [53]). Hence, the non-functional attributes of the product need to be completely redesigned. Given that most manufacturers and retails offer a multitude of products, this process is considered as time and resource consuming. Since these 3D models are replicas of virtual products with considerably different characteristics, they are described in this study as *virtual product replica* [52] (Fig. 2, M5). These virtual product replicas can be adopted as virtual assets for manufacturing and retail firms since they can be used throughout the entire product development process if needed (Fig. 2, M6). Due to the expertise of manufacturers and retail firms regarding the consumption of consumer products, methods may be transferred from manufacturing and retailer domain to the virtual world and game developer domain to foster virtual good purchase. Vice versa, virtual world and game developers draw on methods to specifically prepare 3D models for the usage in virtual environment that might be transferred to the manufacturer and retail firm domain. In both domains, technical artists or design studios

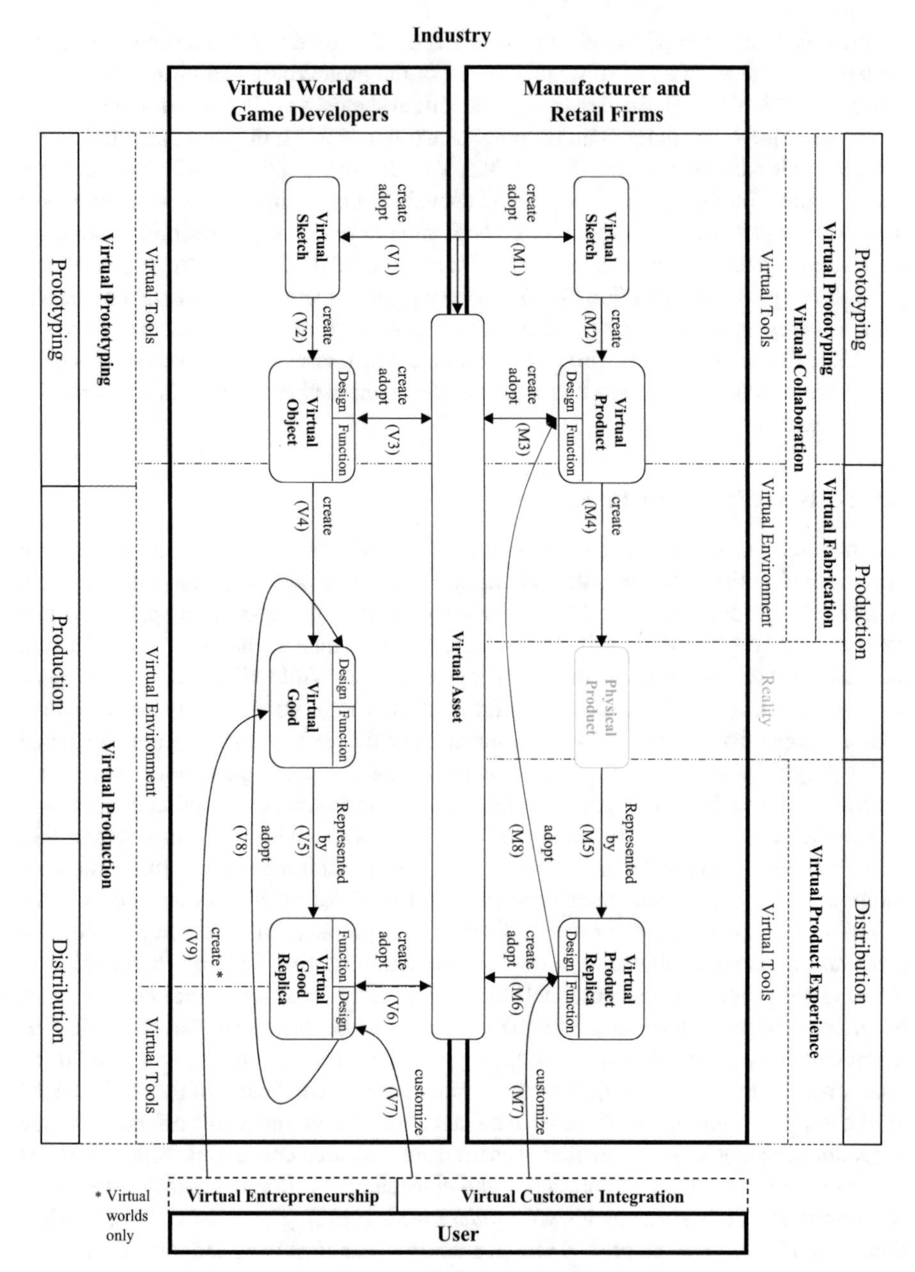

Fig. 2. Product development processes and intermediate 3D models (own figure).

may be required to create non-functional attributes and goods which offers a business opportunity for companies focusing on the creation of even such.

4.3 User Integration

Third, the role of the user changed from a passive customer to an active participator, also driven by the previously described need for non-functional attributes and goods. Both manufacturing and retail firms and virtual world and game developers use virtual tools to integrate the user in their product development processes (e.g., [38, 46]). As manufacturing and retail firms, virtual world and game developers provide replicas of the virtual goods used in the environments to allow the user a customization of the good. Since these replicas do not include all attributes of the virtual goods in the environment, i.e., functionality or textures and materials, these goods are defined as *virtual good replica* in this study which can be adopted by virtual world and game developers as virtual assets and used throughout the product development process (Fig. 2, V5, V6). The virtual good replicas empower the user to customize non-functional characteristics of the object for both virtual worlds and games. In game environments, the game provider is thereby taking mostly the part of the "producer". The production process is conducted by adapting user created, non-functional content and transferring the attributes to the in-game item (Fig. 2, V7, V8). An example for this process is the steam workshop environment which allows users to take part in challenges with the purpose to create non-functional designs (skins) for weapons [54]. The challenge winning skins are afterwards adapted by the game developer for the virtual good. In some virtual worlds, however, the user can act as the creator of the entire virtual good, thus define both functional and non-functional characteristics [46] (Fig. 2, V9). Hence, the user can either create both functional and non-functional attributes of a good inside the dedicated virtual environment or create non-functional attributes of the good outside the virtual environment by using a virtual tool. Manufacturers and retail firms on the other hand use 3D models to provide users with a virtual product experience and allow them to customize the product they intend to buy (Fig. 2, M7, M8). For the virtual product experience, the virtual product replica should correspond with the characteristics known from the virtual world and game developer domain, i.e., user friendliness, user friendly and an enjoyment [12]. Differences between both domains occur due to the specific environments the goods are produced and used in: While virtual goods are produced and used in the virtual environment, manufacturers are required to produce the good physically. Hence, the 3D models are information carrier and recorder that contain necessary manufacturing information. Due to the current developments in additive manufacturing [31], users might be enabled to create entire products and relying on manufacturing firms solely as contractors for the production process. But to date, users can not create and produce entire physical products in cooperation with manufacturers as it is possible in virtual world environments.

5 Limitations and Future Research

The limitations of the study stem from the methodological approach and the analysis of the results. First, conference proceedings were not included in the literature search and selection process. The inclusion of high-quality conference proceeding may not only strengthen the results of the study but provide a better understanding of current research. While the methodological approach does not require the inclusion of conference proceedings, an extension of the study with conference proceedings might be considered in future research. Second, the analysis and interpretation of the results were conducted by a single author. Although the findings were discussed with other researchers, the results remain subjective. Third, since no research was identified that considers the in-house processes of virtual world and game developers, the findings regarding the creation process rely on publications that describe the creation from a user perspective. However, since the results stem from virtual worlds that allow the users to use the scripting environment of the virtual world for the creation of the goods, the processes provide an understanding of how the in-house development process of the corresponding development team might be established.

Due to the sparse research on the creation process of virtual goods, future research may focus on the analysis of these processes based on case studies or expert interviews. Especially the mechanisms and approaches to integrate the user as a customizer or creator of virtual goods constitute an interesting research avenue because the degree of integration may influence the business model of virtual world and game developers. The user as an independent creator and producer of virtual goods in the environment, also in games, may bear a user-based business model that focus revenue share rather than a one-sided producer-dominated market. For research on manufacturers and retail firms, product development processes may be reconsidered. Virtual product replicas meant for virtual product experience and virtual customer integration seem to have more similarities with the 3D models used in the prototyping stage than the rather complex virtual product. Thus, research may focus on the characteristics 3D models considered for prototyping and if they can serve as objects for user integration and virtual product experience. In addition, less research analyzes the interdependencies and knowledge exchange between the manufacturer and retail firm and the virtual world and game developer domain which may lead to the transfer of theory and methods. In the same vein, virtual assets at the intersection of manufacturer and retail firms and virtual world and game developers are not considered in the identified literature. Although public markets exist which offer virtual assets (e.g., [55, 56]), these platforms are largely unexplored. Lastly, the derived product development process model in Fig. 2 is the first model that considers both domains, the dependencies of the corresponding virtual objects and intermediate 3D models. However, the preliminary model needs to be validated and extended by practical empiricism and case studies with companies from both domains.

References

1. Remondino, F., El-Hakim, S.: Image-based 3D modelling: a review. Photogram. Rec. **21**, 269–291 (2006)
2. Schreer, O., et al.: Lessons learned during one year of commercial volumetric video production. SMPTE Motion Imag. J. **129**, 31–37 (2020)
3. Scopigno, R., et al.: 3D models for cultural heritage: beyond plain visualization. Computer **44**, 48–55 (2011)

4. Rengier, F., et al.: 3D printing based on imaging data: review of medical applications. Int. J. Comput. Assist. Radiol. Surg. **5**, 335–341 (2010)
5. Bouchlaghem, D., Shang, H., Whyte, J., Ganah, A.: Visualisation in architecture, engineering and construction (AEC). Autom. Constr. **14**, 287–295 (2005)
6. Pfouga, A., Stjepandić, J.: Leveraging 3D CAD data in product life cycle: exchange – visualization – collaboration. In: Curran, R., Wognum, N., Borsato, M., Stjepandić, J., Verhagen, Wim, J. C. (eds.) Transdisciplinary Lifecycle Analysis of Systems, pp. 575–584. IOS Press BV, Amsterdam (2015)
7. Zhu, D.H., Chang, Y.P.: Effects of interactions and product information on initial purchase intention in product placement in social games: the moderating role of product familiarity. J. Electron. Commer. Res. **16**, 22–33 (2015)
8. Hamari, J., Keronen, L.: Why do people buy virtual goods: a meta-analysis. Comput. Hum. Behav. **71**, 59–69 (2017)
9. Marder, B., Gattig, D., Collins, E., Pitt, L., Kietzmann, J., Erz, A.: The Avatar's new clothes: understanding why players purchase non-functional items in free-to-play games. Comput. Hum. Behav. **91**, 72–83 (2019)
10. Heimo, O.I., Harviainen, J.T., Kimppa, K.K., Mäkilä, T.: Virtual to virtuous money: a virtue ethics perspective on video game business logic. J. Bus. Ethics **153**(1), 95–103 (2016). https://doi.org/10.1007/s10551-016-3408-z
11. newzoo: 2020 Global Games Market Per Device & Segment. https://newzoo.com/key-numbers. Accessed 10 Nov 2020
12. Algharabat, R., Abdallah Alalwan, A., Rana, N.P., Dwivedi, Y.K.: Three dimensional product presentation quality antecedents and their consequences for online retailers: the moderating role of virtual product experience. J. Retail. Consum. Serv. **36**, 203–217 (2017)
13. Bao, J.S., Jin, Y., Gu, M.Q., Yan, J.Q., Ma, D.Z.: Immersive virtual product development. J. Mater. Process. Technol. **129**, 592–596 (2002)
14. Stark, R., Israel, J.H., Wöhler, T.: Towards hybrid modelling environments - merging desktop-CAD and virtual reality-technologies. CIRP Ann. **59**, 179–182 (2010)
15. Webster, J., Watson, R.T.: Analyzing the past to prepare for the future: writing a literature review. MIS Q. **26**, xiii–xxiii (2002)
16. Bordegoni, M., Colombo, G., Formentini, L.: Haptic technologies for the conceptual and validation phases of product design. Comput. Graph. **30**, 377–390 (2006)
17. Israel, J.H., Wiese, E., Mateescu, M., Zöllner, C., Stark, R.: Investigating three-dimensional sketching for early conceptual design - Results from expert discussions and user studies. Comput. Graph. **33**, 462–473 (2009)
18. Makris, S., Rentzos, L., Pintzos, G., Mavrikios, D., Chryssolouris, G.: Semantic-based taxonomy for immersive product design using VR techniques. CIRP Ann. **61**, 147–150 (2012)
19. Park, H., Son, J.-S., Lee, K.-H.: Design evaluation of digital consumer products using virtual reality-based functional behaviour simulation. J. Eng. Des. **19**, 359–375 (2008)
20. Teklemariam, H.G., Das, A.K.: A case study of phantom Omni force feedback device for virtual product design. Int J. Interact. Des. Manuf. **11**(4), 881–892 (2015). https://doi.org/10.1007/s12008-015-0274-3
21. Park, H., Moon, H.-C.: Design evaluation of information appliances using augmented reality-based tangible interaction. Comput. Ind. **64**, 854–868 (2013)
22. Choi, A.C.K., Chan, D.S.K., Yuen, A.M.F.: Application of virtual assembly tools for improving product design. Int. J. Adv. Manuf. Technol. **19**, 377–383 (2002)
23. Heimrich, F., Anderl, R.: Approach for the Visualization of geometric uncertainty of assemblies in CAD-systems. J. Comput. **11**, 247–257 (2016)
24. Rosenman, M., Wang, F.: A component agent based open CAD system for collaborative design. Autom. Constr. **10**, 383–397 (2001)

25. Pfouga, A., Stjepandić, J.: Leveraging 3D geometric knowledge in the product lifecycle based on industrial standards. J. Comput. Des. Eng. **5**, 54–67 (2018)
26. Xiao, S., Xudong, C., Li, Z., Guanghong, G.: Modeling framework for product lifecycle information. Simul. Model. Pract. Theory **18**, 1080–1091 (2010)
27. Zhang, H., Wang, H., Chen, D., Zacharewicz, G.: A model-driven approach to multidisciplinary collaborative simulation for virtual product development. Adv. Eng. Inform. **24**, 167–179 (2010)
28. Abramovici, M., Göbel, J.C., Savarino, P.: Reconfiguration of smart products during their use phase based on virtual product twins. CIRP Ann. **66**, 165–168 (2017)
29. Bohm, M.R., Stone, R.B., Szykman, S.: Enhancing Virtual product representations for advanced design repository systems. J. Comput. Inf. Sci. Eng. **5**, 360–372 (2005)
30. Dangelmaier, W., Fischer, M., Gausemeier, J., Grafe, M., Matysczok, C., Mueck, B.: Virtual and augmented reality support for discrete manufacturing system simulation. Comput. Ind. **56**, 371–383 (2005)
31. Kang, H.S., Noh, S.D., Son, J.Y., Kim, H., Park, J.H., Lee, J.Y.: The FaaS system using additive manufacturing for personalized production. Rapid Prototyp. J. **24**, 1486–1499 (2018)
32. Olsen, K.A., Saetre, P.: Managing product variability by virtual products. Int. J. Prod. Res. **35**, 2093–2108 (1997)
33. Jiang, Z., Benbasat, I.: Virtual product experience: effects of visual and functional control of products on perceived diagnosticity and flow in electronic shopping. J. Manag. Inf. Syst. **21**, 111–147 (2004)
34. Lu, Y., Smith, S.: Augmented reality E-commerce system: a case study. J. Comput. Inf. Sci. Eng. **10**, 21005 (2010)
35. Tao, X., Chen, X., Zeng, X., Koehl, L.: A customized garment collaborative design process by using virtual reality and sensory evaluation on garment fit. Comput. Ind. Eng. **115**, 683–695 (2018)
36. Dahan, E., Hauser, J.R.: The virtual customer. J. Prod. Innov. Manag. **19**, 332–353 (2002)
37. Füller, J., Matzler, K.: Virtual product experience and customer participation - a chance for customer-centred, really new products. Technovation **27**, 378–387 (2007)
38. von Hippel, E., Katz, R.: Shifting innovation to users via toolkits. Manage. Sci. **48**, 821–833 (2002)
39. Artacho, M.A., Ballester, A., Alcántara, E.: Analysis of the impact of slight changes in product formal attributes on user's emotions and configuration of an emotional space for successful design. J. Eng. Des. **21**, 693–705 (2010)
40. Klein, L.R.: Creating virtual product experiences: the role of telepresence. J. Interact. Mark. **17**, 41–55 (2003)
41. Katicic, J., Häfner, P., Ovtcharova, J.: Methodology for emotional assessment of product design by customers in virtual reality. Presence Teleoper. Virt. Environ. **24**, 62–73 (2015)
42. Kim, C., Lee, C., Lehto, M.R., Yun, M.H.: Affective evaluation of user impressions using virtual product prototyping. Hum. Fact. Ergon. Manuf. Serv. Ind. **21**, 1–13 (2011)
43. Bugshan, H.: Co-innovation: the role of online communities. J. Strateg. Mark. **23**, 175–186 (2015)
44. Fairfield, J.A.T.: Virtual property. Buston Univ. Law Rev. **85**, 1047–1102 (2005)
45. Li, S.G., Kuo, X.: The enhanced quality function deployment for developing virtual items in massive multiplayer online role playing games. Comput. Ind. Eng. **53**, 628–641 (2007)
46. Varajão, J., Morgado, L.: Potential of virtual worlds for marketing tests of product prototypes. J. Text. Inst. **103**, 960–967 (2012)
47. Cheung, C.M.K., Shen, X.-L., Lee, Z.W.Y., Chan, T.K.H.: Promoting sales of online games through customer engagement. Electron. Commer. Res. Appl. **14**, 241–250 (2015)

48. Mäntymäki, M., Salo, J.: Why do teens spend real money in virtual worlds? A consumption values and developmental psychology perspective on virtual consumption. Int. J. Inf. Manage. **35**, 124–134 (2015)
49. Jung, Y., Pawlowski, S.D.: Virtual goods, real goals: exploring means-end goal structures of consumers in social virtual worlds. Inf. Manag. **51**, 520–531 (2014)
50. Jung, Y., Pawlowski, S.: The meaning of virtual entrepreneurship in social virtual worlds. Telemat. Inform. **32**, 193–203 (2015)
51. Wu, S.-L., Hsu, C.-P.: Role of authenticity in massively multiplayer online role playing games (MMORPGs): determinants of virtual item purchase intention. J. Bus. Res. **92**, 242–249 (2018)
52. Korbel, J.J., Blankenhagel, K.J., Zarnekow, R.: The role of the virtual asset in the distribution of goods and products. In: AIS (ed.) Proceedings of the 25th Americas Conference on Information Systems (AMCIS) (2019)
53. Lee, K.H., Woo, H., Suk, T.: Data reduction methods for reverse engineering. Int. J. Adv. Manuf. Technol. **17**, 735–743 (2001)
54. Steam: Steam Workshop. https://steamcommunity.com/workshop/about/?appid=730. Accessed 3 Dec 2020
55. Turbosquid: Turbosquid. https://www.turbosquid.com. Accessed 3 Dec 2020
56. CGTrader: CGTrader. https://www.cgtrader.com. Accessed 2 Dec 2020

Designing a Decision Support Tool to Improve the Recylability of Plastic Products

Tobias Prätori(✉), Norman Pytel, and Axel Winkelmann

Chair of Business Administration and Information Systems,
University of Würzburg, Würzburg, Germany
{tobias.pratori,norman.pytel,axel.winkelmann}@uni-wuerzburg.de

Abstract. The scarcity of resources means that recycling is becoming increasingly important to minimize environmental damage and to compete in the global marketplace. However, recycling rates are still relatively low, especially for plastic products. This is mainly because there is an information gap between the product design and end-of-life phases. We want to develop a decision support tool that provides the designers of plastic products with important information and supports design decisions based on ecological, but also economical and functional criteria. To achieve this, we apply a design science research approach and rely mainly on expert interviews results.

Keywords: Decision support · Recycling · Plastics · Circular economy · Product design · Design science research

1 Motivation

Due to the scarcity of resources, both demand and competition for critical raw materials will continue to increase [1]. A possible strategy to solve this problem is a more efficient use of resources. The EU proposes a circular economy, which, in contrast to traditional linear models, does not assume that resources are abundant. Recycling in particular is an important pillar for closing the cycle [1, 2]. Although plastics are omnipresent in our lives, plastic products' recycling potential, unlike metals, paper, or glass, has hardly been exploited [3]. The rates for landfill and thermal incineration of plastic waste are still high. This leads to a variety of negative effects for us and our environment, such as increased CO_2 emissions or marine pollution [3, 4].

The product design phase is especially crucial in the context of the circular economy since the production processes and materials are defined in this stage [5]. These two factors significantly influence how easy it is to disassemble products into their components [2]. However, product developers often lack the specific knowledge that recyclers have [6–8]. To close this gap, we want to develop a digital decision support tool that provides designers of plastic products with important information about their recyclability.

F. Ahlemann et al. (Eds.): WI 2021, LNISO 46, pp. 508–513, 2021.
https://doi.org/10.1007/978-3-030-86790-4_34

2 Related Work

In recent years, several technologies have become established that can enable CE-related decision support. Pagoropoulos et al. [9] identified three architectural layers in which digital technologies can be classified: Data collection, Data integration, and Data analysis. There are various scenarios in which technologies such as Radio Frequency Identification (RFID) and Internet of Things (IoT) are used to collect data to support CE. For example, RFID chips could be used to obtain complete information about the entire life cycle of products and thus enable a closed-loop supply chain [10, 11]. Furthermore, IoT sensors could be used to collect a variety of data on interconnected objects and machines for subsequent analysis [12, 13]. Breakthroughs in areas such as hardware and algorithms also open up promising new possibilities for data analysis [14]. In the past, for example, methods and tools from the field of artificial intelligence were used to promote CE through decision support [12, 15]. Besides the collection and analysis of data, the integration of information plays an important role [13]. Data usually comes from heterogeneous sources, such as sensors, Enterprise Resource Planning (ERP), or Manufacturing Execution Systems.

Several authors developed tools to support decision making in the context of CE, with processes within the supply chain that can be tracked and evaluated. Mboli et al. [16] devolped a decision support system that uses a semantic ontological model to track, monitor and analyze products in real time with the focus on residual value and applied the model in a real-word use case to demonstrate its viability. Lechner and Reimannn [17] built on a case study and presented a non-linear optimization model to support decision-making in reverse logistics. Kinoshita et al. [18] proposed a decision support model of environmentally friendly and economical material strategy for life cycle cost and recyclable weight. The authors used a goal programming approach to solve the underlying multi-criteria decision problems and a case study to analyze environmental and economic aspects among procurement, assembly, and recycling.

In the past, several decision support tools were also introduced that directly address the recycling process. Irie and Yamada [19] introduced a decision support model to support product disassembly to recover material carbon. They extract the bill of materials and then use 0–1 integer programming to determine if the material should be recycled or disposed of. Li et al. [20] performed a multi-criteria assessment of robotic disassembly. The developed decision support tool can compare the results from different recycling scenarios based on environmental, technological, and economical assessment criteria. Yu et al. [21] employed a fuzzy comprehensive evaluation and an analytic hierarchy process (AHP) approach to enable decision support for selecting an optimal method of recycling waste tire rubber. Paraskevas et al. [22] developed a Monte Carlo-based decision support tool to evaluate resource efficiency of secondary aluminium production. The tool identifies all feasible compositions of metal streams prior to remelting and quantifies the environmental effects.

Although some progress has been made in the past regarding decision support in the CE context, the low recycling rate of plastic products is still a problem that has not yet been adequately addressed.

3 Research Objective and Proposed Methodology

Our research objective is to increase the recyclability of plastic products. We want to achieve this by providing product developers with a decision support tool to bridge the gap between design and end-of-life phase. In this context, we aim to investigate the following research question:

RQ: How should a decision support tool for the development of plastic products be designed?

To answer this research question, we intend to design the decision support tool as an IT artifact. We employ a design research approach, as proposed by Henver et al. [23]. The authors proposed a conceptual framework for executing and evaluating Information Systems (IS) research. Following Hevner et al. the research relevance is assured by addressing the needs from the environment and the rigor by drawing from the knowledge base. The environment consists of three main components: people, organizations, and technology [23, 24]. Our research involves multiple stakeholders within companies. In addition to the main stakeholders, the product developers or designers, other functions such as procurement, production, sales and related information systems are also affected. The stakeholder's demands are influenced by personal factors and organizational factors as well as by technological factors. The knowledge base contains foundations like theories methods as well as methodologies like data analysis techniques.

4 Initial Results

To define an initial list of requirements, we held several preliminary interviews with recycling and plastic industry experts. From this, we could already derive first requirements (see Table 1).

Table 1. Initial design features

No.	Feature
1	Data export from enterprise systems
2	Offer intuitive UI with high usability
3	Calculation of relevant ecological, economic and functional measures
4	Prioritization of the measures by the product developer
5	Comparison of the alternatives based on the multiple criterias
6	Feedback on product designs and suggestions for improvement
7	Data import to enterprise systems

To ensure the tools's usability, it must be integrated into an existing IT infrastructure and into existing business processes. For example, it must be possible to export existing bills of material from ERP systems to use them in the tool. A user interface (UI) characterized by a high degree of usability serves to integrate the tool into routine operation. It must then be possible to use the results of the tool in other systems. Furthermore, the tool must be able to calculate various measures. In addition to ecological factors such as the CO2 index and recyclability, importance must also be attached to the product's functionality and cost-effectiveness. The developer must be able to prioritize these indicators so that the tool can show him the best alternatives according to his needs. In addition, the tool should be able to provide feedback to the designer on how to optimize the design with regard to its criteria.

The consideration of several factors results in a multi-criteria decision problem. To solve this complex problem, algorithms from the field of Multicriteria Decision Making (MCDM) are implemented. There is a variety of MCDM methods that differ in terms of required data, their mathematical properties, and other characteristics [25]. To make a pre-selection for the actual implementation in the decision support tool, a preliminary literature analysis of MCDM methods was first carried out. Three criteria were considered: user-friendliness, data input and output, and potential application areas. Thus, we have identified three procedures that are considered for the actual implementation during further research: Technique for Order Preference by similarity to Ideal Solutions (TOPSIS) [26], Preference Ranking Organization METHod for Enrichment of Evaluations (PROMETHEE) [27] and Analytical Hierarchy Process (AHP) [28].

5 Outlook and Contribution

A literature analysis serves as a starting point for our further research. In this way, we want to conceptualize previous academic work in the context of decision support to enable ecological product design. To gain further practical insights into stakeholder demands, we conduct qualitative expert interviews. The experts are either directly product designers, decision-makers in companies that manufacture plastic products, act as consultants or multipliers in the plastic industry, or are know-how carriers in the recycling industry. Through these interviews, we want to gain insights into typical processes in plastics companies and get an overview of the typical IT system landscape within those companies. Since the design process is inherently iterative, the evaluation of the decision support tool will also be iterative [24]. For this purpose, the requirements are continuously compared with the implemented features and evaluated by the experts.

With the decision support tool we propose, it is possible to provide crucial ecological information already during the product development process. This makes it possible to design plastic products so that they can be more easily recycled. Furthermore, it is possible to transfer defined design principles to other use cases, making it possible to address a wide range of companies and industries. In this way, we can make an essential contribution to the implementation of a circular economy.

Acknowledgements. This work has been developed in the project DIMOP. DIMOP is part of the project ForCycle II which is funded by the Bavarian State Ministry of the Environment and Consumer Protection. The authors are responsible for the content of this publication.

References

1. European Commission: A Zero Waste Programme for Europe. Brussels (2014)
2. European Commission: Closing the Loop - An EU Action Plan for the Circular Economy. Brussels (2015)
3. European Commission: A European Strategy for Plastics in a Circular Economy. Brussels (2018)
4. Ellen MacArthur Foundation: The New Plastics Economy (2016)
5. Mesa, J., González-Quiroga, A., Maury, H.: Developing an indicator for material selection based on durability and environmental footprint: a circular economy perspective. Resources. Conserv. Recycl. **160**, 104887 (2020)
6. Poudelet, V., Chayer, J.-A., Margni, M., Pellerin, R., Samson, R.: A process-based approach to operationalize life cycle assessment through the development of an eco-design decision-support system. J. Clean. Prod. **33**, 192–201 (2012)
7. Favi, C., Germani, M., Mandolini, M., Marconi, M.: Includes knowledge of dismantling centers in the early design phase: a knowledge-based design for disassembly approach. In: Proceedings of the 23rd CIRP Conference on Life Cycle Enineering, pp. 401–406 (2016)
8. Romli, A., Prickett, P., Setchi, R., Soe, S.: Integrated eco-design decision-making for sustainable product development. Int. J. Prod. Res. **53**(2), 549–571 (2015)
9. Pagoropoulous, A., Pigosso, D.C.A., McAloone, T.C.: The emergent role of digital technologies in the circular economy: a review. In: Proceedings of the 9th CIRP IPSS Conference: Circular Perspectives on Product/Service-Systems, pp. 19–24 (2017)
10. Govindan, K., Soleimani, H., Kannan, D.: Reverse logistics and closed-loop supply chain: a comprehensive review to explore the future. Eur. J. Oper. Res. **240**(3), 603–626 (2015)
11. Jayaraman, V., Ross, A.D., Agarwal, A.: Role of information technology and collaboration in reverse logistics supply chains. Int. J. Log. Res. Appl. **11**(6), 409–425 (2008)
12. Reuter, M.A.: Digitalizing the circular economy. Metall. and Mater. Trans. B **47**(6), 3194–3220 (2016)
13. Salminen, V., Ruohamaa, H., Kantola, J.: Digitalization and big data supporting responsible business co-evolution. In: Advances in Human Factors, Business Management, Training and Education, pp. 1055–1067 (2017)
14. Moreno, M., Charnley. F.: Can re-distributed manufacturing and digital intelligence enable a regenerative economy? An integrative literature review. In: International Conference on Sutainable Design and Manufacturing, pp. 563–575 (2016)
15. Rojek, I., Dostatni, E.: Machine learning methods for optimal compatibility of materials in ecodesign. Bull. Polish Acad. Sci.Tech. Sci. **68**(2), 199–206 (2020)
16. Mboli, J.S., Thakker, D., Mishra, J.L.: An Internet of Things-enabled decision support system for circular economy business model. Softw. Pract. Exp. pp. 1–16 (2020)
17. Lechner, G., Reimann, M.: Integrated decision-making in reverse logistics: an optimization of interacting acquisition, grading and disposition processes. Int. J. Prod. Res. 1–20 (2019)
18. Kinoshita, Y., Yamada, T., Gupta, S.M., Ishigaki, A., Inoue, M.: Decision support model of environmentally friendly and economical material strategy for life cycle cost and recyclable weight. Int. J. Prod. Econ. **244**, 107545 (2020)
19. Yamada, T., Irie, H.: Decision support model for economical material carbon recovery and reduction by connecting supplier and dissassembly part selections. J. Adv. Mech. Des. Syst. Manuf. **14**(2), JAMDSM0024–JAMDSM0024 (2020)
20. Li, J., Barwood, M., Rahimifard, S.: A multi-criteria assessment of robotic disassembly to support recycling and recovery. Resour. Conserv. Recycl. **140**, 158–165 (2019)
21. Yu, H., et al: Decision support for selecting optimal method of recycling waste tire rubber into wax-based warm mix asphalt based on fuzzy comprehensive evaluation. J. Clean. Prod. **265**, 121781 (2020)

22. Paraskevas, D., Ingarao, G., Deng, Y., Duflou, J.R., Pontikes, Y., Blanpain, B.: Evaluating the material source efficiency of secondary aluminium production: a Monte Carlo-based decision-support tool. J. Clean. Prod. **215**, 488–496 (2019)
23. Hevner, A.R., Salvatore, T.M., Park, J., Ram, S.: Design science in information systems research. MIS Q. **28**(1), 75–105 (2004)
24. Silver, M.S., Markus, M.L., Beath, C.M.: The information technology interaction model: a foundation for the MBA core course. MIS Q. **19**(3), 361–390 (1995)
25. Zavadskas, E.K., Turskus, Z.: A preference ranking organisation method (The PROMETHEE method for multiple criteria decision-making). Technol. Econ. Dev. Econ. **17**(2), 397–427 (2011)
26. Hwang, C.L., Yoon, K.: Multiple Attribute Decision Making: Methods and Applications. Springer, New York (1981)
27. Brans, J.P., Vincke, P.: A preference ranking organisation method (The PROMETHEE method for multiple criteria decision-making). Manage. Sci. **31**(6), 647–656 (1985)
28. Saaty, T.L.: Multicriteria Decision Making - The Analytic Hierarchy Process. Planning, Priority Setting, Resource Allocation. RWS Publishing, Pittsburgh (1990)

Towards IoT Standards Interoperability: A Tool-Assisted Approach

Laurell Popp[1(✉)] and Melanie Schaller[2]

[1] Chair of Business Management and Business Information Systems, University of Würzburg, Würzburg, Germany
laurell.popp@uni-wuerzburg.de
[2] iNDTact GmbH, Würzburg, Germany
mschaller@indtact.de

Abstract. Internet of Things (IoT) applications and ecosystems rely on the integration of numerous sensors and devices. One of the challenges of integration is the broadness of standards and protocols used by the sensors. At the same time, systems generally only support a limited amount of protocols, essentially limiting the choice of sensors and devices for a given scenario. In this paper, we propose a research methodology for building a tool that acts as middleware between sensors and systems, translating standards while maintaining their respective advantages.

Keywords: Internet of Things · Messaging protocols · Standardization

1 Introduction

The IoT is understood as the concept of turning physical objects into smart objects by equipping them with computational intelligence and transmitters and connecting them to the internet [1]. Thus, IoT is not understood to be one specific technology, but rather as a concept which utilizes multiple technologies. One element of this concept is connectivity, which typically follows the TCP/IP reference model. As such, IoT connectivity typically consists of four layers: the link (e.g., ethernet), internet (e.g., IPv6), transport (e.g. TCP), and application (e.g. HTTP) layers [2, 3]. For IoT data exchange purposes, multiple messaging protocols, which are part of the application layer, are designed for several scenarios [4, 5]. Each standard serves a different set of requirements, making them advantageous in bandwidth, latency, and security for different sets of applications [4]. In many cases, practitioners cannot choose sensors or systems according to their advantages but rather if they can communicate by supporting the same messaging protocols. On the other hand, users may have to resort to using the "lowest common denominator" protocol, thus eliminating the advantages of specific messaging protocols.

In this paper, we explore the possibility of removing this problem using Peffers et al. Design Science Research (DSR) methodology [6] to build a tool conversing various messaging protocols while maintaining their respective advantages. In this context, we especially pay attention to future technologies such as 5G mobile radio standards and seek to preserve its benefits such as speed and latency reduction. Therefore, this work

F. Ahlemann et al. (Eds.): WI 2021, LNISO 46, pp. 514–518, 2021.
https://doi.org/10.1007/978-3-030-86790-4_35

is primarily beneficial for practitioners seeking to use the full advantages of messaging protocols without limiting sensor selection.

2 Related Work

To validate the problem and take note of the current state of research in the subject on hand, an exploratory, unstructured literature review was conducted, which is part of phase one of our proposed methodology (see next section).

Several publications analyzed IoT messaging standards in a structured manner. Jaikar and Iyer, as well as Naik, compared messaging standards by several factors, such as speed, latency, security, and transport protocols [4, 5]. Several authors identified the need to unify IoT applications, platforms, and ecosystems, some even referring to them as "silos of proprietary systems" [7]. The approach taken varies by use case and typically tries to enable interoperability between IoT platforms, architectures, ecosystems, messaging standards, or applications on a theoretical or practical level. Iglesias-Urkia and Casado-Mansilla integrated the CoAP messaging protocol and the theoretical standard IEC 61850 in the context of smart grids, thus mapping existing standards to a specific set of requirements laid out by a use case and the theoretical standard itself [8]. Kovacs et al. proposed an architecture for semantic interoperability using a limited set of international standards [9]. Desai et al. developed a semantic translation gateway for CoAP, MQTT, and HTTP protocols using a proxy architecture [7]. For sensing and actuation purposes, Yun et al. developed a platform that incorporates middleware programs for interoperability between the oneM2M standard and a set of other standards [10]. Zarko et al. developed a framework for the cooperation between IoT platforms on an organizational level by proposing so-called IoT platform federations and roaming IoT devices, where devices may switch between IoT platforms and interact with their respective resources [11]. Roth et al. proposed a framework for the interoperability between middleware platforms, thus enabling communication between smart environments [12]. Bandyopadhyay et al. identified and analyzed IoT reference architectures to build an understanding of the extend of interoperability of IoT standards [13]. Overall, these approaches are limited to a specific scenario or, in the case of Desai et al., to a limited set of messaging protocols. Our approach is not confined to a set of standards but instead tries to incorporate most of the currently used standards and thus enabling practitioners to be free in their choice of sensors or systems. In addition, none of the previous approaches paid attention to conserving specific advantages of certain standards, which is especially critical in cases where those advantages must be maintained, such as time-critical applications, for example, industrial wireless sensor networks [14].

3 Methodology

Our proposed methodology follows the DSR methodology introduced by Peffers et al. [6]. The goal of DSR in the field of business informatics is the creation and evaluation of artifacts of information technology to solve identified problems [15]. Thus, this article aims to propose an approach to address the issue at hand. In addition, we contribute to DSR in general by solving a practical problem. The DSR methodology proposed by

Peffers et al. consists of six steps, which are shown in Fig. 1. Each step is supplemented by the specific approach and the generated output. The steps will be described briefly with our proposed approaches for each phase.

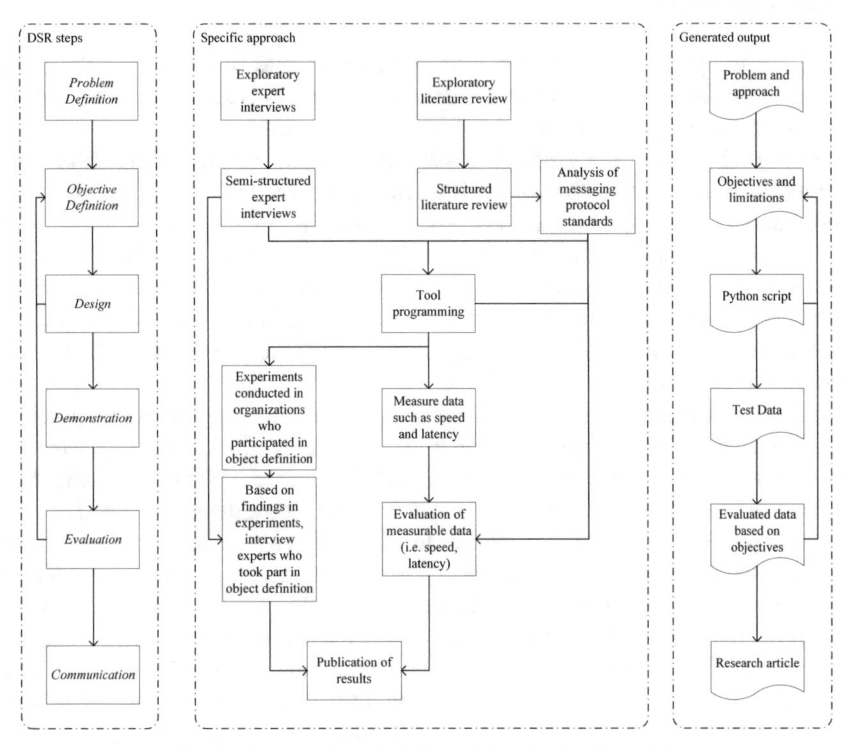

Fig. 1. Proposed methodology following Peffers et al.

Problem Definition: At first, we define the problem by conducting a literature review and expert interviews, targeting experts (such as managing directors, CTOs, or CEOs) of companies in the field of sensor, system or infrastructure design in IoT environments. Both the expert interviews and the literature review serve as a concretization of the problem by identifying cases from both theory and practice, in which messaging protocols hindered the effective development of IoT infrastructures.

Objective Definition: Using the survey conducted in the first stage as a pre-test, we will be able to develop a standardized questionnaire for semi-structured expert interviews concerning usage of messaging protocol standards in practice following the methodology of Bell et al. [16]. By doing so, we intend to identify requirements (for examples, refer to Chapter 4) from practice to define this research's objectives. The study targets approx. fifteen experts of companies in the field of sensor, system, or infrastructure design in IoT environments, thus reaching saturation of homogenous samples [17, 18]. Furthermore, by conducting a subsequent, structured literature review, we identify and analyze currently used messaging standards. This step will yield a list of standards, their respective strengths, characteristics, and use cases. Consequently, we intend to determine which standards are to be supported by the artifact, thus defining further design objectives. By combining both approaches, we intend to define the objectives and limitations of the artifact to be developed.

Design: As a consequence of steps one and two, we develop a tool to convert the most commonly used messaging protocol standards by fulfilling the design objectives.

Demonstration: Due to the design artifact, we will perform experiments within the organizations which participated in the expert interviews of step one and two, demonstrating the feasibility of our solution. By conducting field tests with the designed tool, we will measure data such as speed and latency for a variety of pre-defined scenarios.

Evaluation: To evaluate our artifact, we test it against our defined objectives. Participating interview partners will be asked to take part in an evaluation interview. In addition, the measured data itself will be evaluated by comparing the results to the direct implementation of the respective standards.

Communication: The results will be published as a research article, and the code of the tool will be made available to the public as open-source code.

4 Current Stage and Outlook

First and foremost, we conducted an exploratory literature review, which is part of step one of our proposed methodology. In addition, we conducted two exploratory interviews. During our literature review, we identified the most common messaging protocols, such as AMQP, MQTT, Websocket, and HTTP, their respective advantages and analyzed previous work concerning interoperability between IoT protocols and standards, which were briefly explained in Sect. 2. In addition, we conducted exploratory, unstructured interviews with two CEOs of IoT companies. Both interview partners confirmed the need for such a tool. One partner suggested the importance of upcoming 5G technology (especially its advantages in speed and latency [19]), and as such, 5G support while preserving its benefits will be one of the defined objectives, provided the structured interviews will confirm this need in phase two.

Furthermore, we targeted the Design step by choosing the programming language Python for the development of our artifact. Python was chosen due to its capability of running on SoC-hardware as well as its general hardware independence. Additionally, Python supports multiple encryption standards, offers an extensive library of packages, and enables rapid prototyping due to its characteristic of being an interpreted programming language [20, 21].

The next steps include the identification of common problems associated with IoT messaging standards selection as well as gathering additional information about the needs of practitioners through additional interviews as a baseline for our standardized questionnaire, thus completing the first step of our methodology.

References

1. Whitmore, A., Agarwal, A., Da Xu, L.: The Internet of things—a survey of topics and trends. Inf. Syst. Front. **17**, 261–274 (2015)
2. Braden, R.: Requirements for Internet hosts - communication layers. https://tools.ietf.org/html/rfc1122. Accessed 28 Aug 2020
3. Braden, R.: Requirements for Internet Hosts - Application and Support. https://tools.ietf.org/html/rfc1123. Accessed 28 Aug 2020
4. Naik, N.: Choice of effective messaging protocols for IoT systems: MQTT, CoAP, AMQP and HTTP. In: Presented at the 2017 IEEE International Systems Engineering Symposium (ISSE) (2017)
5. Jaikar, S.P., Iyer, K.R.: A survey of messaging protocols for IOT systems. Int. J. Adv Manag. Technol. Eng. Sci. **8**, 510–514 (2018)
6. Peffers, K., Tuunanen, T., Rothenberger, M.A., Chatterjee, S.: A design science research methodology for information systems research. J. Manag. Inf. Syst. **24**, 45–77 (2007)
7. Desai, P., Sheth, A., Anantharam, P.: Semantic gateway as a service architecture for IoT interoperability. In: Presented at the 2015 IEEE International Conference on Mobile Services (2015)
8. Iglesias-Urkia, M., Urbieta, A., Parra, J., Casado-Mansilla, D.: IEC 61850 meets CoAP: towards the integration of Smart Grids and IoT standards. In: Presented at the Proceedings of the Seventh International Conference on the Internet of Things (2017)
9. Kovacs, E., Bauer, M., Kim, J., Yun, J., Le Gall, F., Zhao, M.: Standards-based worldwide semantic interoperability for IoT. IEEE Commun. Mag. **54**, 40–46 (2016)
10. Yun, J., Ahn, I.-Y., Song, J., Kim, J.: Implementation of sensing and actuation capabilities for IoT devices using oneM2M platforms. Sensors **19**, 4567 (2019)
11. Zarko, I.P., et al.: Towards an IoT framework for semantic and organizational interoperability. In: Presented at the 2017 Global Internet of Things Summit (GIoTS) (2017)
12. Roth, F.M., Becker, C., Vega, G., Lalanda, P.: XWARE—a customizable interoperability framework for pervasive computing systems. Pervasive Mob. Comput. **47**, 13–30 (2018)
13. Bandyopadhyay, S., Balamuralidhar, P., Pal, A.: Interoperation among IoT standards. J. ICT Standard. **1**, 253–270 (2013)
14. Rondón, R., Gidlund, M., Landernäs, K.: Evaluating bluetooth low energy suitability for time-critical industrial IoT applications. Int. J. Wireless Inf. Netw. **24**, 278–290 (2017)
15. Hevner, A.R., March, S.T., Park, J., Ram, S.: Design science in information systems research. MIS Q. **28**, 75–105 (2004)
16. Bell, E., Bryman, A., Harley, B.: Business Research Methods. Oxford University Press, Oxford (2018)
17. Kuzel, A.J.: Sampling in qualitative inquiry. In: Doing Qualitative Research, pp. 31–44. Sage Publications, Inc., Thousand Oaks (1992)
18. Saunders, M.N.K., Lewis, P., Thornhill, A.: Research Methods for Business Students. Pearson, New York (2012)
19. Li, S., Da Xu, L., Zhao, S.: 5G Internet of Things: a survey. J. Ind. Inf. Integr. **10**, 1–9 (2018)
20. Kermarrec, F., Bourdeauducq, S., Badier, H., Le Lann, J.-C.: LiteX: an open-source SoC builder and library based on Migen Python DSL. In: Presented at the OSDA 2019, Colocated with DATE 2019 Design Automation and Test in Europe (2019)
21. Logaras, E., Manolakos, E.S.: SysPy: using python for processor-centric SoC design. In: Presented at the 2010 17th IEEE International Conference on Electronics, Circuits and Systems (2010)

Methods, Theories and Ethics in Business Informatics

Introduction to the WI2021 Track: Methods, Theories and Ethics in Information System Research

Björn Niehaves[1] and Sven Laumer[2]

[1] University of Siegen, Chair for Information Systems, Siegen, Germany
bjoern.niehaves@uni-siegen.de
[2] Friedrich-Alexander Universität Erlangen-Nürnberg, Schoeller Endowed Chair for Information Systems, Nürnberg, Germany
sven.laumer@fau.de

1 Track Description

Information System (IS) Research deals with unique questions and problems. In their specific context, the constant social and technological change requires scientists to critically reflect on the prerequisites and consequences of research paradigms and methods in our discipline. Furthermore, an increasing need arises to discuss ethical questions concerning research objectives and methods. This involves a continuous consideration of methodologies, concepts and theories of research to adapt to changing realities and ethical challenges. Against this background, it is essential for the IS discipline to regularly review all topics of its professional spectrum from a superordinate perspective. The WI2021 Track on Methods, Theories and Ethics in IS Research seeks to address this issue by providing a platform to discuss overarching objectives of research. Three research articles are part of this track and each one of them contributes a distinct perspective to studying this highly relevant phenomenon.

2 Research Articles

2.1 Design of Goal-Oriented Artifacts from Morphological Taxonomies: Progression from Descriptive to Prescriptive Design Knowledge (Frederik Moeller, Hendrik Hasse, Can Azkan, Hendrik van der Valk and Boris Otto)

In their paper, Moeller et al. introduce a framework to guide the transformation of descriptive knowledge about artifacts into design principles reflecting the artifact's objective and its mechanisms to fulfill its objective (i.a), i.e. prescriptive knowledge. Through their work, the authors propose a sound method to transfer meta-characteristics from empirical insights that are agglomerated in morphological taxonomies to practical requirements for design. Therefore, the theoretically derived framework of Moeller et al. contributes to the accumulation of prescriptive knowledge about an artifact by answering the question about how to design an artifact with a specific goal. In its essential contribution for design science research, the authors' framework promise exciting approaches for future research, including its practical application.

2.2 Ethical Design of Conversational Agents: Towards Principles for a Value-Sensitive Design (Thiemo Wambsganss, Anne Hoech, Naim Zierau and Matthias Soellner)

Taking into account the relevance of ethical considerations for the design of Conversational Agents (CA), Wambsganss et al. propose meta-requirements and design principles derived from an extensive analysis of literature and findings from qualitative interviews. By reshaping the interaction between human and technology through their AI-enabled design, CA gain high interest, but are likely to gain even more in the near future. However, through embodying human-like characteristics, these technologies are prone to design biases, e.g. by reproducing racism or stereotypes. Considering these ethical challenges, the authors provide design knowledge as a basis to apply a value-sensitive approach for CA. Therefore, the authors contribute to a highly relevant field of research.

2.3 On Your Mark, Ready, Search: A Framework for Structuring Literature Search Strategies in Information Systems (Thorsten Schoormann, Dennis Behrens, Michael Fellmann and Ralf Knackstedt)

Schoormann et al. provide a framework to counteract challenges regarding an essential step to contribute to the scientific discourse: creating a comprehensible fundament of knowledge to build one's own and future research on. Considering the increasing number of scientific publications, the specific, contextual nature of phenomena, and the intertwining of IS research with adjacent disciplines, the need for structured and transparent processes of systematic literature reviews grows. The authors contribute to this issue by developing a Search Canvas that reflects the understanding of essential components of a literature review. By providing a clear and understandable framework, this paper distinctly supports researchers to integrate their findings in the existent body of scientific knowledge and to overcome theoretical deficiencies of valuable insights.

Design of Goal-Oriented Artifacts from Morphological Taxonomies: Progression from Descriptive to Prescriptive Design Knowledge

Frederik Möller[1,2(✉)], Hendrik Haße[2], Can Azkan[2], Hendrik van der Valk[1], and Boris Otto[1,2]

[1] Chair for Industrial Information Management, TU Dortmund University, Dortmund, Germany
{Frederik.Moeller,Hendrik.van-der-valk}@tu-dortmund.de
[2] Fraunhofer ISST, Dortmund, Germany
{Frederik.Moeller,Hendrik.Hasse,Can.Azkan, Boris.Otto}@isst.fraunhofer.de

Abstract. Morphological Taxonomies are a widely popular tool in Information Systems to systematically deconstruct an artifact into designable dimensions and characteristics. Subsequently, these taxonomies have engraved in them knowledge about the design of artifacts, i.e., descriptive design knowledge. Most studies producing morphological taxonomies refrain from giving prescriptive advice about the design, i.e., the specific morphological configuration of an artifact, but rather stay descriptive. The paper proposes a framework for knowledge and artifact transformation originating in morphological taxonomies and ending in design principles. We develop a framework that assists researchers and practitioners by showing clear paths on transforming descriptive design knowledge engraved in taxonomies to prescriptive knowledge as design principles.

Keywords: Taxonomy · Design principle · Morphology · Design knowledge

1 Introduction

Accumulating prescriptive design knowledge is the chief purpose of *design science research* and a vehicle to ensure transferability of instance knowledge to additional application scenarios [1–4]. Design knowledge, *per se*, is "(…) knowledge that can be used in designing solutions to problems (…)" [5 p. 225] and diverges dichotomously between *descriptive* and *prescriptive* design knowledge [6, 7]. Descriptive design knowledge explains the "what," and prescriptive design knowledge the "how" in artifact design [7, 8]. While both kinds of design knowledge have merit, there is little research on transforming one into another. For example, [6, 9, 10] explain that the dominant transformation mechanism is the introduction of a *goal*, which presents a desirable goal that an artifact is supposed to fulfill. The study picks up from this point and illustrates knowledge transformation of two types of artifacts that are representations of either kind of knowledge,

F. Ahlemann et al. (Eds.): WI 2021, LNISO 46, pp. 523–538, 2021.
https://doi.org/10.1007/978-3-030-86790-4_36

namely morphological taxonomies (*descriptive design knowledge*) and design principles (*prescriptive design knowledge*) [6, 8].

Taxonomies are useful and widely used artifacts to structure a domain of knowledge [11]. In contrast to the conceptual, deductively derived *typology*, *taxonomies* are usually generated empirically [12, 13]. They are used to represent *descriptive knowledge* about a domain of interest or classify objects into categories [14] and can be the basis for analytic theory [15]. Frequently, researchers visualize taxonomies as morphological boxes [16, 17] that comprehensively, illustratively, and intuitively explain and visualize the form or shape (i.e., the design configuration of an artifact [18] or the *Gestalt*[1] [17, 20]) as combinations of design dimensions and design characteristics (e.g., see [21]). In the paper, if we address taxonomies, we mean morphological taxonomies that have a sound empirical basis and illustrate dimensions and characteristics morphologically (e.g., see [21] or [22]). Yet, most taxonomies refrain from advising on which configuration of dimensions and characteristics is better suited to achieve a particular goal [23] (e.g., see [24–27]). The lack of prescriptiveness is even more relevant, as one of the primary goals of design science is the accumulation of prescriptive design knowledge regarding the design of artifacts that achieve specific *goals* [4, 28, 29]. In terms of usefulness for practice, prescriptive guidelines provide instruction rather than mere description and are easier to instantiate [23]. For example, [30] find that only a few taxonomies recommend configurations of artifact design. A suitable tool to formulate, communicate, and codify prescriptive design knowledge for reuse in other instances other than that of their origin are design principles [31–33]. Thus, we ask ourselves whether these two types of artifacts (for that matter, design principles are a meta-artifact [34]) could be conceptually linked to cover a more comprehensive spectrum of design knowledge in artifact design.

Because of the above, we see the need for a framework that bridges that gap and supports researchers and practitioners to extend descriptive knowledge engraved in taxonomies into prescriptive knowledge formulated as design principles. Our paper addresses precisely that issue and aims to uncover how morphological taxonomies can be used to generate prescriptive knowledge about the design of an artifact. Because of the above, our paper pursues the following research objective:

Research Question (RQ): How can descriptive knowledge about an artifact (morphological taxonomies) be transformed into prescriptive knowledge about its design (design principles)?

To close the gap, we draw from the concept of descriptive and prescriptive design knowledge [7], which we will use to illustrate links between the constructs of both morphological taxonomies and design principles. Additionally, next to the transformation of the underlying knowledge, we will explain pathways to change from a generic description of an artifact to a goal-oriented target artifact.

Our paper is structured as follows. After the introduction, we explain the background to our work, i.e., foundations of morphological taxonomies and design principles. Subsequently, we will present our rationale for linking both artifact types by utilizing descriptive and prescriptive design knowledge. Afterward, we introduce specific steps that

[1] *Gestalt* refers to "(…) the arrangement and connectivity of parts of an objects, and how these conform to represent a whole (…)" [19 p. 7].

practitioners and researchers can follow to generate design principles from morphological taxonomies epistemologically sound. Lastly, we address contributions, limitations, and avenues for further research.

2 Background

2.1 Morphological Taxonomies

There are multiple ways to visualize taxonomies. Studies investigating taxonomic research in IS literature find various visualization options, for instance, *mathematical sets, hierarchies, matrices, visually,* or *textually* [30]. Each visualization option can be better suited for a specific task [16]. For example, hierarchies are well-suited to generate tree structure, which enables classification (e.g., see [35]), while mathematical sets have a high degree of formalization (e.g., see [36]). Lastly, researchers visualize taxonomies as morphologies, which are "(...) concerned with the structure and arrangement of parts of an object, and how these conform to create a whole Gestalt." [20 p. 793]. Figure 1 illustrates hierarchies and mathematical sets as visualization options for taxonomies.

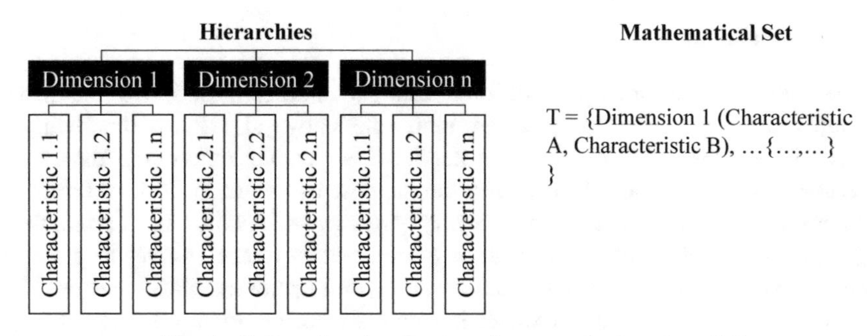

Fig. 1. Options for visualization of taxonomies based on [16].

As the study focuses on artifact design and morphological characteristics, we focus on those taxonomies derived empirically and visualized morphologically that give intuitive, visual aid in discerning central designable elements of an artifact, i.e., their *Gestalt* [17, 37]. In the paper, we consider designable dimensions, as they, rather than mandatory dimensions (e.g., see [38]), are potentials for choosing design options. Our understanding of design task-specific morphological taxonomies is best expressed through the notion of *design phenomenology*, which describes "(...) the study of the form and configuration of artifacts" [18 p. 8] and includes taxonomies [39]. That notion is especially useful as finding (supposedly useful or even optimal) design configurations (i.e., patterns) of artifacts is not a straightforward task but requires the exploration of design options, especially if the underlying problem is ill-structured rather than well-defined [40]. Finding design configurations is the quintessential task of a designer, i.e., to choose design options from a variety of possible alternatives [41]. Thus, morphologies are often used to represent sub-components of artifacts and reflect design configurations of design variables [23, 42] (see Fig. 2). Finding problem-solving combinations of these design dimensions lies at the heart of designing artifacts and is a "(…) game of combinatorics (…)" [41 p. 247]. In the case of taxonomies, for each dimension, there need to be at least two characteristics [43].

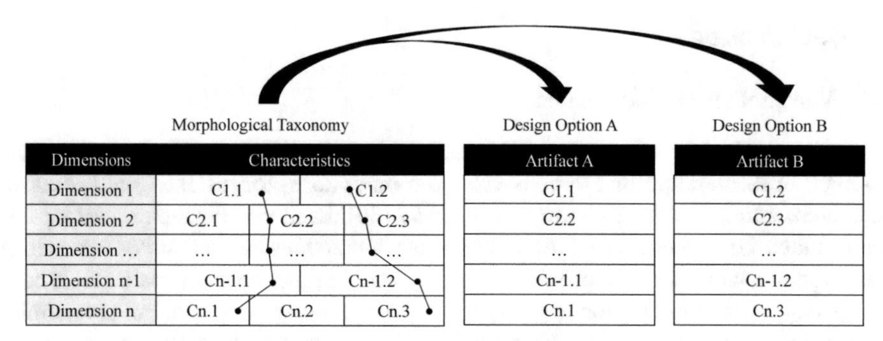

Fig. 2. Extracting design options from morphological descriptions of artifacts.

2.2 Design Principles

Quintessentially, design principles are formalized and codified prescriptive statements that support designers in realizing design more efficiently [31]. Rather than being a guarantee for success, they require, if instantiated, contextualization with the user's experience and the environment that they are supposed to work in [28]. In terms of theory, design principles belong to the category of *design and action*, which, rather than being explanatory, predictive, analytical, or a combination thereof, strives to produce meaning through accumulating and communicating *prescriptive design knowledge* [15]. The literature provides various templates to formulate design principles linguistically [44], e.g., see [31, 45]. An integral part of design principles is the formulation of prescriptive statements that guide the designer in instantiating the artifact [9, 31, 46]. Table 1 gives two examples of design principles.

Table 1. Examples of design principle formulation.

Design principle	Source
"Provide features for an (initial) assessment of a business model (element) to represent the current state and identify improvement potential."	[47 p. 6]
"Provide the system with the ability to query data from multiple sources, so users can retrieve a comprehensive sample, given that, in the specific search context, relevant contributions are scattered over different data source"	[48 p. 98]

3 Bridging the Gap Between Taxonomies and Design Principles

3.1 Domain Constructs

To start our investigation, we first clarify relevant constructs that constitute both artifact types. Table 2 gives descriptions of the constructs that are relevant to link both artifacts types conceptually. In *design science research*, constructs are the conceptualization and shared language of a specific domain [49]. As there is no standard set of constructs in both fields, we draw from established literature.

Table 2. Domain constructs of taxonomies and design principles tailored to artifacts.

Artifact	Construct	Description
Design principles	Solution objective	The goal an artifact is supposed to achieve [46]
	Meta-requirements	Requirements addressing a class of artifacts rather than a single instance alone [50]
	Boundary conditions	An environment that design principles should be applicable in [31]. Boundary conditions are part of the design principles' *context* [8]
	Material property	Describes what the artifact consists of [31]
	Activity	Describes what the artifact should be able to do [31]. Activities are part of the *mechanisms* to achieve goals [8]
Taxonomy	Meta-characteristic	The purpose of the taxonomy, from which dimensions and characteristics must be derived [43]
	Dimension	Designable dimensions that consist of at least two characteristics [43]
	Characteristic	The specific manifestation of a dimension [43]

The focal question of the paper that needs to be answered to develop design principles out of taxonomies is what type of link exists between the two artifacts. For that purpose, we draw from the theory of knowledge; more specifically, we draw from the notion of *design knowledge*. Design knowledge is knowledge about artifacts, i.e., how they are designed and what they should be able to do [51]. For our purposes, we explicitly draw from the dichotomous division of design knowledge into *descriptive design knowledge* and *prescriptive design knowledge* [6]. Descriptive design knowledge refers to descriptions of the *status quo*, i.e., usually at a fixed point in time, the fundamental morphological characteristics of an artifact. On the other hand, prescriptive design knowledge represents design knowledge that is supposed to guide designers on what should be [7].

In terms of knowledge contributions, taxonomies (and classifications in general) are descriptive, while design principles (and design theory in general) are prescriptive [6, 7]. As both types of artifacts are highly useful in their respective field and frequently published in IS publications, and both do concern the design of artifacts at different levels of design knowledge contributions, we ask ourselves how they can be linked and used to yield more useful results. Additionally, intertwining both artifact types enables better coverage of the design knowledge spectrum ranging from descriptive to prescriptive knowledge. Using design knowledge as the primary linking mechanisms, we investigate how the constructs of both artifacts interlink with each other.

3.2 Knowledge Transformation

The primary transformation mechanism between descriptive and prescriptive knowledge is introducing a *goal* that the artifact should fulfill [6, 9, 10]. Fundamentally, mere description, *per se*, does not require a goal. For example, business model taxonomies (e.g., see [25]) frequently shy away from prescribing specific configurations and only describe that generic arrangements exist. While descriptive research is valuable, prescribing configurations to achieve specific goals is highly demandable. The first step for us is to investigate what a *goal* means in the respective domains.

A suitable starting point for that investigation seems the concept of the meta-characteristic in taxonomies, which describes the conceptual origin of all dimensions and characteristics [43]. Insofar, it describes the goal of a taxonomy, an example for a meta-characteristic can read as "(…) relevant for the description of an analytics-based service (…)" [52 p. 5]. Yet, there is no indication that the meta-characteristic must have any reference to a specific purpose or quantification of success. Also, focusing a meta-characteristic too narrowly on a particular purpose for an artifact might pre-empt configurations from the outset and hinder the freedom and completeness of the range of possibly useful configurations. Thus, the meta-characteristic is better suited to guide generic structuring of possible design configurations in artifact design and delimit, generally, what type of artifact the object of investigation is. For the meta-characteristic above, we can stipulate that the generic artifact is an analytics-based service.

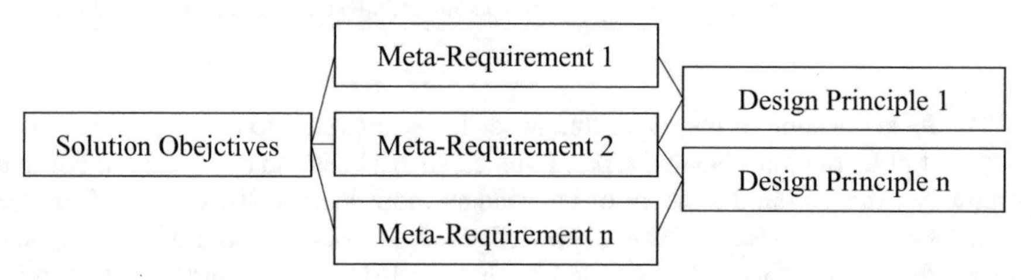

Fig. 3. The intersection of solution objectives with design principles through meta-requirements.

Next, what comes most closely to a traditional goal in design principles is the *solution objective*. The solution objective describes what the artifact-to-be-designed should be able to achieve [46]. Analogueley to the meta-characteristic, the solution objective should be the origin for design principles, from which meta-requirements are derived, and ultimately design principles formulated [46] (see Fig. 3).

Thus, we can view the meta-characteristic of taxonomies as the generic delineation of the type of artifact that is under investigation. At the same time, the solution objective explicitly details what the artifact should be able to achieve. Extending the example given above, the solution objective could assign the generic artifact of the service to a target. For instance, the service is assigned to a specific industry or use case. The solution objective needs to be formulated in the borders of the meta-characteristic and derived from the goal. For example, if the meta-characteristic is expressed as follows:

Meta-Characteristic: Key dimensions and characteristics of **[type of artifact]**.

The solution objective, correspondingly, should integrate the meta-characteristic using the type of artifact specified in it. For example, the solution objective could read as follows:

Solution Objective: How to design **[type of artifact]** to fulfill the **[goal]**?

If we take a more in-depth look at the individual constructs of both domains, we can argue for similarity and transferability. Table 3 juxtaposes contextualizable constructs of both domains and gives short argumentations on how and why they are linkable. Drawing from [8], we use the notion of *mechanisms* as the dominant vehicle to interweave both concepts (see Table 2).

Table 3. The interweaving of domain constructs of taxonomies and design principles.

Taxonomy	Design principles	Linking rationale
Dimension	Mechanism	**Mechanisms** delineate **design dimensions** of design mechanisms, i.e., those activities that need to be executed to achieve a goal
Characteristic	Sub-mechanism	**Sub-dimensions** correspond to design characteristics as lower-threshold **sub-mechanisms**. Mechanisms contextualize a set of activities
-	Activity	A specific course of action, i.e., an **activity,** is central to prescriptive knowledge. Once a goal is introduced, the activity should fulfill **meta-requirements**

Looking at the various conceptual elements of both taxonomies and design principles, one can see similarities. For example, the design principle should give prescriptive knowledge, i.e., guidelines on designing a specific design dimension of an artifact, which, in turn, would represent its mechanisms. Subsequently, as design characteristics are a specification of design dimensions, they, on the other hand, can be translated to lower-threshold sub-mechanisms that the artifact should be designed to be able to let the user fulfill an activity. To illustrate and visualize that way of design principle formulation, we adapt the framework of [31] and integrate the elements *mechanisms*, *sub-mechanisms*, and *activity* (see Table 3). We define three fix points to rationalize our framework, i.e., the *prerequisites*, the *transition threshold*, and the *prescriptive guidelines*. First, the *prerequisite* for our framework is the existence of a morphological taxonomy that describes, comprehensively, designable dimensions, and characteristics of an artifact. Next, the *transition threshold* defines the border between descriptive and prescriptive knowledge through the introduction of goals. Lastly, we show how our framework assists in *formulating prescriptive knowledge*, for which we will use design principles.

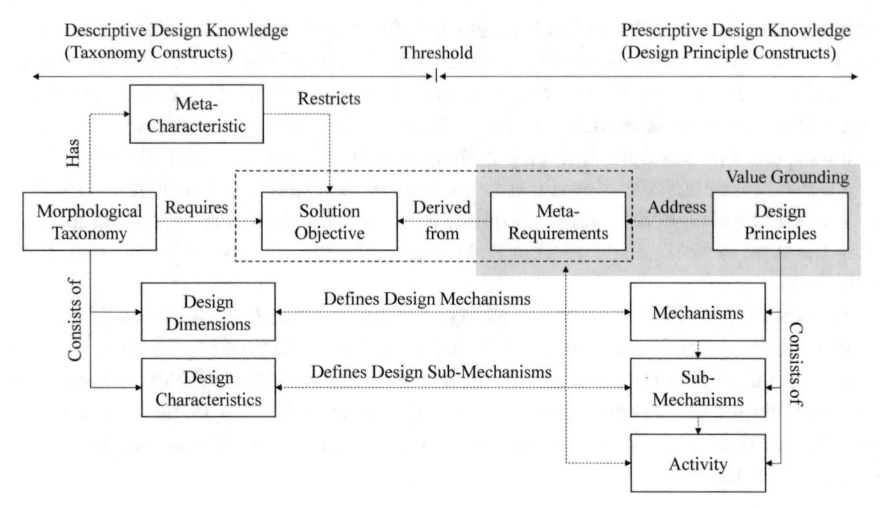

Fig. 4. Entanglement of constructs of morphological taxonomies and design principles on design knowledge level.

3.3 Artifact Transformation

As explained above, the morphological taxonomy hosts a variety of unrealized, potential artifact configurations. A particular configuration, i.e., the final arrangement of all of its parts, is the *Gestalt* of the artifact [17]. In the previous section, we have argued for the transferability of constructs of both domains on a design knowledge level. Yet, as that transformation process also affects the *Gestalt* of the artifact, i.e., its transformation from a generic description to a goal-oriented one, the present section argues how that transformation happens on an artifact level. Thus, as to transform artifacts, we term that state as the *generic Gestalt* of an artifact that resides in the *descriptive design knowledge space*. That *generic Gestalt* consists of design dimensions, which, in turn, consist of design characteristics. On the other side, in the *prescriptive design knowledge space* resides the *target Gestalt*, i.e., a yet unrealized artifact configuration that the designer tailors to achieve a pre-determined goal. The goal must serve as a conceptual starting point to derive solution objectives.

Figure 5 visualizes the interdependencies in the transformation process, conceptually. The individual fragments are no procedural model, but a conceptualization of interlinking mechanisms and are as follows:

(1) The *descriptive design knowledge space* hosts the unrealized finite number of possible artifact configurations, i.e., the generic *Gestalt* of the artifact. It consists of morphological design dimensions, which, in turn, includes more detailed design characteristics. The morphological description requires to be comprehensive so that it is a sound basis to derive goal-oriented configurations.
(2) The *prescriptive design knowledge space* consists of the overarching goal that determines the ultimate purpose the artifact should be able to fulfill. Solution objectives

for the artifact must be derived from the goal. In terms of the *Gestalt*, the *prescriptive design knowledge space* entails knowledge about how to configure the artifact to achieve the goal **(Solution Patterns)** and prescriptions for how to instantiate each design element **(Design Principles)**.

(3) The meta-requirements are derived from the solution objectives. Yet, they must be delimited by one design dimensions (and each design dimension must be addressed) to ensure a comprehensive design that describes the artifact fully. Each meta-requirement must be derived from a suitable knowledge base (e.g., theory, literature, interviews, or case studies [53]). That ensures argumentative strength and reasoning that the meta-requirements originate in a sound foundation.

(4) Finding the solution pattern or a range of potential solution patterns, i.e., a goal-achieving morphological combination is selecting the correct combination of design characteristics. Drawing from organizational configurations, the decision whether an optimal or several *equifinal*[2] solution patterns exist requires evaluation through the designer [55, 56]. In that context, a correct combination is a combination of design characteristics that ensure that the artifact fulfills each design dimension's meta-requirements.

(5) Lastly, once the solution pattern is identified, to give more detail, that just which design characteristics to select, but, more so, to also prescribe how they should be instantiated, design principles must be formulated. There should be at least one design principle for each design characteristic that, per the concept of value grounding, addresses at least one meta-requirement [9, 46].

(6) Finally, if both the solution pattern and design principles are available, the designer should have adequate prescriptive assistance both in selecting design characteristics and corresponding prescriptions on how to instantiate them. As the designer is the user of the design principle, addressing each design dimension is paramount so that comprehensive design is possible [31].

3.4 Synthesis

Given the interweaving of domain constructs, we can now synthesize what one would need to do to formulate design principles from morphological taxonomies and to reach a goal-oriented target *Gestalt* of an artifact.

Step (1): Generate a generic **morphological taxonomy** that comprehensively illustrates the compositional structure of artifacts in design dimensions and corresponding characteristics. It is recommended to follow the method of [43], as it is the *de facto* standard in taxonomy development in Information Systems [14]. That morphology hosts the untapped repository of a finite number of design options, i.e., different configurations and resulting patterns.

Step (2): If a morphology is present, it should represent, generically, i.e., free from a too narrow purpose, the *generic Gestalt* of an artifact. If that is the case, one must

[2] *Equifinality* refers to a concept of *organizational design* and means the existance of multiple potential solution patterns for a design problem [54] In the following, we will refer to the singular of a solution pattern, though we acknolwedge that there can be more than one that fulfills the same purpose.

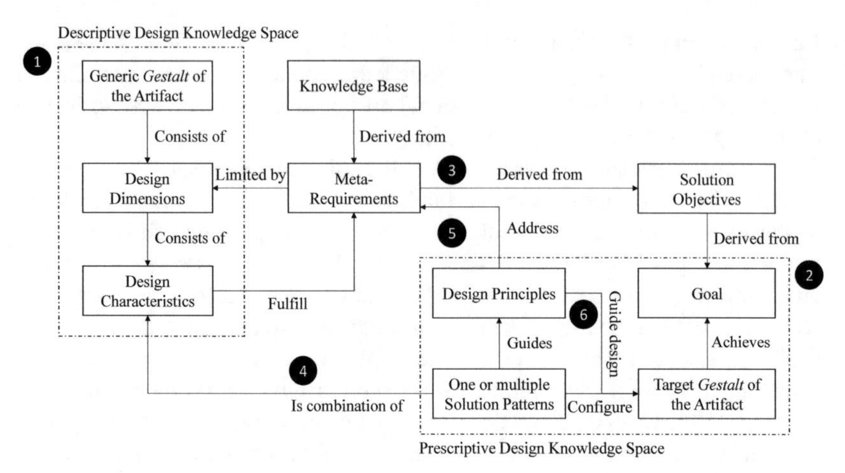

Fig. 5. Framework for artifact transformation from a generic description to a target artifact.

formulate a *solution objective* that specifies what an artifact of a type covered by the meta-characteristic of a possible configuration should be able to achieve. That solution objective needs to be derived from a goal. For example, if the morphology illustrates design options for *digital twins* (e.g., see [22]), a specific, hypothetical goal could be to design *digital twins for collaborative use* (e.g., see [57]).

Step (3): Once the *solution objective* or multiple of them are formulated, one must identify a suitable knowledge base that scientifically supports the formulation of meta-requirements that need to be fulfilled. As the morphology is present and presets delimited design dimensions, it is purposeful to take these design dimensions as conceptual borders to elicit meta-requirements. Meta-requirements can stem from various knowledge bases, typically including, but not limited to, *literature reviews*, *theories*, *interviews*, or *case studies* [53]. These findings should substantiate the formulation of meta-requirements that address the targeted artifact on each design dimension.

Step (4): Once *meta-requirements* are formulated for each design dimension, it is about the designer to argumentatively select and justify the characteristics most suitable to fulfill them. Naturally, one could arrive at the conclusion that no characteristic is fitting, which would force the designer to formulate new ones and extend the taxonomy. The designer must choose at least one characteristic per design dimension, and their combination results in the solution pattern. Identifying and evaluating the right design configuration could be supported by expert feedback or experience from designers.

Step (5): The solution pattern would only prescribe the specific configuration of the target artifact. Yet, it does not give instructions on designing the artifact successfully, i.e., what must be done to realize the target artifact. For that purpose, one can formulate design principles that implicate, linguistically, what the designer should do in each design dimension. As per the entanglement and mirroring of constructs in both domains (see Table 3), we recommend an adjusted template that is consistent with the terminology of taxonomies. The design principle should precisely address how the **artifact** should be designed (i.e., which **characteristics** should be chosen) to achieve the goal defined in the outset. Next, the design principle should specify the **activity**, which should be derived from at least one meta-requirement, that is made possible by selecting the characteristic. Lastly, analog to [31] 's notion of *boundary conditions*, which delimit scenarios for application, the design principles, in the present case, are only ever applicable in the context in that they were built.

Table 4. Adapted template for design principles. Based on [31].

Template of [31]	Adapted template
Provide the system with **[material property – in terms of form and function]** in order for users **[activity of user/group of users – in terms of action]**, given that **[boundary conditions – user group's characteristics or implementation settings]**	Provide the **[artifact with a specific goal]** with **[at least one characteristic]** to enable **[activity derived from meta-requirement]**, given the design of **[dimension]** in **[boundary condition]**

Step (6): Summarizing, in the enclosed design space generated and tailored to achieve a particular goal, one can follow the notion of *technological rule* formulation by [58]. Subsequently, one can see the instantiation of the final set of design principles in a chain of them as the last step to achieve the goal. Thus, one can easily imagine the final artifact as the sum of instantiated design principles:

$$\sum\nolimits_{k=0}^{n} \mathrm{IDPn} = DA$$

Where the desired artifact (DA) is the final product of a chain of instantiated design principles (IDPn) that ranges, as a finite set, from one design principle to, however, many are needed, i.e., *n*-many design principles.

4 Scenario-Based Illustration

As per the relatively large-scale endeavor of our proposed framework, we construct a simple scenario that supports our reasoning [59]. For example, the case of [24] offers a taxonomy of data-driven services in manufacturing. The taxonomy is an excellent example of the deconstruction of a design artifact in generic design dimensions that can be configured freely.

Step (1): The taxonomy of [24] describes data-driven services in manufacturing. We will assume that the taxonomy is comprehensive and thus does not require manipulation of dimensions or characteristics. Their meta-characteristic reads as follows: "key characteristics of data-driven services within the manufacturing industry" [24 p. 5]. The meta-characteristic delimits the formulation of the solution onto the domain of data-driven services in manufacturing industries. Thus, the solution objective must reside in these conceptual borders.

Step (2): Suppose our goal was to formulate design principles for data-driven services that are determined to enhance quality in manufacturing. Subsequently, a possible *solution objective* could be:

Solution Objective: How to design data-driven services to enhance quality in manufacturing environments successfully?

In the present case, as per the previously defined meta-characteristic, steering the objective of the data-driven services explicitly onto a specific value proposition domain seems reasonable and well within the previously pre-determined restrictions.

Step (3): Once the solution objective is formulated, the designer must endeavor to elicit meta-requirements that are tailored for each design dimension. As our illustration is a scenario, we will assume that a suitable knowledge base, e.g., the literature on quality management or qualitative interviews, will produce ample grounds for reasoning the selection of specific characteristics from the taxonomy. For example, if the findings would prescribe that ensuring quality through data-driven services requires the integration of data generated from the machine (i.e., data about the process), which can be supplemented through acquired data from other machines, these characteristics should be selected. Possible, hypothetical meta-requirements derived from the solution objective for the dimension **Data Sources** and **Pricing Model** could be formulated, as shown in Table 5.

Table 5. Hypothetical meta-requirements for the present scenario.

Dimension	Meta-requirement (MR)
Data source	**MR1:** Data-driven services should provide quality through monitoring machine data
	MR 2: Data-driven services should leverage data from comparable machines
Pricing model	**MR 3:** Data-driven services should foster long-standing monetary relationships with customers instead of single payments
	MR 4: Data-driven services should produce recurring income

Step (4): Once all meta-requirements are formulated, one can match them with the characteristics that are most useful to achieve them. In the present case, the (abbreviated) solution pattern is supposedly the most fitting to achieve the overarching goal of generating data-driven services that enhance the quality of manufacturing processes.

Step (5): Lastly, based on the solution pattern, the designer must formulate design principles. Staying with the example of the design dimension *data sources*, a design principle that addresses MR1 and MR2 could be formulated as follows:

Provide the **Data-Driven Service for Quality Enhancement** with mechanisms to integrate **acquired data** to enable **benefiting from analysis of historical data from similar machines**, given the design of **Data Sources** in **Data-Driven Service Design in Manufacturing Industries**.

Provide the **Data-Driven Service for Quality Enhancement** with mechanisms to integrate a **Subscription-based Revenue Model** to build long-term relationships with customers generating recurring income and opportunities for selling additional services, given the design of the **Pricing Model** in **Data-Driven Service Design in Manufacturing Industries**.

The first design principle would address MR1 and MR2, as leveraging data produced by machines that are owned by the manufacturer should not pose any issues of data ownership and draws from the most prominent data source. The second design principle would address MR 3 and MR4.

Step (6): Naturally, the last step would be instantiating the chain of design principles, which would, hypothetically, then lead to the desired *Gestalt* of the artifact.

5 Contributions, Limitations, Outlook

Our work theorizes a way to bridge the gap between two popular IS artifacts that, respectively, have a high amount of value regarding either descriptive or prescriptive design knowledge contributions. We propose the interweaving of both artifacts, with the ultimate goal of mapping the entire spectrum of design knowledge regarding an artifact's design. For that purpose, a generic morphological description of an artifact's design structure is the essential requirement to spur the design and development of more specific artifacts of that same type that are tailored to fulfill particular goals. We argue that our work is a significant contribution to extend and further substantiate taxonomies in IS research and to use them as the basis for further study and comprehensive design knowledge contributions, rather than a finished result. As this implies that descriptive knowledge is transformed into prescriptive knowledge, we contribute to the highest goal of design science, which is the accumulation of prescriptive knowledge.

Our work is subject to limitations. First and foremost, we theorize on argumentation to transform descriptive knowledge to prescriptive knowledge, that we showcase using a hypothetical, illustrative scenario. Thus, both a limitation and a natural opportunity and obligation for further research is testing our framework in practice and studying how design principles for goal-oriented artifacts can be designed from generic, morphological descriptions.

Lastly, our work provides fertile soil for further research, as it, hopefully, spurs discussion on design knowledge transformation. As our framework is yet a product of theorizing, the next steps could include gathering empirical data, e.g., conducting interviews with researchers with experience and knowledge in taxonomy design and design principle development. Additionally, our conceptualization of descriptive and prescriptive design knowledge offers potential for subdividing that process into more distinct design stages.

References

1. Legner, C., Pentek, T., Otto, B.: Accumulating design knowledge with reference models: insights from 12 years' research into data management. J. Assoc. Inf. Syst. **21**, 735–770 (2020)
2. Vom Brocke, J., Winter, R., Hevner, A., Maedche, A.: Accumulation and evolution of design knowledge in design science research - a journey through time and space. J. Assoc. Inf. Syst. **21**, 520–544 (2020)
3. Seidel, S., Chandra Kruse, L., Székely, N., Gau, M., Stieger, D.: Design principles for sense-making support systems in environmental sustainability transformations. Eur. J. Inf. Syst. **27**, 221–247 (2017)

4. Chandra Kruse, L., Seidel, S., vom Brocke, J.: Design archaeology: generating design knowledge from real-world artifact design. In: Tulu, B., Djamasbi, S., Leroy, G. (eds.) DESRIST 2019. LNCS, vol. 11491, pp. 32–45. Springer, Cham (2019). https://doi.org/10.1007/978-3-030-19504-5_3
5. van Aken, J.E.: Management research based on the paradigm of the design sciences: the quest for field-tested and grounded technological rules. J. Manage. Stud. **41**, 219–246 (2004)
6. Barquet, A.P., Wessel, L., Rothe, H.: Knowledge accumulation in design-oriented research. In: Maedche, A., vom Brocke, J., Hevner, A. (eds.) DESRIST 2017. LNCS, vol. 10243, pp. 398–413. Springer, Cham (2017). https://doi.org/10.1007/978-3-319-59144-5_24
7. Gregor, S., Hevner, A.R.: Positioning and presenting design science research for maximum impact. MIS Q. Manag. Inf. Syst. **37**, 337–355 (2013)
8. Gregor, S., Chandra Kruse, L., Seidel, S.: The anatomy of a design principle. J. Assoc. Inf. Syst. **21**, 1622–1652 (2020)
9. Goldkuhl, G.: Design theories in information systems-a need for multi-grounding. J. Inf. Technol. Theory Appl. **6**, 59–72 (2004)
10. Goldkuhl, G.: Design science epistemology: a pragmatist inquiry. Scand. J. Inf. Syst. **32**, 39–80 (2020)
11. Glass, R.L., Vessey, I.: Contemporary application-domain taxonomies. IEEE Softw. **12**, 63–76 (1995)
12. Lambert, S.: The importance of classification to business model research. J. Bus. Model. **3**, 49–61 (2015)
13. Bailey, K.D.: Typologies and Taxonomies: An Introduction to Classification Techniques. Sage Publications, Thousand Oaks, London (1994)
14. Szopinski, D., Schoormann, T., Kundisch, D.: Because your taxonomy is worth it: towards a framework for taxonomy evaluation. In: Proceedings of the Twenty-Seventh European Conference on Information Systems (2019)
15. Gregor, S.: The nature of theory in information systems. MIS Q. Manag. Inf. Syst. **30**, 611–642 (2006)
16. Szopinski, D., Schoormann, T., Kundisch, D.: Visualize different: towards researching the fit between taxonomy visualizations and taxonomy tasks. In: Proceedings of the 15th International Conference on Wirtschaftsinformatik (2020)
17. Ritchey, T.: General morphological analysis. a general method for non-quantified modelling. In: 16th Euro Conference on Operational Analysis (1998)
18. Cross, N.: Design research: a disciplined conversation. Des. Issues **15**, 5–10 (1999)
19. Ritchey, T.: On a morphology of theories of emergence. Acta Morphol. Gene. **3**, 1–17 (2014)
20. Ritchey, T.: Problem structuring using computer-aided morphological analysis. J. Oper. Res. Soc. **57**, 792–801 (2006)
21. Remane, G., Nickerson, R.C., Hanelt, A., Tesch, J.F., Kolbe, L.M.: A taxonomy of carsharing business models. In: Proceedings of the 37th International Conference on Information Systems (2016)
22. van der Valk, H., Haße, H., Möller, F., Arbter, M., Henning, J.-L., Otto, B.: A taxonomy of digital twins. In: Proceedings of the 2020 Americas Conference on Information Systems (2020)
23. Kroll, E.: Design theory and conceptual design: contrasting functional decomposition and morphology with parameter analysis. Res. Eng. Des. **24**, 165–183 (2013)
24. Azkan, C., Iggena, L., Gür, I., Möller, F., Otto, B.: A taxonomy for data-driven services in manufacturing industries. In: Proceedings of the 24th Pacific Asia Conference on Information Systems (2020)
25. Möller, F., Stachon, M., Hoffmann, C., Bauhaus, H., Otto, B.: Data-driven business models in logistics: a taxonomy of optimization and visibility services. In: Proceedings of the 53rd Hawaii International Conference on System Sciences (2020)

26. Möller, F., Bauhaus, H., Hoffmann, C., Niess, C., Otto, B.: Archetypes of digital business models in logistics start-ups. In: Proceedings of the 27th European Conference on Information Systems (2019)
27. Janssen, A., Passlick, J., Cardona, D., Breitner, M.: Virtual assistance in any context - a taxonomy of design elements for domain-specific Chatbots. Bus. Inf. Syst. Eng. **62**, 211–225 (2020)
28. Chandra Kruse, L., Seidel, S.: Tensions in design principle formulation and reuse. In: Proceedings of the 12th International Conference on Design Science Research in Information Systems and Technology (2017)
29. Simon, H.A.: The science of design creating the artificial. Des. Issu. **4**, 67–82 (1988)
30. Oberländer, A.M., Lösser, B., Rau, D.: Taxonomy research in information systems: a systematic assessment. In: Proceedings of the 27th European Conference on Information Systems (2019)
31. Chandra Kruse, L., Seidel, S., Gregor, S.: Prescriptive knowledge in IS research: conceptualizing design principles in terms of materiality, action, and boundary conditions. In: Proceedings of the 48th Hawaii International Conference on System Sciences (2015)
32. Chandra Kruse, L., Seidel, S., Purao, S.: Making use of design principles. In: Proceedings of the 11th International Conference on Design Science Research in Information Systems and Technology, pp. 37–51 (2016)
33. Sein, M.K., Henfridsson, O., Purao, S., Rossi, M., Lindgren, R.: Action design research. MIS Q. Manag. Inf. Syst. **35**, 37–56 (2011)
34. Iivari, J.: Towards information systems as a science of meta-artifacts. Commun. Assoc. Inf. Syst. **12**, 568–581 (2003)
35. Hartmann, P.M., Zaki, M., Feldmann, N., Neely, A.: Capturing value from big data – a taxonomy of data-driven business models used by start-up firms. Int. J. Oper. Prod. Manag. **36**, 1382–1406 (2016)
36. Eickhoff, M., Muntermann, J., Weinrich, T.: What do FinTechs actually do? A taxonomy of fintech business models. In: Proceedings of the 38th International Conference on Information Systems (2017)
37. Tomitsch, M., Kappel, K., Lehner, A., Grechenig, T.: Towards a taxonomy for ambient information systems. In: Pervasive '07 Workshop: W9 - Ambient Information Systems (2007)
38. Guggenberger, T., Möller, F., Haarhaus, T., Gür, I., Otto, B.: Ecosystem types in information systems. In: Proceedings of the 28th European Conference on Information Systems (2020)
39. Archer, L.B.: A view of the nature of design research. In: Jacques, R., Powell, J. (eds.) Design: Science: Method. Westbury House, Guildford (1981)
40. Maher, M.L., Poon, J., Boulanger, S.: Formalising design exploration as co-evolution. In: Gero, J.S., Sudweeks, F. (eds.) Advances in Formal Design Methods for CAD. IFIP — The International Federation for Information Processing, pp. 3–30. Springer, Boston (1996).https://doi.org/10.1007/978-0-387-34925-1_1
41. Simon, H.A.: Problem forming, problem finding and problem solving in design. Des. Syst. 245–257 (1995)
42. Cleven, A., Gubler, P., Hüner, K.M.: Design alternatives for the evaluation of design science research artifacts. In: Proceedings of the 4th International Conference on Design Science Research in Information Systems and Technology. Association for Computing Machinery, New York (2009)
43. Nickerson, R.C., Varshney, U., Muntermann, J.: A Method for taxonomy development and its application in information systems. Eur. J. Inf. Syst. **22**, 336–359 (2013)
44. Cronholm, S., Göbel, H.: guidelines supporting the formulation of design principles. In: Proceedings of the 29th Australasian Conference on Information Systems (2018)
45. van den Akker, J.: Principles and methods of development research. In: Design Approaches and Tools in Education and Training, pp. 1–14. Kluwer Academic Publishers (1999)

46. Heinrich, P., Schwabe, G.: Communicating nascent design theories on innovative information systems through multi-grounded design principles. In: Tremblay, M.C., VanderMeer, D., Rothenberger, M., Gupta, A., Yoon, V. (eds.) DESRIST 2014. LNCS, vol. 8463, pp. 148–163. Springer, Cham (2014). https://doi.org/10.1007/978-3-319-06701-8_10
47. Schoormann, T., Behrens, D., Knackstedt, R.: Design principles for leveraging sustainability in business modelling tools. In: Proceedings of the 26th European Conference on Information Systems (2018)
48. Sturm, B., Sunyaev, A.: Design principles for systematic search systems: a holistic synthesis of a rigorous multi-cycle design science research journey. Bus. Inf. Syst. Eng. **61**(1), 91–111 (2018). https://doi.org/10.1007/s12599-018-0569-6
49. March, S.T., Smith, G.F.: Design and natural science research on information technology. Decis. Supp. Syst. **15**, 251–266 (1995)
50. Walls, J.G., Widmeyer, G.R., El Sawy, O.A.: Building an information system design theory for vigilant EIS. Inf. Syst. Res. **3**, 36–59 (1992)
51. Cross, N.: Designerly ways of knowing: design discipline versus design science. Des. Issues **17**, 49–55 (2001)
52. Hunke, F., Engel, C., Schüritz, R., Ebel, P.: Understanding the anatomy of analytics-based services – a taxonomy to conceptualize the use of data and analytics in services. In: Proceedings of the 27th European Conference on Information Systems (2019)
53. Möller, F., Guggenberger, T.M., Otto, B.: Towards a method for design principle development in information systems. In: Hofmann, S., Müller, O., Rossi, M. (eds.) DESRIST 2020. LNCS, vol. 12388, pp. 208–220. Springer, Cham (2020). https://doi.org/10.1007/978-3-030-64823-7_20
54. Gresov, C., Drazin, R.: Equifinality: functional equivalence in organization design. Acad. Manag. Rev. **22**, 403–428 (1997)
55. Fiss, P.C.: A set-theoretic approach to organizational configurations. Acad. Manag. Rev. **32**, 1180–1198 (2007)
56. Ragin, C.C.: Fuzzy-Set Social Science. University of Chicago Press, Chicago (2000)
57. Ramm, S., Wache, H., Dinter, B., Schmidt, S.: Der Kollaborative Digitale Zwilling: Herzstück eines integrierten Gesamtkonzepts. ZWF Zeitschrift fuer Wirtschaftlichen Fabrikbetrieb **115**, 94–96 (2020)
58. Bunge, M.: Scientific Research II: The Search for Truth. Springer, Berlin Heidelberg (2012)
59. Hevner, A.R., March, S.T., Park, J., Ram, S.: Design science in information systems research. MIS Q. Manag. Inf. Syst. **28**, 75–105 (2004)

Ethical Design of Conversational Agents: Towards Principles for a Value-Sensitive Design

Thiemo Wambsganss[1(✉)], Anne Höch[2], Naim Zierau[1], and Matthias Söllner[2]

[1] Institute of Information Management, University of St.Gallen (HSG), St.Gallen, Switzerland
{thiemo.wambsganss,naim.zierau}@unisg.ch
[2] University of Kassel, Information Systems and Systems Engineering, Kassel, Germany
soellner@uni-kassel.de

Abstract. Conversational Agents (CAs) have become a new paradigm for human-computer interaction. Despite the potential benefits, there are ethical challenges to the widespread use of these agents that may inhibit their use for individual and social goals. However, besides a multitude of behavioral and design-oriented studies on CAs, a distinct ethical perspective falls rather short in the current literature. In this paper, we present the first steps of our design science research project on principles for a value-sensitive design of CAs. Based on theoretical insights from 87 papers and eleven user interviews, we propose preliminary requirements and design principles for a value-sensitive design of CAs. Moreover, we evaluate the preliminary principles with an expert-based evaluation. The evaluation confirms that an ethical approach for design CAs might be promising for certain scenarios.

Keywords: Ethics in IS · Value-sensitive design · Conversational agents · Design science research

1 Introduction

Driven by technological advances in *Artificial Intelligence* (AI) especially in the area of *Natural Language Processing* (NLP), many organizations strive to leverage the potential of Conversational Agents (CAs) for improving *human-computer interaction* (HCI) [1]. CAs such as *Amazon's Alexa, Google's Assistant, and Apple's Siri* are software programs that engage with users through natural language [2]. CAs promise to dramatically enhance user experience by enabling personalization, around the clock availability, and immediate response times [3]. The popularity of these interfaces has been steadily growing over the past few years [3]. Thus, a plethora of positive user outcomes have been recorded, such as engagement [4], trust [5, 6], rapport, and ease of use, in several domains, such as education [7–9], healthcare [10] and customer service [11, 12]. Despite the potential benefits of these agents, there are ethical problems that arise from the use of many contemporary CAs. First, the appearance and behavior of CAs are susceptible to design biases such that certain stereotypes are reinforced and strengthened. For instance, [13] found that most agents are embodied with feminine characteristics, as these are supposed to improve the attitude towards the agents, but also solidify specific gender

F. Ahlemann et al. (Eds.): WI 2021, LNISO 46, pp. 539–557, 2021.
https://doi.org/10.1007/978-3-030-86790-4_37

roles. Second, the knowledge base and respective Machine Learning (ML) models are susceptible to bias, resulting in systematic errors that may create unfair outcomes. For example, they can lead to inaccurate predictions for specific subgroups or may carry the implicit values of programmers and organizations [14]. Moreover, these agents operate with some level of autonomy, resulting in increased opaqueness that highlights questions of accountability and transparency [15]. For instance, [16] has shown that users are more likely to choose financial portfolios that exceed their risk profiles when using a CA compared to non-conversation robo advisors, which may serve as an example of how these agents can be used to manipulate customers. Finally, as CAs operate on user data and may, in fact, be used to collect enormous amounts of (sensitive) data, user privacy becomes an even more important issue [17]. In sum, while CAs have the potential to fundamentally improve user outcomes, developers and providers may need to increasingly follow ethical considerations in the design of these agents to ensure the well-being of their users [18].

However, as the proliferation of CAs has been driven mostly by monetary goals (e.g., [20]), it remains doubtful whether the design of these agents takes ethical concerns sufficiently into account and could rightfully give rise to the skepticism of many users. This sentiment is also reflected in CA research to date, as most authors did not follow a distinct normative approach in deriving design guidelines but rather descriptively analyze user interactions with these agents, which does not allow to draw direct conclusions about the ethical design of these agents (e.g., [21]). In fact, the importance of ethical perspectives on design research on novel IS artifacts has been discussed by IS scholars long before. For example, [22] stated that ethical considerations in the field of IS design should receive a more prominent role. Following this, [23] suggested to include ethical guidelines in the design research of IS artifacts and proposed six ethical principles informing design science research. [24] followed by discussing the philosophical responsibility of IS research. Recently, IS researchers have identified the novelty of AI-based CAs as IS artifacts and called for further work to investigate ethical designs with principles and guidelines for CAs [1, 25]. Also, in practice, value-sensitive design plays a prominent role, i.e., large technology providers of CAs such as Google[1] and Microsoft[2] have recently released ethical guidelines on the design of these AI systems. Moreover, intergovernmental organizations such as the *Organization for Economic Co-operation and Development* (OECD) or the *Group of Twenty* (G20) drive the societal debate by releasing principles for the ethical design of AI systems such as CAs (OECD[3] in May 2019, G20[4] in June 2019). The intergovernmental guidelines and current literature strongly motivate the need for a value-sensitive design of AI-driven IS such as CAs. However, they provide a more conceptual framing with rather general categories for AI-based IS artifacts [23]. Current literature falls short to provide meaningful and evaluated design principles (e.g., according to [26]) to help IS designers and practitioners to 1) instantiate value-sensitive CAs and 2) evaluate currently instantiated CAs from a value-sensitive design perspective based on these principles. Following the *AI principles*

[1] https://ai.google/principles/.

[2] https://www.microsoft.com/en-us/ai/responsible-ai.

[3] https://www.oecd.org/going-digital/ai/principles/.

[4] https://dig.watch/updates/g20-digital-economy-ministers-endorse-ai-principles.

of the OECD, we therefore aim to contribute to the field of value-sensitive design of CA by answering the following research question **(RQ)**:

***RQ**: What are relevant design principles that foster a value-sensitive design of Conversational Agents?*

To answer the stated research question, we overall follow a design science-research approach (DSR). As stated above, there is a lack of concrete design knowledge for the ethical design of CAs. Thus, we intend to iteratively derive and evaluate design knowledge on the baseline of existing normative design recommendations (i.e., OECD AI principles), while focusing on social response theory [27, 28] as a guiding theoretical lens to inform concrete artifact design [29]. Users experience those agents as increasingly human-like, which is why social response theory may represent a new *"foundation for understanding and designing humane anthropomorphic agents"* ([25], p. 1). In sum, we follow a value-sensitive design approach that allows us to translate ethical requirements or imperatives (i.e., OECD AI principles) identified into actionable design guidelines [31]. To the best of our knowledge, there is no study that rigorously derives requirements from both scientific literature and potential users to derive design principles for value-sensitive CAs following intergovernmental guidelines, such as the OECD AI principles. With a value-sensitive CA, we implicate a dialogue-based system that incorporates human and ethical values into its core design and implementation process, e.g., when designing the interaction or when training ML models.

In this paper, we present the preliminary design principles and an expert-based evaluation of those principles according to [32]. Our results suggest that a value-sensitive design of CAs might be a promising approach for different user interaction scenarios, e.g., where privacy and transparency play an important role. With a further evaluation of these design principles, they might serve as a foundation informing CA designers towards an ethical design. In the following, we will first introduce the reader to the necessary theoretical background. Afterwards, we present our methodological approach for creating design knowledge following the three cycle view of [33]. Finally, our preliminary requirements and design principles are presented and evaluated by experts, followed by an outline of the subsequent steps and the expected implications once our research is completed.

2 Theoretical Background

2.1 Value-Sensitive Design of Conversational Agents

Recent advances in NLP and ML bear the opportunity to design new forms of HCI for IS with conversational interfaces, also called Conversational Agents (CAs). CAs are software programs that are designed to communicate with users through natural language interaction interfaces [2]. In today's world, conversational interfaces, such as *Amazon's Alexa, Google's Assistant,* or *Apple's Siri*, are ubiquitous, with their popularity steadily growing over the past few years [34]. They are implemented in various areas, such as customer service [12, 35], counseling [36], collaboration [37] or education [7, 38]. Recently, an overwhelming amount of research emerged in different disciplines that investigated the effect of different design elements and configurations unique to these agents on various forms of user perceptions, such as trust or social presence (e.g., [12, 21]). However, the application of AI usually comes with disadvantages, such as lower transparency, loss of control, and lack of trust by human users [39]. As [25] claim, *current ethical design perspectives fall mostly short of a practical application of design principles for the interaction design of CAs*. Value-based design is a theoretically grounded approach for a technological design that integrates human values in a principled and understandable way during the whole design process [31]. Ethics can be seen as a foundation of value-sensitive or value-based design [22]. Nevertheless, literature strongly motivates the need for a value-sensitive design of AI-driven IS such as CAs but provides a rather conceptual framing with general categories for IS artifacts (such as [23]). Literature only poorly provides meaningful and evaluated design principles to help IS designers and practitioners to instantiate value-sensitive CAs. Thus, we aim to contribute to research by investigating design principles based on the *OECD AI guideline* and therefore follow the recent call for future work by several IS scholars to "*[build] a cumulative body of prescriptive [design] knowledge on methods for the engineering of humane anthropomorphic agents [CAs] as well as generic design principles guiding the design of humane anthropomorphic agents*" ([25], p. 14).

The widespread application of AI-based IS has been driving a recent discussion of their values and ethics (i.e., [25]). Earlier studies already focused on different but singular aspects of ethical values, for example, privacy [40], prevention of bias [41] or trust [42]. However, there is a lack of holistic and actionable design knowledge that supports value-sensitive development of novel AI-based IS such as CAs. Besides, several intergovernmental organizations such as the OECD or the G20 have stated principles for AI. The guidelines are complemented by a discourse in the academic literature (e.g., [1, 15, 29]). The OECD collected five ethical principles for AI-based systems by 50 experts from 20 governments as well as leaders from the business, labor, civil society, academic and science communities:

> *"1) AI should benefit people and the planet by driving inclusive growth, sustainable development and well-being. 2) AI systems should be designed in a way that respects the rule of law, human rights, democratic values and diversity, and they should include appropriate safeguards – for example, enabling human intervention where necessary – to ensure a fair and just society. 3) There should be transparency and responsible disclosure around AI systems to ensure that people understand AI-based outcomes and can challenge them. 4) AI systems must function in a robust, secure and safe way throughout their life cycles and potential risks should be continually assessed and managed. 5) Organizations and individuals developing, deploying or operating AI systems should be held accountable for their proper functioning in line with the above principles."*

Nevertheless, the OECD AI principles are not operationalized in such a way that allow designers to easily translate them into concrete design features (e.g., according to [26]). The principles of the OECD were composed to provide a general perspective on the value-sensitive design of AI-based systems and therefore fall short to provide meaningful and evaluated design principles to help IS designers and practitioners to 1) instantiate value-sensitive CAs (e.g., according to [26]) and 2) evaluate existing interaction designs. Therefore, we aim to address this literature gap and investigate, derive and evaluate design principles for value-sensitive CA design.

2.2 Social Response Theory as a Lens for Value-Sensitive IS Design

Our design approach is anchored in social response theory. According to this theory, humans tend to respond socially to IS that displays characteristics similar to humans (e.g., to animals or technologies) [44]. Behavioral clues and social signals from computers, such as interacting with others, using natural language, or playing social roles, subconsciously trigger responses from humans, no matter how rudimentary those clues or signals are [27, 28]. Following the "*Computers are Social Actors*" (CASA) paradigm, existing research has examined different social clues and their influence on HCI (e.g., [21]). However, a value-sensitive and ethical perspective on designing CAs has been poorly considered in the literature, thus inhibiting the development of truly social actors (i.e., agents that act on moral principles [30]). Accountability, transparency, or trust have been proven to play a major role in trustworthy social relationships but are only minorly engrained in the interaction design of CAs (e.g., [45]). Thus, we follow the value-sensitive model of the humanness of CAs [25] by investigating principles for an ethical CA. We aim to contribute to better user acceptance, experience, and user-centered design according to social response theory [27, 28].

3 Research Methodology

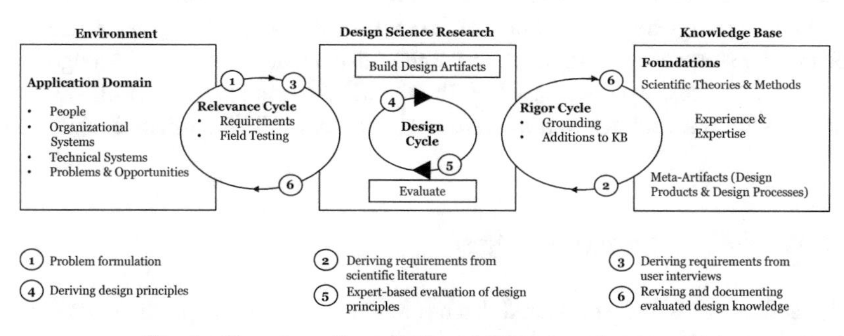

Fig. 1. Overview of our design science research approach

To answer our research question, we follow a DSR approach [33]. We decided to follow this methodology, as it allows us to solve a set of practical problems and to contribute to the existing body of knowledge by designing and evaluating new design knowledge based on a sound understanding of the current knowledge base and user perceptions of a new technological phenomenon [46]. Moreover, this allows us to give a "voice" to the users – a key aspect of value-sensitive design. Figure 1 shows the steps that are carried out.

We focus on translating the OECD AI principles two to five into actionable design principles according to [26]. The first principle depicts rather a meta-principle that encompasses all of the following, which is why we do not include it in this research project that focuses on actionable design knowledge. Overall, our research project aims to contribute to research with a *nascent design theory* that gives explicit prescriptions for a value-sensitive and thus a more ethical design of CAs [47]. We followed a theory-driven design approach by grounding our research on social response theory [27, 28]. The *first step* of the DSR cycle includes the problem formulation. The relevance of the practical problem was therefore described in the introduction of this work. In the *second step*, we derived a set of requirements in the form of *literature issues* (LIs) from the current state of scientific literature for the design of value-sensitive CAs according to the OECD AI principles. Therefore, we conduct a systematic literature review in the fields of Human-Computer Interaction (HCI) and Information Systems (IS) design. Next, we conducted eleven semi-structured interviews with students and professionals using the expert interview method by [48] to capture requirements from users for ethical CAs. Based on the interviews, we gathered *user stories* (USs) as user requirements for the design of a value-sensitive CA. In the *fourth step*, we derived preliminary *design principles* (DPs) addressing the LIs and USs from the prior steps using the structure suggested by [26]. We argue that a CA (and possibly also other AI-based IS) that instantiates our DPs should increase the perceived humanness and thus improve overall user experience and interaction. Our principles should provide designers of CAs with ethical considerations based on implicit values derived from literature and expert interviews. Thus, we aim to enable designers to design more ethical CAs, ultimately increasing the well-being of its users. Accordingly, in *step five*, we perform an expert-based evaluation of our preliminary design principles based on the evaluation framework proposed by [32]. We interview experts from academia and industry to quantitatively and qualitatively evaluate the relevance, robustness, and usefulness of our principles according to the OECD guidelines for designers from the fields of social science, psychology and IS design. At the end of the study, we contribute to research with evaluated design knowledge on how to design value-sensitive CAs based on the OECD AI principles. Overall, we hope to contribute with our findings to *a nascent design theory* [47] for value-sensitive design of CAs.

4 Deriving Design Knowledge

In this section, we will describe and discuss how we derived the preliminary DPs. The problem formulation (step one) described in the introduction serves as the foundation for the derivation of the requirements from literature and users.

4.1 Step 2: Deriving Requirements from Scientific Literature

To derive requirements from scientific literature, a systematic literature search was conducted using the methodological approaches of [49] and [50]. We initially focused our research on studies that demonstrate the successful implementation of a value-sensitive design for IS artifacts. In order to do this, publications on design, ethics and design science of IS and CAs were identified by a systematic search in different search engines and databases, such as *Google Scholar, EBSCO, JSTOR, ACM, AIS Library*. We used the following keywords to find potential hits for our literature review: *"Value-sensitive Design", "User experience", "Chatbot", "Conversational Agent", "Design", "Design Science Research", "Design Artifact", "Ethical AI", "AI Principles", "AI Guidelines"* AND *"Transparency", "Fairness", "Explainability", "Understandability", "Accountability", "Robustness", "Security", "Safety, "Privacy"*. Initially, we received several thousand hits based on these search terms. Therefore, we screened the titles and abstracts of the publications. Our goal was to identify papers that deal with ethical aspects of CAs. Thus, we only included literature that contributes to a kind of ethical perspective on the design of CAs according to the OECD AI principles. We excluded papers that explicitly did not deal with an ethical perspective when deriving design knowledge of CAs (i.e., papers focusing on sales-driven dependent variables). On this basis, we selected 87 papers for more intensive analysis. We have summarized similar topics of these contributions as literature issues (LIs) and formed 15 clusters from them to derive a concept matrix according to [51]. Those topics represent integral design issues that were addressed to increase individual and or social good when using those agents. We allocated those issues to the individual OECD principles, which served as scaffolding divisions for the organization of those issues. The LIs are aggregated and illustrated in Table 1 with exemplary papers.

Table 1. Aggregated LIs for a value-sensitive design of CAs with exemplary papers

Dimension*	#	Literature issues (LIs)
Human-centered values and fairness	LI1	Prevention of bias or discrimination (e.g., [41])
	LI2	Accessibility & Design (e.g., [11])
	LI3	Compliance with human rights & democratic values (e.g., [52])
	LI4	Beneficence (e.g., [52])
Transparency and explainability	LI5	Transparency (e.g., [53]) & Explainability (e.g., [54])
	LI6	Trust (e.g., [42])
	LI7	Traceability (e.g., [55])
	LI8	Communication (e.g., [56])
Robustness, security and safety	LI9	Non-maleficence (e.g., [52])
	LI10	Privacy (e.g., [40])
	LI11	Resilience (e.g., [57])
	LI12	Reliability (e.g., [42])
Accountability	LI13	Auditability (e.g., [58])
	LI14	Reporting (e.g., [59])
	LI15	Responsibility (e.g., [60])

*according to the OECD AI principles two to five

4.2 Step 3: Deriving Requirements from User Interviews

Based on the derived LIs, we conducted eleven semi-structured interviews according to [48]. The interview guideline consists of 29 questions and each interview lasted around *28 to 59 min* (*mean = 40.99 min*). The interviewees were all potential users of a value-sensitive CA and all had used a CA before in different scenarios. Therefore, we followed a literal replications logic. Therefore, we chose participants with different insights based on their background (i.e., different demographics). In order to gain impressions resulting from different user groups, a heterogeneous group of users was interviewed, such as students and professionals. The participants were asked about the following topics: experience with CAs, perception of values and ethics in CAs, requirements for a value-sensitive CA (e.g., functionalities, design), requirements for a CA that aims to follow the OECD principles, such as fairness, transparency, robustness, accountability.

The interviewees were in *mean = 32.91 years* old *(SD = 12.06*). Five participants were students of business administration, one of economics, one of teaching profession, and one a student of nutrition science. Three interviewees were practitioners in different sectors (medical, police, and business), four were male, seven were female. After a more precise transcription, the interviews were evaluated using qualitative content analysis. The interviews were coded, and abstract categories were formed. The coding was performed using open coding to form a uniform coding system during evaluation [48]. Based on these results, we gathered *120 user stories* (USs) as user requirements following [61]. We aggregated the most common user stories, which resulted in 19 USs for value-sensitive CAs (illustrated in Table 2).

Table 2. Aggregated user stories for a value-sensitive design of CAs based on [61]

#	User stories (USs)
US1	As a CA user, I would like to always be treated equally regarding the outcome resulting from collected but not necessarily context-relevant data (e.g., gender, race)
US2	As a CA user, I think it would be helpful if the CA was accessible and available in different language or age groups so that everyone has the same access to benefits/risks
US3	As a CA user, I think that communication and design should suit different requirements and needs, e.g., older people need more assistance than younger ones, so the system has to be reactive
US4	As a CA user, impartiality and equality of opportunities and respectful interaction are key for perceiving a CA as fair
US5	As a CA user, I would like the interaction and communication with the CA to be easy and intuitive
US6	As a CA user, I wish that the process follows certain structures and is always be understandable
US7	As a CA user, it would be convenient if the interaction was like human-human interaction in terms of empathy and flexibility
US8	As a CA user, I expect that the focus is on solving my issues/problems and ensuring this through inquiries and confirmations or exit strategies if necessary

(*continued*)

Table 2. (*continued*)

#	User stories (USs)
US9	As a CA user, it would be helpful to know that only context-relevant data is collected to help me and therewith prevent any sort of bias
US10	As a CA user, it's important that the system is aware of the potential risk of hacking or theft
US11	As a CA user, enlightenment and commitment to privacy and data protection rules is inevitable, e.g., regular reports would give me a good feeling/trust in the system
US12	As a CA user, I would like to have a feedback function and human contact option always available (e.g., as an exit strategy)
US13	As a CA user, in case of an attack, I expect to be directly informed about the attack and what is advised to do, e.g., deleting or changing passwords or that the system is in self-destruction mode and deletes all personal data
US14	As a CA user, I expect that my data is protected against any kind of abuse
US15	As a CA user, I would like to use a CA that embeds control mechanisms through independent third parties to make the system credible
US16	As a CA user, I would like to use a CA that is regularly controlled through independent control organs/institutions for continuous monitoring and improvements
US17	As a CA user, I would like to use a CA that regularly controls both technical control and human control mechanisms, e.g., to control if intended actions are happening
US18	As a CA user, I would like to use a CA that reports every action step and provides access to information
US19	As a CA user, I would like to receive detailed feedback in case something relevant is affecting my data

4.3 Step 4: Deriving Preliminary Design Principles

As illustrated, we have identified 15 LIs and 19 USs as requirements for a value-sensitive design of CAs. Based on these findings, we derived 14 preliminary DPs for a value-sensitive CA that aim to address OECD AI principles two to five. The design principles (and the LIs as well as the USs the particular DP is derived from) are depicted in Table 3. Our DPs were formulated based on the analysis of current issues related to value-sensitive design, design of CAs and requirements of users based on social response theory [27, 28]. We argue that a CA (and possibly other AI-based ISs) that instantiates our DPs increase the perceived humanness of the CA, for example, through more trustworthy design elements and thus improve the overall user experience and interaction. For example, a value-sensitive CA that employs a mechanism to avoid data bias in the training's data and is instantiated in different languages for different cultural and age backgrounds should be perceived as fairer and human-centered, and thus the interaction with the CA should result in a better user experience.

Table 3. Preliminary design principles according to [62]

Dimension	#	Design principles (DPs)	LI	US
Human-centered values and fairness	DP1	For designers to establish a human-centered CA, which is perceived as fair by users, employ a working step that ensures data collection fulfills the minimalism and general data collection regulation to ensure that the user does not feel treated unfairly because of not context-relevant information	LI4	US1
	DP2	For designers to implement fairness in CA, employ a mechanism that checks the training data for representativeness and bias to make the user feel confident while using the CA and sharing information	LI 1,3	US1
	DP3	For designers to build a human-centered CA, employ a chat indicator in the design that signals compliance with democratic as well as moral and ethical values to enhance the users' perceived fairness	LI4	US4
	DP4	For designers to implement a fair and human-centered CA, ensure widespread accessibility and usability to allow users from different language and age backgrounds to easily interact with the CA	LI2	US2,3
Transparency and explainability	DP5	For designers to enhance the perceived transparency and trustworthiness of a CA, employ an indicator (e.g., some sort of certificate) showing that the CA is compliant with national and international laws and standards to allow the user to perceive the rightful design	LI6, 8	US5,6
	DP6	For designers to establish a transparent CA, consider feedback cycles and traceable structures to allow the user to understand internal processes and outcome generation and thus enhance understanding	LI5, 7,8	US8
	DP7	For designers to employ transparent CAs, integrate an indicator/avatar that educates the user about data collection procedures to allow the user to feel involved and well advised	LI8	US9

(*continued*)

Table 3. *(continued)*

Dimension	#	Design principles (DPs)	LI	US
	DP8	For designers to establish transparent and understandable CAs for users, develop a professional wording, flexible (exit strategies, keyword independent solving) and empathetically communicating avatar that creates a convenient and pleasurable user experience	LI8	US5, 6,7
Robustness, security and safety	DP9	For designers to design robust and secure CAs for users, employ an indicator that signals the user protection of sensitive data and implements safety and security standards/laws to allow the user to feel protected against any type of harm or abuse	LI9, 10	US11
	DP 10	For designers to establish robust CAs for users, employ regular security checks and well-elaborated risk management strategies that ensure data and privacy security and therewith enhance overall resilience	LI 11	US10,12–14
	DP 11	For designers to develop robust CAs, employ some sort of official certificates in the design that allow the user to strengthen perceived reliability and safety through serious commitment	LI 12	US11
Accountability	DP 12	For designers to establish accountable CAs employ a mechanism that demonstrates independent audit or control organs are regularly revising the CA to ensure compliance with given laws and standards and signals the user trustworthiness for the CA	LI 13,15	US16
	DP 13	For designers to design accountable CAs, employ an indicator that makes internal reporting strategies and guidelines available for the user and allow for further information and therewith enhance perceived responsibility	LI 14	US15, 18
	DP 14	For designers to design accountable CAs, employ logging and tracking mechanisms to establish clear structures that can easily be retraced and understood by users in order to allow for the correct functioning and clear communication towards the user	LI 14	US17, 19

4.4 Step 5: Expert-Based Evaluation of Design Principles

In the next step, we aimed to evaluate our preliminary DPs with experts from different domains, such as IS, HCI, and psychology. Our primary goal was to both qualitatively and quantitatively evaluate if the design principles would be of use from the perspective of the experts and if they are robust and important for the design of ethical CAs. Therefore, we performed expert interviews following the criteria of [32]. The interview questionnaire consisted of 46 items and was composed of three parts. We started with an introduction about research on CAs and ethical design to provide a basis for a common understanding. In the second part, we sequentially showed the interviewees our preliminary DPs for a value-sensitive design of CAs and asked questions about their relevance, usability, and robustness. (e.g., "*How important/useful/robust is this DP for an ethical design of CAs and why?*"). We quantitatively captured their impression on a 5-point Likert scale from "fully disagree" to "fully agree". Moreover, we documented their qualitative justification of the answer for each DP. The questionnaire closed with a creative task, where we asked the experts to derive concrete design features on how the DP could be instantiated. We aimed to further evaluate our DPs by analyzing if the experts could deduct a specific design feature from the principle. Moreover, by doing so, we received further design knowledge about potential design instantiations. We provided an empty CA box, where the participants were asked to draw/sketch a design feature or write down their ideas in design statements. In total we interviewed ten experts - eight were researchers, while two were practitioners. The mean age was mean = 28.20 (SD = 8.53), seven were female, three were male. In average the interviews lasted mean = 66.8 min (SD = 15.33). The documented results were a) qualitatively evaluated by calculating the mean and standard derivation (SD) for each DP and evaluation dimension (relevance, usefulness, and robustness) and b) qualitatively analyzed by performing a cluster analysis of the provided answers. The quantitative results of our interviews are displayed in Table 4 and the qualitative cluster results along with exemplary quotes are displayed in Table 5.

Table 4. Quantitative results from the expert-based evaluation based on the three evaluation dimensions (relevance, usefulness, and robustness) for each value-sensitive design principle

	Relevance of DP		Usefulness of DP		Robustness of DP	
DP	Mean	SD	Mean	SD	Mean	SD
1	4.70	0.46	4.7	0.46	4.0	0.77
2	4.60	0.49	4.4	0.49	4.1	0.94
3	4.4	0.92	4.3	0.90	4.0	0.77
4	4.9	0.30	4.8	0.40	4.7	0.46
5	4.5	0.81	4.6	0.66	4.4	0.80

(continued)

Table 4. (*continued*)

	Relevance of DP		Usefulness of DP		Robustness of DP	
DP	Mean	SD	Mean	SD	Mean	SD
6	3.8	0.98	4.1	0.70	3.9	0.83
7	4.5	0.67	4.5	0.50	4.1	0.94
8	4.7	0.46	4.8	0.40	4.2	0.87
9	4.5	0.67	4.6	0.66	4.3	1.00
10	4.7	0.64	4.6	0.66	4.7	0.64
11	3.8	1.54	3.9	1.58	3.6	1.50
12	4.6	0.49	4.6	0.49	4.3	1.00
13	4.0	0.77	4.2	0.60	4.3	0.46
14	4.0	1.18	3.3	1.15	3.5	1.29

Our evaluation confirmed that all DPs are mostly positively perceived by the experts in terms of relevance, robustness, and usefulness. The mean values for the DPs are promising when comparing the results to the midpoints of the scale. The relevance of all design principles is better than the neutral value of 3, and all fourteen DPs have normalized values greater than 0.7 (greater absolute values than 3.5), which indicates a high relevance. Regarding the usefulness, only DP14 is evaluated with a mean value lower than 4, which can be explained by the fact that tracing and logging user activities seem to generally be seen sceptical by potential users, which highlights a particularly sensitive area to users that could be meaningfully addressed by value-sensitive design activities. This is reflected in an exemplary expert comment "*Users don't want their actions and habits to be traced in such detail; they would feel supervised in an uncomfortable way*". Twelve DPs are regarded as highly useful with higher normalized values greater than 4.0 (except for DP 6 and DP 11). Regarding the robustness of the DPs, eleven out of fourteen DPs received higher mean values than 4.0. Only DP11 is regarded as less robust by the experts with a mean = 3.6. The SD for DP11 with regards to robustness is quite high (SD = 1.50) indicating that there is a disappearance between the experts judging the DP as not very robust or as very robust. In their qualitative comments, some interviewees elaborated that they perceive certificates and signaling as important and a way to demonstrate compliance with certain values or procedures. Others formed a completely different image, stating that certificates can also be deceptive and should be seen critically and cautiously, as they are not only advantageous. Eleven DPs are judged as highly robust with greater mean values than 4.0 except for DP 6, DP 11, and DP 14.

Table 5. Clustered qualitative results from the expert-based evaluations by representative examples

Group	Quotes
On fairness (DP1–4)	*"Mitigation bias and ensuring representativeness is of great importance because it enhances perceived fairness."* *"It is harmful if the user has to be concerned about being judged because of criteria (gender, age, religion) that need not be relevant for the outcome"*
On transparency and trust (DP5–8)	*"Certificates support perceived transparency and trust in CAs as a signaling effect, (but be also aware of weaknesses)."* *"Engage in understandable structures and consistent regulations to help users follow the outcome process and reassure with feedback questions that intended goals are reached."* *"I think providing information concerning different topics (e.g., data collection/use, internal risk strategies) is crucial for transparency and trust."* *"I think clear and honest communication about data collection and usage is of great importance. If this is not part of the communication process, the user could feel unsure and is not be likely to trust the system."* *"From my experience users value adequate language and questions as key to perceive a CA as capable and trustworthy"*
On robustness, safety, and security (DP9–11)	*"Sensitive data of users have to stay private to make users feel more confident"* *"To enhance trust and robustness, implement regular safety checks and reduce error tolerance"* *"Especially data security and compliance with the DSGVO should be basic elements of CAs"*
On accountability (DP12–14)	*"An accountable CA should be controlled by independent institutions to ensure regular improvement and compliance with legal norms and standards."* *"Users like to be ensured that internal and external structures/organs prevent misuse or harmful action"*

As described above, we also included qualitative questions in our questionnaire to receive the participants' opinions about the DPs and reasons for their quantitative judgements. The general attitude about most DPs was very positive. Especially the principles for trust and transparency were highlighted often by the interviewees. However, the DPs on accountability sometimes seem to be not clear enough. The clustered results are displayed in Table 5 along with the OECD principles.

Moreover, the experts revealed some interesting ideas and concepts for implementing the DPs as instantiated CAs, e.g., for usability and trust, *"Insert an EXIT-Button to stop interaction or to switch to human."*, or for visualization, *"Insert control units for the size of writing or the sound, in general, be adaptive to different user needs."*, and for different user groups "*Use of symbols instead of texts to makes interaction easier and more intuitive for elderly users*".

5 Discussion and Conclusion

Besides a multitude of behavioral and design-oriented studies on CAs, a distinct ethical perspective on CA design falls rather short in current literature. Therefore, in our paper, we presented first insights into how to deduct actionable design knowledge for the design of value-sensitive CAs based on contemporary ethical frameworks for AI design. We document 15 literature issues based on 87 papers and 19 user stories based on eleven user interviews on how to design a value-sensitive CA following the OECD AI principles. Moreover, we derived and evaluated 14 design principles that address them. Our results show interesting findings for the design of conversational interfaces and possibly other AI-based IS.

We, therefore, contribute to the design of CAs based on a value-sensitive approach to ensure an ethical perspective on this emerging technology. We provide researchers and practitioners with requirements and design principles for the design of their own CA to help them to ensure their user manipulations are built based on an ethical grounding. Especially with further advances of NLP and ML (e.g., [63]) and newly available data sets for specific domain-related tasks (e.g., argumentation annotated corpora for argumentation skill learning [64, 65]), design knowledge for a value-sensitive perspective on CAs might encourage designers and research towards a more ethical design of these novel ISs. This might help providers of CAs to communicate to the user how a value-sensitive design approach has been followed based on our principles. Overall, we aim to contribute to a *nascent design theory* [47] for the class of value-sensitive IS artifacts. We systematically deduced design knowledge as documented in Table 1, 2, and 3. Due to the systematic procedure, we aimed at generating a satisfying design contribution [66]. We believe with further empirical evaluation and instantiation of our generated design knowledge; we contribute to a nascent design theory in IS (e.g., such as [9]). We, therefore, hope to encourage designers to focus more on an ethical design of conversational IS.

However, our research also comes with limitations. Since our objective was to derive practical design principles to help designers, we derived the requirements from a certain IS and HCI perspective. Different literature streams or different interviewees (e.g., interviews only from ethics) might lead to different results on different granularity levels. Moreover, we abstracted and derived certain design principles to provide a holistic design perspective of the OECD principles. Therefore, a certain abstraction level was chosen. The question that remains for the individual domain and class of CAs is how to instantiate the design principles as design features for their specific use case. Therefore, we call for future work to provide empirical insights into the effects of specific principles and instantiated design features on human perception.

References

1. Maedche, A., et al.: AI-Based digital assistants. Bus. Inf. Syst. Eng. **61**(4), 535–544 (2019). https://doi.org/10.1007/s12599-019-00600-8

2. Shawar, B.A., Atwell, E.S.: Using corpora in machine-learning chatbot systems. Int. J. Corpus Linguist. **10**, 489–516 (2005). https://doi.org/10.1075/ijcl.10.4.06sha
3. De Keyser, A., Köcher, S., Alkire (née Nasr), L., Verbeeck, C., Kandampully, J.: Frontline service technology infusion: conceptual archetypes and future research directions. J. Serv. Manag. **30**, 156–183 (2019). https://doi.org/10.1108/JOSM-03-2018-0082
4. Winkler, R., Hobert, S., Salovaara, A., Söllner, M., Leimeister, J.M.: Sara, The lecturer: improving learning in online education with a scaffolding-based conversational agent. In: Conference on Human Factors in Computing Systems - Proceedings (2020). https://doi.org/10.1145/3313831.3376781
5. Adam, M., Wessel, M., Benlian, A.: AI-based chatbots in customer service and their effects on user compliance. Electron. Mark. **31**(2), 427–445 (2020). https://doi.org/10.1007/s12525-020-00414-7
6. Zierau, N., Engel, C., Söllner, M., Leimeister, J.M.: Trust in smart personal assistants: a systematic literature review and development of a research agenda. In: 15th International Conference on Wirtschaftsinformatik (WI 2020) (2020)
7. Winkler, R., Söllner, M.: Unleashing the potential of chatbots in education: a state-of-the-art analysis. In: Academy of Management. Meetings Annual Chicago, A O M. (2018)
8. Wambsganss, T., Winkler, R., Schmid, P., Söllner, M.: unleashing the potential of conversational agents for course evaluations: empirical insights from a comparison with web surveys. In: Twenty-Eighth European Conference on Information Systems (ECIS2020). pp. 1–18, Marrakesh, Morocco (2020)
9. Wambsganss, T., Söllner, M., Leimeister, J.M.: Design and evaluation of an adaptive dialog-based tutoring system for argumentation skills. In: International Conference on Information Systems (ICIS), Hyderabad, India (2020)
10. Laumer, S., Maier, C., Gubler, F.T.: Chatbot acceptance in healthcare: explaining user adoption of conversational agents for disease diagnosis. In: Twenty-Seventh European Conference Information System (ECIS2019), Stock. Sweden, pp. 10–18 (2019)
11. Følstad, A., Brandtzaeg, P.B.: Users' experiences with chatbots: findings from a questionnaire study. Qual. User Experience **5**(1), 1–14 (2020). https://doi.org/10.1007/s41233-020-00033-2
12. Zierau, N., Wambsganss, T., Janson, A., Schöbel, S., Leimeister, J.M.: The anatomy of user experience with conversational agents: a taxonomy and propositions of service clues. In: ICIS 2020, pp. 1–17 (2020)
13. Feine, J., Gnewuch, U., Morana, S., Maedche, A.: Gender bias in chatbot design. In: Følstad, A., et al. (eds.) CONVERSATIONS 2019. LNCS, vol. 11970, pp. 79–93. Springer, Cham (2020). https://doi.org/10.1007/978-3-030-39540-7_6
14. Rahwan, I., et al.: Machine behaviour. Nature **568**, 477–486 (2019). https://doi.org/10.1038/s41586-019-1138-y
15. Pfeuffer, N., Benlian, A., Gimpel, H., Hinz, O.: Anthropomorphic information systems. Bus. Inf. Syst. Eng. **61**(4), 523–533 (2019). https://doi.org/10.1007/s12599-019-00599-y
16. Hildebrand, C., Bergner, A.: Conversational robo advisors as surrogates of trust: onboarding experience, firm perception, and consumer financial decision making. J. Acad. Mark. Sci. **49**(4), 659–676 (2020). https://doi.org/10.1007/s11747-020-00753-z
17. Roßnagel, A.: Smarte Persönliche Assistenten gestalten. Datenschutz und Datensicherheit - DuD **44**(9), 565–566 (2020). https://doi.org/10.1007/s11623-020-1324-y
18. Følstad, A., Brandtzaeg, P.B., Feltwell, T., Law, E.L.C., Tscheligi, M., Luger, E.A.: Chatbots for social good. In: Conference Human Factors Computing System - Proceedings 2018, April 2018. https://doi.org/10.1145/3170427.3185372
19. Fuckner, M., Barthes, J.P., Scalabrin, E.E.: Using a personal assistant for exploiting service interfaces. In: Proceedings of the 2014 IEEE 18th International Conference on Computer Supported Cooperative Work in Design, pp. 89–94 (2014). https://doi.org/10.1109/CSCWD.2014.6846822

20. Reddy, T.: Chatbots for customer service will help businesses save $8 billion per year. https://www.ibm.com/blogs/watson/2017/05/chatbots-customer-service-will-help-businesses-save-8-billion-per-year/. Accessed 01 May 2020
21. Feine, J., Gnewuch, U., Morana, S., Maedche, A.: A taxonomy of social cues for conversational agents. Int. J. Hum. Comput. Stud. **132**, 138–161 (2019). https://doi.org/10.1016/j.ijhcs.2019.07.009
22. Mingers, J., Walsham, G.: Toward ethical information systems: the contribution of discourse ethics. MIS Q. Manag. Inf. Syst. **34**, 855–870 (2010). https://doi.org/10.2307/25750707
23. Myers, M.D., Venable, J.R.: A set of ethical principles for design science research in information systems. Inf. Manag. **51**, 801–809 (2014). https://doi.org/10.1016/j.im.2014.01.002
24. Hassan, N.R., Mingers, J., Stahl, B.: Philosophy and information systems: where are we and where should we go? (2018). https://www.tandfonline.com/action/journalInformation?journalCode=tjis20, https://doi.org/10.1080/0960085X.2018.1470776
25. Gimpel, H., et al.: Humane anthropomorphic agents : the quest for the outcome measure. In: AIS SIGPrag 2019 pre-ICIS workshop "Values and Ethics in the Digital Age" (2019)
26. Gregor, S., Chandra Kruse, L., Seidel, S.: The Anatomy of a design principle. J. Assoc. Inf. Syst. Forthcoming **21**, 2 (2020)
27. Nass, C., Steuer, J., Tauber, E.R.: Computers are social actors. In: Proceedings of the SIGCHI conference on Human factors in computing systems celebrating interdependence - CHI 1994, pp. 72–78. ACM Press, New York, USA (1994). https://doi.org/10.1145/191666.191703
28. Nass, C., Moon, Y.: Machines and mindlessness: social responses to computers. J. Soc. Issues **56**, 81–103 (2000). https://doi.org/10.1111/0022-4537.00153
29. Hevner, A.R., March, S.T., Park, J., Ram, S.: Design science in information systems research. Des. Sci. IS Res. MIS Q. **28**, 75 (2004)
30. Mädche, A.: Humane anthropomorphic agents : the quest for the outcome measure. In: Pre-ICIS Workshop 2019 "Values and Ethics in the Digital Age", pp. 1–18 (2019)
31. Friedman, B., Kahn, P.H., Jr., Borning, A.: Value sensitive design and information systems. Hum. Comput. Interact. Manag. Inf. Syst. Found. 1–27 (2006). https://doi.org/10.1145/242485.242493
32. Venable, J., Pries-Heje, J., Baskerville, R.: FEDS: a framework for evaluation in design science research. Eur. J. Inf. Syst. **25**, 77–89 (2016). https://doi.org/10.1057/ejis.2014.36
33. Hevner, A.R.: A three cycle view of design science research. Scand. J. Inf. Syst. 1–6 (2007)
34. Krassmann, A.L., Paz, F.J., Silveira, C., Tarouco, L.M.R., Bercht, M.: Conversational agents in distance education: comparing mood states with students' perception. Creat. Educ. **09**, 1726–1742 (2018). https://doi.org/10.4236/ce.2018.911126
35. Hu, T., et al.: Touch your heart: a tone-aware chatbot for customer care on social media. In: Conference Human Factors Computing System - Proceedings 2018, April 2018. https://doi.org/10.1145/3173574.3173989
36. Cameron, G., et al.: Towards a chatbot for digital counselling. In: HCI 2017 Digital Make Believe - Proceedings 31st International BCS Human Computing Interaction Conference HCI 2017, pp. 1–7, July 2017. https://doi.org/10.14236/ewic/HCI2017.24
37. Elshan, E., Ebel, P.: Let's team up: designing conversational agents as teammates. In: International Conference Information System (2020)
38. Wambsganss, T., Winkler, R., Söllner, M., Leimeister, J.M.: A conversational agent to improve response quality in course evaluations. In: ACM CHI Conference on Human Factors in Computing Systems (2020)
39. Mädche, A.: Humane anthropomorphic agents : the quest for the outcome measure. Pre-ICIS Work. 2019 "Values Ethics Digit. Age", pp. 1–18 (2019)
40. Rosen, J.: Why privacy matters. Wilson Q. **24**, 32–38 (2000). https://doi.org/10.1145/1378727

41. Veale, M., Binns, R.: Fairer machine learning in the real world: Mitigating discrimination without collecting sensitive data. Big Data Soc. **4**, 20539 (2017). https://doi.org/10.1177/2053951717743530
42. Gefen, D., Karahanna, E., Straub, D.W.: Trust and tam in online shopping: AN integrated model. MIS Q. Manag. Inf. Syst. **27**, 51–90 (2003). https://doi.org/10.2307/30036519
43. Nick, B., Eliezer, Y.: The ethics of artifical intelligence. Cambridge Handb. Artif. Intell. **47**, 316 (2011). https://doi.org/10.1016/j.mpmed.2018.12.009
44. Moon, Y.: Intimate exchanges: using computers to elicit self-disclosure from consumers. J. Consum. Res. **26**, 323–339 (2000). https://doi.org/10.1086/209566
45. Pavlou, P.A., Gefen, D.: Building effective online marketplaces with institution-based trust. Inf. Syst. Res. **15**, 37 (2004). https://doi.org/10.1287/isre.1040.0015
46. Wambsganss, T., Rietsche, R.: Towards designing an adaptive argumentation learning tool. In: 40th International Conference on Information Systems, ICIS 2019, p. 1 (2020)
47. Gregor, S., Hevner, A.R.: Positioning and Presenting Design Science Research for Maximum Impact (2013)
48. Gläser, J., Laudel, G.: Experteninterviews und qualitative Inhaltsanalyse : als Instrumente rekonstruierender Untersuchungen. VS Verlag für Sozialwiss (2010)
49. Cooper, H.M.: Organizing knowledge syntheses: a taxonomy of literature reviews. Knowl. Soc. **1**, 104–126 (1988). https://doi.org/10.1007/BF03177550
50. vom Brocke, J., Simons, A., Riemer, K., Niehaves, B., Plattfaut, R., Cleven, A.: Standing on the shoulders of giants: challenges and recommendations of literature search in information systems research. Commun. Assoc. Inf. Syst. **37**, 205–224 (2015). https://doi.org/10.17705/1cais.03709
51. Webster, J., Watson, R.T.: Analyzing the past to prepare for the future: writing a literature review. MIS Q. **26**, xiii–xxiii (2002)
52. Poel, I.: An ethical framework for evaluating experimental technology. Sci. Eng. Ethics **22**(3), 667–686 (2015). https://doi.org/10.1007/s11948-015-9724-3
53. Weller, A.: Transparency: motivations and challenges. In: Samek, W., Montavon, G., Vedaldi, A., Hansen, L.K., Müller, K.-R. (eds.) Explainable AI: Interpreting, Explaining and Visualizing Deep Learning. LNCS (LNAI), vol. 11700, pp. 23–40. Springer, Cham (2019). https://doi.org/10.1007/978-3-030-28954-6_2
54. Mittelstadt, B., Russell, C., Wachter, S.: Explaining explanations in AI. In: FAT* 2019 - Proceedings of the 2019 Conference on Fairness, Accountability, and Transparency, pp. 279–288. Association for Computing Machinery, Inc., (2019). https://doi.org/10.1145/3287560.3287574
55. Spanoudakis, G.: Plausible and adaptive requirement traceability structures. In: ACM International Conference Proceeding Series. pp. 135–142 (2002). https://doi.org/10.1145/568760.568786
56. Rothenberger, L., Fabian, B., Arunov, E.: Relevance of ethical guidelines for artificial intelligence - a survey and evaluation. In: European Conference Information System. ECIS 2019, pp. 10–11 (2019)
57. Sharma, S., Henderson, J., Ghosh, J.: CERTIFAI: Counterfactual Explanations for Robustness, Transparency, Interpretability, and Fairness of Artificial Intelligence models (2019)
58. Millar, J., Barron, B., Hori, K., Finlay, R., Kotsuki, K., Kerr, I.: Accountability in AI promoting greater societal trust. In: G7 Multistakeholder Conference AI, p. 16 (2018)
59. Yan, M., Castro, P., Cheng, P., Ishakian, V.: Building a chatbot with serverless computing. In: Proceedings of the 1st International Workshop on Mashups of Things and APIs, MOTA 2016. Association for Computing Machinery, Inc., (2016). https://doi.org/10.1145/3007203.3007217
60. Dignum, V.: Responsible artificial intelligence: designing AI for human values. ICT Discov. 1–8 (2017)

61. Cohn, M.: User Stories Applied For Agile Software Development (2004)
62. Gregor, S., Chandra Kruse, L., Seidel, S.: Research perspectives: the anatomy of a design principle. J. Assoc. Inf. Syst. **21**, 1622–1652 (2020). https://doi.org/10.17705/1jais.00649
63. Wambsganss, T., Molyndris, N., Söllner, M.: Unlocking transfer learning in argumentation mining: a domain-independent modelling approach. In: 15th International Conference on Wirtschaftsinformatik, Potsdam, Germany (2020). https://doi.org/10.30844/wi_2020_c9-wambsganss
64. Wambsganss, T., Niklaus, C., Söllner, M., Handschuh, S., Leimeister, J.M.: A corpus for argumentative writing support in German. In: 28th International Conference on Computational Linguistics (Coling) (2020)
65. Wambsganss, T., Niklaus, C., Cetto, M., Söllner, M., Leimeister, J.M., Handschuh, S.: AL: an adaptive learning support system for argumentation skills. In: ACM CHI Conference on Human Factors in Computing Systems, pp. 1–14 (2020)
66. Gregory, R.W., Muntermann, J.: Research Note: Heuristic Theorizing: Proactively Generating Design Theories (2014). https://www.jstor.org/stable/24700315, https://doi.org/10.2307/24700315

On Your Mark, Ready, Search: A Framework for Structuring Literature Search Strategies in Information Systems

Thorsten Schoormann[1(✉)], Dennis Behrens[1], Michael Fellmann[2], and Ralf Knackstedt[1]

[1] Information Systems, University of Hildesheim, Hildesheim, Germany
{thorsten.schoormann,ralf.knackstedt}@uni-hildesheim.de
[2] Business Information Systems, University of Rostock, Rostock, Germany
michael.fellmann@uni-rostock.de

Abstract. Researchers often face challenges already in the early stages of a literature review, and thus, struggle in getting started with the search and in organizing the process. This starting point is however of great relevance because design decisions such as in terms of corpus creation have impacts on the entire results of the review. By following the design science paradigm, we present the 'Search Canvas', a generic framework that aims at supporting the (creative) process of exploring, specifying, and visually representing a literature search strategy. In doing this, we contribute to the understanding of what components need to be considered when deriving a search strategy and provide an instrument that enables researchers to iteratively plan and communicate such strategies.

Keywords: Literature search strategy · Keyword-based search · Canvas-based framework · Literature review · Design science

1 Introduction and Problem Awareness

The relevance of conducting rigorous literature reviews in any kind of project is uncontroversial (e.g., [1–6]). Reviewing the literature is a crucial starting point of every research, and thus, used by researchers at different professional stages from students to graduates to become familiar with or deepen their view on a phenomenon [7, 8]. In contrast to narrative reviews, systematic reviews seek to ensure rigorousness through well-defined processes as well as quality criteria such as traceability, systematicity, or reproducibility [2, 9, 10]. Ensuring rigorousness enables other researchers to fully decode the review's path as well as to build on and complement the review's findings.

Even though available methodological guidance (e.g., in the form of quality criteria or procedure models) helps to perform literature reviews, it is however still challenging to get started with the review and to formulate an appropriate search strategy—especially for students and novice researchers. We argue that this can be attributed to three main indications: First, although the review's starting point is of great importance because

F. Ahlemann et al. (Eds.): WI 2021, LNISO 46, pp. 558–575, 2021.
https://doi.org/10.1007/978-3-030-86790-4_38

"[*failures*] have a considerable impact on the resulting review's quality" [11], (IS) researchers often face the 'dilemma at the start' [11] because they have no clear orientation where to begin searching like in other disciplines that have, for instance, established overviews of reference databases [12]. Second, although IS research is often intertwined or linked with adjacent disciplines, conventional corpus creation often focuses on parts of a phenomenon without the benefit of a larger context, which leads to deficits in terms of identifying the majority of research [13]. Third, several authors stated dangers in terms of a review's linearity, particularly with regards to forcing reviewers to strictly apply 'methodological checklists' and not allowing them to adapt search strategies based on an emerging understanding [14, 17]. Methodological flexibility is however demanded, for instance, to make the review's research questions more precise in successive stages [15], develop a search phrase across iterations [16], and to perform an (initial) planning phase not only at a review's beginning [14].

In addition, from our personal experience as researchers, lecturers, and authors, we also observed this discrepancy between the (particularly novice) researcher's expectations and the systematic literature review's degree of difficulty. On the one hand, novices tend to prefer performing systematic reviews because they seem to have an easy to follow set of specified start activities from selecting keywords to summarizing the results in the form of a concept matrix for example. On the other hand, however, asking the researcher about details concerning the decisions they have made, it often becomes evident that there are serious deficits in the review's rigorousness (e.g., search query was changed at a late stage). To bridge these gaps, we aim at deriving a framework that facilitates the (creative) process of specifying a literature search strategy, and thus, helps to divide and conquer the complex task of getting started with a review. Therefore, we raise the following research question (RQ): *How to design a tool that supports specifying and communicating literature search strategies?*

In attempting to answer this, we carried out a design science research (DSR) study in which we iteratively build and evaluate a framework, the 'Search Canvas', which synthesizes the basic components that need to be considered during a literature search. As canvas-based tools facilitate exploration and ideation [18], brainstorming, and collaboration across disciplinary boundaries [19], we believe that this might be a helpful tool to overcome challenges with regard to starting a search as well. Since we adapt known solutions in the form of the canvas (e.g., known from the business model canvas [20]) to new problems, we position our work as *exaptation research* (i.e., "adopt solutions from other fields" [21]). Our contribution seeks to complement available knowledge on how to conduct literature reviews and especially help novices organizing the starting point of a review, for instance, by enabling them to jointly ideate within a team of reviewers, communicate ideas to collect feedback from experts, and document (interim) results. In doing this, we also hope to respond to calls for better documentation of design decisions in IS research, which is a basis for transparency [5].

2 Research Background: Searching for Literature

A well-documented specification of the **search strategy** contributes to the rigorousness of a literature review because it ensures transparency, systematicity, traceability, clarity, and reproducibility [5, 10, 14, 22, 23]. Generally, searching for literature can be carried out through (1) a keyword-based procedure or (2) a systematic personal reading [8]. Both have pros and cons: Personal reading needs a lot of time and keyword-based searches depend on the selection of proper items. The identification of keywords in particular is challenging [2] as certain concepts might have "dozens of completely different words or expressions for designating the same phenomenon" [8]. Hence, the process of planning and conducting a search is highly iterative and requires continuously finding/validating terms [24].

In order to handle the complexity of the search phase, authors have provided methodological recommendations for literature reviews. For example, [25] suggested phases including *conceptualization of topic* and *literature search*, and argued that a review should start with a broad conception of what is known about a certain topic to provide definitions of key terms (e.g., by using seminal books). The search itself should contain information related to databases selected and keywords used. [26] proposed guidelines consisting of steps including *searching for the literature* in which the authors claimed for explicit descriptions of the search process and the justification of how the comprehensiveness can be assured (e.g., journal selection and clear keyword definition). In [27], a procedure model is presented comprising *generating a search strategy* that consists of using various combinations of keywords, drawing up a list of synonyms and alternative spellings, as well as deriving search strings by means of Boolean operators. The author called for explicitly documenting and justifying the entire search. By laying a focus on transparency and systematicity, [14] proposed beginning with *developing a review plan* (e.g., formulate a research question, describe review goals, publish review protocol), *searching the literature* (e.g., define criteria for inclusion, select databases, describe search strategy), and *selecting studies* (e.g., describe screening process, list included studies). [13] explored the creation of a corpus and differentiated between steps for *identifying boundaries* and *construct a corpus*.

In attempting to operationalize such recommendations, so-called **review protocols** are provided that help to structure and document literature searches. Although review protocols are usually employed for systematic reviews, they are according to [11] valuable for all types of reviews. Those protocols aim at minimizing the bias in the study and are a critical element within a review [28]. Especially in the context of software engineering, progress towards a unified protocol has been made: Several authors [27, 29] deduced a *search process template* differentiating between electronic databases (name, search for each database, date of search, years), journal hand search (name, years), conference proceedings, efforts to identify unpublished studies (e.g., researchers contacted), and other sources (date, URL); [30] specified elements for the search process including search strings, inclusion criteria, exclusion criteria, initial primary study selection, and final primary study selection; [28] complemented these ideas through a procedure-perspective and defined the first phase for a review with steps for specifying a research question, develop a review protocol, and validate it. As another example, [31] presented *search planning worksheets* containing elements for databases, grey literature, journals, and experts to contact. In the IS discipline, [11] emphasized the great relevance of such protocols and [26] argued that protocols are particularly worthwhile to have in case of multiple reviewers within a single project to ensure clearness and consistency in terms of the search procedure.

Nevertheless, although recommendations related to the search strategy are available, still various challenges occur—for novice researchers in particular—such as identifying adequate items or combining items into a search phrase [2, 8, 11]. Additionally, as there is a heterogeneous set of protocols, there is a need for a holistic overview of relevant components in IS. In contrast to subsequent phases in the review such as categorizing literature and managing bibliographic data that is well-supported by tools [22], the creation of a search strategy is still more an 'art than sciences' that requires a well-defined structure and a significant amount of knowledge and experience.

3 Research Design: A Design Science Study

3.1 Justification and Overview of Design

In order to achieve our overall goal, we developed the Search Canvas. We decided to derive a canvas for literature searches because of four main reasons: First, visualization in general helps to structure information and allows us to overcome cognitive overloads [32]. Second, so-called visual inquiry tools such as the business model canvas [20] support the joint process of exploration and ideation, are expected to be effective in individual and group settings, and are easy to use [18]. Third, some of the canvasses have experienced worldwide success and great acceptance (e.g., business model canvas has been downloaded more than 5.000.000 times) [19]. Based on a survey, users stated that by means of canvas they achieved, for instance, better conversation, a shared understanding, better brainstorming, better collaboration across disciplines because it is intuitive, visual, and simple [19]. Moreover, [33] identified positive effects on the actual learning and the perceived ease of learning. Fourth, canvasses have been adapted to methodological purposes such as design science [34] as well as in domains as diverse as data-driven businesses [35], service design [36], or sustainability [37]. We believe that these reasons and benefits are also helpful for literature searches, especially to (1) address the iterative and creative character of specifying a search strategy, (2) communicate interim strategies and enable other stakeholders and experts to provide feedback, and (3) enable interdisciplinary teams of researchers to collaborate with the canvas as a so-called boundary object (i.e., provide interfaces for different worlds [38]).

Our overall study is structured by utilizing Hevner et al.'s [39] framework (see Fig. 1). This framework bridges the *environment* and the *knowledge base* with the actual *DSR project*. For building our artifact, the Search Canvas, we adapted principles for visual inquiry tools [26] and relied on different sources: Conceptualization of available methodological guidance for literature reviews to draw on existing knowledge; a systematic review of articles published in high-ranked IS journals to examine how the search strategy is reported/created in 'practice'; think aloud-sessions—as part of an established research paradigm investigating people's cognitive process and behavior [40]—to reveal how researches actually derive a search strategy and which problems occur. For evaluation, we aimed at gathering both qualitative insights utilizing a survey of potential users and quantitative insights through performing an A/B-test that helps to disclose the effects of applying our artifact.

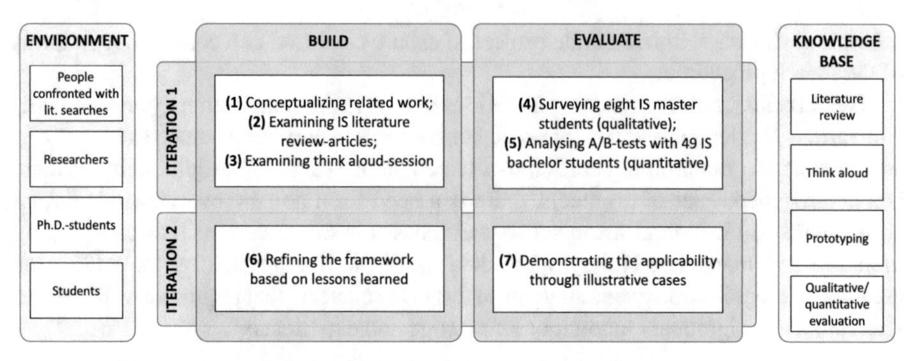

Fig. 1. Research design including different steps (1–7), according to [39]

In total, we ran through two major iterations (i.e., design cycles) of building and evaluating our Search Canvas. Next, both iterations are described in detail.

3.2 Iteration 1 – Initial Search Canvas

Conceptualizing Related Work (1). First, we aimed to build on available knowledge, and thus synthesized methodological guidelines and components that need to be considered during the literature search phase by means of a rather narrative review approach [4]. In doing so, we deduced relevant concepts from methodological work on literature reviews (see also Sect. 2).

Examining Literature Review-Articles (2). Afterward, we analyzed how existing studies in IS research describe their search.[1] Therefore, we conducted a broad search with the following search phrase: *"literature review" OR "literature analysis"*. Since the first popular articles in IS research regarding systematic literature reviews start in early 2000, we limited the results to 'from 2000'. As sources, we selected leading IS journals from the *AIS Senior Scholars 'Basket*. As a result of the rather broad search phrase, we found 999 articles. Following [3], a complete keyword search as well as an evaluation of titles and abstracts was applied. The articles that did not comprise related terms such as 'literature review' or 'literature analysis' were eliminated. The remaining articles (n = 135) were verified by the full text, and non-relevant articles (i.e., the methodology is not described explicitly) were eliminated (n = 51).

We examined the obtained sample according to the following characteristics: 'Search items specified' (are the items defined in a fix or a fuzzy manner); 'no. of items' (the number of specified keywords); 'derivation of search items' (description and justification of why the items are selected); 'search sources' (sources selected in a fix or fuzzy manner); 'search phrase' (logically combination of the items). As an excerpt from the results[2], we found a total of 51 studies with 209 search items and 7 search phrases. Hence, there is an average of approximately 4.09 search items per paper. Nonetheless, the amount of search items and sources that were selected within a review varies considerably.

[1] The entire list of IS articles from the review is available upon request.

[2] For more details on the results of our literature review, see also [16].

As an example, whereas [41] used 21 search items, [42] only one item. Moreover, we found that 27.45% defined their keywords in a fuzzy manner (e.g., with "such as") and only 13.72% described their phrases, which makes it hard to trace the process in detail. Although important to ensure rigorousness, only 54.90% followed a research methodology of which 18 articles refer to Webster and Watson [3].

Examining Think Aloud-Sessions (3). To disclose people's cognitive processes [44], we carried out several think alouds [43]. Following the '10 ± 2 rule' for evaluations [45], we selected eight participants: Six Ph.D.-students (IS, Information Management, and Operation Research) from one to four years of work experiences; two master students (IS). Thus, our selection comprises especially novice and early-stage researchers. The participants came from different universities, and all of them conducted at least one literature review by themselves. All sessions were carried out individually in a separate office with three actors (participant, moderator, and observer). For collecting data, an audio recording was made and observations were protocolled. The workshop was divided into three major parts: First, in the introduction, we welcomed the participants, described the rules of the workshop, outlined the task that has to be executed. Second, the participants received a sheet that summarizes important information related to think aloud and the task to be carried out. The task aims at creating a search phrase for a literature review (here, on 'sustainability and business models'). If a participant stopped talking, the moderator reminds her/him to continue talking. In case that a certain part of a search strategy or at least the entire strategy was comprehensible, the moderator forwarded it to the next step. Third, in the final part, the participants were asked to answer some questions regarding literature reviews in general. In line with our study's purpose, two researchers coded the obtained data independently to determine (a) problems and challenges while setting up a search strategy as well as (b) typical activities that were performed during the specification of a search strategy.

Surveying Master Students (4). To get qualitative (in-depth) feedback on the artifact's applicability and usefulness from potential users, we provided the initial Search Canvas and a short questionnaire to eight IS master-leveled students enrolled in a course in which they had to conduct a literature review (i.e., incentive in the form of a grade). Therefore, the students employed the Search Canvas and answered questions as well as gave general feedback in terms of the canvas's usefulness (see Sect. 4).

Analyzing A/B-Tests (5). Additionally, to obtain quantitative insights and to explore which differences occur when applying the Search Canvas against not-applying it, we performed an A/B-test with 49 bachelor students enrolled in IS (incentive: bonus points for the exam at the end of the course). In doing this, the artifact is investigated in a controlled environment with potential 'real users' and 'real tasks' (here: to create a search strategy). 24 students completed the task with the help of the Search Canvas and 25 students completed the task without using the Search Canvas (see Sect. 4).

3.3 Iteration 2 – Refined Search Canvas

Refining the Framework (6). Based on the lessons learned from the evaluation episode in Iteration 1, we refined (i.e., built) the Search Canvas (see Sect. 4 for refinements).

Demonstrating the Applicability (7). Following Peffers et al. [46], *illustrative scenarios* that apply "an artifact to a synthetic or real-world situation aimed at illustrating suitability or utility of the artifact" are among the most frequently used approaches for evaluating frameworks. This is further emphasized by [39] who stated that "detailed scenarios around the artifact [*should be constructed*] to demonstrate its utility". In line with this, we selected two different published IS literature review-articles and apply the refined Search Canvas to (re-)document the literature search performed by the authors (see Sect. 5).

4 Iteration 1 – Initial Search Canvas

4.1 Building the Initial Search Canvas

Drawing on the findings derived in steps 1–3, we built our Search Canvas. Initially, the canvas differentiates between the following components[3]: Purpose of search, related domains, seminal work, search item candidates, search items, search sources, combination candidates, final search phrase, and project management (see Fig. 2).

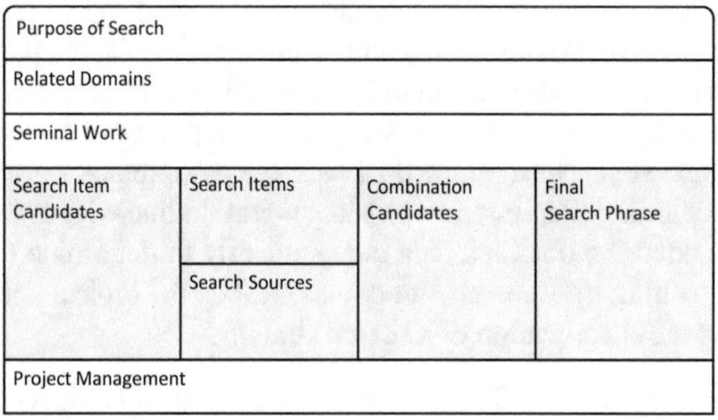

Fig. 2. Our initial framework for search strategies (Search Canvas, Iteration 1)

4.2 Surveying Master Students (Qual. Evaluation of Initial Search Canvas)

In step 4, to get feedback on the artifact's usefulness from potential users (e.g., novice researchers), we provided the canvas as well as a short questionnaire to eight IS master-leveled students with (a) closed questions that should be answered through a Likert-scale and (b) open questions that should be answered through text fields. By analyzing the closed questions, two observations emerged (see Table 2): First, documentation is the highest-ranked purpose of the Search Canvas (5.0). Second, the overall helpfulness of the Search Canvas is quite high (4.62). In terms of open questions, we obtained positive feedback referring to the framework's ability to structure the search process (P2, P6, P7, P8), the framework's simplicity (P5), and the support of brainstorming keywords (P5). In contrast, one improvement could be deduced: Ambiguous difference between 'search item candidates' and 'search items' (P5). In Iteration 2, we have merged and renamed these components (see Sect. 5) (Table 1).

[3] For space reasons, we described the components of the refined Search Canvas—see Sect. 5.

Table 1. Questionnaire results (Likert-scale from 1 low to 7 high)

	P1	P2	P3	P4	P5	P6	P7	P8	AVG
I am familiar with lit. reviews	6	4	1	2	4	4	5	6	**4**
I am familiar with procedure models for literature reviews	6	3	1	2	4	4	4	5	**3.62**
I am familiar with tools for lit. reviews	5	3	1	2	5	4	5	6	**3.87**
I think the framework is helpful	6	5	5	3	4	4	5	5	**4.62**
Documentation of the search is easier via the framework	6	6	–	4	4	4	4	6	**5**
Specification of the search strategy is easier via the framework	7	3	–	4	6	4	5	6	**4.83**

4.3 Analyzing A/B-tests (Quant. Evaluation of Initial Search Canvas)

Step 5 sought to gather insights about potential effects occurring from the usage of the framework. Therefore, we conducted a preliminary A/B-test that distinguishes between two groups (i.e., experiment and control group) each with a set of randomly assigned students. The test was held within an obligatory course for (IS) research methods. The participation was anonymous and voluntary, and thus, there was no direct incentive in the form of a grade/credits but participating helped the students to successfully pass the overall course. The task (~30 min) that had to be solved was formulated as follows: 'Systematically create a search strategy (i.e., the first phases of a literature review in particular) that seeks to identify articles providing extensions for the process modeling notation BPMN 2.0'. All of the participants were familiar with at least one procedure model for literature reviews (e.g., [25] was discussed within the course) and with process modeling (part of the curriculum). A total of 49 IS bachelor students participated in the test, 24 students in **Group A** (i.e., with the Search Canvas and a short description) and 25 students in **Group B** (i.e., without the Search Canvas). The results of the demographic and experience data are summarized in Table 2.

Table 2. Demographics/experiences (scale: from 1 low to 5 high; group averages reported)

	Group A	Group B	Difference	Median
I am familiar with BPMN (domain of review)	2.78	3.18	0.40	2.98
I am familiar with lit. reviews	2.83	2.82	0.01	2.83
I am familiar with the procedure model [25]	1.67	1.27	0.39	1.47
I am familiar with additional procedure models for lit. reviews	2.61	2.59	0.02	2.6

Table 3 reports (a) the frequency in percent (%) of how often a typical search strategy component is addressed by the groups (e.g., how often did participants refer to 'related disciplines') as well as (b) the number of items within a component (e.g., how many 'seminal works' are specified, accumulated across the answers). As this evaluation task was executed individually, the component 'project management' has not been used.

Table 3. Results from the A/B-test (Group A = with canvas; Group B = without canvas)

Components	Group A (n = 24)		Group B (n = 25)	
	% addressed component	No. of elements	% addressed component	No. of elements
Purpose of search	55%	–	88%	–
Related disciplines	50%	6	0%	0
Seminal works	33%	8	11%	1
Search item collection	61%	46	22%	7
Search sources	50%	22	44%	4
Preliminary combination	5%	1	0%	0
Final search phrase	0%	–	33%	–
Project management	n.a.	n.a.	n.a.	n.a.

Based on the results, five main observations emerged: First, the group with the canvas has addressed more components of a literature search (e.g., 33% specified 'seminal work' in contrast to 11% from the non-canvas group; 61% specified 'search items' in contrast to 22% from the non-canvas group). Second, the component 'related disciples' is only addressed by the canvas-group. Third, in addition to these advantages, the results indicate that the 'purpose of search' is described more frequently in the non-canvas group (88% against 55%). Fourth, two components were addressed rather low, namely 'preliminary combinations' (5% with canvas against 0%) and 'search phrases' (0% with canvas against 33%)—this might be due to the given task during the think aloud-sessions that focuses primarily on the first steps of creating a search strategy. Fifth, even though the component 'search source' is addressed equally (50% with canvas against 44%), the number of potential search items is considerably higher within the canvas-group (46 items against 7 items).

Furthermore, we could observe that the component 'related domains' often contains websites, so the term 'domain' was misunderstood. To overcome this shortcoming, we revised the wording in Iteration 2 (see Sect. 5).

5 Iteration 2 – Refined Search Canvas

5.1 Refining the 'Search Canvas'

Based on the lessons learned from Iteration 1, three major refinements have been made (step 6): First, we have merged 'search item candidates' and 'search items' to 'search item collection' because participants mostly did not use both components. Second, we have renamed 'related domains' into 'related disciplines' because some participants tended to provide websites. Third, we have renamed 'combination candidates' into 'preliminary combinations' and have added more guiding questions for the usage. Moreover, we decided to rename the component 'project management' into 'collaboration' as this is quite broad and users might think of controlling, etc., which is not meant. Overall, in line with the 7 $\pm$ 2 heuristic [47]—the magical number that describes the number of chunks handled through the short-term memory—, the refined canvas comprises nine distinct but interrelated components (see Fig. 3).

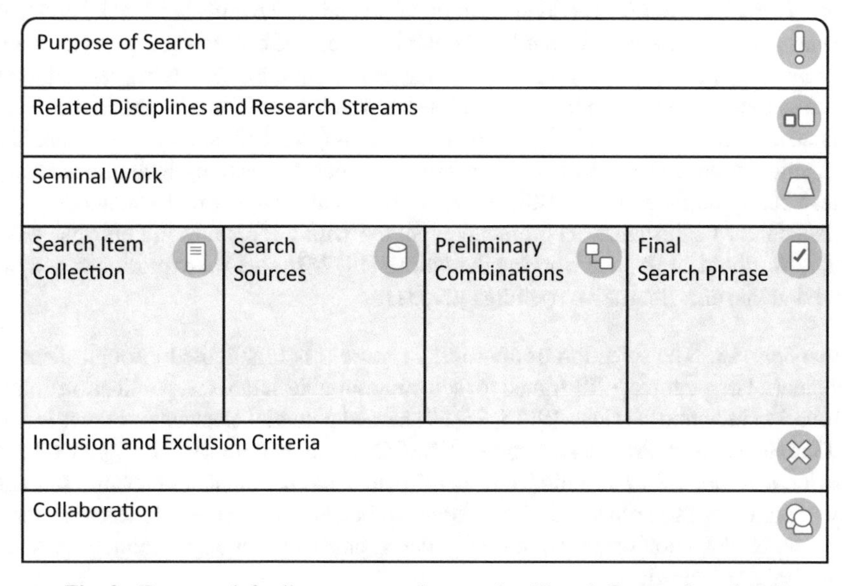

Fig. 3. Framework for literature search strategies (Search Canvas, Iteration 2)

In the following section, the components of the Search Canvas are described in more detail. To do so, we refer to the three sources examined during the artifact building (steps 1–3) as well as to selected evaluation episodes (steps 4–5).

Purpose of Search. The structure of the review to be conducted highly depends on the overall goal and the research questions that are formulated within a project [11]. Thus, the review's key questions [14, 27, 28] and purposes should be clearly stated [22, 26] as well as the actual problem that is addressed by means of the review [9].

*Related Disciplines and Research Streams**[4]. Describing the specific researcher's perspective on the phenomenon of interest is helpful because the readers might more easily follow why specific decisions are made during the review. [13] pointed out that reviews often see only a part of the phenomenon for which reason it would benefit from the larger context. Particularly in emerging fields in IS such as digital transformation or artificial intelligence, phenomena become increasingly interdisciplinary. Furthermore, by determining interfaces to other disciplines and research streams, potential search terms and sources can be deduced.

Seminal Work. The participants of the think aloud-sessions emphasized that they usually start with a review by exploring seminal authors and co-authors, seminal publications, and seminal books from a certain phenomenon of interest. This is further evident by methodological literature, for instance, "a preliminary search for seminal publications can help researchers to identify and select search terms" [11] and identification of relevant literature can be grounded on 'main authors' [24].

*Search Item Collection**. The identification of potential keywords is a crucial and iterative part of the search process. During the think alouds, we observed different strategies for identifying possible search items: Looking up translations, synonyms, related words in dictionaries, as well as modifications of a term like the base form of a certain word (e.g., lemmatization). After identifying potential keywords (mostly in the form of a 'candidate list'), suitable ones were selected. To foster this process, creativity techniques such as brainstorming might be worthwhile to apply. This is also supported by methodological guidance that, for instance, recommend engaging with a topic through encyclopedias, textbooks, edited books, and working definitions [11, 26] as well as exploring synonyms, abbreviations, and alternative spellings [27, 31].

Search Sources. The selection of appropriate sources is highlighted through plenty of statements. For example, [22] argued for selecting suitable databases, publication outlets, and citation indexing services. [9, 15, 26, 29] named potential electronic sources including Google Scholar, ProQuest, Scopus, EBSCO, IEEE Xplore, ACM Digital Library, Elsevier, and the AIS Electronic Library. [27] clustered potential sources into journals, grey literature such as reports, and conference proceedings. [13] listed possible sources including books, book chapters, journal articles, conference articles, monographs, and unpublished manuscripts.

*Preliminary Combinations**. To combine selected search items researchers should (a) consider Boolean operators and additional logical operators that are implemented by a search engine or dataset used for the review [1, 28, 31] as well as (b) verify various alternatives of combining the search items [27]. During the think aloud-sessions, participants also combined their search items by applying logical connectors such as AND, OR, and NOT as well as by using specific search expressions such as "-" for the exclusion of items, or "*" as a placeholder for unknown words/endings (truncation).

Final Search Phrase. Since some participants argued that "[..] the hardest step in a search is actually putting together the keywords", we decided to split this step into two components for potential candidates and the final search phrase. Doing this, we hope to foster creativity by suggesting a separate first step that should allow an easy collection of combinations of terms (i.e., divergent thinking). Afterward, in a second step, the user can select appropriate combinations (i.e., convergent thinking). Available recommendations on literature reviews support this, for instance: [11] stated that most literature reviews in IS research are conducted through a search phrase, which helps to determine the review's scope and objectives, [22] argued for specifying a search strategy with a precise set of search terms used, and [14] emphasized to report the 'full electronic search strategy' to contribute to the review's transparency.

Inclusion and Exclusion Criteria.* During the qualitative evaluation (step 4), we could obtain feedback in terms of the importance of appropriate approaches that help to filter the sample to be collected. Therefore, we added a component for inclusion and exclusion criteria, which is also supported by methodological guidance, especially for *scoping reviews* [4]. In more detail, [27] specified inclusion criteria based on a specific time span (e.g., 01/2004–06/2007), [27] excluded articles that did not define a research question, and [1] suggest aligning such criteria along with the research question.

Collaboration. Often research is not an isolated endeavor, so that different researchers collaboratively work on a certain project—in particular in highly interdisciplinary fields. Since there is an increasing amount of available publications that need to be reviewed, a team of researchers is required to handle this amount [26], which needs to be coordinated [28], for instance, during the screening steps [4]. It might also be helpful to consult (domain) experts that, for example, verify or suggest a set of relevant keywords or relevant search sources [31].

5.2 Exemplary Guiding Questions

In addition, to guide the application of the framework, we propose exemplary key questions for each of the components (see Table 4).

5.3 Demonstrating the Applicability

According to [46], *illustrative scenarios* are among the most frequently used approaches for evaluating frameworks. Following this, in step 7, we selected two IS studies from our sample of literature review-articles and described them through our Search Canvas (Fig. 4): First, [48] who sought to identify structuring themes within 20 years of IS-enabled organizational transformation (*purpose*), which was inspired by Scott Morton in 1991 (*seminal work*). At the intersection of strategic management and IT-enabled business transformation (*related disciplines*), the authors lay an IS-view on that phenomenon. Thus, they searched in IS outlets such as EJIS and JIT (*sources*) by employed several keywords including 'strategic transformation' (*search items*), which were combined utilizing an OR-operator (*phrase*). During the search, [48] particularly included

Table 4. Exemplary key questions for guiding the framework's usage

Component	Exemplary key questions
Purpose of search	What is the overall goal of the study? What is the actual problem or need to be addressed?
Related disciplines	Which are related disciplines of the phenomenon of interest? Which streams of research/genres exist on the phenomenon?
Seminal work	Which seminal articles, books, etc. exist? Which seminal authors and co-authors exist?
Search item collection	Which synonyms, translations, hyponyms, hypernyms exist? Which abbreviations and alternative spellings exist?
Search sources	Which are the key outlets of the review's field? Which databases and citation indexing services can be used?
Preliminary combinations	Which Boolean operators are supported by a search source? Which (syntax) expressions are supported by a search source?
Final search phrase	Which combinations would have the most promising results? Which combinations are suitable for which search source?
Inclusion and exclusion criteria	When to include or exclude a paper to be reviewed? Does a paper to be reviewed seem to be relevant for the review?
Collaboration	Who is your research collaborator and what is his/her role? Which experts can be contacted/consulted?

empirical studies and excluded studies linking transformation to enterprise systems, etc. (*inclusion/exclusion*). Second, [49] examined IS studies employing Grounded Theory to disclose the specific role of axial coding (*purpose*). The topic, placed within the field of qualitative research methods (*related streams*), is well-grounded on previous work such as from Strauss & Corbin and Glaser (*seminal work*). Hence, [49] searched for the keywords 'strauss', 'corbin', and 'axial' (*search items*) in the AIS Senior Scholar's Basket (*source*), which were combined through a Boolean OR (*search phrase*). The authors excluded articles that do not refer to the specified seminal authors or do not employ axial coding (*inclusion/exclusion*). Both studies are conducted by several authors (*collaboration*).

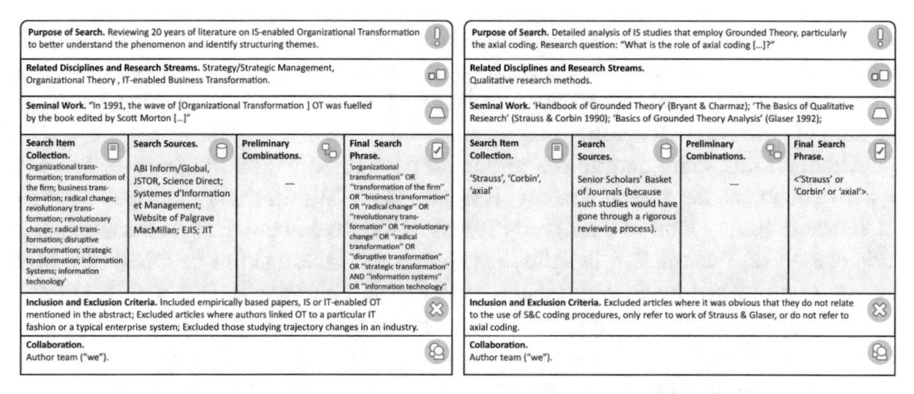

Based on Besson & Rowe [48] Based on Seidel & Urquhart [49]

Fig. 4. Illustrative scenarios demonstrating the framework's applicability

6 Discussion and Conclusion

The sources examined in this study revealed challenges for searching literature and demands in terms of standardized templates that help to document the search strategy in a flexible manner. As an example, although methodological guidance stressed that the entire process has to be documented [5], our analysis of state-of-the-art reviews in IS indicates that this is fulfilled by limited studies: Only 7/51 articles specified a search phrase, there is great heterogeneity in the number of keywords used (between 1–21 terms), and only 28/51 articles followed a systematic procedure. Furthermore, as disclosed through the think alouds, even though the participants were familiar with review procedures, they struggled with the search process, thus asking for "guidance on the derivation of a search phrase". Against this backdrop, we examined the main components of keyword-based searches in IS to design a supporting framework. Therefore, we conceptualized available methodological guidance on literature reviews, literature review-articles, and think aloud-sessions to deduce a set of main review components. Drawing on this conceptualization, we iteratively developed and evaluated the Search Canvas across two major iterations.

Our **contribution** is threefold: *First*, we contribute to an understanding of what are essential components that should be considered and reported during the early stages of a review, and thus help particularly novice researchers to get started with the search. We present a framework for structuring and visualizing search strategies, which importance is emphasized by various authors in IS such as [11] who emphasized that "a search protocol is a useful way to guide and organize the literature search". Although documentation is a major aspect of ensuring transparency (e.g., "quality of a review is rather reflected by the thoroughness of the documentation of the search" [4]), steps for searching and screening are often (still) underrepresented in IS-reviews [5]. *Second*, since the canvas facilitates exploration and ideation [18, 19], our artifact allows for methodological flexibility [14, 15] through refining a search strategy across several iterations, for example, by communicating ideas and collecting feedback from experts. *Third*, the canvas might help facing challenges in terms of the corpus creation [13] because (a) researchers might pay more attention to critical aspects such as adjacent disciplines and the broader phenomenon's context utilizing the canvas (e.g., as shown during the evaluation) as well as (b) brainstorm on and validate strategy aspects such as search terms and sources through the help of collaboration across disciplines.

Although this study contributes to how to get started with a literature review and how to document the search strategy, it is not free of **limitations** that open avenues for future research. First, we primarily report descriptive findings from the evaluation and focused on quantitative insights, neglecting the investigation of whether a high amount of keywords leads to ultimately better search phrases. In line with Parè et al. [4], "we must also bring the 'quality' element to the discussion of conducting literature reviews" for which reason further steps might be concerned with analyzing 'precision' (i.e., correctness, quality) in addition to 'recall' (i.e., completeness, quantity). Second, even though all reviews require a minimum level in terms of being systematic [14], we did not evaluate the applicability across different review types such as theoretical, narrative, or descriptive reviews [4], especially quantitative-based reviews might demand additional canvas components [5]. Third, whereas a canvas is intended to be the boundary object that is continuously revised within a team of collaborators over a period of time, our evaluation is restricted to a specific timespan and individual use. Further research is required that explores the usage over time, for instance, through a case study or longitudinal study. In doing this, researchers might examine when review teams stop with the actual specification of a search strategy (e.g., adapting concepts such as 'theoretical saturation') to provide guidelines on how to apply the iterative nature of the canvas. Fourth, our study is limited to the group of users, namely IS students. As indicated by the questionnaire (step 5), there seems to be a tendency that more experienced researchers gave higher rankings for the framework's usefulness—maybe because they did already face several challenges during reviewing the literature. Hence, future endeavors can focus on the target user groups and investigate for which groups the framework is suitable (e.g., IS education). Fifth, referring to the framework's design, the artifact is based on own decisions and interpretations (e.g., in terms of the components and their arrangement) as well as on the underpinning research methods that have been applied, which both have limitations.

In conclusion, we hope to complement the valuable stream of research on literature review guidance that is already available for the IS discipline as well as shed light on the first steps of deriving and documenting a search strategy. The initial evaluations indicate promising results, especially in supporting novice researchers to perform, specify, and document search strategies with a higher level of transparency.

References

1. Boell, S.K., Cecez-Kecmanovic, D.: On being 'systematic' in literature reviews in IS. J. Inf. Technol. **30**, 161–173 (2015)
2. Levy, Y., Ellis, T.J.: A systems approach to conduct an effective literature review in support of information systems research. Inf. Sci. Int. J. Emerg. Transdisc. **9**, 181–212 (2006)
3. Webster, J., Watson, R.T.: Analyzing the past to prepare for the future: writing a literature review. MIS Q. **26**, xiii–xxiii (2002)

4. Paré, G., Trudel, M.-C., Jaana, M., Kitsiou, S.: Synthesizing information systems knowledge: a typology of literature reviews. Inf. Manage. **52**, 183–199 (2015)
5. Templier, M., Paré, G.: Transparency in literature reviews: an assessment of reporting practices across review types and genres in top IS journals. Null **27**, 503–550 (2018)
6. Schryen, G., et al.: Literature reviews in IS research: what can be learnt from the past and other fields? Commun. Assoc. Inf. Syst. **41**, 759–774 (2017)
7. Schryen, G.: Writing qualitative IS literature reviews – guidelines for synthesis, interpretation and guidance of research. Commun. Assoc. Inf. Syst. **37**, 286–325 (2015)
8. Rowe, F.: What literature review is not: diversity, boundaries and recommendations. Eur. J. Inf. Syst. **23**, 241–255 (2014)
9. Thomé, A.M.T., Scavarda, L.F., Scavarda, A.J.: Conducting systematic literature review in operations management. Prod. Plan. Control **27**, 408–420 (2016)
10. Cram, W.A., Templier, M., Pare, G.: (Re)considering the concept of literature review reproducibility. J. Assoc. Inf. Syst. **21** (2020)
11. vom Brocke, J., Simons, A., Riemer, K., Niehaves, B., Plattfaut, R., Cleven, A.: Standing on the shoulders of giants: challenges and recommendations of literature search in information systems research. Commun. Assoc. Inf. Syst. **37**, 205–224 (2015)
12. Boell, S., Wang, B.: www. litbaskets. io, an IT artifact supporting exploratory literature searches for Information Systems Research. In: Australasian Conference on Information Systems, Perth, Australia (2019)
13. Larsen, K.R., Hovorka, D., Dennis, A., West, J.: Understanding the elephant: the discourse approach to boundary identification and corpus construction for theory review articles. J. Assoc. Inf. Syst. **20**, 15 (2019)
14. Paré, G., Tate, M., Johnstone, D., Kitsiou, S.: Contextualizing the twin concepts of systematicity and transparency in information systems literature reviews. Eur. J. Inf. Syst. **25**, 493–508 (2016)
15. Wolfswinkel, J.F., Furtmueller, E., Wilderom, C.P.M.: Using grounded theory as a method for rigorously reviewing literature. Eur. J. Inf. Syst. **22**, 45–55 (2013)
16. Schoormann, T., Behrens, D., Fellmann, M., Knackstedt, R.: Sorry, too much information design principles for supporting rigorous search strategies in literature reviews. In: 20th Conference on Business Informatics, pp. 99–108. IEEE (2018)
17. Boell, S.K., Cecez-Kecmanovic, D.: Debating systematic literature reviews (SLR) and their ramifications for IS: a rejoinder to Mike Chiasson, Briony Oates, Ulrike Schultze, and Richard Watson. J. Inf. Technol. **30**, 188–193 (2015)
18. Avdiji, H., Elikan, D., Missonier, S., Pigneur, Y.: A design theory for visual inquiry tools. J. Assoc. Inf. Syst. **21**, 3 (2020)
19. Strategyzer: The business model canvas: why and how organizations around the world adopt it (2015)
20. Osterwalder, A., Pigneur, Y.: Business Model Generation: A Handbook for Visionaries, Game Changers, and Challengers. Wiley, Hoboken (2010)
21. Gregor, S., Hevner, A.R.: Positioning and presenting design science research for maximum impact. MIS Q. **37**, 337–355 (2013)
22. Bandara, W., Furtmueller, E., Gorbacheva, E., Miskon, S., Beekhuyzen, J.: Achieving rigor in literature reviews: insights from qualitative data analysis and tool-support. Commun. Assoc. Inf. Syst. **37**, 154–204 (2015)
23. Tate, M., Furtmueller, E., Evermann, J., Bandara, W.: Introduction to the special issue: the literature review in information systems. Commun. Assoc. Inf. Syst. 37, 5 (2015)
24. Boell, S., Cecez-Kecmanovic, D.: A Hermeneutic approach for conducting literature reviews and literature searches. Commun. Assoc. Inf. Syst. **34**, 12 (2014)

25. vom Brocke, J., Simons, A., Niehaves, B., Riemer, K., Plattfaut, R., Cleven, A.: Reconstructing the giant: on the importance of rigour in documenting the literature search process. In: 17th European Conference on Information Systems, Verona, Italy, pp. 2206–2217 (2009)
26. Okoli, C., Schabram, K.: A guide to conducting a systematic literature review of information systems research. Sprouts: Working Papers on Information System, vol. 10 (2010)
27. Kitchenham, B.: Procedures for performing systematic reviews (2004)
28. Brereton, P., Kitchenham, B.A., Budgen, D., Turner, M., Khalil, M.: Lessons from applying the systematic literature review process within the software engineering domain. J. Syst. Softw. **80**, 571–583 (2007)
29. Kitchenham, B.A., Brereton, O.P., Budgen, D.: Protocol for Extending An Existing Tertiary Study of Systematic Literature Reviews in Software Engineering. Keele University, Keele University (2006)
30. Kitchenham, B.A., Mendes, E., Travassos, G.H.: Protocol for systematic review of within-and cross-company estimation models. Keele University (2008)
31. Booth, A., Sutton, A., Papaioannou, D.: Systematic Approaches to a Successful Literature Review. Sage, London (2016)
32. Täuscher, K., Abdelkafi, N.: Visual tools for business model innovation: recommendations from a cognitive perspective. Create. Innov. Manage. **26**, 160–174 (2017)
33. John, T., Szopinski, D.: Towards explaining the popularity of the business model canvas: a dual coding approach. In: Multikonferenz Wirtschaftsinformatik. Lüneburg, Germany (2018)
34. Morana, S., et al.: Research prototype: the design canvas in MyDesignProcess.com. In: International Conference on Design Science Research in Information Systems and Technology, Chennai, India (2018)
35. Kühne, B., Böhmann, T.: Requirements for representing data-driven business models - towards extending the business model canvas. In: 24th Americas Conference on Information Systems, New Orleans, USA (2018)
36. Poeppelbuss, J., Lubarski, A.: Modularity canvas – a framework for visualizing potentials of service modularity. In: Wirtschaftsinformatik (WI), Siegen, Germany (2019)
37. Schoormann, T., Behrens, D., Kolek, E., Knackstedt, R.: Sustainability in business models–a literature-review-based design-science-oriented research agenda. In: 24th European Conference on Information Systems, Istanbul, Turkey (2016)
38. Star, S.L.: This is Not a Boundary Object: reflections on the origin of a concept. Sci. Technol. Hum. Values **35**, 601–617 (2010)
39. Hevner, A.R., March, S.T., Park, J., Ram, S.: Design science in information systems research. MIS Q. **28**, 75–105 (2004)
40. van Someren, M., Barnard, Y.F., Sandberg, J.A.: The Think Aloud Method: A Practical Approach to Modelling Cognitive Processes. Academic Press, London (1994)
41. Mindel, V., Mathiassen, L.: Contextualist inquiry into IT-enabled hospital revenue cycle management: bridging research and practice. J. Assoc. Inf. Syst. **16**, 1016 (2015)
42. Roberts, N., Galluch, P.S., Dinger, M., Grover, V.: Absorptive capacity and information systems research: review, synthesis, and directions for future research. MIS Q. **36** (2012)
43. Ericsson, K.A., Simon, H.A.: Verbal reports as data. Psychol. Rev. **87**, 215–251 (1980)
44. Jaspers, M., Steen, T., Bos, C., Geenen, M.: The think aloud method: a guide to user interface design. Int. J. Med. Inform. **73**, 781–795 (2004)
45. Hwang, W., Salvendy, G.: Number of people required for usability evaluation: the 10$\pm$2 rule. Commun. ACM **53**, 130 (2010)
46. Peffers, K., Rothenberger, M., Tuunanen, T., Vaezi, R.: Design science research evaluation. In: Peffers, K., Rothenberger, M., Kuechler, B. (eds.) Design Science Research in Information Systems. Advances in Theory and Practice, pp. 398–410. Springer, Heidelberg (2012). https://doi.org/10.1007/978-3-642-29863-9

47. Miller, G.A.: The magical number seven, plus or minus two: some limits on our capacity for processing information. Psychol. Rev. **63**, 81 (1956)
48. Besson, P., Rowe, F.: Strategizing information systems-enabled organizational transformation: a transdisciplinary review and new directions. J. Strateg. Inf. Syst. **21**, 103–124 (2012)
49. Seidel, S., Urquhart, C.: On emergence and forcing in information systems grounded theory studies: the case of Strauss and Corbin. J. Inf. Technol. **28**, 237–260 (2013)

Author Index

F. Ahlemann et al. (Eds.): WI 2021, LNISO 46, pp. 577–578, 2021.
https://doi.org/10.1007/978-3-030-86790-4